For my sister Jen Peacock,
her husband George Peacock,
and their son Robert Peacock.

CONTENTS

Illustrations follow page 312

ACKNOWLEDGMENTS

⌀ Since Mrs. Inchbald's story certainly could not have been told without the resources of many libraries, both here and abroad, I would like to thank the following:

The Folger Shakespeare Library for their kind assistance in making available manuscript materials, especially Mrs. Inchbald's pocket-books; the British Library and the York Minster Library in England; and the Emory University Library, the Georgia Tech Library, and the Oglethorpe University Library here in Atlanta.

I would like to thank Paula Backscheider, the late Philip Griffith, and Betty Rizzo, all of whom read the manuscript and offered valuable directions and suggestions.

For help and encouragement over the years, I would like to thank Martha Bowden, Nancy Grayson, J. Patrick Lee, Heather McPherson, Byron Wells, and Calhoun Winton.

I also thank all the members, both past and present, of the Southeastern American Society for Eighteenth Century Studies for listening to me read and talk about Mrs. Inchbald and her friends over many years and in many places.

And finally, I want to thank a very important group of people who helped prepare the manuscript, for without their help there would never have been a book. They are Kathleen Doig, Larry Furse, Jessica Ellis, Dawn Jackson, Avigail Schimmel, Paul Schnell, and Richard Wetmore.

ONE

In London to Find a Fortune

✷ On April 10, 1772, Elizabeth Simpson packed up her things, left her mother a note, walked some two miles to the turnpike, and took the stagecoach to London. Only about thirty miles from her home in Standingfield, it was a journey she had made before. Four of her sisters lived in London with their husbands, and the year before she had spent some weeks with them enjoying London life, especially her visits to the theatres. This time, however, she had come on her own to find a place as an actress. Independent and determined, she would not leave until she had succeeded in finding an assignment.

The story of her first days searching for a company that would take her turned out to be full of adventure as she told it later, even though some of her story is false and some very exaggerated.[1] She already knew several of the players in the Norwich Theatre Company, and since it was the end of the season, when the players gathered in London to make summer plans, she began to contact those she knew.

Her brother George had been a member of the Norwich Company for two years, and she had visited him at the theatre there. She knew the Norwich manager, Richard Griffith, who, in fact, interviewed her but did not hire her. She called on Mr. Reddish, a friend of her brother's who had at one time been in the Norwich Theatre also but who had just completed the winter season at Drury Lane; she called on Mr. King, a popular comedian at Drury Lane who had recently sold his share of the Bristol Theatre to James Dodd. She knew that all of these actors knew each other and that they had been in companies both in London and in the provinces.[2]

Her experience from the beginning with London and the theatres illustrates an important point that Elizabeth never forgot: that the players, the managers, the writers, and the performers were all mutually dependent, all dependent on the skills and experiences of one another. From the time she went to London to seek a place to act with some group, she was always a part of the company of players. This account of her association with hundreds of theatre players and friends became her life, a part of her personal life as well as her professional life.

One actor she knew slightly was James Dodd, who was a friend of Reddish's; she called on Dodd even though perhaps she knew his reputation was not altogether that of a proper gentleman. He was a fine actor, but he did not always act properly either in private or in public. For example, in July of 1769 he quarreled with his wife, Martha, and went off with the actress Mary Bulkley. He insisted that Martha and he be separated, and while she was in Richmond, Surrey, he wrote to the manager to discharge her, threatening to take her by force; going to Richmond with a pistol in hand, he stopped a post chaise in which he thought she was hiding. She was not hiding as he had thought, and he was taken before a magistrate and put in jail for two nights. Such behavior was much discussed in theatre circles, and the sympathy was all for Martha, especially when she fell ill and died at Bury St. Edmunds in October. As well known as Dodd and Bulkley were, it is hardly possible that Elizabeth would not have known about the altercation and Martha Dodd's death in Bury. In any case, she went to see him, and he gave her enough encouragement for her to return a second time. At this beginning of the summer season, Dodd was preparing to go to Bristol to assume his place as manager; no doubt Elizabeth wished to have a place there in the summer.

After her second interview, she thought she understood him to offer her a place, but as she turned to leave, he tried to detain her, to make love to her; she would have none of it. She snatched up a basin of hot water and threw it in his face and fled.[3] She should have known that a beautiful young girl without experience could not find a place merely because she wished to find one; moreover, she had a serious handicap—she stuttered. Wandering about for almost a week, now without money and frightened by the city, she wrote a note to one of her sisters and went to stay with her, continuing to contact various people.

The year before, she had corresponded with Joseph Inchbald, an actor who had been at Norwich with her brother. He had proposed to her and had written to her mother, and she had refused him. Now that she was in London, however, he began to call on her two or three times a week. Conversation was better than correspondence. In the evening of June 9, Elizabeth Simpson and Joseph Inchbald, both of whom were Catholic, were married by Mr. Rice, a Catholic priest; the morning after, they were married again to conform to the laws of the Church of England.[4] Joseph Inchbald had an engagement to act at Bristol for the summer, and on June 11 they set off to join the Bristol troupe. No one at that point could have imagined the years to come. Hardly a decade later, Mrs. Inchbald had a successful play produced in London and was thus beginning a professional career that made her the leading woman playwright of the eighteenth century, made her novel *A Simple Story* one of the most important pieces of fiction in the 1790s, and gave her the knowledge to write criticism of the plays in *The British Theatre*, establishing a precedent for all the theatre criticism that followed in the first half of the nineteenth century.

In the last two decades of the eighteenth century and the first of the nineteenth, Elizabeth Simpson Inchbald was at the center of the world of the theatre and the world of publishing. She was also one of the leading social figures in the intellectual group that made up the writers and artists in London. Because London was the center for all the theatrical activity of the country, Inchbald knew virtually everyone—players and managers—in all of England and Scotland. Because she had friends in Dublin, she also knew the theatres in Ireland. In fact, from reading the accounts of the theatres in Scotland, Ireland, and England in the years from 1772 to 1810, it is obvious that there was actually no separation between the theatre groups.

When I was completing a study of the playwright Nicholas Rowe, I came across Elizabeth Inchbald's *Remarks* on his play *The Fair Penitent;* I was immediately struck with how relevant they were to the present. She wrote of Calista, the Fair Penitent: [she] "feels deeper sorrow from her lover's abated passion . . . than from motives of contrition"; "since the ladies of Great Britain have learnt to spell, and have made other short steps in the path of literature . . . there is scarcely a woman in this country who can sympathize in the grief of the fair penitent."[5] I wondered about the ladies who had "learnt to spell" and who had "taken short steps in the path of literature" and about the ladies of our present who have lost their sympathy for the traditional role of becoming overcome with "passion." When I began to learn about Mrs. Inchbald herself, I realized that I had discovered a strong, very independent person who became a successful playwright and novelist, who knew the leading figures in London society of the late eighteenth century, and who knew and cared about a host of ordinary people.

When I read her manuscript pocket-books, tiny little memorandum books, I discovered the world in which she had lived: the domestic pleasures and problems, the expenses of food and drink, the daily association with friends and family, her marriage, her studies, her ambitions, her fears and successes. I began to feel that I should introduce her to others as a fascinating, independent woman. She was one of the most important writers of the years 1784–1808; she was the "Celebrated Mrs. Inchbald" in literary and social circles, but her public life failed to reveal the complexity of her personality or the richness of her society. In the world of the late eighteenth century, the use of "Mrs." for a married woman and "Miss" for an unmarried woman was still socially correct. Mrs. Inchbald called her husband Mr. Inchbald even when she used his name in her very private pocket-book.

Thus I have retained an occasional Mrs. in this study. These pocket-books, like those kept by her sisters, were annuals with small spaces to record under each date of the week the memorable happenings of that day, the books they read, the plays they attended, and the people who came and went in their households. It is exceedingly unfortunate that so few of the pocket-books are extant, but the ones we have give us significant details of life in the theatres and of the social lives of the men and women who fashioned the world of the theatres.

Inchbald has been written about in her own time and ours. She herself worked on her memoirs for three decades, only to destroy them on the advice of her confessor. In our time she has been examined for her views of the role of women and for the commentary in her plays about her contemporary society. James Boaden, her younger contemporary, arranged the *Memoirs of Mrs. Inchbald* from the pocket-books and her letters in 1833, more than a decade after her death, offering his own views of her life and achievements.

After Inchbald's death in 1821, her papers and letters were given to her friend Mrs. Phillips, who wrote to the publishers Colburn and Bentley offering her papers:

[Mrs. Phillips] agrees to place in the hands of . . . Henry Colburn and Richard Bentley all her papers, letters, & documents of & relating to the late Mrs. Inchbald, and the said Henry Colburn and Richard Bentley agree to procure the assistance of a literary gentleman to be selected by themselves for the purpose of writing and preparing a Life of the late Mrs. Inchbald from the said materials, the amount of the pecuniary remuneration for whose services is to be left to the discretion of the said Henry Colburn and Richard Bentley and which amount is to be included in the charge incurred on account of the said work, and after deducting their charge for printing, paper, advertising & all other incidental expenses, including the usual allowance of Ten percent on the gross amount, for risk of Bad Debts, the profits remaining of every Edition that may be printed of the work, are to be divided into two equal parts, one moiety to be paid to Mrs. Phillips & the other moiety to belong to the said Henry Colburn & Richard Bentley the books to be accounted for at the Trade Sale Price 25 as 24, unless it be thought advisable to dispose of copies or the Remainder, at a lower price, which is left to the judgment and discretion of the said Henry Colburn & Richard Bentley.[6]

Mrs. Phillips continues in her letter to say that her wish is "to perpetuate Mrs. Inchbald's fame"; she considers her "to have been the cleverest self-educated woman that ever lived." She would hope that whatever benefit might accrue from the publication would be given to George Huggins, Inchbald's nephew, and Ann Jarrett, Inchbald's niece. The date of this letter is 1832. Colburn and Bentley chose James Boaden to prepare the *Memoirs,* which appeared in 1833.

Boaden was an obvious choice, since he had already written books on Dorothy Jordan, John Philip Kemble, and Kemble's sister Sarah Kemble Siddons, all "stars" in the theatres; it was especially appropriate for him to write one on Mrs. Inchbald, since she had been intimately connected with Jordan, Kemble, and Siddons. Moreover, he was a quite successful journalist and playwright who knew most of the circle of friends and acquaintances associated with Inchbald; thus he was able to give background information not found elsewhere.[7]

Boaden held strong opinions about the theatre and the players in all three London theatres—Drury Lane, Covent Garden, and the Haymarket—and although he sometimes is rather verbose, he is, nevertheless, always knowledgeable.[8] The details he includes in his discussions reveal a vast amount of gossip and theatre lore not to be found elsewhere, information that makes the world of London and the theatres exciting and important. It was a world so much a part of London and the English provinces that the ideas and events portrayed help to fashion the social history of the last quarter of the eighteenth century.[9]

The most recent biography of Elizabeth Inchbald is *Elizabeth Inchbald: A Biographical Study* (1987) by Roger Manvell; the subtitle is *England's Principal Woman Dramatist and Independent Woman of Letters in 18th Century London.* Manvell's biography is a short but appreciative essay supporting the thesis of the subtitle. In 1921 S.R. Littlewood published *Elizabeth Inchbald and Her Circle* on the one-hundredth anniversary of her death; William McKee's *Elizabeth Inchbald, Novelist* (1935) was the first full-length study of her novels. G. Lewis Joughin's indispensable bibliographical listing of her work was published in *Texas Studies in English* (1934). Patricia Sigl has done extensive research on the papers Boaden used in his *Memoirs of Mrs. Inchbald* to identify the present location of this material.[10]

The material for Inchbald's *Memoirs and Familiar Correspondence,* edited by James Boaden and published in two volumes in 1833, may be found in the British Library and in the Folger Shakespeare Library. She kept pocket-book diaries from her early years until her death in 1821. The Folger has those of the years 1776, 1780, 1781, 1783, 1788, 1793, 1807, 1808, 1814, and 1820. The Folger also has a collection of miscellaneous materials, including, for example, receipts for some of her plays and a copy of her will. Other manuscript material may be found in the British Library in the manuscript department—numbers 46611 ff., 260–63; 27 925f 24, 28 558.

These manuscript materials are not only interesting for Inchbald's own life and career; they also contain a wealth of material about the people in her world, especially the world of the theatre. The details that cover her daily activities reveal the relationships of her friends and acquaintances, the events in the government, the books published, and many of the books she read and discussed. In the early books, she kept an account of the money she spent, including how much she paid for washing and wine; in the 1776 book she records the events of her trip to France, and in the 1783 book she records the details of her time in Dublin for the brief period when she acted at the Smock Alley Theatre.

In 1780 she joined the Covent Garden Company. The books for 1780, 1781, and 1783 show her determined struggle to make a place for herself as an actress. The 1788 and 1793 books are about the success of her plays and her novel *A Simple Story*. The books for 1807 and 1808 were kept during the time she was writing her *Remarks;* those for 1814 and 1820 are about her life after she retired. A check of the pocket-books and the information in Boaden indicates that he followed her record very closely for the material he selected to discuss. But a careful look at the pocket-books that survive reveals many details that he simply passed over, and always, as is to be expected, his selection and his reading of the material reflect his own personal views.

Writing biography for anyone is a difficult task, because it requires a multitude of facts and opinions: facts about the subject's life and friends and the social milieu, knowledge of the political events and views of a specific time span, and ultimately a judgment of the subject of the biography. Writing the biography of Elizabeth Simpson Inchbald is both difficult and exciting, because she reveals so much of her social and professional life in the pocket-books that are extant, a source we find very broken. Nevertheless, she is too important to our understanding of the years of her life—1753–1821 in England, Scotland, Ireland—not to collect and examine all the sources we have.

For this biography the chief sources of information are the *Memoirs* that Boaden edited, the pocket-books, and various manuscript materials from the Folger Shakespeare Library and the British Library. The material found in those sources about her friends and acquaintances is supplemented by information from various contemporary memoirs and such accounts of the theatre world as Tate Wilkinson's *Wandering Patentee;* additional information about her friends and acquaintances in the world of the theatres comes from *A Biographical Dictionary of Actors, Actresses, Musicians, Dancers, Managers, and Other Stage Personnel in London, 1660–1800,* by Philip H. Highfill Jr., Kalman A. Burnim, and Edward A. Langhans.

Recent studies of Inchbald's work, viewed as a part of the body of work of the women novelists in the late eighteenth century, have taken very little account of the context out of which she wrote or the context of her world—the world of London and the theatres in the late eighteenth century and the first part of the nineteenth. Such a narrow view of her life and her work creates a false picture of her as a person and of her work in the theatre. After the production of her first play in 1784, she was viewed for the most part in conjunction with the Colmans, father and son, and with Thomas Harris, patentee of Covent Garden. She also had a long association with the publishers G.G. and J. Robinson and their successors, the Longmans. From 1777 she was a friend of Sarah Kemble Siddons and her brother John Philip Kemble. As a result of their early association, she formed friendships with all the Kemble-Siddons family, the family that dominated the world of the theatre from the 1780s until the mid-nineteenth century. She also knew hundreds of other people, not only in the theatre but also in the periodical world, the political world, and the social world; reviewing her life gives the reader an insight into all these quite different aspects of the late eighteenth century.

Elizabeth Simpson Inchbald was beautiful, witty, and independent. Even in her teens, she declared that she would rather die than not live in London. In the end she did live in London for over forty years, for most of that time as the celebrated Mrs. Inchbald. This biography is her story, the story of her personal and professional life, of her family and friends, of her associates in the theatre and the publishing world, and of many of the small details that make up a life in London from 1780 to 1821.

AT HOME IN SUFFOLK

Elizabeth Simpson was the daughter of John and Mary Simpson, who also had five other daughters and two sons. She was born October 15, 1753, at Standingfield, a small hamlet near Bury St. Edmunds in Suffolk.[11] Her father was a farmer, from all the evidence a quite successful one. The Simpson farm spread out at the bottom of a slight hill. There was a substantial red brick barn as well as the house. There were fruit trees, fields of grain, vegetable gardens, and the usual domestic animals. Standingfield lies just on the border of Suffolk, some five miles from Bury St. Edmunds, its market town. Although the settlement itself is not so ancient as Bury St. Edmunds, it has a church, St. Nicholas, that dates to the 1300s.[12]

The family was devoted to one another and very supportive of family enterprises. Mary Simpson, who before her marriage was Mary Rushbrook, daughter of William Rushbrook of Flimpton, must have been a remarkable person for her time and circumstances. She conducted a household that not only fostered the activities of a busy farm but was also the gathering place of the local society, a society typical of the prosperous rural areas that supported the city of London. One writer, reviewing Inchbald's early life, remarked that her "family had a very large circle of visitors, and her own pocket-book exhibits the names of at least a hundred persons who called upon them." Mrs. Simpson read to her daughters, encouraged their reading of plays and romances, and went with them to Bury to see the plays put on at the tiny theatre there, which was a part of the Norwich circuit.[13]

When she left for London that day in April, Elizabeth had been living with her mother and her sister Deborah. Her father had died in 1761, when she was seven. By the time she was sixteen, four of her sisters had married and moved to London with their husbands. Two of them, Anne and Dorothy, were married to men named Hunt, another to Mr. Huggins, and another to a Mr. Slender. Another sister was married to a Mr. Bigsby. Her older brother worked on the estate of the duke of Norfolk, and her younger brother, George, had already become an actor. Elizabeth and her younger sister, Deborah, were the only ones living at home with their mother. The family was comfortably well-off, living as they did on the farm, and after her husband's death, Mary Simpson continued to manage the farm quite successfully.

Farming in Suffolk was special: the climate was mild, and the soil, although it had been cultivated for hundreds of years, remained fertile because of the farming methods that had begun to be practiced in the early eighteenth century and which made farming in Suffolk among the most advanced in all of England. The agricultural revolution that occurred in England in the early years of the nineteenth century had already taken place in Suffolk in the second half of the eighteenth. This national movement and the improved conditions brought about by rotation of crops had already become a part of the Suffolk practice by the time the Simpsons cared for their land in the fifties and sixties. Moreover, in the late eighteenth century, the farm implement industry was being established in Suffolk. Robert Ransome, son of a schoolmaster and apprenticed to a Norwich ironmonger, had set up his foundry in Ipswich and taken out a patent for cast iron plowshares.[14]

Suffolk is bordered on the west by Cambridgeshire and on the north and east by Norfolk, its seacoast looking toward Europe. Mrs. Inchbald's contemporaries—John Constable, Thomas Gainsborough, and George Crabbe—all celebrated their land, giving Suffolk a distinctive place in the landscape of the south. Lavenham was celebrated for its cloth industry in the fourteenth and fifteenth centuries; Ipswich was an Anglo-Saxon town, chartered in 1200, with at least ten of its churches dating from the early days; Bury St. Edmunds had an abbey dating from 1065–1098 and a massive abbey gate built circa 1327; Sudbury, another market town, was mentioned in the Doomsday book and in the eighteenth century was the birthplace of Gainsborough. All of these served to give distinction to a time and place that were part of Elizabeth Simpson Inchbald's world from the early days of her childhood until the turn of the century, when her brother finally gave over the farm. Perhaps the artist who captured her world and countryside in Suffolk most directly was Constable, her younger contemporary.

The Simpson farm, at the bottom of a hill, was viewed below from the medieval church. The church has a "doom painting" behind the altar and a monument to Thomas Rokewode. The Simpsons did not attend this nearby church but instead went across the fields to worship in the Roman Catholic chapel, a chapel built into Coldham Hall, the seat of the Gage family. The Simpsons must have been regular attenders at Mass, for in the years after she left home, Inchbald went to Mass whenever she returned home even though at times in her life she was not devout. And in later years she continued to see members of the Gage family both in Standingfield and in London.

As the scenes and routines of the farm remained a part of Elizabeth Inchbald's life, so did her close family ties and her love of books and the theatre. She learned to read very early, having been taught at home, as she herself pointed out: "it is astonishing how much all girls are inclined to literature, to what boys are. My brother went to school seven years, and never could spell. I and two of my sisters, though we never were taught, could spell from our infancy."[15] And throughout the pocket-books, Mrs. Inchbald records her reading and her digests of information that served to provide her with a reference library. One account of the family says that all the girls wrote memorandums that were "well written and well spelt" and that Mrs. Simpson read Samuel Richardson's popular novel *Clarissa* to her daughters at leisure times and played cards, loo and whist, with them. Although there are no direct comments about Elizabeth's speech, it was quite obvious to everyone who knew her that she had a severe speech impediment; no one seemed to mind.[16]

Mrs. Simpson seems not to have offered any opposition when her son George and her daughter Elizabeth decided to follow a career on the stage. She kept in touch with all her children, who were devoted to her, according to the evidence of letters, returns to Standingfield, and gifts from the farm to the daughters and sons. And the constant social entertainment of going out to tea, visiting, and receiving visitors must have been very early set by Mrs. Simpson. This frequent visiting among the sisters and the acquaintances from Standingfield and its surrounding areas continued even after two of the sisters, Anne and Dorothy, had gone to London and Elizabeth had married and become a strolling player. In later years Inchbald's pocket-books are filled with references to her visits to her mother and to the produce sent from the farm to her in London.

From an early age Elizabeth was attracted to the outside world. The trip to Bury, only five miles away, was merely the daily routine of the post or errands for the farm. She longed to see the world, as she declared at thirteen: "she would rather die, than live any longer without seeing the world."[17] Her brother George had joined the Norwich Company of players in 1770, and Elizabeth, already enamored with the stage, went to visit him alone, taking the stagecoach by herself, an early example of her independence.

From all accounts, one of the favorite things for the Simpsons to do was to go to Bury to the fair in the fall and while there attend the season of plays put on by the Norwich Company. During this festival time, spectators could go to rehearsals in the morning and the plays at night. The Simpsons must have spent the days of the fair in the theatre. They were very early familiar with the players and the manager, Richard Griffith; and long before Elizabeth went to London on that day in April, she had determined that she would become an actress, certainly a bold decision for a teenage girl who stuttered.[18] She also had a very special feeling for Griffith and wrote to him for an interview.

Richard Griffith was the son of an Irish actor, Thomas Griffith. After the rather usual experience (for a young actor) of acting at such theatres as Edinburgh, Bath, Dublin, and both Covent Garden and Drury Lane in London, he became the manager of the Norwich Theatre in 1766. By some three or four years later when the teenage Elizabeth Simpson wrote to him asking to join the company, he had become quite successful. As manager he remained for fifteen years, resigning then only because of ill health. He was said to be scrupulously honest, careful with the company's money, and generous to the players. Elizabeth had been to Norwich many times when she made up her mind to have an interview with him and to ask for a place in the company. He did grant her the interview; although he did not hire her, he was polite and evidently encouraging. She had quite a crush on him, recording in her pocket-book that she stole his picture.[19] One of the players in the company called Griffith "a perfect beau of the old school, a Sir Philip Modelove in real life; a man who to the end of his career remained young at heart."[20]

Another of the members of the Norwich Company was Joseph Inchbald. Elizabeth had known him with the company long before her trip to London. Very little is known about him, but he seems to have been a competent actor as a member of the company, not playing the principal parts but supporting others in the cast. He was a painter as well, and at Norwich he probably worked as an artist in the town painting portraits of the townspeople and scenery for the theatre. There is also a reference to his son, whose name is not recorded, as being a part of the company. In the season of 1770–1771, he was a member of the Drury Lane Company in London, where he was playing such minor parts as Oswald in *King*

Lear. In the season 1771–1772, he continued to play supporting roles such as Capulet in *Romeo and Juliet.* He had earlier been with a troupe of players at Stourbridge Fair, and he had been in Norwich from 1768 to 1770. There is some indication that he was rather careless of his appearance. After his marriage to Elizabeth Simpson, we know about him through her references.

When he married Elizabeth, he was thirty-seven and she eighteen. He had two sons, Robert and George; the younger one was said to be illegitimate, and perhaps the older one was also, but there is very little information about them in 1772. Not even their ages are known, though Robert was perhaps the younger, and it is certain that he was the one who went with them to Scotland. There is very little known about Joseph Inchbald and his sons except in relation to Elizabeth. For most of their married life, one or the other son lived with them. Some of the commentators have suggested that Elizabeth married for protection, for an older man to take the place of the father she had lost at so early an age. But following the two of them as they became players in the provinces, it seems obvious that he was very much in love with her and that for both of them it became a love match quite exceptional in theatrical circles. After his death in 1779, she went to Covent Garden, where she acted from 1780 to 1789; she remained in London until her death in 1821.

In 1784 she had her first play, *A Mogul Tale,* produced at the Haymarket, and from then until her last play in 1805, she became virtually the playwright in residence at Covent Garden in the winter and at the Haymarket in the summer. She wrote or adapted some twenty-one plays; eleven of these were original, the others adaptations of French and German plays. Two of her plays, *Lovers' Vows* and *The Wise Man of the East,* were adapted from the German playwright Augustus von Kotzebue, whose plays Richard Brinsley Sheridan also used for his own adaptations. She wrote two novels, *A Simple Story,* published in 1791, and *Nature and Art,* published in 1796. From 1806 to 1808 she published a series titled *Remarks,* critiques of the 125 plays in *The British Theatre.* Her commentaries were so successful that she was asked to select the plays in *The Modern Theatre* and those in *A Collection of Farces and other Afterpieces.* Everyone agreed that she was the leading authority on drama in the last years of the eighteenth century and the first decade of the nineteenth.[21]

She knew everyone in the theatre from 1780, when she came to London, until 1810. Moreover, she knew most of the figures in the political world. She was a close friend of William Godwin; and she, Godwin, and the actor and writer Thomas Holcroft were central figures in the liberal press in the 1790s. Her plays and novels were published by G.G. and J. Robinson and Company, and she had a hand in several periodicals, supplying and writing material, sometimes without using her name. In the twentieth century, she has been viewed as a friend of Sarah Siddons and John Kemble, the two most celebrated players in the late eighteenth century, but in her own time she was as well known and celebrated as the two of them. She was an extremely independent person, and the ideas she uses in her plays and novels and the views she expresses in the *Remarks* are clearly those of an independent thinker and writer.

The record in her pocket-books and letters and the evidence from her friends and associates all support this view. She was determined to write. She was also determined to live by her own standards, and she guarded her private life fiercely. It is from her letters, her pocket-books, and commentary from friends and acquaintances that a portrait of her may be constructed. Boaden, for all his care in using the material in his hands, could not view her or her world without his own perspectives and prejudices. The other material is not simply useful; it is necessary for a true picture of her character and accomplishments.

Being independent did not always bring Inchbald comfort or happiness, and her determination to do things her own way frequently caused her anxiety. It is in the pocket-books that her fears are evident; there also, with the account of her work, is revealed an amazing picture of her determination. With Boaden and the extant pocket-books and letters, it becomes possible to assemble a description of her and her world to delight and instruct.

AMBITION AND INDEPENDENCE

After the rituals of being married first by a priest and second, the next day, by a clergyman in the Church of England, and after Joseph Inchbald performed in a play the evening they were married, the Inchbalds set off to Bristol, where he had an assignment for the summer; he was in the same company she had hoped to be a part of when she had been interviewed by Dodd.[22] They met Dodd on their way to Bristol, but he ignored them, and they gave no notice of his presence in the company; nonetheless, the world of the stage for the summer people, which included the Inchbalds, was a very narrow, close-knit one. The players spent most of their time in one another's company, living in the same houses, eating together, spending time rehearsing, and finding amusement together during the hours they were not in the playhouse. Elizabeth Inchbald joined the others for tea, made new friends, and began to write out the part of Cordelia in Shakespeare's *King Lear*.

This first summer must have been an interesting one for Elizabeth. Her husband, assuming the male role and being of a rather independent nature himself, frequently went his own way. They could not escape Dodd, who was certainly an important member of the troupe this summer, and his presence and behavior as he resumed his liaison with Mary Bulkley lent a certain unstable moral quality to the whole group. This was the first summer that Dodd was a partner in the management of the Bristol Theatre, but there was a great flurry of reports in the papers, much opposition against him from the local patrons, and much unrest in the theatre. Although Martha Dodd, his wife, had died in 1769 in Bury St. Edmunds, her death did not stop Dodd from resuming his affair with Mary Bulkley, who was the wife of George Bulkley, the leader of the Bristol Band. Dodd's obvious and public affair with Mary Bulkley in the company where her husband directed the band did little to commend him to the public; he managed to keep his interest in the Bristol Theatre for only two summers before he sold it and went to Dublin. This summer in Bristol, the Inchbalds were no doubt aware of all the gossip about Dodd and others in the company; for Elizabeth it was the beginning of her accumulation of theatre gossip, and since the players continued to see each other in various places and circumstances, it was also the beginning of her knowledge of how to deal with her fellow players.[23]

Another couple the Inchbalds knew this summer were Mr. and Mrs. Hartley. Mrs. Hartley was very beautiful, and, like Mrs. Inchbald, she was tall with golden hair. According to Boaden, Joseph Inchbald "seemed particularly attached to them," but Mrs. Inchbald did not like or approve of them: he reports, "she most likely means that the lady took the liberties of beauty not well shielded by principle, and the husband saw them without pain."[24] But whatever the Inchbalds thought about the Hartleys or Dodd and Mrs. Bulkley, they all four became a part of their story.

Determined as she was to become a professional member of the acting company, Elizabeth Inchbald was faced with long hours of study for the many parts required of the beginner; added to this was the fact of her severe speech impediment. At this time, in the summer and fall of 1772, just short of her nineteenth birthday, she was strikingly beautiful. Tall and slender with red-gold hair and gray eyes, she had a kind of youthful freshness that contrasted, no doubt, with the appearance of her thirty-seven-year-old husband. Mrs. Inchbald retained her beauty—her striking good looks—throughout her life, for even when she was in her sixties, her figure, her complexion, and her hair were remarked upon. She seemed in her early days to have been relatively unaware of her appearance, being much more occupied with her stage presence, but later, when she had become a London celebrity, she records in her pocket-books her concern with aging, lamenting the loss of youth, however, rather than of beauty.

Soon after they arrived in Bristol, and before he could play his part as Lear,

Joseph Inchbald became ill; giving up her plan to study the part of Cordelia, Elizabeth nursed him, and when he recovered, she fell sick. The conditions under which the players worked were, even in the summer, very difficult, and illness was an all-too-common occurrence. This first experience for Elizabeth was an introduction to one of the chief problems of her profession—her health. After they both recovered, Joseph coached her in the part of Cordelia, and on September 4, 1772, she played it, with her husband as Lear.

From the beginning of her stage career, Mrs. Inchbald worried about her performance. Her severe speech impediment made her reluctant to practice in the presence of anyone, even her husband. Finally, Boaden says, "although not fond of repeating her parts before him, she became at last obedient to his wishes, and they *spouted* (as she plainly calls it) at home and in the open air, till at length she hit upon a better tone of declamation than she had set out with."[25]

When the Inchbalds had finished their summer season in Bristol, they went to London, for London was a kind of employment pool for assignments for the next theatrical season. Because Elizabeth had been so unsuccessful in London in the spring, she surely must have let her husband make the arrangements, especially since she herself was hardly more experienced than she had been in the first place, having acted only a few times at Bristol. Joseph Inchbald did set up an engagement for them to join West Digges's company in Scotland, where they began an entirely new chapter of their lives.

TWO

SCOTLAND AND THE PERILS OF TRAVEL

❧ **B**y the fall of 1772, when the Inchbalds joined his company, West Digges had already had a great deal of experience on stage as an actor and as a manager. He was the son of Thomas Digges, his mother, Elizabeth, was the daughter of John West, sixth baron De La Warr, and his sister was married to the first earl of De La Warr. The Digges family did not entirely approve of West's profession. Moreover, he was much gossiped about: his private life was hardly private, since everyone knew that he had had a series of amours and that he was always in debt, a fact that made it certain that he could not remain in one city for any length of time. He had begun his acting career in Dublin. The date of his birth is uncertain, but by the time the Inchbalds met the company in Glasgow, he had been associated with the theatre in Scotland since 1752, when, as a stroller, he had helped put up a wooden booth in the Bishop's Palace in Castle Yard, Glasgow. This, the first theatre in Glasgow, was torn down almost at once by George Whitefield, the Methodist, and his followers, but after 1752 Digges returned to Scotland again and again. In 1756, as manager of the Cannongate Theatre in Edinburgh, he produced the premiere of the Reverend John Home's tragedy *Douglas,* in which he also played Douglas. The play was a cause célèbre and created all kinds of problems in the church, including the resignation of Home and the disciplining of several of the clerics who had attended the performances.

For much of the time in these early days in Scotland, Digges had lived with Mrs. Sarah Ward, a well-known actress, but by 1759 he was back in Dublin, where this time he became enamored of George Anne Bellamy, another quite well known actress, and was again deep in debt. One writer described their relationship this way: "they quarrelled energetically and entertained extravagantly." When Digges's mother, Elizabeth, died, she stipulated in her will that her elder son, West Digges, should quit the stage if he were to inherit her estate. Considering his constant need for money, he evidently observed the terms of her will for some time. By 1771, however, he was in Edinburgh again, and this time he held the lease of the theatre. In the summer of 1772, shortly before the Inchbalds arrived in London to seek a contract, Digges had been arrested for an old debt; fortunately, he had escaped by legal provisions involving Scottish law.[1]

The company Digges had assembled left a good deal to be desired. One critic from London wrote: "[Digges] is now at the head of a company who seem intended as foils to himself, and though they change every year, I am informed they never change for the better. The smallness of the salaries accounts for this. There is only one or two whose pay exceeds a guinea a week, nor can the receipts of the house afford more, while the rent is so high."[2]

On October 10 the Inchbalds, with their friend Richard Wilson, embarked on a ship for Scotland; they had a stormy passage for a week until October 17, when they landed at Leith and went to Glasgow to report to Digges.[3] When the Inchbalds and Wilson arrived in Scotland, the company had been put together, and Digges was already performing with the company assembled. On October 23, however, Mr. Inchbald and Wilson went to see Digges and arranged for Mrs. Inchbald to play Cordelia on the Monday following; thus she too became a member of the company. It was here in Glasgow that she was introduced to even more of the hardships and problems of the profession than she had found in Bristol. Perhaps the greatest single difficulty was that encountered in travel. In Scotland— as indeed everywhere—the roads were virtually impassable in the winter, the sea was stormy, the theatres the companies played in were far apart, and frequently the audiences were slim and rowdy. It was not a very comfortable way to live. In spite of such problems, however, by the fall of 1772, when the Inchbalds began their new assignment, the conditions in the theatres of the principal towns in the provinces had improved over the twenty years since Elizabeth's birth in 1753.

This improvement was especially evident in Norwich, the theatre Elizabeth knew as a child. Sybil Rosenfeld, in her book *Strolling Players and Drama in the Provinces, 1660–1765*, finds that the Norwich players, those who had supplied Elizabeth with her first theatre experience, had a long and varied history by 1750. Norwich had entertained strolling players soon after the Restoration and continued to do so until more formal companies were formed in the early eighteenth century, when, as Rosenfeld says, "here at last was a permanent company which played almost every winter season and in Assize week."[4] Moreover, the plays offered included new plays fresh from the London stage.[5] Players from London came to join the company, and the revival of such plays as Garrick's version of *Romeo and Juliet* were done almost as soon as they appeared in London.[6] And although the towns on the circuit varied in some years, Bury St. Edmunds was one town that remained constant; its season ran in September and October during the fair. Norwich did not lack variety in plays or players. "Actors from London did not scorn to play in the company, and scenery and costumes were from time to time obtained from London theatres. The city was well served, not by an itinerant band of impoverished strollers, but by a company capable of showing its citizens the best in old and the latest in new drama."[7]

Thomas Gilliland, writing about the Norwich circuit, called it a "profitable circuit" and gave an outline of how the circuit operated. It was a life the Inchbalds were soon to live: "The year is made out thus: first Yarmouth; then Ipswich, a distance of fifty-three miles; forty-three more to Norwich [for the assizes]; back to Yarmouth twenty-two; then to Stirbritch [Stourbridge], eighty-six to Bury twenty-eight; Colchester, twenty-two; to Ipswich again, eighteen; to Norwich, forty-three; Lyme, forty-four; back again to Norwich, forty-four; and again to Yarmouth, twenty two: making in the whole a twelve month's tour."[8]

No doubt Elizabeth Inchbald's early association with the Norwich players determined her subsequent ambition of going on stage herself, and her association with her brother and his friends gave her the information she needed to try for a place in some company; her husband completed her quest. The circuit in Scotland that Digges managed was long established; that is, although it was not so stable as the Norwich circuit, Edinburgh and Glasgow had long had a season of plays, and the opportunities to play in such places as Aberdeen and Greenock were frequently available. Unfortunately, some of the towns in Scotland were not as prosperous as those on the Norwich circuit, and some of the places in which the plays were to be performed were barns—shabby ones at that.

At first Mrs. Inchbald did not play in many real parts; for example, she was a witch in *Macbeth*, and she "walked" in a pantomime while the scenery was being changed behind the flat. She spent a good many hours writing out parts and memorizing them. She was very discouraged about her acting; after all, she had had very little experience, but she was then—and always—very impatient. Then there were domestic matters. Evidently their friend Wilson boarded at the same place they did, and he and Joseph frequently went out together. Moreover, Bob, Mr. Inchbald's young son, lived with them and was a real problem. Children were always a part of the company. They were used to play children's parts in the plays, and—perhaps more important—their salaries, however small, added to the parents' income. New both to marriage and the practices of strollers, Mrs. Inchbald was very unhappy with the circumstances. Considering the kind of extended family the company made up, it is not surprising that there were frequent disagreements between husbands and wives; nor is it surprising that when the members of the company shared all the hours of the day and the night, there were frequent quarrels about such things as parts, costumes, and, most of all, money.[9]

When they left Glasgow, the Inchbalds went to Edinburgh, and here Elizabeth persuaded her husband to work with her as he had done during the summer in Bristol. They walked as she spoke her parts aloud, repeating their walks until she became more proficient. Her first important role was that of Jane Shore in Nicholas Rowe's play *Jane Shore;* she also played Cordelia again and added Calista in *The Fair Penitent,* another very popular Rowe play. Both roles were popular pathetic heroines, standard roles in frequently performed plays both in the provinces and in London. For Elizabeth Inchbald these were roles she repeated many times.

This first season found Elizabeth obliged to become not only an actress but a wife as well. And although there is no doubt that Joseph Inchbald was an indulgent husband much in love with his beautiful wife, he was typical of husbands who also indulge themselves. And Elizabeth, being young and beautiful, had a great many admirers, one of whom was Mr. Sterling, an actor in the company who called on her whenever Joseph was away. It is not very clear why Mr. Inchbald was absent so frequently, but Elizabeth seems to have tried to discourage Sterling without much success. Sterling continued to call in Mr. Inchbald's absence; he insisted, according to Elizabeth, on passing his evenings reading to her. She records such items in her pocket-books; over the years she had one admirer after another who wished to spend the evenings with her—not always wishing to spend them reading, however. Mr. Inchbald's frequent absences and his son Bob's presence resulted in her insistence, more than once, upon their having separate chambers. When they left Edinburgh for Glasgow again, their friend Wilson going along, Elizabeth began to correspond with Sterling; he was among the first of her admirers whom she kept as a friend on her own terms. Because the players lived so closely with each other, it is not surprising that relationships changed from time to time. Given that the company moved frequently without establishing any permanent center for playing or living, it was only natural that they should become intimate with each other. Both Sterling and Wilson, Joseph Inchbald's frequent companion on "rambles," remained friends of Elizabeth Inchbald.

It is easy to understand why Mrs. Inchbald would resent her husband's frequent absences, but it is not so easy to understand about his son Bob. Bob had been with his father in Norwich in 1769, although the only mention of his being a member of the company is in a memorandum indicating that Inchbald and son were rehired. Bob would have added to his father's income by playing children's parts. He is recorded as playing Lucius in *Julius Caesar* on December 15, 1773, and on January 5, 1774, he played Robin in *The Merry Wives of Windsor.* Because he had been with his father before they went to Scotland, it is not surprising that he was a member of the company. But he was a child, and Elizabeth probably found him difficult to deal with. In later years he continued to be difficult and demanding to her, even though she frequently gave him money; perhaps he felt he deserved some support because of his father; he remained for her a remembrance of the past and a problem.

When they had been in Glasgow for a few days, Joseph Inchbald and Wilson went on a day and night "party of pleasure." Boaden's account, taken no doubt from Mrs. Inchbald's pocket-book, reads: "On the following day Mr. Inchbald came home, very sick of the excursion, and ashamed of the almost repentant limping, which a fall he had met with obliged him to display on his entrance. Perhaps the best tempered wife in the world might have deemed, or even pronounced the accident a *judgment* upon the sufferer, for resisting her lawful authority in at least all parties of PLEASURE."[10]

Wilson evidently had been a friend of Joseph Inchbald's for quite some time. He was perhaps a good example of the ordinary player of his time—never a very distinguished actor, always seizing the moment. He was, however, a competent performer, and over the years he was sometimes in the provinces, sometimes in London; he had a rather checkered career. When he and the Inchbalds joined the Digges Company, he already had a colorful past, having been in an itinerant company that played at Leeds in 1767 and having been in Belfast in 1770 in July. In August of that season he was at Norwich, where he, no doubt, began his friendship with Joseph Inchbald, so that when he went with the Inchbalds to Scotland in the fall of 1772, they were already familiar with each other. At this point it is not clear whether Wilson had a wife (even though in one account of their travels, a Mrs. Wilson is mentioned). In another account of his career, it is said that he had had at least five "wives," but in the fall of 1772 he may have been between "wives." Boaden does not suggest that any "wife" of his kept Elizabeth Inchbald company as she waited for them to return that cold night.[11]

During this first season in December and January, Mrs. Inchbald began to play a number of characters. Boaden lists them: "she was the Calphurnia to her husband's Caesar; Lady Anne in 'Richard the Third'; Lady Percy in 'Henry the Fourth'; Lady Elizabeth Grey in 'The Earl of Warwick'; Fanny in 'The Clandestine Marriage'; Desdemona to her husband's Othello on their benefit night; Arpasia to his Tamerlane; Anne Bullen [in *Henry VIII*]; Mrs. Strickland in 'The Suspicious Husband.'"[12] In addition to these important roles, she played in the masquerades—she was the Tragic Muse in *The Jubilee*, and she was one of the Bacchantes in *Comus*. In June they were in Greenock, lodging in Port Glasgow; this time Digges was away acting on his own invitations. Here Elizabeth began to play almost every night. She was Angelica in *The Constant Couple* and Violante in *The Wonder*, in addition to her other roles.

After a month in Greenock, they set out to go to Edinburgh again, where they were to perform a summer season. And as they returned to their same lodgings, Sterling reappeared, and the Inchbalds began to see Digges and his "lady" Miss Witherington again. Elizabeth seems to have been a favorite of theirs; they took her to and from the theatre, gave her an airing in their chaise, and in July Digges employed her brother George Simpson and his wife.

Their next engagement in this first summer season was in Aberdeen; consequently, they set out in the evening of August 2 from Leith by ship, but the wind was foul; they made no headway, and by the next evening the captain put to shore again. Mrs. Inchbald was never a good "sailor," although she was obliged to be a traveler by both sea and land. This time their journey illustrated the terrible hazards of travel in Scotland, where to go by land was perhaps as difficult as by sea.

The first night ashore, the Inchbalds found a small inn, where they took a walk by the seashore; but by the next day, with no prospect of traveling by ship, they, along with the Wilsons and Bob, set off by land. Boaden's account of their experience, probably taken from Elizabeth's pocket-book, shows clearly the difficulties of such a hazardous journey.

> They ... set off on foot. ... They dined in a garden; rode a little way on coal carts; drank tea at St. Andrews; hired a cart part of the way to the ferry, where they slept. Early in the morning ... they crossed the river, and walked eight miles. Mrs. Wilson however, having tired, they took a cart to Aberbrothick, where they dined. Another cart took them all to Montrose. They set off late in the evening to walk the next stage; but a farmer whom they met on the road recommended a half way house to them, where they slept; and early in the morning Mr. Inchbald and she ... set out to walk alone to Bervie, which they reached by breakfast-time. They went in a cart to Stonehaven, and, having joined their companions, at length reached Aberdeen, Mr. Inchbald and Mr. Wilson going before.[13]

Some two weeks later, Elizabeth Inchbald developed an ague and fever; she was ill for over two weeks, and afterward she had a "swelled" face. It was at this time that she was attended by Dr. Brodie, who afterward remained her friend for many years. Boaden says he saved her life, for she was so ill that Mr. Inchbald sent for a priest to give her the last rites. Such small details as those of the journey, her illness, and the friends who were a part of her life make her story very real and allow us to feel her experiences and understand her circumstances.

The season at Aberdeen having closed, the company set out to return to Edinburgh, this time in two chaises. They breakfasted the next morning at

Montrose, where they had thought to perform but were disappointed; they ate and slept at Arbroath, breakfasted at Dundee, and took the ferry there. Once across, however, they could get no chaise. Again they had a difficult time of it. Elizabeth Inchbald rode in a cart to Cupar, where they all had tea. "At night they set off in a cart again—it was a dismal night—perfectly unsheltered, they were all wetted to the skin, and in this chilled and miserable state, slept at a small public-house. On the morrow they had, in defiance of rheumatism, to put on their wet clothes; but, however, they were driven in a cart very fast to Kirkaldy. They crossed the water to Leith, and took a coach to Edinburgh, overjoyed to arrive at their old lodgings."[14]

By the end of the year 1773, Mrs. Inchbald had become an experienced actress and an experienced traveler. Being an experienced traveler, however, did not mean she could avoid the hardship of their precarious existence. Sometime during 1773–1774, Digges being absent, Joseph Booth, a member of the company, became the temporary manager. A versatile man, he was a portrait painter as well as an actor. Although he was usually quite ingenious, he failed once: the company was denied permission to play in Glasgow, and having no funds, "they were all in the utmost distress. The whole stock was detained for rent and board, & at an inn. From this awkward situation they were liberated by a young Scotchman, who had just joined the company in a kind of frolic, and who paid their score, and set them off to Kilmarnock, and from thence to Ayr, where they had a brilliant run of good fortune." In the 1780s when Booth became the assistant prompter at Covent Garden, he remained a friend of Mrs. Inchbald's.[15]

A DECLARATION OF INDEPENDENCE

In the beginning of the year 1774, Elizabeth began to study French; Joseph again listened to her rehearse at home and on their walks by the sea or on the hills; the boy Bob played cards with her, and on January 10 her brother George arrived. During the cold and damp of January and February, both she and her husband were ill. During this time she began to write, although she does not record what she worked on. She seems to have written from the time she was a child; when she began to think she could make such writing useful for others is not clear. The French she had begun this year was in the end essential to her professional career, as we shall see. And about this time she records that she quarreled with her husband about "parting" of salary. She had not yet been married for quite two years, but she had already declared her independence; she had also in many ways established her character. Determined, volatile, loving, she did not mind working at her professional duties; she was willing to be a part of the company even though that meant she was constantly surrounded by people; and even though she much depended on her husband, she wanted a "parting" of their salaries. Joseph Inchbald himself was a rather relaxed, affable person. He was sometimes away with Wilson, leaving his wife in solitude, but he also was her willing partner and teacher in rehearsing her parts. Theirs was a good marriage.

The Inchbalds remained with the company until the end of the spring season in 1776. During these years there were times when Mr. Inchbald and Mr. Bland were the managers while Digges attended to his own affairs—both professional and personal. And at times the company was split, acting in two different places. This was evidently the case in 1775 when Mr. Inchbald, Mr. Webb, and Mr. Smith shared the responsibilities, since Digges was away all summer until September 18. Managing a company involved a variety of problems, not the least of which were the relationships among the families. For example, George Simpson, Mrs. Inchbald's brother, quarreled with Digges, and Mrs. Inchbald was obliged to help him and his wife become reinstated after they had paid a forfeit of five pounds, quite a significant sum for them.

During the summer of 1775, Elizabeth Inchbald was dangerously ill again, unable to act until October, when she played Jane Shore at the request of the ladies in Dumfries. Never one to be idle, she studied French and read even though she did not have strength enough to act—she always read; this summer she read accounts of Spain, France, and Italy, and she used all such knowledge in the future. In Scotland during these years she was faithful to her duties as a Catholic, and since Christmas 1775 was on a Sunday, she went to prayers three times. She also had an interview with the priest as the year 1775 came to an end. On December 30 she played Violante in *The Wonder*, and Digges made her a present of a beautiful pair of earrings and a necklace to match.

Boaden does not give any information about how much the Inchbalds were paid. They, like the other members of the company, counted on a double salary, plus some extra for his son Bob, who played children's parts. Just what was expected of Mrs. Inchbald for the expense of her costumes is not clear either, though she probably was expected to provide her own. Later in her pocket-books she records the sums she spent on providing her costumes; sometimes it was a considerable amount of her weekly salary. Once Digges gave her a silk gown, and once he wrote her a note requesting that she "dress in a matron-like manner." When she was well, she acted three or four times a week, as did her husband. In addition, he supplemented their income by painting, and more than once he painted a portrait of her.

During these years Elizabeth was a regular attendant at Mass, wherever she happened to be; in Scotland, where there were many Catholics, the chapels were easy to find. In England, however, the government and the church restricted Catholic worship to private chapels. In these years in Scotland, Elizabeth was in constant touch with her family, writing to her mother, receiving letters in return, and hearing from her sisters in London. Her sister Mrs. Slender wrote to report the death of her husband; her sister Debby, she heard, had gone to France; and the work on the farm continued as usual. Living in our world, it is difficult to understand how important letters were to Elizabeth Inchbald and her world. Her pocketbooks are filled with the records of the letters she sent and the ones she received.

THE YEAR 1776: A TURNING POINT

In 1776 the Inchbalds left Scotland and looked for new work. It was also a year in which Mrs. Inchbald was again frequently ill. In January she records in her pocketbook that she had such a bad cough that she was unable to play her part of Juliet; her sister-in-law Mrs. George Simpson played for her, and on January 12 Mrs. Inchbald lost her wedding ring as she acted Imogen to her husband's Iachimo. It had slipped off probably when she washed her hands; she paid Mrs. Waterson for finding it, but it was a kind of symbol of the problems they faced, most of them having to do with family. Now not only were George Simpson and his wife members of the company—sponsored by the Inchbalds—but Mr. Inchbald's older son, George, had been added to the family group as well. Young Bob was still there, now four years older than in 1772 when he and his father and his stepmother had become members of the company. By now Mrs. Inchbald's pocket-book makes it clear that she, rather than her husband, managed family matters. Four years after her marriage, she seems to actively manage their relationship and their responses to both his family and hers, as well as having an important voice in their professional decisions with Digges.

Her 1776 pocket-book also reveals all kinds of information about the company, about Digges, about her family, and about finances and how the company was handled. For some reason she was even more depressed about her acting; she was never satisfied, but in early January she was more upset than usual. She wrote in her pocket-book, "Mr. Inchbald said Miss Mills was worth more than me," but two days later she records, "I was at the reading of Philester while my hair was dressing Mr. Inchbald heard me in my part." She played Rosalind in *As You Like It*, and she finished her entry for the day with "I went to bed crying c&c for playing very ill." On the following day she drank tea with her brother George, but her husband called at her brother's and had words with him; she adds, "after I cry'd c&c." During all this time there seems to have been an ongoing discussion about finances, about her brother and his wife as members of the company, and about the relationships with her husband and his sons. She says she worked by herself and "was cross." She was at this point studying French and reading *The Sufferings of Christ*. Mr. Woods, the manager, sent Mr. Inchbald a note that she answered, and she was in Digges's box at *The Fair Penitent* while Mr. Inchbald played Horatio, the part of the wronged husband in the play.

In addition to answering her husband's note, she managed his money—or at least she tried to do so. On the Thursday and Friday of the second week in January, they evidently had a great quarrel. Her entry tells the story: "Was at Reh. of Philaster then Mr. and Mrs. McPherson sent for Mr. Inchbald to borrow money of him. We had words about it. I play'd Lady Percy he Henry the 4th. . . . After Mr. Inchbald came home we had high words about what he said to me in the Green room c&c." In early January she worried about their salaries. Her comment about being "uneasy about our salary" reveals a concern of hers. She was, however, working with a "French master" almost every day. Some of these early entries about money are very revealing, for they show her concern and show also a kind of pattern among the players. The finances of all the companies in the provinces were dependent on the whims and pleasures of local audiences, audiences who felt they could dictate the choices of plays and could reject players whenever they chose. Already at this point in her marriage she was determined to manage her finances, whatever the situation about "our salary" might be.

Her account of expenses in the 1776 pocket-book, the first we have, gives a vivid picture of the "necessities" of a person in her position in Scotland. One item that is a constant is "washing"—March 4–10 it amounted to 3 shillings 6 pence; she paid her French master 1 pound 1 shilling for twenty lessons; she bought a pair of white leather gloves for 1 shilling 6 pence; the next week washing was 3 shillings 5 pence 2 farthings; there is never any explanation for the variations. Two items she continually records are the letters she paid for—those sent to her— and the money she spent on shoes. Since the roads were almost impassable, the footpaths and streets must have been very rough; in one entry after another, she pays for shoes of various kinds and for repairing shoes. She paid 3 shillings 6 pence for a pair of "black stuff shoes"; three weeks later she paid 4 shillings 6 pence for a pair of black shoes. She spent 7 farthings for having her petticoats mended, 10 shillings to have a muslin cap made, and 11 shillings for ribbon for the cap.

One interesting document is a receipt for shoes, covering January, February, and March, signed by Geo. Williams and marked "paid in full." On January 11 the item was "one pair shoes for Geo. Inchbald"; the second item, on January 20, was "one pair soling." The first cost £1 5s. 6d.; the "soling" cost 2s. On February 10 the item was one pair of nankins (a kind of soft shoe) for Elizabeth Inchbald for 4s. 6d. On March 5 the charge was again for "soling," 1s.; on March 16 one pair of shoes was purchased for Joseph Inchbald at 5s. 6d., and on March 20 one pair of nankin shoes for Elizabeth at 4s. 6d. Surely shoes would have been a constant item of expense because of the weather and the conditions of the streets and walkways.

From the brief entries in the account, it is difficult to tell which items might be stage expenses. In March Elizabeth bought seventeen yards of gray silk for a gown and a petticoat at 4s. 4d. a yard for £3 18s. 9d., and the next week she bought a lining for the petticoat, body lining for the gown, and ribbon. She paid 1s. 3d. for the gown and petticoat "making," she spent 4d. for black lace for her apron, 10s. for ribbon for a cap, and 8d. for "my riding sleeves making." In May, after Joseph had been ill, she entered 1s. for his "chair" to the house and hers from the house. Evidently he was too ill to play, and she needed to be at rehearsal. She records, "Mr. Inchbald very ill and my cold very bad—The doctor called twice in the morning—I went to Rehearsal. . . . we were both better after we came home." These expenditures were recorded for the second week of May.

The records of her expenses are important not only to indicate how much money she spent; they also give information about clothes, food, and expenses in Scotland in 1776. Elizabeth had a dressmaker, but she herself had selected the material for the dress and petticoat and for the trimmings as well, and the amount she spent for these items is an interesting record of costs. She certainly could not have been extravagant, for she had little money, but these entries make valuable comments on the places where she lived and the times; years later, when she was in Ireland, her records show that materials were much more expensive.

As the month of May went on, the Inchbalds became quite unsettled. For some reason that Elizabeth never makes clear, they seem to become more and more dissatisfied with their situation. Race Week was the first week in June; the first day was wet, and Joseph Inchbald spent it at the house, she at "the French." On Tuesday she records: "Mr. Inchbald was at rehearsal in the time I was at French. After we had words about Mrs. Mills. He was out all afternoon with Mrs. Claggert. . . . I answered my mother's letter. . . . he had high words with me in bed." On Wednesday the entry reads: "was off with Mr. Inchbald and to bed while he was at rehearsal. . . . Was in Mr. Digges's box at the 'Journey to London.' We came home before the Lying Valet." She walked alone, and on Sunday she "rose before

Mr. Inchbald" and had her hair dressed. When she got to church, the sermon was already finished. This week Joseph was doing a picture of Mr. Claggert while she continued to work on the French. On Wednesday of this week, there were two items of great importance—"Was a little off with Mr. Inchbald and I at the French—then he came home told me of the dispute with Mr. Digges about my Jane Shore and I went through it to myself." On Friday of this week, there was more trouble; Joseph continued to work on Mr. Claggert's picture, and Elizabeth worked on French. Although she was called to rehearsal, she says she "had a great mind not to go." That evening their friend Mr. Webster called to tell Joseph that the audience would riot on his account. She says, "I was very uneasy."

The next day, a Saturday, Mr. Inchbald went to see Digges, and she followed him only to go through a single scene at rehearsal. That night, as she had feared, "there was a riot as we had expected on Mr. Inchbald's account I was present at the conclusion—and after was very uneasy and hardly slept all night." She gives no explanation of the reason for the riot, but audiences frequently created a disturbance with very flimsy excuses. Since there was always an interaction between the audience and the players, any small disagreement could bring on a riot. In this case it is even more puzzling: evidently Digges had returned and was again the director of the company, but given the circumstances, he could do nothing. As strollers, the Digges Company was entirely dependent on the audience for support, and the audience knew it could demand and control its choices of both plays and players. Boaden suggests that Mr. Inchbald had become overconfident and did not show enough respect for the audience's wishes; as Boaden said, "offence is given to those, who will not be offended with impunity."[16] Wilkinson, in his *Wandering Patentee,* gives one report after another of the riots he had observed, sometimes on his own account. After telling of one such occasion, he remarks that in the country, as opposed to London, the "performers are looked on as entirely subservient and dependent. The most trifling offence to one is immediately espoused by the whole, and the performer has very little chance for relief, unless he proclaims his humility and sorrow for offences past."[17]

The Sunday entry in the pocket-book reads: "I slept toward morning and then was angry with Mr. Inchbald and went to prayers without speaking to him— a very wet morning—when I came home from prayers he was out—when he came home was easy and satisfied—Mr. Johns called and dined and drank tea here—after he was gone Mr. Inchbald and I talked of leaving Scotland next Tuesday." But on the next Tuesday she wrote: "I was almost of the mind not to go away Tuesday next with Mr. Inchbald and went to the house to tell Mr. Digges so and he persuaded me to the contrary."

Evidently Joseph Inchbald did not go on stage again after the riot; he continued to paint, however, and to go about, sometimes without her. She writes in her pocket-book: "Mr. Inchbald went to the Webbs while I was at the French. . . . Mr. Inchbald sent word he dined at the Webbs. . . . I was angry—Bob called in the afternoon and drank tea with me—in the time Mr. Inchbald came home. I was a little off with him—At the French after we walked to Mrs. Wells and called on the Thompsons." The Webbs were longtime friends, Mr. Webb having been with the company from the beginning, when the Inchbalds and Wilson joined the company in 1772; sometime afterward Mr. Webb had married. In the beginning he was one of those young actors who flirted with Elizabeth Inchbald, which of course did not please her husband, but now four years later, the Inchbalds and the Webbs were friends.

On Friday, June 28, Joseph, going to make arrangements for their sailing, found that the ship did not leave until the following Wednesday. During these last days, Elizabeth went to prayers almost every day, studied French, and as the time drew near she packed; they had new boxes and they "tryd" them before they packed them to ship. She wrote letters to friends and family, and she "looked over old love letters." She does not say whether she kept or destroyed them; considering the unsettled life they lived, it is difficult to see how she could keep anything, but she evidently kept not only her pocket-books but various letters and other documents as well. On Monday, July 1, after breakfast, a lady called with a letter to France; they went to see Digges and "had much talk," and after they dined, they finished packing. She says they went to many places and saw friends, and at two o'clock the next morning, they left Edinburgh. In many ways they left behind a chapter in their lives. And this year of 1776 continued to be one problem after another for them. Unfortunately, we have no way of knowing just when and why the Inchbalds determined to seek another and better place in France. Had they heard from friends? Did Elizabeth think she could find some kind of employment? Were they simply so naive that they thought Joseph could support them with his painting? Perhaps they had planned to go for quite some time, and the riot simply gave them a reason to make the break; perhaps she had begun to study French as a part of a plan. She does not mention such a scheme in her pocket-book, but the couple had become increasingly restive. Perhaps she really did think her mother would help by sponsoring their plans, even though in the early spring she records that her mother sent a letter back, unread. She does not say what the contents of the letter were, but she does say that it had been approved by both her brother and her husband.

Mrs. Inchbald had changed, had learned, since the time she was interviewed by Dodd on that spring day in London in 1772 when she threw the basin of hot water in his face. Nevertheless, she must have been very unsophisticated indeed to suppose that they could live for a year in Paris on the money they had in hand. At this point it is also evident that she depended on her husband to make plans for them. As independent as she was about their money and domestic arrangements, she was still the conventional wife looking to her husband for direction.

Moreover, it turned out that they encountered all kinds of difficulties on their journey. They took ship on July 7, but the elements did not favor them; they were becalmed; Elizabeth was very unhappy, and nothing her husband or the captain of the ship could offer made her happy. The crossing to France turned out to be very difficult.

Judging by the independence that Mrs. Inchbald had begun to express about her own money and social life, it must have been very strange for her to spend the days and nights as a wife. Her own account of the trip, in her pocket-book, is filled with small details that add to the picture of her frustration—all the way from the weather that delayed their passage from England to France to her dependence upon her husband for the pattern of their daily life in Paris. Mrs. Inchbald, always seasick, was very cross with her husband while they were on the ship, and the passage from Shields to St. Valleri, which should have taken them no more than four or five days, took two weeks; during the week of July 15–21, they spent some several days "anchored seven miles from Yarmouth." There are only two entries in her account for this week—1s. 8d. for washing and 9d. for "fruit and flowers Mr. Inchbald bought on shore for me." When she was not violently ill, she read in *Paradise Lost* while he was reading *Saloman's Geography*. He played on a fiddle, and during the second week, when the wind "blowed hard," she was very frightened and was sick again. On fine days she sat on deck; it was very hot some of the time, and she records, "Mr. Inchbald was angry with me for not shifting—I laid in bed late then cryd much." The captain and Mr. Inchbald went ashore, but she did not.

Writing about this trip, Boaden gives his own view: "The Inchbalds were come to France to fraternise with its arts and its language, and their plan was for the husband to take lessons in painting, and the wife in French, as soon as they were a little settled at Paris." Boaden continues, "and to be an English Catholic, reconciled in a great degree the people of France to two not very splendid travellers from England."[18] They had no difficulty in making friends; some of their English friends who were already there came to call, and they met a Friar Jerningham, who helped them see the great churches (as was often the case, he remained friends with Mrs. Inchbald long after their visit to Paris). They were also befriended by an *abbé* who helped them see the city; that is, Elizabeth found his knowledge of the theatre and opera fascinating, but Joseph was hardly so enchanted, and she was obliged to hear her friend tell about the opera rather than go to see for herself.

The visit to Paris was all too brief. While they were there, she records in her accounts various charges for being shown the monuments, especially the churches; she records money spent for fruit and nuts in the gardens. In the week of September 9–15, she paid five shillings for a pair of black slippers and one shilling for "my riding hats cleaning." On September 18 they returned to England; their trip that was to have lasted for a year or so was over in less than three months. They had no money; she cried because she had to leave without her cat, and they walked in the fields, without food. Boaden says they went without dinner or tea and "once went into the fields to eat turnips instead of dining." While they were in Brighton, they went to the theatre, no doubt with "orders," free tickets, that is, given by some friend acting in the theatre. "Eating turnips in the fields" is a frequent remark about impoverished actors, but in this case it must have been literally true since Mrs. Inchbald records it in her pocket-book.

On September 30 they left Brighton and went to London. There they found friends—Mr. Inchbald's friend Dick Wilson and their former manager Digges. But nothing developed for them in London. Perhaps Joseph Inchbald knew that there would be more opportunity in the country; consequently they went first to Chester, where again they met friends, and from there they went to Liverpool, where he arranged for them to act with Joseph Younger.[19] It turned out to be a fortunate assignment, for it was there that they met the Siddonses, and shortly after they arrived, Digges appeared. Elizabeth Inchbald played Lucia in his version of Addison's *Cato* and Anne Bullen to his Wolsey in Shakespeare's *Henry VIII*. And again she began to correspond with members of her family, not having done so since the trip to France.

It was also here in Liverpool that the Inchbalds had word that their boxes shipped from Greenock, some six months before, had been lost off the Isle of Man; a month later the boxes arrived. Boaden's comment is worth quoting, for it underscores the problems of travel: "—the well-timbered trunks, that were doomed to lie wind-bound, for weeks together, in some unpassable roads, on board vessels not so fortunate as to be lost, (for insurance can make that easy to their owners,) but out of time and short of provision, rotting for want of action, and losing all passengers that could *afford* to lose their patience and get into a stage."[20]

The Inchbalds had certainly had enough bad experiences with ships and water, roads and post coaches, in 1776. After that unsettled year, 1777 proved equally varied, though by the end of 1777 they were with Tate Wilkinson and his

York Company; they could ask for nothing better—that is, nothing better in the country. Neither of them talked of London, perhaps because she continued to be unhappy with her acting, and perhaps he thought they would be better off for the two together to remain in the country than for him to try to return to Drury Lane.

They arrived in Liverpool on October 10; on the eighteenth she played Juliet and her husband played Capulet; on the twenty-first she was very upset about her performance in *The Mourning Bride*, but Younger himself had said to Mr. Inchbald that she had played "well." She had not been on stage since the summer just before they left for France; it is not surprising that she felt unsure of herself. Boaden's report comments, "The family harmony seems once more re-established, though she does not feel herself quite settled in her profession. Liverpool and Manchester were resting-places for a time." But even so, they continued to have adventures in their travels.[21] Mr. Inchbald played constantly in December of 1776; she did not play so often, but she began to make friends among the Catholics in the community, and several times, she records, they played cards. As the year came to an end, she performed two of her usual roles in *Jane Shore* and *The Mourning Bride*.

Joseph Younger, with his friend George Mattocks, was the manager of the theatres in Liverpool and Manchester during this season of 1776–1777. He had had experience in Edinburgh in the 1750s, and in 1760 he became the prompter at Covent Garden, where he also acted, in spite of the fact that he had a severe lisp. By the time the Inchbalds joined him, he had been manager at Birmingham in the 1760s and in 1776 in the summer at Hull. George Mattocks, his partner in Liverpool and Manchester, was an actor, a dancer, and a fine singer in his early career, but by the time he and Younger became partners, he seldom acted. Instead he was featured as a singer at Covent Garden in the winter season. Both Younger and Mattocks serve to illustrate the roles of managers and those who were important members of the theatrical community even though they were not very skilled at acting. In the case of Younger and Mattocks, they also serve to illustrate the uncertain affairs of those actors who became managers. In many cases they were not successful.

On December 17 the company went from Liverpool to Manchester, leaving at about eight in the morning in a post coach; by ten o'clock they were overturned, but no one was hurt, and by six in the evening they were in Manchester. Such detail came from Mrs. Inchbald's pocket-book, as did the information that on January 18, 1777, the Inchbalds met Sarah Siddons's brother John Philip Kemble. In the days and weeks following, the Inchbalds and the Siddonses became close friends as they all enjoyed each other in a domestic situation, John Philip frequently reading to them in the evening.

The company they joined with Joseph Younger was an interesting group, quite unlike Digges's company and the company in Scotland. Younger had not had so much experience in managing a company as had Digges, and the company itself was a rather young group of players. Many of the members became very distinguished in the years afterward, and among those destined to become celebrated were Sarah Siddons and her husband, William. The Siddonses had already had a rather eventful career in various companies before this summer and fall of 1776.

Mrs. Siddons was the daughter of Roger and Sarah Kemble. The Kembles were a family of actors. Sarah Ward Kemble's father, John Ward, was a player, and after she and Roger married in 1753, they remained in her father's company. Their first child, Sarah, was born in Wales while they were touring in 1755, their second, John Philip, in 1757. Sarah married William Siddons in 1773. He and she acted in her father's company. Sarah was baptized a Protestant, as were her younger sisters; the sons, Sarah's brothers, were baptized in the Roman Catholic Church, and both John Philip and Charles were designated for the priesthood. John Philip was sent to the English College at Douai, but finding that the priesthood was not his vocation, he returned to England and joined a company of strolling actors.

After their marriage and before Mrs. Siddons went to Drury Lane in 1775, the Siddonses had acted with various companies, and in fact Sarah had been in Younger's company when she went to London in December of 1775. David Garrick had hired her in the summer of 1775 upon the advice of friends, but because she was pregnant, she did not make her debut until December 29, when she played Portia in *The Merchant of Venice*. Her debut was a disaster, and although she played during the remainder of the season, she was not given a contract for the next year. Garrick's last season was 1776, and perhaps he could not support her any longer; in any case, she was very bitter about the whole experience.

As soon as the London season was over, the Siddonses had returned to Younger and his company in Liverpool for the summer; they were there when the Inchbalds joined the company in October. Boaden, using Mrs. Inchbald's 1776 pocket-book, follows the Siddonses and the Inchbalds from October 11, when Mr. Inchbald made an agreement with Younger, until the summer of 1777, when the Inchbalds went to Canterbury and the Siddonses went back to Liverpool.[22]

Another family associated with Younger were the Farrens—Margret, the mother, and her three daughters, Elizabeth, Kitty, and Peggy. Elizabeth, the eldest of the three, had by 1776 acquired quite a reputation. Born in 1762, she began acting as a child; in 1774, when the family joined Younger, he cast her in several important roles, even though she was only fourteen, such as when she made a memorable success in playing Rosetta in the popular *Love in a Village*. When the Farrens came to Younger, they were desperately poor. John Farren, the father, had hoped to have his own company, but he was never successful, and the family had strolled from one place to another until his death in 1770. Younger was instrumental in getting Elizabeth Farren to London, where she was signed by Colman for the summer season in 1777.

It is a strange but remarkable fact that in 1776–1777 four of the most important figures in the London theatres of the future were in Younger's company, where they acted together and shared the adventures of travel from Liverpool to Manchester and back again. Elizabeth Farren became a celebrated actress especially notable in "fine lady" parts, and in 1797 she became the countess of Derby upon her marriage to Lord Derby. Sarah Siddons and her brother John Philip dominated the theatres in London from 1782 until 1815, and Mrs. Inchbald was a leading playwright for Covent Garden from 1784 until 1805. Their time together was brief, but later in London all of them were closely associated with one another.

In February Elizabeth Inchbald began a novel.[23] She had been reading *Lord Chesterfield's Letters* and *Gil Blas* in French and Pope's *Essay on Man*. In Liverpool she had read *Man of Feeling* and *Man of Nature* as well as a translation of Horace in English. She kept a commonplace book and recorded in it a digest of what she read, a practice she continued throughout her life.

During this spring Boaden finds Mrs. Inchbald very "unsettled." He immediately suggests that John Philip Kemble was the cause of her problems, that she had fallen in love with him, found her husband quarrelsome, and found refuge in being with Kemble. No doubt she was frequently upset with her husband—she had recorded their frequent disagreements in her 1776 pocket-book—but it was at this time that she began to question her religious faith. It is tempting to put together John Philip's leaving his training for the priesthood and her uncertainty about the church as being a part of their conversations, a possibility certainly as likely as a developing romantic attachment between them. John Philip was twenty, and later he was an extremely handsome man and quite enamored of the ladies. At this time, however, he must surely have been more interested in joining the company than in creating trouble between the Inchbalds. It was not until June 1777 that he became a formal member of the company, but then he remained through the winter and spring of the next season.

Sometime during this spring when Elizabeth Inchbald was "unsettled," she wrote to her Paris friend Friar Jerningham about a case of conscience; her letter, as related by Boaden, reads in part: "Can a person be admitted to the sacraments of the Roman Catholic Church, who confesses he has strong doubts of revealed religion; yet who, acknowledging his own incapacity to decide upon a question of such magnitude as the truth of the Scriptures, humbly submits his reason to the creeds of the Church, and promises to strive against any future disbelief as against any other temptation to sin?" Boaden in this same passage includes two prayers that he found in her papers: "No other actual sin, but great coldness and imperfection in all my duties, especially in my religious ones, as in prayer and fasting." And another even more poignant: "Almighty God! look down upon thy erring creature. Pity my darkness and my imperfections, and direct me to the truth! Make me humble under the difficulties which adhere to my faith, and patient under the perplexities which accompany its practice."[24]

Always in uncertain health, Elizabeth Inchbald was frequently ill and despondent, and the memory of her disappointment in the failure of their French journey must have been especially strong in these months. Remembering also her husband's behavior when he would not allow her to go to the opera and his inability to succeed as an artist in Paris must have still caused her pain. And in addition to her dissatisfaction and worry about her performances, she must have worried about the rather unstable company she found herself in. Quite aside from any response she made to the Siddonses or Kemble, or indeed to her husband, it is no wonder that she considered going home to Standingfield.

On March 24 the Inchbalds, the Siddonses, and Kemble, with two friends, Mr. Lane and Mr. Jefferson, went on a short excursion: they spent a few days at Northwick and then took country lodgings on Russell Moor. Boaden's account of this brief respite no doubt came straight from Mrs. Inchbald's pocket-book: "While her husband paints, Mrs. Inchbald reads with Mr. Kemble. In the afternoon they all walk out, and in the evening play cards, and sometimes get more infantine in their sports: these clever people go out upon the moor to play at 'blindman's buff' or 'puss in the corner.' Amid all the opening scenes of ambition or wealth, it is highly probable that every member of the party, at times, heaved a silent wish to be there again."[25]

Boaden, who always had an opinion of his own, not only presumed upon the future; he also found material to "place" Mrs. Siddons and remark that when she returned from London she "almost threw away ambition, and, buckling to her hard lot, passed many a day washing and ironing for her family; and, at the conclusion of her labours, regaled the society with a song, and lured her brother to join her in a duet."[26] At Easter the Siddonses went to York, at Wilkinson's invitation, Sarah making her debut there on April 15. She was very successful and remained in York until her benefit in May; after that she returned to Manchester, where the Inchbalds and Kemble had remained.[27]

While the Siddonses were in York, the Inchbalds and Kemble continued their association. Again Boaden uses Mrs. Inchbald's pocket-book: "Kemble began a course of reading now, that passed the time very profitably—the History of England; and Mrs. Inchbald wrote her notes of the important facts as he proceeded. But he was moreover, little as we should expect it, the very genius of kickshaws, and a master in all the tricks that could be done upon cards. His fair friend and he play together daily, (as she records, without fear of her fame,) with wax dirt thread, wire—any thing, in a word, that fancy could apply to the purposes of exercise and amusement."[28]

On their Sundays, though players, they did not forget that they were Catholics; and when not near a chapel, Mr. Kemble read the Mass in French to the Inchbalds. With great humility he put aside the scholar and the original Latin, which Douai had for years been riveting to his memory, and neither wished nor affected to be wiser or better than his companions.

Just how Boaden knew that Kemble "put aside the scholar" is not clear, but the use of Mrs. Inchbald's notes adds reality to these days and weeks when the Siddonses, the Inchbalds, and Kemble were in the provinces. Birmingham, Manchester, and Liverpool were already in the 1770s important cities in the developing industrial world of central England. According to one estimate, Birmingham had a population exceeding 70,000 at the end of the century, Liverpool 80,000 by 1800, and Manchester almost 100,000. Although by 1800 Mrs. Siddons, Kemble, and Mrs. Inchbald had long resided in London, they no doubt remembered their time in the three cities.[29]

According to Boaden, in her pocket-book Mrs. Inchbald writes on May 26: "I rose at three in the morning, and left Manchester in a post-chaise with Mrs. Siddons and her maid. The gentlemen rode on the stage-coach. They breakfasted at Macclesfield; after which they proceeded on their journey to Birmingham; Mr. Inchbald on horseback—Mr. Kemble was taken into the chaise by the ladies; till very late in life he was an indifferent horseman." Boaden continues: "At Birmingham, in their usual style, the Siddons and the Inchbald families lived together; and sometimes Mr. Inchbald painted in the apartment of Mrs. Siddons. . . . His wife went through her parts with Mr. Kemble, and, there will be little doubt, benefited much by his critical remarks."[30]

However compatible the Inchbalds, the Siddonses, and Kemble were in this association, they were suddenly informed against and forced to disband and go their separate ways. Both Younger and Mattocks, their managers, were respectable gentlemen, but in this instance they evidently did not have license from the authorities to act. Players were still considered to be "rogues and vagabonds," and when the magistrates chose to consider them such, they could forbid them the town. There was nothing to be done but for the whole group to leave and find other work.[31]

The Siddonses and Kemble went first to Warwick and then to Wolverhampton; the Inchbalds went to Canterbury, where they remained for some two months. This Canterbury summer "season" proved to be one of those ideal periods for both of the Inchbalds. They made friends with the Catholics in their neighborhood, and it was here that they renewed their friendship with Thomas Holcroft, who had been in Scotland with them and who became, like the Siddonses and Kemble, Mrs. Inchbald's lifelong friend. Boaden says that "The Inchbalds passed two months at Canterbury profitably and pleasantly."[32] She shared a benefit, and so did he, and with their two months' salary in addition to their benefits, they probably left Canterbury happily, especially since on August 16 Joseph Inchbald had a letter from Tate Wilkinson inviting them to join his company—the York Company.

Their friend Holcroft was not quite so fortunate; he continued to have difficulties making his way in the world of the theatres. Born in London in 1745, the son of Thomas Holcroft, a shoemaker, he was taken by his family on a wandering tour of England, sometimes as beggars, sometimes selling various wares; he called it "tramping the villages." Exposed to all kinds of severe weather even as a child, he, like Elizabeth Inchbald, was affected by various severe illnesses all his life. When he was still a child, his father sent him to work in the coalfields, driving the asses from the mines to the villages; as a teenager he was a stable boy at Newmarket, where he remained for three years even though he had a severe riding accident.

Holcroft's father was alternately abusive and indulgent with him, but he taught his son to read and encouraged him to educate himself. In 1764–1765 he was with his father in Liverpool, where he taught school for a few months and where at nineteen he married for the first time. He was then—and he remained—desperately poor, and the story of his marriage and his attempt to become an actor is the classic one of hardship and despair. He was in London briefly as a writer and even more briefly as a secretary to Granville Sharpe, the abolitionist, a post from which he was dismissed for attending a "spouting" club. He examined the possibility of joining the East India Company and going to India; instead, through a series of happenstance encounters, he became a strolling actor. By the summer of 1777, he had had some experience, acting in the Kemble Company in the early 1770s. His son William was born in 1773, and in 1774 he and his wife, with their infant son, joined the strolling company of J.C. Booth.[33] In the fall of 1777 he arranged a contract with Drury Lane, but for most of the season of 1777–1778 he did little acting; instead, he sang as a member of the chorus. He had a fine voice, could play a violin, and was a better musician than an actor. The summer at Canterbury was for him, as for the Inchbalds, an interlude before his career in London.[34]

After their time in Canterbury, on September 22 the Inchbalds went to Standingfield to visit her mother and other family members. During all these months, Joseph Inchbald had used his leisure time to paint. At Canterbury he finally succeeded in doing a portrait of Elizabeth to his satisfaction, and while they were at her mother's house, he painted a portrait of Mrs. Simpson's grandson.[35] Then on October 13 they went to Hull to begin their contract with Wilkinson and his York Company. They were at last stable professionals in a stable professional company.

THREE

WILKINSON AND THE YORK COMPANY

✍ When the Inchbalds joined the York circuit, they found many of their friends there, and in the months to follow they made new ones who were to remain their friends for the rest of their careers. Again their experience reaffirms the idea that the companies operated as organized entities, not as showcases for individual performers. The Inchbalds fit neatly into Wilkinson's schemes, and by 1777 Wilkinson had a very profitable circuit with competent players. In 1769 he had obtained a royal patent for York and Hull—the only other patents that had been granted outside of London were for Bath and Norwich, granted in 1768. Wilkinson's four other playhouses were never granted royal patents.

By the time the Inchbalds joined the company, the calendar year and the theatre season did not match; it is difficult to tell just how the "season" was counted. It did not follow the London practice; there Drury Lane and Covent Garden were the only patent theatres playing in the fall, winter, and spring, and the Haymarket was the summer theatre. In York Wilkinson offered the players the opportunity of playing during the whole year except for special occasions, such as Lent and official mourning times for public figures who had died. Moreover, his organization of the various theatre seasons in the cities on the circuit was carefully planned and publicized. There were subscription season plays, "bespoke" plays, and benefits, and the selection Wilkinson made for the subscription series in the various places where the troupe went very much reflected his clever selections of the traditional and the new: plays like Nicholas Rowe's *Fair Penitent* (1703) and Mrs. Hannah Cowley's *Belle's Stratagem* (1780).[1]

When the Inchbalds joined the company in Hull in October 1777, the year had been the usual round of places and times. In general it went like this: York, February–May; Leeds, June–July; York, August Race Week; Pontefract, August–September; Wakefield, September; Pontefract, October; Hull, October–January. Not only were the times set; the travel and lodging also proceeded on a regular basis—this was quite unlike some of the circumstances the Inchbalds had experienced before. For Joseph and Elizabeth Inchbald, the York circuit was, as Boaden put it, "a permanency . . . under that 'father of the fatherless.'"[2] Wilkinson was to be their friend for the rest of their time in the theatre.

Wilkinson had not always been the "father of the fatherless." In 1766, at age twenty-six, Wilkinson had been made a partner with Joseph Baker in the management of the York Theatre Company; he remained there until his death in 1803. His adventures as an actor are legendary and are recorded in great detail in his *Memoirs* and his *Wandering Patentee.* He not only tells where and when he acted and the characters he played; he also includes names and judgments about dozens—indeed hundreds—of other actors and actresses, and these places covered the major theatres in the provinces and in Dublin.[3] So complete are the details that Wilkinson himself gives that it has been difficult for later writers and critics to do more than use his judgments as a basis for the history of the York circuit.

Wilkinson was the son of the Reverend John Wilkinson, who was "her Majesty's chaplain of the Savoy, Chaplain to the Prince of Wales and rector of Coyty in Glamorganshire." Tate grew up listening to his father's sermons; he said, "My whole delight was in praying, preaching, burials, &." Tate was especially talented in mimicry, which more than once got him into trouble. In one of the most memorable such incidents, he was falsely accused of mimicking Peg Woffington. Samuel Foote also became very upset when Tate was part of a pirated production of Foote's farce *The Minor.* Both Woffington and Foote were important members of the theatre in London. Tate's impudent behavior was quite unacceptable, for he was very good at imitating facial expressions and body language as well as speech, and Tate's mimicry of Peg's body language and speech made clear she was no "lady." Peg Woffington, although she played "fine" ladies, was not one.[4]

When Wilkinson became a partner of Baker in 1766, he continued to act in addition to his work of refurbishing the York Theatre. The scenery was in a deplorable state, the costumes were dirty and worn, and the theatres in the circuit were as dismal and dirty as York—or more so. He worked to make more dignified the manner in which the actors solicited tickets for their benefits, he stopped the practice of allowing performers to "own" their roles, and he would not tolerate performers who did not learn their lines.[5]

In 1768 he married Miss Jane Doughty, and in 1769 their first child was born. In 1774 he built a new theatre in Leeds. In September 1776 he opened a new theatre in Doncaster. While he was attending to the expansion of the circuit, he was acting in various places; in May 1772 he was acting in Dublin at the Crow Street Theatre. In 1774, at the invitation of Digges, he was at Glasgow for a week. It was at this time that he must have become acquainted with the Inchbalds, who were also in Glasgow then.

The city of York had had a long history as the center of commerce and government. First under the Danes and then under the Romans, it anchored the north. During the thirteenth and fourteenth centuries, the great medieval walls and bars were constructed. York Minster, one of the world's great cathedrals, was built between 1220 and 1472. By the last quarter of the eighteenth century, when the Inchbalds came there, the city flourished not only as the center of commerce but also as a center of the arts and as the social center of the north. London was some two days away by stagecoach; thus, it is not surprising that theatre lovers attended the plays given on the York circuit—going to London involved a long and hazardous journey.

A brief look at a newspaper, Sherington's *York Chronicle or The Northern Post and General Advertiser*, reveals the kind of public and social events the citizens had at hand.[6] In the January 3, 1777, issue, there is a long account of the American Revolution, reported from the "lately arrived" Captain Gardner, who was General Howe's aide-de-camp. His report detailed the British action near Rochelle and Eastchester, New York, and was followed by a list of the dead and wounded given by rank, not by name—the Hessian Corps had a separate listing.

There were the usual notices: a list of prizes in the lottery; a list of those who had deserted from a recruiting party; and advertisements for tailors, furniture makers, carpenters, and joiners. There were various items advertised for sale— houses, horses, books. The announcement for the plays in the February 7 issue was followed by a "wanted" ad: "A Curacy wanted immediately, by a person in Deacon's orders, of unexceptionable character—for particulars inquire of the printer of this paper."[7]

There was an announcement in the Friday, February 14, paper for "An apprentice—Boy—13—absconded from his master, a farmer. Anyone who employs or harbors the said apprentice will be prosecuted." And on the twenty-first there was a long column about a masquerade: "near twelve o'clock near 600 masks were assembled in the upper suites of apartments where refreshments of every kind were served with great plenty." The writer goes on to describe some of the partygoers and their dress, including a "fair Quaker, a mask as a bill taker from the theatre," who "bore a great bill on his pole and cushion, poorly ridiculing the new troop of French dancers." Supper was served on the level below the first level; it was hot and delicious, and the wine was delicious, too. At seven in the morning, guests were still there—some drinking below and others dancing upstairs.[8] Such an account is simply a single example of reports repeated week after week. Reading them reminds us of the material of plays and novels, material that Mrs. Inchbald was to use in the future.

Whatever she found in the newspapers, she could not have foreseen her association in the distant future with the advertisements for *Bell's British Theatre*. They ran in every edition of the *York Chronicle* in the early part of 1777 and are especially interesting when we realize how they must have seemed to people like the Inchbalds. The advertisement began in bold type: "bell's british theatre is now publishing in weekly numbers with magnificent embellishments, Price 6s each on fine paper, with fine first proof impression of prints. The Dramatic characters which accompany each play painted from life by Mr. Roberts of the Royal Academy by permission of the different performers on the London stages and afford the most pleasing descriptions of the individual persons and characters. The vignette Subjects for the title to each volume are furnished by the justly celebrated Mr. Mortimer, are most beautiful and picturesque excelling any other book embellishment executed in the kingdom."

According to the advertisement, some seven volumes of a proposed twenty-five had been completed. Some of the players in the illustrations are listed, including Mrs. Hartley as Lady Jane Grey. Considering the association the Inchbalds had with the Hartleys in the summer of 1772, which was something of a "look into the future"—the time when Mrs. Inchbald later did *Remarks* for *The British Theatre*—the advertisement is a kind of presentiment of that future.

When the Inchbalds joined the group in Hull, they found some of the friends they had known elsewhere as they met members of the troupe with whom they were to form lasting friendships; some of the actors had been with Wilkinson for some time, some remained with him for their whole careers, and some moved on to other assignments, especially if they had an opportunity to go to London. In any review of the actors and actresses who at one time or another were with the York circuit, it is quite remarkable that almost all of them had respectable careers—some of them, like John Philip Kemble and Elizabeth Farren, had quite extraordinary careers after they went to London. The Inchbalds' future no one could have predicted.

The Inchbalds began to be on stage at Hull immediately. Here they began an association with the other members of the group that was professional, not social. Joseph Inchbald began to play some of the principal parts, and Elizabeth Inchbald, too, began to do more than Jane Shore or Cordelia. She first appeared on a Tuesday evening, October 28 (the fourth night of subscription), in "A Tragedy, call'd The Roman Father / (written by William Whitehead, Esq; Poet-Laureate)." Wilkinson was "The Roman Father"; Mr. Cummins, Publius Horatius; and Mrs. Cummins, Valeria; in capital letters the playbill announced "HORATIA, MRS. INCHBALD, / (From the Theatre-Royal Edinburgh)." The play was followed by "Publius Horatius's Entry into Rome, In a triumphal Car." The entry was followed and accompanied by "vocal Parts." There were then a two-act farce, *The Irish Widow*, in which the Hitchcocks played, and finally dancing by Mr. and Miss West.[9]

This evening's program introducing Mrs. Inchbald was typical of the kind of entertainment Wilkinson offered his audience. The variety of spectacle, including music and dance, the combination of drama and pantomime, the play by a famous playwright—the poet laureate—all contributed to the success of the company. Wilkinson's choices and combinations for the entertainment of his patrons were very skillfully made. A review of his playbills shows that he was no ordinary manager and director. The Inchbalds certainly profited by their experiences with him.

On November 4 Elizabeth played the countess of Somerset in *Sir Thomas Overburry*, a play listed as "The last Tragedy. . . . This tragedy was written by the late unfortunate Mr. Savage and often performed last season at the Theatre-Royal, Covent-Garden, with great success." The "late unfortunate Mr. Savage" was Dr. Samuel Johnson's friend whose life Johnson memorialized in his *Lives of the Poets*. Johnson certainly did more than Savage himself to ensure his lasting fame—more than the play, which was a second version of an earlier one Savage had written. Johnson writes, "he had taken a resolution to write a second tragedy upon the story of Sir Thomas Overbury, in which he preserved a few lines of his former play, but made a total alteration of the plan, added new incidents, and introduced new characters; so that it was a new tragedy, not a revival of the former. . . . In the execution of this scheme, however, he proceeded but slowly, and probably only employed himself upon it when he could find no other amusement."[10] Johnson's comments about Savage were the comments that could be made of many of Elizabeth Inchbald's contemporary would-be playwrights, but not for her—she never "employed" herself "slowly . . . when [she] could find no other amusement."

On November 7 Joseph Inchbald played Oliver Cromwell in *King Charles the First; or, The Royal Martyr*. It is interesting to remember that Joseph was a Catholic; to play Oliver Cromwell must have required him to see the play/history as simply a play on stage. For most of the references Mrs. Inchbald makes about history, she followed the practice of her time and saw the plays, the playhouse performances, as enactments of the very real pageant of history.

On November 14 one of the first of the benefits was given for Miss Mucklow, a "Revised Hamlet," though how and to what degree the revision made the play different from Shakespeare's *Hamlet* is not clear. Mrs. Inchbald's friend Mrs. Hitchcock played Ophelia; she played the queen. The queen in *Hamlet* was a role Elizabeth played frequently, but this was the first time she played it as a member of the York troupe. The next evening she was Semiramis in *Semiramis, Queen of Assyria,* a performance followed this time by

> a new comic Dance, call'd
>
> The IROQUOIS as performed by Mr. and Miss West before their majesties and the Royal Family at their Palace at Kew.
>
> Their performance in this Dance as well as in the Comic Dance, call'd the
>
> Cow-Keepers, gave the highest Satisfaction,
>
> and was by command of his Majesty repeated twice in the same Evening by Mr. and Miss West,
>
> they are to be dressed in new Dresses, the Habits of their Country, as worn by the IROQUOIS INDIANS in AMERICA
>
> To finish with a comic Jig after the manner of the Iroquois Dance at their Festivals. The music is all Italian,

as printed on the playbill. Elizabeth played in *The Inconstant or the Way to Win Him* on November 18, and on November 25 she played Amestris in a revival of Rowe's *Ambitious Step-Mother.*

In Hull the Inchbalds lived on Finkle Street near the theatre; in York they lived in Stonegate, one of the ancient, narrow streets near the York Minster. That location was only a short distance from the theatre. Stonegate was also one of the streets that led to St. Helen's Square and St. Helen's Church, two of the oldest parts of the city. The theatre, opened in January 1765, was quite near the Minster. It had been enlarged by Baker, Wilkinson's predecessor, to hold some 550 spectators. All that remains today is the back wall, which almost touches a Roman Catholic church, an early-nineteenth-century building. But the remaining wall gives a sense of location, since it is clear that the front was just within Botham bar and just across from the Minster itself.[11]

The Inchbalds had their first benefit, a joint one this time, on a Tuesday, the "Last night but Two" of the Hull season. The play was *Cymbeline,* and the playbill is an unusually interesting one. Joseph Inchbald played Posthumus and Elizabeth Inchbald, Imogen, an assignment they had long been familiar with.

> End of the third act (by particular desire)
> An Interlude taken from
> LILLIPUT
> Between the Play and the Farce will be presented institution of The Order of the

Garter. Never performed but at the Theatre Royal Drury Lane, and then at the request of several people of Fashion, on account of the vast number of Nobility and Gentry who were Disappointed at Windsor, occasioned by the great concourse of people that were present at the grand ceremony, Mr. GARRICK added to the exact Representation several imaginary Characters, which met with general Approbation, and was performed upwards Fifty nights, with all the Machinery and Dresses proper to the piece.

The GENIUS of ENGLAND will descend in a CHARIOT encircled with Four TRANSPARENT Paintings. First Britannia presenting the MAGNA CHARTA; Second, The STAR and GARTER; Third, The EMBLEMATICAL Silver Anchor; Fourth, the George and Order supported by CHERUBINS in the CLOUDS.

The Genius of England, Mr. Cummins, First Druid, Mr. Inchbald, Second Druid, Mr. Leng, Third Druid, Mr. Buck.

Prince of Wales, Master Hitchcock
King Edward, Mr. WADDY.
Knights by the rest of the Company.
First Ariel Spirit, Mrs. Inchbald,
Second Ariel Spirit, Miss Holmes,
Third Ariel Spirit, Miss Mucklow.
Singing Bards, Mr. Wood, Mr. Butler, Mr. Suett, Mr. Eyles, Mrs. Beynon, Mrs. Leng, Mrs. Butler and Mrs. Hitchcock. To which will be added a musical Entertainment, called
The DESERTER
Henry, Mr. Wood
Simpkin-Suett
Flint, Mr. Colby,
Russet, Mr. Buck
Serjeant, Mr. Butler,
Skirmish, Mr. Inchbald.
Jenny, Mrs. Leng
Margret, Miss Phillips
Louisa, Miss Hitchcock.
Tickets as usual, and of Mr. Inchbald, at Mr. Hayton's in Finkle Street.

Their benefit was played during the season of Christmas, and the use of all the company suggests that it was indeed a festive occasion, made more so by the pageantry and the music. The next night, December 31, the Inchbalds played in *King Charles the First; or, The Royal Martyr,* she as the queen, he as Cromwell. This being the last night of the season in Hull, the company went to York to begin the season there on January 6, 1777; they remained there until May 18.

The Inchbalds played three or four times as often for Wilkinson as they had for Digges or Younger. Such activity seems to have pleased them both. Wilkinson's York circuit was certainly equal to the London theatres in the selection of plays, farces, and "entertainments" he offered. And the other members of the troupe were an interesting and varied group. They were playing with the Hitchcocks, the Cumminses, Dick Suett, and a whole list of others, as is evident in the playbill for their benefit performance.

The Cumminses were among those who spent most of their careers with Wilkinson. Dick Suett, or Dicky, as he was called, joined Wilkinson's company in 1771 upon the recommendation of Charles Bannister, a popular actor at Drury Lane. Suett had in fact been a "child" star in London, performing at both Ranelagh Gardens and Marylebone Gardens.[12] He was very talented, a singer as well as an actor, and his roles on stage were many and varied. He was especially good in low comedy characters; he played almost all such roles in the Shakespeare plays. He was, for example, always applauded in the role of the grave digger in *Hamlet,* a situation he made comic, not sentimental, as he appeared with a dozen waistcoats that he removed one by one. A review of his place in the York Company confirms his multitalented roles; he and the Inchbalds were frequently on stage together.

The family of the Hitchcocks were all friends of the Inchbalds, and again, as we have found with others, they all must have known each other long before York. Robert Hitchcock and his wife, Sarah, were members of the Norwich Company in 1769 after Griffith had become manager in November 1766. It was Griffith to whom the young Elizabeth Simpson appealed for a place in his troupe, where her brother George was already acting; it was he also who inspired her "crush" as a teenager when she stole his picture. Griffith remained manager of the Norwich Company until 1780, long after the Hitchcocks left. In the fourteen years that he managed the company, he developed it into one of the most important of the companies outside of London. Moreover, it was the Norwich Company in which Joseph Inchbald had acted and had become enamored of Elizabeth. Obviously the Hitchcocks, the Inchbalds, and Griffith and his family all knew each other.[13]

Although the Hitchcocks, the Inchbalds, and Griffith were acquainted, their careers only occasionally came together. Miss Hitchcock, the daughter of Robert and Sarah, was only slightly younger than Mrs. Inchbald, and she, like Suett, had acted as a child, appearing with her parents at York as early as 1772. Among others in this 1777–1778 season who became friends of the Inchbalds were the Kennedys, Mr. Waddy, the Lengs, the Phillipses, Mr. Buck, and the Wilkinsons themselves.[14]

The first night of subscription in York, Thursday, January 8, 1778, a tragedy, *The Roman Father,* was presented; Mr. Inchbald was not in it, but Mrs. Inchbald played Horatia and was announced as being from the Theatre Royal, Edinburgh, at the bottom of the playbill. On the fourth night of subscription, January 20, Mr. Inchbald played Hardcastle in *She Stoops to Conquer; or, The Mistakes of a Night.* He was introduced as making "his first appearance on this stage," which meant, of course, that the "never acted here" could be a repeat of a play in another theatre on the circuit. The playbill of January 20, 1778, reads in part:

Mr. Wilkinson's respects to the public, begs leave to assure them (whatever misconception or misunderstanding may have unhappily subsisted between him and the Gentlemen Proprietors of the Theatre) whether he has the Honour to continue as manager, or retain his property (on an equal footing) or not, he never shall lose sight of the Gratitude for Favours already received. As a proof, he has prevailed on Mr. Digges, manager of the Theatre-Royal Edinburgh, (a Gentleman whose merits are well known in the Theatrical World) to perform four nights at the York Theatre. Mr. Wilkinson hopes to be at York immediately, and doubts not but matters will be so adjusted between him and the Proprietors, as to render any future Dispute impracticable.

Digges then did perform for the Hitchcocks' benefit, which was *All in the Wrong*, with Elizabeth Inchbald playing Lady Restless and Joseph Inchbald the Quaker in the "comic opera" *The Quaker* that followed the main piece. For his own benefit, Digges played Falstaff in *Henry IV*; and for the fourth night, he played Sir John Brute to Elizabeth's Lady Brute in *The Provok'd Wife*. Boaden says that while Digges was there, he "seems to have had some confidential communication with her," which rather upset her husband, who, Boaden says, "seldom fancied any thing of this sort matter of mere indifference." Boaden explains that "the fact was, that she had always a very teasing love of admiration and attention."[15] Boaden, writing more than forty years after these events, could hardly be qualified to make such statements; he must have found something in her pocketbook that she herself had written. Since Elizabeth was young and beautiful and a friend of Digges, it is not surprising that they talked to each other; nor is it surprising that her husband should resent Digges's attention to her.

At York they lived in the same house as Mr. and Mrs. Waddy, continuing the kind of living situation that was usual for those on the circuit, who could hardly have commanded a house every time they moved from one place to another. Moreover, independent living would have been far too costly, and Mrs. Inchbald was already beginning to send money to her mother and her sister Dolly in Standingfield. There is no mention of Mr. Inchbald's son, who had lived with them in Edinburgh in 1772, but her correspondence and attention to her family was a constant part of her life. She had two aunts living in Hull, one of the cities on the circuit, and when the Inchbalds began their duties in September 1777, they visited with them.

Boaden, reviewing the year 1778 at York, remarks, "Her professional course at York had no particular features, except the personal intimacy of the manager's family; a matter of enviable distinction in this case."[16] From all accounts the Inchbalds became close friends of the Wilkinsons, the two families seeing each other socially as well as in the theatre.

On March 7 the Inchbalds' benefit was a production of *The Battle of Hastings,* with this notation added to the playbill: "Now performing at the Theatre-Royal Drury Lane, with great applause." The main piece was followed by the "Institution of the Garter—(by particular desire)" and a "new comic opera *The Quaker.*" The directions for tickets read, "Tickets as usual, and of Mr. Inchbald, at Mr. Cape's in the Mint-Yard." Wilkinson had worked to change some of the practices of the theatre. He had tried, not always successfully, to keep spectators from coming on stage or backstage during the performances. He had also tried to make the selling of tickets for benefit performances more professional, suggesting that friends of the performers go to the particular actors or actresses having the benefit rather than the reverse, as it had been in the past, when those whose special night it was would go about knocking on doors, promoting themselves and selling tickets.

On April 21 Wilkinson's own benefit was *School for Scandal,* "never acted here."[17] Joseph Inchbald was Oliver, Elizabeth Inchbald Lady Sneerwell. Elizabeth had declared repeatedly that she would not play Lady Sneerwell, but evidently she was willing to do so for Wilkinson. Boaden seems to imply that Lady Sneerwell was not the only part that she would not play except for Wilkinson's benefit. Before they left for Leeds on May 2, *Hamlet* was presented. Wilkinson had altered *Hamlet* in 1772; the playbill does not indicate whether this performance was Shakespeare's or Wilkinson's, probably Wilkinson's.

On May 18 the company left York and went to Leeds. It was here that Joseph Inchbald began to paint again—that is, he painted scenes. He had been rather too busy as an actor to have much time to paint portraits, but scene-painting combined his talents, making him more valuable to Wilkinson. On the playbill for May 25, a note informed the reader that Mr. Wilkinson was ill and obliged to defer the play *Tamerlane,* but shortly thereafter, for Mr. and Mrs. Leng's benefit, *Tamerlane* was done with Wilkinson playing the part of Bajazet, a stock part in which the character, representing the "wicked" Louis IV, is the villain. Tamerlane, representing William III, is the hero. The play by Nicholas Rowe was presented in 1701 by Betterton and his company in Lincoln's Inn Fields; it was immediately popular, and when the Whigs gained power after the death of Queen Anne in 1714, *Tamerlane* was presented each year on the fourth or fifth of November (the fourth being William's birthday and the fifth the day he landed in England) as a tribute to him and as a celebration of Whig party loyalty. It was a play frequently performed as a benefit.

From Leeds the company went to Halifax, and from there to York for Race Week; during Race Week there were no benefits, since this week was the most important one for ensuring the finances of the company. And during this week the town expected new or special plays. On Saturday, August 29, Wilkinson presented Burgoyne's *Know Your Own Mind*, with Mrs. Inchbald in the principal part as Miss Neville.[18]

On September 11 Mrs. Inchbald played the queen in *Hamlet*, and on September 14 she played Lady Sneerwell in *School for Scandal*. She did so again on September 18, "by desire of William Serjeantson and Peregrine Wentworth, Esqrs." Then the company went to Doncaster, where they were billed as "their Majesty's Servants"; the theatre at Doncaster was not a "patent" theatre.[19]

At the bottom of the playbill for October 2, 1778, a note read, "The School for Scandal being particularly desired, by several Families, and as it would be prejudicial to the Interest of the Theatre to repeat the comedy more than once, Mr. Wilkinson thinks it necessary to inform the public, it will be acted (on positively for the last time) on Mon. Oct. 12th being the last week of performing." Wilkinson, in planning the plays to be given, tried to please his audience with new plays and answer requests when it was possible, since his "bespoke" plays were supported by the patrons who requested them. Reviewing Wilkinson's playbills, it is easy to see how carefully he directed his company—even though financial success did not always follow.

From Doncaster the company went to Wakefield, where on Wednesday, October 21, Kemble was announced as Captain Plume in Farquhar's *Recruiting Officer*, "his first appearance on this stage." Joseph Inchbald was Sergeant Kite, and Elizabeth Inchbald, Sylvia. The friends were together for the first time since they had left Birmingham after the company had been informed against. The Siddonses and Kemble had gone first to Warwick and then to Wolverhampton; from there they went to Liverpool and joined the company directed by Younger.

From Liverpool Kemble had written to Mrs. Inchbald about the riot that occurred when the audience refused to attend to any players who had not played before the king. The Siddonses were shouted off the stage, the lights in the theatre were put out, the stage was trashed, and Younger was forced to return the ticket money. The letter is dated June 18. On June 21 Kemble wrote to Wilkinson seeking a place in the company. Given Kemble's recent experiences and his rather limited time on the stage—he had begun to act in January of 1776 with a group of strollers hardly to be called actors—it is to Wilkinson's credit that, recognizing Kemble's promising talent, he hired him.

Once he had joined the company, Kemble very quickly became the leading actor. When the company moved to Hull, Kemble's tragedy *Belisarius, or Injured Innocence* was presented. This was the play he had worked on when the Inchbalds and he had been together at Birmingham and she had begun her novel *A Simple Story*. He had written to her about his work, saying, "My tragedy has long been finished—long in Mr. Harris's hands, who sent it back to me a month ago unopened, with an assurance that it *would not do.*"[20] He also reported that he had written a farce called *The Female Officer* that had been played in Manchester "with great applause." Inquiring about her novel, he wrote: "Pray how far are you advanced in your novel?—what new characters have you in it—what situations? how many distressed damsels and valorous knights? how many prudes, how many coquettes? what libertines, what sentimental rogues in black and empty cut-throats in red?" His list certainly suggests that distressed damsels, prudes, libertines, and sentimental rogues were the popular characters in a novel. "I must know all this," he continued, "whenever you write to this quarter again, . . . write often. You would, if you knew the pleasure I receive from the good style, lively ideas, and polished manner of your letters."[21]

Mrs. Inchbald had indeed worked on her novel. She finished the first hundred pages in two months, showing from the beginning that when she set about to write, she did so rapidly, at least making a first draft. Completing her *Simple Story* turns out to be one of the major concerns of Elizabeth Inchbald's own story.

After Kemble's benefit of *Belisarius,* for the Inchbalds' benefit Wilkinson wrote: "For my friend Inchbald I got up the play 'Bonduca' as altered the preceding summer by Mr. Colman, in which I undertook the part of Caratach, and my son John, then only nine years of age, took the child's part of Hengo, which had been so well sustained by young Edwin in London. I need not say that my boy was well received and cherished, as all audiences on such occasions are ever liberal to the first start of endeavor and wish to give stability to the tender sapling."[22]

Both of the Inchbalds and Kemble were in *Bonduca,* as well as Wilkinson and his son. Again, Wilkinson's comments reveal more to us than to his own audience. His son's playing a part is, of course, the usual way the children of the players functioned as part of the production, and the "young Edwin" he refers to was the son of John Edwin the elder of Covent Garden and the Haymarket. "Young Edwin" made his first appearance at the Haymarket when he was ten years old. In later years his father created several roles in Mrs. Inchbald's plays.[23]

After he joined the company, Kemble began to play a variety of roles. One estimate suggests that he played some thirty roles from October 30 until the middle of January 1779. Kemble and the Inchbalds were frequently in the same performances: for example, on January 20, 1779, Kemble was Orestes in the *Distres'd*

Mother and Mrs. Inchbald was Andromache. On January 26 Kemble played Ranger in *The Suspicious Husband* while Elizabeth played Jacintha. On February 9 *School for Scandal* was given, with Kemble as Joseph and Elizabeth as Marie; although Joseph Inchbald was not listed in the cast, he was given credit for "the Picture Scene painted by Mr. Inchbald."

The Inchbalds and Kemble were frequently together with the Wilkinsons, and Boaden remarks that the Inchbalds "had now considerably enlarged their visiting circle, and at the close of the year she found herself able to read little more than the newspapers."[24] The spring season in Leeds was a busy one. One playbill announced that *School for Scandal* "cannot be performed for a considerable time on account of Mr. Wood and Mrs. Hitchcock being obliged to perform their contract with Mr. Colman at the Theatre Royal in the Hay-Market." Joseph Inchbald was in *The Funeral* on May 26 and in *Henry V* on May 31, and Elizabeth was in *School for Lovers* on June 3.

MR. INCHBALD'S SUDDEN DEATH

On June 4 the Inchbalds, along with several others in the company, went to Halifax on a party for pleasure; but, in Boaden's words, "as usual with the fraternity, they had an eye to profit in their pleasures, and performed there that evening." The next day they returned to Leeds. Suddenly on June 6 Mr. Inchbald died of an apparent heart attack. Mrs. Inchbald was devastated. She never forgot that "day of horror."[25]

Boaden's comment about her loss is significant not only with regard to Joseph Inchbald's death but also because it reveals Boaden's view of Elizabeth Inchbald and her marriage, a view written more than forty years later. No doubt by the 1830s, with the changing views of marriage and the family, a marriage such as the Inchbalds', between a couple of players in Wilkinson's York Company, was not seen in the same way as it was in the 1770s in Yorkshire. From their marriage in 1772 until his death 1779, theirs was, at least for the public, a quite conventional relationship.

Anyone reading Mrs. Inchbald's pocket-books finds that she is very candid about herself and about her husband. Always independent, she was frequently annoyed when he did not agree with her. Very early in their marriage, she claimed her own money, which she then spent as she pleased. She was not extravagant; nevertheless, she bought her own clothes, paid for her own washing—not his— and bought an occasional beer. But he always remained the head of the "household," even though she refused to live with him as long as his child lived with them. We do not know how long they lived apart, but they somehow worked out the problem, and by the time they were in York there is no mention of friction about Bob. The question of money, however, was frequently discussed; it was a subject that was especially complicated since, very soon after they were married, she had begun to give money to her family, a practice she continued for the rest of her life.

About Inchbald's death Boaden wrote: "That he was the object of her *romantic* love, we have before put at rest; but he had all the best influence of father, brother, counsellor and friend: that she had sometimes given pain by a rather too unweighed indulgence of her vanity, would no doubt be often felt by her, in her hours of retrospection; and all his fondness for her person, and zeal for her professional success, return to her, bitterly regretted, in the periods of her solitary struggle to make her way in the metropolis."[26]

Boaden, of course, was wrong; she made her way quite nicely. Under the circumstances, had he not died, they likely would have stayed with Wilkinson indefinitely, as did their friends the Cumminses. Boaden's picture of Elizabeth Inchbald's reaction to the loss of her husband takes no account of her independence, thinking that without him she could not continue to make her way in the world of the theatre. In spite of the materials he used, Boaden never understood her; he could not take the measure of her strength and persistence.

Her grief over her husband's death was quite natural, and everyone did what they could to console her. Kemble wrote an inscription to Inchbald's memory:

The Remains of
Joseph Inchbald, Comedian,
lie interred here;
a most worthy man,
who, leaving behind him
a very affectionate wife,
died
in his 44th year,
June 6th,
1779.[27]

Kemble also wrote a Latin inscription and sent it to the *Biographia Dramatica*.

Many years later Wilkinson wrote a special tribute to Mr. Inchbald in his *Wandering Patentee:*

Mr. Inchbald was my friend, my worthy man, my esteemed actor, in all my long "Pilgrim's Progress." For the time he was engaged with me, I never experienced more ingenuousness, honor, and integrity, nor did I ever know an actor of such universal worth, who confessed at least weekly, (if not daily) the comforts he felt in his Yorkshire situation, and ardently expressed an anxiety for the success and life of me, his manager, whose interest he, by every means, endeavored to support. He soon grew into great favour. . . . his painting (to which he had I believe been bred) also aided his popularity: His picture-scene, now in full sight, whenever the School for Scandal is represented, proves his talents, execution, and design.[28]

On June 14 a play was performed for Mrs. Inchbald's benefit; she stayed with the Cumminses and began to work on her writing again. On the twenty-sixth of the month, her husband's son, George Inchbald, came to Leeds, and upon her solicitation Wilkinson engaged him. George was Inchbald's older son and was already an experienced actor; according to Wilkinson he was a "young man of great service in a theatre, though not so attentive always as he should be, but of good behaviour."[29] After some time of mourning, Elizabeth Inchbald went with the company to Pontefract, where she lodged in an inn where George Inchbald and Kemble also lodged. She spent hours talking about her deceased husband, asking Kemble about death; after all, he and she were Catholics, and he, trained for the priesthood, would have been able to speak the language of the church with her. Boaden, an Anglican, remarks that she talked "no doubt as to the predisposition that led to so alarming and fatal a result."[30] Boaden makes no mention of any of the sorrow she must have felt about "Sudden Death," a condition of which she must have been acutely aware.

"Sudden Death" was a subject widely feared and much discussed throughout the seventeenth and eighteenth centuries. John Dunton, writing in "The Post-Angel" in 1701, warns: "Reader, let us live so, that we may not be surpriz'd by Death, and then 'tis no matter where, when, or how suddenly it comes." Sudden death in the eighteenth century came by means of an accident frequently, but the instances of those who "fell down dead, and never spake one word" were many and tragic. Dunton told his readers, "let sudden Death put us presently upon setting our House in order," lest we have "not so much as Time to say, Lord have mercy on my Soul." Dunton gave a set of directions to "prevent being surpris'd" by "Sudden Death."[31] Alas, no one in Mr. Inchbald's circle had given any attention to such a grave subject. Moreover, Mrs. Inchbald must have been completely overcome with the fact that "Sudden Death" gave no time for the priest to come and administer extreme unction to the dying "sinner." She must have remembered that her husband had summoned the priest when she had been at the point of death in Aberdeen, but in the end it was he who had been overtaken with "Sudden Death." For days and weeks she was inconsolable. She was only twenty-six, and her life had ended in one way and must begin in some other.

The playbills for July 1779 begin to list George Inchbald as Mr. Inchbald; it was not until several weeks after her husband's death that Elizabeth Inchbald began to act again, but she was reminded of him everywhere, as for example on July 7, when, for a performance of *School for Scandal,* the comment "The Picture Scene painted by the late Mr. Inchbald" gave him credit for the work he had done. No doubt the "Picture Scene" was used over and over, but surrounded by friends, supported by the kindness of Mr. Wilkinson and his wife, Mrs. Inchbald gradually began to return to her duties on stage.

Her life away from the stage continued to be centered on family and friends. She talked at great length with her stepson George Inchbald, and she received letters from family and friends. Dr. Brodie, the physician who had helped her recover from the dangerous illness she had suffered in Aberdeen, wrote to her. All her life she was attracted to doctors, who in turn treated her with special kindness. Sir John Whitefoord wrote to her, and a Mr. Waylett sent her a profile of her late husband. And while she continued her correspondence with her family and friends, she also began to write again.

By the last of August she had finished yet another version of her novel. She showed it to Kemble, to George Inchbald, and to the Hitchcocks; Kemble wrote her at length about it, but what he said is not extant. Considering that later, when it was published as *A Simple Story,* Kemble was said to be the principal character in it, his comments at this point in its composition would be very significant; the literary critics, however, will never be able to have such firm evidence, especially since there are no copies of the various states of this novel, a work she was to revise again and again before its publication in 1791.

On October 5 she sent her manuscript off to London, addressed to her friend Dr. Brodie, who, in turn, offered it to the trade. Again, it would be very gratifying if we could know to whom he offered it—to several different publishers, or only to Mr. Stockdale, who refused it. This novel was not published until some twelve years later; by that time Mrs. Inchbald was already a popular playwright, her plays published by the Robinson firm.

WORK BEGINS AGAIN

During the winter months of this year, Mrs. Inchbald read a great deal, and in early December she began a farce that she read to her friends. She was never one

to work in solitude, never one to be secret about her ideas—her plots and characters. Over the years she received a great many criticisms of her work, sometimes
adverse as well as favorable. She always considered comments, but most of the
time she made her own decisions as to how much her friends caused her to modify
her work. It is important, however, to realize how constantly she worked and over
how long a period. It is, of course, very frustrating not to have more of her early
manuscripts; the pocket-books reveal her emotions and her daily activities but
very little of the content of her writing. And these months in early 1780 were very
important in her gradual resolution to go to London, thus slowly making herself
even more independent and self-reliant than she had been.

In January of 1780 she went from Hull to York with the company and lodged
with a Mr. Tyler. The account of these weeks as recorded in her pocket-book gives
an interesting glimpse into the domestic life of the players. Several members of
the company, along with Elizabeth Inchbald, lodged in the same house—George
Inchbald, Miss Hitchcock, Miss Mills, Mr. Chalmers—and both Mr. and Mrs.
Tyler, who were their fellow players. Elizabeth paid twelve shillings a week for her
room and board; exactly what this entitled her to as a boarder is not clear. Did she
have a room of her own? A bed chamber? Most likely all the household shared the
dining room, using it also as a kind of reception room. Later, when she lived in
London, her accommodations varied widely depending on her financial and psychological state at the moment. In January 1780 she depended on the comfort of
her friends and shared with them the expenses of a boardinghouse.

In the early months of the year, she was very busy with rehearsals, performances, and her writing of one kind or another. Beginning with her pocket-books
for 1780, 1781, and 1783, we have an opportunity not only to follow her own
experiences but also to see the theatre world of London, because in 1780 she left
York and went to London to act at Covent Garden and the Haymarket. Moreover, these are the years that record her repeated efforts to have a play accepted for
the stage and then published. Denied repeatedly, she refused to give up, and the
record of her determination to succeed becomes a major feature of her life. Her
first play, *A Mogul Tale,* was not presented until the summer of 1784, but when it
succeeded, she became the "Celebrated Mrs. Inchbald"; she continued in that role
for the rest of her life.

On January 9, 1780, the company was in Hull, where she played Harriet in
The Guardian, and in the margin of her pocket-book she writes, "my night," meaning her benefit. In her accounts for this week, she records £12 1s. 6d. "after all
expenses," a tidy sum for a benefit in Hull. Having been in the company now for
some three years, she had made friends; she reports that the day before her ben-

efit, Miss Wilberforce and other ladies called for places and tickets. She saw Mr. Kemble in the evening, and an officer had come in the afternoon for tickets. On the day after her benefit, she played again and afterward "sat up very late reading in a magazine." She talked of going to London, and the next day she wrote to her friend Wilson. Wilson had been in London for quite some time by January 1780; he had had a varied and interesting career since the days in Scotland when he and Joseph Inchbald had stayed out all night, leaving Elizabeth to sit up until dawn worrying about their safety.

Wilson had been Mr. Inchbald's friend when they had acted together in Norwich in 1770 at the time when Mrs. Inchbald (then Elizabeth Simpson) had become acquainted with them; then in 1772–1773 he was with the Inchbalds in Scotland. Samuel Foote, after performing in Edinburgh for some weeks in 1774, engaged Wilson for the Haymarket in 1774 and 1775, and Wilson began acting in Covent Garden in 1775–1776, where he remained for the next ten years. Like most of the actors during these years, he frequently played in various places in the summer; most often, however, he was with Colman at the Haymarket. When Mrs. Inchbald wrote to him in January 1780, he was at Covent Garden; in June of 1780 he created the role of Lord Oldcastle in Colman's *Separate Maintenance,* and later that same season he created the role of Governor Harcourt in John Lee's *Chapter of Accidents.* By the time Elizabeth Inchbald began to ask for his help in her plan to go to London, he was well established there.

One of the problems during those early weeks of 1780 was that she had several interests moving along at the same time. She had parts to learn and re-hearsals to attend, she had tea with the Cumminses, and she talked of Mrs. Cowley's new comedy—it must have been *The Belle's Stratagem*—a play that was to become very familiar to her. She played in *The Mourning Bride* and afterward talked to Miss Hudson about a dress; after the play they talked of London, and Miss Hudson, she says, "told me about Mr. Harris." Thomas Harris was the proprietor of Covent Garden; George Colman the elder was the proprietor of the Haymarket. She was very soon to know a great deal about both men and both theatres.

On March 12 she sent her farce to Colman in London; that is, she sent it to a sister, probably Anne Hunt, who in turn took it to Colman. In her accounts for the week, she included the expense of sending the letter. During this week also she was much concerned with preparing her dress for Bellario; she calls it her "boy's dress." The part again had far more significance than she realized, for it was to be the first part she played in London. It was a role well suited to her, with her slender figure and golden hair; she was quite often cast in "breeches" parts.

All this spring she was very much aware that various gentlemen were giving her special attention. She continued to correspond with Dr. Brodie, now in London. What the relationship developing with Kemble during these months may have been is difficult to assess. One incident she found puzzling: when Kemble called one day and found her with company, he came back later saying "he came on particular business." His particular business seems to have been to caution her against her familiarity with Miss Wilberforce. Whatever reason he had "to have observed her conduct with a strong degree of interest," his behavior illustrates the way a gentleman thought to protect a friend. This episode is reported by Boaden; in the pocket-book Elizabeth writes of Kemble several times in a rather cryptic way. Once she writes, "Mr. Kemble rather petulant in what he said to me behind the scenes." She also records an incident about Kemble that happened when she was not present. It seems that Kemble had "words" with Mr. Anderson not once but twice, and George Inchbald reported the altercation to his stepmother. George also reported what Mr. Wilson said about her performance as Bellario; as the days go by, she writes that Mrs. Anderson has spoken up in defense of her husband. The references in the pocket-books confirm the view that Mrs. Inchbald was very much a part of the whole group of the players, that they were actually a "family"; and along with the comments about people, she continued to follow the performances in the theatre.

On March 23 Kemble came to take leave of her; he was on his way to London. But the following day he appeared again; she says she "was called to see Mr. Kemble who came to take his leave—he sat some time," and two days later, after having tea with Mrs. Taylor, she writes: "She told me what the people said of Mr. Kemble and my marrying." The rumors continued for a very long time.

All along these weeks in the spring, she talked to various people about her wish to go to London; gradually she developed a plan and began to seek a place at Covent Garden with Harris. "A gentleman sent by a Lady came to ask me if I was going to leave York." Kemble had gone to London briefly to debate at Cornely's House on "the Question Whether the representatives of the people ought to be answerable in a private capacity for what they may say in their official ones."

Mrs. Theresa Cornely had come from Germany and taken a mansion in Soho Square that she used for various public events, such as balls, concerts, masquerades, and other public occasions.[32] For a time she was very successful; she advertised the events in the press and passed out handbills. Conveniently located near the theatres, her mansion offered accommodations for a variety of events that, by the 1780s, could be staged by renting the facilities. It was here that Kemble "debated," probably sponsored by a "spouting" club.[33] In the entry of April 14, Elizabeth Inchbald says that she heard Kemble was ill, but the next week on

Wednesday she "heard in bed that Kemble had come." Two weeks later, in the midst of recording her reading—this time in Pope's poetry—she saw Kemble, walked with him, and talked again of going to London. The day following she "scolded" him, but as she was out walking again, he overtook her and told her of Smith's affair, a puzzling reference because it is almost impossible to determine which "Smith" it might have been; but of the two possibilities, especially since Kemble had just returned from London, it must have been the Smith who had gone away with Mrs. Hartley, only to be abandoned when she returned alone to Covent Garden. In the spring when Kemble was in London to hear the gossip, Mrs. Hartley had created the role of Lady Frances in *The Belle's Stratagem*, a part, though she could not have known it, that was to be very important for Mrs. Inchbald.

Throughout these months in the spring of 1780, the gossip and happenings of Wilkinson's company are of special interest to anyone concerned with the way his troupe operated. In the entries of the week of May 14, Mrs. Inchbald records a sharp disagreement that she was having about a part in *The Belle's Stratagem;* then Wilkinson told her she must go with the troupe to Edinburgh (by this time Wilkinson was operating two troupes—one in York and the other in Edinburgh); all this time she was trying to decide what she should do about signing articles to stay with Wilkinson or taking her chances in London. Joseph Inchbald, although no doubt instructed by her, had always made the arrangements with the various managers; now without him the situation was very different, very uncertain. Elizabeth, who was always ambitious, by the spring of 1780 was ready to move on, to go to London, to work on writing and publishing.

On Monday, May 14, she records in her pocket-book that she stayed up until five in the morning with Mrs. Hitchcock reading *The Belle's Stratagem;* later in the week she says that she had words with Mrs. Hitchcock "about our dresses." On Thursday, at the rehearsal of *The Belle's Stratagem,* she and Mrs. Hitchcock "changed our parts there." She continues, "I at mine and rather dull about it." On Saturday she says she dined by herself in the kitchen and afterward "Laid late and at my part in bed." She then packed her books and was behind stage at *The Jealous Wife,* but before the play was over, she left and walked out to Bothem Bar, where she met Mr. Wilson and told him of her quarrel with Mrs. Hitchcock; afterward she "made it all up with her at Mr. Wilson's."

The next week she continued to pack, to study her part in *The Belle's Stratagem,* and to rehearse; on Thursday of this week, she says she talked of Mr. Wilson and Mrs. Melmurgh in Edinburgh. There are some interesting observations to be made about all the items of these two weeks. For one, we are talking about Mrs.

Cowley's play *The Belle's Stratagem*, which was to become one of the most popular plays from its premiere in London on February 22 at Covent Garden.

Lady Frances Touchwood's role was created by Mrs. Hartley, the Mrs. Hartley that the Inchbalds had been with in Bristol that first summer after their marriage. She, like Elizabeth Inchbald, was tall and beautiful, with golden hair very much like Elizabeth's. Shortly after she performed the part of Lady Touchwood in the premiere, she retired from the stage after playing Lady Frances again on May 29, 1780. Her career had been filled with good parts, much praise for her beauty, and much gossip. In the summer of 1773, the next summer after the Inchbalds played with her, she was involved in a fracas at Vauxhall Gardens when the man she was with, Henry Bate, growing tired of what he considered the insults of some "gentlemen" who considered themselves her "admirers," engaged in a fight for her "honour."[34] Three of these "gentlemen"—Thomas Lyttelton, later known as the "wicked" Lord Lyttelton; George Robert Fitzgerald, called Fighting Fitzgerald; and Fitzgerald's servant, Captain Crofts, who served as a kind of bodyguard, were behaving in a very ungentlemanly fashion. Bate thrashed Crofts handily; there were duels, but no one was killed. Bate, who was the editor of the *Morning Post*, afterward was called the "Fighting Parson." The whole episode created a flurry of commentary in periodicals, newspapers, and a dozen or so pamphlets. No doubt all the attention helped to put Mrs. Hartley in the public eye. Sometime between the time when the Inchbalds knew the Hartleys and when Mrs. Hartley appeared in London, Mr. Hartley disappeared.

In 1774, after the end of the season, Mrs. Hartley created a sensation again when she ran away to France with her fellow actor "Gentleman Smith." William Smith had played with her as her lover in a new production of *Henry II*. Evidently the play inspired the lovers. When they returned from France, they went to Dublin, where they both acted at Smock Alley. In the fall they returned to London, but Harris refused to have both of them at Covent Garden, and Smith began to play at Drury Lane in 1780; from the entries in Mrs. Inchbald's pocket-book, Mrs. Hartley had finished the season at Covent Garden. She had created the role of Lady Frances in the first performance of *The Belle's Stratagem* on February 22, 1780, and she played it for the last time on May 29; after that she left the stage.

The dates are very puzzling here. How did Wilkinson get a copy of the play to use? Did Mrs. Cowley give him a copy, or did she give him permission to copy out the parts? Copying "parts" was tedious business and was usually done by someone paid to do it, sometimes by one of the actors who needed extra money. Wilkinson regularly went to London and frequently returned to York with new plays.[35] It is likely that Wilkinson acquired his copy from Harris, who, as the proprietor of Covent Garden, would have had the right to give it to him. It seems that the proprietors had control of the use of the plays until they were published and in the public's hands; that is, only after the plays were published could various groups in the provinces have copies, and of course such acquisitions would then be widely advertised.[36]

For several reasons the use of the London plays in the provinces was always a risky business; some years later, Wilkinson had a great quarrel with Elizabeth Inchbald about his use of one of her plays for which he had not asked her permission. The use of plays that were published but could not be used in the regular season because of the monopoly of the two patent theatres continued for decades in the eighteenth century. The dates here for Mrs. Inchbald's and the Wilkinson troupe's use of *Belle's Stratagem* come very near the last performance of Mrs. Hartley at Covent Garden. Her performance on May 29 came only three days before Elizabeth records that she played Lady Touchwood in the theatre in York.

During these weeks while Mrs. Inchbald continued to perform and to work on her farce, she spoke of Colman, George Colman the elder, who by 1780 was the sole proprietor of the Haymarket Theatre. That was the summer theatre, which, although it could not play in winter because of the monopoly of the two patent theatres, Drury Lane and Covent Garden, had become a very successful operation.[37] She and Kemble talked about Colman after Kemble's return from his "debate" at Mrs. Cornely's rooms at Carlisle House. Elizabeth Inchbald was not one to suppose that she would have the good luck to be called to London to play; she quite understood that she herself would have to create the circumstances of finding a place there. It is interesting to remember her experience with searching for a place in 1772, when she encountered Dodd and refusal, when she married and went with her husband to Bristol. Now in 1780 she knew more people to help her and knew far more about the London theatre world. It was this knowledge that in the end made her successful.

In London Colman opened the Haymarket on May 30, 1780. It is evident from various sources of these spring months of 1780 that Colman was being talked about. Because she read all the papers she could get her hands on, Mrs. Inchbald kept up with the gossip in London, as well she might, since throughout the spring she talked and wrote constantly about going—or not going—to London. In early June she recorded that she had read about Mr. Colman in the news. In May it had been reported in the *Morning Chronicle* that "A formidable combination seems to be forming against Mr. Colman's campaign this summer." According to the *Chronicle,* such an assessment was due to Colman's losing two of his principal players—Parsons of Drury Lane and Lee Lewes, who proposed to "revive the Lecture upon Heads at Covent-Garden."[38] Such a "lecture" would not be forbidden, since it was not a play. The *Chronicle* was quite mistaken; Colman lost no "campaign." The summer season of 1780 was among the most successful for Colman and the Haymarket.

The first play of the season on May 30 was his own *Manager in Distress,* a satire on debating societies, especially that of Mrs. Cornely in Carlisle House— this, one of the most recent ones, Kemble had participated in while he was on his first visit to London. It is tempting to conjecture what Kemble told Elizabeth Inchbald upon his return, but she records only that they had conversation.

The last play of the Haymarket season, *The Temple of Health,* was another farce, again a satire, this time on the quack Doctor Graham, whose "Temple of Health" promised everything from wealth and good fortune to sexual pleasure and a fountain of youth. By the season's end, Colman had staged ninety-one nights of plays and after-pieces. Colman's success this summer seems quite extraordinary considering the events going on in London in May and June.

In June London had been the scene of the Gordon riots, one of the most destructive uprisings of the century. The immediate cause of the riots was a bill giving Catholics slightly more freedom. This enraged the leaders of the London Protestant Association, who in turn organized a march to Parliament to protest. The bill gave the Catholics so little more freedom that it had passed in Parliament with very little opposition: it simply relieved Catholics in the army from part of the attestation oath. But the government was losing the war in America, and there was widespread fear of both France and Spain: "it became easy again, as it had been in the past, to earn a cheap popularity by speaking out against English papists as untrustworthy representatives of a dangerous international conspiracy and members of a foreign and traitorous religion."[39]

The president of the Protestant Association was Lord George Gordon, younger son of the duke of Gordon and a member of Parliament. Very eccentric, he was almost mad, demanding an audience with the king and behaving in a very disgraceful manner. He had several audiences, but finally, when the king refused to answer him and he was refused admittance, he returned to the leaders of the association, and together they organized a protest march. On June 2 a gathering of marchers, said to be more than fifty thousand, assembled in St. George's Fields; they were orderly at first, but the mood quickly got out of hand, and the marchers were taken over by looters and criminals, who began to attack innocent people, burning Roman Catholic chapels and destroying prisons, distilleries, and the houses of those who were unpopular in the government and Parliament. The king was appalled at what he called "the great supineness of the civil magistrates."[40] The troops were called out, but they in turn had to deal with the civil authorities, who refused to do anything. In the confusion there was another night of violence, but by Friday, June 9, the disturbances were over. The consequences were not: Gordon was arrested and tried but acquitted; twenty-one ringleaders were found guilty of treason and hanged.

In June Mrs. Inchbald recorded in her pocket-book that she read about the riots in London, but she gives no view; perhaps because her source of information was the newspaper, she did not quite understand how dreadful the riots were. In later years, however, she was to be closely associated with two of those present in London during the riots—her friend Holcroft, who saved the life of a young man falsely accused of doing mischief, and Edward Topham, one of the King's Guards, who evidently did little more than sit on his horse in great splendor before the palace. Both Holcroft and Topham were soon to become players in Elizabeth Inchbald's search for success.

Aside from being upset about her parts and about her ongoing attempts to leave Wilkinson and York to go to London, she was concerned about two other subjects over the months of the spring and summer. She continued to work on her writing, especially a farce that she eventually sent to Colman and her novel, which she had revised, read to everyone, changed, and copied, and now was ready to send to London. Her other "problem," if it may be called so, was that she began to receive proposals of marriage. That is not surprising, but the men who suggested she should choose them as mistress or wife make an interesting study in terms of their attitudes to marriage, and her responses begin to reveal just how independent she was becoming. Most of the people who knew her certainly gossiped about whom she might select, even though in her pocket-book she never gives details. Dr. Brodie, who had attended her in her near-fatal illness in Aberdeen, had now gone to live in London. She received long letters from him, and no doubt they contained some kind of a proposal. She records in one entry that the people in the company as well as in town expected her to marry Kemble. She writes: "George came in and talked, he went out after and Mrs. Tyler with me. She told me what people said of Mr. Kemble and me marrying."

Boaden writes: "Those who settle everything in country towns gave them to each other so heartily, that it seemed like disappointing their patrons to avoid or even defer the union."[41] One of her admirers in the company was Dick Suett, who enlisted both Kemble and her stepson George to plead his suit. He was one of the most valuable of the players; he had a fine voice and was already a very fine comedian—he later became one of the most celebrated comedians on the London stage. Boaden writes: "However, she had discharged the duties of a wife with so much theatrical applause that . . . her hand was again solicited in wedlock; and the reader will laugh as she did at the notion of changing her name for that of Suett."[42] Her entries in her pocket-book do not suggest that she in any way ridiculed him, and she remained friends with him all the years in London until his early death.[43] As the year went along, it became evident that Suett would be leaving and going to London. He had been a favorite of Wilkinson; Wilkinson had brought him up and trained him from the time he had come to the York Company as a teenager. He had already been a child actor in London, where he had also sung in various productions. For the manager of a company he was very important, and in the summer of 1780 Wilkinson was reluctant to let him go.

As for Mrs. Inchbald and her scheme to get to London, Wilkinson was even less cooperative. She herself found it extremely difficult to understand that some of the players had to fill the secondary roles, that the "star" player must be supported, that it took the whole cast to make up a successful performance. As the summer progressed, she became more and more dissatisfied with the roles she was assigned. Her disaffection about her roles was not enough for her to leave Wilkinson, but when she found that Mrs. Smith, a new player whom Wilkinson had hired, would be given lead roles, she became even more dissatisfied. Boaden writes of Mrs. Inchbald: "The manager's attention to her was unfailing: George Inchbald's salary was raised at her desire; but she was not contented, and disputed with him as to some character that he wished her to act: he promised an increase of her *own* salary, but the day following she had a fresh dispute; and honest Tate, in explanation, said many very flattering things as to her talents, and, not the least flattering, as it went beyond words, absolutely offered, if she staid another year, to make her salary one guinea and a half per week."[44]

From the evidence of the earlier time, when Joseph Inchbald made the contracts for them, it is easy to see that she was now completely alone; there are a great many places in her records that show her very real despair of ever finding a way to leave York and go to London, indicating clearly that she almost gave up. But even at this time when she was new at making decisions, she persisted. Her husband had not been ambitious; he had accepted his place among the secondary characters, and he certainly was content with Wilkinson. Wilkinson found it hard to understand Elizabeth Inchbald, but through all the discussions with friends and with Wilkinson, she was determined to go her own way.

She seemed never to have any real trouble learning her parts, though she worked at doing so constantly. She did worry about her "dress," for the actresses were still required to provide their own costumes; she began to be reluctant to pack and go from one place to another, and when Wilkinson planned to send the company to Edinburgh, she protested vigorously. The entries in her pocket-book for these weeks in April and May show how unhappy she was and how impossible it was to please her. She quarreled with everyone. She wrote to Wilkinson; she wrote to her friend Wilson in London; she wrote again to Wilkinson and again to London, this time to George Colman. The entries in her pocket-book about going to London continue almost every day. In the meantime her domestic life went on. She wrote that she talked to Mr. Wilkinson about going to Edinburgh, and the next day she wrote, "Laid very late in bed and was very melancholy, heard Miss Mills had taken the dining room in the afternoon, read a little out of many books, drank coffee in the kitchen, it thundered the time—after at Matilda till dark then Mrs. Hitchcock just called who came with Miss Mills—went for letters but there were none."

In spite of the continuing problems about her future, she, of course, continued to be a part of the company, and she continued to play in a variety of roles. For example, she continued to play in *The Rivals,* a play she very much disliked, especially the role of Mrs. Malaprop; but whether she liked it or not, she could not refuse. And on Wednesday, March 14, she played Bellario in *Philaster.* On Tuesday she had recorded that "after supper Mrs. Tyler with me fitting my Boy's dress," an entry to be remembered, for this was to be the first role she played when she finally got to London. On Thursday of the week before, she records that she called on Mr. and Mrs. Cummins and heard about Mrs. Cowley's new comedy— another entry to be remembered, for in September the "new comedy," *The Belle's Stratagem,* was performed by the company, showing again that Wilkinson kept his offerings in fashion: the play had opened in London only two weeks before the Cumminses and she "talked" of it.

Mrs. Inchbald's entries about Kemble were frequent during the weeks and months of the spring of 1780, and some of the entries are as significant for Kemble as for her. He had continued to be a part of Wilkinson's company since he had appeared in Doncaster in December 1778. On Wednesday, March 21, she records that Kemble came and "wished me well"; on the Saturday following, she writes, "Mr. Kemble took his leave of me." But it seems Kemble could not part with her, for the next day, Sunday, she writes, "he sat sometime." She does not report their conversation. This was the point at which Kemble was leaving for London and his engagement at Mrs. Cornely's Carlisle House. Kemble returned and, as it turned out, remained with Wilkinson until the 1781 season, when he went to Dublin, engaged at Smock Alley with Daly.

The whole company evidently thought that Elizabeth Inchbald and Kemble would marry. Later in the week, her stepson George, who was still in the company, came to supper and told her that Wilkinson had returned and "of Mr. Kemble's School for Scandal Scandalized." Kemble had tried various kinds of writing since that time when he worked on his play *Belisarius* and she on her novel, as yet unnamed, while they were "vacationing" on Moor; they were then with Younger's company. Mrs. Inchbald's entry, however, has to do with the fact that on March 27, 1779, he had played in *Belisarius* again, had played the master in *The Toy Shop*, and had had the role of the colonel in his own "interlude," *School for Scandal Scandalized*. Her entry on Friday, March 29, indicates that the "School" had been presented at Covent Garden on March 18, and although Herschel Baker questions that the manuscript in the Huntington Library is actually Kemble's work, Mrs. Inchbald's entry in her pocket-book gives proof that it is indeed Kemble's.

That spring before Mr. Inchbald's death, Kemble had worked on several adaptations, an alteration of Massinger's *New Way to Pay Old Debts*, for example, and a miscellany called *An Attic Evening Entertainment*, selections he put together from William Collins, Laurence Sterne, Shakespeare, and the Bible. In reading Mrs. Inchbald's pocket-books for 1779–1780, it is quite evident that both she and Kemble continued to work at writing and their profession of acting. Neither she nor he spent time being "romantic."

During the first weeks of April, she talked back and forth to Wilkinson about staying with him and about going to London; at this point she certainly did not have a firm offer at Covent Garden, and the talk of her staying at York or leaving kept her very much upset. On Monday, April 2, she wrote that she had "agreed to article from Christmas." On the next day, after playing Mrs. Candor, she was "poorly and had whey after and at Horatio in Bed." On Thursday her entry reads, "played in The Roman Father—had wine with Mr. Wilkinson and told him of my London offer the time of *Widow and No Widow*," a comment that not only gives information but shows just how business was conducted. After all, the players not on stage had many opportunities for conversation during the long evening performances. The next day she had a letter from her friend Wilson in London, and on the following day she wrote, "After I was in bed wrote the copy of a letter to Mr. Wilkinson."

During all the weeks and months from April to the end of August, Inchbald was very tense and unsettled. As always, she wanted things to happen immediately, which was, of course, not possible when so many people were involved with her in the theatre. She could not suddenly leave and go to London. On April 9 she played Hamlet for George Inchbald's benefit. The playbill read:

HAMLET:

PRINCE OF DENMARK

HAMLET, by MRS. INCHBALD

(Her First Appearance in that Character)

Her stepson played Horatio; Suett, as always, played the double role of Rosencrantz and one of the grave diggers, appearing—much to the delight of the audience—after he had been killed as Rosencrantz. Wilkinson played the ghost.

Mrs. Siddons had played Hamlet in Liverpool during the 1777 season, when she and Kemble had left the Inchbalds in Manchester. She, too, like Elizabeth Inchbald, later played the role in a benefit, an occasion when the actors selected their own parts. Siddons's letter to Inchbald reporting the incident is filled with gossip and observation about this "benefit." She writes: "I played Hamlet in Liverpool to near a hundred pounds, and wish I had taken it to myself; but the fear of charges, which, you know, are most tremendous circumstances, persuaded me to take part of a benefit with Barry, for which I have since been very much blamed; but he, I believe, was very much satisfied, and in short so am I." Siddons had played Hamlet before when she and her husband were strolling. The Reverend Henry Bate, sent by Garrick to see Sarah, reported on her very favorably and added, "nay beware yourself *Great Little* Man, for she plays Hamlet to the satisfaction of the Worcestershire Critics."[45]

Siddons kept the role, but she never played it in London.[46] Since *Hamlet* was the most popular of the Shakespeare plays, it is not surprising that actresses sometimes played the part, especially in benefits, when they could choose for themselves. In the years after Inchbald and Siddons, two other contemporary actresses played the part, Jane Powell and Julia Glover. Many years later Siddons played Hamlet again, this time in Dublin in the summer of 1802. One spectator wrote, "the audience was rapt in admiration of her excellence."[47]

Jane Powell, like Elizabeth Inchbald, was tall and beautiful. One writer observed, "This lady's person is majestically beautiful." In Lady Macbeth, one of her important roles, she was said to be second only to Siddons in that part. With her figure suited to breeches parts and her knowledge of Shakespeare, her first performance of Hamlet for her benefit at Drury Lane in 1796 was quite a success, with receipts of £466 11s. 6d., less the house charge of £212. Her second time, for her benefit on May 25, 1797, was far less financially successful, with only £87 against £220 charges. One critic, writing about her first Hamlet, said she "looked the character remarkably well. . . . if we make allowances for embarrassment and imperfect study, the performance of Mrs. Powell was by no means indifferent." And after her second performance, in 1797, she played "with as much spirit as before, and more correct as to the text." Like Siddons's and Inchbald's earlier, her performance was for a benefit, this time her own. In 1822 Julia Glover played Hamlet for her benefit, though there is no record of how she played the part or of how profitable it was. That the actresses played Hamlet in benefits when they could choose to do so is an important statement of their independence.[48] By the time Inchbald played the part in 1780, she was already determined to go to London in the fall.

Kemble evidently did not see Mrs. Inchbald play Hamlet, since she records on Thursday that she had heard "Mr. Kemble was ill and in Bath." His sister Mrs. Siddons was in Bath this spring making her reputation as a star player—or perhaps we should say recovering from her disappointment about Drury Lane and beginning to be the self-assured actress that she became upon her return to London two years later. By April 23 Inchbald records: "heard in bed that Kemble had returned." Her entries continue to be filled with the details of her days, which make them interesting and which also support the facts about Kemble, Wilkinson, and the other players in the company. The pocket-books are never merely an account of her personal activities; they are much more.

During these difficult weeks and months, Elizabeth Inchbald felt herself in a kind of limbo. She very much trusted her friend Wilson to attend to her interests in London, but in the meantime she had to deal with Wilkinson and to be associated with Kemble, Suett, Miss Mills, Mrs. Smith, George Inchbald, and all the others in the company while she tried to remain independent in her choices and judgments.

In a letter to Wilkinson dated April 10, she makes herself quite plain:

Dear Sir,

I can now no longer neglect another post writing to Mr. Harris and therefore hope you will pardon my mentioning particulars to which your reply must determine me in what manner to write, and I beg you will be so kind as to answer them immediately.

If I resign my London offer it can only be for your first salary, the liberty of giving up the following parts, the promise of Miss Younger's part in the "Belle's Stratagem," the choice of my York Benefit next after Mr. Cummins and Mr. Kemble, and if I go to Hull (which I have not the smallest inclination to do) the last night. Now I hope Sir, you will not think any of these conditions extravagant as they are only necessaries to render my services (in the way you now regard them) of consequence. The salary you have before promised. As to my catalogue of parts I have omitted fifty most disagreeable ones; but as they go under the title of first parts [I] am content with them—the part in the "Belles Stratagem" is to repay me for Lady Sneerwell in the "School for Scandal." My permitting two Gentlemen to make choice before me in our York Benefits . . . proper humiliation, and my desire of the last night in Hull of no consequence as I had rather article only from Xmas, and know a place I shall do much better in for that time—but if you shall have real occasion for me there, I think I shall deserve that sixth as well as any other Lady nor can afford (knowing my weak interest) to go without it.

Now Sir, as I profess these proposals are made with a consciousness that (should you refuse them) I shall be reduced in a year to accept terms much inferior I hope you will not call me impertinent; yet I will not give up my London offer (fatal as I make no doubt it will be to me) for anything less—and consider as a favorable circumstance I am not situated (Like almost all my sister Heroines) to extort a double salary. Moreover consider how Peaceable I am—how Good-natured—how tall—and how pretty.

Eliz: Inchbald

The moment your answer arrives (which I beg may be before night) I can conclude for the Summer.

Monday Morning
3rd April, 1780.[49]

We have no exact date for an answer from Wilkinson, but his report written many years later is revealing both for her and for him. Lewis, the manager at Covent Garden, was with Wilkinson and his players that summer in Edinburgh, and it is to him that Wilkinson refers when he writes: "While Mr. Lewis was with me, he with the powerful assistance of Mr. Harris, with large offers from his hand, and Mr. Lewis as liberal with an offer in the other hand, seduced my dear friend Mrs. Inchbald from me. . . . But then Mr. Harris offered me his friendship . . . till at length depending on a little bribe for the day, and a large promise for the morrow, I yielded up my fair one, and she was conducted to the royal tent at Covent-Garden."[50]

Throughout the spring Inchbald read books as well as worked on her parts. She was reading Pope the last week of April as she records, "read Eloisa to Abelard and many other poems out of Pope." Again the next day she "read many poems," and the next "read in Pope." Into the next week she was still reading Pope. This day she happened on Kemble, and they talked of London. All during this time, she was working on parts while she began to pack to go to Leeds. The last weeks in May were filled with a flurry of preparing to leave. She packed on Sunday, spending all day in her "bed gown" while the little Robinson girl visited her. Her accounts show the preparation for the journey. She spent 6d. for "box mending." She spent 5s. for "riding dress making," and she spent 4s. for "cloth for a bed gown and making."

The last week in May, the company left for Leeds. Her accounts now reflect her new situation. She now paid 10s. for board and lodging (she had been paying 12s.). Her journey, with all expenses, she records as costing her 11s. 6d., and then she records, "had on my arrival here with 20 owing to me 7s/6." Later, after she had been in London for some years, she left off keeping her accounts in her pocket-books, and we can no longer tell how she managed her money. Still later, of course, when she had her plays bought and published, she records in great detail the money she received and how she managed it, as she records her daily activities.

On the Thursday before she left with the Cumminses, she talked to Miss Hitchcock, who had had a letter from her father. The entry reads, "had been poorly in the night and woke very unhappy when Miss Hitchcock called with a letter from her Papa with an account of my Farce which pleased me much." Even in the days when she had been very upset about going to Edinburgh, she contin-ued to work. The next night after she had received the letter from Hitchcock praising her farce, she records that "Mr. Wilkinson spoke against my farce." And on Tuesday she wrote, "Was very busy with my washerwoman then mending till Mr. Wilkinson call'd about my bill—then began to write my farce." Several times in these weeks she "read till daylight." One day she did not go to rehearsal "but was all the morning and afternoon at my farce but did not like it." Two days later she wrote, "As soon as it was light settled the plot of my Farce to my liking." But she was never satisfied, for a day later she wrote, "a little at my farce but could not please myself—very dull—wrote letters—read the paper, studied parts and to bed early."

She traveled with the Cumminses to Leeds; they dined on the road, drank tea, and supped together; arriving, she unpacked and "Looked my farce over & began Garrick's Life." During these weeks in Leeds, she continued to discuss going to Edinburgh. She continued to protest that she did not want to go. The situation was indeed no ordinary one, because it resulted from the fact that Wilkinson was now managing the theatre in Edinburgh as well as his York cir-cuit. About Christmastime in 1779, he had gone to Edinburgh, having rented the theatre there; he had returned on March 28 just in time to see Mrs. Inchbald's performance of Hamlet and about the time she began to mention her displeasure at the prospect of going, perhaps because she did not wish to remember the past. According to Wilkinson's report, they went to Edinburgh, where the "Edinburgh races were brilliant as to an assemblage of persons of fashion."[51] Some of the York players had been there all winter and spring, and some had come from London for the summer season, for example, Lewis from Covent Garden. The Hitchcocks had been there although their daughter had been in York.

As one entry after another during these weeks in Leeds reveals her displea-sure about going to Edinburgh, she continues to write about her farce, and in

these entries she records various comments about her acting. She was never satisfied with her acting, and the entries during these weeks of the spring and summer
of 1780 are especially revealing as they appear with her comments about going to
London. Many years later, when she wrote criticism, she shows clearly that she
understood much more than she could perform. She never mentions her speech
impediment, nor does anyone else writing of these years in the York circuit, but
the comment most frequently given about her acting was that it was, still, more
artificial than natural.

After being absent from her entries for some time, Kemble reappears during
the week of June 18; on Saturday, June 23, she was at rehearsal and after dinner
turned "to my farce when Mr. Kemble call'd to hear me through his part but I would
not . . . news came of General Clinton." The Sunday entry that follows reads, "Laid
late—then dress'd myself marked Mr. Kemble's Poems c&c, dinner read the news
then carried my wine and sat with Mr. and Mrs. Cummins." Later that day she
talked to Mr. Wilkinson about "Edinburgh dresses c&c." The next night, Monday,
was Kemble's night; she played Bellario and spoke the epilogue. They "supped below and Mr. Cummins had wine. The High Street was illuminated."

The poems she mentions in her entry were those in Kemble's book that had
been recently published in York. Entitled *Fugitive Pieces,* it was a rather slight
gathering of random verses that included the epitaph he had written for Joseph
Inchbald's tomb as well as poems addressed to a "lady." Kemble's later biographer,
Baker, finds the preface to this little volume pompous and the "love-lyrics" "pal-
lid" and concludes that "His volume of verses is among the slightest productions
of an age notorious for slight poetry."[52] Baker, having very little real or even cir-
cumstantial evidence, judges that if the "lady" was Mrs. Inchbald, their interest in
each other had cooled. Reading her pocket-books and Kemble's compositions, it
is difficult for anyone to find any real passion. But since Baker had no evidence of
"passion," it is interesting that he, too, like their friends, thought Mrs. Inchbald
and Kemble extremely "interested" in each other. In the summer of 1780, Kemble
was still a very inexperienced actor, almost more interested in writing than in
being on stage, and Inchbald was completely involved in her own career and professional matters, not interested in having an emotional attachment with Kemble
or anyone else.

After she had played in Kemble's night, she was sick and did not go to rehearsal, and after dinner when Mrs. Cummins found her, she was dizzy and crying. Mrs. Cummins stayed with her until dark, persuading her to go to Scotland.

This unusual trip to Scotland evidently upset several of the players; for some
it gave an opportunity to be better known, which was the case with Kemble, but

for Elizabeth Inchbald it must have been quite emotionally disturbing—after all, she had been on the circuit in Scotland until the summer of 1776, and although the troupe played in several cities, Edinburgh was certainly the chief one; there must have been several of the theatre's patrons who remembered her and her husband.

This last week before she left York, she records another significant occurrence: she says simply, "Mr. Suett offered himself to me again and received his engagement from Drury Lane." She had already been sick, and this conversation with him made her no better. She did not go to rehearsal, either on Friday or Saturday, when she says, "Mr. Southwell called to let me know I had been forfeited." A review of the times she was ill during these weeks when she was seeking a place in London and when she was reluctant to go to Edinburgh suggests that she must have had what we now know as migraine, severe headaches with nausea. Her reports of being ill may also be noted as occurring when she was under pressure either about her acting or her writing. This summer of 1780 was, even for her, unusually stressful. She was so intense about her acting and so frustrated about having her novel and her farce accepted that she continued to be especially vulnerable to infection. And all her life she had headaches and pulmonary problems.

In the first week of July, the company finally went to Edinburgh. Wilkinson writes about the season in his *Wandering Patentee:*

I took the greatest part of the company to Edinburgh races, securing the Scotch part of the company in the north, under the direction of the sensible, trusty, and steady good actor, the respectable Mr. Woods. Mr. Lewis, of Covent-Garden Theatre, was added also as a strong cannon to secure my castle during the Edinburgh races. . . . Edinburgh races were brilliant as to an assemblage of persons of fashion, and have greatly increased from that year. . . . A very good week I had, so as to afford genteel profits, notwithstanding the distance of 200 miles to Edinburgh, and 200 miles back to York races.[53]

Until the very last, Inchbald was unhappy about going to Edinburgh and about the uncertainty of her place in York and in London. Shortly before she left, she again played in *The Belle's Stratagem.* And when they came to Edinburgh, that was one of the plays Wilkinson presented. Wilkinson reports the occasion by saying, "'The Belles Stratagem' was new, and Mr. Lewis was the Doricourt."[54] He does not mention Inchbald, who played Lady Touchwood. This kind of neglect was the usual situation in the male-dominated society of 1780 and was one of the reasons Inchbald quarreled with Wilkinson.

Perhaps also one of the reasons for Mrs. Inchbald's reluctance to go to Edinburgh was the recent disturbances about the Roman Catholics. In his journal entry for February 2, 1779, James Boswell wrote, "On my return home from a consultation . . . I found Signora Marcucci, the Italian dancing-mistress who lives in our stair, had taken refuge with my wife, there being an outrageous mob against the papists." Boswell, not having heard of any disturbance, went out into The High Street and found that the mob was burning the Catholic chapel. He says he saw them throwing fuel on the fire; the house was in flames, and as he watched he saw a large book, "perhaps some venerable manuscript, come flaming out at one of the windows." Boswell tried to reason with the mob, but no one could stop them. In his entry for Wednesday, February 3, he wrote, "The mob pillaged Bishop Hay's library in the forenoon with impunity."[55]

Mrs. Inchbald knew Bishop Hay very well; she had corresponded with him when she was in Edinburgh in 1773, and when she was in Edinburgh with Digges, she had attended Mass regularly. Although this mob scene was in February 1779 and the trip to Edinburgh a year later, there had been the Gordon riots in London in June 1780, just before Inchbald and the Cumminses left York. Inchbald was certainly aware of all that had gone on, even though she did not discuss the Gordon riots in her pocket-book. It was about this time also that someone wrote about Mrs. Inchbald to Dr. Alexander Geddes. It is likely that she herself instigated the inquiry about just what the church's position may be for her as an actress. In part Dr. Geddes's reply reads, "If then Mrs. Inchbald is conscious to herself that the theatre is, either directly or indirectly, to her the immediate or even remote cause of sin, she is surely too reasonable not to see the necessity of leaving it: but if she has never found it dangerous to her virtue, or incompatible with her Christian duties, I cannot well see that she is under an obligation of quitting it from any natural principle of moral rectitude I am acquainted with."[56]

When Wilkinson continues his report about this summer of 1780, he says, "York races immediately following, we all jogged back again across the Tweed." Again at York he writes, "we opened the theatre on Saturday (August 19th) previous to the race-week, 1780, with Mr. Lewis in Doricourt."[57] Again no mention of others in the cast, and again Mrs. Inchbald was Lady Touchwood. Reading Mrs. Inchbald's pocket-book gives a rather different view of the plays and the performances. In Edinburgh on Monday, August 23, she played Mrs. Sullen; it was the first race day, and there was a "good house," but she was "displeased with my dress." The next day, Tuesday, her entry reads, "At rehearsal heard I dressed remarkably well—talked to Mr. Lewis about the London season c&c—was drest before dinner . . . played Mrs. Racket—a great house—was well pleased." She played on Thursday, on Friday, and on the Monday following. She had been to prayers on Sunday; she had given rather infrequent attention to her religious duties these weeks and months. The next Sunday entry was quite different: "did not go to prayers but read my farce and was much pleased with it—Mr. Sterling called—after dinner sent for and read many newspapers. Mr. Sterling call'd again drank tea and staid supper—read my farce to him c&c . . . wore my long gown all day." Mr. Sterling was her friend from the earlier days, when she and her husband had been in Edinburgh. She continued to play the following week, but on Monday she "was all morning writing in my farce and got very forward." On Tuesday she promised Mr. Wood that he could see her farce; on Wednesday she says, "Mr. Sterling here and finished reading my farce to him." On Friday Mr. Wood went home with her after rehearsal but "declined to hear my farce."

There are frequent references to various gentlemen who came to speak to her. She continues to see Mr. Sterling; Sir John Whitefoord called and "sat sometime" on Sunday, and in the afternoon "I drank tea and supp'd at Mr. Woods he read many of his works to me—a foggy evening." (Perhaps the reason he had refused to read any more of her farce was that he wanted to read his "works" to her.) She and Kemble were not the only scribblers in the company.

Being in Scotland—in Edinburgh—was quite different from being in York and the York circuit. Several times during their brief stay, Inchbald and her friends went sightseeing. On the first Sunday after arriving in Edinburgh, she reports, "thought of going to prayers but did not." Instead she went with Mrs. Wilkinson and others in a coach and four to Rosslyn Castle and came home by Dalkeith and Musselburgh. The next week they went on another excursion, to Holyrood House, where they dined and had tea. On this occasion Mr. Lewis and Mr. Cummins were along, and afterward Mr. Lane, Mr. Mason, and Mr. Ross joined them for tea and a walk in the square.

On August 13 the company set off for York and the Race Week there. She finished packing and with the Cumminses began the journey at nine o'clock in a diligence; they had supper at Haddington and traveled all night; they had breakfast at Berwick-upon-Tweed. Her entry continues, describing "a very fine morning—after happened of George then who rode with us—went round the Duke of Northumberland's House and dined . . . slept a few hours at Newcastle." The next day, Wednesday, she continues: "A very fine warm day—breakfasted at Durham, dined at Northampton, drank tea in the Castle at Easterwold, at dark arrived at York . . . supped at Mrs. Tyler's—slept over the way—saw the newspapers I wanted to see." Thursday she "read parts in the morning had dinner and breakfast brought over—went to my lodgings to tea then had my hair dress'd and called at my shoe makers and on Mr. Wilson."

On Friday and Saturday she continued to catch up from her stay in Edinburgh—she began a long letter to her sister Anne Hunt, and George came;

her head was "poorly." She continued to feel "poorly," perhaps a result of the inevitable reaction to the stress of her trip. It was another fine day, but hot, and she says she read Pope's history of Abelard and Eloise. Saturday she rose early, finished her letter, "put on my cap with the thought of London," and after tea she brushed her things and read the news. The account of these two weeks, significant for Mrs. Inchbald, is also a view of the circumstances and activities of Wilkinson and his company. His version in *The Wandering Patentee*, although it is concerned more directly with the business side of the season, includes comments about the various members of the troupe who went to Edinburgh and back to York. Putting two Race Weeks together, as he did, was quite an undertaking, requiring that he plan seasons far in advance.

WILKINSON AND THEATRE MANAGEMENT

Wilkinson's account of this period is important not only for what we learn about his experience but also for the information it offers about the management of the two theatres and his decisions that pertained to the players in his company. In December of 1779 Wilkinson had become the manager of the Edinburgh Theatre, a theatre that had had a rather uncertain direction in the seventies.[58] During that unstable period, the Inchbalds' experiences between 1772 and the summer of 1776, when they left for France, must have been typical of the troupe's uncertain financial and theatrical situations. Wilkinson gives a summary of the managers and the dates:

The managers of the Edinburgh Theatre within my time, as near as I can recollect since the year 1758, have been Mr. Lee, Mr. Love, Mr. Ross, Mr. Callender, Mr. Dowson, Mr. David Beat, Mr. Ross, Mr. Digges, Mr. Corri, Tate Wilkinson, 1780, Mr. Heaphy, 1781, Tate Wilkinson the races, 1781, Mr. Jackson, 1782, Mr. S. Kemble Mrs. Esten, and now Mr. S. Kemble and Mrs. Esten. . . . When I survey the picture of being enthroned and dethroned, of a king and no king, at Edinburgh; surely reader, you will agree in the opinion, how sensibly happy I ought to feel and think myself possessed of every decent comfort of life, and a family rejoicing in the smiles of content, and receiving every friendly service in Yorkshire.[59]

In this same passage, Wilkinson lists the players he took with him. He reported that although the players were very good, his scenery especially fine, and the plays he presented, in which he played leading parts, all important, all celebrated, "it was above one month before business grew tolerable, nor were my troops left in garrison quarters at Hull in a flourishing state by any means, either the remainder of Hull season, or the beginning of York, where they received orders to march after I had left them. . . . Bad houses at Edinburgh, bad houses at York, made the campaign very disagreeable, hazardous, and fatiguing."[60]

Wilkinson returned to York in April and found his company "very dull and glum. . . . It was indeed a bad time for plays every where. It was . . . the very distressing juncture of the American, French, Spanish, and Dutch war, against old England. Edinburgh was drained not only of cash, but of most of its principal inhabitants." And upon returning to York, he found that "the inhabitants were not in the best of tempers; for the theatrical entertainments, from the same cause before hinted, the American war, money was invisible, not any winter visitors."[61] Hitchcock was left in Edinburgh to manage the company until Wilkinson returned.

All of these matters affected the company in personal as well as in professional ways. For example, Elizabeth Inchbald's friend Miss Hitchcock remained in York while her parents were in Scotland. With Wilkinson in York, Inchbald wrote even more letters than she did when Wilkinson and she were in the same town. Several new players were added, some for the York circuit and some special ones from London for the summer season, that is, for the two Race Weeks, the one at Edinburgh, the other at York. Among these special additions was Mr. Lewis, a close friend of Harris and the prompter at Covent Garden. Lewis was to be very important for Inchbald and her plan to go to London. In such a small group, gossip was always part of their social life, and in one entry Mrs. Inchbald comments, "At rehearsal Mr. Wilkinson desired I would not go to Mr. Ross's"—a slight comment but far more important than it might seem. Wilkinson had contracted with David Ross to manage the theatre for the seasons 1779–1782. In the end Wilkinson lost money, and Ross was obliged to assume the financial responsibility he had handed over to Wilkinson. The whole short comment by Mrs. Inchbald suggests that she very probably knew about the problems between Ross and Wilkinson.

David Ross was the son of Alexander Ross, vicar of Easterfearn. Born in 1728, he was sent to Westminster School, where for some reason his father became angry with him and disinherited him. The first record of his acting was at the Smock Alley Theatre in Dublin in 1749. He was at Drury Lane in 1751–1757 and at Covent Garden from 1757 to 1766. During the summers Ross began to manage various companies in the provinces. In 1767 he took over the management of the theatre in Edinburgh. The royal patent had just been awarded, and the proprietors selected him in spite of considerable opposition to his appointment.

The rent for the theatre was four hundred pounds a year for the old theatre in Cannongate Hall. For the next two years, Ross was very deep into the planning and financing of the new theatre being built in "new town," to be known as Shakespeare Square. Ross encountered a series of disasters. The opening of the new theatre in 1769 had to be postponed because of the collapse of the North Bridge; he financed the building in a complicated series of arrangements, and when his first seasons were failures, he wished to go back to London. In the end, after renting the theatre to Wilkinson in 1779–1780, he sold it to John Jackson on November 10, 1781. Ross was a good actor, and Mrs. Inchbald certainly knew him from the days when she and her husband had been in Scotland. He seems to have been one of those men who, although handsome and talented, are rather indolent.[62]

Hugh Kelly in *Thespis* said that Ross had all the qualities of a fine actor—voice, charm, elegance, ease—but that he "continued negligent in his art, sacrificing his prime years to a slothful stillness, dissipating his talents and skill by lack of will."[63]

Wilkinson was glad to be relieved of his bargain when the theatre was sold to Jackson. Jackson, too, was well known in Edinburgh, and there is no doubt that Mrs. Inchbald knew him as well as Ross. During the 1770s he had acted regularly in Edinburgh with his wife. In 1780 he began to take a company to play in Glasgow—he had already had plays performed in Dundee, Aberdeen, and Dumfries. For most of the decade of the 1780s, he was successful, and when he put the theatres of Edinburgh and Glasgow up for auction in November of 1791, he turned the lease over to Stephen Kemble. In that decade of the 1790s, Inchbald's interests were entirely centered in London, but she knew Stephen Kemble and his wife very well: he was John Philip's younger brother, and she was Mrs. Inchbald's friend the former Miss Satchell.

AUGUST AND SEPTEMBER 1780

In the last weeks of August, Inchbald's London plans remained unfinished. On August 20 she writes that Lewis called "to ask if I had heard from London c&c." She would not let him in. On Tuesday she was finishing and copying a letter to Harris, and on Wednesday she says again that she was working on a letter to Harris. By this time in August she was very upset about her plan, but suddenly on Friday of this week she says, "at rehearsal Mr. Wilkinson told me he had wrote to Mr. Harris he would part with me—my head poorly." On Saturday she wrote to her friend Wilson in London, went to rehearsal, was "in good spirits" and saw Kemble, played Lady Frances Touchwood, and concluded her entry, "my cold and throat poorly—tho looked well." She spent Sunday at leisure. She wore her long gown all day, read the newspapers, her head still "poorly."

Inchbald's whole campaign was quite difficult and, for her, quite remarkable. Since her marriage she had always depended on her husband and his friends to give her a place. Although she knew people in London who encouraged her, she did not know either Thomas Harris at Covent Garden or Richard Sheridan, the manager at Drury Lane. The months from the death of her husband to her move to London were filled with self-doubt, illness, both physical and psychological, and frantic letters and messages to anyone who would listen. It is at this point that we see her becoming more and more determined to find her own way and to persist in her determination to achieve her goal. Her doing so is the story of the next forty years.

The last week in August was filled with letters back and forth to Harris, to Wilkinson, to Harris again. But more significantly, she was sick. This time she summoned the doctor, Mr. Wallace, who, she says, "bled me"; then she "sorted [her] things," and Mr. Wallace called "the time," as did Kemble. The entries in the pocket-books about illness show Inchbald to be typical of her time and place, both in terms of her symptoms and in terms of the prescriptions to relieve them. She really never got over the years when she and her husband had been strollers— although they had thought of themselves as being members of Digges's Edinburgh Company. And she never got over the problems left from the illness when she almost died in Aberdeen, the time when Mr. Inchbald sent for the priest. Moreover, when she was under stress, all the old problems returned. This was the case during that last week in August.

Although she looked forward to London, she was still under contract to Wilkinson, which meant she was required to play until the very last days before she left for Covent Garden. On Saturday, September 8, she left York at night with the Smiths, traveled all day, dined and drank tea at their lodgings in Leeds, and went to Wakefield, arriving there about six. They looked for lodgings. It is not surprising that she ends this entry again, "my head poorly, supped at the Inn, came to my lodging—very low spirited." The next day she says, "Rose late—read in the Bible of David c&c . . . talked to my Landlady of my disorder." She was following the company as she was required to do, from York to Leeds to Wakefield.

This second week in September, she talked of London, took long walks, and drank tea with the Smiths. On Friday she was "low spirited"; it was a wet market day, and she "read much." The next day she took a long walk with Mrs. Smith, and they talked of Reddish; Mrs. Inchbald says she was "melancholy tho my head quite well." Reddish was her friend from the early days, one of those she con-sulted in 1772 when she came to London to seek her fortune. By 1780 he had fallen into great difficulties. In 1778 he had received assistance from the Drury Lane actors' fund, and he died in the York Asylum some five years after this conversation between Mrs. Smith and Mrs. Inchbald, leaving several children by several different wives. It is no wonder that Mrs. Inchbald was affected, for he had been in York in 1779 for a brief time when he was, as Boaden put it, "infirm," that is, quite out of his mind. Moreover, he had been a friend of her husband, and she was always concerned with any of his friends.

On Sunday she dressed in her "riding dress," but the rain prevented her walk. Kemble called in the afternoon and again after supper. He thought she was about to leave for London, but she did not do so for another ten days. And in the week of September 17 she continued to act—on Monday in *The Belle's Stratagem,* on Thursday in Rowe's *Jane Shore,* on Friday in *The Belle's Stratagem* again. Through-out these last two weeks, she recorded the gossip that floated about, usually that the various members of the company did not believe she was indeed going to London. Some of her friends, however, did realize that she was leaving. On Sun-day she finished *Thompson's Travels,* received her salary, put on her "riding dress," and "walked on the heath with the Smiths—Mr. Kemble c&c—were very merry—it rained."

It is interesting to notice these friends she walked with on this last Sunday. Mrs. Smith was certainly not her favorite friend. During her dispute with Wilkinson over whether or not he would release her, she wrote a very revealing letter, which is not dated:

Sir, You surely forget that I am articled and will stay with you just as long as I please, therefore don't affront me or perhaps out of spite I may stay with you all the winter—however, I believe I shall go away on the 8th. . . . I have nothing against Mrs. Smith, she is a woman I admire very much—but I will make this observation, that had she been com-pelled to play second parts in the tragedies with me, as I have in the comedys with her, she might have been thought as little of as I am at present—so far does the success of an actor depend on the partiality of a manager—under you I never could be a favorite anywhere. Give me leave to acknowledge the many favors and great civilities I have received both from you and Mrs. Wilkinson as Mrs. Inchbald but as an actress.[64]

Unfortunately, her parting was very bitter, and Wilkinson's comments, when he wrote about her and Mrs. Smith later, are revealing. About Inchbald he said: "While Mr. Lewis was with me, he with the powerful assistance of Mr. Harris, with large offers from his hand, and Mr. Lewis as liberal with an offer in the other hand, seduced my dear friend Mrs. Inchbald from me, though actually under article from August 1780 until May, 1781. . . . Nor was that my only loss at that crisis; for be it known, that whenever any provincial actor or actress makes any stride in the opinion of the audience . . . immediately sets a London manager to level his dart, and say, that bird is mine—I will have it."[65]

The other loss Wilkinson refers to here was Suett, a player whom, as we have said, he had trained and supported since Suett was very young. Wilkinson did have some justification for his comments.

The Smiths remained with Wilkinson until 1786. Wilkinson was unusually patient with them, for Mrs. Smith was very difficult. And when Dorothy Jordan came along, the two—Mrs. Smith and Jordan—were great rivals. Mrs. Smith was excessively jealous of anyone and everyone. She injured herself permanently when she returned to the stage too soon after the birth of her child in the fall of 1782, refusing to allow Jordan to take her place. Finally Wilkinson could no longer tolerate her, and he wrote, "we agreed to part at the expiration of articles, the end of May 1786, and never were friends again in Yorkshire." Their story again illustrates the difficulties managers had in attempting to keep all the players happy and amiable.[66]

FOUR

LONDON AT LAST

☙ **O**n her first day in London, a Thursday, Mrs. Inchbald wrote, "A fine day—unpacked then dressed and dined below with my Landlady talked of Mr. Davis c&c, then laid down and was dull—at dark walked with my Landlady to many shops—found there was a play at Covent Garden—supped with her and read the paper." The next day she "had [her] hair dressed and liked the hair dresser much." She saw William Thomas Lewis and Richard Griffith, and she had hoped to see Thomas Hull, but she "was disappointed by Mr. Hull's not calling me"; Mr. Harris promised to call the next day. But the next day, although she "Dressed and waited sometime for Mr. Harris's calling," he did not come. She found her way to her sister's, and when she returned, Mr. Hull "calld and I spouted a little to him." Afterward she went to Drury Lane with Mr. Wilson of York and another gentleman. The play was *The Tempest*, followed by *All the World's a Stage*. After she went home, she reports, "Mr. Wilson the actor supped with me. After Mr. Griffith calld."

The gentlemen she had hoped to see as soon as she had arrived were the ones who administered Covent Garden; we have found them in her pocket-book as she was planning for London, and we have found them mentioned by everyone who advised her about her obtaining a place at Covent Garden. Harris, as the proprietor of Covent Garden, was the ultimate authority; Hull was in 1780 the acting manager.

These early days in London include most of the activities she was to engage in for the next decade. Although she did not know all the players at Covent Garden, she knew many of them, and she was always delighted to see her friends from elsewhere; her sister was to be her constant companion; she would wait on Harris many times, and she would continue to work on her acting—to "spout" to someone. Hull, who, like Harris, she "waited" for, was at this time acting manager for Lewis. Hull made his debut at Covent Garden in the fall of 1759, and according to the *Biographical Dictionary,* he continued there in the winter season for the next forty-eight years. He was an accomplished, though never a brilliant, actor. Seldom playing leading roles, he was nonetheless very valuable in that he frequently played night after night, week after week. He once remarked that he had missed the prompter's call but once in fifty-four years. Beginning with the season 1775–1776 through 1781–1782, he served as acting manager; in this position it was proper for Mrs. Inchbald to "spout" to him before she saw Harris. In fact Lewis, who was the manager, filled the role of what we would call an artistic manager, selecting the plays and serving as director as well. As I have explained elsewhere, the type of acting at Covent Garden was more rhetorical than natural, more formal and artificial than the dramatic style Mrs. Siddons was to practice when she returned to the London stage in 1782.

The day after her work with Hull, Mrs. Inchbald had an especially busy time. She rose early and brushed her things; her hairdresser came for a short time; her friend Davis came unexpectedly; and as soon as she was dressed, Harris sent for her to come to the House. She went over parts to him and, she writes, "came home very happy at his approving of my Belario." She ends her entry, "went to bed early but did not sleep." And this entry on Sunday, September 30, completed her transfer from York and Wilkinson to London and Harris. This entry did not, however, tell the whole story; her life in London was not her life in York.

On Monday, October 1, she began to attend to her duties. She called on Hull at the House and then went to see the wardrobe attendant. She called on Lewis and on Charles Macklin, but neither was at home. Afterward she says, "then at my parts." She went to *The Beggar's Opera* with Mr. and Mrs. Lewis, and when she got home, she discovered a message with a part in *Measure for Measure.* She was sorry; she does not explain why she was sorry, but much later she criticized the play for its lack of an orderly plot and for the corrupt characters portrayed.[1]

After indicating concern about the weather and her health, Inchbald discusses the universal problems of food and lodging. By 1780 in London, food was plentiful, but housing was something of a problem.

The first place where she lived in London was typical in many ways of housing in the area around the Haymarket, Drury Lane, and Covent Garden. She had a room for herself, but she shared the house with her landlady, using the drawing room and the dining room with the household. In all the pocket-books, she reports about domestic matters. For example, the dining room was also used as a reception room, and by Thursday of this first week that she was in London, September 11, the weather had turned chilly, and she had a fire in the dining room.[2] This accommodation was very much more elegant than the rooms the Inchbalds had had in York, where they lived in the Shambles.[3] In London, as she continues to report, she had a fire several times during the fall and winter, sometimes in the dining room, sometimes in the parlor; in January there was a fire in her dressing room in the theatre. And although the climate in London was not so uncomfort-able as in the north, the uncertainty of cold and rain, the short days of winter, and the heat of summer prompted her to continue to record the weather throughout her pocket-books, even to her last entries, when she recorded that she was cold during the night in the next-to-last entry in the 1821 book before her death two days later.[4]

In these first days after her arrival in the city, when she saw Wilson and Suett, her friends and suitors, we have information about them as well. Evidently, soon after Suett arrived in London, he told Inchbald that he was about to marry and asked if she would like to board and lodge with him and his wife, but of course she refused. The invitation is another clue to the way "housing" worked for them in London. Suett did marry the dancer Louisa Margareta West, whom he had known when they were in Wilkinson's company; Inchbald also knew her, for she is listed in the playbills with the Inchbalds. Again it is interesting to notice that Suett had lived in the same household with the West family when he first went to Wilkinson in 1772. Certainly there was more opportunity in London to have a place of one's own, but even so, privacy was a luxury few could afford. As for Inchbald, she must have remembered the crowded accommodations of the early days, for she never again lived under such unpleasant circumstances.

When she had a place of her own, she entertained visitors in her parlor, and in her pocket-books she records a host of visitors for both teas and suppers; but when she lived on the Strand in very cramped quarters, she had to go down to the shop, her landlady's millinery shop, to see her visitors. Her friend John Taylor, who was in the habit of visiting her every Sunday for many years, said, "I then [at the Strand] only saw her when she came down to me in the shop, or when she called on me at the Sun office in the same street."[5]

In her accounts she always enters the money for domestic matters, for wash-ing, for example; and after her return from Ireland, she usually had a dresser at the theatre.[6] She always took responsibility for the domestic tasks needed in her rooms and apartments, and over the years she records a great many simple household tasks that she performed, all the way from sending for the bricklayers to stop up a mouse hole to washing her bed hangings and scrubbing her floor; and when she lived on the Strand, she not only scrubbed her floors, but she also had to buy her coal from the collier and take it up the stairs to her tiny room at the top of the house.

Soon after she arrived in London, she began to go to plays at Drury Lane on the nights when she was not playing at Covent Garden; her friends Suett and Wilson were at Drury Lane. This practice of the players' visiting from one theatre to the other was a common one, and Mrs. Inchbald records dozens of times when she went to Drury Lane while she was acting at Covent Garden. But of course after she was free, she went to both theatres whenever she pleased. And although she already knew a great many people—friends and family—she began to make many more friends, and over the years she lived in London, she knew all the players in both theatres.

Several times during her first season, Mrs. Inchbald mentions about her "dress." Here again, the situation was far different from the early days, especially in Scotland, when she was required to supply her own dresses. One of the most interesting sets of figures in her 1776 account pages has to do with her costumes for the stage; there were dresses, shoes, gloves, all obviously bought to be used on stage and carefully distinguished from the dresses and shoes she wore offstage. Just how much attention to costume she was required to pay when she came to Covent Garden is difficult to determine. She made her cap for her first appearance as Philaster, a "breeches" part.

Hairdressing was among the most frequently mentioned activities that Inchbald records in her books. Her friend Mr. Davis was the hairdresser of several actresses, and as a friend to all of them, he not only dressed their hair but frequently passed on news and gossip also. Inchbald had known him in York, but he soon appeared in London; and although she frequently told him she would never see him again, he always came back. She was among the first of the actresses to wear her own hair on stage; in the late 1790s she began to remark that she spent very little on clothes.

Mrs. Inchbald was quite striking in appearance, with her auburn hair[7] and a fair, sandy complexion, and during the early years in London, she continued to be very aware of her appearance, both the way her hair was dressed and the clothes she wore. For example, when she returned to Covent Garden for the second season in the fall of 1781, she wrote in one entry, "drest and looked remarkably well," and when she played her favorite role of Lady Touchwood, she wrote, "drest in the room that was Miss Catley's . . . admired my dress." When she went to hear the reading of Holcroft's new comedy, she wore her "white," and after having conversation with Harris behind the scenes, she reported that "he took my spying glass from me." She was very nearsighted and without her glass could hardly see.

Some of the entries in the pocket-books suggest interesting information about fashion. Her accounts in the 1776 book when she was in Scotland are filled with notations of expenses for material and "making" of various dresses and coats. In the entry for March 25–31, 1776, she records that she bought seventeen yards of "grey silk for a gown and petticoat at 4 shillings, 4 pence a yard and 1 shilling for lining for the petticoat" and another shilling for "body lining." In 1783 in her entry for February 24–March 2, when she was about to leave Ireland, she lists that she spent £1 15s. of English money for twenty-five yards of Irish cloth and 4s. 6d. for two yards and a quarter for "slieves [*sic*]." She selected her dresses carefully. Once when she went to the House to fit her dress, she came home and put on her hat before she saw Harris. It was upon this occasion that he told her he would consider her farce. The pocket-books show clearly that she was careful of her appearance and that she understood the importance of fashionable dress. It is not surprising that later she was asked to be a part of John Bell's periodical *La Belle Assemblée*.

Even in these early days, Mrs. Inchbald saw her friends socially and through them made other friends. She knew Mr. and Mrs. Lewis as friends; he had helped her secure her place with Harris, and the Lewises were friends of Charles Macklin—although Inchbald knew him only slightly.

Mr. and Mrs. Lewis played an important part in Inchbald's life in London, from these first days until she quit the stage. In the early days, Lewis, as acting manager at Covent Garden, was her direct link to Harris. Lewis had come to Covent Garden from Dublin in 1773; when Inchbald came, he was the acting manager, but in 1782 he became deputy manager, carrying out those duties while he continued to act; he remained for thirty-five years. He had been sponsored by Macklin, the celebrated actor who by 1780 had had a very distinguished career for some seventy-five years, having acted in London by 1725. He created quite a sensation with his interpretation of Shylock in the season of 1740–1741 at Drury Lane, and afterward he became more and more celebrated. According to the *Biographical Dictionary*, he was "entitled to rank, with Garrick, as one of the two most 'revolutionary' performers between Betterton and Kean."[8] In 1780 Macklin, in his eighties, was engaged at Covent Garden, and he continued to act until his death in 1797 at age 98.

The day after her evening with Macklin and the Lewises, Inchbald spoke to Harris about her dress. The costumes at Covent Garden must certainly have been more attractive than some she had had available earlier. Over the years she was to be much admired for her taste in dressing, especially because she was not extravagant but rather careful to look appropriate for her parts. The part of Bellario was a breeches part and one she had played many times before. Perhaps she already had all or at least part of her costume. On Wednesday she was "at her part" and was fitted for her boy's clothes.

As happy as she was to be in London, Inchbald was not without worries. She was never, even when she became the "Celebrated Mrs. Inchbald," quite pleased with herself. She always worried about her acting; she realized she was not as accomplished as her own judgment told her she should be; she was a perfectionist all her life, but, aware of her problems, she never stopped to feel sorry for herself. Instead she worked away, seeking advice from friends—both personal and professional. The other constant references in her pocket-book during these last months of 1780 are the references to the people in the company at Covent Garden and the other friends and relatives she knew in London. In the first weeks she was there, she went to Drury Lane more than once; after she began to have roles assigned for her to act two or three times a week, she had no time to see the plays at Drury Lane, even though some of her friends were there, Suett and Wilson, for example.

On Tuesday, October 9, she appeared for the first time on the London stage. The play, an adaptation of Francis Beaumont and John Fletcher's *Philaster*, had a character, Bellario, who actually was a beautiful young girl but who appeared disguised as a young man. The part suited her exactly. Tall and slim, she was well suited to breeches parts. This first one was not the last. She had worked on her cap for two days before playing the part, but in the actual performance she forgot to remove it as she should have; being on the London stage for the first time, she was understandably very tense.

The play had been adapted by George Colman, and his advertisement, preceding the printed version, is an interesting example of the way the eighteenth century viewed Jacobean drama, the way such drama influenced the dramatist, and the way such adaptations were made. Colman begins by saying:

This present Age, though it has done Honour to its own Discernment by the Applause paid to Shakespeare, has, at the same Time, too grossly neglected the other great Masters in the same School of Writing. The Pieces of Beaumont and Fletcher in particular ... abound with Beauties, so much of the same Colour with these of Shakespeare that it is almost unaccountable, that the very Age which admires one, even to Idolatry, should pay so little Attention to the others. The Truth is that Nature indeed is in all Ages the same; but Modes and Customs, Manners and Language, are subject to perpetual Variation. Time insensibly renders Writings obsolete and uncouth, and the gradual Introduction of new Words and Idioms, brings the older Forms into Disrepute and Disuse. But the intrinsic Merit of any Work, though it may be obscured must forever remain; As antique Coins, or old Plate, though not current or fashionable, still have their Value, according to their Weight.[9]

The story line of *Philaster* tells of a king who wanted to arrange a marriage, of unhappy young people who wished to make their own love matches, and of the power of a ruler to impose his plans on family and subjects. The part Inchbald played was that of the young girl who heard such reports of a young man that she disguised herself as a boy and became Philaster's page. The complications in the story line are the usual ones of defiant young people and their elders. Much of the action takes place in the woods, an expansive place that can accommodate a number of characters all searching for the princess, who runs away to avoid a marriage that she cannot face. Bellario, the beauty disguised as a page (the part Inchbald played), finds the princess and is wounded when she steps between her and her former lover. In Colman's version no one is killed, but Bellario, admitting that she is a girl, shows that the princess could not have lost her "virtue" and thus can marry her prince. The foreign suitor is sent away; Bellario goes away on pilgrimage.

Colman's adaptation shortens some of the scenes of the original, leaves out one scene entirely, and makes another less violent. Colman himself explains:

> The Scene in the Fourth Act, wherein Philaster, according to the original Play, wounds Arthusa and Belario, and from which the Piece took its second Title of "Love Lies Bleeding," had always been censured by the Criticks. They breath too much of that Spirit of Blood, and Cruelty, and Horror, of which the English Tragedy hath often been accused. The Hero's wounding his Mistress hurt the Delicacy of most; and his maiming Bellario sleeping in order to save himself from his Pursuers offended the Generosity of all. This part of the Fable therefore so injurious to the character of Philester, it was judged absolutely requisite to alter; and a new Turn has been given to those circumstances: But the Change has been affected by such simple means, and with such Reverence to the Original, that there are hardly ten lines added on Account of the Alteration.[10]

There are some interesting points to be made about some features of the play that make the turn of the breeches part rather more realistic than Shakespeare's use of the device in *As You Like It*. There is no comment in the pocket-book about Inchbald's performance or her failure to remove her cap; instead, according to the next day's entry, she was asked if she wanted to play Mrs. Strickland instead of Bellario; she accepted the assignment, as we discover two days later when she records, "played Mrs. Strickland after wrote a copy of a letter to Mr. Harris." The players did have some choices, and she continued to write letters.

All along during these weeks there are comments in her book about her domestic and social life. On the day after her performance of Bellario, she saw Suett and Mr. and Mrs. Lewis.

Suett, who had been among the first to propose to Mrs. Inchbald after her husband's death, was now at Drury Lane, he too having left Wilkinson for London. She records that he "told me he was going to marry—they (the Lewis's) offered to board and lodge me—after settled to stay here." Her entry compared to that in the *Biographical Dictionary* about Suett is rather puzzling. According to the *Biographical Dictionary*, Suett married a Miss West, a dancer, in York in the summer of 1781 while he was there for the summer season, before he returned to

London in the fall. Perhaps his comment to Inchbald was rather premature. The offer of lodging raises an important point. In London, as in York, many of the players shared accommodations; that is, they boarded in the same residences. Just where Inchbald lived this first season is not clear; later she discusses her landladies and their houses, sometimes in great detail. This entry about Suett and the Lewises' accommodations does once again give us a detail of how the players lived outside of their time in the green room and on stage.

Suett had made his London debut two days before Inchbald's, on October 7 in the part of Ralph in *The Maid of the Mill*. In the spring of 1782, he was living in Gloucester Street, Queen's Square, in Bloomsbury. The *Biographical Dictionary* reports that Suett married Louisa West, a dancer who had been with Wilkinson in 1779–1780 and that the marriage took place in York at St. Michael le Belfrey. Inchbald certainly knew West, though the difference between the pocket-book entry and Suett's marriage date is puzzling. Did Suett have another disappointment about his wedding plans? The *Biographical Dictionary* gives the dates from December 20 to January 14 as an engagement West had played with her brother in Derby. The lives of the players were always uncertain, regulated as they had to be by the demands of their engagements. In the end Suett's marriage to Louisa was not happy. He and Inchbald continued to be friends, and they both remained in London for the rest of their professional careers, Suett at Drury Lane in the winter and at the Haymarket in the summer, from 1793 on. Again we are reminded of the way the players knew each other and were a part of the professional life in all three theatres.

Continuing her report of happenings, Inchbald says she went with Davis to *Jane Shore* and that she "bespoke" a cap and had a fire in the dining room. In most of the houses where the players boarded, the dining room was also a kind of parlor where they could entertain visitors, and by the middle of October the weather in London could be quite chilly.

During these days she also read the newspapers; the London papers reported on the theatres quite differently from the way Yorkshire papers did. Writers who came to the theatres night after night wrote as critics even if they had done no more than attend the plays as members of the audience. From the beginning of her time in London, however, Mrs. Inchbald was keenly aware of their comments. In the end, of course, she became an important member of their ranks when she wrote her *Remarks*. But in October 1780 it was her friend Davis who brought her the paper, which, she said, "I liked very much." Davis brought her the paper almost every day, and once she was "greatly alarmed" by a line she read in a paper that said she would be addressed the next day; the next day she makes no comment about herself, but two days later Wilson brought her Woodfall's paper with a letter addressed to her. She does not include it in her pocket-book, but a day or so later she "had Mr. Woodfall's paper and heard all the others were equally hard on Mrs. Ward." Woodfall was one, an important one, of the proprietors of the great many periodicals flourishing at this time. This was Sarah Ward, whom Inchbald had just seen in *Jane Shore;* Sarah, with her husband, had been at Liverpool in 1776 when the Inchbalds were there, and thus it is not surprising that Inchbald would follow her closely. After she played Lavinia in *The Fair Penitent,* she says there was "only one paper concerning my Lavinia." The same entry indicates that she "read some of my farce." Her own writing was always at hand, and when she was in good spirits she worked away at it.

In the entries in the weeks before the end of the year, she repeatedly records gossip about various players both at Drury Lane and Covent Garden; perhaps we should call it "comments" rather than gossip, for at this point in London she was the "new" player. On October 17, after a day at the rehearsal of *The Fair Penitent,* in which she was to play Lavinia, she had walked to her sister's, where she ate broth (she had been dizzy at rehearsal the day before). Then after dinner Mr. Davis made her two caps, Mrs. Bates called and fitted her jacket, she wrote a note to Mr. Palmer, and then she "was at Jane Shore and the Camp at Drury Lane— Mrs. Ward's appearance."

The Wards had been in London, but their contract with Covent Garden had not been renewed in the spring of 1777 and they had been in various places, including Birmingham and Liverpool. For a brief time Mrs. Ward had returned to Drury Lane, where on October 17 she played in *Jane Shore;* this was one of Nicholas Rowe's "she tragedies," as was *The Fair Penitent,* for which Mrs. Inchbald had been rehearsing. These plays of Rowe's were "classics" known to every theatre patron. By some they were considered to be very old-fashioned and out of date; to others, they were so familiar that seeing them over and over provided a special opportunity to make judgments about the players. Evidently the audience at Drury Lane was not pleased with Mrs. Ward's performance—at least according to Woodfall they were not. After her comment about Woodfall and Mrs. Ward, Inchbald says, "at my parts—dined while my hair was dressing—play'd Lavinia . . . not pleased till Mr. Davis came home said he sat with Mr. and Mrs. Crawford and what they said of me." Again she does not explain, but the comments from the Crawfords were probably complimentary. This fall found the Crawfords at Drury Lane after being at the Haymarket in the summer. Recently married, they were much gossiped about. Mrs. Crawford was well known as an actress and as Mrs.

Ann Spranger Barry, but upon Barry's death in 1777 she had married Thomas "Billy" Crawford, who was some sixteen years her junior. This summer and fall was the first time she had been in London since her marriage, and Mrs. Inchbald would have been very interested in any comment from the Crawfords.

The entry in the pocket-book the next day read, "a wet day—only one paper concerning my Lavinia . . . alone and in good spirits at what Mrs. Booth told me of Mrs. Hartley." Later in the week she played Constinata, but she did not stay the farce for she feared she had played "ill." But the next day she says, "I uneasy till I saw the paper—then all the rest of the evening at my farce and easy." The entries in her pocket-book were certainly for her own use; thus they are full of unfinished puzzling comments that only she could understand. What did Mrs. Booth tell her of Mrs. Hartley? The *Biographical Dictionary* says that Hartley had retired in the spring of 1780, and now it is late October of the next theatre season. Why were Woodfall and the other writers "hard" on Mrs. Ward? The periodical press was very active in the decade of the 1780s, and the journals were filled with comments and speculations about the theatres.[11]

The accounts of her activities during these first weeks in London are filled not only with new friends but also with the people she already knew, among whom perhaps the most familiar one was Davis. He had been with her and her husband in York, where, Wilkinson says, "Mr. Davis, well known for his fashionable taste in all tragedy geer, made a stage trial in Edwin, in 'Matilda' on Friday July 3, 1778; but he and the Muses did not agree. The York stage, and indeed the London and Dublin Theatres have been much indebted for his pains in embellishing Kings, Queens, Princes, Emperors, and Ladies of Quality: I have purchased in the year I am now scribbling, a variety of dresses, which have been universally approved, made in London under the direction of the said gentleman."[12]

Her comment in the pocket-book that Davis sat with the Crawfords places him in that group of theatre people; although they did not act, they performed many of the very necessary tasks to make the plays possible. Davis had not only been her hairdresser, but, as Wilkinson observes, he also designed costumes. He seems to have gone from place to place and to have known even more gossip than Mrs. Inchbald. She frequently quarreled with him, though we are never told the reasons. She would write in the pocket-books that she sent him away *forever*, but in the spring he invariably reappeared.

Some of these entries in the last two weeks of October mention Harris. Taken together, these early entries about Harris reveal a growing acceptance of each for the other. Inchbald from the early days had had a special place in the troupe with the manager: in Scotland with Digges, in York with Wilkinson. Her long campaign to come to Covent Garden had not always been smooth, as we have seen. Wilkinson really needed her to stay with him, to take the "second" parts[13]; and even though we may understand her pique, Wilkinson was right in terms of managerial policy, and she was wrong. It was her persistence, in spite of everything—or anything—that found her in London in Covent Garden. One writer to Harris chided him for hiring her, saying she would never be worth a sixpence. In the pocket-book entries for October, November, and December there are repeated, though usually slight and cryptic, comments about her encounters with Harris. We have noted the first of these when, as a new player, she went to be interviewed for the parts she would play. This day, the Sunday after she had arrived in London, concluded with the assignment of Bellario. It is interesting to observe that on Friday, October 18, she played Angelina in *The Fop's Fortune*. Boaden comments: "In this lovely part she was highly complimented. Mr. Harris himself saw her performance, and it was the first time of his seeing her act."[14] Her account in the pocket-book reads, in part: "received the part of the Abbess [in *The Comedy of Errors*] and sat below most of the day—played Angelina. Mr. Smith of Drury Lane complimented me and Mr. Harris the first of his seeing me on the stage was happy."

The mention of Smith and Harris as seeing her performance reminds us that Smith of Drury Lane had come to Covent Garden to see the performance. Smith was the Gentleman Smith who had gone away with Mrs. Hartley to France. This episode had extended from France to Dublin and had been much discussed in the press; but by this fall of 1780, Smith was back at Drury Lane and Hartley was gone from Covent Garden. Hartley acted no more in London.

The day following her report of the two distinguished gentlemen, Inchbald called at the House and talked to Wilson about her farce; she "just saw Mr. Harris." In the next week in almost every entry there is some comment about her farce—or farces—that she read over herself, that she read to someone else. On Sunday, October 28, she says she "sent and Received my farce from Mr. Colman." On the Tuesday following she says Wilson "took my farce," and on the following Thursday she was "at my farce and parts . . . was at Hamlet then behind a little and saw Mr. Harris." The next day her entry reads: "At rehearsal of Anne Bullen then at my sister's a very fine and cold day—walked in Grey's Inn Gardens—dined and drank tea and supped at my sister's at candlelight began to copy my farce and wrote after I got home." Such an entry brings together the details of life in London: her time at the theatre, the weather, her dinner and walk. Typical of many of the entries, it shows clearly the variety of interests she had at hand in London.

And we are reminded again of the great variety of work and pleasure that a player in the London theatres could indulge in.

The theatre people and her family were not the only people Mrs. Inchbald saw in London. One weekend in early November, her friend and suitor Dr. Brodie wrote her a note, and she replied evidently saying she would see him; he came and spent some time with her. She also saw Francis Twiss with her brother and sister-in-law. Twiss had long been a friend of George Simpson and the Simpson family. He was a circuit judge who went regularly to Norwich and usually stopped by to see the Simpsons on his way. He became not only a friend but also one of Inchbald's closest advisers and critics; he was one of the few people to whom she went for advice, and she usually followed his advice. She does not indicate at this point that she submitted her work to him, though she probably did. She talked to everyone about her writing. She was never secretive about it at any time in her career. It is quite amazing to find, through reading the pocket-book entries for these last weeks in 1780, that she was doing so much work on her writing while she continued to play a variety of roles on stage.

The Sunday she saw Twiss and her brother, she also saw her friend Griffith, the manager of the theatre at Norwich. He had just resigned because of ill health after some fourteen successful years. He was the Griffith whom she had a crush on when, as a teenager, she went to see him. He treated her kindly, and she and her brother had been his friends for all the years since 1770. In fact, it was in the Norwich Company that George Simpson began his career, and it was here that Joseph Inchbald and his friend Wilson had met Elizabeth Simpson, who two years later became Mrs. Inchbald. George Simpson and his wife had, since the time they were in York with Inchbald and Wilkinson, come to London evidently without an assignment. Mr. and Mrs. Simpson had been with Griffith and the Norwich Company in 1778 and 1779, and, as is typical of provincial players, they were in London to see plays and find a next assignment.

Wilson, another of this circle, had been at Norwich with Griffith and Inchbald; it was he who had "partied" with Mr. Inchbald in 1772 when they were first in Scotland and Mrs. Inchbald had stayed up all night waiting for them. But by November of 1780, such events were far in the past, and all the Norwich friends had been in many other places. Wilson had come to Covent Garden in 1775–1776, where he was associated for the next ten years, until 1785. It was from this vantage point that he had helped Mrs. Inchbald with her contract for Covent Garden and had served as her "messenger" for her repeated submission of her writing to Colman. He was the original Lord Oldcastle in Colman's *Separate Maintenance* on June 13 in 1780 and Sir James Juniper in *Summer Amusement* later on the seventeenth. And while she was writing to him about London from York, he was very busy. He created two more original roles that summer at the Haymarket—Tremor in Andrews's *Fire and Water* on July 8 and Governor Harcourt in Lee's *Chapter of Accidents* on August 5. He was very attentive to and supportive of Mrs. Inchbald all summer and fall.

On December 20 Wilson, as cited by Boaden, wrote Inchbald a proposal of marriage:

Dear Madam,

I most earnestly intreat you will not take offence at my addressing you on a subject upon which my happiness so materially depends; as it is a matter I have well considered, before I could gather courage, I hope I shall not offend you by saying I sincerely love you, and will by a uniformity of conduct convince you how much I am attached to you. I have a great many faults, not one of which but is easily erased. I have unfortunately been acquainted with ladies who have had as many faults as myself, therefore a reform there was not to be expected: with you, should I ever be so happy, I would be everything you could wish me; my conduct, in every respect, should be framed to your wish; my whole life should be devoted to render you happy. For God's sake, whatever is my doom, do not let me lose your friendship. Honour me so far as to let me know my fate as early as possible: a state of suspense is of all states the most miserable. I know your prudence will not suffer you rashly to enter on a second marriage, without minutely deliberating on the consequences. Give me but leave to speak to you on this subject, and I shall then hope, by time, to convince you it is my wish to do every thing that can render me worthy your attention. I am, sincerely,

Your devoted friend and well-wisher,
Rd. Wilson
Wednesday morning, 10 o'clock.
No. 15, King Street, Soho.

The next day he wrote another letter:

Dear Madam,

I hope you will believe me, when I assure you I had a very uncomfortable night, in consequence of the letter I sent you. I was out this morning before your answer came; I returned at eleven and found it. So far from alleviating my passion, it has increased it: your letter breathes the spirit of virtue and good sense and makes me more conscious of your inestimable worth. You say, "your temper is uncertain, and that nothing but a blind affection could bear with it." I think the man that is honoured with your hand must be totally blind to his own happiness, if he could not overlook and humour an infirmity of that kind, to secure so many lasting virtues. I will allow the loss of a worthy, loving, and attentive husband, is not soon to be reconciled to a lady who thinks and feels with that goodness of heart that you do; and that the hazard in venturing on a second is great. I will confess, that

I have not conducted myself through life with that degree of prudence and discretion, that your late worthy husband did; but this I will be bold to say, that my *heart* is good; so is my temper. I feel with you I could be every thing you would wish to mould me to, and know no pleasure without you. Only give me leave (in hopes your present sentiments may remove) to convince you, your friends, and the world, in time, by my deportment, that I have no wish on earth but what is centred in you. As to worldly matters I will not presume to enter on that subject, till I dare flatter myself with the *smallest* part of your esteem: that once gained, I will venture to say I never will forfeit it. Believe me anxious to do every thing in my power to render your life happy, and that I am, with sincerity,

Your real friend and devoted servant,
R.W.
Thursday. No. 15, King Street.

Whatever her feelings or his were at the moment, they remained friends, very close friends, as he continued to help her place her manuscripts; and on the twenty-fifth for a Christmas present he sent her a book.

Dear Madam,

I have sent you the "History of England;" and have troubled you with this for no other reason than—to wish you a merry Christmas; a happy new year—a great many of them; that you may be married before this day twelve months; that I may have the choosing of your husband—it would be a difficult matter to find a good one, but I think I could find one that loves you dearly. This is all in friendship; and I am, most sincerely,

Your devoted humble servant,
R.W.[15]

It is certain that Wilson's "choosing of your husband" was a reference to himself. Wilson's personal life was rather varied; according to the *Biographical Dictionary,* he had had "relationships": the first was with Elizabeth Elrington at Leeds in 1767, and then in 1775 he lived with Maria Weston, who had left her husband, a tradesman. It was she who was with Wilson when they were with the Inchbalds in Edinburgh, and they were together when they came to London in 1775. How long they continued to live together is not certain, but Wilson certainly would not have written a proposal to Inchbald if in the last weeks of December he had been living with someone else. In many ways Wilson was a typical player: he always was in need of money, always in debt. The *Biographical Dictionary* points out that he moved from place to place. By 1786 it was reported that he had left London in order to escape his creditors. He went to Edinburgh, where again he became a great favorite.

During this 1780–1781 season, however, Wilson continued to be Inchbald's adviser about professional matters with both Harris and Colman. And Inchbald continued to write and send work to Colman and to write to Harris about her salary and her parts. Harris kept tight control of the finances; because he and Lewis found her "useful," Harris gave her good roles, for the most part secondary roles like, for example, the part of Lavinia in *The Fair Penitent,* but paid her very little. Moreover, after the new year, during Lent the playhouses were closed two nights a week for the Oratorios and the players' salaries cut until after Easter. Harris understood that she was an experienced actress who already knew the roles in the standard plays, but he was not one to give anything away without exacting a price. Inchbald and the other players were required to "walk" in the pantomime—an assignment she despised—and for all the persistence she exercised, he would not accept one of her farces.

Sometime during these various attempts to do as she pleased and to have her work accepted, Wilson wrote again to her. The letter is undated, but the advice that he gives places it in this early period when she had not yet learned to deal with Harris. She had evidently refused a character in some play that she considered not worthy of her, and Wilson writes:

I am sorry Mr. Harris attempted to send you a character that you must, in justice to yourself, refuse. I would wish you to be particular in the mode of refusing it. Remember, my dear Madam, how ardently you wished for London! what flattering reasons you have to wish to continue it! You have had in your theatrical situation, every thing you could wish for, but money; but then you have got possession of characters that will hereafter demand money. Whatever is the dispute, treat with no deputies. See Mr. Harris—reason with him; he is ever ready to redress grievances, when the parties make their own complaint: if it come through any other channel, circumstances are not always properly related; and, too frequently, advice is given before the manager has time to form his own judgment. I hope to God it will terminate to your entire satisfaction.[16]

Wilson, of course, was right, though the pocket-book entries show that she continued to ask for more salary and continued to read her farces to everyone—as she continued to work on them, revising them and copying them out. Her handwriting was rather difficult to read; she must have made her "copies" more legible than her pocket-book entries, but the entries in the pocket-books that record her work always include entries about copying. The work in the theatre was always to be done; parts were assigned, rehearsals attended, and sometimes she was in both the main piece and the farce or after-piece.

On November 14 she played Lady Frances Touchwood again in *The Belle's*

Stratagem, this for the first time in London. Before she began to rehearse it, she had seen Cowley, and on Monday, November 12, she says that after rehearsal she talked with Cowley again. On the Wednesday following she played Lady Touchwood, and on Saturday she played Lady Touchwood again. Having played it in York for Wilkinson, she was already familiar with the role and the play. Both the play and her role became favorites with her, and many years later in her *Remarks* she speaks again of her pleasure. She found Sir George and Lady Touchwood ideal: "The love of Sir George and his wife is fervent, yet reasonable; they are fond, but not foolish; and with all their extreme delicacy of opinion, never once express their thoughts either in ranting, affected, or insipid sentences."

The cast of the play was a fine one. Richard Wroughton was Sir George Touchwood; Lewis was Doricourt; Lee Lewes played Flutter; Saville was done by Aickin; and Villiers by Whitfield. Mrs. Racket was played by Mrs. Mattocks; Miss Ogle by Mrs. Morton; and Letitia by Miss Younge. Both Mattocks and Younge were favorites with the London audience.

Lewis was Inchbald's friend with whom she had gone to the theatre when she first came to London; Wroughton had been at Covent Garden since 1768. He had created the character Sir George in the season before (1779–1780) and playing Lady Touchwood's husband again in this production. Lewes had created the role of Flutter in the first production, and he, like Wroughton, had been at Covent Garden since the sixties. The play had been a success for Cowley in its first production, and it remained her most frequently acted play. She is sometimes compared to Inchbald, since they were contemporaries and both successful— though Cowley was not so successful as Inchbald.

Cowley's first play, staged by Garrick at Drury Lane, was entitled *The Runaway.* In this production in 1776, Siddons was cast as the ingenue, but this year, which proved to be so unsuccessful for Siddons, turned out to be quite successful for Cowley. Nonetheless, *The Runaway,* as successful as it was—it was played ten times— was not so successful as *The Belle's Stratagem,* which was played twenty times in its first season. As already noted, in the spring of 1780 *The Belle's Stratagem* was presented at Covent Garden with Hartley creating the role of Lady Frances. In Inchbald's pocket-book entries for November 1780, there are two interesting comments about Hartley, who was at Bristol that first summer after the Inchbalds were married and who, as we have said, resembled Inchbald physically. Hartley had golden hair like Inchbald and was tall with a fine figure. The mention of Hartley in this fall season is not surprising; indeed, Inchbald's pocket-book includes information not found elsewhere, and the combination of Cowley, Inchbald, and Hartley brings up some interesting questions about the three in the theatre. Hartley did not perform in London after the spring season of 1780; Cowley's next play was not so successful as *The Belle's Stratagem,* and Inchbald's first success did not occur until four long years later. Theatre managers were very demanding.

At rehearsal, shortly after she arrived, Inchbald had written, "Mr. Lewis told me of some faults. Mr. Wilson there and told me what Mrs. Hartley said of me who was there but did not speak to me." Some two weeks later an entry began, "A wet day . . . only one paper concerning my Lavinia . . . saw two acts of Much Ado and the new farce of the Election . . . alone and in good spirits at what Mrs. Booth told me of Mrs. Hartley." Another two entries extend the story. In the week of January 21, in the midst of discussion about her salary and her entry of playing in the pantomime even though she was ill, she says, "heard Mrs. Hartley was to be in the New Comedy." On Saturday, February 1, 1781, after she had played Lady Frances again, she says, "received a part in the new comedy and heard Mrs. Hartley would not play all the season." The "new" comedy was evidently Cowley's *World As It Goes;* it was unsuccessful. Presented as *Second Thoughts Are Best,* it was again rejected. Boaden's report of this play is worth repeating: "It should however be remembered, that in a new comedy called 'The World As it Goes,' by Mrs. Cowley, she [Inchbald] was complimented by a part called Sidney *Grubb,* but had no chance whatever of becoming a *butterfly;* for the play being condemned the first night, and also when tried again under the title of 'Second Thoughts Are Best,' Miss *Grubb* never survived to her *chrysalis* state."[17]

In the *Memoirs* Boaden wrote of Mrs. Siddons, he examines Cowley's play in some detail:

> Mrs. Cowley on the fame of her Belle's Stratagem hurried again upon the stage. But her present offering was of a very different description from the delicate comedy just named. There is unity of design, great simplicity, and strong though refined effect, in The Belle's Stratagem. The audience was indifferent to The World as it Goes and voted the party at Montpelier exceedingly disagreeable. The fair author took a month for alteration, and brought her play again before the town under the title Second Thoughts are Best. The audience did not reverse, but confirmed the original judgment. It was a total failure from hurry and want of intelligent structure.

In a footnote he continues to discuss his view of drama. Here again we are invited to consider the paradox of national character. "The grave meditating Englishman begins to build without a plan; the volatile Frenchman lays his design deeply, and excels all nations in dramatic fable. We have a wide field of observation—in no country does character or humour present a more abundant harvest—but we are not sufficiently attentive to the homely instruction of honest Touchstone—'They that reep must sheaf and bind.'"[18]

The entries about Cowley and Hartley in Inchbald's pocket-book reveal her association with Cowley and her feeling about Hartley; she evidently remembered her husband's response that first summer in Bristol when, as Boaden remarked, she disapproved of his response to the Hartleys. That she should be so interested in Hartley from the fall to February confirms our view of how interrelated productions, players, and writers were. Boaden's analysis of the problem of Cowley's play is the kind of analysis Inchbald later made of her own plays; she was acutely aware of "structure," and although sometimes she did not achieve her goal, she was always aware of it.

All through the season after the pantomimes began around Christmas, Inchbald reports that she played in them—many times, according to one report—when she was not playing in either a main piece or an after-piece. On Monday, February 4, she played in *The Gamester* and in the pantomime. Then she says, "vext on hearing the Pantomime was to be played every night with the new tragedy." The pantomime required that she dress and be at the theatre whether she played or not. On the Wednesday following, she played in the pantomime again; this time her entry includes the comment, "Sent to ask Mr. Harris for a Masquerade Dress c&c." And the next day she says, "Miss Satchell calld. I went with her to look at masks and to my hair dresser." And on the next day, in an entry filled with the usual sundry items, she writes, "Wrote a note to Mr. Sheridan . . . in the Pantomime—after some consideration went to the masquerade." In the next entry she says, "Not till morning in bed . . . saw Miss Satchel and her sister—went together to the play . . . in the pantomime." On the next day, Saturday, she was at rehearsal of the new comedy at eleven and was in the pantomime again. On Sunday, after writing letters she began to work on her farce; her sister sent for her to come to dinner, where they "dined off a turkey—after I came home was sleepy and drunk tea—then finished the first act of my farce." On Monday she continues: "was till near Dark at my farce—liked it much and near it completed. Dined at my sisters and she told me what Debby said about my salary."

Inchbald's entries about her family are frequent and sometimes puzzling. As in all families, there were frequent differences, but she seldom explains. Her sister Hunt helped her by going with her to the theatre, by taking notes to various people, by dining with her sometimes at her own place and sometimes at Inchbald's. In several places Inchbald records that she was angry or that they quarreled. Boaden, writing almost fifty years after these entries, simply ignored them, remarking only now and then about "important" people she came to know after she came to

London. About her family he says only that her sister Hunt lived in very lowly circumstances. The question of where Inchbald lived in places near the theatre is also rather a puzzle. Did she live near enough to get home before the streets were deserted? Other players lived nearby—did they sometimes go home together? The plays were not over until near midnight, and usually the actresses had a maid or a family member to accompany them home. The Covent Garden area had, by 1780, become a slum. The elegant terrace houses that had been built in the early part of the 1700s had now become pubs or rooming houses or, in some cases, houses of prostitution. In one of these entries in February she says, "a man took hold of me as I came home."

From the pocket-book it is not clear whether her family depended on her for financial support this first year; later she actually supported her sisters. Her brother George Simpson and his wife visited several times during the 1780–1781 season. The Simpsons had been in several places after Edinburgh in 1776. They had returned to Norwich in 1777, and in 1781–1782 they were with Wilkinson. During this 1780–1781 season they were probably still at Norwich. The *Biographical Dictionary* quotes an agreement reported in the Norwich papers that "Mr. and Mrs. Simpson's Salary be advanced to £2/12s/6p week."[19] In one entry in October, Inchbald says, "Mr. Wilson called for a bird my brother sent me," and in her accounts for that week she paid eight pence for getting her bird. George Simpson, if he were with the Norwich circuit, could very well have been in Bury very near his mother and the farm, and hence sending the bird would have been easy to do. The fair in Bury was always in October, and it was at this time that the Norwich troupe came to town. One resident in 1773 reported, "This fair is now become rather a Place of Amusement than a temporary Mart, as most of the Merchandises now brought thither are chiefly Articles of Luxury and Curiosity." As Elizabeth Grice put it, the fair had actually become "a resort for gingerbread sellers and cheap jewellery, for family reunions and scandalmongering on a magnificent scale."[20]

The playhouse at Bury was at first a huge theatrical booth in the Abbey Gardens. In 1734 the Clothiers' Hall in the upper story of the Market Cross became a playhouse, and in 1778 Robert Adam remodeled the Market Cross to make it into a proper theatre, described at the time as "no mean specimen of his taste and architectural skill. The body is of white brick, but the ornaments are of freestone." It remained the town's theatre until 1819, when a new one was built by William Wilkins the younger, who designed it and insisted that the Adam theatre be turned into a public room, not a theatre, and that he be given the sole right to be licensed for plays.[21]

THE NORWICH TROUPE: FRIENDS AND FAMILY

The Sunday before Mrs. Inchbald began to rehearse *The Belle's Stratagem,* her brother was in the gathering of her friends—his friends, now hers, Griffith and Twiss, all associated with the Norwich troupe. Although Griffith had resigned as manager, he remained as an actor, and Twiss, Simpson's friend, was not only a circuit court judge in the Norwich circuit but also an ardent supporter of the theatre at Norwich. Another visitor to town was Palmer, the Bath manager who was there in the time of the Oratorios.[22] Palmer was John Palmer the younger; his father, John Palmer the elder, had organized the Orchard Street Theatre in Bath, and in 1775 Palmer the younger had renovated it; it was here that Sarah Siddons was currently acting. Inchbald sat in the same box with Palmer and "liked him excessively." At this point she probably would have transferred to Bath, as Boaden suggests, but she never had the opportunity to do so; later, when her first play was successful, she turned to Palmer again, only to discover that he, Harris, and Colman were close friends and associates, not to be "played" against each other.[23] In spite of her knowledge and experience at Edinburgh and York, she had, even at this point, not learned the degree to which she must be dependent on the managers, men who, although they found her useful as an actress and attractive as a woman, were still the dictators of the theatre—of Covent Garden, Drury Lane, and the Haymarket.

The entries about her salary and about her writing continue all through the spring until the season was over on June 4. Boaden gathers the various entries about her salary to conclude that she received £2 for the first week of the year; £3 until February 27, including the extra pound for walking in the pantomime; a salary cut of 10s. in Lent; later, because of the Oratorios twice a week, a cut of £1; and on April 21 she had her full salary of £3 again.[24]

Boaden, always interested in her suitors, continues to speculate, especially about her relationship with Dr. Brodie. Boaden and a great many other people viewing her and her career have had opinions about what she should have done. Most of her friends and family also must have found it strange that she did not encourage any of her suitors. Boaden says: "Mrs. Inchbald, though she could laugh at the serious addresses of Suett, and very steadily decline those of Wilson, seems not to have any repugnance to a second hymen, provided it elevated her condition in life, and the person was a gentleman agreeable in his manners."[25] Boaden and Inchbald's friends and family quite underestimated her independence and her driving passion to become a writer, however. It may be true that later the question of money was of paramount importance, but in this 1780–1781 season at Covent

Garden, her chief concerns were having some control over the parts she played and her untiring efforts to have a farce accepted. Although she records the daily events, even the weather, in her pocket-books, the repeated activities at this time are not the conversations she had with friends, not the food she ate, not the amusements of going to the theatre at Drury Lane or "in front" at her own Covent Garden, not stories of the green room or of the men who came to court her, but always, from one week, one day to another, that she was "at her part" and "at her farce." It is astonishing that she could work so steadily on her writing while she performed at the theatre.

In January and February she records many days as cold and wet; sometimes she says she had a fire in the dining room. Her pocket-book entries show that she clearly used this room as a reception room. When people called on her, they were shown into the dining room; for example, there is the amusing entry that says the marquis of Carmarthen called while her family was there and she sent them hastily into her bedchamber. These various details of her domestic arrangements suggest the social situations that arose when, as one of several occupants of a kind of boardinghouse, she wished to be alone. Such circumstances also account for her dining with her sister and going for tea at various places. In her pocket-book she frequently enters sums for wine, occasionally for brandy. She records that she paid nine shillings for her apartment, and several entries show that she arranged the furniture to her own satisfaction, making another comment about the circumstances for entertaining such visitors as Dr. Brodie and the marquis of Carmarthen. Evidently the dining room was where she used to read her farces aloud to her visitors. Reading aloud to each other was a favorite social pastime; the problem for Inchbald's visitors was that they were expected to respond. It somehow seems doubtful that Dr. Brodie or the marquis would spend their evenings listening.

During these cold wet months, Inchbald got sick in spite of the fire in her dining room. In the week of January 21 she was sick and "low spirited." The next day the doctor came and stayed all morning. She continued to play in the pantomime and on Wednesday in *Measure for Measure,* but she also continued to be ill and to see the doctor. The stress of her various activities, the weather, and her erratic eating habits all combined to keep her feeling "poorly," and she kept being upset with some of her visitors—this time Dr. Brodie. Around Christmastime he had brought her "many presents"—she does not say what he gave her, but on February 2 she returned them. In April he saw her almost every day: he called, had breakfast with her, or "supped" with her, until the middle of the month, when Dr. Grey, the doctor she had consulted, sent her home to Standingfield. Her entry on Sunday reads: "my sister and nanny came, drank tea and packed up my things—walked to the House and the Doctor went to the Stage Coach with me—the coach full." She paid sixteen shillings for her carriage and left her sister the money to pay her rent. On Monday at about eight o'clock she arrived at her mother's. She found her brother and sister and "little George" there and "after breakfast drest and then we walked—was very merry and happy but not quite well." The next day her sister Bigsby, who lived nearby, came to dine and stay to tea, after which they all went "round the wood." She wrote to Dr. Brodie. On Wednesday her brother read and they "told Laughable Storys." She was "not quite well." Thursday was a wet day, and they were prevented from visiting her sister Bigsby, but her sister Dolly told her fortune, and after supper they disputed about religion. Saturday was a fine day, but she was "poorly all day." Poorly or not, she was obliged to return to London. On Saturday she rose at three, went on horseback to Bury, breakfasted at Sudbury, and arrived in London at three. She disputed with a porter and then called at her sister's. It is no wonder after such a journey that she recorded on Sunday, "very dull and not well."

The next week she resumed her usual duties. She played Anne Bullen and walked in the pantomime. She records that the duke of Gloucester was in the audience that night. Before going home she had seen Wilkinson several times, he having been in London for some time; and as soon as she returned, she wrote to him. Apparently he had invited her to come to York for the summer, but she had declined.[26] On Friday she reports that "Mr. Webb called with an offer for me from Birmingham."

All through the spring she continued to write to Harris, this time about her farce, not about her duties on stage. She wrote to him about her books, that is, about the parts in the plays she needed. During March, while Wilkinson was still in town, she saw him frequently. On March 9 she was "in front and behind" at *Merry Wives* and *Flitch of Bacon*. For most of the time when she was at the theatre and not on stage, she sat in the pit—"in front"—but she also had access to go "behind," where the players were. On coming home she "found a letter from Mr. Harris to me." On the next day, a Sunday, she "sent a note to Mr. Wilkinson after wrote an answer to Mr. Harris." The Monday following she sent her cousin Hunt with a note to Harris, but he was not there, and afterward she and Wilkinson went to see De Loutherbourg's exhibition; "exhibition" is her word—De Loutherbourg called his show "Eidophusikon, or Representations of Nature," or sometimes "Various Imitations of Natural Phenomena, Represented by Moving Pictures."[27]

The show had been presented for the first time in February to a select group of some 130 people at De Loutherbourg's house in Lisle Street. The setting was luxurious, and the little theatre he had constructed was splendid. One spectator, as cited by Altick, at the opening wrote: "The room is the most beautiful that can be conceived; the panels painted in the richest style with festoons of flowers, musical instruments, etc. heightened in gold; where taste seems to have banished tawdriness and elegance takes complete possession. The seats for the spectators are crimson stuff, and at the upper end is a seat of state between two pillars of the Ionic order, fit for a princely visitor."[28]

Inchbald does not comment on their response, but she must surely have been impressed, remembering how her husband had worked at designing scenery for Wilkinson. On the Tuesday following she wrote: "A very fine Day went to Mr. Harris's breakfasted with him c&c came home by the Park and calld on Mr. Wilkinson—then at my sister's . . . playd Lady Frances Touchwood and the pantomime, in the afternoon received my Antient Law . . . went to my sister's at dark and supped off elles." Two days later, on Thursday, she wrote, "A dullish Day. . . . Mr. Wilkinson calld and took his leave—sorted my things . . . was in the green room at part of Jane Shore. . . . Dr. Brodie supped with me—he had sat with Mr. Harris c&c." It is tempting to wonder if Brodie and Harris talked of Inchbald as they sat together. Boaden is quite wrong in saying that she "could laugh" at Suett or that she would make a marriage to "elevate her condition in life." She seems never have wished to do anything to "elevate her condition in life." And she was always kind about Suett, especially later when everyone realized that Suett was very ill. As time went by and Sheridan and the Kembles began to be among the elite, she went with them sometimes when they asked her, but she never wished to be "elevated."

With all the people she knew and all the persistence and determination about her farce—or farces—it seems unfortunate that neither Harris nor Colman accepted one at this time. It has always been true that the beginning writer has a difficult time starting a career. Some three years later, both Colman and Harris commissioned her to write for them after her first success. The farce she had back from Colman on this March 13 she had called "Antient Law." Boaden remarks, "We are apt to conjecture that this was a *farcical* treatment of the subject already handled by Massinger and others, and by them called 'The Old Law,' *e.g.* that there should be no 'long withering out a young man's revenue;' but that every man at four-score, and woman at three-score, if found living, should be put to death; because being useless either in counsel or generation, they filled a place 'which would be better supplied when they had made it empty.'"[29] It was much later before she wrote a farce about age again.

Wilkinson had been in London for quite some time, and when he went home to York, he prepared a very special theatrical piece. Kemble had remained with Wilkinson this season of 1780–1781, and he was the principal actor in a kind of collection of "beauties." Wilkinson wrote of this piece in the York winter season, 1781:

> I produced a Theatrical Fête, which was conducted well, and in general much approved at York. It was also acted at Hull. The first division consisted of the speeches of Brutus and Mark Anthony, in the 3d act of "Julius Caesar." The second division was from Massinger's "Roman Actor:" To those who have not read that noble defense of the stage, they have much pleasure and improvement to come. Mr. Kemble appeared to infinite advantage in Paris: It was indeed on his account I had taken the pains of selecting the scene. . . . The third division was the 4th act of Shakespeare's "Henry IV," where I pleased myself with acting the King; and all the parts were completely attended to. The last performance was three acts from Dr. Young's "Brothers." The whole received much approbation.

Wilkinson called it

A Selected Entertainment,

Taken from

Shakespeare, Massinger, and Dr. Young,

Intitled

HUMOURS AND PASSIONS.[30]

The whole evening must have been "rhetorical," a style that fit Kemble exactly. He was still very young and inexperienced. He would have to wait quite some time before finding success, before becoming the leading actor of his "age." It would be quite some time also before Inchbald achieved success as a writer; she was never successful as an actress.

The morning after their evening at De Loutherbourg's, Inchbald says, "Wore my Hat—calld on Mr. Wilkinson. . . . I wrote to Mr. Harris and a copy to Mr. Colman." On Monday, March 18, she played Lavinia in *The Fair Penitent*. She saw Wilson and talked of her farce and Scotland. They both certainly remembered the Scotland of their past, but this time it is probable that Wilson was considering whether he should leave London and his debts and escape to Scotland—as he very shortly did. In this entry she says also, "Dr. Brodie in the stage box"; the stage box was quite literally overlooking the stage and thus was one of the most desirable places to be. The stage boxes could accommodate several people and were, therefore, used frequently for social gatherings of friends. After she was no longer on stage, Inchbald arranged a box for herself and her friends.

The next day, Tuesday, she sent her cousin to Colman, who returned her farce and sent her a letter. She went to the market with her cousin, and afterward Dr. Brodie called and brought her a pencil, a welcome gift. That night she played Lady Frances again. She received a new part this week—the queen in *King Charles;* the next day she was at the reading of *King Charles* and received another part, Lady Danvers. On the Sunday following, her entry is filled with detail: "then Dr. Brodie and I walked to Batesy [Battersea] Bridge—eat Broth at Chelsey Hospital and drank chocolate with several at Ton Coffee House . . . happend on Mr. Harris at my door and had much talk with him . . . sent Lady Danvers to Mrs. Wells."[31]

Her afternoon at Chelsea Hospital was only one of the entries she makes concerning various walks about the city. The day following she went with the Webbs to walk in Grey's Inn and Lincoln's Inn Gardens. The next week she walked with the Whitfields in the park, and they saw the king go to the Parliament House. On the following Sunday she and the doctor walked over Westminster Bridge and to Bagnege Wells. These walks were to the monuments of London—that is, all these were places frequented by Londoners when they walked about their city. Chelsea Hospital—Royal Hospital Chelsea—was built by Charles II in 1682 for veterans of war who were wounded, disabled, or had become too old to take care of themselves. The gardens were from the beginning a special feature, and Inchbald's walking there with her friends, having a bowl of soup in a nearby pub, and going with "several" to the Ton Coffee House would have made for a pleasant excursion.

The walks she took with the Webbs were to two of the London's Inns of Court—the inns where the law students came to study after coming down from Oxford or Cambridge. Lincoln's Inn had a beautiful garden and walks; Grey's Inn, situated on the north side of Holborn, was much smaller than Lincoln's Inn, but it too had a garden. The park she walked in was probably St. James, for the king would have been driven by there when he went to Parliament House.

By the second week in April, the benefit nights had begun. After she played the queen in Lewis's night, she saw Harris in the green room and he offered her a "half night." Of course Inchbald acted in all of the benefits when she was asked. Sometimes the plays were new or favorites of the actor whose benefit it was, even though it might be a difficult play or a not-quite-successful one. She continued to see Dr. Brodie; he brought her the *Herald* that had a comment about her "Queen," though she does not say what the comment was, perhaps because in the next sentence she says he told her "that Miss Farren was going into keeping." Perhaps he wished to "keep" Mrs. Inchbald.

Miss Farren, now a "star," was the little girl who had gone with her mother and her little sisters to Manchester in January of 1777. Since that time she had been helped by Younger to go to the Haymarket in the summer of 1778, but she returned to Liverpool for the 1778–1779 season. In 1779–1780 she returned to London, where she acted at both Covent Garden and Drury Lane. Then in 1779–1780 she began a seventeen-year engagement at Drury Lane that lasted until her marriage to the earl of Derby. This year of 1781, she was still only eighteen—her birthday was July 6, 1762. The gossip from Dr. Brodie says perhaps more about him and the green room than it does about Farren. In the end Farren, Inchbald, and Siddons were three of the actresses who guarded their private lives and their reputations concerning men and money with great pains.

During May Inchbald continued to be unwell, she continued to play Lady Frances, she continued to play in "benefits," and she continued to see the marquis and Dr. Brodie. She reports in one entry that she wrote to the marquis, and in another entry she says that Dr. Brodie called about a masquerade ticket. She ends this entry, "my head poorly."

Living in London was quite unlike living in Yorkshire, especially for the variety of pleasures offered. By spring Inchbald had become a close friend of the Whitfields; Boaden says they were "her most intimate acquaintance." They introduced her to their friend Mr. Babb at his country house on Sunday, May 6, and Boaden says that "he became her very steady and valuable friend."[32] On the next Sunday she dined in the country and saw Mr. Griffith's country house; she returned to London in the same coach with him. The Whitfields had been with Griffith in 1772–1773, and although the Inchbalds had gone to Scotland in 1772, there is no doubt that Inchbald knew the Whitfields before she came to London. George Simpson (Inchbald's brother) and his wife knew the Whitfields and Griffith and Babb. This group remained good friends for many years in the 1780s, forming a kind of support group for each other.

On Wednesday, May 22, Inchbald called on Harris and "was sometime with him . . . playd Lady Allworth." This is the role she played in *Sir Giles Overreach* to Henderson's Sir Giles. Henderson was the "star" of the company, having come to the Haymarket from Bath in the summer of 1777. A great success, he made some forty-five hundred pounds for Colman that summer season at the Haymarket. He had played Shakespeare—Shylock, Hamlet, Falstaff, Richard III.[33] After such success he was employed by Harris at Covent Garden and by 1780–1781 had become the leading actor in the company.

Miss Satchell, who had gone to the masquerade with her, was among those people who remained friends with Inchbald for many years. There were several Satchell sisters: the one who went with Inchbald was Elizabeth, who became Mrs. Stephen Kemble; Catherine Satchell became Mrs. John Lewis Duill, and Susanna became Mrs. Robert Benson. Elizabeth had, like Inchbald, come to

Covent Garden in the fall of 1780. Her debut was as Polly in *The Beggar's Opera* on September 21. Boaden called her "the only *real* Polly of 'The Beggars Opera,' and whose tears *filtered* through the very stones of Newgate."[34] The entry in the pocket-book about the masquerade is not very clear—did two of the sisters go? Inchbald saw two of them the next day. What did they wear? Did Inchbald go to another masquerade with the marquis? Perhaps she did. Her family chided her for going—for going with him. But what about the ticket Dr. Brodie spoke about? Perhaps there has been too much emphasis on these entries by Boaden and other critics. Boaden saw her own experience as foreshadowing the use of the masquerade in *A Simple Story*. By the time Boaden was writing in the 1830s, the restrictions governing the conduct of women had become more and more rigid. The masquerade described in the pocket-book was a kind of frolic—a party that we would celebrate as carnival, but in a rather mild form—since, after all, they went for one night only and returned to work on stage the next.

Most of the time the masquerades were simply parties—all-night celebrations given in great houses as we would give an autumn or spring celebration, gathering all our friends once a season to repay their hospitality. Inchbald must surely have read about many such events when she was in York. There was the one in the *York Chronicle* that we reviewed. The report describes some of the masks— a "fair Quaker" and a "bill taker"—but that report actually concluded:

—but the entertainment of the evening was singularly insipid—the profusion of good wines had no effect on the spirits of the company, for however wonderful it may appear, the more they drank, the more insufferably dull the generality of them grew.—Fitz W—s, and Con—g, it seems had made an oath to Temperance, which they repeatedly observed throughout the evening; at two supper was served down below; the food was hot and of all the "varieties of the season" and the wines were "better than are generally given at such public entertainments." At seven in the morning some of the guests were still there drinking below and others dancing upstairs.[35]

Perhaps the attention given to Inchbald and masquerades has somehow been overemphasized.

Inchbald's entries in the pocket-book are so casual that it is difficult to make any judgment about their significance. Moreover, to equate her own experiences with Miss Milner's in *A Simple Story* is hardly justified. Going to a masquerade was common, and no doubt many a masquerade ended in as dull a fashion as the one reported above. And after all, Inchbald had been playing Lady Frances in *The Belle's Stratagem*, where a masquerade is the central device of the play, the way in which the plot moves forward, and the way in which the conclusion is worked out in the very last few lines of the play. It is very doubtful that Inchbald paid more than passing attention to the whole episode. As for the marquis, although he does not figure prominently in the pocket-book of the 1780–1781 season at Covent Garden, he was a friend of Inchbald's for many years to come. Boaden's—or her family's—attempts to raise the class issue failed completely. In fact, Inchbald always took people—especially her friends—for what they were, not for whether they were "stars" in the theatre or important writers or prominent figures on the London scene. The evidence in the years after this first season in London clearly supports her independent judgment about people as well as her independence in making her own decisions about what she would or would not do.

Several entries in the last few weeks of May are rather puzzling. She paid her accounts to both her dresser and her hairdresser. She paid Barker, her hairdresser, £12 12s. 4d. Earlier there were two entries about arranging a loan. She had called on two pawn brokers one day and a Mr. Thomas. This entry was on the first of May. On the accounts for May 6 and the days following, she paid 1s. 6d. for a seal, £3 for a watch, 4d. for having silk stockings washed, 4d. for figs, and 8d. for a stage coach to the "Hope." At the top of this page she has entered an extra note, "Saturday evening, Mr. Wilson rather in Liquor said much to me of marriage." And on May 21 she "calld at Mr. Harris but he was come to town—came home by the water in the Park . . . calld twice at the play. . . . Mr. Rienhold made a serious offer of lending me a sum of money." Why did she need the money? Was it because she had a low salary and London had proved to be even more expensive than she had thought? Boaden speculates that she had quite a tidy sum when her husband died, and she was certainly not one to spend her savings and live beyond her income. Perhaps a more logical reason was that with the end of the season she was without work for the first time since she and her husband had returned from France in the summer of 1776. Was one of her visits to Colman a request to play at the Haymarket? She did so in the summer of 1782, but if she did wish to play at the Haymarket, she certainly had waited too late to arrange a contract.

By 1781, when Inchbald ended her first season in London, the Haymarket was the only theatre in London to offer licensed plays in the summer. The continuing monopoly of Covent Garden and Drury Lane in the winter was replaced by various forms of entertainment in the summer—the pleasure gardens, fairs, and by this time the circus, but for those patrons who wished to attend the theatre, the Haymarket was their only choice. And by this time George Colman the elder was in firm command there. His kindness to Inchbald some three years after this season of 1781 was the beginning of Inchbald's career as a playwright. But this day, at the end of her first season at Covent Garden, when she took the stagecoach to Bury, she was very upset and frustrated about her acting career, about making choices in her personal life, and about her still unsuccessful attempt to have a play accepted. On May 28 she had written a letter to Wilkinson, which, we may assume, refused his offer to come to York for the summer. It seems somewhat strange that she did not accept his invitation, but she knew that the "impossible" Mrs. Smith would still have the leading roles; perhaps it was not worth the long journey, the expense of returning to the circuit, only to be confronted with the same old problems. Kemble was still with Wilkinson, but she certainly would not have returned merely to be associated with him.

On Thursday, May 30, she had played Lady Allworth for the last time, and she records all this week that she was copying parts, a revealing task since she was surely not copying all these parts for herself; she was also seeing Mr. Hitchcock, and on the Sunday following she says she "copied many parts" for him. Hitchcock was about to go to Dublin to become assistant to Daly at the Smock Alley Theatre, and her "copying many parts" was for him to take with him, no doubt. It is difficult to comprehend how tedious were some of the tasks involved in the assembling of the theatre promptbooks.

During this last week she also wrote to Wroughton. "Unhappy—wrote my letter to Wroughton."[36] Whether her unhappiness and the letter to Wroughton are to be considered together is not clear. She and the Hitchcocks were very close, but she did not know Wroughton before she came to Covent Garden. However, Wroughton had the reputation of being very kind to his fellow players and being very persuasive for himself and for them. Perhaps Inchbald wanted him to speak to Harris for her.[37]

The Summer of 1781

As the days of the closing season passed, Mrs. Inchbald became very unhappy. She was facing weeks and months without employment, since she had evidently refused Wilkinson's offer to go back to York for the summer races. On the Tuesday before she left on Thursday, she writes: "Polly and Nanny and after Mr. Wroughton called—cryd—calld and dined with Mr. and Mrs. Hitchcock—walked with him after—he showed me a letter concerning me from Ireland—drank tea there—at Separate Maintenance."

It was almost two years before the Ireland scheme took place, but the early mention here is significant both for Hitchcock and for Inchbald. Moreover, this Ireland reference had many ramifications. We remember that in June Kemble was still with Wilkinson, still learning his "art," still a leading member of a provincial company, however we may view Wilkinson and his company. Most biographies of Kemble credit Wilkinson with turning him into a competent actor; those same two years passed before Kemble appeared in Ireland along with Hitchcock and Inchbald. All these cross-references of dates and places support the view that the whole of the theatre business was so completely intertwined that a very false and incomplete picture would result from considering what happened to one player and not another in London, Ireland, and the provinces, especially York, Bath, and Edinburgh, the companies Inchbald, Kemble, and Wilkinson were concerned with. The theatre was a business, a national institution, and a great pleasure for hundreds of people. To confine the view of it to a few principal players and managers is to represent it poorly indeed. Because there were only the three theatres in London, and because Sheridan, Harris, and Colman were in complete control of their theatres, it should not be surprising that an unknown writer would find it very, very difficult to have work accepted and staged. Inchbald's determination is to be remarked upon, but it is hardly surprising that even on location in London she had still not succeeded in having her pieces accepted.

The journey to Standingfield was overnight, from the time she left at eight until the next day after breakfast. She found all well at home; it was a showery day; her box came in the evening. Such a journey from London to Standingfield must have seemed very pleasant after the travel of the past. However she felt about the York circuit, she certainly did not wish to return to the constant moving from place to place, and she no doubt remembered that she did not wish to return to Edinburgh, where Wilkinson remained in charge this summer of 1781, exactly as he did the year before.[38]

The months in London from September to June had not been very productive in advancing Inchbald's career. Her parts, though they were not all merely supporting ones, were not the "star" parts of Yates or Mattocks; and although she worked diligently on her writing, she still had not had a piece accepted. She does not seem to have been discriminated against because she was a woman, but she had to pay for the fact that everyone wanted to write a play, have it produced, and enjoy the financial success that resulted. It is difficult to overestimate the number of plays submitted to the two London theatres and to Colman at the Haymarket. Everyone, except perhaps the king and queen, wanted his or her play read, accepted, acted instantly, and published. Inchbald's repeated letters to Colman and Harris, her reading her work to everyone who crossed her path, her constant work, revision, and copying all added to Colman's and Harris's awareness that she was not only serious but also persistent. When her first play was successful, she never again was without a play on the stage until her last one in 1805. This is not to say that all of the plays and after-pieces were equally successful or that all of them remained on stage in London until the turn of the century; but this first season in London, although it did not give her all the success she had hoped for, provided the knowledge of the context necessary for the success of the years to come.

The record of her time in the country is not significantly different from her life in London except that she did not have to go to rehearsal, study her parts, and act on stage in the evening; that is, the pattern of her daily life of reading, writing, visiting with friends, having tea, and walking continued, only this time instead of walking in Hyde Park, she walked in the home field and went to Coldham with her sister, where she saw her friends the Gages.

The Gage family lived just across the fields, and it was here that the Catholics held Mass, since, of course, they could not do so in the old church just up the hill from the Simpson farm. The Gage family was an ancient one, and Rookwood, their house, was designed to incorporate a chapel in the building. There were a great many Catholics in Suffolk, and the Gage "chapel" was one of several where services could be held. Inchbald had not been a faithful attendant of divine service in York or London, but now she attended regularly for the weeks in the summer, along with her mother and her sister.

The weeks on the farm give a picture of the routine of such a village as Standingfield. While her days were filled with reading and writing letters, the farm chores followed the season. In the third week in June, an entry reads "worked . . . walked with Dolly . . . a fine day, the men took their harvest." In several entries the next week, she records that she shelled peas, probably to help her mother, who was obliged to feed the harvesters. Mr. Webb, the farm manager, brought newspapers and letters when he went to Bury, as he did frequently. Once she records that Mr. Webb and her mother "had words." She records the first Monday in July that she "walked—then shelled peas . . . after dinner (making) beer washing day— after worked." She continued to shell beans and peas while she read, wrote letters, and worked on a comedy. This combination of work and reading and writing continuing in her home surroundings within the daily living of family and friends gives an accurate account of families like the Simpsons: "sister Bigsby," who lived nearby, came for tea unexpectedly, and afterward Inchbald and her mother "talked of her time." As devoted as the family members were, they sometimes quarreled. On a Sunday Inchbald writes: "Coldish morning—wore my black—no sermon—after dinner while my mother slept and Dolly read George and I quarreled." George and his wife came and went several times during this summer, adding two adults to the household. Inchbald writes in several entries of "little George," who vexed his grandmamma. She talks to Dolly about her "situation" and another time "about men." Dolly tells her about Miss Webb and her "intrigues" and "after of her adventures in Kings Place, of Ld. Littleton and Ld. Harrington."

The work in the fields followed the pattern of the seasons. In late July Inchbald walked in the home field. On August 9 the "harvest" began. On the following Friday she and her mother went "to the Harvest fields—saw many Gleaners." The next day she walked in the home field where the men were reaping. The Sunday following, August 11, she writes: "Wore my white silk, prayers began very late. . . . While my mother slept said all I could to Dolly concerning her conduct—read in Think well on't—from tea to supper looking over and mending my comedy and liked it much . . . my mother bottled off the gin." Dolly, the only one of the sisters left at home, was unhappy; she was not married, and unlike Inchbald, she seems not to have used her time wisely. Remembering Inchbald's comment, it is easier to understand Dolly when later she did become a "fallen woman." Inchbald's comment about her comedy here was a rare declaration of satisfaction.

All the time since June, when she had come home, Inchbald had worked at her writing. Along with the walks, the domestic duties of shelling peas and beans, seeing her sisters and her brother, having tea, going to service, wearing her white silk and her hat, she had been writing a comedy. We are never sure what happened to the farces and comedies she worked on—in York, in London, and now this summer at home. It was three years yet before her first play was produced, but there is no clearer record of the way she worked than in the pocket-book she kept this summer while she was living with her family surrounding her. The ideas Virginia Woolf suggested more than a century later in "A Room of One's Own" would never have occurred to Inchbald; and the process of producing a manuscript to submit to Colman or Harris was complicated beyond our understanding, involving handwriting, hand copying, on paper the writer bought, and once the manuscript was complete, there was no guarantee that it would ever be read by anyone, not even the committee who went through the submissions before they were handed to Colman, or Harris, or Sheridan. Inchbald was quite aware of all these matters, and her running account of her work on this comedy makes an interesting review of the process.

Less than a week after she arrived home, she says her mother read her farce and she began her comedy, and as the days went by she recorded the places where she worked. Sometimes she worked in the parlor, sometimes in her room, sometimes in the closet. In one entry, for example, she says, "I wrote till Supper in my own room from a thought I began in the morning for my comedy." Two days later she "worked below, talked of Miss Farren &c. in the evening at my comedy." The next day, in a very mixed entry, she says, "sick and could not eat—before tea very sick,—showery evening—settled the first act of my comedy." It is difficult to tell just how fast she worked on a piece. Later, when she wrote commissioned pieces, she worked very fast, but that kind of writing was still far in the future. These comments from her pocket-book remind us that creative work such as she was doing was pleasure for her as it is for any writer, and even in these entries, while she was at home with no one except her family to discuss it with, it is clear that writing was literally her life. And the reports of her work that are embedded in her daily life make very real her circumstances, not the easiest to foster creativity: after she went to the fields to see the reapers, she returned to work on her writing.

From the very beginning of her professional career, Inchbald had been a perfectionist, constantly unhappy with her acting, constantly rejecting and re-writing her work. Her speech impediment kept her locked into a quite rigid kind of performance on stage, but her constant revision of her writing allowed her to gain more and more control to shape her plays. Reading them aloud to everyone she could find to listen gave her a basis for judgment even though the people she knew—her family and friends—were not professional critics; they were, however, very familiar with the theatre and plays, both old and new, and were thus an audience for Inchbald. Inchbald herself was her most severe critic.

Early in July, as she began to write her comedy, she wrote, "A very wet day and evening—all the day at my comedy but in the evening disliked what little I had wrote." Two days later she says, "wrote but did not please myself." The next day, in an entry filled with farm business, she writes, "A very fine and hot day—low spirited in the morning walked in the home field and then for George to the Hayfield—the Rent Day—read while my mother slept—then went for George again—in the evening at my comedy but did not like it." Two days later she writes, "wrote a scene in my comedy that I liked better." She is not always specific about how her work is progressing, but day after day she indicates that she worked, and most of the days when she could, she walked. In the entry for July 27 she records a variety of items: "A fine day—Mr. Talbott calld in the morning and borrowed 3 guineas of me . . . after tea wrote in my comedy in the Little Passage—my head very well—carting hay in the home field." Three days later she writes, "after break-fast read my two acts of my comedy and liked them." And the next day, "from tea till supper settling and writing in my comedy got forward." The next day she "wrote a scene in my comedy I liked." The Sunday following she writes, "Wore my white hat—Mr. and Mrs. Gage at Prayers . . . then at my comedy and wrote half a scene." This was now the first week of August, and the harvest was continu-ing all week; and all week she continued to work on her comedy. On Thursday of this week she says, "drest and walked with my mother in the Harvest fields then worked. The harvest men dined here." And as the work continued, she walked in the harvest fields, saw many gleaners, and was "at my comedy in the Passage." As the week ended on Saturday, she wrote, "Began to read my comedy and did not like it . . . walked in the home field, the men reaping there . . . read one scene in my comedy to Dolly." The repeated entries about her writing along with the domestic details make her situation very real. Her creative work was immersed in daily activities, and her judgments about liking or not liking it must surely have been prompted at least partly by the duties she performed for her mother. If on the Sabbath she wore her white hat and came home from prayers to write half a scene in her comedy, she must have had that rare gift of concentration that enabled her to move instantly and smoothly from the reality, the "men reaping," to working "at my comedy in the passage."

The next step after completing the writing of her comedy was to copy it, which took somewhat more than a week. All the while she walked and continued to work on her comedy. Sometimes she got "forward," sometimes she worked on the fourth act, and on Friday, August 30, "after dinner Sir. Tho. sent for Mr. Webb to meet him at the Great Gate." The next morning while she was dressing, Dolly came to tell her that one of the harvest men had just fallen from a tree and was killed. The next day, Sunday, after coming from prayers, she and Dolly "Looked at the Fountain and where poor Annas was killed." The next day Annas was buried.

As August came to an end and September began, George and his wife were there. Everyone was preparing for the new season. Wilkinson described George's wife as "little but delicate in the extreme; She is a very pleasing elegant actress, both in tragedy and comedy, but not powerful or great . . . but she is always sure to gain the good word of gentlemen and ladies, and all the parts of a good-natured theatre."[39] In these days just before everyone departed for the new season, the house at Standingfield must have been very crowded. Inchbald, who was extremely sensitive to any affront, however slight, did not understand why her "sister" kept to herself upstairs in her own room, and as usual Inchbald writes in her pocketbook, "I spoke cross to my Sister thinking she meant to affront me—George went to Bury." But the next day she wrote: "A cloudy day—breakfasted in the Parlor and then left Standingfield in a post chaise with my Brother and Sister—very good-natured, dined and supped at Colchester with many of the Norwich Company—a little uneasy at finding Mrs. Yates played Lady Allworth." No doubt she had already begun to hear news of the theatre; Lady Allworth was one of her parts.

They were on their way back to London. On Wednesday they left Colchester and arrived in London about four in the afternoon. She went to her old lodging, wrote a note to Mr. Hitchcock, walked and had supper with Mr. Twiss. She closes this entry with "My sister had a fit." And the next day, "My brother calld, then I there and very sorry to hear my sister [George's wife] had been so ill." Neither she nor her sister would have known what caused a "fit"; perhaps she had a mild stroke, or more likely she fainted. As devoted as Inchbald was to her family, she is extremely vague about their lives. Added to the lack of details is that Inchbald seldom gives precise names; after all, she had three sisters in London and a cousin whom she saw frequently, both a sister and her cousin were referred to as "Nanny," and she called her sister-in-law "sister."

The references to illness, whether Inchbald's or that of her friends and relatives, are never clear and are sometimes very puzzling. Inchbald's use of the word "fit" could mean many things or nothing. Her sister-in-law was younger than she, and perhaps she had fainted—had a small seizure—for whatever reason. Inchbald records such episodes about herself and her friends throughout the pocket-books. Mrs. Simpson recovered, though Inchbald gives no other details than that she dined at her brother's the next night. The family as always is mentioned in almost every entry. A day later, on Saturday, her cousin Hunt called to tell her that her "brother" Bigsby had broken his leg. Later that day she walked with her brother and sister in the park and dined and drank tea at Dolly's Chop House with them.

THE RETURN TO LONDON AND THE NEW SEASON

Then on Monday, September 23, she returned to Covent Garden; she called at the house and found that her dressing room had been given over to the mantua makers. The next day, while she was at the rehearsal of *The Belle's Stratagem,* she heard something—she does not say what—of *Romeo and Juliet;* then she writes, "very dull and thought of Ireland . . . at the house about my dress—had my hair cut." The next day she played Lady Frances; she said Harris "admired my dress." The question of dress—of what she should wear in the various parts she played— is rather puzzling. At this point she seems not to be altogether responsible for furnishing her own costume, a point of great contention among the actresses. We remember that she spent quite some time on her "boy's cap" when she first came to London and was assigned the part of Bellario. The "dress" of the actresses was very much a part of their personal image, and as interested as she was in her own personal dress, it is likely she was very careful about her stage "dress." The "dress" of the actresses and actors in the prints of such publications as *Bell's British Theatre* served as fashion plates in much the same way as the illustrations in fashion magazines of our time do.

On Thursday she received a part in a new comedy, and on Friday she went to the reading of Mr. Holcroft's comedy *Duplicity;* afterward she had "much talk" with Mr. Harris "behind the scenes and he took my spying glass from me." Her relationship with Harris this fall is quite different from that of the year before, as is clear from several entries, and on into the future they became good friends even though she was always wary of his gifts. He had the reputation of admiring pretty women—actresses—but his reputation was quite unlike that of Daly, whom Inchbald was about to encounter in the next season. The next day, a Sunday, was very cold; she stayed in bed late, and her landlady sent her a basin of tea. When she got to chapel, she could not get in; she returned to her lodging and then in the afternoon had tea and supped with Mr. Babb along with Mrs. Whitfield and Mrs. Morton. They went in a coach, and she says she was "charmed with his house."

Mr. Babb was her brother's friend, introduced by him to the Simpson-Inchbald circle. He had a house where he entertained frequently. He evidently knew the Whitfields and others associated with the theatres, and for many years he had supper or tea as open house for his friends. He was Inchbald's friend for many years to come, though this is her first reference to him in the pocket-books.

She had been so busy that she had not had time to unpack her boxes until this Tuesday, over a week after she had arrived. And it was not until Thursday that she mentioned "her comedy." Her brother and sister left on Saturday; and on Sunday, after seeing her sister Hunt, she read over her comedy and "liked it much." The pattern of her days continued as it had been in the season before; now the walks in the fields were replaced by the visits of friends, rehearsals, and concern about Harris and her "parts." But along with anything—with everything—she worked away on her comedy.

She was more and more unhappy with her position—with her parts, her acting, and the rigid rules Harris imposed. She had no dressing room of her own; she continued to be in the pantomime—when she did not go to rehearsal of it, she was forfeited. She was given a part in the new comedy, a comedy that turned out to be Holcroft's *Duplicity.* Holcroft was an old friend, but how much she had seen of him in London is difficult to determine. He was associated with both Drury Lane and Covent Garden, and although she must have seen him in London, she does not record such a meeting until after she began to rehearse his "new" comedy. She was very pleased to be assigned a part, and at the first rehearsal she saw Mr. Harris. She continues to record the dresses she wore—this time her "white" (her own, not a costume), and afterward she was very unhappy; she called in the green room and walked in the pantomime. Her continued reporting of her unhappiness must have been prompted by her continued frustrations, but frustration simply meant for her that she would continue to work at her writing and her career. In the future Holcroft was a part of her personal life, but in this season of 1781–1782 he was simply the friend who had acted with her in Canterbury in the summer of 1777 before she and her husband went to York and Tate Wilkinson.

The next day she walked in Lincoln's Inn Gardens, thinking of a letter to send to Mr. Harris. As if she did not have enough troubles to worry about with Harris and her parts, she had a letter from her sister about her rent, and on her way home after rehearsal, she saw Dr. Brodie at her house; she turned aside, but when she went home, she found a note from him; she does not report its contents. Boaden had dismissed Dr. Brodie in the spring before, but evidently Boaden was more interested in the reason Inchbald refused to see Brodie than in their continuing relationship. Boaden is probably correct, however, when he concludes that Brodie did not propose marriage but a relationship on his terms. Certainly Inchbald would have none of it. At the end of this week she received her salary and shook hands with Harris.

Her part in *Duplicity* lasted for only seven performances, performances that had been interrupted by the success of *The Count of Narbonne*, adapted by Jephson from Walpole's *Castle of Otranto*. Inchbald had no part in it, and Boaden says that it "succeeded so greatly, as even to suspend the pantomime itself." Boaden continues, "It was astonishingly acted; Miss Younge, Miss Satchell, Henderson, Wroughton, Lewis, left nothing either to be wished, or *surpassed*, even by the great people who succeeded them in their respective characters."[40] Inchbald's roles at Covent Garden were almost always in comedy, and this gothic "romance" would not have suited her. While it was playing, she had almost nothing to do during the whole of November.

Harris was preparing a version of *The Beggar's Opera*. Inchbald had once told Wilkinson that she would play a "thief" in *The Beggar's Opera,* but she would not play the whore. In this version at Covent Garden, she had the part of Wat Dreary in an all-female cast. She did not mind the breeches role, but she had to devise her own costume; and she reports that Harris laughed at it. The next day she saw Wroughton, and he "spoke kindly" about the performance. At the end of the week she writes: "Mr. Ledger brought my Salary and told me to be ready in Lady Allworth—very happy and sometime sorting my things—walked for tooth powder." Her moods change with the assignment of parts and with the approval of Harris or Wroughton or Ledger. Always sensitive, she became even more so this second season in London. The first, 1780–1781, had the novelty of being her first; this second was simply dull and unprofitable.

Boaden includes a letter she wrote to Harris revealing another very serious problem. In a company so constantly together, it is not surprising that gossip should be frequently reported, especially if that gossip suggested that the bearer of it could find favor with the manager. Mrs. Inchbald, like all of her colleagues, was certainly guilty of spreading rumors. This one about her evidently hurt her deeply, and she wrote to explain. Someone, though she does not say who, had told Harris that she had ridiculed him. Her letter reveals much more than her message to Harris. The speaker had ridiculed not only her but also the whole of Covent Garden, and he had especially marked her stuttering, a very cruel thing to do. Moreover, Inchbald could match anyone in satiric repartee; evidently in this instance she discovered that her opponent had no sense of humor or understanding of witty conversation. A part of Inchbald's explanatory letter is worth quoting:

Mr. ————, unprovoked, first takes an opportunity to say, "Every actor and actress there is an object of ridicule—is fit only for *York*—would do very well at *York, &c.*" He says *I* am only fit for Queen Sheba; mimicks my stuttering; and says he told Mr. Harris, the first night I played, that I was not worth a farthing, and he [Mr. Harris] was *taken* in. . . . Says, "he read my 'Polygamy;' it was indecent, and not a word spelt right." These things (pleasant man!) he declares publicly. I forgive him, because I think he is joking; and, in the same manner, think *he* will not be offended if I joke with him. But I have sometimes found the contrary, and then have begged his pardon, and he has promised to THINK NO MORE OF IT: but, I believe he has often broke that promise, for I challenge the whole world to say that I ever spoke disrespectfully of Mr. Harris to any soul living but to him; and then I was urged to it, by being first provoked by himself. Perceiving, after our first or second conversation, that nothing but turning his beloved friend into ridicule could draw his attention from making *me* the object of *his*, I used *you*, but as a defensive weapon. I confess my obligations to you. And had you never *wantonly* made me unhappy, by business you forced me to do, purely to show your power, and make the poor piece of bread you gave me bitter to me, your name, even in sport, should have been spared.[41]

Boaden, commenting on this letter, says that Harris "was not without feeling as a gentleman, to correct the occasional harshness of management." Besides, Boaden points out that Inchbald was still an obscure actress, not yet the "lady able to invent the 'Simple Story,' and to contest the palm of novel-writing with even the most accomplished of her countrywomen. The exterior garb of her candidate farces, ragged paper, rude penmanship, and careless orthography, was not at all prophetic of a Dramatic Muse, who should become one of the best supports of comedy, and rank with Centlivre and Cowley."[42] If her sharp tongue had gotten her in trouble with Harris, it was later to make her known as a witty, sharp conversationalist. Harris, it seems, accepted her apology.

In the spring she faced an even more serious piece of gossip when it was whispered about in the green room that she had spent the night in Mr. Harris's house. Evidently her friend Mrs. Whitfield had listened and reported to her husband, and he in turn helped Inchbald trace the source to Miss Ambrose. Inchbald's pocket-book entry is an interesting footnote to her action. On Sunday, April 28, her sister and her brother Hunt came and told her of Debby's jealousy. "[I]n the evening went over and asked Mr. Whitfield who had told him of my being a night at Mr. Harris's. Mr. Morton being there I came back directly and did not mention it." But Mr. Whitfield did find out that Miss Ambrose had started the story, and needless to say, Inchbald wrote to Ambrose and received an apology from her and from Mrs. Whitfield. Boaden remarks, "The staring malignity, folly and falsehood of supposing that a beautiful woman, and that woman a widow, would surrender herself and her character thus idly, and without a cue from interest or passion to boot, hissed itself soon out of credibility even in the Green-room."[43] Thus to win in the green room, full of players who each looked to his own place, by displacing another was to make a small triumph. Ambrose was an even more "humble" player than Inchbald, and her small triumph became defeat. Even though she had been at Covent Garden for some time, she ended her career there in May of 1782.

As the season of 1781–1782 continued in January, Inchbald was required to play some rather unsavory parts. Boaden says that she was required to play Lady Touchwood, a "monster of adultery and unbounded lewdness," in *The Double Dealer* and the countess of Nottingham in *The Earl of Essex*.[44] All these circumstances help to explain her frequent pocket-book comments that she was unhappy, very unhappy, and that she cried herself to sleep; under such constant pressure, she was frequently ill. The characters she played during this period were supporting characters, some of them quite wicked. For example, the countess of Nottingham betrays both Essex and Queen Elizabeth when she tells a false story about the ring the queen had given Essex. If Nottingham had returned the ring to the queen, Essex would have been pardoned. Instead, her speech telling the queen that "never pride insulted mercy more" seals Essex's fate. But in the end, when Burleigh tells the queen of the betrayal, she cries out, "Oh, barbarous woman!" Inchbald would have found Nottingham's character wicked indeed.

Inchbald's unhappiness about her parts amounted to unhappiness about her acting, about her increasing realization that she would probably never have the leading parts, never become a "star," never command the salary of Mrs. Pope, who is listed as playing the part of Queen Elizabeth in *The Earl of Essex*. Mrs. Pope was one of the "stars" and was paid handsomely, making some twenty pounds a week in the season 1779–1780.

In late November and early December, while she had no assignment on stage, Inchbald went to Drury Lane frequently. She continued to write to Colman, and in one entry she says she saw Mrs. Wilson and Miss Satchell and walked with them to Little Briton. Miss Satchell was to be married to Stephen Kemble, who was then in Ireland, having gone there before his brother John Philip.[45] Inchbald and Satchell became close friends and were friends for the rest of their lives. Another time in late December, Inchbald and Satchell walked to Oxford Road and met Mr. Twiss. Mr. Twiss, a friend of the Kembles and of the Simpsons, was a circuit judge whose territory included Suffolk. When he traveled the circuit, he always stopped by to see the Simpsons; he and all the Simpson family were very close, especially he and George Simpson. He was even at this time engaged in making a concordance of the Shakespeare plays, a project not completed for some years to come. He was also in the future to marry one of the Kembles.

Elizabeth Satchell was the daughter of John Satchell, a maker of musical instruments. She studied voice with Thomas Baker, a singer at Covent Garden for over thirty years. Elizabeth had made her debut at Covent Garden on September 21, 1780, as Polly in *The Beggar's Opera*. She had three sisters who were also on stage: Susanna, who married the actor Robert Benson; Catherine, who married John Duill first and after his death John Taylor; and a sister who married James Bland and played in the provinces.

As the year ended, Inchbald played Millwood in *The London Merchant* and was in the new pantomime *Harlequin Free Mason*. As in the past, Inchbald hated to "walk" in the pantomime, and her entries for the last of December and the first of the new year are filled with notations about "walking." On December 26 she "walked in the new pantomime—not very happy after." The Saturday following she was in the pantomime again. The next week she still "walked." On Monday she wrote, "a dark wet day—went to my sisters about a turkey—walked in the pantomime," a notation she continued all week. The next week she continued to be unhappy about her assignment. On Tuesday she wrote, "After some consideration wrote a note to Mr. Harris concerning the pantomime—in the pantomime." She continued to be in it, and on Friday she wrote, "in the pantomime and heard Mr. Harris would not suffer Mrs. Martyr to go out of it etc." For several days after this entry she was ill, but when she was back she wrote, "playd the Abbess in the Pantomime—was very well." The pantomime continued day after day until on Monday, February 12, she wrote, "playd in The Gamester and pantomime . . . vext on hearing the pantomime was to be playd every night with the tragedy." Her entries about the pantomimes continued through the spring until she went home to Standingfield in April by the doctor's orders.

The pantomimes were always a part of the festivities during Christmas and the New Year. A form of entertainment that included elaborate costumes, scenery, and music, the procession sometimes reflected classical myth, sometimes included the tricky Harlequin of the commedia dell'arte. Boaden, although thinking pantomimes "trash," points out, "The manager of a theatre, however, looks at Pantomime as the grand source of emolument; and so entirely is this taken for granted, that the forecast of a season divides itself into but two parts—'how to get on till the Pantomime' and, after it has done its duty, 'till the Benefits.'"[46]

In the summer of 1782, Inchbald's first summer at the Haymarket, she was in a pantomime that Colman wrote called *Harlequin Teague, or the Giant's Causeway,* in which, Boaden says, Colman "satirised the absurdities of modern masquerades."[47] Lasting from August 17 to September 14, it was a speaking pantomime with songs and beautiful scenery. It attracted crowds of spectators. She had been in pantomimes at York—one in August of 1779 called *Harlequin Salamander,* in which her friend Suett played the clown. She, of course, understood the important place the pantomimes played in an evening's entertainment; her objection to them was simply that she herself wanted no part in them. Many years later she discussed writing one at Harris's suggestion, but she never did.[48]

But to return to Covent Garden, on Friday, December 28, she had played in *Duplicity.* She records, "Mr. Wilson's part read he not coming or being found." The truth of the matter was that Wilson was ill, as he frequently was; this time his brother John, who was at Drury Lane, read his part.

Mrs. Wilson, Wilson's current "wife" in 1781–1782, was Sarah. She and Wilson had acted together in Edinburgh, and now in London they were both employed at Covent Garden and in the summer at the Haymarket. Mrs. Inchbald's entry in the spring of 1781 that she heard the Wilsons were reconciled must have been true, because she has several entries about seeing Mrs. Wilson. Sarah was in Holcroft's *Duplicity* along with her husband and Inchbald. Mrs. Wilson was formerly Mrs. Weston, acting in Edinburgh in 1772 when the Inchbalds were there and when Wilson and Mr. Inchbald enjoyed their "freedom" to stay out all night. Both she and Wilson left the Edinburgh company long before the Inchbalds did, going first to York and then to Covent Garden. Mrs. Inchbald was certainly closely associated with both of them, and her refusal of Wilson's proposal of marriage in the fall of 1780 has an extra quality of the pathetic. The players and their domestic arrangements were far more related to the late twentieth century than to the eighteenth. Mrs. Wilson had three children; perhaps they were Wilson's, although there was some evidence that one of them was Harris's.[49]

While Inchbald continued to speak to Harris, she began a new campaign;

this time she wrote to Palmer at Bath and she talked to the Hitchcocks. Boaden says of her letter to Palmer that "she did not reflect, or she did not know, that the two managers were such close friends, that unless Mr. Harris really wished her away, Palmer would not have dared to take her. He replied to her letter, and she saw him when he came to town; but nothing arose out of it."[50] The discussions with the Hitchcocks turned out to be more important. Both Mr. and Mrs. Hitchcock were close friends of Mrs. Inchbald, as was their daughter. They had all been with Wilkinson, and the Hitchcocks had known Mr. Inchbald before the Inchbalds were married, because they were a part of the Norwich Company with him; they then joined Wilkinson's company in 1771 and remained with him until the summer of 1777, just before the Inchbalds joined Wilkinson at Hull. Hitchcock served as Colman's manager in the Haymarket, but after the summer season in 1781, the summer just ended when Inchbald was at home in Standingfield, the Hitchcocks went to Dublin, where he became Daly's assistant and prompter. Moreover, Hitchcock had been given the power to recruit players, an assignment that he proved very successful in fulfilling.

Sometime in the spring, Inchbald wrote to Wilkinson. The letter is not dated, but it is clear from its contents that she was making plans for the 1782–1783 season:

It is not more than six weeks since you wrote for me—has any alteration taken place since? Not that I am certain I can come—I shall certainly leave Covent Garden some time in the winter—that is the moment I can get an engagement I like—but then if Mr. Daly advance me the money I have wrote for [fifty guineas] I am engaged to him,—but as I shall not go unless he sends it me, which perhaps he will not, or cannot do why then I shall be happy once more to call you manager.

My terms must be the same as when I left you, with forty pounds for my York and Hull Benefits whether I clear it or not, this was our agreement, you remember when I left you; and a very reasonable one, considering I might get much more provided you could give me such nights as some of your performers come in possession of. As to clothes I say nothing about. Dress me as bad as you please, I am sure to look better than any other person—but remember this—I buy no decorations for your clothes—such as they are given to me such I wear them neither my time or income will admit of my dressing any more than my head and feet . . . send me an answer immediately and the moment I have the letter from Ireland . . . I have been pressed to go to Norwich (for they are distressed for a woman) but they objected to my leaving them in the summer but no consideration should bribe me to quit Mr. Colman and I know 'tis an engagement you will have no objection to for by next year perhaps I may be able to Steal you something.

If you take me I can come when you please, either at the close of Mr. Colman's House or not till Christmas for I am engaged at Covent Garden and shall play there till I get an engagement I like—but as Mr. Harris has broke his word with me (which he will not deny) I can leave him when I please, of which if you want proofs I can immediately give them.[51]

The Kembles were already in Ireland. John Philip had left York in the fall of 1781 just about the time Inchbald returned to Covent Garden. Kemble's first appearance on the Smock Alley stage was in *Hamlet*, a role he was to make entirely his own at Drury Lane. In Dublin he was successful, but not notably so, and when he played in *The Belle's Stratagem*, he was not successful at all. Tragedy was his milieu; comedy was not. John Philip's brother Stephen George was with Wilkinson in the season 1781–1782 and in the summer went to Ireland, to Cork and in October to the Capel Street Theatre in Dublin. When Mrs. Inchbald arrived in Dublin in the fall of 1782, she found both Stephen and John Philip there.

During this spring of 1782, while she worked on a new engagement for herself in the winter, she had managed an engagement with Colman at the Haymarket. The season there began on Monday, June 3; her first part was Ben Budge in yet another performance of *The Beggar's Opera*. One account of this production, quoting from George Colman the younger, claimed that his father must have

been extremely keen when the sacred hunger for gold induced him to bring upon the stage the indecorous catchpenny of the reversed Beggar's Opera. . . . Many of the actresses, for instance must have been conscious of their want of symmetry for male attire; trousers were not then in fashion; nor were boots furnished for gentlewomen upon low salaries; those females, therefore, who could not afford the last articles appeared not only "en culottes" but in silk stockings, and certes, among the she-highwaymen belonging to Macheath's gang, thus accoutered there were to quote the song of Jemmy Jumps in the Farmer

Six feet ladies
Three feet ladies
Small legg'd ladies
Thick legg'd ladies all with horse pistols in their hands, screaming "We take the road"—
a feminine phalanx which constituted, as Macheath himself says of the Judges in the Old Bailey, "a terrible show."[52]

The Wilsons were in the cast as well as Inchbald. In the first performance, however, Mrs. Wilson had to have Miss Norris take her part as Filch because she was very pregnant. It was said she was "too far advanced in her pregnancy to dress *en homme.*"[53]

Also during the spring Inchbald had a new correspondent: S.J. Pratt wrote to her from Bath. It is an interesting letter, considering the fact that Inchbald was still an ordinary actress acting rather secondary parts. Perhaps Pratt had seen some of her unpublished work, but it is more likely that he had talked to the Siddonses about her. The letter is dated February 22, 1782. Inchbald must have received it the next week, and as usual she answered it. For Inchbald, the letter flattered her; for Pratt, the letter made another "connection."

There are fifty thousand reasons why I wish to know Mrs. Inchbald. Her worth, elegance, and ingenuity, are of themselves motives sufficient to excuse the awkwardness of this uninvited overture. Has she a place in her mind for a new friend? In such a mind, there must be 'many mansions;' and, till I am proved, I will accept the lowest—rising in gradation to the bosomed affections as I support the trial. I am myself surrounded by correspondents—to sustain which, without drawing upon the night to answer the deficiencies of the day, is not possible. Yet I am strongly tempted to invite one more. Mrs. Inchbald is a powerful attraction; I know that I admire, and I think that I can serve her.[54]

As an actor, Pratt had taken the stage name Courtney Melmoth; as a writer he used his own name, Samuel Jackson Pratt. He had been ordained as a clergyman, but sometime in the 1770s he had eloped to Dublin with a schoolgirl whose name was Charlotte. The *Biographical Dictionary* suggests that Melmoth was perhaps her family name. Needless to say, her family did not approve of such behavior, and the two—Charlotte and Pratt—became strolling players for the next several years. He made his debut, listed as "A Young Gentleman," at Smock Alley on February 22, 1773, Charlotte on May 8 listed as "Mrs. Melmoth." In February 1774 she appeared as Calista in *The Fair Penitent* at Covent Garden, and in October he appeared there playing the role of Philaster.

Never successful as an actor, Pratt was said to have lived off his wife's earnings. The accusation, although partly true, did not take into account the years they traveled together over England and Wales, sometimes giving public readings and lectures. Mrs. Melmoth was engaged in Dublin from 1780–1781 until 1788–1789. Pratt began his writing career in 1774 as a miscellaneous writer, but his five-act tragedy *The Fair Circassian,* which was performed on November 27, 1781, at Drury Lane with Farren in the cast, made his name; it was the hit of the season, acted a total of twenty-one times. Pratt was, however, a rather questionable character, seeing himself as deserving attention from everyone whether or not he offered anything in return. He once borrowed money from the Siddonses and, refusing to repay the loan, he publicly accused Mrs. Siddons of avarice.[55] Inchbald had known about Pratt before receiving this letter, but she could not have foreseen her next encounter with him and his wife. Pratt was never successful after his

Fair Circassian, but he continued to expect Siddons to promote him in the theatre, even after his accusation. His acting as a strolling player had taken him to Edinburgh, to York, to Covent Garden, and it is quite likely that at some of these assignments Inchbald and he had been in the same company; without specific evidence it is difficult to place him, but in the December before the letter, Inchbald has an interesting entry about him.

In the December pocket-book, there are two interesting entries, one about her parts, the other about Pratt. While she was still at the rehearsal of the "Opera," she was given a new part in a play called *The Banditti;* it was condemned; in the next entry she was "pleased to find we did not do the Banditti—calld on Mrs. Whitfield &c was with her in the pit at Drury Lane—Fair Circassian—calld at our house." Inchbald had seen Farren and her mother several times, but this is the first time she records seeing Farren play. The play's being performed so many times meant that it was approved of by the audience; but at a time when every playgoer fancied himself a critic and at a time when any comment about a popular actress could find a publisher, the comments about Farren's acting in the part of Almeida, the heroine, did not find favor with everyone. One critic wrote, "went to see the new Tragedy at Drury Lane *The Fair Circassian;* the Heroine by Miss Farren—old Drury has no other Tragic Queen at present and I can't say I admire her."[56] Pratt and the manager, however, were vastly pleased, and three editions of the play were published before the end of the year.

Having seen the play, Inchbald obviously knew about Pratt's success, and when she was sent the letter from him, she paid for it even though she was puzzled. Her expense accounts record over and over the postage she paid for the letters sent, and she received a great many, but she seldom reports their contents and almost never says anything about her replies. She did reply, however, to the letters from family and friends, and her correspondence with someone like Harris prompted another and another from her. On Wednesday she records that it was a "fair day—walked with Miss Satchell and for the pictures Mr. Pratt gave me." Pratt was a friend of Angelica Kauffman, the artist, and it is quite likely that the "pictures" were hers.

Inchbald certainly never left a letter unanswered, and she never left an account unpaid. When she began at the Haymarket for the summer of 1782, her first summer there, she was paid very little, not even so much as she had been making, and thus she felt obliged to move into smaller quarters. The day before she played in the Haymarket for the first time, her cousin came and took her things to her new lodging. Here she paid 8s. for "Lodging and maid" and 6s. for eating and drinking with the company.

GEORGE COLMAN THE ELDER AND THE HAYMARKET

When Inchbald joined the company at the Haymarket, Colman senior was the proprietor, having been in sole control since the death of Foote in 1777. The Haymarket, as the summer theatre, was officially to be open between May 15 and September 15, dates not always observed for various reasons. Although the limited season precluded the long seasons of the two winter theatres, it had many advantages. For one, it was the only theatre operating, and therefore the company was made up of actors from Covent Garden and Drury Lane as well as those who came from elsewhere. It was somewhat less expensive to put on a production; the audience liked to be entertained, not instructed, and in 1777, when Colman took control, it became very successful, perhaps because Colman had had experience as an actor, a playwright, and a manager. Now as a proprietor he made use of all these experiences.

A man named John Potter, a carpenter, built a theatre in the Haymarket in 1720. Why he did so is not known, but he must have realized that the playhouses then in use were in need of repair or had been pulled down. There were really only two in use, that of Drury Lane and the one in Goodman's Fields. The Haymarket, as its name designates, was in fact a market for the produce that came from the country, and in the 1720s and 1730s it was very much in the country. The way to it was a dark lane frequented by footpads. It began under the patronage of the duke of Montagu. The first announcement, on December 15, 1720, read in part: "At the new Theatre in the Haymarket, between, Little Suffolk Street and James Street, which is now completely finished, will be performed a French Comedy as soon as the rest of the actors arrive from Paris."[57] There seems to have been little reaction from the other theatres until some two years later, when Drury Lane and Lincoln's Inn required their players to sign agreements that they would not leave or change—"no poaching and no desertions."

The theatre itself was quite small and plain. There was no lobby, the corridors were very narrow, and the ground floor was all pit with plain wooden benches. There were boxes at the rear, and the side boxes were actually on the apron of the stage. The first season with the French players was not a success, and in the following years there were only occasional performances—concerts, amateur performances, and such. But in 1729 Mr. Johnson of Chester, a dancing master, put on an entertainment. It was called *Hurlothrumbo, or the Supernatural.* Johnson himself played the principal character and provided most of the action. It was a remarkable production and a very great success. Moreover, along with his "entertainment," Johnson put on favorite plays, such as *The Orphan, Venice Preserved,* and *Oroonoko.*

George Colman the younger wrote about the Haymarket's condition when his father took possession. Aside from the decay of the structure, there was the deplorable state of the wardrobe and the props:

With the Theatre, certain decayed and moth eaten articles, which Foote dignified by the collective name of a wardrobe and which might have produced altogether at a sale, if well puffed by a knowing auctioneer, about twenty pounds at the utmost, were made over to the lessee. . . . When he wanted more habiliments than he possessed, he resorted to a frippery in Monmouth Street, not to purchase but to job them by the night; and so vilely did some of the apparel fit the actors that he was often obliged to make a joke of the disgrace. . . . There was a skeleton of a man belonging to his company who performed a minor part in the scene of a debating club, in which Foote acted the president; this anatomic vivant was provided with a coat which would not have been too big even for the late Stephen Kemble,[58] the arms were particularly wide and the cuffs covered his hands. Foote, during the debate, always addressed this personage as the much respected gentleman in the sleeves.[59]

But supplying new costumes was not the most pressing problem; Colman had to form a company. In the years after this first season, Colman never had to think about filling the company, but in the beginning he needed to have new "stars" if he could find them. And he did find them. This first season both Farren and Henderson were new members of the company, along with Digges, who came to act in London for the first time—an interesting comment on Digges and the theatres, since he had had a very distinguished career in Ireland and Scotland even after the early time when the Inchbalds were in his company, but he had never acted in London. Farren acted Kate Hardcastle in *She Stoops to Conquer* and became the sensation of the summer. Henderson, coming from Bath, played Shylock. He, like Farren, was a great success when he finished the part before a crowded audience that included Garrick and Macklin. Macklin, before Henderson, was the best-known Shylock; Garrick disliked Henderson but had to admit, as one commentator said, "the jealousy of the actor on the verge of retirement for the actor just beginning . . . a great career."[60]

By this season of 1782, and with the hit version of *The Beggar's Opera*, Colman had made the Haymarket into a theatre as important as the two winter theatres. He had improved it by a complete redecoration; the summer audience had increased, and with the success of the first seasons, he had no problem filling the cast. Henderson left in 1782, but his place in the company was taken by such competent actors as John Bannister, son of Charles Bannister, a leading actor at Drury Lane, and Farren remained. Colman had given her her first chance in

London, and she continued to perform in the summer after she joined Drury
Lane in 1784. All of these players were to remain as players whom Inchbald
knew; several of them were to act in her plays.

After her part in *Beggar's Opera,* Inchbald played in *Separate Maintenance,* in
The East Indian, and in *The Fair Penitent.* Colman frequently presented his own
work—this summer a pantomime called *The Nonsense of Genius.* As at Covent
Garden, Inchbald walked in it. This time she did not mind so much as she had
when Harris refused to release her from a task she hated.

The play *The East Indian* has had perhaps more importance in the present
than it did in the summer of 1782. It was written by Frances Burney, accepted by
Colman, and played only nine times; and when it was revised, it was no more
successful than at first. Writing about it, Boaden finds that Burney "conceived
that the drama was likely to afford her an easy accession of fame and fortune."
But, he says, "However excellent the materials which the novelist affords to the
dramatic writer, the habit of composing the longer work is somewhat unfriendly
to great celebrity in the shorter, and the inventor of the subject does not usually
best dress it for the theatre." He felt that in general "the comedies of the novelist
are commonly weak and heavy; there is too little business and too much conversation, and a very admirable painter of the manners is guilty of an indifferent play."[61]
Moreover, Burney "knew nothing of India and, wanting local manners, was voted
a misnomer, and expired as Johnson says, under frigid indifference." Another problem Burney had, when later her tragedy *Edwy and Elgiva* was accepted by Harris
and presented in 1795, was the fact that she did not understand the process of
helping to stage her own play; she allowed her brother to attend rehearsals, and
she did not revise parts that the players thought unsuitable.[62]

One newspaper critic, complimenting Mrs. Inchbald on her performance in
The East Indian, stated that her performance was as excellent as Mrs. Bulkley's
and that he had "never heard sentences uttered more from the heart, than the
tones of Mrs. Inchbald conveyed to his ear;—that no *impediment* at all was dis-
cernible through the whole night,—and that none such existed in the lady *professionally;* and that if the winter theatres were anything more discerning than mere
money speculations commonly are, any competent manager would find her equal to
a share of first-rate business in his community."[63]

It was during this summer season in August that Mrs. Inchbald appeared on
stage with her natural hair, still elaborately dressed, but her own.

FIVE

To Ireland with Hitchcock

The entries in Mrs. Inchbald's pocket-book for this summer of 1782 are filled with her frequent conversations with the Hitchcocks, good friends whom she had known in York, and sometime during the summer Harris kept one of her farces that she had sent him and gave her an advance of twenty pounds. Now finally there was some reason for her to continue to write. And at the end of the Haymarket season, with a contract Hitchcock had arranged for her, she prepared to go to Ireland, to Dublin, to Smock Alley. In November Hitchcock himself accompanied her there, and on the way she acted for several performances at Shrewsbury, where she was treated kindly by the proprietor, Miller. He paid her a guinea a week and allowed her a benefit. She played in *Jane Shore* and *The Fair Penitent,* plays very familiar to her; for her benefit she chose *The Mourning Bride,* not one of her usual plays. Indeed, a survey of players' benefit-play choices reveals an interesting view into the plays they would choose for themselves if they were free to dictate to the managers. For their benefit the players could select their own play, provided their friends agreed and were willing to act for them. Inchbald's choice reveals, rather clearly, that she really wished to have leading parts in tragedy, a wish never fulfilled.

Hitchcock remained in Shrewsbury while she was there, and together they left for Dublin at six o'clock on the morning of November 5. Her pocket-book entry reads, "At six left Shrewsbury with Mr. H.—A snowy day—breakfasted at Ofwesty stopped at Cozen and dined about seven at Kenicozy Manor—Slept—very late at company." The next day, Wednesday, was "A very fine day—breakfasted of my cake at Bangor Ferry. Arrived at Holyhead at eight in the evening dined and found there would be no boat for Ireland till Friday." She walked with Mr. Hitchcock the next day for most of the morning and talked of the Irish theatre. Her pocket-book entry continues on Friday. "A very fine day—at 12 went on board a Packet for Dublin—a fair wind but little of it till towards night—went to bed at dark." On Saturday she continues: "At ten o'clock left the ship and at 12 landed in Dublin—Looked at many Lodgings dined and drank tea at Mrs.

Hitchcock's came to my Lodgings about nine—Eat no supper." The Hitchcocks were already in Dublin.

On Sunday she wrote, "Liked my lodgings—Mrs. Hitchcock calld—a little expected Mr. Daly—wrote to my mother, my Bro, my Sister, Aunt and Mrs. Whitfield—at dark Mr. Kemble calld—sometime after Mrs. Hitchcock Master and Miss and all staid till after 10 o'clock." She was among friends. The next day her "great box" had come and she unpacked. Mr. Daly and Mr. Hitchcock called, and Mr. Kemble came and stayed "a long time." The next day she was at rehearsal of *Which Is the Man?* at twelve and again at seven, where she found the House "lighted." And on Friday she began her Dublin season by playing Julia in *Which Is the Man?*

Dublin was certainly not London, and Smock Alley was not Covent Garden; they were different in a great many and important ways. Kemble, who had been there for some time, had found Dublin filthy, full of "idleness, drunkenness, and dirt" at Smock Alley.[1] There were two other theatres—Crow Street and Capel Street. Richard Daly had acquired the Smock Alley Theatre through a kind of subterfuge. It was his way never to be quite honest. He was a thoroughly disreputable character. Son of a farmer in County Galway, he attended Trinity College but dropped out without taking a degree. While he was in school, he boasted of the number of duels he had fought and of the pranks he played with his fellows, a group of wild ruffians who had killed two watchmen. In 1779 he appeared listed as a "Young Gentleman" at Covent Garden playing Othello. He was not a success. He was, however, befriended by the Crawfords; Mrs. Crawford, the former Mrs. Spranger Barry, had married Thomas Crawford shortly after the death of Barry, and they had been at Covent Garden in 1778; she was then the leading tragedienne at Covent Garden. Her husband, some sixteen years younger than she, played on occasion with little success. They were at Drury Lane in the season of 1780–1781 and returned to Dublin before the next season. Daly returned with them. The Crawfords were at Crow Street Theatre, and there Daly met and married Jane Barsanti in September.[2]

Daly allowed everyone who would to do his work for him, but one way and another he put together an excellent company at Smock Alley, many of the members coming because he had persuaded Hitchcock to recruit them for him. The Kembles and Inchbald were among these, as well as Mrs. Melmoth and her husband. Daly considered himself irresistible to women, young or old, and the story of his exploiting them was a familiar one both in Dublin and in London. The actresses in his company were all his prey; one account speaks "of the young actresses he [Daly] lured to his company and then blackmailed into submission by threats of canceled contracts and humiliating roles."[3] Perhaps the most notable example of his behavior was that he got Dorothy Phillips (later Dorothy Jordan) pregnant; Jordan subsequently became the mistress of the duke of Clarence, the future William IV. In 1781 Dorothy Phillips, called Miss Francis in Dublin, had acted in the company that first year when Kemble came, but by the time Inchbald came, she had gone to York, where Wilkinson, kind manager that he was, had taken her in along with her mother and sister. It was there, too, that Wilkinson suggested she call herself Mrs. Jordan after the birth of her baby. After all, she could hardly remain *Miss* Francis. During the season of 1781–1782, when she played with Kemble, she acted Adelaide in *The Count of Narbonne,* Charlotte in *The Gamester,* Selina in *Tamerlane,* and Miss Ogle in *The Belle's Stratagem.*

Kemble's experiences in the months before Inchbald came were among the most important of his early career, for he met Robert Jephson and was given a part in Jephson's play *The Count of Narbonne,* which had been very successful the year before at Drury Lane and had been scheduled in Dublin soon after Kemble arrived. Fortunately for everyone concerned, Daly invited Kemble to a dinner party where he met Jephson. Herschel Baker's account of this occasion reads: "he [Jephson] fancied himself something of a theatrical arbiter in the Irish capital. He was surprised, at Daly's dinner party, to discover that the unpromising new actor possessed all the requisites of a great tragedian, and 'above all' he marveled at his 'classical knowledge.' He immediately envisaged John Kemble as Raymond in *The Count of Narbonne,* then in preparation at Smock Alley, and undertook to groom him for the part."[4] Having decided to take Kemble into his care, he hired a dancing master and a drill sergeant as tutors for Kemble, and he himself worked with him on voice production. Wilkinson had thought Kemble already competent, but Wilkinson was much prejudiced in favor of those he had trained. The York Company was really the only one Kemble had known for any length of time; he very much needed the experience of working with Jephson, who was already an experienced playwright before he wrote *The Count.*[5]

Kemble and Miss Francis were the chief players in Daly's troupe that season. Later she played comedy almost entirely and he played tragedy, but this season in 1781 in Dublin, they both played in tragedy and in comedy, that is, whatever they were assigned. Neither of the two admired Daly. Kemble had difficulty with him from the beginning, and his attention to Miss Francis resulted in her flight to York before their child was born. In reviewing Kemble's relationship with Daly, Baker says: "Daly was a man of great talent, but he was a rounder and an unscrupulous entrepreneur. As it happened he met his mate in his new star."[6]

When we remember the later careers of Kemble, Jordan, and Inchbald, we find it difficult to imagine them in any context other than their eventual success. This is particularly true of Kemble and Jordan, as they came to be among the most celebrated players of their time. Their experiences in Dublin were invaluable; Inchbald's experience in Dublin did not lead to any change in her acting; given her speech impediment, it could not have done so. But Kemble's and Jordan's time with Daly became a part of their apprenticeship, both of them becoming more and more sure in their stage presence.

As the "star" actor in York, Kemble was not one to be instructed by Daly, who had had much less experience and certainly had much less understanding of acting. The story is told that when Kemble played Sir George Touchwood in *The Belle's Stratagem* to Daly's Doricourt, Daly "thought Mr. Kemble did not display sufficient spirit in his part, and told him so behind the scenes, and that he must exert himself more and take pattern from him. This imperious conduct did not suit our hero's temper at all; he warmly resented it, immediately changed his dress, and told Mr. Daly he might get some one else to finish the part, nor would he resume it till the manager had asked his pardon."[7]

In the summer of 1782, John Philip Kemble toured Ireland with Daly's troupe, though he and Stephen Kemble were back in Dublin when Inchbald arrived on November 9. But while Inchbald was on her way, and Kemble was preparing for the new season beginning on October 10, Sarah Kemble Siddons made her thrilling—indeed sensational—appearance at Drury Lane. The evening and her performance as Isabella in *The Fatal Marriage* was one of those famous nights in theatrical history that endure long after the play and the players. It was equal to that of Garrick in *Richard III* and certainly that of her brother John Philip the next year in *Hamlet*. For the moment, as the performance and its fame were being talked about in London, it took a few days to reach Dublin, communication in 1782 not being what we now expect it to be.

Kemble must have known about it soon after it happened, however, and he certainly would have told Inchbald. She records in her pocket-book that he brought her papers to read. Then on Wednesday, December 27, she records that "Mr. Kemble calld with a letter to engage him at Drury Lane and after sent me one with the same offer to him at Covent Garden." Neither Kemble nor Inchbald realized the importance of the two letters. For Kemble the letters meant that he need not seek a contract with Daly; for Inchbald, Siddons's sudden fame that promoted Kemble meant that her two friends and colleagues would never again be her fellow players. But in December in Dublin at Smock Alley, no one could read the future. Daly perhaps more than anyone else saw an opportunity to profit, and before the spring ended the season, he had engaged Siddons for the summer along with Kemble, and he had released Inchbald.

In the early weeks of 1783, Mrs. Inchbald reported that Daly had gone to London, a report that signaled the beginning of Daly's campaign to employ Mrs. Siddons for a season devoted exclusively to her, but in February no one in the Smock Alley troupe foresaw Mrs. Siddons's future stardom, certainly not Mrs. Inchbald.

In her entry for February 9, Mrs. Inchbald wrote, "A very warm day—at rehearsal of Barbarosa Mrs. Hitchcock told me the contents of Mr. Daly's letter from London—at dark calld on Mrs. Toplin and Mrs. Melmoth [Pratt's wife] for her turban—drank tea in the dressing room then read and worked." On the Wednesday following, she reported, "A very fine day—read c&c playd in Barbarosa—a very great house." And on Saturday the entry reads, "A wet day—at 12 rehearsal of Alexander—playd in it . . . saw Mr. Daly . . . read accounts of Mrs. Siddons—my Landlady very ill." On Sunday she wrote, "As soon as I had breakfasted carried home the accounts of Mrs. Siddons to Mr. Kemble." The next day she reported, "a fine day—calld at the House and Mr. Kemble told me of Mrs. Siddons's behaviour to him . . . read most of the evening then in the Greenroom Mr. Kemble there." Such an entry about Kemble shows that the two were close enough for him to talk about his sister; Inchbald was very close to all the Kembles, and an entry about Siddons's "behaviour" reminds us of the days when the Inchbalds met the Kembles, when Mrs. Siddons, her husband, her child, and her brother John Philip were in Liverpool. The Kemble-Siddons family were later to become the most important "family" in the theatre from the 1780s until the mid-nineteenth century. Charles, the youngest of the Kemble brothers, and his daughter Fanny continued the family's fame.

On Wednesday Inchbald's entry reflects another association that she had with Kemble, an association that was to continue throughout their professional careers and throughout their lives. Kemble had written a play, and on this day Mrs. Inchbald wrote, "A fine day—read—then happened of Mr. Hitchcock and took a very long walk with him—after Mr. Kemble calld with my part in his play and staid some time—dined late." And on Thursday, after being at the reading of *Timon* and playing in *Love for Love*, she says she "Laughd with Mr. Kemble on the stage—he came to my dressing room with English papers after." The next day she says, "then read Mr. Kemble's farce which he sent me with a note . . . in Mrs. Kennedy's box with her c&c at Hamlet playd by volunteers—had much talk with Mr. Kemble." On the following Wednesday, after she had been to a rehearsal of *Timon* and called at Mrs. Melmoth's, Kemble called on her with his *Life* and stayed while she read it. That night she played Desdemona. From her constant references and casual comments—almost asides—it is quite clear that she was involved with the whole Kemble family, not merely with John Philip. On the Friday after the Wednesday reading of his *Life,* she reports, "Mr. Kemble seemed angry about his Brother [Stephen]," but on Saturday she adds, "talkd Mr. Kemble in a good temper about his Brother." She was to remain in all the years to come a friend of the Kemble family, and she and John Philip would continue to discuss their work just as they had done in 1777 during their "vacation."

In the small circle of the theatre, Mrs. Inchbald undoubtedly saw the Kembles constantly, and since they had already been friends, her frequent comments about them in her pocket-book are to be expected, but her entries reveal other people and other interests as well; she reports on her reading, her social calls, and her constant attendance at the theatre. She had had a letter from Sir Charles "which pleased me much"; she had sat up late one night writing to Mr. and Mrs. Whitfield. One day she wrote to her mother and to Mrs. Kemble. All the comments in her books indicate that although she did perhaps favor John Philip, she also was a friend of his family.

Baker, writing about Kemble and Inchbald, observed about Kemble that "during the winter he played at Smock Alley, the tedium of the provincial capital was for the most part unrelieved. True, Mrs. Inchbald, signed by Daly to act in his company, arrived on November 9. Apparently the lady, still hopeful, resumed operations on Kemble, but with no success.... But Mrs. Inchbald was a woman not easily deterred. Such coquetry, no doubt, was more amusing than perplexing to Kemble."[8] Such a comment must be taken for what it is—the male chauvinistic comment about Kemble, who became—much later—the male chauvinistic image of the consummate male stage figure. As for Mrs. Inchbald and her stay in Dublin, John Philip's behavior was only one of several interesting developments.

Another way Mrs. Inchbald's Dublin season has been viewed has been as a drama of the virtuous maiden attacked, the virtuous maiden adamant, and the virtuous maiden triumphant but deprived. Boaden and all those who have used his *Memoirs of Mrs. Inchbald* have found Daly the villain and Mrs. Inchbald the heroine. No doubt Daly made advances to her, and no doubt Mrs. Inchbald repulsed him. Daly was a womanizer—the whole story of his career confirms such a statement. He "ruined" Miss Francis, the future Mrs. Jordan, who moved on to a more celebrated womanizer—no less than the duke of Clarence. It is true that Frances bore Daly's child, but what exactly transpired between the two has never been very clearly established. It is also true that Jane Barsanti, whom Daly married, was an admirable person and should certainly not have had to countenance his philandering ways. In her pocket-book entries Mrs. Inchbald frequently mentions the Dalys. She reports about both of them, and although her entries in the pocket-books are never explicit about her emotional—or sexual—experiences, after one has read dozens of comments about various persons it is usually possible to make a judgment about her involvement. Mrs. Daly was pregnant when Mrs. Inchbald came to Dublin. On April 7 Inchbald records that Mrs. Daly was "brought to bed"; her whole entry this day is significant: "A very fine day—walked at rehearsal of Love Makes a Man—Mr. Daly told me of many actresses that had wrote to him c&c—Mrs. Daly brought to bed—playd Angelena." She records in various entries that Daly had spoken to her and read letters to her about other women. And, moreover, she had been told such about Mrs. Melmoth and Mr. Daly. Mrs. Hitchcock then had told her that Mrs. Melmoth "had complained to Daly of what I told her." This entry is in early March, during a week in which Mrs. Inchbald read, sorted her things, spoke to Mr. Daly about a dress, talked with Mr. Digges, and so forth. On the Saturday of this first week in March, she records: "At rehearsal of Timon—calld at my milliners and with a letter to Mrs. Melmouth from Mr. Pratt which she read to me . . . behind at the Beggars Opera. . . . Mr. Kemble read a letter from Miss W— to me c&c then Mr. Daly and he had a great quarrel—after I wrote to my Bro. about Mr. Davis's sickness."[9] Mrs. Melmoth was Pratt's wife, and the combination here of gossip about her and Daly and the fact that Inchbald says she called with a letter from Pratt to her suggests that Inchbald was somehow a messenger between husband and wife. This entry also adds to the evidence that Kemble would not be dictated to by Daly.[10]

As we see from her entries, whatever Inchbald's personal experiences with Daly might have been, she was also deeply involved in the gossip and infighting of the troupe, and her record of small details hardly argues for any great confrontation with Daly. A much more likely explanation of her position is that as the spring went along and Kemble began making plans to leave Daly and go to London, Daly became even more aware of making plans for the future of his theatre, a future he wished to center around Mrs. Siddons. About this time also Mrs. Inchbald has a series of entries in which she records the fact that some of her parts were changed, given to Mrs. Melmoth, or changed because of the change of the play. The benefits for various players began in March, too, and this interrupted the usual calendar of performances. On March 16 Mrs. Inchbald records, "A fine day—at rehearsal of Roman Father—Mr. Kemble came after told me he and Daly had agreed c&c showed me an old letter of mine. After dinner met Mr. Hitchcock and went with him to Mr. Butler—drank tea at Mrs. Hitchcock's— my benefit offered." And on Tuesday she writes: "Wrote to Mr. Daly concerning my night and Lady Louisa Connolly . . . playd in Roman Father. . . . Mrs. Melmouth's night—after my part had a long dispute with Mr. Daly and were friends at last." And on Wednesday: "went to Lady L. Connollys with my Letter—then calld at the house and Mr. Daly offered to buy my night." The reference to "Lady L. Connollys with my letter" is actually a reference to Sir Charles and his former wife, Sarah, and her daughter—his "supposed" daughter, Louisa. In 1781 Lady Sarah had married again, this time to George Napier, an officer in the army, and by 1783 they were living in Dublin. The entries in Inchbald's pocketbook continue to be detailed and complex.

Whatever the personal problems Mrs. Inchbald had had with Daly, the entry about "my night" and his offer "to buy my night" was simply a professional decision, even though the "long dispute with Mr. Daly" was probably her attempt to get for herself some extra time or money or both. Her record of such professional exchanges gives an important insight into the way she handled herself professionally, a way not always followed by other players. She was always willing to advance her interests, but she also knew how to compromise.

The closing days of March found her recording the weather, her reading, and the list of those who were having benefits. Sunday was a "brown day"; Tuesday a cold one, and on Thursday she writes, "at rehearsal a showery day—after dinner received a beautiful note with a book from Mr. Kemble—playd in Beaux Stratagem." And the following day, "All the day reading in Mr. Kemble's book wrote to him and returned it—in the morning Mr. Hitchcock just calld drank chocolate Mr. Digges's night." And the next day, "read received a book and a strange note from Mr. Kemble which I answered—Mr. Daly sent for me about my salary and I sat some time." Then she says, "sent a note to Mr. Daly about a dress—sorted my things—a cloudy afternoon—drank tea at Mrs. Hitchcocks— went with her and suppd at Mr. Cardiffs Mr. Hitchcock came to supper and we talked of his making love to me at York." These entries are significant for her continuing friendship with John Philip—she always calls him Mr. Kemble—and their rather puzzling relationship. She certainly had not gone to Dublin to be with him, but the time she spent there seems to have been the conclusion of any personal, romantic ties between them.

On April 6, a Monday, she has an entry that includes everything—it reads, "A cloudy day—at my dress . . . playd Adelaide—farce Pantomime—Lord Temple's command—heard Lynch had just killed his wife—dull." Later this week appeared the notice that Mrs. Daly was "brought to bed." On the Tuesday following, she again records that Mr. Daly read her a letter, this time "of Mrs. Cowley's about her comedy c&c." The day after Mr. Hitchcock came to speak about her benefit, she says, "I wrote a resignation of it and calld with it." On the Sunday of this week, there is another very revealing entry. She writes, "A fine day—Miss Hitchcock called me and I drest very Smart and sat at her house sometime—Mr. and Mrs. Cardiff there and saw a Letter from Mr. Wilkinson about Miss Hitchcock."

Within this entry we are reminded of how intricate the theatre network was for Inchbald and her associates. The letter from Wilkinson about Miss Hitchcock, the Hitchcocks' daughter Mary Anne, meant that eventually Miss Hitchcock would return to Wilkinson and the York circuit. However, she remained in Dublin until 1787 before she returned to Wilkinson, where she stayed for only two years. She then went back to Dublin and married a barrister, Jonas Greene, who became a recorder and was knighted in 1821, whereupon Mary Anne became Lady Greene. The reference about Mrs. Cowley in Daly's conversation is difficult to place. It might have been her comedy *Which Is the Man?* (1782) or *A Bold Stroke for a Husband* (1783); in any case such details confirm our observation of Inchbald's knowledge of the theatre even before the publication of her first play in 1784.

Having given up her own benefit, Inchbald seems to have been less involved with the House and more concerned with social outings and shopping. She bought a dress and went to shops, and in one entry she says, "then all the Evening we playd at many games." She continued to act in various plays, however, and to attend the "benefits" at the theatre. Once there was "A Dancer's night," once "a Mrs. Kelly's night," once "a family's benefit," once "a Lady in distress Benefit." One typical entry of this period reads, "A fine windy day—wore my new gown—calld at the House at Mr. Cardiffs and went to shops with her and Mrs. Hitchcock—drunk tea at Mrs. Hitchcocks and workd Mr. Cardiff there and talkd of my acting—in the Pit with Miss Hitchcock at Zenobia—farce Rival Candidates." Earlier this week, as a part of an entry, she says, "Mrs. Hitchcock calld and sat a long time talking of ———," a sentence she did not finish but simply left blank. Talk and work were both inclusive words; Mrs. Inchbald used them frequently.

The Monday entry of the first week in May is an especially memorable one in that it suggests several views of Mrs. Inchbald's life, both in the list of things she did that day and in the comment about Daly. It reads: "Answered Mr. Kemble's Letter—at rehearsal of Henry 8th Found I could go home by Bristol—went a jaunt in a chariot—Mr. and Mrs. Hitchcock dined and drunk tea with me—Mr. Cardiff calld I calld at the House after walking on the Flags with Mrs. Hitchcock— Mr. Daly made love to me—after dull and at Mrs. Cardiffs. After supper drank Punch below—play Royal Shepherd & Rosina." Is this account the end of Daly's "attention" to her—is this the final assault after the reading of the letters from other actresses? She had already agreed to "sell" her benefit; it is quite unlikely that she would "sell" or "give" her favors. Her relationship with Kemble must still have been an ambivalent one for both of them. He must have been glad to see her when she arrived that November day in 1782. For even though Mrs. Siddons's triumphant return to Drury Lane did undoubtedly create a stir in Dublin, the far-reaching consequences of that event as far as Mrs. Inchbald and John Philip were concerned were hardly to be dreamed of. By May of 1783, when Daly returned from London, having signed Mrs. Siddons for the summer season, shortly to begin, Mrs. Inchbald must have felt she would sell her benefit partly because she was willing to allow for a change of schedule. That she would have made a great sum of money from it seems unlikely.

The complications of Daly's financial arrangements were intricate. He was a shrewd businessman, and in the years to come he was to make quite a fortune from his profession. In May 1783 he was only beginning, and the formula for benefits that he had demanded of the players required that they have a certain amount withheld from their weekly salaries to guarantee that they would be able to underwrite their benefit when their turn came. By May Mrs. Inchbald certainly would have had some observation about how the benefits were proceeding. Perhaps the thirty pounds she settled for when Kemble called with it on Friday, May 23, was a better financial settlement than a benefit would have been. Another interesting observation on this point is that in the weeks immediately preceding this Friday, she had begun again to make comments about her acting. Always sensitive about it, she seems to have commented on it in her pocket-book when her concern became either that she had "many compliments" or that she "thought they did not like me." Never really satisfied with herself as an actress, she sensed, no doubt, that her manner of rather stiff rhetorical speaking set her into a type of acting that her speech impediment demanded and thus made her much less flexible than she wished to be. This last-of-the-season experience of feeling that she was something of a failure and her continuing uncertain relationship with Kemble must have made her unhappy indeed. In the second week in May, she again records that she saw Kemble in the green room, the next day that she had a book from him in which she found a letter from York, and on the day following that he "caused" her to cry. She played on the Thursday in a farce called "Hotel" and records the next day that she was "happy at the praises I Received." She played a week later on Monday night, and on the following Wednesday she comments, "Surprised to find I playd—dined at Mrs. Hitchcocks—dressed my own hair—playd Lady Frances Touchwood—farce Agreeable Surprise—Mr. Young's night." This was her last performance in Dublin. On the following Sunday, May 15, she left for England.

Inchbald's record of her last weeks in Dublin is quite revealing, confirming again the way the theatre and the players were a part of the community. Startling performances, great occasions, and memorable benefits occurred seldom. More usually Inchbald and her friends went to rehearsal, explored the local "sights," employed local tradesmen, and were a part of the local scene. Her accounts reflect the local economy as well as her own personal frugal habits. As the time came for her to leave, her accounts reflect her preparation for the trip home. She had a dress made—she records in early March that she bought twenty-five yards of Irish cloth. The following week her purchases reflected the stage as she spent 6d. for "washing for the Stage, a Hat for the stage at 5d, and hair dressing at 1d."

In May she and her friends went on various local excursions; she took a "jaunt in the circular road and park," walked to the Green on the flags, walked to Phoenix Park, walked to the Barracks, and once went with Mrs. Hitchcock to the waxworks. Just before she left, she bought material and had a greatcoat made, and some two weeks later she says, "worked some time and then went to the Taylors about my great coat—at rehearsal of some of the Hotel and Which is the Man—calld and went through my part at Mrs. Hitchcock's my coat came home—after dinner slept—playd in Hotel and was very sleepy—." And the next day, a Sunday, she reports that she wore her new coat. Her entries in the pocket-books about clothes give another series of details that not only describe Inchbald's daily life; in addition, the ways she and her friends lived, the social life, the way they dressed, and the tea and coffee they drank while they had conversation help us understand their work, especially Cowley's and Inchbald's social comedies.

As the week came for Mrs. Inchbald to depart, her entries reflect her regret at leaving her friends. Mr. Hitchcock, who had been responsible for her coming to Daly, went with her to the Bristol ship to make a reservation. Two days later, she spent all day packing, a day when she also records that "Mr. Kemble spoke an Ode." On Sunday she writes, "Very low spirited—many people calld—finished packing—dined at Mrs. Hitchcock's—they came with me to the Inn—I went in a Boat to the fly packet—a cloudy evening—got on Board about nine—not much wind at first." Her time in Ireland was over; so far as we know, she never returned.

Boaden devotes little space to these months Inchbald spent in Ireland. As usual, he makes general remarks about her relationships with men—this time Kemble and Daly, of course; he reviews in general her parts and finally concludes that she left because she would not tolerate Daly. Of Kemble he observes:

Mr. Kemble expressed himself to be her warm admirer; and she often heard his praises from people who wished her happiness; but whatever he felt, he appears to have cautiously abstained from any thing by which it could be supposed he stood pledged to any connexion nearer than friendship. There appear some ingenious wishes on her part that he would declare himself in form. She reads his books; writes to him, has notes, sometimes beautiful, and at others *strange*. When he calls, she either welcomes or refuses him admittance: he yields to her humour for the time, but returns, and is again in favour: and thus the matter stood until she quitted Dublin.[11]

Evidently referring to the entry where she records that Daly "made love" to her, he says:

at another [day], she was presented with the addresses of Mr. Daly, the manager. He had a *wife;* so that the profligacy and impudence of his proposals were without palliative. How she treated him, we can readily imagine; and how such a beast received her rejection and the indignation which, as she felt it, we may be sure she did not suppress. It is probable that it became impossible to stay with him after he was exposed; for he bought up her benefit, and her friend Mr. Kemble was the messenger who, on the 23rd of May, 1783, brought her heavy guineas for the payment.[12]

But the situation was hardly so simple or so precise. Her season of 1782–1783 was over. She had gained little professional advantage and even less money. Her two seasons in London had not suggested that she was rising steadily in the ranks of those who, beginning with minor parts, would be trained to major ones. She had managed evidently from her accounts to live on her meager earnings, but to do so she had had to live on the edge of real poverty, with nothing for security. And although Harris had given her twenty pounds for a farce a year before and Colman had a play in hand that he had not returned, she had had no success at all in having her productions put on stage or appear in print. All the work and flurry of leaving York in September 1780 and becoming a member of the Covent Garden troupe had come to nothing—or to very little at least. The remaining months of 1783 did not improve her position in any viable way.

Her trip home found her seasick as usual. She went to bed but "rose at one and staid on Deck till night—a beautiful day but a calm in the evening which obliged us to anchor—Laid in one of the State Beds—slept well." On Tuesday she says, "rose about nine went on Deck was obliged to anchor again several hours for the tide which brought us to Liverpool about Eight in the Evening—a Brisk wind against us all day—suppd c&c at the Cross and Keys." The next morning she went to the custom house, called on an acquaintance, "Lent Mr. Connely [an Irish player she hardly knew] ten pounds—after dinner took coach for London— a wet evening—Mr. Butler in the coach." The next day her entry reads, "A very wet day—breakfasted early—dined at Litchfield where Mr. Butler left us and I sent a letter by him to my brother—a Captain that came by the packet in the coach and we talked much—slept well." Friday she continues, "a fine Day—the Captain very good company arrived in London about seven dined at the Inn—came to Mrs. Whitfields—heard my mother was better—and my sister well."

This account of her travel contrasts sharply with the trip she made to France, when the ship was becalmed for days, and of the times in Scotland when the winds were so contrary that they had to land and go on foot. In the past she certainly would not have had ten pounds to lend to anyone. Her repeated reports of the weather give a vivid picture of the wet coach, the talk with "a Captain that came by the packet." The pocket-books are far more than mere social entries.

LONDON AGAIN

The day after her arrival in London, a Saturday, she records that she was "not happy" and that she "calld at the door of the Haymarket." The following day she was with her sisters, many people called, and at ten o'clock she set out for Standingfield to see her ailing mother. She arrived there about eight in the morning, found her mother "poorly—very happy—after walkd." The next day her mother was better, and on Wednesday her entry reads, "A Beautiful morning—Left my mother's about Seven—breakfasted at Sudbury—arrived in London about Seven—Mr. Davis calld on me—Mr. and Mrs. Whitfield supped out—play at Haymarket Love in a Village." The next day she went into the city and Mr. Davis called. And on Friday, "a fine day—drest—calld at the Haymarket—then saw Mr. Dine and Mr. Harris . . . drest again and behind the scene at Hamlet . . . saw Mr. Colman."

Her first Sunday in London again suggests the variety of her daily life: "A Fine day—Whitsunday—after breakfast Mrs. Hunt [her sister] calld and I made breakfast again—Lookd over Mr. Whitfield's Library c&c Miss Allen dined and drank tea out . . . at dark received a letter from Mr. Pratt then calld at my sisters and suppd there—Mr. Davis came there to me and came home with me and suppd again—unhappy."[13] Two breakfasts and two suppers, letters, a library, and Mr. Davis. It is not quite clear why she should have ended the day with "unhappy," but she continued to be upset—not surprising, since her experience in Ireland had given her neither money nor professional advancement.

In spite of her unhappiness, she began to go to rehearsal at the Haymarket and act; immediately, on Tuesday of the next week, she was at the House to rehearse *Separate Maintenance,* even while she was still unpacking. It was fortunate that she could resume her place in the Haymarket, but in her domestic life she needed to reestablish herself. Pratt and Davis came again, and she says she was "very unhappy." She saw Davis every day, was at rehearsal of *Separate Mainte-nance,* and "went with Miss Allen to many shops—in the wardrobe and behind a little at Spanish Barber and Agreeable Surprise."

Her mention of Pratt reminds us of those "connections" various people kept with her. Inchbald had just been with Pratt's wife, Melmoth—now former wife (perhaps they had never been married)—in Dublin; she had just written about her in her pocket-book, had just heard gossip about her and Daly, had changed roles with her, had had tea and conversation with her. This is the last time we hear of her, but not the last time we hear of him. Melmoth remained in Ireland until 1793, when she went to New York. She remained there until her death in 1823.

Davis had been Inchbald's good friend since the beginning of her stage ca-reer. Along with Wilson, he had arranged her transfer from Wilkinson to Harris and Covent Garden. She had been out of town all the winter season; that she should see Davis upon her return seems expected, but evidently there were other reasons for his repeated calls. He needed money; she probably owed him some, and her generosity was well known. If she would lend Connely ten pounds merely because she happened upon him on her journey from Dublin to London, it is no wonder that she would listen to Davis. Although her accounts do not make it altogether clear why she owed him money or, indeed, whether it was her debt or his, the fact is that she paid him.

Davis and his problems were not the only ones she had to consider. Bob Inchbald appeared, this time with a wife. On Sunday, June 3, she wrote, "then Miss Allen went out and slept out—Mr. Davis calld—Bob Inchbald drank tea and suppd with me—surprised me about his wife—a very wet afternoon & evening."

All during these weeks, she is living in the Whitfields' house, that is, she was staying there, seeing to the care of the house and directing their maid while they were away. She includes a sum in her accounts for provisions; she shells peas, makes breakfast; she enters payment for a maid at 2s. 5d. one week and 2s. an-other.[14] The maid, Etty, made her a bonnet and took her letter out to send to Mrs. Whitfield. She records that she gave various people orders. A Mrs. Johnson from Dublin was given one; Davis had one; the hairdresser called and was given an order. She resumed her practice of going for her salary on Saturday, and she records several times in one week that she had seen Colman and not Harris; Harris actu-ally was the one who sponsored her career, but their work together was still more than a year in the future. At the moment, in July and August of 1783, she was back in the routine of the summer season at the little theatre in the Haymarket. The plays were very ordinary, and Mr. Colman was frequently "not there."

On a Wednesday, "a very fine and hot day," she "read much" and afterward "went with Etty and came home by Vauxhall." Etty was not well sometimes, but she washed the parlor, and one night Mrs. Inchbald was up at night because Etty heard a noise. Inchbald mentions Mrs. Siddons occasionally—once someone told her about Mrs. Siddons's "lame sister." The "lame sister" was Ann, the seventh child of the Kembles, who was not only lame but squint-eyed as well, obviously not suited to become an actress. For years she embarrassed Mrs. Siddons with her public demands for money. Although Inchbald knew the Kemble family, she probably had little association with Ann.[15]

And over a week after Inchbald had been at Vauxhall, she records that her visit had been reported in the *Post*. She went to see a rowing match, and Mr. Babb had Etty bring her a gift of tea things, evidently the china for her afternoon tea, which he frequently shared with her. These reports indicated her increasing popularity.

On Wednesday, August 19, she had unexpected visitors. It was a "fine cool day," and she had been to hear the reading of a play by Mrs. Bulkley[16]; afterward, "Mr. Kemble from Ireland with Master Siddons brought me a letter from Mr. Hitchcock." Master Siddons was Sarah's son, Henry, who had shared in her memorable performance of Isabella, taking the part of Isabella's son.[17] Inchbald always saw and enjoyed the Siddons-Kemble group. Master Siddons had tea with her a day or two later, although his uncle did not. John Philip did come on the Saturday following and "staid some time—told me of Connely's poverty and many things." There is no record that Mrs. Inchbald ever was paid back the ten pounds she had given Connely.

During the last weeks in August, Mrs. Inchbald was looking for lodgings. The benefits began, and her friend Mrs. Wells came to town. Her mother, Mrs. Simpson, was evidently somewhat better, for Inchbald had a letter from her, but she continued to worry about both her mother and the farm. Her brother thought the overseer, Mr. Webb, did not behave properly, and now her mother certainly could not "oversee" him. Her mother sent her a parcel, and George and his wife came up to town. And in the midst of all these happenings, Mr. and Mrs. Whitfield came home. The Whitfields were her point of stability, and even though she moved to new lodgings, she continued to see them daily and continued to help with their household. She records more than once that she "went to many places for Mrs. Whitfield—dined drank tea and supped there."

The season at the Haymarket being over, Inchbald returned to Covent Garden. She also returned to the same pattern of rehearsal, the same talk in the green room. She continued to read the newspapers and to write and receive letters. On Wednesday, September 16, she writes: "A fine but cold day—at Rehearsal till late—My brother calld after and told me his intention of taking my mother's farm c&c playd in Separate Maintenance and Agreeable Surprise read c&c an Eclipse of the moon." Her pocket-book is now filled with comments about her family, the farm, and her friends. On Friday, September 18, she writes: "Finished Hume's Essays—Mrs. Wells calld dined and drunk tea with me—my Bro. then my sister and Mrs. Twiss calld the time playd in Volpone, farce Son-in-Law— suppd at Mr. Twiss's. . . . Mr. Wilson offered to get me a coach."

As was often the case, this entry contains significant details. Her brother is leaving to go back to Standingfield, Wilson is back at Covent Garden, and Mrs. Wells has appeared, all details that are to be significant in the future. Mrs. Wells became and remained one of Inchbald's good friends; or perhaps we should put it another way—Inchbald became and remained one of Wells's good friends. In the weeks to come, each played an important role in the other's professional and personal life.

Mrs. Wells was Mary "Becky" Davies, whose father, Thomas Davies, was a woodcarver and gilder in Birmingham. It was he who, employed by Garrick, dug up the root of the mulberry tree at Stratford-on-Avon and created the famous box for Garrick. Mary's father became ill about the time she was six, and her mother became a tavern keeper. Many actors frequented the tavern, and Mrs. Davies eventually attempted to become an actress, playing minor parts. Mary at fourteen acted at York with Wilkinson, and at sixteen she married Ezra Wells, an actor who played Romeo to her Juliet. He deserted her soon after, but Mary continued to act as Mrs. Wells. She was at Bristol in the summer of 1780 and in June 1781 came to the Haymarket. On September 4 she created the role of Cowslip in O'Keeffe and Arnold's *Agreeable Surprise*. On September 14, 1781, she played Macheath in *The Beggar's Opera*—in the production in which Inchbald also played when the men played the women's part and the women played the men's. In the season of 1781–1782, she was at Drury Lane, where she acted an impressive list of parts. Like Inchbald, she knew everybody, and everybody in the theatre world of London knew her after the summer of 1781. By the time Inchbald reappeared from Dublin and began acting at the Haymarket, Wells was acting many of the leading roles.

She was a superb mimic, rivaling the fame of Wilkinson himself; as Wilkinson did, she brought both fame and censure upon herself. On stage she created a list of roles, most of which were in comedy, many requiring songs. In the fall of 1783, she and Inchbald were frequent companions; they became close friends, each helping the other during a friendship that lasted until Mrs. Wells retired and left London.

Because Inchbald was obliged to find accommodations after her return from

Dublin, she again went from one place to another until the summer was over, searching for a permanent address. The Whitfields had been away for a good part of the summer, but on September 20 she says the Whitfields came home, and after supper with them she went to her new address. In her accounts she lists 10s. 6d. for a porter to carry her boxes to her new lodging. The summer had been a very difficult one for her, especially since she really did not have a proper place of her own. When she had arrived from Dublin, the Whitfields had had guests, and she spent a day or two with her sister until both of them went to Standingfield to see her sick mother. Upon their return she spent the rest of the summer either with the Whitfields or with her relatives until she went to St. Martin's Lane and her new lodgings. It is no wonder that for this September she wrote "Unhappy" in her list of Septembers.[18]

Having moved into her new quarters, she began to see the Kembles. She "sat by Miss Kemble" at the Whitfields; she had dinner and tea with Mr. Kemble and heard that the Siddonses had come to town. Three days later she "happend on Mrs. Siddons and walked together." She wrote Kemble for an order, and on Monday, October 5, she and Kemble were at the Whitfields and he gave her the order; the next day she wrote him a note and that night went to Drury Lane to see him in *Hamlet.* She wrote him another note the next day. Stephen Kemble called on her several times this fall, for he was engaged at Covent Garden and they were to see each other frequently at the theatre.

The Kembles and Mrs. Siddons were having a remarkable success in 1782–1783. After her success at Drury Lane in October, Siddons placed two of her sisters with her at Drury Lane, Frances—later to be Mrs. Twiss—and Elizabeth, later to be Mrs. Whitlock. And in the summer after the season at Drury Lane ended in early June, Siddons, her sister Frances, and two other actors, William Brereton and Francis Aickin, went to Dublin, arriving there on June 16 after a very rough crossing from Holyhead. They were met by John Philip Kemble, and together they acted for Daly in Dublin and afterward briefly at Cork. This was the summer season after Inchbald had left, and when they came to town, John Philip lived for a while in Inchbald's quarters at No. 2 Leicester Court while she stayed with the Whitfields.

On September 24 Stephen Kemble made his Covent Garden debut in *Othello;* his Desdemona was Miss Satchell. The two of them were married in St. George Bloomsbury on November 20. As members of the company, they were both in the green room when Inchbald was there, and on several occasions Inchbald and they were in the same performances. Inchbald was at the performance of *Othello* when Stephen made his debut. In the pocket-book entry that mentions that she "happend of Mrs. Siddons," she says, "in the front at Othello—farce Quaker—behind in my dressing room c&c—Mr. Stephen Kemble appearance—suppd at Mrs. Whitfields." Miss Satchell and Inchbald had long been friends; in fact Satchell was the friend who went with Inchbald to one of the masquerades in 1780, Inchbald's first year in London.[19] Satchell had played Polly in *The Beggar's Opera* in 1780, and she had played Adelaide in the first performance of *The Count of Narbonne;* four days after her marriage, billed now as Mrs. Kemble, she played Miss Dormer in *The Mysterious Husband.* She was a valuable member of the company at Covent Garden.

Stephen Kemble was not so successful as his wife: after the season of 1782–1783, his contract at Covent Garden was not renewed. There were several reasons for his lack of success in London. For one, the comparison with his brother was really unfair, since John Philip's style was unique and Stephen could not have imitated it. Moreover, from his early years Stephen was obese, a fact that created many jokes, sometimes cruel ones.

Boaden wrote of Miss Satchell before she married: "The stage never in my time exhibited so pure, so interesting a candidate as Miss Satchell—her modest timidity, her innocence, the tenderness of her tones, and the unaffected charm that sat upon her in the public regard, which she cultivated long and extended under the appellation—Mrs. Stephen Kemble. This young lady carried into a family abounding in talent powers of so peculiar a kind, so perfect, so unapproachable, that, if they were inferior as to their class, they shared a kindred pre-eminence."[20]

John Philip made his debut at Drury Lane on Tuesday, September 30, in *Hamlet.* He repeated his performance four times before playing in *Edward the Black Prince,* his sister Elizabeth acting Mariana. Inchbald went to *Hamlet* on October 6. On the Thursday following, her entry reads, "A hot day—wore my shift—at my parts—at dark Mr. Davis calld on me—then I at Mrs. Whitfields drank tea and read much about the Kembles there—behind fixing my glass c&c . . . eat no supper—not well." Her comment about reading "much" about the Kembles was a comment repeated all over London, because with the whole group of Kembles playing both at Covent Garden and Drury Lane, it is not surprising that the papers should be filled with comments about them. They were compared to other actors and actresses, they were praised, they were analyzed, and sometimes they were criticized adversely; but after this 1783–1784 season, the Kemble-Siddons group dominated the theatres in London for the next two decades.

John Philip and Stephen had been in Dublin together, although not in the same company. It is interesting to realize that Stephen's playing at Covent Garden on September 24 preceded John Philip's at Drury Lane; his debut was not until September 30; and Mrs. Siddons did not return to Drury Lane until October 8, when she acted in *Isabella* by royal command. Sarah and John appeared together in *The Gamester* on November 22. The fall season of 1783 belonged to the Kemble-Siddons family, to John Philip, Stephen, Elizabeth, Frances, and, of course, Sarah Kemble Siddons.[21]

ANOTHER FALL SEASON AT COVENT GARDEN

For Inchbald this fall of 1783 was a very difficult period of time. True, she was back at Covent Garden, where she was now at "home" and where she could count on a "usual" income, where she could talk to Harris and to Colman. The prospects for a career in the theatre, never very great, became even less so with the advent of the Kemble-Siddons group. It was not that anyone at the time could foresee the future, but for all her good wishes to the Kembles and the Siddonses, it must have been discouraging to consider that the Dublin venture had not advanced her worth as an actress and that in spite of Harris's advance of twenty pounds, she had heard no more of a production of her farce.

Discussing this period of time, Boaden includes not only her meager salary: "she was to drudge on upon a salary of sometimes £2 frittered away by stoppages on one account or another . . . she had lent her money to an Irish actor, and that did not return. She had remitted money to her sister Hunt."[22] She had paid Davis the forty-three pounds he claimed, and she gave money to other "connections." Then she learned that her mother had died on October 6. Mrs. Simpson's death was not unexpected, but to her devoted family it was a very sad occasion. Inchbald and her brother George Simpson went to Standingfield, where they visited her mother's grave and went to the Catholic service on Sunday at Coldham.

The entries in her pocket-book during these days in October show clearly the dependence she and everyone else had on letters. She had known for some time—from the time she had returned from Dublin—that her mother was ill—but she did not learn of her death until the thirteenth. In several entries she had repeatedly recorded that she had heard how sick her mother was—Mr. Twiss told her "how bad my mother was"; and calling on her sister she found a letter from her nephew George Huggins that "affected me much." She and her brother spent the night at her sister Hunt's, and on Saturday morning at four o'clock they left London in a post chaise and got to Standingfield at three. The next day, Sunday, they went to Coldham for Mass with their sister Bigsby, who lived nearby. Afterward she and George walked "under the wood." On the next day she wrote, "A beautiful day—George went to Jack Simpsons's I to Mrs. Bigsby's—after dinner to my mother's grave—after tea to Bury with George—calld at many places—supt and slept at my cousin Wilson's."

The following night, Tuesday, they went to the Bury Theatre and were "behind," where they evidently were asked to perform the next night—that is, Inchbald's Wednesday entry reads, "At rehearsal of Spanish Friar—then calld on my Sister and dined there—happend of Mr. O'Brian and he walked with me—playd in Spanish Friar." The next day: "At 3 left Bury—breakfasted & suped on the Road—drank tea in town at my Sister Hunt's playd in B Opera-farce 3 weeks—had words with Mrs. Pitt and Mr. Lewis—vext at many things—suppd at Mrs. Whitfield's."

It seems fitting that Inchbald should play in the Bury Theatre in a kind of memorial for her mother, who always went to Bury for the season. George Simpson and his wife were living nearby—at least temporarily. The careers of the George Simpsons were rather uncertain. Mrs. Simpson—Inchbald calls her "sister" just as she does her own siblings—was a better player than he was, and at times she had a contract when he did not. George Simpson, like Inchbald's husband, Joseph, was a rather easygoing, not-very-ambitious actor who depended on his good looks and good nature to find friends and to get engagements. Mrs. Inchbald helped him go to Edinburgh and to York with Wilkinson. He had been to Norwich when she decided to go on stage, and he had preceded her to Dublin, acting at the Crow Street playhouse in 1773–1774, the season just after the Inchbalds were married. During these years of the 1780s, the Simpsons were frequently in London for one reason or another, and Inchbald saw them with various friends for tea, for dinner, or for pleasure excursions to the parks.

Sometime during the fall of 1783, Inchbald began to write items for Woodfall's periodical; that is, she, like many other readers, sent in letters, what we would call "letters to the editor." The entries in the pocket-book are tantalizingly cryptic. The day after she returned from Standingfield and Bury, she wrote, "A fine warm day—Mr. Davis calld—at Mrs. Whitfields heard what was in the paper on Mrs. Pitt calld at the House on Mr. Twiss—saw Mr. Kemble." On the next day, a Friday, she says, "wrote about Mrs. Pitt—." The next day she writes: "More in the papers against me of Mrs. Pitt—went for salary. . . . I dined and drank tea in the Kings Bench Prison with Mr. Davis he suppd with me in the kitchen at Mrs. Whitfields."[23] The next entry begins, "Mrs. Wells calld and sat while I drest. . . . Mr. Twiss and Mr. Benton came in the evening—Mr. Twiss staid supper and brought me home."

These entries again cover the theatre, the papers, the King's Bench Prison,

Mr. Twiss, the kitchen, and the dressing room. And the item about Mrs. Pitt suggests a new activity for Inchbald—writing letters to the periodicals. Mrs. Pitt was Harriet Pitt, the illegitimate daughter of Ann Pitt. She had begun dancing and acting while she was very young; by 1765 she had borne two children by George Mattocks—Harriet and Cecil. After Mattocks deserted her and married Isabella Hallam, Harriet soon became the "wife" of Charles Dibdin, by whom she had two sons—Charles and John. Dibdin also deserted her. These two sons became actors and singers, following their father. What Inchbald meant when she wrote "against me of Mrs. Pitt" is a puzzle, since although Pitt was at Covent Garden, she seems to have had no reason to write about Inchbald.

The mention of Davis and the King's Bench Prison meant that Davis, having been arrested for debt, was living under the rules of the prison but was free to go with Inchbald to have supper in the kitchen. The next day she had supper with Twiss. Twiss and Davis, two of her good friends that were far apart in class and circumstances, were representative of the great diversity of her friends. Both remained her close friends even after she became the "Celebrated Mrs. Inchbald."

On Monday, November 9, in an entry filled with a variety of activities that included a walk to "Lister Fields" with Mrs. Whitfield, she "—had words with her about Etty's breaking [she mentioned the mug]. I read Caesars Commentarys after—he [Mr. Whitfield] at home at supper—wrote of Mrs. Siddons temper [was this an item she sent to Woodfall?] Play Richard and Pantomime." Then on the Saturday following, in the midst of a number of activities, she writes, "then at home till dark writing to Woodfall about females."

Pitt and Inchbald were rivals, no doubt, for some of the secondary roles, and no doubt Inchbald wanted some of them, for she, Inchbald, was always dissatisfied with her assignments. Pitt had come to Covent Garden from Drury Lane in 1780 at the same time Inchbald had come from York, but now in November 1783 the reasons for Inchbald's quarrel are not clear; perhaps it had to do with the comment she had written about "females," or it may simply have been that Inchbald chose to quarrel with her over some incident that had occurred in the green room. These items about Pitt and "females" show Inchbald's tendency to caustic response; she was never amiable and compliant.

All during these last weeks of the year, she continued to see her friends the Whitfields. She records carefully their daily association. Mrs. Whitfield did not easily forgive her husband for his escapade of staying out until three in the morning; Inchbald says he "found our consequences," and in the several entries in the pocket-book she records that he did not "sup" at home; sometimes he was there with Mr. Babb, or he was at tea and afterward read to them, or Inchbald read.

One Sunday late in November, her entry reads, "A cold cloudy day—worked and wrote to Mr. Cardiff—followed Mr. and Mrs. Whitfield to Mr. Babb's—dined and drank tea there—Mr. Tom Whitfield there—happened of Bob Inchbald and his wife—suppd with Mrs. Whitfield and Read poetry to her—he out—thought and talked of going to India." And the following Friday she writes, "A beautiful day had no paper went an errand for Mrs. Whitfield and happened of Sir Charles Bunbury he walked with me and I asked him about India."[24] Inchbald was at this time very frustrated. She did not like her assignments, she does not seem to be working at writing—she was not even writing letters. This entry about "going to India" is important for examining her plays and the political contest of the 1780s and 1790s and for the way all her connections with political events would reappear in her work. It is also important as yet another indication that she was never satisfied with herself or her work. Already by this date many young people—both men and women—went out to India and returned with a fortune. She used this situation in her play *Such Things Are* in 1787, but now she was no doubt asking for herself.

The last entries in the year were written while the debates were going on about the East India Company, debates that continued for a very long time. She does not record her conversation about India, but later she was to hear the debates about the company and its ruler, Warren Hastings, and later still, when Sheridan spoke against Hastings at the trial, she was present. On December 11, after Mr. Davis called on her, she "set out to go to the Guild Hall but calld on Mr. Twiss he read the debates to me and my Bro. came the time." This debate was no doubt the bill Charles James Fox had put forward to reform the East India Company. The next day, Thursday, she and her brother walked, met Mr. Harris, called on Mrs. Wells, and went to a coffeehouse in the city. On Monday, December 14, she notes that Kemble had a letter in Woodfall's paper. She supped with Mrs. Whitfield while her brother, Mr. Whitfield, and Mr. Kemble were at the House of Commons. Without realizing it, perhaps, she was learning about the political and economic realities of her world in the 1780s. Mr. Whitfield, Kemble, and her brother would surely have reported what happened in the House of Commons.

During these last weeks in December, she saw Sir Charles Bunbury several times, and he began to call on her; their association became a major chapter in her life in the next few years. Sir Charles was the son of Sir William Bunbury; the Bunbury property was in Suffolk, and Mrs. Inchbald certainly knew him, since his home at Barton was no more than a dozen miles from Standingfield and he was the member in Parliament from Suffolk. But before the eighties, they lived in two very different worlds; that is, Inchbald did not live in his. In the summer of

1783, while she was acting at the Haymarket, she mentions him several times, and in the fall when the Covent Garden season began, she saw him on the street or in the theatre. In the 1783 pocket-book she still refers to him as "Sir Charles Bunbury"; later she calls him simply "Sir Charles."

Inchbald's references to Mrs. Wells and Woodfall's paper suggest another connection that was to become very important for her, for by this time—1783— Mrs. Wells was living with Edward Topham—Captain Topham—who was sometimes called "Epilogue" Topham because he was much applauded for his epilogues written for one after another of his playwright friends. Stanley Morison, in his biography of Topham, says: "Captain Epilogue was a public character, dressing, speaking, play-writing, printing, fox-hunting, living his own life in a way distinctly his own in an age of eccentrics; an aristocrat, born more scrupulous than squeamish, a dilettante yet not a butterfly, a pursuer of freedom, and therefore more loyal above all to himself and to his notions of what became an English Gentleman of taste and fashion."[25]

The three of them—Becky Wells, Inchbald, and Topham—had the will and the skill to play an important part in the theatre in the 1780s and 1790s. They all three were creative; that is, by their definition they created "situations," both personal and for the stage; they wrote plays, prologues, epilogues, letters to the newspapers, and each pushed forward her or his own agenda, each in her or his own way, but each in partnership with the others.

Edward Topham was the son of Francis Topham, judge of the Prerogative Court of York. Topham went to Cambridge, entering in 1767 and leaving in 1770 without taking his degree. His father died in 1770, and thus he had the money to travel. He went to the Continent on the Grand Tour, and after his return to Scotland, he published *Letters from Edinburgh*. He secured a commission in His Majesty's troop of Horse Guards. And in June of 1780, during the Gordon riots, he was commander of the troops who guarded the palace. Afterward he became involved in political journalism, in the theatre as a playwright, and, finally, in journalism, promoting his version of the theatre and making a success in editing.

Topham wrote a pamphlet deploring Edmund Burke's American policy.[26] He wrote a farce entitled *The Fool,* and his prologues and epilogues were much sought after; one prologue was said to have brought Colman five hundred pounds, and after that Topham was given the "freedom of Covent Garden." He had a home in Suffolk and a house in Bayston Street near the Marble Arch, where he entertained. It was here that he met Mrs. Wells, who came to rehearse an epilogue.

In December 1783 the experiences and successes of Inchbald, Wells, and Topham were in the future, but the entries in the fall of 1783 in Inchbald's pocket-book begin to show their close association. This association also begins to reveal how complex and important the world of Inchbald and Wells was to London and the whole of England in the last two decades of the eighteenth century. The theatres—Drury Lane and Covent Garden—the opera, and the pleasure gardens not only provided entertainment and a social context; they also addressed the problems and fears pertaining to George III and his government, to the country's reaction to the American War for Independence, and to the events in France that finally, in the case of America, ended with the Treaty of Paris and, in the case of France, resulted in the final triumph over Napoleon. An understanding of Inchbald's life and work must take into account such people as Topham, Sir Charles, Lord Derby, who at this time in 1783 was already said to be "engaged" to Farren, and General Burgoyne, now returned to London after his disgrace in America, whose plays were regularly produced at Drury Lane and the Haymarket. These men were all intimates with Colman, attended the theatre virtually every evening, and were regularly in the green room; there is no question but that Inchbald frequented the green room herself and that she took part in the conversations and events there.

General Burgoyne, one of the generals sent to take Boston, had been allowed to return to England in 1777 after his defeat at Saratoga, and he had become again an important presence in Drury Lane. Lord Derby also was in Parliament and, with his association with Farren and his frequent appearance at the theatre, added another political dimension there, especially since he and Sheridan were close friends. Being a part of green-room circles at the theatres meant being in the center of the London world.

In January 1784 Inchbald lived in very humble lodgings in a house belonging to a Mrs. Smith in No. 2 Leicester Court, Castle Street, Leicester Fields, Kemble having moved to better quarters. It was not the kind of place for her to receive visitors, either for social pleasure or for business. To make matters worse, she quarreled with Mrs. Whitfield during February and did not become reconciled until the last day of March, when Twiss had them both to dine with him. The Whitfields went to Birmingham in June, and Mrs. Inchbald was again left to oversee their house. It was here that she and Colman made ready her farce.

Perhaps this is an appropriate place to point out just how special her experience as a playwright was. Especially since her farce was only the beginning for her, and since it turned out to be very successful, it made it easy for her to submit other farces and plays. It is difficult to exaggerate the number of plays that were submitted to the managers each season. There were hundreds and hundreds, which perhaps is not surprising because the theatres were the center of the world of writers and theatre patrons. Virtually everyone in the intellectual and social circles of London wished to have a play produced. Hundreds of writers did have at least one play accepted, and hundreds of these plays failed. Many years after this 1784 season, George Colman the younger, in his *Random Records,* reports: "People would be astonished if they were aware of the cart-loads of trash which annually are offer'd to the Director of a London Theatre: The very first manuscript which was proposed to me for representation, on my undertaking theatrical management, was from a nautical gentleman, on a nautical subject:—the piece was of a tragic description, and in five acts;—during the principal scenes of which the Hero of the Drama declaim'd from the Main-Mast of a Man-of-War without once descending from his position."[27]

Many of Mrs. Inchbald's close friends were to try their hand at writing plays; William Godwin, who became her friend in the 1790s, Amelia Opie, and even Frances Burney failed. Being a successful writer in other fields did little to assure a success in the theatre.

SIX

1784

✒ Inchbald had represented the manuscript that she gave to Colman as being by a Mrs. Woodley; he very soon discovered that it was her work, though he kept her secret until she gave him permission to acknowledge that it was hers. Colman's attention to revising her piece and her willingness to work with him attest to the skill of Colman's writing and his understanding of the necessary elements for a piece to be successful; Inchbald's working to understand and please him shows her willingness to learn the ingredients of a successful piece. Each accepted the other in professional terms. He was not her mentor, nor was she his student; they worked together as partners.

We are not quite sure of the date and circumstances of Colman's accepting her farce *A Mogul Tale*, but Boaden reviews the progress of the negotiations. On March 4, 1784, she sent her piece to Colman in her own name. On March 7 he agreed to purchase it for one hundred guineas. On the seventeenth Colman began to write to her about it. That Inchbald finally had a farce accepted and that Colman helped her make it ready for the stage is a kind of miracle, considering all the circumstances of the way such an event came about. It was very fortunate indeed that her subject was a popular topic, that the Haymarket was just the place for *Mogul*, and that she had the choice of actors from both Covent Garden and Drury Lane. And it was even more fortunate for her that Colman took it, for the problem in the winter theatres was that there were so many plays submitted by insistent would-be playwrights that the managers spent more than half their time dealing with determined authors who refused to take no for an answer. And frequently—very frequently—the plays were not successful and the disappointed writer wrote yet another play, and the process was repeated.

Colman's attention to *A Mogul Tale* is instructive regarding the methods he used to select plays for his audience at the Haymarket. He is said to have observed, upon first seeing the manuscript, that "he never met with so cramp a hand in his life, nor was ever so much puzzled to make out a piece."[1] One of his notes speaks to the problem of handwriting—his, not hers, but anyone who has tried to read her pocket-books understands what Colman means by "so cramp a hand," for hers was a more "cramp" hand than his. He writes: "Dear Madam, If you can't make out my scrawls on the blank leaf, pray do me the favor of calling on Thursday morning, and I will explain my dark hints to you. Your very humble servant, G.C." In another note he says: "I wish to have the farce completed as soon as possible. The idea is droll, as well as temporary; and, with a little care, I think it can't fail. Success attend it!" Inchbald at once gave it that "little care," and he wrote again: "Mr. Colman is very sorry he could not wait on Mrs. Inchbald before he left town. He has taken the *Mogul* with him. He is not yet quite the thing; but Mr. C. will try to bring him back the better for his excursion." Another letter addresses her rather than her piece: "Mr. Colman presents his compliments to Mrs. Inchbald, and assures her that he never mentioned her name to any person whatever on the subject of 'The Mogul Tale,' and was yesterday extremely surprised at his son and Mr. Jewell both suggesting her as the author, which suggestion however he did not in the least confirm, nor was it in the green-room. He really thinks it better for the author not to be avowed at present, though he thinks the piece can not be injured; and to attempt to injure the reputed author would be infamous."[2]

The season of 1784 at the Haymarket was a memorable one, not only for Inchbald's first play, but for several other reasons as well. Colman's son, George Colman the younger, had his first successful play performed that season. The Haymarket provided first-rate entertainment in the summer, which is the most difficult time of the theatrical year. Colman had by this time completely redecorated the interior, making it "elegant, gay, and it appeared to be 'well dressed.'"[3] The theatre itself had had some strange physical abuse a couple of times. One such incident occurred in the spring of 1780, when Colman rented the Haymarket to Charles Dibdin for a puppet show. The audience, expecting live actors, rioted when the curtain went up, and the whole interior of the theatre was destroyed. By 1784, however, the theatre had been repaired and redecorated.

The first play of the 1784 season was Colman's own, called *The Election of Managers,* a play that was really far too topical, for it followed immediately a real General Election. The license to put it on had at first been refused but later granted. Moreover, the actors and actresses were made up to look exactly like the real-life characters they portrayed. Elizabeth Farren, for example, was made up to resemble the duchess of Devonshire, who was said to have secured votes for Charles James Fox by rewarding the voters with kisses.[4] At first the audience liked the play; then one man, "a very fat 'Buck' Bob Monckton, son of General Monckton," began to shout "Off! Off!" disrupting the show.[5] The play was continued the next night, but when Monckton was joined by other "bucks," it was withdrawn. Perhaps

Colman did not wish to provoke a riot. The prologue, written by Colman himself and spoken by Palmer, gives a kind of review of the Haymarket with such comments as:

> What though our house be threescore years of age
> Let us new vamp the box, new lay the stage
> Long paragraphs shall paint with gay parade
> The gilded front and airy balustrade.

The verse continues, naming such playwrights as Lillo, Fielding, and Foote and ending, "With hearty welcome tho' but homely cheer / May our old roof its old success maintain." Inchbald's play fit exactly the phrase "homely cheer."[6]

In this summer season, Colman put on fifty plays, and nine of them were new pieces. Aside from Inchbald's play and young Colman's *Two to One*, the new ones included *Lord Russel*, a tragedy by Hayley; *Peeping Tom*, by O'Keeffe; *Hunt the Slipper*, by a clergyman, the Reverend Harry Knapp; *The Noble Peasant*, a comic opera by Holcroft, with music by Shield; *The Two Connoisseurs; A Peep into Elysium;* and Colman's own *The Election Managers*, which created a great stir.

Colman had been quite successful from the beginning of his proprietorship, but this season of 1784 was special, since both Inchbald and Colman the younger were introduced with their first successes. Both later became very successful playwrights, and Inchbald's *Mogul* became a classic. An after-piece, *The Noble Peasant*, became a standard piece, and O'Keeffe's *Peeping Tom*, based on the Godiva legend, was a huge success. In short the 1784 season at the Haymarket was quite remarkable.

Inchbald's play *A Mogul Tale* opened on July 6. Colman wrote the prologue for it, just as he had done for his son's play. In this first play, Inchbald made use of the latest interest, written about in the periodical press, talked about widely, and very soon to be the most sensational national interest since the American war. Her constant attention to the newspapers and her interest in her own world rather than the world of the past helped to make her first several plays memorable. *A Mogul Tale* was about the balloon craze. The dates of the various balloon incidents show that Inchbald and Colman had made a shrewd guess in staging her play in 1784, shortly after the success of the Montgolfier brothers in France and before Lunardi succeeded with his balloon on September 15, after Inchbald's play had closed. Certainly with all the publicity in France and the rivalry and secret preparation that rocked the French court in the fall and winter of 1783, the miracle of flight had made a tremendous impression in both England and France in the months of June and July and later in the fall when there were several attempts to conquer the air.

One account of these months points out that "People had been talking about it for several months, and not only in France but in every branch of the international club of inventors and savants, where the latter habitually jeered at and pooh-poohed the former." For the triumph of Inchbald's first play, it is somehow fitting that she and the Montgolfier brothers succeeded after months and years of experiment and work. The Montgolfier family had a paper manufacturing business, including mills, factories, and a distribution system. The younger of the two brothers, Etienne, was an architect who lived in Paris and by a stroke of luck was asked by M. Reveillon, the paper-maker in Paris, to work with him in making fine paper.[7] Joseph Michel, the older brother, was by November 1782 in charge of the family business in Annonay.

The Montgolfier mill was a very fine one, turning out beautiful paper. The family had long been established there, and the workers in the mill were well trained, well paid, and loyal. The brothers had an ideal situation; with Etienne contributing the design and Joseph providing the technical features, there was little doubt that together they would succeed in constructing a balloon. At the same time there were others—in France and elsewhere—working on somewhat different designs. It was a paradigm of the space race between the Soviet Union and the United States. Alexandre Charles and his sponsors the Robertses were in Paris while the Montgolfiers were in Annonay, a small city in Vivarais, and like the twentieth-century race, the eighteenth-century one had many players.

The balloon the Montgolfiers constructed was made of cloth-covered paper and sent aloft with hot air. Their first public demonstration took place on June 4, 1783; it was quite successful, rising "in to the air, where its accelerated motion carried it, in less than ten minutes, to a thousand fathoms of elevation. It then described a horizontal line of 7,200 feet." The second machine, on September 19, was much larger, weighing one thousand pounds. The first trial of this amazing machine was halted by the weather, but on November 21, in the presence of thousands, the balloon was successful. It was the first manned flight.[8]

Rivaling the Montgolfiers were Alexandre Charles, with his sponsors the Roberts brothers, and Jean-Pierre Blanchard. The construction of Charles's balloon was quite different from that of the Montgolfiers'. It was made of silk cloth covered with a substance the Robertses had devised to coat fabrics for use in cloth-hung walls and ceilings. Made out of rubber, a new and rare substance from the colonies, it made the cloth impermeable to gases. To inflate his balloon, Charles used hydrogen, a substance fourteen times lighter than air. At five o'clock on

August 27, 1783, on the Champ de Mars, the balloon rose rapidly before an immense crowd of spectators and disappeared in a rain storm; the gentlemen and ladies of the court and the crowd of French citizens remained in the pouring rain. It was the beginning of a new world.[9]

With so much excitement in Paris in August of 1783, while Inchbald was acting at the Haymarket, it is not surprising that she should use a balloon as her point of reference. This was only the first of many times when the latest popular incident served as the basis of a play of hers. The device of an English couple and their dotty friend the doctor ascending in a balloon and floating to earth in an unknown foreign land created a certain excitement from the very beginning of the play.

To add to the reality of the play, the problems of the balloons were obvious to everyone, for there was no way to predict how high or how far a balloon would go, or where the machine would go down. In July, when Inchbald's play was first acted, there were still many questions of design, many problems of mechanics, and few facts about flight other than the exciting demonstrations in France.

Balloon mania was everywhere. Frederick Reynolds, a contemporary playwright friend of Mrs. Inchbald, gives an account in his *Life* of his own knowledge and perception. Reynolds was intimate with George Biggin, "an ingenious chemist" who employed Vincenzo Lunardi to build a balloon for him. As a friend of Biggin, Reynolds had the opportunity to make small "Montgolfiers," and one day at a dinner party in Greenwich he took a small Montgolfier with him. When Lord Effingham, his host, found he had it with him, he was invited to bring it inside. He reports, "I obeyed, and then, for the *first time*, he, his friends, the landlord, and the waiters, beheld the *wonderful machine*." The whole town found out about the machine, and his father suggested that he gratify "public curiosity," so he and Lord Effingham went out into the middle of the river to give a demonstration. At first the balloon would not rise, but when it rose and vanished from sight, Reynolds was quite the hero. The successful operation was not the end of the matter, however, for the balloon fell in a farmer's yard, terrifying him and destroying his property; he demanded and received twenty pounds.[10]

Early in the spring of 1784, Lunardi, who was a secretary to Prince Caramanico, the Neapolitan ambassador, wrote and published a prospectus for his plan to ascend from the hospital grounds in Chelsea. He offered subscriptions to those who wished to come see the preparation of his balloon, and when it was finished, he exhibited it suspended from the dome of the Lyceum. Some twenty thousand people paid admission to see it, but since we do not have Inchbald's 1784 pocket-book, we do not have evidence that she was among those who went.

Considering her interest in all that went on in London, it is certainly likely that she was there.

Lunardi's balloon was "a red and white-striped bag made from 520 yards of oiled silk thirty-three feet across, and with a gondola eleven feet long and four feet wide."[11] It was powered by hydrogen and helped by Dr. George Fordyce, who himself helped fill it on September 15. Lunardi, accompanied by a cat and a dog, made a successful flight, landing in a field near Ware. Lunardi knew how to create publicity as well as how to construct his machine, and after the flight he advertised that his balloon would be on exhibition for one shilling at the Pantheon. John Bell published *Lunardi's Grande Aereostatic Voyage Through the Air . . .* , and accounts were in the periodicals, for example, in the September issue of the *European Magazine.*

Another balloonist in London during 1784 was the Frenchman Jean-Pierre Blanchard. He and his balloon, along with Lunardi and Lunardi's balloon, attracted attention especially when the duchess of Devonshire gave a dinner at Devonshire House for both Blanchard and Lunardi. Lunardi expressed his thanks by wearing a silk coat to court with her design in a color that she called "Devonshire Brown," and she organized a party when "The Prince of Wales and a hundred Whigs and their ladies braved the chill air to join the crowd who had bought tickets to watch Georgiana release the ropes of Blanchard's balloon."[12]

All these events and publications surrounding Inchbald's play certainly enhanced its value, illustrating Colman's remark, "The idea is droll, as well as temporary." With all the opportunities for Londoners to see Lunardi's balloon at the Lyceum, the audience would have been familiar with the way a balloon looked. Even though it is doubtful that a large one could have been on stage, a small one like the one Reynolds described probably would have been part of the "machinery." Colman had advertised in the playbill that the "New Piece" was presented with "new Scenery, Machinery, and other Decorations" in two acts "(never perform'd)," "the Principal Characters by/Mr. Parsons, Mr. Wewitzer, Mr. Gardner, Mr. Swords, Mr. R. Palmer, and Mr. Williamson./ Miss Morris, Mrs. Inchbald, Mrs. Cuyler, and Mrs. Wells."

Mrs. Wells, Inchbald's friend who played the role of Fanny, gave an account of the introduction of the play in the green room:

> She presented Mr. Colman with a farce called "The Mogul Tale," which she told him was written by a lady, a friend of hers. If it had merit, she wished it to be brought out if not, she requested it might be immediately returned. He soon perceived its worth; and it was accordingly given among the performers to study. What surprised us all—at the rehearsal

Mrs. Inchbald seemed in great agitation, and corrected me in some of the passages which I did not speak to please her; which was by no means agreeable to me at the time, for I then conceived her very inadequate to the task. . . . The piece was received with great applause: at its conclusion she came into the green room and begged us to wish her joy. Her former mysterious conduct, and her present very great appearance of joy, led us to suppose she had an affection of the brain and this was a paroxysm. Mr. Parson asked her what he was to wish her joy for: was it some great aunt who had died and left her a large fortune? Or was she about to be married? Or had she captivated the heart of some dear swain? She turned round of him and replied, "No, Sir, it is none of these circumstances you mention, but what I prize far more—I am the authoress of the farce you have just played and I must confess I am very happy at its success." We were all very much astonished, as we never considered her abilities to reach mediocrity.[13]

Wells's use of the term "mediocrity" was again a comment on the fact that as an actress Inchbald was very ordinary, filling roles of little consequence; it was also an indication that by this time Inchbald was becoming a professional, not reading her work to just anyone who would listen.

Mogul Tale was the after-piece to the tragedy *Fatal Curiosity*, which the play-bill has as "Written by Lillo, Author of George Barnwell." The players acting the characters in this main piece were not in *Mogul Tale* except for Mr. R. Palmer, who after *Fatal Curiosity* spoke "an Occasional Prologue," and at the end there was a "Dance called The Medley"; these features came before the beginning of the after-piece. The main piece was changed for every performance, since it was, in most cases, the selection that was a part of the regular repertory. The presentation of the after-pieces, songs, dances, and so on that made up the evening's entertainment was changed daily to encourage patrons to come night after night. A review of the dates of Inchbald's play and its accompanying main pieces is a lesson in Colman's skill as a "director."[14]

After the first performance of *Mogul* on July 6 as the after-piece for *Fatal Curiosity*, it was done again on the seventh with *Love in a Village*, on the ninth with *The English Merchant*, again on the thirteenth (*Mogul*'s fourth night), on the sixteenth (its fifth night), and on the twentieth, along with *Chapter of Accidents* (its sixth night). On the sixth night, at the top of the playbill was the notice "(For the Author of the Farce)." It was the "Author's night": if a piece was presented six times, the sixth night's money was the author's. On July 21 Colman's *Two to One* and Inchbald's *Mogul Tale* were played on the same evening—for Colman's play it was the thirteenth night; for Inchbald's, the seventh.

On August 2 "A New Opera (never PERFORM'D)" was presented. It was written by Inchbald's friend Holcroft, with music by Shield.[15] The Colmans, father and son, used Arnold as their composer. Colman's play *Two to One* was filled with songs that Arnold had supplied, and given the rather slight situation and the conventional plot, Arnold's music was an important feature in making the little farce a success. Holcroft's opera was another matter, and in spite of the fact that Arnold was a kind of composer-in-residence for the Colmans, Holcroft was allowed to use his own music designed by Shield. On August 4 Holcroft's opera and Inchbald's farce were played on the same night.

Boaden does not include from her pocket-book many of the entries for the period when she and Colman were working on the final version of the play. As usual, she was not really satisfied at some of the final rehearsals, but after the success of the first night—Boaden calls it "its most brilliant success"—she wrote, "I played in 'The Mogul Tale,' my own farce; it went off with the greatest applause." Afterward she continued "to speak of great applause and full houses the 'ten times of its representation, in the months of July and August.'"[16]

Kemble sent her a letter from Liverpool dated July 17, evidently as soon as he heard of her success. Boaden prints it in its entirety, remarking that it was "very characteristic"; it is so indeed. After the first part of the very first sentence of congratulation, he turns to himself and his writing, his own ambitions. It also is remarkable in its tone of "depression"; by this time in 1784 Kemble had had a second very successful season at Drury Lane. Moreover, his comments show again that he and Inchbald had worked together, had talked at length of their work. He begins: "Next to your *self,* nobody can be more inclined to think highly of your *productions* than I am; but, alas! my poetical days, I believe, are gone by. In my best pretensions, I was but an indifferent rhymer; nor in my vainest moments ever thought any thing I did fit to be called poetry. I have ransacked my brains for apt parallels, but to no purpose. I cannot pay you a compliment in verse too high for what I truly think of you in prose." Kemble had been working on a translation of Ovid and had shown her some of it when he was in town. He continues, "I thought to have finished the Epistle in the country; but no such thing. I have laboured and laboured so long in vain at it, that it is now thrown aside from an absolute conscience of wasting so much time to no manner of purpose. The truth is, my health declines every day: I have neither spirits (in which I never abounded) nor genius (of which inclination, perhaps, wholly supplied the place) to attempt any thing for my improvement in polite letters."[17]

After such a complaint, he turns to speak directly to her, giving her the kind of praise she treasured, the kind of praise that at this juncture she treasured more, perhaps, than the poetry he had written for her—or to her—in the days at York or the mysterious book he had presented to her in Dublin and then asked her to return. He continues: "You know me, I believe, well enough to feel for me when I say, that with all my ambition I am afraid I shall live and die as a common fellow." Just how Kemble sees himself, as the letter continues, would suggest that he had already become a romantic, melancholy figure of the kind beginning to be popular in the novels. In complimenting her, he implies that he is already in the years of decline: "Your regular and continent life gives you assurance of many healthful years; and your uncommon talents, having now forced themselves into notice, will crown you with growing reputation. If I could write, I would: I cannot—so you must receive esteem instead of flattery, and sincerity for wit, when I swear there is no WOMAN I more truly admire, nor any MAN whose abilities I more highly esteem."[18]

Inchbald's friend Twiss was at Norwich when *Mogul* was presented. Seeing only an account in the newspapers, he found that the *Morning Herald* had "marred a curious tale in telling it"; he suggested that next time she should write the piece herself. In the *European Magazine* the report read:

> Monday evening, the 5th inst. a Farce of two Acts was performed the first time called the Mogul Tale. / Aristotle has defined Tragedy and Comedy. We his disciples, the critics of magazines, have, therefore, some phrases and terms, if not principles and rules, to give plausibility and effect to our own imaginations and feelings & if we should happen to have any. Farce is an unlimited region of happy absurdities, antitheses, puns, and repartees. These should be brought together by a Fable as improbable, and characters as extravagant as possible. Accordingly, in the Mogul Tale, the Dramitis Personae are conveyed from Wapping to the Mogul's Seraglio, where they assume the parts of Ambassador from Great-Britain, the Pope, and a nun. They escape death by the clemency of the Mogul, and receive admonitions, for the use of their countrymen, on India pecularions and cruelties, which will be nearly as effectual in remedying the evils as the celebrated India Bills of Mr. Fox or Mr. Pitt. The Farce was introduced with becoming expense and attention, and the performers succeeded in affording the Galleries a hearty laugh.[19]

Boaden gives an account of this first performance, pointing out the result of the concealment of the author. Inchbald played Selima; in the second scene, hearing a cue from Atkins the shoemaker, she was supposed to speak. The cue was "Since we left Hyde Park Corner," and she was to reply, "Hyde Park Corner!" But she could not speak, overcome with stage fright about her own play. At length she stood without a sound and then stammered "Hh-yde Pa-ark Co-orner!" her stammer an obvious identification.[20]

The characters are not listed with the players on the playbill, but no doubt they were easily identified in performance. Johnny Atkins, the shoemaker, was played by Mr. Parson, an actor who, like many others, had been in a variety of places with a variety of companies. He had been in Edinburgh, but in 1762, after he married, he and his wife came to London to act at Drury Lane. He remained there for some thirty-two seasons, going back to Edinburgh for the season of 1769–1770. He began acting at the Haymarket in 1773 and was there every summer from 1782 to 1788. He was a useful actor, especially in playing old men, and he was to play just such a role in Inchbald's next play, *I'll Tell You What*, in the summer of 1785. One writer reviewing the Haymarket during these years says that Parson was a "fine performer . . . one of the best low comedians of his day."[21] Ralph Wewitzer created the part of the doctor. He had a long career both at Covent Garden and Drury Lane, playing at the Haymarket from 1780 to 1787. Born in London and apprenticed to a jeweler, he became an actor in 1773; like many others, he was at Dublin for a short while to escape his creditors. He returned to Covent Garden, where he remained until 1789. In the summers he played in various places— Liverpool, Birmingham, Brighton, Richmond. He was much sought after to play in comic parts of old men, the kind of actor suited to the role of the doctor. He was especially skillful in playing eccentrics—the doctor was, of course, a charlatan, a characterization Inchbald treats rather lightly, but clearly.

William Swords played the part of Omar. He had been in Ireland in 1781, but returning to London, he was at the Haymarket in 1781–1782; he was a singer as well as an actor, and in the fall of 1785 he went to Covent Garden. Evidently he, like many others, played the secondary roles so necessary to present any play. John Gardner was another of the actors who wandered about and played more frequently at the Haymarket than in the winter theatres.

Mr. R. Palmer was the younger brother of John Palmer, known as "Plausible Jack," and William Palmer; they were the three sons of a doorkeeper at Drury Lane. The next year, 1785, John Palmer was deep into a scheme to establish a theatre in Wellclose Square. The cornerstone for the building was laid in December 1785, but his scheme was blocked by the patentees of Drury Lane, Covent Garden, and the Haymarket. Palmer's building was ready, however, and, opening on June 20, 1787, he was brought to court by Sheridan, Harris, and Colman. For almost a year, until April 1788, the theatre was used for "entertainments." Palmer sold shares to raise money for the building, and he and his partner, the Reverend William Jackson, thought they had made the proper legal arrangements—only to fail completely. This summer of 1784 saw the beginning of some of the plans. In the end Inchbald was not among those whom Palmer signed, but her brother George Simpson was, and so was her friend Becky Wells.

Wells, in the part of Fanny, was properly cast, since Fanny carries the play both in the action and as a central character. Inchbald was one of the "ladies" in the garden of the Seraglio; the other two ladies were Miss Morris and Mrs. Cuyler.

Very soon, after the end of the season, Miss Morris went away to Gretna Green with Colman the younger and was married there. She had been at Covent Garden in 1780–1781, and Inchbald certainly knew her there, for she and Inchbald were both in the notorious performance of *The Beggar's Opera,* that is, the performance of the men as women and the women as men. In *Mogul* she was Zaphira. The third "Lady" was Mrs. Cuyler; born into a wealthy family, she had had by the summer of 1784 enough amours to have furnished a multivolume novel. By this time she was said to have been the mistress at one time or another of both R.B. Sheridan and Thomas Harris. According to the *Biographical Dictionary,* she was living in easy circumstances—"resident in lavish quarters at No. 7 St. Albans Street."[22] She was Sheba.

From the very beginning, in this first play, Inchbald displayed some of the characteristics found in all her others. The dialogue rather than the action is the center of interest, and the conversations reflect the current interests of the audience.[23] Also some of the devices found in popular entertainments are usually included: in this case the men, as expected, stray after women not their wives, and the women complain; the setting, though it is said to be exotic, is actually very English and local; and here as elsewhere concerns about the royal family, the church, and the current debates in Parliament are all very much a part of the fabric of the play. The year 1783–1784 was the beginning of the period in which the government began to restructure and reform the East India Company, and much of the dialogue and many of the situations comment on the present situations and the contest over who would control the company.

Mogul opens with the stage set in a garden, and as the balloon descends, two of the ladies are arguing about who is the emperor's favorite. The first lady says, "Who do you think is the Emperor's favourite now: whilst I continued his favourite myself, I had no occasion to make any enquiry."[24]

The second lady replies, "You may be the Emperor's again: as to me, I shall never enjoy his favor—But here she comes." The third lady enters and speaks: "So, here you are musing and plotting mischief against me, because the Sultan loves me; well, the woman who possesses his heart, is sure to have every woman in the Seraglio against her: but there was a time when you was kind to me."

The first lady replies, "Yes my dear Sophie, when you was in distress: and I assure you, that if ever that time should come again, we will be as kind again, and love you as well as ever." To which the third lady replies, "You think so—however our sex are seldom kind to the woman that is so prosperous, their pity is confined to those that are forsaken—to be forsaken and ugly, are the greatest distresses a woman can have."

This conversation about women suggests, in this very first play, Inchbald's rather cynical views. Later, when Johnny abandons Fanny after he has found the "Ladies," Fanny's loyalty is in sharp contrast to his weakness as her husband and protector; such observations about the situations in the play are not made as part of a didactic examination of the play, but simply to show that in subtle ways, even in this first play, Inchbald's satiric comments establish a kind of realism that is characteristic of all her work. These rather cynical views of human relationships were a continuing feature of the plays.

The action of the play moves along swiftly. The travelers, puzzled about where they are, suggest that they may be in Scotland, Denmark, Norway—or Limbo.

Fan, pleased to be out of the balloon, exclaims, "Oh! Lord! I am so glad to set my foot on christian ground again," while Johnny says, "O! dear! O! dear!—The devil take all balloons," and to Fan he responds, "Christian ground you fool! why we're in Limbo—it must be Limbo, or Greenland. Doctor what say you, it is Greenland, is it not?" But the doctor has no idea where they are, and in his reply shows he really knows nothing: "Why man, Greenland is cold, quite reverse of this climate; this is either east, west or south, but which I cannot tell. I am sure it is not north, by the heat, other conclusions I draw from other causes . . . we may be amongst people, who pay no regard to genius, science, or invention, but may put us all to death, taking us for three witches that ride in the air." They are hungry, and although the doctor says the pure air they breathed above the earth supplied all their needs, Johnny points out, "you know you eat heartily of the ham and chickens, and drank more of the wine than Fan and I."

When the first lady appears and asks if they are gods, Fanny and Johnny learn they are in the dominion of the Great Mogul, that is, to be specific, in the Seraglio with his favorite concubines, where no man is allowed, no one "except our wretched sex, and Eunuchs who are our guards." Johnny replies: "Eunuchs! Lord madam they are of no sex at all—we have often heard madam of the Great Mogul. Why Lord he can't be jealous of me, and as to the Doctor there he is nobody—it is all over with him, he has no longer any inflammable air about him, either in his balloon or himself, its all gone, isn't it Doctor?"

The lady warns them that they will be asked to give an account of themselves, but the doctor cannot "contrive" anything to say; Johnny thinks it is all over for the three of them, but the first female says, "As to that female, she has nothing to apprehend for herself, she will be saved from death and most likely exalted to the embraces of the Great Mogul." To which Fanny replies, "I had rather not madam, if its all the same to you."

When the eunuch enters, he tells them they must appear before the Great Mogul; as he leaves, Johnny turns to the doctor and asks, "what shall we do? what the devil shall we do?" Johnny blames his wife and says he will pretend to be a woman. Such little bits of dialogue—the husband blaming his wife, who only came because he asked her to, the pretense of a woman in men's attire—make the play bright and amusing, and although Inchbald never achieved the kind of humor found in early-eighteenth-century plays, her wit is the ordinary obvious kind that her audience would respond to. She knew her audience and was always mindful of it.

As the scene changes, the mogul appears and speaks to the audience: "Admirable! incomparable, most excellent! in a retreat of the gardens I saw the wretches fall—overheard their conversation. We were amazed at the miraculous manner of their arrival, but such acts I knew had been lately discovered in Europe—I am resolv'd to have some diversion with them." The mogul instructs the eunuchs to "Aggravate their fears, as much as possible, tell them, I am the abstract of cruelty, the essence of tyranny; tell them the Divan shall open with all its terrors. For tho' I mean to save their lives, I want to see the effect of their fears, for in the hour of reflection I love to contemplate that greatest work of heaven, the mind of man."

The eunuch, escorting Fanny, Johnny, and the doctor, speaks to Johnny: "Unhappy man I pity you, I was once in Europe, and treated kindly there!—I wish in gratitude I could do any thing to serve you—but the Mogul is bloody minded, and cruel, and at present inexorable." He goes on to admonish them to "be firm and bold before him—seem to know yourselves of consequence—seem to have no fear."

The scene draws to reveal the mogul on his throne, surrounded by slaves and eunuchs, giving orders: "Let those who refused the presents I demanded, be impaled, the Nabob who refused his favourite wife, be burnt alive—and let the Female who broke my favourite dish, and thereby spoiled my dinner, be torn to pieces."

The eunuch introduces Johnny as an ambassador from England, lost, who needs to meet the king, his master, who is within two days' journey of the mogul's realm. He turns to the doctor to ask what the machine is called as he—the eunuch—says it is invented for the use of man. All through this dialogue there are references to current ideas. The balloons successful in Paris were not designed to be used to spy on armies, but very soon they were to be used in just such a way. And perhaps Inchbald's audience had heard that Benjamin Franklin had witnessed the flight and when asked what use such invention would be put to, replied, "What is the 'use' my friend of the child that was born today?"[25]

The mogul demands to know about the king the doctor represents, instructing the eunuch to read the roll identifying the vast realm of the mogul, which includes all of Asia and Africa and ends with "King of eight thousand Islands, and husband of one thousand wives."

The eunuch then tells the doctor to pretend to read a roll about his king. The doctor takes the roll and reads: "The King his master, is by the Grace of God, King of Great Britain, France, Ireland, Scotland, Northumberland, Lincolnshire, Sheffield, and Birmingham: giver of all Green, Blue, Red, and pale Blue Ribbons, Sovereign of the most surprising Order of the Bath, Sovereign of the most noble Order of St Patrick—Grand master of every Mason Lodge in Christendom, Prince of the River Thames, Trent, Severn, Tyne, New-River, Fleet-Ditch, and the Tweed: Sovereign Lord, and master of many loyal subjects, husband of one good wife, and father of eighteen fine children."

Read loud and clear by Wewitzer as the doctor, the list must have delighted the audience in its mixture: "King of Great Britain, France, Ireland, Scotland, . . . Prince of . . . Fleet-Ditch." For the audience hearing the roll of the mogul and their king read, with the item of his eighteen children, he being the "husband of one good wife" must have made the play very timely and amusing. George III and his numerous children with his "good wife" Queen Charlotte were frequently the subject of popular caricatures. Inchbald's use of it here, even in this first play, is an example of her commentary on popular views and her freedom to ridicule political figures, even the royal family, especially since everyone knew the Prince of Wales and his brothers were already much discussed with regard to their mistresses and their extravagant lifestyles.[26]

When the mogul asks the eunuch who Johnny is, the eunuch replies that he is the pope. The doctor intervenes to say that Johnny is not interested in women and that Fanny does not belong to Johnny but to him and that she is now a nun. Left alone, Johnny and Fanny lament their situation and in doing so give a nice vignette of London low life, revealing in the use of detail Inchbald's skill in making real the imagined situation on stage. Fanny says, "Oh Johnny, Johnny, Johnny, will you leave me here in a strange land, amongst tigers, land monsters, and sea monsters." And Johnny replies: "Oh Fan, Fan, if we were at Wapping again, mending of shoes, in our little two pair of stairs room backwards—with the bed just turn'd up in one corner of the room." Fanny: "My Johnny and I sitting so comfortable together at breakfast, where we had pawn'd your waistcoat to get one, with one child crying on my knee, and one on yours; my poor old mother shaking with the ague, in one corner of the room—the many happy mornings Johnny that we have got up together shaking with the cold—No balloon to vex us."

The second scene opens with the eunuch reading a letter the doctor has written; in it he says he has been able to procure some inflammable air, and he invites the eunuch to come with him to Wapping, provided he bring with him a female with "black eyes, neither too large or too small." The eunuch reads it to the mogul, giving the mogul an opportunity to assert his power and continue the suspense. He tells the eunuch to "seize this Doctor Ambassador and drag him immediately to the place of execution," and the "Cobbler holiness already half drown'd in liquor" to be supplied with even more liquor and like the doctor brought to the place of execution.

The scene now changes to the garden, where Johnny is drunk and tempting the ladies. The one lady says that their religion "tells us we have no souls." Whereupon Johnny says "you have a very pretty body . . . and I am a sweet soul, and what is a body good for, without a soul." Johnny makes disparaging remarks about wine and the restrictions of the mogul and his religion; he is tricked into selecting one of the ladies and denying that Fanny is his wife. When he leaves and Fanny enters, dressed richly, the ladies tease her. One of the ladies says, "my dear English lady—I have been told in your country, every woman had a lover a piece, but here we have but one between us three and ninety seven of us." And when Fanny asks about her "Pope," one of the ladies says, "He was here just now, and making love to me." Fanny refuses to believe her, but when Johnny comes in drunk and begins to exclaim at the extravagant dress Fanny is wearing, he is overcome, giving her the handkerchief the eunuch has designated for him to select the lady he wishes to make love to.

The mogul is not done with his trickery, however; they are all taken to the throne room, where they find the mogul seated on his throne, and Johnny, Fanny, and the doctor stand before him. He is about to pronounce a sentence of death upon Johnny and the doctor and take Fanny for his Seraglio, when Fanny and Johnny reveal their true identity. When he pronounces judgment, however, he speaks of himself and his country:

You are not now before the tribunal of a European, a man of your own colour. I am an Indian, a Mahometan, my laws are cruel and my nature savage—You have imposed upon me, and attempted to defraud me, but know that I have been taught mercy and compassion for the sufferings of human nature; however differing in laws, temper and colour from myself. Yes from you Christians whose laws teach charity to all the world, have I learn'd these virtues? For your countrymen's cruelty to the poor Gentoos has shewn me tyranny in so foul a light, that I was determined henceforth to be only mild, just and merciful.—You have done wrong, but you are strangers, you are destitute—You are too much in my power to treat you with severity—all three may freely depart.

With everything ready for their departure, each of the three speaks characteristic sentiments:

> *Fanny:* Sir, we are very much obliged to you, and please give my compliments to the Great Mogul, and tell him I am very much obliged to him for not killing my husband.
>
> *Johnny:* And I am very much obliged to him, for not ravishing my wife.
>
> *Doctor:* And present my compliments to him, and let him know that I will explain the generosity of his conduct in a Mogul Tale, that I intend to publish, giving an account of our adventures in our grand Air Balloon.

The success of *A Mogul Tale* was not solely based on its novelty. In this first success, Inchbald combined several elements in the text that were to characterize her later pieces—a sympathetic portrayal of an English husband and wife, a celebration of English patriotism, including several witty remarks about the pope, and an assumption throughout that no matter how exciting strange places and exotic customs might be, England, Hyde Park, was the best place to be.

With the balloon craze as a point of reference, Inchbald clearly pictures the world of London. Johnny is a cobbler, and when he and Fanny lament what they think is to be their lost past, he comments, "Oh Fan, Fan, if we were at Wapping again, mending of shoes," where in spite of their poverty, their crowded room with children and her mother, they were happy. There is no intrigue here of unfaithful husbands and wives, only comments about men and women; there is no "serious" message, only the pleasure of an exotic setting that allows the costumes to be splendid, full of color and rich fabric, and a setting far away to enable political comments as part of a play.

In the spring of 1784, there had been a great political campaign for seats in Parliament, a contest between William Pitt and Charles James Fox. Many of the differences between the two had to do with Fox's bill to set up a commission to run the East India Company. Inchbald certainly knew about the campaign, and her use of setting here in *Mogul* is the first but not the last for her to make a political comment. The mogul shows himself far more compassionate than the popular perception of a mogul as a tyrant.

Another feature of the success for Inchbald was the contrast of her play with the other plays as they were presented in sequence. Colman the younger's play was a much more conventional situation—of two young men seeking to marry the same beautiful young woman—than Inchbald's play, featuring husband and wife; and Holcroft's comic opera *The Noble Peasant*, which was really musical entertainment, suitable for summer in the Haymarket, was not sharp and amusing as was *Mogul*. These contrasts made the situation of Inchbald's play even more memorable than if *Mogul* had appeared alone. Inchbald played in several of these plays this summer. In addition to playing Selima in *Mogul*, she played Lady Margaret Russel in *Lord Russel* and Lady Frances in *The Two Connoisseurs*.

The *European Review* calls Inchbald's play a farce, a term usually used to describe a two-act after-piece. Our casual use of the term to mean an amusing light comic performance does not take into account that a "farce" could also be serious. Inchbald was to do two more two-act "farces," *The Widow's Vow* and *Appearance Is against Them*. *The Widow's Vow* is, like *The Beggar's Opera* she and Wells had played in, produced in a situation that allows the audience to understand that a trick is played, whereas disguise and pretense are mixed for those who are the characters in the play. *Appearance Is against Them*, however, is quite serious and ends, as do many of her plays, on a very ambivalent note. Working on the plays, however, Inchbald paid little attention to any definition of farce, and with the help of Colman, her conclusions became more acceptable in both after-pieces and main pieces.

Both Colman and Harris knew how to select plays that complemented each other; thus Inchbald was in good hands, a circumstance especially important for her first plays, these first farces. It is always important to remember the sequence of the main piece, the after-piece, and the various bits of music, dance, or "entertainments" that made up the rest of the evening program.

Inchbald was to repeat variations of certain elements in *Mogul*, such as the "dotty" doctor and the weak husband, but perhaps the most frequently repeated creation was the character of Fanny. She became the first "Inchbald woman," independent but loving, with far more common sense than her husband; the "Inchbald women" were, with few exceptions, always independent, and almost always they showed sense, not sensibility.

With the season at the Haymarket over, Inchbald went back to Covent Garden, but although she continued to play "second lady" parts, her salary was raised, and she had the courage to write to Colman about a comedy he already had in hand, anonymously sent to him even before her *Mogul*. Boaden, in his usual roundabout way, but with her pocket-book before him, writes, "She now resumed her literary labours with avidity; and heaps together her notices of '*writing*' at her '*play*,' at a '*farce*,' at some '*plot*,' for one or the other, as it might work out: but such memoranda of pieces begun, leave an uncertainty as to which they were."[27] Boaden does include a very interesting letter from her friend Twiss, evidently in answer to a letter of hers. A part of Twiss's letter reads:

Dear Madam,

   As I found you anxious to have your comedy returned this day, I have just now read it through; and indeed, after I had once dipped into it, I found sufficient attraction in the piece to induce me to peruse the whole of it immediately. As far as my poor judgment goes, I think the comedy, upon the whole, does very great honour to your talents: as I am not in the habit of paying compliments, you will not suspect me of insincerity.

Having complimented her on her talents, he begins to analyze her play to make it suitable for the stage. He thought the fifth act "infinitely inferior to the others"; the catastrophe he thought improbable—not managed with "that adroitness which I should have expected from your pen"—and having given such general judgments, he continued, giving quite specific ways the play could be improved. His analysis shows how clearly he understood the demands of the stage.[28]

As a close friend of hers, he felt no hesitancy in being frank, in telling her exactly what he thought of her work. He was a friend of her brother George and a very good friend of Kemble's; in May 1786 he married Kemble's sister Frances. Twiss was at this time working on the concordance to Shakespeare's plays that he was to publish in 1805; thus it is not surprising that he was very much aware of structure and language in any play he read. No doubt Inchbald took his advice seriously.

Twiss wrote the letter quoted above on November 19, 1784, from his residence in Caroline Street, Bedford Square, and it was sometime that month that Colman wrote for her to return the altered play to him. He evidently liked the fifth act better than Twiss did, and by the first of April he wrote from Soho Square:

In the last page you will see my idea of the plan of this act. If you don't like it, or don't comprehend it, let me see you to-morrow, or Saturday, or Sunday morning; or come, if you can, at all events. If not, I hope at least to receive by the middle of next week the four first acts again—if not a new sketch of the fifth. I believe I shall go out of town to dinner on Sunday, and not return till Monday, which I mention to prevent your having any needless trouble. I most heartily wish you success, of which I think there can be no doubt.[29]

The Twiss letter and the Colman one suggest more than their instructions to her, for they both reveal knowledge of the theatre in the 1780s, Twiss's understanding of structure and Colman's knowledge of what was required for his stage at the Haymarket. Colman had written in the evening after midnight—his postscript, "Thursday night—I believe I may say Friday morning; and if I send you a foolish note, remember it is the *first of April*!"[30]

Inchbald set to work immediately, and by April 20 she had sent another revision; he in turn wrote again, returning his revision of the fifth act. Without the original manuscripts it is not possible to reconstruct the original or Inchbald's and Colman's revisions; what is clear, however, is that for Colman to present a play it must be worthy of his stage; he did not present a new play simply because he favored the writer.

Colman's letter on April 20 is short but precise: "Mr. Colman presents his compliments to Mrs. Inchbald, and returns the fifth act, begging her to look it over as revised; and, after any new graces she may bestow on it, to add the conclusion and send it back, that the transcript may be added to the rest of the copy."[31]

Again, such a letter reveals the procedures that playwrights needed to follow to prepare copy for the first reading. The comment about "copy" reminds us of how much people in the eighteenth century depended on handwritten transcripts. Inchbald was constantly entering the notation "copying" or sometimes "copying all day" in her pocket-books. Her friends teased her about her handwriting; indeed it is difficult to read, and of course for important documents she was more careful than with the copies she kept for herself. Considering the primitive circumstances of duplication and her frequent moving from place to place, it is surprising that any of the letters she wrote or received are still extant.

Colman wrote her one more short note: "The licenser wants a title for your play: I have thought of a whimsical one, that I think will not displease you; and, if you will favour me with a call about eleven in the forenoon tomorrow or next day, 'I'll Tell You What!'"[32]

Boaden says she did not like the title, but she followed Colman's suggestion, and he, in the prologue, made good use of it; Colman also wrote the epilogue, giving her play his entire support. It was read in the green room to the players on July 13, and Inchbald was delighted with its reception.

I'll Tell You What was presented on August 4, 1785, and again, as in the case of *Mogul,* it was a great success, playing twenty-eight times before the end of the season. The players this time were the most important in the company, and the five-act comedy gave them an opportunity to perform to their own pleasure. One, Parson, who played one of two brothers, rather objected to the fact that his part was of little consequence in the plot. It is true that his is a rather minor role compared to that of the brother's part, played by Palmer; the brother was a major character in developing the incidents in the play. Colman must have persuaded Parson to take his assigned part, for the cast remained the same for the whole of the run.

Parson's objection reminds us that the production of these plays involved many people and many factors. The plays were read to the players long before they were put on stage; the play had to be cleared by the lord chamberlain's office; then the proprietor assigned parts to the players, arranged rehearsals, and assigned duties to the stagehands, the dressers, and the prompter for the particular play he was producing. Inchbald's *Mogul*, for example, undoubtedly had a balloon in some form on stage. And although the players could express their views, it was the proprietor who ultimately made the decisions.

I'll Tell You What, like *Mogul*, begins with a witty confrontation between two men talking about women and happiness. The incidents in the play are quite intricate, as was the usual pattern of comedy in the 1780s. Moreover, if *Mogul* represented Inchbald's interest in the latest spectacular event, *I'll Tell You What* showed her interest in the contemporary social scene, a social scene she quite clearly marked out for her interest in exploring realistic relationships between men and women. She bases her central theme on a young man who divorces his wife and remarries happily, leaving his first wife to regret her frivolity along with her new husband, who is consumed with the jealousy he thought to provoke in her first husband. Inchbald has been criticized for using stock situations and devices. She does use whatever is conveniently at hand and useful to explore her interests—especially her view that as persons, men and women are equal: they have the same emotions and strengths, the same foolish weaknesses and indiscretions. Throughout her plays runs this thread of social patterns; the relationships between men and women serve to reveal and support comments on Inchbald's social world. She examines what these universal patterns say about society in general and the family in particular. She was not alone in using these relationships, but her unique stamp is clearly evident in her plays. Like Sheridan in *School for Scandal* (1777), she uses family skillfully and makes the plot turn on an independent woman.

The other general interest found in the Inchbald plays is the relationship of the children in a household to the behavior of the adults. Even in this first comedy, one of the subplots is focused on the child, whose mother has married for love without a dowry and whose father who has been disowned by his father. This subplot allows Inchbald to provide a comment about marriages that are arranged and marriages that are for love. The situation is not developed as a major theme, but it offers an important contrast to the other marriages examined in the play. When one considers Inchbald's work in its entirety, it is clear that the themes of family and society, which are major concerns of hers, define her contribution to the social and political discussions of the 1780s and 1790s.

In *I'll Tell You What* two brothers, Mr. Charles Euston and Mr. Anthony

Euston, are absent and thought shipwrecked in the West Indies. They return, quite surprisingly, to find that their nephew Sir George has divorced his wife Harriet and married again. The second Lady Euston is clever and forthright, sure of herself and her virtue, and when Major Cyprus, the second husband of Harriet, the first Lady Euston, attempts to seduce her, that is, the present Lady Euston, she exposes his scheme and ridicules him before his wife Harriet, Sir George, and all Major Cyprus's friends and acquaintances, who are sure to hear of his ridiculous behavior and his miserable failure. With her common sense and independence, she becomes the first of Mrs. Inchbald's fully developed "Inchbald women"; Lady Euston is clever as well as independent, and it is she who is the center of the action.

As the play opens, Charles Euston and Sir George Euston appear on stage in Sir George's town house. Charles has already discovered the situation and is very upset. He and Sir George converse:

Sir George: But, my dear Uncle, why in such a passion?—

Mr. Euston [Charles]: I can't help it—I am out of all patience!—Did not I leave you one of the happiest men in the world?—

Sir George: Well, and so you find me, Sir.

Mr. Euston: 'Tis false—you are not happy—you can't be happy—'tis false—and you shan't be happy.

Sir George: If you are resolved to make me otherwise, Sir—

Mr. Euston: No, I am not resolved—'tis yourself that is resolved—Did not I leave you one of the happiest of men?—married to one of the most beautiful women in the world?—Did not I give you my blessing and a large fortune, and did I not stay and see you father of a fine boy?—Then only just stept over to visit my estate in St. Kitts, and, now I'm come back, here I find you married to another woman—and your first wife still living—and, egad, she is married to another man.

As the conversation continues, we discover that Anthony Euston has disowned his own son and intends to make his nephew his heir, but Sir George points out, "I should derive very little enjoyment from the possession of a fortune which his son, my poor cousin, (but for a single act of imprudence) had a right to expect." To which Charles Euston replies, "You silly young rogue, I am not angry with you for getting rid of your wife—(for that I dare say is what every sensible man in the world wou'd do, if he cou'd) I am only angry with you for getting another—Cou'd not you know when you were well off, you blockhead?"

As they talk of Anthony, we discover that Anthony knows nothing about the changed situation and that Sir George himself must explain; we also learn that "the single act of imprudence" of his son, Sir George's cousin, was that he married a wife without a dowry, without his father's consent.

Sir George has an engagement, and the scene closes without any resolution of how Anthony will be informed of Sir George's new situation and his new wife. The second scene shifts to the former Lady Euston, now Lady Harriet Cyprus. She is conversing with her maid Bloom who has just told her that her former husband, Sir George, has married, indeed has been married for some three months, and that he and his wife have returned to London and live nearby. In the dialogue that follows, we understand that Lady Harriet is very sorry for herself, bitter at the circumstances that pushed her into a divorce, and very unhappy in her present situation.

She had herself through her own indiscretions been compromised in such a way that her "honour"—as her brother saw it—"compel us to a divorce." Bloom leaves and Lady Harriet speaks her true feelings: "And so Sir George has been married these three months to another, and entirely forgot me—To be so soon forgotten!—I shall never now forget him, I am certain. He has behaved like a man of resolution and spirit in casting me from his heart, and I feel the irreparable loss. Why were we divorced? I shou'd have disliked him still had he been my husband; and yet how tender, how patient to my failings to what Mr. Cyprus is—His cruel and unjust suspicions of me are not to be borne."

In another part of the house we find Cyprus greeting an old friend, Colonel Downright, who has just come to town. Downright is puzzled, asking who the lady is that he has married. Cyprus says she was Sir George's lady, and upon further questioning Cyprus recounts his version of what happened: "Let me describe a scene to you, where poor Sir George's situation must affect the most obdurate heart. Lady Harriet Euston (now Lady Harriet Cyprus) was, when I first became acquainted with her, a very loving wife . . . a very loving wife indeed; and but for my insinuations—artful insinuations I may call them—had continued her conjugal regard—she had been to this hour an example to wives, if I had not tempted her to stray."

With Downright interrupting him, he continues, "Hear me out," and he describes the incident that prompted the divorce. "One evening we had prolonged the *tête-à-tête* rather beyond the usual time; when, unexpectedly, Sir George and a party of beaux and belles were rushing up stairs." Lady Harriet in great haste pushed him into a closet, and he continues the story, pointing to "that closet":

Major Cyprus: That very identical closet, which you see there—for Sir
    George never loved the house after, and so settled it on her Ladyship—

Screwed up in that closet, I believe I remained ten minutes; when old
Lady Downfall, who was of the party, called for drops, the door was
opened,—and out dropt your humble servant.
Colonel Downright: Zounds, it was enough to make you wish yourself—
Major Cyprus: Nay, it was Sir George's place to wish. Every beau in the room
was round me in a moment; and, in a whisper, "Give you joy Major"—
"The happiest man in the world"—"An Alexander"—"A conqueror
every where."—Even old Sir Samson Shrivel, shook his head and wished
to be in my place . . . he [Sir George] said nothing. You may depend
upon it, he heard and saw all the half stifled laughs, and was wise enough
to know to whom they were directed—so poor fellow he turned pale—
bit his lips—looked at her Ladyship—looked at me—looked at his
sword—and then cried, "Heigh ho!" . . . And do you know I said—Faith
it was an odd speech, and has been laughed at since in a thousand
fashionable circles—the conclusion of it has been particularly marked. . . .
"Dear Sir George," said I (half stifling a laugh, for by my soul I could not
help it, though I pitied the poor devil too) Dear Sir George, said I, "I'll
tell you what"—you will find nobody to blame in this affair—I protest
my being in that closet was entirely owing to "I Tell You what"—In
short to an—undescribable something—"

In this scene, as the first act comes to a close, we have had a scene within a
scene as Cyprus has dramatized the event of the assignation. He ends his little
drama within the drama by observing that "Sir George, out of despair, is just
married again—and Lady Harriet's affection for me is such—yet faith I must
confess . . . that notwithstanding I am so very happy in my marriage—my wife is
very beautiful and so affectionate—yet I am a sad wicked fellow; I have not forgot
my old ways—no, I am going tomorrow evening to meet a Lady of untarnished
reputation—a married lady—Faith 'tis wrong—I know it is—but I cannot with-
stand the temptation—no, I cannot forget my old ways."

At this, the end of the first act, all the situations of the play have been set.
The divorce and remarriage of Sir George; the divorce and remarriage of his first
wife, Lady Harriet; the return of the two brothers Charles and Anthony, uncles of
Sir George; and the situation of Anthony's son, Sir George's cousin, who has been
disinherited for a single mistake—he has married for love and now finds himself
without funds, unable to take care of his family.

The second act opens much like the first, although this time it is Anthony
Euston, not Charles, who is surprised; and this time the audience, apprised al-

ready of the situation, finds the scene doubly amusing. The encounter between Anthony and the new Lady Euston is very short and confusing. Anthony refuses to understand that the mistress of his nephew's new house is Lady Euston. The servant who admits him in answer to his request to see the "Lady" of the house is told simply to say he is a relation whom she will be glad to see, and as the servant goes to announce him, he remarks, "This house is a handsome one—yet, I wonder Sir George shou'd leave his other—for I remember my niece was remarkably fond of its situation." When Lady Euston appears, the confusion increases, for when he is about to greet her, he realizes she is not Lady Harriet. His mistake in simply asking for the lady of the house leads her to declare, "I have the honour to be mistress of this house, Sir." Since no names have been exchanged, Anthony is not told the true situation and Lady Euston, after Anthony leaves, remarks: "This is certainly an Uncle of Lady Harriet's, who is unacquainted with her divorce— and I cou'd not inform him of it; 'twould have led to such disagreeable explanations, and such a long round-about story it must have caused—'Sir, I am *second wife* to your *present* niece's *first husband.*' Lud! Lud! how ashamed I shou'd have been—Lady Harriet had better explain it by far."

The devices Inchbald uses to confound the confusion are certainly not new; rather, they are stock situations dressed up to fit the play. The unique twist is the mixed relationships caused by the divorce and the remarriages. Not content with the suspense of Anthony and the two women—Lady Harriet and Lady Euston— Inchbald introduces another character to the discussion of relationships. Sir Harry Harmless, in conversation with Colonel Downright, again gives a picture of wives and husbands as he gossips about Cyprus. Sir Harry is hardly more than a harmless fop, though he sees himself as a man about town and pretends to have assignations with every beauty.

Sir Harry tells Downright that Cyprus is far from happy and that he is extremely jealous, and when Downright asks the cause, Sir Harry replies: "Nay, I assure you he has no cause—Nor is he jealous of one, alone—he is so of every body—and will be so of you—therefore, I tell you, that you may be on your guard.— I am constantly with his Lady and him, and, because the poor woman once shut him up in her closet, he now suspects a lover concealed in every part of the house— and I have known him, when the mad fit has been upon him, search for a supposed rival even in her drawers and bandboxes." Questioned further about the situation, Sir Harry declares: "I have seen such things! Enough to terrify me from marrying—for wives are sometimes so provoking, I am sure I cou'd not keep my temper—Now, here is Lady Harriet Cyprus—you cannot think how provoking she is—she sometimes says such terrible things to her husband that, I am sure, if she was my wife—"

Downright: Why you wou'd not beat her, would you? or lock her up?
Sir Harry: No—but perhaps I might kick her lap dog, or do some outrage to her dress.

Even as they speak, they see Cyprus and Lady Harriet, and as they go out, husband and wife appear; they are quarreling. He addresses her: "So, madam, I have followed you home, and now shou'd be glad to know, what unusual whim brought you into the Park so early?" She replies, "How can you be so teazing as to ask questions?" They blame each other for their unhappiness, each seeing the cause of their personal pain brought about by the other's fault. Lady Harriet declares: "How dare you, Major Cyprus, upbraid me, or think, because my unhappy partiality for you *once* betrayed me into indiscretions, I am not now an altered woman?—I am sure I have most heartily repented of all my faults, and wished a thousand times I had never seen you." Major Cyprus, in his turn, cannot believe that she would talk so, "Repent you ever saw me! . . . I believe you are the only woman who cou'd call me her husband, and be insensible of her happiness."

She now thinks her former husband, Sir George, was in every way superior to the major. She tells him so directly, and in the ensuing dialogue she lists these "superior" qualities:

Cyprus: And in what quality pray did your first husband, your first husband, madam—in what quality did he eclipse your humble servant?
Lady Harriet: (After a pause.) He danced better than any man I ever saw.
Cyprus: Danced better!
Lady Harriet: And his bow was exquisite.—
Cyprus: (Bowing.) O—your most obedient!
Lady Harriet: Then, sometimes, he was the most entertaining—
Cyprus: You would have a husband entertain his wife then?
Lady Harriet: Certainly—and entertain himself, at the same time.

Cyprus has had enough and declares that he will suffer no more such talk: "I have done with you—you are below even my resentment." She replies by giving Sir George's "virtues": "He seldom asked me where I was going; or who visited me in his absence?—Where I had been walking?—What made me so remarkably cheerful, or why I looked so very ill-natured?—In short, he was truly and literally, in every respect, a fashionable husband."

These speeches and the characters they define created situations and dialogue that Inchbald was to use repeatedly. Cyprus is a caricature of the fashionable beau, a caricature illustrated in dozens of prints from the early 1770s. Diana
Donald says that in the 1770s "social satire as a distinct genre of caricature attained currency." William Cowper said, "Bunbury sells Humour by the yard, and
is, I suppose, the first Vender of it who ever did so." Henry Bunbury had in the
1770s done a series of "macaronia," in one of which "The St James Macaroni" fits
Cyprus with his wig and his sword, suggesting the frivolity, the emptiness, of a
man whose chief pleasure in life was seducing vulnerable women, not women
with sense and virtue.[33]

The quarrel is interrupted by a servant announcing a "gentleman"—the gentleman is Mr. Anthony Euston. As he walks in, thinking he has found Sir George
and his wife, Lady Harriet is the one who must tell him about the divorce and her
remarriage. Anthony Euston is very upset to learn that it was Sir George who "on
some frivolous suspicion" sued for it. Anthony is appalled by the whole situation,
especially when Cyprus says, "but you know that is no reason, now-a-days, why
the Lady's first husband shou'd be dead," and Colonel Downright remarks, "I had
forgot that a man in England might marry his neighbour's wife, and his neighbour
living in the next street.—And 'tis not the wives of their neighbours, only, these
generous gentlemen assail, but more especially the wives of their *friends*," a very
direct and harsh comment on Inchbald's part that leaves no doubt that Downright is "right."

We are next returned to a room at Sir George Euston's, where the conversation concerns Charles, Anthony Euston's son, who we are told is a lieutenant
stationed in the East Indies. He has left his wife and two small children in England. She is now destitute and has written Anthony a "pleading" letter. Sir George
promises to look into the matter. The lieutenant represents both the plight of
being in the army with so little to support a family and the consequences of marrying for love. All the husbands and wives have problems.

After Euston leaves, Lady Euston and Sir George have a serious discussion
about themselves. We find that the major has insulted Lady Euston, and Sir George
is preparing to challenge him—as well as that "wretch," Sir Harry:

> *Lady Euston:* Oh, pray have pity on poor Sir Harry. . . . Do, my dear Sir
>   George, suffer me to revenge my own cause this once—and ever
>   after—
> *Sir George:* I positively must!
> *Lady Euston:* Nay, Sir George, in a year or two, I may, perhaps, have no

objection to your fighting a duel—but only three months married—I
do wish to keep you a little longer.

Sir George: Depend upon it, Lady Euston, death had never half the terrors I
have beheld it with since I called you mine—but that life you have
endeared to me—

Lady Euston: You wou'd throw away immediately in my service—No, no,
Sir George, a fond wife will never suffer her husband to revenge her
wrongs at so great a risk. Besides, the exertion of a little thought and
fancy will more powerfully vindicate innocence, than that brilliant
piece of steel, I assure you.

As the conversation continues, she suggests to him the various scenarios of
fighting a duel:

Lady Euston: Now suppose a gentleman makes love to me—I divulge the
affront to you, you call my insulter to an account—Your ball misses; he
fires into the air; and, to the fame of having dared to wound your
honour, he gains that of presenting you with your life—

Sir George: But, why must these circumstances take place?

Lady Euston: Well, then, we will suppose he kills you; how do you like that?

Sir George: (Smiling.) Hem!

Lady Euston: Or, we will suppose, you kill him—Even how do you like that?

Sir George: Well I confess that, if a severe punishment could be thought of,
for such insolence—

Lady Euston: There is as severe a punishment to men of gallantry (as they
call themselves) as sword or pistol; laugh at them—that is a ball which
cannot miss; and yet kills only their vanity.

Sir George: You are right.

Lady Euston: Let me see—we have been now only three months married;
and, in that short time, I have had no less than five or six men of
fashion to turn into ridicule.—The first who ventured to declare his
passion was Lord William Bloomly—his rank, joined to his uncommon beauty, had ensured him success; and, wherever I went, I was
certain to hear his distress whispered in my ear—at every opportunity
he fell even upon his knees; and, as a tender earnest of my pity for him,
begged, with all the eloquence of love, for "a single lock of my hair,
which he wou'd value more than any other woman's person; the wealth
of the worlds; or (he is a great patriot you know) even the welfare of his
country."

Sir George: I am out of patience!
Lady Euston: You will be more so—For I promised him this single lock.
Sir George: You did not!
Lady Euston: But I did—and added, with a blush, that I must insist on a
few hairs from one of his eye-brows in return—which he absolutely
refused;—and, on my urging it, was obliged to confess, "he valued that
little brown arch more than the lock he had been begging for; consequently, more than any woman's person; the wealth of worlds; or even
the welfare of his country."—I immediately circulated this anecdote,
and exhibited the gentleman, both as a gallant and a patriot; and now
his Lordship's eye-brow, which was once the admiration, is become the
ridicule of every drawing-room.

Lady Euston has persuaded her husband to allow her to deal with the insults
that have been made by Cyprus and Sir Harry as she says, "And, indeed, Sir George,
it is my fixed opinion that, the man who wou'd endeavor to wrong a virtuous wife
shou'd be held too despicable for the resentment of the husband, and only worthy
the debasement inflicted by our sex."

This scene with her husband is our introduction to Lady Euston. She is not
in any way like Lady Harriet; as she tells her husband the story of her recent
encounters with the beaux, we find her a woman not only of sense but of wit as
well. She is in some ways the most attractive of the "Inchbald women."

The scene shifts, and we find Colonel Downright and Anthony Euston together. Anthony has come to ask Downright a favor. Downright thinks the favor
is to be his second should he, Anthony, be challenged to a duel by Lord Layton,
his friend and host of the day before. The story of Lord Layton and the day before
introduces yet another situation into the story. When Lord Layton and Anthony
begin their journey to Lord Layton's house in his coach, Lord Layton has just
seen a beautiful girl, whom he gave "a look of solicitation." Anthony, moved by
her beauty and her story of being "a poor, indigent, forlorn mother," rescues her
from Lord Layton's "intention" and takes her to his house, leaving her in the care
of his housekeeper.

By the end of the third act, Inchbald has introduced not only the divorce
story but the troubling situation of an abandoned wife and children. Act 4 opens
in a room in Anthony's house, his brother Charles announcing, "Wonders will
never cease! Who wou'd have thought it! . . . My brother Anthony to bring home
a girl!" Charles cannot get Anthony to tell his story, and only after Charles leaves
do we discover that Anthony has received a challenge from Lord Layton. Anthony, so prompted, turns to consider his son: "when I consider myself as shortly

to be an inhabitant of another world, and without the power to assist him—." He sends for the lady he has rescued, and when she comes, he asks for her story. She refuses to give her name, but after some conversation she does tell her story.

She had met her husband when she was "friendless . . . forlorn and destitute." Their love came about from his compassion and her gratitude. She had nothing; her husband, born to wealth, gave up all his fortune when they were married. The husband went abroad with his regiment, and her supplication to his father proved useless. She resolved to come to London to face his father in person, only to learn that his father had been lost at sea.

The story is too much for Anthony; he acknowledges that he, Anthony Euston, is her husband's father and that she is safe and her husband forgiven.

The picture Inchbald draws of the tragedies young couples face when they marry without paternal blessing was a familiar one for the stage and novels, but in this scene Inchbald reveals her use of subtle detail. The husband and wife did not fall desperately in love and then go to Gretna Green to be married; instead, she was friendless, he compassionate. The situation, as the "Lady" recounts her story, portrays both husband and wife as deserving commendation—not condemnation. Moreover, in spite of the elements of sensibility here, Inchbald does not use language to underscore the pathos of the situation; she does not extend the scene. Anthony quickly discovers that the lady is his son's wife. As awkward as this element of the play may seem, Inchbald has been clever in handling both Anthony and the lady. The situation of the disinherited child is a stock device; Inchbald's variations consist of presenting Anthony, the stern, unforgiving father, as actually a caring and humane man who would consider defending to Lord Layton his action in rescuing a beautiful, innocent girl, and the lady as being unsentimental and realistic in speaking of her actions and situation.

We learn very soon that there will be no duel between Lord Layton and Anthony. Instead, Colonel Downright, coming back from Lord Layton, has encountered a young man who will challenge him; the young man is, of course, Anthony's son, the lady's husband. After a few moments of suspense before Charles sees his father, all is forgiven—father and son weep and embrace. The lady, Mrs. Euston, entreats her husband to kneel to his father—"Kneel for me! . . . Kneel to him for us all!"

With the resolution of the father-son story, we turn again to Major Cyprus and Lady Harriet, a bitter relationship filled with recriminations not easily resolved.

Lady Harriet has found a letter that Lady Euston has sent to her husband, consenting to meet him. Bloom, sent to Sir George by her mistress, informs him, "I am not the only object deserving his resentment—but that even his wife of a few months—she whom the world says he doats upon, and who has driven me from his remembrance, is indiscreet as I have been—." Bloom, returning, declares that the only way she could persuade Sir George to come was by swearing that Lady Harriet was dying—"suddenly taken ill; and cou'd not leave the world in peace till you had communicated something from your own lips to him."

All is confusion when Lady Harriet finds that the letter from Lady Euston is addressed not to her husband but to Sir Harry Harmless; and when a few minutes later Sir George knocks, Bloom is sent to meet him; she cannot face him and sends a servant to answer the door. Bloom, entering, has to admit to Sir George that her mistress is a great deal better. Sir George is leaving when Cyprus returns home; Bloom pushes Sir George into a closet, and Cyprus, entering, speaks: "Ridiculed, baffled—laughed at—disappointed! How Sir George will enjoy this! A fine figure I cut on my knees to Sir Harry, when the Colonel and his family were shown in! And then my ridiculous vanity is wishing him to be unmasked, confidently expecting it was Euston's wife!"

When Bloom and Lady Harriet reappear, Cyprus and Lady Harriet, each wishing to entrap the other, have an amusing exchange. Lady Harriet says she has been asleep. She had been reading a "miserable dull book." She returns to her nap, and Cyprus orders some music—he orders the French horns, and as Bloom leaves, Lady Harriet says: "And do you imagine your horns will disturb my repose?—I shall like them of all things—." He replies, "Like them or not—I will have them," and she, "You shall—you shall have them." The reference is to the "horns" of a cuckold, a rather too obvious device but popular with the audience no doubt.

A servant appears to announce to Cyprus Colonel Downright and the Euston brothers. Anthony speaks first: "Major Cyprus, I beg your pardon—but I have received intelligence that my nephew, Sir George Euston, is in this house, and I am come to conduct him safe out of it." Cyprus, knowing nothing of the scheme that Bloom has helped Lady Harriet execute to entice Sir George to the house, does not believe Anthony. Suddenly everything comes together. Anthony is there to rescue Sir George; Sir George, bursting out of the closet, speaks to Cyprus's challenge—"Why then I assure you, Major—and I assure you all—upon my honour—and on the word of a gentleman—that my being here—was—entirely—owing—to—to—" Cyprus: "—To what?—To what, Sir?" Downright: "'I'll tell you what'—to 'an indescribable something'—to be sure!" Repeating the title of the play underscores the words, and remembering them, Cyprus is much confounded.

In the fifth act, the whole scheme of Lady Harriet and Lady Euston, of Cyprus and Sir George, is concluded. Lady Euston apologizes for the letter she wrote to stir up Cyprus; Cyprus accepts Sir George's explanation that he had come to the house thinking that Lady Harriet was on her deathbed. Both Cyprus and Lady Harriet make concluding resolutions.

> *Cyprus:* Lady Harriet, from this moment we separate—And we had been wiser, as well as happier, if we had never met.
>
> *Lady Harriet:* Most willingly separate—Your unkind treatment—and my own constant inquietude—have long since taught a woman of the world too feelingly you to acknowledge, "No lasting friendship is form'd on vice."

Lady Harriet's calling herself "a woman of the world" reminds us—and the audience—that those who are "of the world" are frequently unhappy, lonely women. Lady Harriet is not an "Inchbald woman."

Mr. Euston, Charles, is not yet satisfied about the "relation the child of a first husband is to his mother's second husband, while his own father is living." He concludes, however, "let us apply to the *kindred ties* of each others passions, weaknesses, and imperfections; and, thereupon, agree to part, this evening, not only *near relations* but *good friends*."

The players were very good—"incomparable," Boaden says—and "the ladies were all clever women." On the two last nights, *A Mogul Tale* was the after-piece and Inchbald herself played Selima; she was much applauded. Boaden says, "the moment she made her appearance she was welcomed with shouts of applause that lasted some minutes. . . . She was actress enough to perform the authoress properly on this occasion, and enjoy the sensation she had excited with seeming humility, but proud delight."[34]

The players in *I'll Tell You What* were all experienced, competent, and, for the most part, suited to the parts they played. One, however, created rather a discussion; Farren, who played "the Lady" who turned out to be Anthony's daughter-in-law, got rather mixed reviews in the press. Twiss wrote: "Of the acting, I can at present only say, that the chief part deserved praise; always, however, excepting Miss Farren, who is beyond all description despicable." In a footnote to this quote from Twiss, Boaden remarks, "The *comédie larmoyante* was not suited to her. Nature had dressed her countenance in *smiles,* and her beautiful features looked *sullen* in grave expression."[35]

Farren's recent biographer takes some trouble to justify her, repeating at length the report in the *Morning Chronicle* of "Lines Addressed to Miss Farren," the last stanza of which read:

Yes, I'm in love, nor words, my dear,

Can what I feel declare,

Somehow (I'll tell you what) 'tis—Here

And There! And Everywhere![36]

One contemporary account of *I'll Tell You What* is interesting for the "reading" of a writer familiar with the circumstances, the players, and the audience at the Haymarket:

Mrs. Inchbald already known to the public as an actress and the authoress of a farce called "A Mogul Tale, or the Descent of the Balloon," produced a comedy this season. Before her farce was written, this play had been in the hands of the manager, who seemed not very solicitous that it should be performed. After "The Mogul" had by its success given some strength to the lady's pretensions, she reminded Mr. Colman of the comedy. He said in answer to her note, "If you will call upon me, I'll tell you what it is." This expression occurs in two or three very interesting periods of the play: and the notion having struck the manager much more forcibly than the author, it was announced and produced under the name "I'll Tell You What." It was a complete success being played in its first season twenty times. One part of the plot turns on the unhappy circumstances incident to the marriage of a seducer with the divorced wife whose infidelity he has occasioned, he retaining his old libertine inclinations, and endeavoring a second time to make shipwreck of matrimonial happiness by an attempt on the second wife of his own lady's first husband; the circumstance might easily have been made introductory to tragic scenes, or at least to solemn lectures; but by a much more happy and not less moral contrivance, it ends in exposing the gallant adventurer to ridicule and contempt. Judiciously connected with this plot is the story of Charles Euston, who having by an imprudent love-match incurred the displeasure of his father, is obliged to leave his wife in great distress and open to the attempt of a titled seducer, but she is protected by a benevolent stranger, who turns out to be her husband's father: Charles returns, his offended parent is reconciled.[37]

The idea that the materials of the play could be tragic, that the "seduction" of the young lady could be by a "titled seducer," and the assertion that the moral lessons of the play could have been a "solemn lecture" suggest the response of Mrs. Inchbald's world. Here, in one of the early plays, is seen that dual interest that she was to establish as her own—in this case the divorce plot and the pathos of the distressed wife. It was a characteristic that she was to display in both of her novels and in many of the plays. In *I'll Tell You What* the two story lines are held together by the family relationships; in other instances of this duality, the relationships are not so clearly drawn, and even here there are several awkward spots where the shift from one to the other is not very smooth, as for instance when

Anthony discovers that the young lady is his daughter-in-law, the son-husband appears, and all is forgiven, concluding that plot before the divorce plot and its consequences are completed. Inchbald's problem here reminds us of Boaden's observation about *The East Indian* that the suspense is over by the third act.

Both Twiss and Colman had given Inchbald adverse criticism of the fifth act; that is, they had told her that it was flawed and needed revision. Colman took it and worked on it, but to what extent is not clear. Twiss felt that the end of the fourth act, where young Charles Euston is reconciled with his father, was flawed. To quote Twiss: "Young Euston is not ill *introduced*, but his *dismission* is most shamefully abrupt"; and in the fifth act, "We are now arrived at the fifth act; to which I am sorry to say I have many objections to make; though I do not know that I shall at this moment be able to recollect. . . . To my having read your play in its original state am I indebted for understanding the disappointment of Major Cyprus, the masquerade affair, &c.&c.; for without that I most certainly should not have been able to develope what you seem determined should remain a mystery to the spectators of your play."[38]

Twiss, like Boaden, thought all the plotlines should be brought together and explained. Whatever its faults, *I'll Tell You What* was a great success as a play, and that success made Inchbald's reputation as a playwright.[39] Thus, unlike her experience on stage, where she was never really important, this play established her as a playwright to be reckoned with. Her next two theatrical pieces followed quickly. Kemble, who had returned from his summer in Ireland, and Twiss went with her to the city, where, with the three hundred pounds that Colman had given her, she purchased stock. The spectacle of having her two friends go with her to the city is a fitting tableau; they all three were to remain friends and supporters of each other. For Inchbald the whole experience was very gratifying; she really was on her way to being an established playwright. From this time on until she finished her career as a playwright, she was never without funds or without future promises to use her work. It should be noted also that she invested her funds. From the time of the "parting of funds" with her husband in Scotland, she was always concerned to be independent financially.

SEVEN

NEW PLAYS AND A PUBLISHER

❦ *Appearance Is against Them,* a farce, was already in Colman's hands, but when he refused it, Harris promptly accepted it. Harris seems to have been delighted to have it, for he called on Inchbald himself the day after he received it; it was rehearsed on October 4 and played on October 22, 1785. It, too, was a success—the king commanded it and the Prince of Wales went to see it. Very fond of the theatre, the king and queen could command a performance at Drury Lane, Covent Garden, or the Haymarket. The lord chamberlain made known the king's wishes to the theatre manager, who then arranged to have the play presented. Needless to say, the king's presence filled the playhouse.[1]

Inchbald was quite aware of the ways in which managers made money. And again she was paid well, but she was beginning to understand how the new plays were handled by the managers. When she approached Colman to buy the copyright of *I'll Tell You What,* he refused. Knowing that the play, when it was printed, could be acted anywhere, Inchbald thought, according to Boaden, that this might be done for her benefit with her farce at Covent Garden; but Colman was rather annoyed, writing to her: "Your right to your own property I never disputed; but knew that, were your play even in print, neither of the theatres could in honour represent it, without my concurrence, during the present season . . . but, your right out of the question, I have no objection to its being done one night for your benefit."[2]

Accordingly, on Saturday, May 20, 1786, the playbill read:

For That Night Only
For the Benefit of Mrs. Inchbald
At the Theatre Royal in Covent Garden,
(By Permission of Mr. Colman) will be performed
the Favorite Comedy of I'LL TELL YOU WHAT.

This time Inchbald played in it, and some of the characters were reassigned. Farren was replaced by Mrs. Wells; Parsons was not in it this time, but Bensley was, listed as "From the Theatre Royal, Drury Lane."[3]

The use of divorce, which had given the play its distinctive feature, seems not to have been suggested by any one of Inchbald's friends; she never mentions it in the pocket-books, and since it is not certain just when and under what circumstances she wrote *I'll Tell You What*, any speculation about the source of the idea is conjecture. There is, however, one divorce action that Inchbald was very familiar with, that of Sir Charles Bunbury. By the time of the play, she was seeing him regularly, and they were much talked about in the green room and elsewhere.

Sir Charles had married Sarah Lennox in June 1762, and it was a marriage that turned out to be a total disaster for everyone. Lady Sarah was the younger sister of Caroline Lennox, who married Henry Fox, later Lord Holland; Emily, who married James Fitzgerald, Earl of Kildare; and Louisa, who married Thomas Connolly. Lady Sarah had spent a good part of her time in Ireland while she was growing up, with her sisters Emily and Louisa. Emily had a large and loving family, and Sarah felt that she was very much a part of Emily's family. Caroline, as the eldest sister, was looked to by the younger sisters for advice and direction.

In the months immediately before the king's arranged marriage to Charlotte of Mecklenburg, Lady Sarah and all her family had had great expectations, for the king had indeed given them cause to think he could choose his own bride. In conversation with Lady Sarah, he had hinted at a declaration of love, telling her that he would like to select an English queen. Such a conversation led Sarah and her family to believe he would choose her. But the king could not make his own choice; it was made for him by his mother and his adviser, Lord Bute. His future wife was to be Princess Sophie Charlotte of Mecklenburg. Sarah's family and most of the court knew about Sarah and the king, however, so that when the time came for the wedding, she was very reluctant to be a bridesmaid, "especially because, as the eldest unmarried Duke's daughter, she would be premier bridesmaid and well within the sight of the King throughout the proceedings."[4]

Once the king's marriage was official, Sarah's two older sisters, Caroline and Emily, began to seek a husband for her. Their family letters tell a pathetic story of what could and did occur in such families when, joined with pride and politics, the family must retreat and turn to their own resources to provide a young aristocrat suitable for someone like Sarah, who at age sixteen, if not provided for, would be left "to marry for love" or to remain unmarried. Her position in a close—indeed loving—noble family suggests several facets about love and marriage, especially since in the end she married Charles Bunbury. During the "season" of 1761–1762, Bunbury came often to Holland House to see Sarah. He wrote poetry to her and went to all the social and court events where he would see her, and by the end of January there was serious talk of a marriage. By February a marriage settlement had been drawn up between Henry Fox, the duke of Richmond, and Sir William Bunbury. Her family, learning of the rather slender fortunes of his family, found Charles "not rich enough."[5]

Charles and Sarah had little to say themselves; one observer "discovered that the lovers themselves seemed cool and distant." One relative found that "Lady Sarah is just the same as she was; but neither she nor Mr. Bunbury seem to be much in love according to my notion of being in love."[6] Nevertheless, Charles and Sarah were married on June 2 in the Chapel of Holland House by Dr. Francis, using the traditional Anglican service.

In *I'll Tell You What*, Inchbald treats the seduction of Lady Harriet in a rather casual fashion, in no way blaming her or her husband but simply suggesting that Lady Harriet was deceived and tricked into a compromising position by a "beau" who had assignations for the pleasure of bragging about the women he had seduced. The story of the Bunburys was quite different, especially Charles's part; since his actions then revealed a great deal about his character and about the person Inchbald was to deal with over the several years of their association, perhaps it is fitting to continue his story.

After the marriage it was immediately evident that Charles was more interested in his horses and in Newmarket than he was in his bride. He sent Lady Sarah to Barton to live in a house far from London where she knew no one except his family. From the beginning of her life in Barton, Sarah was extremely unhappy, lonely without her family and among people she did not know, people who, although kind to her, lived in a world totally unlike hers in Ireland or London. Her letters are filled with her reports of attempting to be a part of her husband's life, but Bunbury evidently abandoned her entirely and went his own way, paying far more attention to his horses than to his new wife. He had never been a passionate lover, and his neglect and indifference soon became evident. In October Charles went on a house party, leaving Sarah at Barton with his sister. It became increasingly clear that Bunbury "neither loved nor desired her."[7] One recent biographer, writing about this summer and fall, observed, "At the heart of Sarah's life was a blank space where her love for her husband and his for her might have been; a no-go area of anxiety and unhappiness carefully cordoned off from mention or examination."[8] In December 1762 Sarah went back to Holland House with Bunbury, who, as a member of the House of Commons, returned from his summer in Suffolk to London in the winter.

There was some hope that Bunbury could be appointed to a government post, but all attempts of Fox to arrange an appointment came to nothing, and "Sarah and her husband stayed in England, she to dream of Ireland, he of training a Newmarket winner. Gradually she came to realise that her husband's first love was for horses; the more indifferent he became to Sarah's body, the more absorbed he was by horseflesh."[9]

During the summers in Suffolk, Sir Charles attended to his horses, for he was one of the most widely known horsemen in all of Britain. He was a founding member of the Jockey Club, and as the story goes, he and Lord Derby tossed a coin to see who would name the most important of the races at Newmarket; Lord Derby won, and since that time the race has been called the Derby—not the Bunbury. Sir Charles's horse Diomid won this first Derby, and as is the usual case, he was thereafter put out to stud; he proved totally inadequate. He was sold and shipped to America, where he revived and founded the line of thoroughbred horses that became the bloodlines for the Kentucky Derby in the United States. Sarah loved horses, but she could not compete with the whole complex operation of Newmarket.

In the spring of 1768, Sarah's cousin Lord William Gordon was at Barton with her when her sister Louisa came from Ireland; he stayed until the end of May, and soon thereafter Sarah wrote to the family that she was pregnant. The child was Gordon's, not Bunbury's. One version of the birth of little Louisa, Gordon's child, stated that "Something had always been wrong in his [Bunbury's] sexual relationship with Sarah. Whatever it was, it precluded conception. Bunbury was either impotent or uninterested or both. Gordon and Sarah were neither."[10] By the 1780s, when Inchbald and Bunbury were seen everywhere together, he talked of his "supposed" daughter to her. And she, of course, knew that Gordon and Sarah had gone to Gretna Green in Scotland to marry, that eventually Gordon had abandoned Sarah, and that Sarah had listened to her family and returned to them. The whole story suggests a novel rather than a play; but in 1785 in *I'll Tell You What*, Inchbald was not repeating an old scandal. Bunbury's divorce in 1776, however, was certainly known to her audience, and the handling of the subject in the play, with all its details of family and friends, would surely have been partly responsible for the audience response, especially since, as one authority reports, there were no more than one hundred parliamentary divorces granted between 1750 and 1800.[11]

APPEARANCE IS AGAINST THEM

Since the novelty of using divorce as a device proved so successful, Inchbald frequently chose some contemporary circumstance or idea around which she could build incidents and dialogue. As we have seen, she did so in *A Mogul Tale*. Another device Inchbald uses in many of the plays is to have the servants provide plot incidents and the main characters develop ideas rather than actions. For example, in *Appearance Is against Them,* Miss Angle's maid Fish is a principal participant in the action, leaving Miss Angle simply to follow her instructions. Moreover, the conclusion of the play depends on another servant, Clownly, who offers to satisfy Lady Mary "for whatever loss" she has sustained. *Appearance* also uses current fashion to motivate the plot, which is centered around the gift of a shawl, an item that was quite in vogue.[12]

Lady Mary is to be married to Mr. Walmsley, and Miss Angle has been invited to be present, even though she is no more than an acquaintance Lady Mary has made in the country. Lady Mary declares that Walmsley admires "virtue, in us females" and that Miss Angle's behavior toward Lord Lighthead in asserting her virtue has been brought to Walmsley's attention. The two couples, Lady Mary and Walmsley and Miss Angle and Lord Lighthead, are at the center of the discussion of men and women, of beaux and suitors. Lady Mary is the chief spokesperson and Angle the chief actor, but Fish, Angle's maid, asks the questions and moves the plot along. Fish also serves as a foil to the two women.

The play begins with Lady Mary showing the shawl and inquiring why Miss Angle is a "most altered creature" since she came to town. When Fish replies, "Your Ladyship does not think my mistress has lost any of her beauty, I hope?" Lady Mary makes a speech about London.

> *Lady Mary:* As for that, Mrs. Fish, I dare say your Lady has made observation enough to know, that beauty is of little weight here;—of no signification at all!—Beauty in London is so cheap, and consequently so common to the men of fashion, (who are prodigiously fond of novelty) that they absolutely begin to fall in love with the ugly women, by way of change.— . . . As soon as the vulgar lay hold of any thing, the people of ton leave it off.—Such is the case with young women.—The vulgar have laid hold of them, and they are quite out.—

> *Fish and Miss Angle left alone discuss their situation.*

> *Angle:* Oh Fish, that woman's nonsense, at which you laugh'd, was graced with sentiments of the strictest truth!—Young women are no longer thought of here.—How rashly did I give credit to our foolish country people!—They told me, that, "Tho' only admired by them, in London I shou'd be adored—that beauty here was rare—that virtue"—
> *Fish:* Well, madam, and that is rare, every body knows!
> *Angle:* But is it valued?—No.—As soon as I gave Lord Lighthead proofs of my possessing it [virtue], what was the consequence?—I have neither seen nor heard of him since.

The ensuing conversation makes clear that Lighthead has paid Angle marked attention, and Fish thought it odd that he should "all of a sudden never to come near you for a whole month." She continues, "I should not mind losing him, neither, if some duke or other great man would come instead of him; or even that strange young man we met on the road, as we came to town, and that was so kind to us when our chaise broke down."

Fish is convinced that the young man and his servant were immediately in love with Angle and herself, and she says, "But we, I thought, were coming to town to make our fortune, and so I was above making it on the road." But Fish finds "his Lordship runs most in my heart—Perhaps he is sick?"

Fish suggests to Angle that they take the shawl, pretend to Lighthead that he had given it to her, and say that she is returning it because her "virtue" forbids accepting so valuable a gift without compromising herself. Then Lord Lighthead will respond to her letter and the return of the shawl and see her again. Nothing works out as planned. Lighthead's mistress, Miss Audley, finds herself in Lighthead's chamber in his absence; his servant Thompson, fearing Lighthead's uncle, puts her in the bedchamber. Walmsley and Lighthead come in together, and it is immediately obvious that neither is anything more than an empty-headed rake. Walmsley is speaking of his impending marriage: "I know well enough what marriage is—'Tis a poesy of thorns—nobody knows where to lay hold of it—'Tis a stormy sea, where nothing is to be expected but squalls, tempests and shipwrecks!"

The situation is a much-overworked one, but Inchbald's use of it to make comments is very clever. Walmsley's speech about marriage, the presence of Lighthead's mistress, and the behavior of Thompson all underscore the situation of the beaux and their empty disregard of serious relationships with women. In *Mogul* Johnny would be unfaithful to Fanny if he could; in *The Widow's Vow*, Inchbald's next play, the "widow" at fifteen insists that she be married to a handsome young fellow much inferior in rank and fortune, who turns out to be so bad a husband that when he dies, she vows never to see another man. The beaux in *Appearance* are empty-headed, unprincipled young men.

When the servant brings in the shawl, Lady Loveall has been announced, and, coming up, she is determined to see who is in the bedchamber; Walmsley, within, hides under the bed, not visible when Lady Loveall and Lighthead come in, but Loveall discovers Miss Audley. Into all the confusion enters the servant with a parcel—the shawl—and delivers it to Lighthead. He does not even remember Angle's name. He does up the parcel again and sends it this time to Lady Loveall.

Scene 4 turns to Clownly and his servant Humphuy, who are remembering their journey and the ladies they rescued when the chaise broke down. But romance is never without danger, and both are drawn into the mystery of the shawl. When Lady Mary discovers that her treasure is missing, she is beside herself, declaring that she will not marry. Walmsley, delighted to hear such a declaration, decides, however, to find the missing shawl and accuses Clownley and Humphuy. But before the constable takes Humphuy, Angle confesses to the whole scheme. In the end the shawl is returned, and Walmsley consents to marriage after all, and it is hinted that Clownly will attend Angle.

Since *Appearance* is a two-act after-piece, it does not have an epilogue; Angle's last speech serves, however, as a fitting one.

Mr. Clownly, while you imagine you are giving your protection to a thief only—you are protecting a more despicable character.—Had poverty seduced me to the crime of which I am accused, less wou'd have been my remorse, less ought to have been the censure incurred—But vanity—folly—a mistaken confidence in that gentleman's honour, and my own attractions, prompted me to avail myself of a contemptible scheme, in order to regain his acquaintance, which (admitting what he profess'd to me real) he himself wou'd have rejoiced at.—But the event has proved and discovered both our hearts—nor can I reproach him with the cruelty of his, while I experience the most poignant reproofs of an inward monitor for the guilty folly of my own.

This speech contains several of the features Inchbald uses repeatedly. Vanity and folly are frequently displayed in her characters, and she herself was said to be vain. Vanity as one of the seven deadly sins was a part of her Roman Catholic heritage; it is not surprising that she should be aware of it. She almost always has at least one man who is a fop, who is not sincere, a fashionable beau. She also presents women as foolish and silly or gullible, quite as much as men.

Appearance, unlike *I'll Tell You What,* is tightly constructed; but like *I'll Tell You What,* it has an ambivalent conclusion. Not one of the characters is without fault, and though in the end we suppose Walmsley and Lady Mary will be married, the episode of the shawl and the behavior of Lady Mary about its importance certainly reveal both of them as silly creatures. When Miss Audley and Walmsley are discovered by Lady Loveall in the bedroom, the situation is not only farcical but a very cynical example of propriety. Lady Loveall remarks, "I am bound by no secrecy.—Mr. Walmsley has never been sparing of my reputation, nor will I of his—the world shall know it." Angle and Fish are such foolish creatures that they command no sympathy; we are left, therefore, with both Lighthead and Walmsley admonishing us: "who in company has not, throughout the adventures of this day, appeared culpable?" and "These adventures shall then be a warning to us, never to judge with severity, while the parties have only appearances against them."

After the success of *Appearance,* Inchbald's next piece was *The Widow's Vow.*

Set in Spain, it was the first of the plays to use an earlier play as a source. The advertisement in the printed version acknowledged the source: "The Author of the WIDOW's VOW is indebted for the Plot of her Piece, and for the Plot only, to *L'Heureuse Erreur,* a French Comedy of one Act, by M. PATRAT, but to the Excellence of the English *Performers* alone is she indebted for its very flattering Success."

Like the three earlier plays, *The Widow's Vow* was a great success when it was performed in June; the performers were all experienced, and the plot, using stock devices, was pure farce, entertainment of the kind the audience enjoyed, without serious questions of any kind.

Colman wrote to Mrs. Inchbald this time asking to see her play, and she sent it to him in Bath. The correspondence about it was short and complimentary. Colman wrote: "Dear Madam, I have just run over your farce, and I think I never received or read any piece on which I could so immediately and decidedly pronounce that it would *do;* and do, as I think, with little or no alteration. . . . I am afraid to injure the piece by proposing any variation or departure from its present pleasantry and simplicity."[13]

There was some discussion about a title—Inchbald no doubt had read and discussed the play with everybody in her circle, and everybody, including Twiss, gave her advice. In answer to a letter from her, Colman wrote:

Dear Madam,

Though I cannot account for your *panics,* and think I am no unlucky godfather, e'en christen your child after your own liking; and be assured that I will still remain a sponsor for its success, in spite of the terrors of your *friends.* But why would you write so much about it and about it? Call it what you please, but call me, and believe me,

Your real well-wisher and humble servant,

Geo. Colman.[14]

Colman had suggested that it be called "The Neuter" because, as Boaden puts it, "The business arises from an ambiguity of sex."[15] It was eventually named *The Widow's Vow,* the vow being that of a beautiful widow who, having had an unhappy marriage, vows never to marry again; the plot works out a happy conclusion of "A vow to Love, Honour and Obey," another vow altogether.

Everything in *The Widow* is made for entertainment, from the prologue written by Holcroft and spoken by Bannister to the cross-dressing and tricks used to entrap the widow and trick her into breaking her vow. The list of "entertainments" in the prologue reads like an advertisement for summer pleasures, ending, "Our farce may in its turn amuse the town; / And, smiling thus on Folly's vast career, / Sure not on us, alone, you'll be severe!" *The Widow* was, as Colman expected, vastly successful.

One contemporary summary tells the story, and in doing so it reveals the ideas the audience found appealing:

The subject is that of a young widow, who, having made an oath (at Highgate perhaps, or some place where oaths are equally binding, for the scene is in Spain) never to change her state, fortifies it by resolving to avoid altogether the dangerous society of the other sex. Her friend Donna Isabella, justly thinking such a vow will be "more honored in the breach than in the observance," gets it intimated to the fair widow that she is coming in men's clothes to visit her, to make an experiment on the permanence of her resolution. The widow, fearless of any consequence from the address of one of her own sex, however attired, receives her guest, who is not Donna Isabella, but her brother the Marquis: her icy resolution is thawed by the time the discovery is made; and the conclusion, as might be expected is her union with the lover who has pretended such a disguise.[16]

John Bannister created the role of the marquis, a memorable role for him since, according to his biographer, it was the first original character he created. Both John Bannister and his father, Charles, were favorite performers in London over a long span of years, from 1762, when Charles acted for Foote in his production of *The Orators* until John's final benefit at Drury Lane in June 1815. Charles had been associated with the Norwich Theatre in the 1760s until going to Drury Lane in 1767. Both Bannisters played at the Haymarket in the summers, and both were in the transitivity production of *The Beggar's Opera,* Charles as Polly Peachum, John as Jenny Diver. John acted at Drury Lane from 1778 on, after he abandoned his art instructions. He had been a pupil at the Royal Academy along with Rowlandson. Not having the funds to remain with his instructor, De Loutherbourg, he followed his father into acting.

In June, when *The Widow* was read, Bannister was there for the reading of the part of the marquis and performed it on June 20 with much success. Becky Wells played the part of Flora and Mr. Edwin that of Jerome, both servants. As the play opens, Jerome is explaining his mistress's aversion to men, a melancholy story; he says: "When my Lady was only fifteen she fell deep in love with a fine handsome young fellow, inferior to her both in rank and fortune; but my good old Lord, her father, who doated upon her, was afraid a disappointment might break her heart, and so consented to her having him; but he proved so bad a husband that my poor old Master soon died with grief. . . . My Lady, on this, took such a dislike to her husband, that he died of grief too."

Flora asks how long the countess has been keeping her vow; Jerome replies, "Eighteen months."

Flora: Eighteen weeks! what a time!

Jerome: Months.
Flora: Months! she has certainly lost her senses.
Jerome: Not she.
Flora: O but I am sure she must have lost some of them.

From the beginning the servants set the tone: the idea that "the widow" would not see a man for all of eighteen months meant that she had lost her senses.

At this point we are introduced to the only man who is admitted—the widowed countess's uncle Don Antonio. Jerome explains that there is no fear of him, since he is a relative, and when Flora points out that Jerome is no relative, he replies: "Why, as you say, she might fall in love with me—Stranger things have happened—and to tell you the truth, she does not seem positive she shan't, for she bids me keep out of her sight as much as possible, for fear I should put her in mind of that handsome villain that brought her to this retirement."

The idea that Jerome himself would tempt the widow adds another remark to the absurd and witty situation. At this the "old Gentleman" is coming; Jerome continues: "Then I must go, for he'll be wanting to say something to you—he is for ever running after all the maids—I am sorry to leave you—I am, indeed, Flora; indeed I am—Oh it would be a happy thing for me if I could bring myself to care as little for the women, as my Lady does for the men."

As he leaves, Flora says, "A fine sweetheart, truly, I have got—and if this old fright proves another, I'll be even with him." The servants Flora and Jerome, like Fish and Betty in *Appearance,* have important roles, roles that although they are traditional add to the amusement of the situation. This is especially true here, since both Flora and Jerome are very much a part of the discussion of "The Vow."

Antonio, the "old Gentleman," accosts Flora immediately and struggles with her until he kisses her. Flora escapes only when Jerome comes to call her away. Left on stage, Antonio plots to bring Donna Isabella, the countess's neighbor, to see her along with Donna Isabella's brother the marquis.

We are next introduced to Donna Isabella and her brother; there on a visit to her, the marquis wants an introduction to the "rich widow, the charming Countess," whom he has seen walking in her garden. When asked how that could be, he replies that he has seen her "From the top of our house, through a telescope— ... do bring us a little nearer, or I'll purchase a speaking trumpet, and make love to her through it, though my passion be heard by every soul within a quarter of a mile."

Donna Isabella persuades the countess to let her come to see her disguised as a man; thus the countess will again be introduced to "men." Instead, Donna Isabella sends a real man, her brother the marquis, and his servant, who, as it turns out, is the only one disguised. On stage there is much confusion, but the audience, seeing both reality and disguise, enjoys all the misunderstandings, including a near duel between the marquis and Antonio. The duel is comedy as part of the action, but again, as in *I'll Tell You What,* it is important.

As the run of *The Widow's Vow* came to an end, Inchbald received the money for her sixth night; in addition, at some time this summer, she had sold her comedy *I'll Tell You What* and her farce *Appearance Is against Them* and thus had begun one of the most important relationships of her career. The firm of G.G.J. and J. Robinson became the publisher for all her work, and the senior member of the firm became one of her best friends.[17] Publishing now added to her salary as an actress, and her income from the plays made her quite comfortable financially, but she could never feel so. She continued to deny herself while she supported half her family, and unlike most of her friends, she never owned property in London. When she felt especially "poor," she would move from one cheap lodging to another.

Her newfound financial situation made her more independent than ever, and when Harris sent to ask for another comedy—or farce—she attempted to bargain with him for a seven-year contract in the theatre. Boaden gives some interesting dates to show that she had overstepped her ambitions to make her own decisions. When Harris sent Dive to ask for the play—she no doubt had told everybody what it was, perhaps a comedy again, or an opera she was working on—she refused. On the first of June, Lewis wrote at Harris's direction to tell her that she would be discharged if she did not send her work. Just what their compromise turned out to be is not clear, since we do not have her pocket-book for 1786, but evidently she and Harris came to mutual terms, for she continued on the stage rolls; and although it was not until the end of the year that the work was ready for Harris and the Covent Garden stage, she continued to write for Harris and Covent Garden. Earlier in the spring, Harris had sent Dive to her to ask that she write a pantomime, but she hated any association with a pantomime; she never attempted to write one. Boaden, using her pocket-book, says she was writing a farce that she called "The Necklace," her own life, and an opera; none of the three ever became public, although the writing of her own life occupied her for many years after the spring and summer of 1786.[18]

SUCH THINGS ARE

With the seasons spanning the new year, it is difficult to determine just how her time was spent and how her work went from one week to another. By the beginning of 1787, Harris had her next play in hand, although alterations were still being made. On Saturday, February 10, her new play, *Such Things Are*, was performed. Boaden, speaking of its phenomenal success, says the "house was crowded to excess" and that Inchbald said, "The play was received with uncommon applause," and added "I was happy beyond expression."[19]

The play's chief character, Haswell, is based on John Howard, the prison reformer, who by this time was known all over the world; he was in England even as the play was presented, having recently returned from France. The play is a fine combination of broad farce and serious topics. Boaden remarks that Inchbald was perhaps the only dramatist that "would, or could, have introduced him [Howard] into a play, which was to divert as well as to refine an audience. . . . Mrs. Inchbald alternates, and even mixes her gaiety with her pathos; and the tear is scarcely dry, when you are summoned and willing to join in the most irresistible merriment."[20]

The exotic setting, the comic characters, the discussion of tyranny, and the horrors of prison all make material for a properly constructed five-act play. The advertisement, which appeared when the play was published, gives two interesting points:

The travels of an Englishman throughout Europe, and even in some parts of Asia, to soften the sorrows of the Prisoner, excited in the mind of the Author the subject of the following pages. . . . The uncertainty in what part of the East the hero of the present piece was (at the time it was written) dispensing his benevolence, caused the Writer, after many researches and objections, to fix the scene on the island of Sumatra, where the English settlement, the system of government, and every description of the manners of the people, reconcile the incidents of the Play to the strictest degree of probability.[21]

The comment about "reconcil[ing] the incidents of the Play to the strictest degree of probability" reveals the way Inchbald worked as well as one of the reasons for the distant setting. By the time of the play, England's control of overseas properties was becoming the empire of the nineteenth century. And the use of characters easily recognized by the audience as friends and acquaintances made the exotic setting seem very near. In 1787 also the impending trial of Warren Hastings, the former governor general of the East India Company, lent a kind of authenticity to the people and ideas that the play examines.[22]

The play opens with Sir Luke and Lady Tremor, who have been at the sultan's court for some years—just how long they dispute, because the number of years would set Lady Tremor's age:

Sir Luke: I tell you, Madam, you are two and thirty.
Lady Tremor: I tell you, Sir, you are mistaken.
Sir Luke: Why, did not you come over from England exactly sixteen years ago?

Lady: Not so long.

Sir Luke: Have not we been married the tenth of next April sixteen years?

Lady: Not so long.—

Sir Luke: Did you not come over the year of the great Eclipse? answer me that.

Lady: I don't remember it.

Sir Luke: But I do—and shall remember it as long as I live—the first time I saw you, was in the garden of the Dutch Envoy; you were looking through a glass at the sun—I immediately began to make love to you, and the whole affair was settled while the eclipse lasted—just one hour eleven minutes, and three seconds.

Lady: But what is all this to my age?

Sir Luke: Because I know you were at that time near seventeen—and without one qualification except your youth—and not being a Mullatto . . . yes—I forgot—you had two letters of recommendation, from two great families in England.

Lady: Letters of recommendation!

Sir Luke: Yes; your character—that, you know, is all the fortune we poor Englishmen, situated in India, expect with a wife who crosses the sea at the hazard of her life, to make us happy.

Lady: And what but our characters would you have us bring? Do you suppose any lady ever came to India, who brought along with her, friends, or fortune?

Sir Luke: No, my dear—and what is worse—she seldom leaves them behind, either.

Already in this brief conversation we have a glimpse of a courtship and a marriage, a reason for coming to Sumatra, and the setting of time. Sir Luke's precise recollection of their courtship, which includes the reference to the "great Eclipse," which lasted exactly one hour, eleven minutes, and three seconds, and a reference to the Dutch, reflects Inchbald's combined interest in natural phenomena, geography, and current English affairs. The Dutch had been rivals of the English since the sixteenth century in seeking to control commerce on the high seas. By the time of this play, England had gained a part of the lucrative trade in India and some part in the China trade. The Portuguese were the first and the Dutch the second to trade extensively; they were followed later by the English. For example, the English were far behind in trading for tea and porcelain, as they were also far behind in discovering the method for making porcelain themselves. A survey of Inchbald's pocket-books and plays reveals her wide knowledge of her contemporary world, a knowledge that is seen throughout her work. And in this play, as in several others, she includes representatives from various layers of society.

With the entrance of Mr. Twineall, "*in a fashionable undress,*" Sir Luke reads the letters of recommendation that Twineall has brought from England, from Sir Luke's friends Lord Cleland, Sir Thomas Shoestring, and Colonel Fril, and then introduces him to Lady Tremor and Lord Flint. Together the four of them represent the English in Sumatra, although Sir Luke remarks that "Lord Flint, brought up from his youth amongst these people, has not one *trait* of an Englishman about him—he has imbibed all this country's cruelty, and I dare say wou'd mind no more seeing me hung up by my thumbs—or made to dance upon a red-hot gridiron—." With these four characters, Inchbald presents her audience with three of her favorite subjects: the pretense of society, the pretense of dress, and the pretense of language. One of the things she most sought was reality—the reality of her own world; she had no patience with an artificial society, and she certainly poured scorn on the kind of empty, artificial character that Twineall represents.

When Twineall first appears in his "fashionable undress," Sir Luke cannot believe his eyes; he says: "I must own I took you at first sight for something very different from the person you prove to be—for really no English ships have arrived in this harbour for these five years past, and the dress of us English gentlemen is so much altered since that time." To which Twineall says, "But, I hope, Sir Luke, if it is, the alteration meets with your approbation."

> *Lady:* O! to be sure—it is extremely elegant and becoming.
> *Sir Luke:* Yes, my dear, I don't doubt but you think so; for I remember you
>   used to make your favourite monkey wear just such a jacket, when he
>   went   mout a visiting.

The reference to dress allows Inchbald to discuss "fashionable" dress in an amusing way, but for her audience it was a very important subject, and her use of it here would have been noticed and remembered. She herself records her "dress" in her accounts and in the pocket-books. She says she wore her "white" or that she put on her hat to see Harris. For her to do so was really only to reveal that she, like her friends in the theatre, was very much aware of the advantages of being in fashion. Indeed, the plates in *Bell's British Theatre* served as fashion plates to be copied. Hats and hair decoration became very elaborate during the 1780s; the fashion recorded in many of the portraits even overshadows the faces of the sitters.

Lord Flint is next brought into the conversation and finds such a comment "ridiculous," a word that brings up a new subject, the subject of language.

Lady Tremor: Sir, his Lordship has made a mistake in the word "ridiculous," which I am sure he did not mean to say—but he is apt to make use of one word for another—his Lordship has been so long out of England, that he may be said in some measure to have forgotten his native language.

Twineall: And you have perfectly explained, Madam—indeed I ought to have been convinced, without your explanation, that if his Lordship made use of the word *ridiculous* (even intentionally) that the word had now changed its former sense, and was become a mode to express satisfaction—or his Lordship wou'd not have made use of it in the very forcible manner he did, to a perfect stranger.

Sir Luke: What, Mr. Twineall, have you new modes, new fashions for *words* too in England, as well as for dresses?—and are you equally extravagant in their adoption?

Lady: I never heard, Sir Luke, but that the fashion of words varied, as well as the fashion of every thing else.

Twineall: But what is most extraordinary—we have now a fashion in England, of speaking without any words at all.

Sir Luke thinks such an idea should be adopted by Lord Flint and his wife; Twineall continues:

Twineall: Why, Madam, for instance, when a gentleman is asked a question which is either troublesome or improper to answer, you don't say you *won't* answer it, even though you speak to an inferior—but you say— "really it appears to me-e-e-e-e-[*mutters and shrugs*]—that is—mo-mo-mo-mo [*mutters*]—if you see the thing—for my part—te-te-te-te—and that's all I can tell about it at *present.*"

Sir Luke: And you told nothing!

Twineall: Nothing upon earth.

Lady: But mayn't one guess what you mean?

Twineall: O, yes—perfectly at liberty to guess.

Sir Luke: Well, I'll be shot if I *could* guess.

Twineall: And again—when an impertinent pedant asks you a question that you know nothing about, and it may not be convenient to say so—you answer *boldly,* "why really, Sir, my opinion *is,* that the Greek poet—he-he-he-he-[*mutters*]—we-we-we-we—you see—if his idea was—and if the Latin translator—mis-mis-mis-mis—[*shrugs*]—that I shou'd think—in my humble opinion—but the Doctor *may* know better than I." . . . Or in case of a duel, where one does not care to say who was

right, or who was wrong—you answer—"*This*, Sir, is the state of the
matter—Mr. F—came first—te-te-te-te—on that—be-be-be-be—if
the other—in short—[*whispers*]—whis-whis-whis-whis"—
Sir Luke: What?
Twineall: "There, now you have it—there 'tis—but don't say a word about
it—or, if you do—don't say it came from me."—
Lady: Why you have not told a word of the story!
Twineall: But that your auditor must not say to you—that's not the fashion—he never tells you that—he may say—"You have not made
yourself *perfectly* clear;"—or he may say—"He must have the matter
more particularly pointed out somewhere else;"—but that is all the
auditor can say with good breeding.

Inchbald's use of fashion in dress and speech must have pleased her audience, for there had been much discussion in the press and elsewhere about language. Inchbald herself did not use dialect, thinking it was vulgar; she did not, for
example, approve of Mrs. Malaprop in Sheridan's *Rivals*. And she was always
interested in fashion, a very important matter at this time in London. Thus in
featuring fashion in dress and speech, Inchbald created an opportunity to ridicule
such contemporary nonsense. Like the silly empty-headed Walmsley and
Lighthead in *Appearance*, Twineall is an example, along with Lady Tremor, of how
silly and meaningless current fashion could be. As I pointed out in discussing
Appearance Is against Them, the printmakers used the exaggerated fashions of the
day to satirize both the upper class and the rising middle class, "the middling
class" of the elaborate wigs and decorated gowns. Lady Tremor, as we shall see, fit
such a character exactly.

After this comic scene, Haswell is introduced. He knows Twineall's family,
his father and his uncle, about whom he inquires:

Haswell: Mr. Twineall, I have the honour of knowing his Lordship, your
father, extremely well—he holds his seat in Parliament still, I presume?
Twineall: He does, Sir.
Haswell: And your uncle, Sir Charles?
Twineall: Both, Sir—both in Parliament still.
Haswell: Pray, Sir, has any act in behalf of the poor clergy taken place yet?
Twineall: In behalf of the poor clergy, Sir?—I'll tell you—I'll tell you,
Sir.—As to that act—concerning—[*shrugs and mutters*]—em-em-em-
em—the Committee—em-em—ways and means—hee-hee—I assure
you, Sir—te-te-te— [*Sir Luke, Lady, and Lord Flint laugh.*] My father
and my uncle both think so, I assure you.

Haswell: Think *how,* Sir?

Sir Luke: Nay, that's not good breeding—you must ask no more questions.

Haswell: Why not?

Sir Luke: Because—we-we-we-we—[*mimicks*]—he knows nothing about it.

Haswell: What, Sir—not know?

Twineall: Yes, Sir, perfectly acquainted with every thing that passes in the house—but I assure you that when they come to be reported—but, Sir Luke, now permit me, in my turn, to make a few inquiries concerning the state of this country.

Sir Luke is suddenly aware that Lord Flint is present and is frightened when Lady Tremor begins to question Haswell.

Lady: But, Mr. Haswell, I am told there are many persons suspected of disaffection to the present Sultan, who have been lately, by his orders, arrested, and sold to slavery, notwithstanding there was no proof against them produced.

Haswell: Proof!—in a State such as this, the charge is quite sufficient.

Lady: . . . and so, Mr. Haswell, all this is true?—and some people, of consequence too, I am told, dragged from their homes, and sent to slavery merely on suspicion?

Haswell: Yet, less do I pity those, than some, whom prisons and dungeons crammed before, are yet prepared to receive.

Haswell is to see the sultan, and the scene and the act end. Almost every idea mentioned in this first act is extended and developed. The fashions of the time, the language of the beaux, the uncertainties of the reports of what transpired in Parliament. Did the use of Twineall's Uncle Charles conceal a reference to Sir Charles Bunbury? It is tempting to think so. Sir Charles served in Parliament with little distinction—perhaps everyone knew he would not know or remember a bill "in behalf of the poor clergy," even though his own father had been a clergyman.

Twineall's self-importance is more than amusing, for he sees himself as making his fortune by flattery, by becoming indispensable to all those he meets. As the second act opens, he is speaking to Meanright, a friend he has not seen for some six years. Without a thought of asking about Meanright and his plans, Twineall asks him to "inform me of the secret dispositions, and propensities of every one in this family, and of all their connections.—What Lady values herself upon one qualification, and what Lady upon another?—What Gentleman will like to be one of his accomplishments? or what man would rather hear of his wife's, or his daughter's?—or of his horses? or his dogs?—now, my dear Ned,

acquaint me with all this—and within a fortnight I will become the most necessary rascal—not a creature shall know how to exist without me."

After such a request, Meanright remarks "Why such a man as you ought to
have made your fortune in England." The speech Twineall gives to explain his
"genius" and the reason he is in Sumatra instead of exercising his plans at home
makes a significant comment about the structure of London society, a subtle comment on families and social success in the small London—family—dominated
world, and a witty bit of satire that Inchbald uses effectively.

Twineall continues:

> *Twineall:* No—my father, and my three uncles monopolized all the great
> men themselves; and wou'd never introduce me where I was likely to
> become their rival—This—this is the very spot for me to display my
> genius—But then I must penetrate the people first—and you will
> kindly save me that trouble—Come, give me all their characters—all
> their little propensities—all their whims—in short, all I am to praise—
> and all I am to avoid praising,—in order to endear myself to them.

Sir Luke is to be praised for his personal bravery; Lady Tremor for her birth;
Meanright goes so far as to say that she has a "A large old-fashioned wig—which
Malcolm the third or fourth, her great ancestor, wore when he was crowned at
Scone, in the year—." Lord Flint, Meanright says, though he is very much at
court and pretends to be a man of principle and sentiment, is perhaps not so
much a friend of the sultan as he pretends. With this information Twineall leaves
the stage, and Meanright in a long soliloquy reveals to the audience that Sir Luke
is a real coward, having fled from his place in the army in the midst of an engagement; Lady Tremor's father was a grocer and her uncle a noted wig-maker, advertising "Periwig-maker on a new construction"; and Lord Flint, "firmly *attached* to
the *interest* of the Sultan, will be all on fire, when he hears of open disaffection."

Anyone viewing the prints of the period will find dozens featuring the enormous wigs—one with the candles setting it on fire, another of the farmer's daughter
returning home with her hair made up so high that she is caught in the door and
cannot enter to greet her father.[23] Lady Tremor's uncle, "a Periwig-maker on a
new construction," and Twineall's being told that she had a wig from her ancestor,
Malcolm the third or fourth, which he wore when he was crowned at Scone, are
too obvious to be in any way serious; but as Inchbald uses this scene, it becomes a
comment to her audience. They must have found the combination of farce and
social situations that allow for satirical comment, cynical commentary on London, all set as a background for Haswell, and the pathos of the prisoners a proper

setting. And if Inchbald is better at cynical farce than she is at pathos, the dialogue, the situations, and the ideas are cleverly handled, making the plot tightly organized and even the prison characters believable. Thus the success of the combination is not surprising.

Again, as in the earlier plays, Boaden chooses certain scenes to compliment. He begins a kind of summary of the action by saying, "But we must exhibit some of the striking points of the business, that it may appear how original and profound this great woman was in her art, and how highly she merited the rewards that awaited her genius." Boaden, and perhaps most of the audience, was especially interested in the episode of the slave who steals Haswell's pocket book to purchase his freedom by paying ransom. The thief then cleverly blocks Haswell's way, thus taking away suspicion for what he has done. But when Haswell promises him aid and money, he is overcome with remorse and throws himself on his knees before Haswell. Of this action Boaden says, "Nature in a moment bursts through the villainy which slavery had taught her . . . the effect was electric. Fearon, a rough but valuable man, struck it by his action into every heart; and Mrs. Inchbald must have trembled under the severe delight of applause that never was exceeded in a theatre."[24]

The prison scenes were very effective and are handled carefully. Haswell is shown in by the keeper with lights to let them see. The keeper says the prisoners are unruly people, unthinking men. Haswell asks, "And wou'd not gentleness, or mercy . . . reclaim them?" The keeper: "That I can't say—we never try those means in this part of the world."

The prisoners are there for a variety of reasons, none of which should have been punished. We learn that even for very small crimes, people are put to death. These prisoners, for "disaffection" or for some trifle, may pay to have better quarters, or those who may be supposed to have friends or family may pay ransom money. One is there who, accused of leading an insurrection but proved innocent and acquitted, could not pay the debt he contracted in proving his innocence. Some are natives; some are not. Two of the prisoners are given special attention—the one an old man, the other a "female prisoner," "without a friend or comforter." Inchbald uses these two prisoners very cleverly to plot her incidents and to present ideas about Haswell and the prisoners. The old man's son attends him, paying a fee each day to come to the prison and bring cordials, for the father, who was strong and healthy when he was imprisoned, is now ill. The son, Elvirus, has petitioned the sultan to let him take his father's place, but to no avail. Haswell promises to intercede. The lady has been in prison so long that the keeper knows nothing about her except to say that she does not complain, only moans to herself.

Inchbald's picture of the prison is quite realistic, considering the circumstance of the stage scene and the plot incidents that she works out. She uses Haswell with the prisoners and their stories to make a powerful statement about the contemporary world, and in doing so she makes clear that Haswell shows mercy but requires justice as well. Inchbald herself never faced going to prison for debt, but many of her friends did. Both Colman and Sheridan were deep in debt several times, and both Digges and Wilson were repeatedly threatened and had to flee London to escape their creditors. The comments about money in these scenes certainly added a realistic note to the plot, for no doubt there were many in the audience who quite understood.

In speaking to the prisoners, Haswell comments about the condition of the prison—the son says of his father, "but three months has he been confined here; and yet—unless he breathes a purer air—." The lady is very weak—so weak she can hardly speak, speaking only when she tells of despairing of a ransom. When Haswell suggests that he will pay her ransom, she begs him not to deceive her, when "the sun, the air, fields, woods, and all that wondrous world, wherein I have been so happy is in prospect." And when Haswell asks her name, she replies, "'Tis almost bolted from my memory."

From the prison we are returned to Sir Luke's apartment, where Sir Luke enters with a young lady about whom he has had a letter from his friend, informing him that she had had her "affections . . . improperly fixed upon a young gentleman." But Aurelia, the young lady, in tears denies that she has come to seek a husband; she says to him, "Dear, Sir Luke, how can you imagine I am in tears because I have not a husband, while you see Lady Tremor every day in tears for the very opposite cause?" Before the conversation proceeds, Lady Tremor and Twineall appear. It is this scene in which Twineall uses the false information he was given by Meanright. Both the script and, no doubt, the acting make it very effective. Sir Luke is certainly pretentious, as is Lady Tremor, but they really are harmless creatures; they do not deserve to be unmercifully teased, as Twineall attempts to do when he would gain Sir Luke's favor by praising his valor in battle and Lady Tremor's approbation by praising her family as descendants of Scottish nobility.

Twineall, however, has made a much more dangerous mistake in thinking there is a rebellion about to be mounted against the sultan. Lord Flint consults Sir Luke about Twineall, who, it seems, has implicated Sir Luke as being a party to the disaffection against the sultan. It is in this scene that Inchbald has prepared the incidents to engage everyone, and with the introduction of Aurelia, she has added the material for a love story and a marriage. In *Such Things Are* the details of characters and plot incidents are tightly woven, in contrast to *I'll Tell You What*, where several incidents and characters are never resolved.

After the introduction of Aurelia and the material set to implicate Sir Luke and Twineall by Lord Flint, we are returned to Haswell, who is conducted into the sultan's palace. Haswell is thanked for restoring the sultan's troops by his care; the sultan would like to reward him, but the reward of releasing the prisoners, which is what Haswell asks for, is answered by the sultan's "Amazement! retract your application—curb this weak pity; and receive our thanks." Haswell refuses and speaks of justice. The sultan has never found anyone with his sentiments, as he speaks: "Sir, your sentiments, but much more your character, excite my curiosity. They tell me, in our camps, you visited each sick man's bed,—administered yourself the healing draught,—encouraged our savages with the hope of life, or pointed out their *better* hope in death.—The widow speaks your charities—the orphan lisps your bounties—and the rough Indian melts in tears to bless you.—I wish to ask *why* you have done all this?—What is it prompts you thus to befriend the wretched and forlorn?"

Haswell, feeling that an explanation is beyond his power, suggests that he read a book, *The Christian Doctrine*. The sultan is amazed; he dismisses the guards and admits to Haswell that he is a Christian. His story, recounted to Haswell, is in itself the plot for heroic drama.

When Haswell asks what made him a Christian, he replies:

My Arabella,—a lovely European, sent hither in her youth, by her mercenary parents, to sell herself to the prince of all these territories. But 'twas my happy lot, in humble life, to win her love, snatch her from his expecting arms, and bear her far away—where, in peaceful solitude we lived, till, in the heat of the rebellion against the late Sultan, I was forced from my happy home to bear a part.—I chose the imputed rebels side, and fought for the young aspirer.—An arrow, in the midst of the engagement, pierced his heart; and his officers, alarmed at the terror this stroke of fate might cause amongst their troops, urged me (as I bore his likeness) to counterfeit it farther, and shew myself to the soldiers as their king recovered. I yielded to their suit, because it gave me ample power to avenge the loss of my Arabella, who had been taken from her home by the merciless foe, and barbarously murdered.

So intent had he been to avenge her death that he continued to pretend that he was the young "aspirer" and to wield absolute power, "with such unsparing justice on the foe, that even the men who made me what I was, trembled to reveal their imposition; and they find it still their interest to continue it." All Haswell can say is, "Amazement!"

The sultan's story concludes act 3, but the threads of the plot are still to be worked out. In the opening scene of act 4, we learn that Aurelia is beloved of Elvirus and that she is only now discovering what has happened to Elvirus's father. When Elvirus tells her that he has asked to take his father's place in prison, they must plot to keep their love secret. Their situation is no more serious than that of Sir Luke and Lady Tremor, who are so upset by Twineall that they plot to get him implicated as a dissident, having been terrified and mortified in his references to her ancestors and his "courage" in battle.

In act 5 Haswell is again in the prison speaking with the female prisoner, hearing her confused story of becoming a part of the group fleeing the war that has been thought to be among the sultan's enemies. He discovers that she is a European and a Christian. As they conclude their talk, she asks Haswell to plead for her freedom, but Haswell tells her she must go herself to tell her story.

As Haswell leaves, he encounters Elvirus. Elvirus, having discovered Haswell's true identity, is more overcome than when he confessed in the garden that he had lied about his true name and situation. Hardly has their conversation ended when the prison keeper comes to plead with Haswell to speak to another prisoner—one just entering. The prisoner is Twineall. Twineall's plea to Haswell adds another dimension to his tale, even as he continues to act his part of a fool.

He says to Haswell: "Dear Mr. Haswell!—Dear Sir!—Dear friend!—What shall I call you?—Only say what title you like best, and I'll call you by it directly—I always did love to please every body—and I am sure at this time I stand more in need of a friend than ever I did in my life."

> *Haswell:* What has brought you here?
> *Twineall:* Trying to get a place.
> *Haswell:* A place?
> *Twineall:* Yes; and you see I have got one—and a poor place it is!—in short, Sir, my crime is said to be an offense against the state; and they tell me no friend on earth but you can get that remitted.
> *Haswell:* Upon my word, the pardons I have obtained are for so few persons—and those already promised—
> *Twineall:* O, I know I am no favourite of yours—you think me an impertinent, silly, troublesome fellow, and that my conduct in life will be neither of use to my country nor of benefit to society.

Haswell's reply to this speech adds another quality to his character and his role.

> *Haswell:* You mistake me, Sir—I think such glaring imperfections as yours are, will not be of so much disadvantage to society as those of a less faulty man.—In beholding your conduct, thousands shall turn from the paths of folly, to which fashion, custom, nature, (or call it what you

will) impels them;—therefore, Mr. Twineall, if not pity for your faults,
yet a concern for the good effect they may have upon the world (shou'd
you be admitted there again) will urge me to solicit your return to it.

Twineall: Sir, you have such powers of oratory—what a prodigious capital quality!—and I doubt not but you are admired by the world equally for that—

At the conclusion of the play, all the people and their problems come to a
proper end. Twineall is not executed; the sultan and his wife are reunited, thanks
to Haswell; Elvirus's father is released and his lands restored, leaving Elvirus and
Aurelia free to marry; and Zedan, the native prisoner who stole Haswell's purse
and then restored it, has been given his freedom. Lady Tremor had hoped to see
Twineall's head cut off; she says, "Oh! if his head is off, pray let me *look* at it?—"

The last person "rescued" is Twineall. He begins at once to say flattering
things about Haswell, who has brought about his release by showing the sultan's
signet, only to have Haswell interrupt him: "Seize him—he has broken his contract already." Haswell will have none of Twineall's extravagant speech: "utter anything but flattery—Oh! never let the honest, plain, *blunt* English name, become a
proverb for so base a vice.—"

In the last speeches, everyone offers Haswell encomiums; Twineall asks, "will
you suffer all these encomiums?" and Elvirus in the last speech answers: "He *must*
suffer them—there are virtues, which praise cannot taint—such are Mr. Haswell's—
for they are the offspring of a mind, superior even to the love of fame—neither
can they, through malice, suffer by applause, since they are too sacred to incite
envy, and must conciliate the respect, the love, and the admiration of all."

Since this was a five-act main piece, there was an epilogue, written by Miles
Peter Andrews, a wealthy young man who made a name for himself by writing
prologues and epilogues. The first lines of the epilogue for *Such Things Are* return
to the comments about class as they were represented by Lady Tremor. Mrs.
Mattocks, who played the part, includes lines addressed to "Our Author":

> Our Author, then, correct in every line,
> From nature's characters hath pictur'd mine [Lady Tremor's];
> For many a lofty fair, who, friz'd and curl'd,
> With crest of horse hair, tow'ring thro' the world,
> To powder, paste, and pins, ungrateful grown,
> Thinks the full periwig is all her own;
> Proud of her conquering ringlets, onward goes,
> Nor thanks the barber, from whose hands she rose.

After Inchbald's skillful handling of Lord and Lady Tremor and Twineall, the epilogue seems very slight; but Andrews was one of the important green-room attendants at Covent Garden, and no doubt his epilogue added to the pleasure of the audience, pleasure that was a very important part of the success of any comedy at Covent Garden.

Boaden reports that Bow Street was full of people who could not get in to see the play. On the sixth night, Monday, February 19, the king ordered the play and came with the queen and the three princesses. They were delighted with the whole performance.

Inchbald said she realized 900 pounds from the play, but Boaden, not quite accepting that figure, says she bought into the funds by buying into the long annuities, for which she paid 410 pounds, yielding 18 pounds a year. He suggests that perhaps she had had other gifts that she thought "improper to minute down." It is interesting to speculate about such matters, however, for by this time she had become celebrated; moreover, she had become a very valuable asset to Covent Garden and Harris.[25] And by this time she and Harris had formed an amiable partnership—in the theatre at least, if not in person. Harris was known for his attention to the actresses in the company, although he was not at all like Daly. When he first acquired a part of Covent Garden, his quarrel with Colman had to do, in large part, with the fact that Colman refused his request to give his (Harris's) mistress a leading part in the company. Ever since then, Harris had evidently been known as having relationships with the actresses in his company. Boaden remarks that after the success of *Such Things Are*, perhaps he (Harris), like Colman, "pressed the fair muse to *his* bosom."[26] Perhaps, but if so, nothing came of it, although their relationship was at times very close. One of the stories repeated in almost every memoir of those who knew Mrs. Inchbald is about how she burst into the green room all out of breath, saying she had just escaped Harris's amorous attentions by pulling his hair when he had attempted to kiss her.

THE MIDNIGHT HOUR

Whatever their personal relationship, Inchbald and Harris continued to work together professionally. In March, after the great success of her play, Harris brought her *Guerre Ouverte; or, Ruse contre Ruse*, by M. Dumaniant. It was originally in French, and she translated it—or, as Boaden remarks, she adapted it—"for she used her original always freely on such occasions."[27] In her usual fashion, she turned her attention to work, and by April 24 she had completed, copied, and returned it to Harris. In spite of her successes, she was still—and always—uncertain. Harris's letter to her about this play reveals, in addition to his assurance to her about her work, an interesting view of how knowledgeable he was about selecting and presenting plays. Perhaps an excerpt will explain how Harris conducted so successful an operation:

> Be satisfied you have done the translation excellently. I approve, very much, every thing but your criticisms. Be assured nothing can be more comic than the Marquis's entrance in disguise, while all the group are assembled to prevent him. The watch-word, &c. is all absolutely necessary to illustrate the character of Nicholas. Rely that the whole is so excellently constructed, that any mutilation of business would essentially injure. I also am clear 'tis too full of bustle and intrigue for a musical piece. It will be much best to keep it in three acts, and it will not be too long—not longer than "Catherine and Petruchio."
>
> The business appears to me as clear as need be, and I have no doubt you find it so. . . . All you have to do is to get a prologue, which must say much of its great celebrity in Paris;—and I think you finish rather too abruptly. The Marquis, Julia, and the General, certainly should have each one more speech. . . . I shall certainly be in town long enough before this can be produced. You have done well to lay the scene in Spain. Look at a map for a maritime Spanish town. Would not Cadiz do, or Barcelona? I think it might be called, "All Fair; or, the Wager Won."[28]

The title, as it turned out, was *The Midnight Hour,* making time an integral part of the business. The scene is listed as simply "A Country Town in Spain," though within the action the town is referred to as a seaport. The prologue does, as Harris suggested, refer to the popularity of the play in France:

> A Frenchman's fancy gave the bantling birth,
>
> Which now, in Paris, source of constant mirth,
>
> Reigns the dramatic idol of the day,
>
> And from its rival pieces bears the palm away.

The Midnight Hour is fast-paced farcical action in spite of its label as a comedy. There is nothing serious in it except a kind of game to outwit the general, who, because he is his niece's guardian, has arranged her marriage with a man who is wealthy, a man no one has met or seen; thus no one can identify him. Such a situation makes possible a series of tricks when a young marquis comes along and wishes to marry Julia. The tricks used to carry Julia away from her locked chamber include all kinds of disguises and clever entrances—men carried in and out in a chest, characters climbing out of windows and hiding behind the shrubbery against a garden wall. The key to the suspense is the fact that the general tells the marquis that he can have Julia if he can get her consent and leave with her before midnight.

On stage the action is swift and the tricks engaging. The marquis is obliged to depend on servants to gain admittance both to the household and to Julia, so the servants are of great importance; indeed, the action of the play turns on the servants and their responses. The general is autocratic and surly, suspecting everyone of being disloyal, an attitude necessary to move the action along when he accuses Cecily, his longtime domestic, of disloyalty. In fact, Cecily is the duenna, more attached to the general than any other servant he has. She is old and ugly and does not respond to the flattery the marquis attempts. She tells the marquis: "if you come hither after my young lady, I have the pleasure to inform you, you won't get her—she is disposed of—her uncle has so ordained it, and I would not be the cause of her disobeying her uncle for the world—I am true to him, because he gives me the power to use every body else as ill as I please—and now I wish you a good day; having the satisfaction to leave you in utter despair."

As the marquis attempts to bribe her, the general overhears the marquis say, "You have won my esteem and friendship for ever," and as he offers her a purse, he poisons her mind against the general; knowing that the general hears him, he brags, "all my wishes must succeed—Oh, General, where are you now, with your boasted confidence?" The general dismisses Cecily, saying: "Go you about your business immediately—you never set your foot into my house again—in pretty hands, truly, I had confided my niece! a pretty duenna I had chosen!" Cecily cannot believe him; the general continues: "Never let me see your face again—take care of that—take care I don't even find you lurking about any of my premises, with a love letter under your apron—."

The general evidently thinks that Cecily has been seduced by the young and handsome marquis, as he says to her, "a'nt you ashamed?—you ought to blush. . . . I always thought it of you—I have suspected you these twenty years." And when she says, "—when I go—your good genius forsakes you," the general taunts her: "Why, you are hated and detested by every body—*I* was the only person on earth that *ever* could endure you—and now you are found out by *me*—you have not a friend in the world." As the general leaves, she tells the marquis, "I will do you all the good I can, out of *spite*." Inchbald has been clever here in showing how quickly the general accuses Cecily, old and ugly as she is, of having fallen for the young marquis.

Cecily is not the only servant to play an important role; the general has Nicolas, Ambrose, Mathias, and Flora, all of whom pledge their support to him; but none of them do support him except poor Mathias, who is deaf. Nicolas, the general's man, should have been the one to carry out the general's orders; he tries to do so, but everything goes wrong. The marquis gets into the house in a chest after his own servant, Sebastian, disguised as Don Carlos, appears to Nicolas.

Nicolas is the dupe blamed and put upon by both the general and the marquis. At one point he says, "Oh, the blessing of being faithful!—I have this day been beaten by all parties—friends and enemies all have kicked me; !—and the bitterest foes agree in using me like a dog."

Flora, while she pretends to be loyal to the general, is at the center of the plans for the young lovers to escape before midnight; but when Nicolas tells the general about the chest trick, Flora thinks all is lost. In the end the marquis supposed to be hidden in the garden is actually Julia, dressed as the marquis; thus Julia can escape, and just as the clock strikes midnight, Nicolas comes running, thinking he has escorted the marquis to his hotel, only to discover it was Julia in disguise. He exclaims, "Oh, heaven, do I see double, or have I lost my sight?"

In the end, when all are gathered, Nicolas inquires: "And pray, who will recompense me for all the injuries I have suffered for my fidelity?" The marquis replies, "I will repay every servant, who either by their genius have aided, or by their fidelity obstructed my designs; for possessed of such a blessing as my Julia, I shall ever remember with gratitude the adventures of this day, and never cease to reflect with rapture on the Midnight Hour."[29]

Lewis played the marquis, John Edwin played Nicolas, and James Fearon, who had played Zedan in *Such Things Are*, was the deaf Mathias. Mrs. Wells played Julia, Mrs. Brown played Flora, and Mrs. Webb played Cecily. Since this comedy was presented at Covent Garden, all these players were members of the company and certainly familiar with the kind of farce *Midnight Hour* represented. The "tricks" were very old, traditional ones, but the intrigue, the way they were put together, kept the audience's attention, and no doubt the servants in Inchbald's version of M. Dumaniant's play gave great delight.

Inchbald seldom repeated situations in her plays, and although *The Midnight Hour* was adapted from the French, it was her own. Lady Wallace, a writer of fashion, had also translated it, and Boaden reports: "when she [Lady Wallace] published, complained of being forestalled. The complaint was idle: she could have no exclusive right to M. Damaniant's comedy: besides, she rendered it less entertaining by being more literal. Mrs. Inchbald knew how to use her materials."[30]

Harris knew what he was doing when he brought her the play in the first place, and he must have known that other people found it a suitable play to translate. Another one of the writers who had selected it for himself was Inchbald's friend MacMahon. He wrote her a letter of congratulation, nevertheless. His letter, though it acknowledges her skill, is interesting for revealing the writer and the theatre: "It was but yesterday I was informed, by an advertisement from Covent-

Garden Theatre, that you had undertaken to produce Guerre Ouverte in an English dress. The French author must be proud of this circumstance; but I cannot help acquainting you with the strange fate that hath, of late, presided over my literary undertakings—if I can dignify with that name the weak attempts of a pen by no means practised, in a career which you have run over with so much fame to yourself and credit to the British drama." MacMahon says he has given his manuscript to his snuffman, since he was sure that had he printed his version he would have given a copy to the snuffman. He concludes, "yet give me leave to insist on one condition—namely, that you will favour me with a printed copy of 'The Midnight Hour,' which cannot fail of being heard with delight when it is struck by you."[31]

For Inchbald and Harris *The Midnight Hour* was as successful as it had been in Paris; Boaden remarks, "And here it would have been well if her dramatic adventures had closed on this most auspicious year; but Harris had little confidence in any manufacture but her own; and accordingly, her old friend—who at length discovered that there were writers who composed better than they spelt, as well as myriads who could spell and never composed a decent line—came in the month of September, and absolutely forced from her the comedy which the sagacious Colman had discovered was too slight even for summer wearing."[32]

Boaden's "summer wearing" is a pun on the title of this new play, called *All on a Summer's Day*. It was played once on December 15 with Inchbald behind; that is, she was fearful of the play's success and remained backstage, very uncertain of its reception. It was condemned and never printed until it was included in the Backscheider edition. Inchbald wrote a letter to the *London Review* in which she protested that Harris had insisted on producing the play, "contrary to my inclination, and even contrary to my most earnest entreaties." Her friend Lewis, who had played Twineall in *Such Things Are,* also had expressed disaffection about it. Considering all the discussions after the single performance, it is not surprising that Robinson did not publish it. It is, however, a very interesting play when it is read as a part of Inchbald's whole oeuvre.

The prologue of *All on a Summer's Day* makes some significant comments about women and playwriting:

> When haughty man usurp'd fair learning's throne
> And made the Empire of the stage his own
> He rul'd a realm where Genius seldom smil'd
> And Nonsense hail'd him as her darling child . . .
> Bard follow'd Bard, yet few coud justly claim

The laurell'd trophies of a lasting name
'Till gentle woman seiz'd the pen and writ
And shone not less in beauty than in wit.

Following this appraisal, the characteristics of a "gentle woman" are listed.
Again the comments are in general terms but obviously meant to be a compliment to Inchbald. The declaration that follows the compliment is not only in
praise of women but is also a statement about Inchbald's plays and her thesis for
the characteristics of any play. The prologue continues:

Woman! by honest emulation fir'd
By sense directed & by wit inspir'd
Sportive, yet elegant; tho' pointed, chaste,
To mend our manners & refine our taste:
Man from her learnt the fascinating art
To please the fancy, captivate the heart
And paint the scenes of happiness and strife
The various scenes that checquer human life.[33]

Quite aside from the compliments to Inchbald, the prologue also suggests in
its list what the play is not. It is a list that suggests some of the other things on
stage elsewhere. There are "no dragons," no phantoms, no "Light'ning flashes and
no Thunder rolls." By this time the gothic had become very popular both on stage
and in the novels, and by this time Kemble had developed very elaborate stage
settings that frequently contained phantoms and thus used lightning and thunder
to create a proper gothic atmosphere. That the play was, nonetheless, unsuccessful speaks as much to the audience as to the play's ideas and subjects. There was no
entertainment in it, and the prologue's "'Tis hers, the tale of sorrow to impart / And
melt to sympathy the feeling heart" was too much a detailed study of the perfidy of
both men and women. In this play Inchbald went beyond divorce and stolen shawls,
beyond silly women and cowardly men in far places. In this play the women and the
men are featured in a variety of very reprehensible acts. Moreover, the plotlines are
even more convoluted than those of *I'll Tell You What*. Perhaps, although her audience delighted in "incidents," there were too many to keep in mind here.

The first scene of the play is in a room at Sir William Carrol's, where his wife
speaks to Mrs. Goodly, who, entering, says, "For shame Lady Carrol! how can you
say such severe things to your husband? you know he does not like it." To which
Lady Carrol replies, "But he knows I do, & therefore he ought to like it; he ought

to take pleasure in every thing that pleases me." With this opening statement, we are introduced to another of Inchbald's analyses of marriage.

Mrs. Goodly is Lord William's sister, and although she sees Lady Carrol as having some good qualities, she thinks Lady Carrol lacks the "virtue of prudence." But Lady Carrol says, "And prudence in me would be nothing else—I can't feel prudent, & at best it would be only affectation."

Lady Carrol was her husband's ward before she became his wife. Her view of her duties as his wife is again, as in most of Inchbald's work, full of satire: Lady Carrol: "and as to conjugal affection, I protest that notwithstanding I know I am no overfond ridiculously attentive Wife, yet I am still not that insensible monster some people represent me:—for instance, I shoud be sorry any misfortune shoud happen to Sir William—I mean any serious misfortune—And, my dear Sister, I perfectly remember, that once when he had a Violent fever, I never omitted enquiring after his health constantly every night & morning; & always answer'd 'I was very sorry,' or 'I was very glad.' According as they told me, 'he was something better.' or 'Something worse.'—Now if this is not tenderness & conjugal affection, why, I know nothing of it, that's all!"

In the following dialogue, Lady Carrol gives the description of the man she could "doat" upon, someone entirely different "in Shape, features, air, & temper." She imagines a "delightful Creature . . . so charming in my own mind . . . that I shoud soon grow quite tired of Sir William & not even be able to look at him." To which Mrs. Goodly observes, "And from this painting of the mind & Ideal accomplishments, half the husbands in London have Rivals in their own wive's esteem, whose perfections have no more of Substance, than the pretty Gentleman your fertile Imagination has just given form to." Lady Carrol: "No, no, no! No Sentiment—my dear Creature, no Sentiments, they are out of fashion—they are not fit to be introduc'd in private Conversations now-a-days.—Here comes Wildlove; leave us, will you?—He has affronted me, & I have a mind to Scold him—Dear me! & yet Wildlove,—Wildlove!—I do think he answers the description of that fanciful thing I made up just now, So unlike Sir William."

Wildlove is a rake—and a fool; he is neither clever nor witty, but he, like Lady Carrol, plays the fashionable games of assignations, writing forbidden love letters, and in general behaving outrageously. Lady Carrol is jealous because he has made love to the maids and not to her. He is promised to meet Lady Henrietta, who we find has "nerves." Lady Carrol has written love letters to a young man she met at a dance where she pretended to be her husband's daughter.

Into all these intrigues the former governor of India appears. Sir William announces his immediate appearance and that he is bringing with him his (the former governor's) daughter and her fiancé. The daughter, Louisa, lived in the household of Sir William and Mrs. Goodly for many years before she went to her father, and Sir William and Mrs. Goodly are very excited about their unexpected return. Wildlove and Lady Carrol are very upset.

In the end Louisa reveals that she and Wildlove were secretly married and that he has deserted her; Lady Carrol, confronted with the fact that she pretended to be Sir William's daughter, is shamed before the whole group; Lady Henrietta is left in the woods waiting for Wildlove to keep the assignation. To conclude so many "situations" proves too much even for Inchbald's skill.

In spite of the failure of *All on a Summer's Day,* there are several witty touches—places where Inchbald's satire shows clearly. Wildlove's speech justifying his behavior to Louisa and their marriage is very awkward—not realistic in the least, not even acceptable as satiric comment against sentimentality. Lady Carrol's trick of the love letters introduces one of the few comic elements in the play when the father of the young man to whom she wrote the letters appears. He is Sir Ralph Mooneye, a friend of Sir William; as the name suggests, he is very nearsighted. He is without his "glass." (Inchbald herself was very nearsighted, losing and mislaying her glass frequently.) The use here is both amusing and realistic. At one point Sir Ralph says, "I wish I had brought my Spectacles with me—Indeed I used formerly to wear 'em constantly; but when I was in London about two years ago, I found that Spectacles were a kind of dress with many of the young fops, and so I have not worn them since, but on particular occasions; for you know I hate new fashions."

To which Sir William remarks, "Hate most of all—the fashionable disregard that women pay their Husbands." Sir Ralph replies, "I do condemn it—but not as a new fashion, that is an old fashion—at least I know it has been in vogue ever since I married."

The conclusion of the play does bring Sir William and Lady Carrol together, even as he is about to return to India. She stands before the door, and when he turns her aside, she kneels before him and asks for "one Salute at parting—for the first you knelt—I kneel for the last." Sir Ralph can hardly believe his eyes: "But is she actually upon her knees—I am afraid you don't see right."

Henley, Louisa's intended husband, sums up the sentiments of those who witnessed the events of the play when he concludes: "And now Sir William & Lady Carrol, I hope you will pardon me; but having been a witness of your conduct as man & wife, for one day only; I have seen so many sorrows & tormenting passions of every kind, incumbent on the State of Matrimony, that I here abjure the thought of Wedlock, and bestow my intended Bride on Mr. Wildlove."

All on a Summer's Day, for all its problems of content, is dramatically one of the most tightly controlled of Inchbald's plays. The setting is in one place, Sir William's estate. The events on stage take place from morning in Lady Carrol's dressing room to just after dinner. There is very little explanation of situations or scenes, with the exception of the appearance of Governor Moreton, Louisa, and Lord Henley. The action, though it does not conform to the classical unity, does center around Lady Carrol and Wildlove and their mischief, thus completing the idea of "time, place, and action" and giving a unity that Inchbald does not always achieve.

On December 8 Inchbald's friend John Philip Kemble married Priscilla Brereton, the widow of William Brereton, who had died in February. Priscilla was the daughter of William Hopkins and his wife Elizabeth. Hopkins was the prompter at Drury Lane, and Elizabeth was an actress there. Inchbald certainly had known Priscilla for quite some time, and in the years to come they were to become special friends.

When *All on a Summer's Day* failed on December 15, the year was coming to an end. Christmas was filled with the pantomime, and the usual familiar plays all brought 1787 to a close.

ANIMAL MAGNETISM

The spring of 1788 continued the great success of 1787 and the two plays *Such Things Are* and *The Midnight Hour.* In March of 1788 Le Texier and Harris brought Mrs. Inchbald a comedy that they called *Animal Magnetism;* it proved to be one of the most popular and frequently performed plays of all of Inchbald's work. Le Texier brought it to her on March 3, and she finished it on March 19; it was put in rehearsal at once; like *The Midnight Hour,* it was by Dumaniant. For *Animal Magnetism* we have Inchbald's own account of the way she worked. In the entries of her 1788 pocket-book, she says she worked on translating. She was always working, but on March 3, when Le Texier brought *Animal Magnetism* to her, she began to translate it at once, and she sometimes did not like what she had done and revised it the next day. In the case of this play, it would seem that she spent as much time copying it as she did translating, and during this whole time—some two weeks—she wrote, "denied to everyone." When it was finished, she wrote: "Fine and not cold—went over my French piece before I read the news. Mr. Texier came for it. After dinner and in the evening I cleaned out my closet drawers &c. . . . Mr. Davis just call'd and Etty brought me a piece of fish—read after supper." At the end of such a task, she frequently cleaned her "closet drawers" and had someone bring her supper. This pattern of professional work and domestic life is an interesting and significant feature of the pocket-books. Inchbald was not able to separate her daily life from her daily work.

Having done the play and given it to Le Texier, Inchbald went to the first reading. Afterward she wrote, "Liked it much." Inchbald was always a part of the reading and production of her work, even though she did not always play a part on stage. This time Le Texier came once more; she said, "Mr. T. called with my piece just as I dined—at dusk carried it to the house—talked with Mr. and Mrs. Lewis at their window." Becky Wells had the female lead in *Animal Magnetism,* and on the Monday after Inchbald turned in the play, Wells and Topham came to talk "sometime."

Animal Magnetism is a three-act farce concerned with a quack doctor and his ward, Constance, whom he intends to marry. She has no intention of marrying him, however; instead she falls in love with a young marquis who haunts the street under her window. Constance has a maid, Lisette, and the marquis has a servant, La Fleur. The four young people are more than a match for the doctor, who is never given a name other than the doctor. Constance, confined to the house, must find ways to communicate with the marquis and La Fleur. Lisette is not only her confidante; she is also involved with La Fleur and he with her. The devices Inchbald uses to plot the story are traditional—concealed letters, conversations at windows, plots to disguise. A wand said to be magic—to have animal magnetism—is the chief device of the play and is used by the young people to entrap and then defeat the doctor.

The contemporary interest in this play centers around the much-discussed theories of the Swiss physician Anton Mesmer, whose work coined a word, *mesmerism,* and who suggested that there was a force emanating from animals that could be used as "animal Magnetism" to have a hypnotic effect. In the case of the Inchbald play, the hypnotic effect was brought about by Constance, the marquis, and their servants.

The usual devices are the substance of the plot: letters are exchanged under great difficulty, and the doctor's servant Jeffery wants to "salute" Lisette in exchange for the key to the garden and then, after kissing her, refuse her the key. The doctor, as the epitome of the charlatan, is nicely drawn. He has been refused a diploma, and as he enters, he complains: "They [the faculty] have refused to grant me a *diploma;* forbid me to practice as a physician, and all because I do not know a parcel of insignificant words; but exercise my profession according to the rules of *reason* and *nature*—Is it not natural to die? Then, if a dozen or two of my patients *have* died under my hands, is not that natural?"

Lisette: Very natural, indeed.

Doctor: But, thank Heav'n, in spite of the scandalous reports of my enemies; I have this morning, nine visits to make.

Constance: Very true, Sir, a young ward, has sent for you to attend his Guardian;—three nephews have sent for you to attend their uncles, very rich men; and five husbands have sent for you, in the greatest haste, to attend their wives.

Doctor: And is not that a sign they think what I can do? . . . I have made overtures to one of their most profest enemies, a man whom they have crush'd, and who is the chief of a sect just sprung up, of which, perhaps, you never heard; for simply, by the power of *Magnetism,* they can cure any ill; or inspire any passion.

Constance: Is it possible!

Doctor: Yes—and every effect is produc'd upon the frame, merely by the power of the Magnet, which is held in the hand of the Physician, as the wand of a conjurer is held in his; and it produces wonders in physic, equally surprising.

After such a speech as this, Inchbald's audience would undoubtedly have thought of two "Doctors" in London that had practiced just such a trick. One was James Graham and the other Katterfelto; both practiced in London in the early 1780s and in the provinces a few years later. A print shows them confronting each other, each extolling their own abilities and instruments "as [bringing] all good things of sex, health, and well being."[34]

James Graham, a Scotsman, appeared in London in 1779 after having lived in America, where he had offered milk baths, electrical treatments, and such. In London he found a house in Adelphi Terrace and established the "Temple of Health." It was a spectacular place, with guards at the entrance dressed in livery and inside a suite of beautifully furnished rooms, where there were in attendance goddesses of youth and beauty dressed in silk robes. One of these attendants was in the future to become Lady Hamilton.

Inside his "Temple" Graham gave lectures about health, which included the topics of sex and procreation. The most dramatic offering he provided was Graham's Celestial Bed, a construction twelve feet long and nine feet wide with a domed canopy "supported by forty pillars of brilliant glass of the most exquisite workmanship in richly variegated colors." Said to have cost two thousand pounds to build, it could be had for a night for fifty pounds, with the assurance that the scientifically constructed apparatuses would, as he said, make the barren "cer-

tainly become fruitful when they are powerfully agitated in the delight of love."
The other "doctor," Katterfelto, identified himself as being "the greatest philosopher in the kingdom since Sir Issac Newton." He gave lectures and showed experiments using trick illustration with a microscope, and he sold Dr. Bato's medicine
at five shillings a bottle after his lectures. In his lectures he claimed that he instructed on "mathematics, optics, magnetism, electricity, chemistry, pneumatics,
hydraulics, hydrostatics . . . and such obscure knowledge as 'proetics' 'stynacraphy,'
and 'caprimancy,'" entirely invented out of his head.[35]

The doctor in *Animal Magnetism* is not quite so "learned" as Graham and
Katterfelto; indeed, he must be instructed: when he asks, "Will you indulge me
with the smallest specimen of your art," La Fleur replies, "there is an universal
fluid, which spreads throughout all nature—."

> *Doctor:* A fluid!
> *La Fleur:* Yes—a fluid—which is a fluid—and you know, Doctor, that this
> fluid—generally called a fluid—is the most subtle of all that—is the
> most subtle.—Do you understand me? . . . It ascends on *high,* (*looking
> down*) and descends on *low,* (*looking up*) penetrates all substances, from
> the hardest metal, to the softest bosom—You understand me, I perceive?
> *Doctor:* Not very well.
> *La Fleur:* I will give you a simile then.
> *Doctor:* I shall be much oblig'd to you.
> *La Fleur:* This fluid is like a river.—You know what a river is?
> *Doctor:* Yes, yes.
> *La Fleur:* This fluid is like a river, that—that—runs—that goes—that
> gently glides—so, so, so—while there is nothing to stop it.—But if it
> encounters a mound, or any other impediment—Boo, boo, boo,—it
> bursts forth—it overflows the country round;—throws down villages,
> hamlets, houses, trees, cows, and lambs.—But remove this obstacle
> which obstructs its course, and it begins again softly and sweetly to
> flow;—thus, thus, thus—the fields are again adorned, and every thing
> goes on, as well as it can go on.—Thus it is with the *Animal Fluid,*
> which fluid obeys the command of my art.

La Fleur tells the doctor he can give him the most "excruciating rheumatism,"
or the gout or a raging fever to show him how the animal magnetism works; the
doctor declines the demonstration. And when La Fleur suggests further that he, La
Fleur, is attending a dying man who might be brought to the doctor to show the
healing powers, the doctor asks, "Pray, Doctor, is it true what they report, that he,

who is once in possession of your art, can, if he pleases, make every woman who comes near him, in love with him?" La Fleur answers, "True—certainly it is."

The guardian/doctor, however, is not the only problem the young people have to solve; after all, neither Constance nor Lisette has spoken or written to the marquis or La Fleur; but La Fleur, posing as the cult doctor, after "instructing" the doctor manages to communicate with Constance and Lisette. They make elaborate plans to deceive the doctor. The marquis will be brought in as a patient and the doctor given a "magic" wand. All proceeds as planned.

In the second act the doctor appears with the wand in his hand. Constance is ready and Lisette with her. This scene must have been hilarious on stage in the hands of skillful players. The doctor ogles Constance; Lisette prompts her to sigh and return his look, sighing all the while, and the ensuing dialogue is interspersed with asides to the audience after almost every speech. When Constance, pretending to respond to the wand, declares that she loves him, Lisette declares, "And I adore you." The doctor is completely overcome.

As the doctor becomes more and more frightened, Lisette kneels and declares: "Ah, sir, behold the state to which you have reduced a poor innocent—If I am treated with kindness, I am naturally soft, gentle and tender.—But if I am neglected—by all that's great and precious, I will do some strange thing—either to you, or to my rival!"

When Jeffery appears and the doctor gives him the wand, the girls repeat their declarations of passion. The doctor is more frightened than ever—"This is worse and worse.—Where is the Doctor, if he does not come, and give me some relief, I am a ruined man." Even as he speaks, La Fleur, still dressed as the cult doctor, comes in leading the marquis. Again the scene is full of comic action as La Fleur not only plays with the doctor but also attempts to speak to Lisette and to Constance. This double action brings the audience into the plot, especially as they see the marquis, as the pretend patient, have a pretend fit, a seizure, that frightens the doctor even more than the effect of the "love" scene.

The third act continues the devices of the disguises; the marquis has La Fleur change places with him and feign death, at which point the marquis brings in two more pretend doctors from the tavern in the next street. The doctor, when confronted by the marquis and the two disguised doctors, stands in front of La Fleur, now pretending to be dead, and knows he is responsible for the death of his first patient. When the marquis reveals himself and the whole scheme, the doctor agrees to anything: "Only deliver me from this trouble, and I will sign it without reading it at all."

There must, however, be a coda to the action. Constance pretends that she is still in love with the doctor—"how cou'd I wed another while he [looking at the doctor] is the object of my love?" The doctor replies, "But consider, my dear Constance, that I am old, ugly, jealous, and infirm—indeed I am—I am, I protest, Constance." It is at this point that La Fleur rises up from the "dead." The doctor has been twice tricked. Youth, love, and beauty have triumphed as the marquis has the last word: "for believe me Doctor, there is no Magnetism, like the powerful Magnetism of Love."

THE CHILD OF NATURE

The theatre year—season—was not the calendar year, and in the fall Harris brought her yet another piece; this time it was by Madame the Marchioness of Sillery, formerly countess of Genlis. She received it in early November and in ten days had it ready for performance. It was given on November 11 and, like *The Midnight Hour* and *Animal Magnetism*, it was a great success.

The Child of Nature was in four acts, and when it was printed, the title page called it "A Dramatic Piece." In the advertisement, which is reprinted in the Backscheider edition of the plays, the translation is explained:

ZÉLIE, the French piece, from which the Child of Nature has been taken, was, with great taste, selected from the dramatic works of the Marchioness of Sillery (late Countess of Genlis) by a Lady, who presented the Manager of Covent-Garden Theatre with a *literal translation*—but however correct or elegant, *a mere translation* must have precluded all prospect of success—the Manager therefore sent the play of *Zélie* to the present translator, who with much care and attention, prepared it for the English stage—That care has been amply recompensed by the reception the piece has met, and more especially in those parts of it which she has taken the liberty to add from her own invention.

For Inchbald the "add from her own invention" is the key to this play, as to the others she adapted. In some cases she added characters (*Lovers' Vows*); in some cases the manuscript shows how she marked through and changed words and passages. In *The Child of Nature*, the comedy of Count Valantia, his schemes and views, she added.

He is Inchbald's usual young man, full of tricks to have the women he fancies. As the first scene opens, we discover that an accident has left his carriage with a broken wheel, but as soon as the servant has gone to have it repaired, it turns out that he has broken it himself. His friend Granada speaks sharply to him:

All this stratagem and mystery looks very much like some scheme contrived by love; yet that's not probable, as you are on the point of marriage with a lady of fortune, family, and beauty, and of whom you have always professed to be enamoured—and yet, within a few weeks of your union, you quit Madrid and her, come post to this village, and as soon as you arrive in the sight of the castle order me to break one of the wheels of your carriage, and then run to the house and ask for assistance to mend it—which they kindly grant, and your Lordship rejoices at the progress of your adventure—which, if not love, is something like madness.

The count confesses that he is there for "Love." Granada asks, "Do you then not love your intended bride, the beautiful Marchioness?" The count replies: "The Marchioness Merida is a charming creature! and I loved her passionately! to distraction!—till I found she loved me, and that satiated my desires at once. . . . I do not say I shall not marry the Marchioness—perhaps I may—yes, I may take her fortune—for you know, Granada, I have none of my own. . . . I once loved; doated upon Merida—but the first time she kindly condescended to declare her passion for *me,* I fell asleep."

Inchbald's variations on "the silly young man" seem endless; Count Valantia is one of the most amusing and one that fits the comments of the other characters and helps to move the plot along.

The adventure the count has come to seek is a strange one. He has written to Amanthis, an orphan who has been sheltered and brought up by the Marquis Almanza, who has never let any living creature behold her or speak to her. She has never been seen except by the marquis and the old duenna who cares for her. The fame of her beauty has gone abroad, and the count wants to "find out whether she was that prodigy or not; and *if* she was, to share the honour of her belonging to me, as well as to him [the marquis]."

The count and his "Adventure" makes only a very small part of the story; Amanthis and her story are far more important. She is seventeen when we meet her. She has had no contact with the outside world, having been taught entirely by the marquis and the books he has selected for her to read; and indeed, everything about her has been a great mystery, kept secret even from the marquis's family. Duke Murcia, the marquis's uncle, asks: "But what kind of an education can she have received in such a confinement?" The conversation turns to books—"books of every kind." It seems the servant has never heard her speak, but he receives in writing every morning her written orders for the day. The servant reports that the marquis, when he is in town, sends her books—all handwritten—books of mortality, divinity, history; he is unwilling for her to see printed books. She also gives orders for pens and papers and orders for different pieces of music. The household is properly appointed with "Dinner and supper at the usual hours—and coffee at six o'clock."

The duke inquires of the servant about the situation, and when the marquis appears with two ladies, he is surprised; but one of the ladies is the Marchioness Merida with a female attendant. The marchioness has been told about Valantia and knows about the broken carriage. The servant confirms, "Yes, Madam; but I hope your Ladyship will pardon me—I have since learnt that his attendant was seen to take a large ax from a portmanteau, with which he chopped in pieces the wheel, and then called for help." There is no secret about Valantia.

After the marchioness leaves the stage, the duke and the marquis have a conversation in which we discover that the duke adopted the marquis upon his father's death and gave him a most "rigorous" education. The duke asks, "did I suffer you to squander your money? . . . did I ever let you have any? . . . did I ever comply with any of your foolish weaknesses?—Is there a single indulgence you can lay to my charge? . . . Then do you not feel for me that respect, that reverence, that fear, and that love, which is due for all my kindness to you?" The marquis assures him that he does give him thanks and credit. The duke, however, wants proof, proof that the behavior of the marquis toward the young woman is honorable. The marquis explains that she has been in his care for thirteen years, since her father, his friend, had to flee the country, leaving an infant daughter. The duke does not understand, asking why the marquis has locked her up. The marquis's speech is the center of the play.

In replying to the duke, he says: "The mode of her education has been an after-thought entirely—Alberto, with all the virtues for which I esteemed him, was a jealous, suspicious nature; and, in respect to female reputation, rigorously romantic—As Amanthis grew up I saw with dread the charge I had undertaken, and the reported death of my friend increased my apprehensions for my trust—I had vowed to protect, to guard her; to whom could I transfer the oath?"

The marquis admits that he has fallen in love with the beautiful Amanthis but that he is about to release her to her own life and choices. The second act reveals the marquis in the garden leading Amanthis to the outside. She protests, "Why will you take me from my retreat? did not you say I should stay here as long as I was pleased with it?—and as long as I loved you? Ah! I expected to stay here for ever."

In his reply the marquis says, "I must show you to the world—we were born for society, and you will be the ornament and delight of that which you shall make your choice." At this strange change in him she is upset: "You did not talk thus to me always—nor do you look with such tenderness upon me as you used to do—while you speak I can see you are not pleased, or not happy; and it gives me a sorrow I hardly know how to bear." She declares, "And you are the *only* object I love—and the only one I ever can love."

Marquis: Do not promise that—when you have seen the world, some other, more deserving—

Amanthis: Oh! do not go on—I cannot bear you should have such unjust suspicions—do not *you* see the world? and yet I believe you prefer me to all the universe besides—when I am there; why cannot you then confide in me, as I have done in you?

The scene is not over. The marquis tells her that she is about to meet a young man, and she replies that she has seen a young man she has not told him about. When the marquis asks her to explain, she replies: "It was only about a week ago, as I was sitting by the little bower near the garden wall, suddenly I heard an unknown voice call me by my name—it seemed to come from the air—I looked up, and beheld a young man upon the wall—the moment I recovered from my fright, I asked him what he wanted—he said he came 'to look at me'—but that appeared so strange!—I could not think it true—and then he gazed on me so wildly, I ran away and hid myself—on which he drew a letter from his pocket, and threw it after me—I would not take it up till he had gone—then I caught it, and flew to my apartments; pleased beyond expression."

The letter is a clever spoof of the rising romantic view of "love" mixed with the silly affectations practiced by the "smart" young beaux about London. In some instances it is hardly exaggerated. It reads: "Know, beautiful Amanthis, there is no retreat, however hidden, into which love cannot penetrate—The hope of beholding you has made me brave every danger, and overcome every difficulty—if you will but kindly pity a passion, pure as it is extreme, it shall soon inspire me with the means to release you from the tyranny of that barbarian, who keeps you secluded from every joy that's waiting to attend you in a happy world. Conceal this adventure from the jealous tyrant, and reflect, that the most tender lover waits impatiently for the happy moment to prove himself your deliverer."

The tyrant holding her away from a "happy world" will be overcome by an unknown lover—tender, passionate, pure. The marquis, returning the letter, asks what she thinks of it.

Amanthis: That the poor man is mad—and yet it is a kind of madness I never heard of before. [*Reading part of the letter.*] "There is no retreat into which love cannot penetrate."—what does he mean by love? he has left out a word—there is—*love of virtue*—*love of duty*—but love all alone by itself, means nothing at all—Then again, [*Reading.*] "Conceal this adventure from the jealous tyrant"—Who does he mean by tyrant?
Marquis: He means me.

Amanthis: You? I never should have supposed it—perhaps you know also
  what he means by a "lover." He says, "the most tender lover"—read,
  and tell me what he means by a tender lover—Ah! you laugh—you are
  puzzled—you don't know yourself what a "lover" is.

Amanthis is very like Shakespeare's Miranda in *The Tempest,* for, like Miranda,
she has never had any contact with the outside world, never any knowledge of
men, either worthy or unworthy. Miranda, seeing Ferdinand for the first time,
exclaims, "What is it a spirit. . . . Believe me, sir, it carries a brave form. . . . I might
call him a thing divine; for nothing natural I ever saw so noble." And later when
she asks him, "Do you love me?" he answers "Beyond all limit of what else i'th'
world / Do love, praise, honour you."[36] Like Miranda, Amanthis has been not
only protected but also instructed by the only man she knows, and when he tells
her she must leave her sheltered place and go to the part of the castle that is
inhabited, the dialogue between them becomes serious and passionate.

Amanthis: But shall I have the liberty to return sometimes and look at
  this—my heart aches to leave a place I have been so happy in.—Oh,
  my dear, dear Lord, you know not half I feel." [*Puts her hand before her
  eyes to hide her tears.*]
Marquis: Beloved Amanthis, be not thus uneasy; I cannot bear to see it—
  for your happiness is dearer to me than my life.
Amanthis: Say that you love me then—will you repeat it often too? as often,
  when I am in the world, as you have done here?
Marquis: Ah, do not doubt it—you are all to me—I have no other thought,
  no other wish—object of all my cares, of all my schemes, of all my
  hopes—and I prefer, to every other blessing, that most delicious one, to
  see, to hear you speak, and to suppose you love me.

As she leaves and he is alone on stage, he says: "With what difficulty have I
restrained myself from falling at her feet, and unfolding (in a language, of which
she is ignorant) the secret transports I mean ever to conceal."

Even as he speaks, the Marchioness Merida appears and says, "I have seen
her; I have just had a peep at her—but I see nothing extraordinary—She wants
powder, rouge, and a thousand adornments."

Marquis: To change one atom, would be to lose a charm.
Marchioness: By no means—I think a girl of seventeen may very well have
  an affection for a man of forty.
Marquis: I am not forty, Madam.

Marchioness: The lover again—one moment lamenting his age, and when
reproached with it, proclaims himself a youth—the whole matter is, my
Lord, you are not too old to be in love, nor she too young to understand it.

Marquis: She knows not what it is—never heard of love, as you would
explain it—but calls, by that name, Gratitude.

The conversation between the marquis and the marchioness continues as they
see Valantia coming. The marchioness is upset with Valantia. She knows he is there
under the pretense of a broken wheel, but she suspects there is some other reason as
well. She resolves to quarrel with him. The marquis is aware of Valantia's scheme.

Acts 3 and 4 continue the discussions about love—and passion. In passage
after passage, the discussion between various characters tries to define love that is
gratitude or love as passion or indeed love as fashion. Amanthis in several of the
scenes is the protagonist for the highest and most ideal qualities of response, for
although she does not understand how to define love in the terms of the other
characters, she knows in her heart, in her natural response the meaning of true
love; the others—the marquis, the marchioness, Valantia, Duke Murcia, all define
love in different and flawed terms.

As act 3 begins, Duke Murcia and the marquis are discussing Amanthis and
her situation. She has no family, and her father is in exile, a fugitive who, the
count reminds the marquis, "may return home to disgrace you."

Marquis: The misfortunes of Amanthis can never make her less dear to me.

Duke: But would you ally yourself with such a family—would you plunge
your own into shame and sorrow?

Marquis: My Lord, I have often promised, and believed, that to the respect
I bear my family, I would sacrifice every selfish consideration; but, on a
farther trial of my strength, I own to you, it is only from the idea I am
not beloved by Amanthis, I can ever resolve to yield her up; for could I
suppose she loved me, all other happiness, all pride, all ambition, all
enjoyment, but in her, I would forego with transport.

Duke: And as all lovers are apt to believe what they so ardently wish—I see
what your family has to expect.

Marquis: You mistake—hope never was more distant from my heart than at
this moment.—All the affection she expresses, although the most
ardent, tender, and endearing, I can see is but inspired by gratitude—of
love, she knows nothing.

Duke: Whose fault is that? were not you her tutor?

Marquis: Certainly.

Duke: And taught her every thing but what you wanted her to learn—but now if any body else should teach it her, what would you say to that, would you give your consent to their union?

Marquis: The instant she makes a choice worthy of her, from that instant I stifle my love for ever—Do you imagine I would oppose her happiness? No—I was her father, before I was her lover.

The marquis's sentiments in this speech are echoed later for Inchbald in *A Simple Story* when she examines and develops the love and growing passion of Miss Milner for her guardian. The questions asked in *The Child of Nature* were much discussed or—perhaps a better word—presented in the novels of the 1780s and 1790s. Inchbald is using Genlis's original, but she is also making characters suitable to her audience. The marchioness and Valantia are stereotypical, but Amanthis is not, and the marquis, revealing his sentiments, is more than the usual sentimental "fool."

The conversation between the duke and the marquis has presented yet an-other item in the contemporary view of love and marriage, that is, that money and family are quite as important as any feeling of love or passion. Amanthis under-stands nothing of the practical aspects of marriage, nor can she understand the actions of the count. She has still—into the third act—been only introduced to him, still sees him as a kind of madman "with that strange kind of wild behaviour"; she asks, "is he admitted into company?" Their conversation, like the conversation between the marquis and Amanthis, is at cross-purposes. Even so, we learn more about the "child of nature" as Amanthis exclaims: "Oh! I am very unhappy! . . . all my pleasures turned to sorrows. . . . And what is liberty when it takes from me the company of him that was dearer to me than life—or brings him to me with a clouded brow, and a heavy heart?—But this moment he flew away abruptly, and frowned when I asked to follow him, although he knows how I have been fright-ened by a young man some time ago, who is now in the house."

When the marchioness realizes she means the count as the young madman, the marchioness advises her to say she hates him. But Amanthis refuses lest she make him "uneasy," and when she says she pities him, the marchioness tells her that that would be the worst of all because it will make him "outrageous."

Amanthis: Will it?—*You* then have told him so? . . . I'll *stay* and tell him what I think of him.

Marchioness: And what *is* that?

Amanthis: That he makes me tremble.

Marchioness: You must not say *so*.

Amanthis obviously understands nothing of the behavior of "lovers," and when she is left with the count in the following scene, he misunderstands her quite as much as she misunderstands him. He thinks that when she says "I wish to give you hope" and that she will send for a priest "to comfort" him, she is giving him her favor. The ensuing dialogue shows again how naive she is.

Count: A priest—will you then make me blest?
Amanthis: If I can—for I assure you I like you very well—and, did you not
    behave so strangely, I should like you better; for you are very hand-
    some—therefore be not uneasy, and think you are not admired; for I
    can see that would vex you more than anything.
Count: You admire me then? transporting happiness!
Amanthis: Oh! now you are going to fright me again. [*Aside.*] I must steal
    away!
Count: You tremble and look pale—may I interpret these sweet emotions in
    my favour?
Amanthis: Yes, if you please.
Count: You then will make me happy?
Amanthis: I will do all I can.
Count: . . . Then know, angelic creature! you shall find in me, all that truth,
    that constancy, that everlasting flame—
Amanthis: Oh, terrible!—don't be in such a passion, pray.
Count: These moments are precious—Vow never again to shun me; never
    more to look unkindly; and I here swear the most perfect love—.

Upon this declaration she thinks again that he must be mad. She holds out a smelling bottle to him and says, "Here—smell of this bottle—it will do you good— it will relieve your head." When we next hear about their behavior, we have their conversation reported by the duke to the marquis. Here again, the report taken seriously by the count is the most absurd kind of scene. The duke saw the marquis and Amanthis together and heard the count "beg for compassion" and remind Amanthis of a promise she had given to make him happy, "on which she started and wept; and he fell upon his knees, and would have wept too, if he could; but as he found he could not, he did something more; and drawing his sword, pointed it at his heart. On this she shrieked more violently than if it had been aimed at her's; and, seizing hold of it, fell motionless into his arms."

The duke then describes how the marquis and he, having recovered her from her swoon, hear that the count has told the duke "that she had given him every hope she would be his, but had merely refused to name the time; which had enraged and drove him to such extremes." And when the count turned to her, the duke continues, the count cried, "'Pronounce, shall I live or die?'—She in a transport cried, 'Live, live by all means.'"

Upon this recital from the duke, the marquis is sure Amanthis has chosen the count and that his fate is sealed. In fact, knowing that the count has no money, he says he will give him half his own fortune. This, however, is no resolution of the problem, for Amanthis does not yet understand. The duke undertakes to instruct her about love, as she says, "I am, indeed, ignorant of what you mean."

> *Duke:* And 'tis so long ago since I felt it, I must recollect a little before I can tell you.—Amongst the passions, is one more troublesome than all the rest, and yet more pleasing than any of them—it sometimes burns you with heat—and sometimes freezes you with cold—it creates in your mind a constant desire to be with one particular person—and when you *are* with them, you generally look like a fool—you think them handsome, though they are frightfully ugly—you think them well made, though they are crooked—wise, though they are simpletons— and you hope they love you, though you are *sure* they do not.

After this speech Amanthis understands that she has the disorder herself, and when the duke says she must cure them and herself by marrying one of them, she says she chooses the marquis—never would she marry the count. Her declaration to the duke must be made to the marquis as well. In their conversation the marquis also speaks of love:

> *Marquis:* You are first to learn, there is a sentiment which governs the human heart with more tyranny, more force, more outrage, and yet more softness, than any other—it is called love—and why its name and nature I have thus long concealed from you, was from the apprehension that in the solitude where you lived, the sensibility of your heart might cause dangerous illusions—I feared you might take the tender, calm ties of friendship for love's superior passion; and seeing none but me, I should consequently become the object of your error. . . . For these four years I have concealed a passion for you of the tenderest, truest, kind— but your heart decides for another. . . .

The marquis is so deeply involved within himself that he cannot perceive any situation for himself. She is indignant, and her speech in which she accuses him of degrading her, of insulting her feelings, adds to the complexity of the discussion here: "Learn, my Lord, to be less suspicious—affect less generosity and moderation, and be less ungrateful and unjust." When he does begin to understand, she declares: "Yes, that passion, though unknown for what it was, has been the joy, the happiness of my life—it reconciled me to my solitude, and now could make the hardest lot with you a blessing." But love declared by the marquis and Amanthis is not enough; we must consider the families. Amanthis is considered unsuitable since her father is in exile and in disgrace. At this point two strangers dressed as peasants enter, and we are confronted with yet another eighteenth-century dilemma.

Following the tradition of an infinite number of problems and situations, we are now, almost at the end of the "love" plot, confronted with an entirely new question, or set of questions. Should Amanthis, confronted with a man, her father, in rags as a beggar, accept him and go away with him? It is this final part of the play that is completely sentimental and remote from later views of filial response. Having learned about passion, must Amanthis go back to the traditional absolute loyalty. She does so and leaves with him, thinking that he is as he appears to be. He, of course, is not, and in the end he reveals that he has been in India, has been exonerated, and is possessed of a fortune. We have concluded with an excessively sentimental scene, one that does not fit, one that is simply tacked on to include the "moral" of filial "love." After the reconciliation of father and daughter, friend and friend, the last situation of the play finds the duke approving of the marriage of the marquis and Amanthis and the witty agreement that as long as the marchioness does not "love" the count, he will marry her.

In the epilogue, spoken by Mrs. Mattocks, who played the part of the marchioness, the first lines are revealing:

> Men are strange things—'twere happy cou'd we scout 'em,
> Make up our minds, and fairly do without 'em.
> The cautious dame prefers a single life,
> The antient maiden to the anxious wife. . . .
> Trace the gay circles, and you'll rarely prove
> That wedlock suffers from immod'rate love.

The epilogue, probably commissioned by Harris, is by Miles Peter Andrews. He draws a contrast between the "Child of Nature" in the past and the present. The epilogue continues an invention Andrews uses in several plays. He describes a family, the Dripping family, used here to satirize the middle class. In the past:

> The simple dress, the bloom that art wou'd shame,
> The frank avowal, and the gen'rous flame;

The native note, which, sweetly warbling wild,
Told the soft sorrows of the charming child—
Turn to a modern Miss, whose feather'd brow
Speaks the light surface of the soil below,
Whose little nose its due concealment keeps,
And o'er a muslin mountain barely peeps,
Taught by Signor to squall she knows not what,
Thumping the harpsichord, is all she's at.
"Papa," a true John Bull, cries, "Nancy, sing—
Give us my fav'rite tune, 'God save the King.'"
Miss, simp'ring says, "Pa,' now I'm grown a woman,
I can't sing English music, it's so common;
But, if you please, I'll give you a bravara,
For Signor says I soon shall equal Mara."

The epilogue ends:

Thus are the feelings of the youthful day,
By fashion's raging tempest whirl'd away:—
May I, but with no wish to under-rate her,
Entreat you to prefer our Child of Nature?

Miles Peter Andrews, like his friend Topham, was well known for his epilogues; he had created a family—the Dripping family—to use as a basis of his
comments. The father was a merchant, the mother very ambitious for herself and
her daughters to "rise" in society. Such a situation made a nice comment on some
of the plays. He supplied epilogues for *Such Things Are, Every One Has His Fault,*
and *Animal Magnetism* as well as for *The Child of Nature.*

EIGHT

1788–1789

✏ The years 1787–1788 were the years of Inchbald's great success, and in 1789, when she left the theatre as an actress, she continued that success. She acted very little during the 1788–1789 season, spending her time on writing or translating plays for Harris and Texier. Her pocket-book for the year 1788 documents her busy professional and social life. She sees friends she has known since before she came to London and Covent Garden, and she records those friends she has made after her successes. The entries about the theatre and her work on plays and translations not only are a valuable record for theatre history, but these many references also show her constant attention to her work and her professional willingness to work with other people. This constant writing and revising mark her as a true professional, willing to consider suggestions, willing to discard or to change her version of a play or a farce. It is not surprising that she was called upon repeatedly.

The report of her social life in the 1788 pocket-book is interesting for the people and places she records, but it also gives a kind of close-up view of the interaction between the players and their audiences. The connections and interconnections, the stories of triumphs and scandals, the combinations of playwrights and politics. By this time Sheridan was in Parliament, and both Kemble and Harris were keenly aware of both the audience and the government. The perception of the events of national concern seems more real and understandable from her entries than from any newspaper or periodical record.

The pocket-book beginning in January always divides the theatre season into two parts and therefore, in this case, indicates which plays Inchbald has done for 1788 and which ones she is working on for 1789. In January of 1788 *Such Things Are* was playing, as was *The Midnight Hour.* Harris was out of town, gone to Bath; she was reading the *Rambler,* and she was seeing Sir Charles, who called twice but did not come up until her brother, who was with her, had left. Sir Charles and his attention continue to be mentioned throughout this 1788 pocket-book, adding an interesting subplot to her other activities.

In 1788, long after the events of 1769, when Bunbury was seeing Inchbald almost every day, they must at some point have talked of his marriage. In 1776 he received a divorce by order of Parliament, but at first, soon after his wife, Lady Sarah, went away, he asked for a judicial separation in Doctors' Commons; that is, his lawyers filed a suit for libel asking for a separation. Such a case required that witnesses testify to the fact of Sarah's adultery. With Sarah in Scotland and with much of the case public knowledge already, it was easy to call the servants from Barton to testify; the evidence was uncontested, and Bunbury was granted a legal separation. Not until 1776 did Bunbury file in Parliament to be granted a divorce, a very costly procedure; then in 1781 Sarah married again, this time by her own choice, to George Napier, an officer in the army, and in 1785 Louisa Bunbury, living in Ireland with her mother and stepfather, died of consumption.

The entries in Inchbald's 1788 pocket-book about Bunbury are scattered throughout the weeks and months, except when she records that he has left London for Barton or when he goes to Newmarket. If he had neglected Lady Sarah and their marriage, leaving her to go to house parties and horse races, he had by 1788 become almost entirely identified with the Jockey Club and racing. There are several references about races and Race Week in the pocket-book. In May Inchbald went with her friends the Whitfields and the Lewises to Epsom Downs. They left early, went to the morning races, dined there, and went to the races again in the afternoon, returning in time to see her *Animal Magnetism*, which was then playing. The next day, a Saturday, Sir Charles called after tea, and the next day on her way to dinner and tea at Mr. Babb's, she saw Sir Charles in Kensington Gardens.

Sir Charles called upon her frequently after tea or in the evening while she worked, sometimes coming from the city, and one Friday he "came from the City and Old Bailey." Several times he came from the theatre—either Drury Lane or Covent Garden—between the plays. Once he came after seeing the last two acts of *Jane Shore* at Drury Lane. Her *Midnight Hour* was playing the third week of January, and on Tuesday of that week she was in the box and then in the pit with Mr. Marlow and saw Sir Charles in a stage box. The next week on Monday Sir Charles called between the play and the farce at Drury Lane, and on Thursday, while her *Midnight Hour* was playing by "King's Command," Sir Charles was with her "from eight to ten reading while I worked."

All these entries about how she spent her evenings indicate a pattern in her relationship with Sir Charles and suggest the kind of "at home" evenings she and her friends spent. Evidently her relationship with Sir Charles at this point was one of easy familiarity as she worked and he read. Sometimes with other friends she read aloud as they passed the time pleasantly.

The entries in the pocket-books are always short and frequently cryptic, which, of course, means that they were simply reminders to her of people and events she remembered in detail; the pocket-books are simply memoranda, but there are phrases she uses that suggest more than they explain. During these winter and spring weeks of 1788, she records more than once that Sir Charles was "violent." On a Saturday night she says, "While I worked [Sir Charles] was violent before he went." The following week on Monday, January 28, Sir Charles told her of his "supposed" daughter. Then the next night he attended the play, sitting in a box near the stage while she played. And on the following night Sir Charles was "here all evening claimed my promise." Her promise must have been making love.

Inchbald is very discreet even in her little books. She never mentions anything personal about sexual behavior, either about herself or the men with whom she was friends. It seems very likely, however, given the circumstances of Sir Charles and Inchbald at this time, that they were having an affair. He was seeing her almost every night, and she was expecting him. On a Wednesday in early February she remarked, "and not till ten and I had given him over Sir Charles came—company had detained him." On February 11, "Sir Charles came at eight and staid till ten . . . told me he was going to Suffolk tomorrow— . . . very dull when he left me till Davis came and suppt."

When he was in town Sir Charles went to the theatre almost every night or to Mrs. Inchbald; sometimes he did both. The references to the theatres in this pocket-book are further proof of the way people of all ranks and classes attended the plays. The king and his family attended usually once a week. He liked comedy and attended Covent Garden regularly; Sir Charles and his friends went to both theatres, sometimes on the same night, since they could choose to see a main play at one and a farce at another. Mrs. Inchbald, still acting at Covent Garden, went to Drury Lane when she was not required at her own stage; even when her plays were being performed, she did not always go to see them either from the front or backstage.

Inchbald reports about both theatres in quite a casual way. At Covent Garden she went to hear Lady Wallace's play read. On Tuesday, April 8, she "was in the Gallery Slips with Mr. Marlow at Lady Wallace's new comedy condemned." The next day, however, she says, "saw Lady Wallace's comedy advertised again," and the next day after, a Thursday, she was behind at the second condemnation of Lady Wallace's play, *The Ton*. All through the spring, she continued to go to the theatres and to work on translations and plays, translations for Harris and Texier and plays of her own.

Whatever else she recorded, Inchbald recorded her work. Sometimes she was translating, sometimes she was "amending" her translation; sometimes she was pleased, sometimes not. On Monday, January 14, she says she "met with a gentleman at his house about a French piece"; Tuesday, "All the morning was reading the French piece"; Wednesday, "All the morning was translating the French piece." Sir Charles came in the evening while she worked, and "after translated till late." The next day she translated all morning, and on Friday she translated all morning and evening; on Saturday she "translated all." By the next Monday she evidently had finished translating, for she says, "Began copying and copied all evening till late." This week she continued to work, but she saw various people, and it was not until Saturday that she "copied all the morning"; this time she worked on Sunday copying again. She says, "I copied much after I came home." Earlier in the morning, young Chambers came and "spouted" to her, and she says Lord Pembroke was there at tea.

Reading her entries, we realize quite clearly the process of her work. Her handwriting was "cramped," and working at night by candlelight must have added to the physical strain. She was also acting during these days. On Monday, January 28, a dark and cloudy day, she went to rehearsal, on Tuesday in the morning she "overlooked" her translation, and that night she played. When she went home after the play, she says, "I sat up very late overlooking my last act." The next morning she sent her French piece to Harris, and Texier "call'd and staid sometime on business." On Wednesday she says she "received the French piece from Mr. Harris with Remarks." Her entry for the next day is significant: "was all day trying to amend the French piece but could not—slept after tea—then read the poem of Sympathy—very dull—try'd after supper but could not work." The next day she was still troubled, "did some improvement to the French piece—very dull at my disappointment—read and worked till tea then suppd."

Tuesday after the weekend when she had played in the "Positive Man," she turned to her "last written comedy." The French piece was not mentioned again until Friday when Harris called and "seemed to give up my French piece." Two days later Texier called with another French piece, which she immediately "sat up to read." The next day, Monday, February 18, she records that she read the French piece again and that Lewis sent for her to tell her that Harris returned her first French piece. This rejected piece was *Hue and Cry*. In February 1788, however, Inchbald did not give up easily.

The story of her work on *Hue and Cry*—her response to the difficulty of pleasing herself and Harris or Colman and her work with Texier—gives a vivid picture of her professional conduct. She quite understood the system: if Harris returned it, she would try Colman; if he too rejected it, she would put it aside and try at some later time. She was a writer, a professional writer, not a dilettante, and she understood that the theatre and the plays presented had to be pleasing to an audience, an audience Harris understood better than she. She was sometimes very upset with him, and she sometimes quarreled with him, but in the end he was the one person whose judgment she would accept.

Shortly after her disappointment about *Hue and Cry,* Texier left her another French piece. This piece was perhaps one for Texier himself, or at least a piece he wished for her to evaluate, since she says Texier called "to tell me he approved of my remarks on the comedy." Her entries are sometimes impossible to place, but Boaden, with more information before him, could be more specific. Sometimes even he does not identify all the pieces she worked on, pieces that show clearly her constant attention to the tasks she was given and those she set out for herself. Reading and evaluating the entries in her 1788 pocket-book is a very frustrating task. Did she do more than one for Texier that he commissioned for his own use? As we have said, she probably did. Did he pay her directly? She records that he came to her with his little girl; sometimes he is clearly a messenger from Harris, and sometimes Harris is not mentioned.

While she was writing and playing various roles on stage during the spring, she was looking for new lodgings. Inchbald, unlike many of her friends, never found a permanent lodging, moving about for various reasons; this time she was living in Great Russell Street, but for some reason she was looking for another lodging. On April 1 her sister Hunt came early to tell her about a lodging, but Inchbald said, "I found I need not leave this." This entry in the pocket-book is typical in its jumble of activities and visitors. After her sister left, "young Woodfall calld and we were correcting his prologue when Sir Charles calld and staid an hour—then Mr. Marlow call'd—after dinner young Woodfall again at dinner Mrs. Whitfield—I drank tea there—call'd on Mr. Lewis at the house—went back to supper he [Mr. Whitfield] at home. . . . Quick's night."

This Tuesday entry is followed by another equally interesting one: "Fine & dry—at 10 at the reading of Animal Magnetism pleased with the reception— call'd and saw many lodgings I liked—in the evening the new landlord of this house called on me and I partly agreed—call'd at the House—Fountableau and Midnight hour—Mrs. Mattocks night—a riot about Edwin."[1] "Quick's night" and "Mrs. Mattock's night" were their benefit nights, and since both of them were very popular players, they probably had good audiences. Mrs. Mattock had created the role of Flora in *The Midnight Hour* and was very soon to play Lisette in *Animal Magnetism.* Just what the "riot" was about Inchbald does not say. Edwin was frequently drunk, but that hardly seemed to matter on stage. He and Mattocks played together frequently; in fact, he was Nicolas in *The Midnight Hour* and was to be La Fleur in *Animal Magnetism.*

More than a week after the first reading of her *Animal Magnetism,* she was at the second reading; the day following, a Saturday, she was at the first rehearsal, and on Monday at another rehearsal. She was translating a speech for Edwin, but he did not come for it, so she left it at Texier's. She continues to record the rehearsals. On Monday, April 28, she wrote: "Very fine—in the front boxes at rehearsal of my piece. Mrs. Harris there and I vexed all the day." Her entry is as usual cryptic. It is probable, however, that she was vexed about Harris's paying her only 130 pounds for her work.

On Tuesday, April 29, she wrote: "Fine and warm—sick at rehearsal of my piece—several people call'd on me. Mrs. Hunt at dinner—behind at Animal Magnetism which went off with applause other pieces Rosina and Omar—supp'd with Mr. and Mrs. Whitfield." The play was a great success, and on Thursday she saw it from the members' box. On the Saturday following, she went to the bank with Mr. Marlow and Mrs. Whitfield; her friends always supported her, and it is interesting that she usually took someone with her when she went to the bank, since it was in the city, quite far from Covent Garden.

Mrs. Whitfield's brother, Mr. Lane, was visiting her in London, and on Sunday Mrs. Inchbald, Mrs. Whitfield, and Mr. Lane went to dinner and tea at Mr. Babb's, where they found Mr. and Mrs. King and Miss Baker. The Whitfields remained her best friends, and she saw the Kings frequently, and their Sundays at Mr. Babb's had come to be a tradition. The Whitfields had been out of town in the summer of 1784, when Inchbald had her first success with *A Mogul Tale.* They had returned to London in 1786, and Mr. Whitfield was hired at Drury Lane during the winter season; Mrs. Whitfield, however, did not act again in either Covent Garden or Drury Lane; instead, she acted at the Haymarket when she did not go with her husband to various places in the summer.

Inchbald saw the Whitfields almost every day for tea or supper, and Mrs. Inchbald and Mrs. Whitfield went on "excursions this summer," as they had done before. Once Mrs. Whitfield and Mrs. Inchbald went with William, the Whitfields' little boy, to King Street and New Street and rapped on doors and ran away before they were found. Boaden finds such a prank rather childish, but Inchbald loved games, and this must have been fun with William.[2] Inchbald entertained all the children, the "young" ones. Young Hitchcock was sent a ticket to her *Animal Magnetism* the first week of May; "young" Hitchcock was the son of her friends in Dublin.

Hitchcock, after 1782 when Inchbald went with him to Dublin, remained there as Daly's prompter and assistant. During the summer of 1788, he moved with Daly from Smock Alley to the Crow Street playhouse, and during the year Hitchcock published his first volume of *An Historical View of the Irish Stage*. Inchbald's visitor was perhaps Robert, who had acted with his mother and father in Dublin until he entered Trinity College at age fifteen in 1783. He had probably come to London on holiday; in the entry she says she saw Davis. He, too, had just come from Ireland. The next week she says Master Siddons called on Monday, and on Tuesday when she went to the Whitfields for dinner, there were two young Russians there. On Friday she went with the Hitchcocks and Mr. Marlow to Drury Lane and saw Sir Charles sitting opposite. It is clear from her entries that she never lacked for visitors and that she and the players, her friends, moved in a special circle; for although they followed the schedule of their assignments on stage, they had the leisure to go on excursions, dine together, talk to each other—gossip about each other. Her entries in the pocket-books continue to show an intimate picture of her own life and in addition interesting details about her friends and acquaintances.

During these weeks in early May, when *Animal Magnetism* was playing, she wrote to Lewis about her sixth night and to Harris, evidently about publishing her play; that is, she "took a letter to Mr. Robinson and Mr. Lewis," and in the evening she called on Lewis again and "after pleased with Mr. Harris's reply." And she says she corrected her piece for the press. On the next day, a Tuesday, she writes: "very fine and warm rose betimes call'd on Mr. Robinson and though I did not see him settled about my piece—call'd on Mrs. Whitfield then on Mrs. Morgan. Saw her house. Many people call'd for orders and George Inchbald wrote for one and after dinner Mrs. Hunt and Mrs. Wells call'd Sally went to the play & I drank tea with Mr. and Mrs. Crisp my new landlord and lady—in the member's box at Rosina & Animal Magnetism—at night eat a cold supper with Mr. and Mrs. Whitfield and Mr. Lane."[3]

Animal Magnetism continued to be played all the next week until Saturday, when the play was Goldsmith's *She Stoops to Conquer*. On Sunday morning she worked and at noon went to Mr. Babb's by walking through Kingston Gardens, where she saw Sir Charles and walked with him a "little time."

The week of Monday, May 26, was Ascot Race Week; her Monday entry is especially interesting: "Very fine and hot—Mr. Topham, Mr. Taylor, young Hitchcock call'd from breakfast to dinner and Ledger here with my money for Animal Magnetism Mr. Davis here after dinner—Mrs. Wells drank tea and supp'd here—Mrs. Whitfield call'd before—I behind at Animal Magnetism, other piece

Marian & Maid of the Oaks—a person sent me a paper with me and Sir Charles coupled in A."[4] Inchbald had by this spring become quite well known outside her immediate circle, and during Race Week, when Sir Charles and the Jockey Club were featured, it is not surprising that they were written about in the public prints. Certainly Sir Charles had been in the public prints before, but this is the first time she records that their association had been publicly noticed. She was very careful of her reputation, and as an actress she needed to be extra careful; for although the reputations of the actresses had by this time in the eighties been viewed with less disapprobation than earlier, Inchbald, Farren, and Siddons were especially careful. In most circles the three were considered quite virtuous. By now in London there was little privacy for her—for anyone in her circle. The list of her callers included friends from the theatre, the press, and politics. Even though we only have a list, anyone interested in examining the year 1788 will find significant material, and following her daily entries reveals information about not only her professional life but her social life as well and that of her friends. And no doubt when they gathered, they all gossiped and afterward gossiped with other friends.

On the Saturday of this week, she went with the Whitfields "on the Thames at Somerset House"; earlier she had been to the Haymarket and was much vexed to find that Colman was not there. No doubt she wished to discuss the ill-fated *Hue and Cry* and perhaps to discuss her contract for the summer.

On Sunday her entry was short and precise: "Denied to everybody—busy sorting my clouths writing my will &c dined with Mr. and Mrs. Whitfield—came home to tea and to write—Davis came to supper." On Monday she had a great many visitors: Dr. Wolcot, a popular writer of satiric verse and the sponsor of the painter Opie; her friend Mr. Taylor, the proprietor of the *Sun;* Mrs. Whitfield; Mr. Lane; and young Hitchcock. On Tuesday: "Waked at seven with a ticket for Hastings Trial (June 9) refused it and very uneasy when I rose and found Sheridan summed up the evidence . . . after I worked Mrs. Wells called & gave me an account of the trial."

June of 1788 marked the beginning of the trial itself; the prosecution had won the right to have the trial earlier, in 1787, with Sheridan's surprising five-hour speech when he had moved the House of Commons so completely to his views that "As soon as Sheridan sat down, the whole House, reportedly for the first time in history, erupted in a tumult of cheering and applause."[5]

On Thursday she says she "worked—from Breakfast to dinner—persons called and Sir Charles left a ticket." *Animal Magnetism* was the play that night, and she says it was a "great house," and on Friday both *Midnight Hour* and *Animal Mag-*

netism were on. Friday was fine and warm, and she went to hear Sheridan against Hastings—"met Sir Charles as I returned with Mr. Marlow."

The Haymarket opened the first week of June, and Inchbald's play *I'll Tell You What* was playing the second week of the season. Mrs. Hunt, Inchbald's sister, was planning to go to Bury, and Inchbald expected to see Sir Charles but did not. She ends her Monday entry with "my face very bad." All during the spring she had had what she called a "face ache." During several entries in February she had written "my head and face very bad." A week later she wrote "my face poorly as for some days," and again the following Thursday "Read and was dull— . . . my head and face very bad." According to her comments, her problem must have been a toothache. It persisted off and on for several weeks. In the last week of July, she wrote that she finished reading the *Rambler* and "at ten Mrs. Wells came to supper. My face poorly for several days."[6]

This Haymarket season found Inchbald playing in Home's *Douglas* one night and in her *Mogul Tale* the next. Mrs. Kemble, Stephen Kemble's wife, played in *I'll Tell You What,* and Inchbald says she came to the playhouse just as the play was over and went to supper with the Kembles, the Taylors, and "old Kemble." In the 1780s Stephen and his wife, the former Elizabeth Satchell, were in various places during the winter months and returned to London and the Haymarket in the summer. The elder Kembles lived in London after 1781, when Roger Kemble retired, having given over the stock in his company, and found a place to live in London. In August Roger Kemble played for his daughter-in-law Elizabeth's benefit. Inchbald's entry for that day, August 26, reads: "Fine at rehearsal of Good Natured Man—saw old Mr. Kemble rehearse. . . . I overlooked my piece of 'The Hue and Cry' behind at some of Inkle and Yorkle then in the front to see old Mr. Kemble in The Miller of Mansfield—Mrs. Kemble's night."

The whole country was set in a frenzy when in the summer of 1788 the king became ill. And in spite of all that his doctors did for him, by October he had become worse and worse both physically and mentally. We now know that he had porphyria, a hereditary disorder that resulted in madness for a time, but in 1788 no one could imagine that he was ill—he was clearly mad. Among those who treated him was Inchbald's friend Dr. Richard Warren, the Prince of Wales's physician. As the king's condition became progressively worse in the months following the first signs of his illness, Warren was one of the doctors who thought the king would never recover, and thus he was one of the advocates for the prince to become regent. But by early March of 1789, Warren and the other physicians declared the king recovered, and the country celebrated with balls, fetes, and parties of all kinds. On April 23, St. George's Day, there was a service of thanksgiving in St. Paul's Cathedral. Inchbald was present in one of the houses in the churchyard and saw the procession from an upstairs window.[7] But in the summer of 1788, St. George's Day was far in the future.

We have no precise date of when Inchbald became acquainted with Dr. Warren. He was Sheridan's physician as well as attending such notables as Charles James Fox and the dukes of Devonshire and Portland. It is not surprising that, given her special feeling for doctors, she developed a "crush" on him. He became one of the special people in her life.

Several pocket-book entries during the Haymarket season say that Inchbald saw the Kembles. During July and early August, while Inchbald was still working on her *Hue and Cry*, a "French gentleman call'd to ask me to adapt a play. Young Hitchcock call'd from the country—then Mr. Harris call'd and staid sometime . . . played in Mogul Tale play Inkle and Yoric—cross and dull." Her work and the theatre always prompted her emotional reactions. Sir Charles had left London for Barton, and the next day she found she could not go to Windsor; Harris had asked her to read "old Inkle and Yarico"—she did so, and finally, she says, she walked home with Stephen Kemble and his little girl—"he told me what young Colman said of his acting &c."

At this time Inchbald was still living in Great Russell Street, and on Monday, August 4, she had a number of visitors, the Taylors and Dr. Wolcot among them. They had come to see Lord Johnny Townshend "chaired." Because Townshend had won the Westminster election, he would be "chaired" as a victory celebration. A Whig, Townshend was a friend of Sheridan and Fox, and the celebration turned out to be quite large, with some two hundred carriages going from Covent Garden to Pall Mall and two hundred Whigs on horseback following.[8] The maid, Sally, was ill—was "poorly," that is—but on Saturday Sally was well enough to help Inchbald put on her "new toilet." There had been an earlier victory march for the Whigs in 1784 in the election when Georgiana, duchess of Devonshire, joined by several of her friends, had campaigned, one of the first times the women had publicly canvassed. The Whigs at that time were in opposition to the king and his ministers. By 1788 Fox, the leader of the Whigs, had lost considerable power, but nevertheless the Whigs won and celebrated their victory.

Inchbald's account in her pocket-book is not exactly a happy one. In the week July 14–20, on Thursday she wrote, "continuous showers till the evening . . . the street and garden filled with people on the business of the Election for Westminster." On Friday she continued, "first day of polling for a member of

Westminster . . . the street very riotous." The next week on Monday there was "continual riot of the election"; on Tuesday she wrote, "Mr. Texier from the hustings told me what had passed between Mr. Sheridan and him—and that two men were killed at the election . . . in the evening a great mob and the soldiers call'd in." No doubt Inchbald and her friends talked politics as well as theatre as they watched the parade.

She continued talking about her piece; she called on the Whitfields and talked of his benefit, and afterward she says, "Mr. Colman told me he should soon begin my piece." Although *Hue and Cry* was not played, in her entry it is clear that she and Colman were working together on it. Inchbald always behaved like a true professional about her work—she was in no way a "sensitive romantic" who felt nothing could be changed or left out of her plays. One of the things made most emphatically clear in the pocket-books is the way she worked with Harris and Colman and within the context of the organization of the theatres.

On the Sunday of this week, she found that Mrs. Whitfield had fallen down the stairs and was hurt. After supper she went and sat up with her all night. And between seven and eight the next morning, she went home and to bed. After tea Texier call'd with one act of his piece for her to begin, and she says she "had reason to think my piece would not be done this season." Her frequent comments on "not liking" took many forms, though usually she was dissatisfied with herself. Sometimes, however, she simply did not like what was brought to her to translate. Working on Texier's piece, she says, "finished translating one act—Mr. Texier here sometime—disliked the second act he brought me." On Sunday she wrote, "Texier here some time talking of his former life."

Texier was by 1788 firmly established in London, though he was French and, by the time of this entry in Inchbald's pocket-book, had had quite a varied and somewhat sensational past. Born in Lyons, he seems to have become enamored with the theatre after participating in amateur theatricals. Soon after these amateur performances, he began to give readings in which he took all the parts. This kind of semiprofessional performance on his part became quite popular, so much so that he left Lyons and his post as cashier in the office of the Ferme general and went to Paris, where for a time he became quite a sensation. However, although he was a gentleman, born of a good family, he began to be very arrogant. The story is that once while he was reading before the French king, he was angered that the king went to sleep. Texier slammed his book on the lectern, thus waking him, whereupon the king said Texier's performances were too noisy. After this episode Texier left Paris, performed some plays before Voltaire in Ferney, went to Belgium, and in September 1775 came to England. Upon Texier's arrival in England, he made friends with Garrick, who sponsored him for a time. Just what happened to their relationship is not clear; perhaps Garrick did not approve of the way Texier began to organize theatrical performances, first for the opera and the King's Theatre, by importing actors and dancers from the opéra comique. Garrick did not care for rivals. Texier was not successful in either of these projects, however, although he brought a suit against Carlo Badini, the librettist at the King's Theatre. There is no information about any settlement of the suit, but both Badini and Texier continued to be a part of theatre production in London. Texier assisted at both Drury Lane and Covent Garden, and for a time in the 1780s and 1790s, he assisted in amateur theatricals, this time in England; he did not return to France.[9]

Harris evidently used Texier in supplying the French plays to be translated by Inchbald. Since obviously Texier could obtain the plays easily, and, as Boaden commented, "Le Texier had himself very excellent judgment in these matters; and, besides using his connexions with Paris to purvey for Harris, he had his own transcendent French *readings* in Lisle Street."[10] Boaden's reference to Lisle Street is a comment about another of the enterprises Texier was engaged in. From the early 1780s on, Texier arranged evenings of entertainment where, as in his early days in France, he read plays, taking all the parts himself. One account of these "entertainments" described the company and the room:

> The company was of the genteelest kind; it is not a place for the million [*sic*]. The room (the same where the eidophusicon was exhibited last year) is neatly fitted up & illumi-nated with wax—the reader has seven lights on each side. Previous to the reading Mons. Le Texier receives his company in his Library, fitted up in a singular rustic taste—the chimney seems a hole in a rock; over it a small whole length figure of Voltaire in alabaster, which Le T. says was presented to him by that great genius. After the reading une petite comedie was presented—*the actors, two pretty little French girls & a lad,* played with much spirit & propriety. After the reading the company were served with tea & after the comedie with lemonade."[11]

The reference to Lisle Street and the date of the account (1783) reflects the way "entertainments" were a part of the London scene in the 1780s and 1790s. In 1781 at his house in Lisle Street, Leicester Square, De Loutherbourg, the artist and scene designer, presented what was called "Eidophusikon, or Representations of Nature"; the alternate title was "Various Imitations of Natural Phenomena, Represented by Moving Pictures." He added motion devices to scene paintings to simulate, for example, dawn, sunset, and a storm at sea. "The company was select (130 persons at five shillings each), the setting luxurious."[12] De Loutherbourg's viewings lasted until the spring of 1782, when the exhibition was moved. Texier, living in Lisle Street also, took over the "stage" for his readings, readings that at one place or another continued into the early 1800s. Moreover, Texier was not the only one who did such "reading entertainment"; John Henderson, one of the leading actors in the 1780s, also read for visitors, although the settings for his performances were doubtless less elegant than Texier's.

In the 1788 pocket-book, Texier is mentioned very frequently; he brings Inchbald translations to do for himself, an opera she does not like, a play he needs for some gentleman. Since he worked for both theatres, he knew "inside" gossip, which he and Inchbald loved to talk about. One Sunday she wrote, "Busy—Mr. Texier call'd and told me Mr. Sheridan knew the translation was mine . . . my sister brought the last of the piece—Mr. Texier called for it after." On the Friday following (August 29), she wrote: "from 2 till 3 rehearsing & cutting my piece and had a very bad opinion of it . . . then Mr. Texier with his little girl called. . . . I read a French Comedy perceived a violent cold coming." Which translation Sheridan knew as hers is not given, for at this time Sheridan was deep into the Westminster election, not the theatre.[13]

Still working on her *Hue and Cry* in the last days of August, she says on Sunday that she "wrote for a new comedy." Just what this means is not clear. Is this one time when she offered to do a translation—not having one at hand? Her entry ends, "my piece was positively put off till next season." The next entry, September 1, reads in part, "then Mr. Harris with a French comedy for me to translate . . ." The next day, she "Laid late with my cold poorly excused myself going to Mr. Babbs. Mr. Texier called and in plain terms told me I might go to Drury Lane . . . finished reading the French comedy & liked it much—at dark walked out with many letters." Again Inchbald leaves many details out; after all, she was writing only for herself. But why did Texier tell her "in plain terms" that she could go to Drury Lane? Did Kemble tell him to tell her, or did Texier serve Drury Lane as well as Covent Garden as a kind of agent? From Inchbald's entries in this 1788 pocket-book, there is no specific evidence, but the references to Texier and his professional conversations and to Harris and his requests make a strong case for the way plays were selected, translated, and presented. Playwriting for the theatre was, of course, professional business, and Inchbald's entries show how valuable she was to Texier and Harris for her skill as a writer. The entries also show how closely associated the two theatres were.

This new comedy that she liked "much" was *The Child of Nature*, which turned out to be her second in this year of wonders—1788—and a very successful production. Boaden uses her work on this play as an example of her absolute attention to the task she set for herself. With the comment that she needed a "new Comedy," Harris had obviously obliged himself.

Boaden's comments underscore the items in the pocket-book about her work:

Mr. Harris was again at her door with a French comedy for her to prepare for his theatre; it was the fascinating "Child of Nature," taken from the "Zelis" of Madame Genlis. No time was to be lost; she immediately locked herself up, closed her shutters, and was denied to every human being till she had completed her translation in four acts. In ten days this indefatigable spirit accomplished it, and on the 11th of September wrote to Mr. Harris stating her terms. They met afterwards to consult about the cast of it. She pursued her other designs without an hour's pause; but on the 11th of November the "Child of Nature" was read, and brought out on the 28th of the month with the greatest effect, and to the entire satisfaction of the author.[14]

Inchbald was very pleased about the reception of *Child of Nature*, but the pocket-book records some problems about it. For one thing, her payment for this piece was only fifty pounds, far less than for *Midnight Hour* or *Animal Magnetism*. Boaden remarks about her payment, "Perhaps there was some middle person whom the manager had also to pay, and he might have learned to consider mere translation as entitled but to slender remuneration."[15] By this time Inchbald does not include her accounts in her pocket-book—did she keep a separate book? As careful as she was about her finances, she must have kept an accurate record. In the entries for late October and early November, just before *Child of Nature* was presented, she comments on several disagreements with Harris. On Friday, November 7, in the midst of a list of visitors, she writes: "Mr. Harris calld he would not stay a moment because I spoke ill of last night's piece—slept afterwards then saw the last act of the Highland Reel in the front saw Mr. Topham behind and found he liked it—I liked it better." The next entry, on Saturday, reads: "Very dark wore my riding coat and fixed a plot that I hoped would complete my comedy. Mr. Harris unexpectedly calld to beg me let the French piece be playd and by Miss Brunton."

The mixture of concerns in this entry for Saturday is typical, but this time the two casual comments about "my comedy" and "Mr. Harris unexpectedly calld" reveal again her pattern of work. Harris would not present her play without consulting her, and evidently she had made some comment to him about casting it; her comment about Miss Brunton—that Harris had "begged" her—is also significant, since obviously by this time she and Harris had quite a different relationship from the days when she had appealed to him to read and consider her work.

Since in fact Miss Brunton turned out to be the original Amanthis in *Child of Nature,* the comment about Harris takes on added meaning when viewed with regard to his relationship with Brunton. Harris had "discovered" her when she was acting in Bath and had brought her to Covent Garden in the fall of 1785, hoping that she could rival Siddons. He mounted a very vigorous campaign of "puffing," but although she was quite successful in her debut season, she certainly did not match Siddons. Mrs. Wells, Inchbald's close friend, had created the principal roles in the *Mogul Tale* and Julia in *The Midnight Hour,* and it is probable that Inchbald intended the role of Amanthis for her. Wells's career in London included both Drury Lane and Covent Garden as well as the Haymarket. In 1787, while she was articled at Covent Garden, she was to play Rosalind in *As You Like It* at John Palmer's Royalty Theatre, but Harris refused to allow any of his employees to perform for Palmer's new venture, which was shut down by the authorities as a playhouse, only to open for entertainments. Wells performed in September in a "scene" in which she gave "Extracts from some of the principal Female Performers." Perhaps Wells's performing a "scene" had helped Harris to decide not to allow Wells to act Amanthis. Inchbald had seen Wells several times during this summer of 1788, and on Wednesday, October 15, Inchbald wrote, "Ledger came to tell me to be ready to play in the Belle Stratagem for Mrs. Wells— drest and just as I got to the house she arrived drank tea in the wardrobe."

Inchbald mentions Topham several times during these months. The year before (1787), Topham had started a paper, the *World,* with "Parson" Este as his partner. It is frequently said that Topham began the *World* to puff Mrs. Wells, but considering the fact that Topham promoted himself both before and after his association with Wells, it is hardly likely that the *World* was begun merely to praise Wells. The *World* was a vehicle to promote a variety of interests, including the theatres, which it did quite successfully from 1787 to 1790; it included advertisements, political comment, society news, and almost everything in "the world." Both Topham and Este were quite capable of producing such a periodical, but to do so required more than merely "puffing" Wells or Inchbald or any other theatrical figure.

One writer discussing the *World* gives a long review of Este.[16] Born in 1752, Este was educated at Westminster School; afterward he studied medicine and surgery, but he never practiced. Instead, he read for divinity and was ordained in 1777. He was a friend of Woodfall, the proprietor of the *Public Advertiser,* writing for this very popular journal in the eighties until he and Topham undertook the *World.* Este wrote under a pseudonym instead of using his own name, although his identity was well known. His style was very much his own, a rather eccentric one. John Taylor commented on "the peculiarity of his style, that often rendered his criticism unintelligible to those who had not attended to his manner."[17] The "stars" of the theatrical criticism were Kemble and Mrs. Siddons, Este being the first of the critics to celebrate Mrs. Siddons for her role as Lady Macbeth. By the time Este was writing for the *World,* his first favorite, Henderson, had died in 1785, and he turned to Kemble. Charles Harold Gray found that

> He [Este] had a feeling for imaginative acting. His chief defect was that he inclined towards hero worship; while Henderson was in the ascendancy, Henderson could do no wrong and Kemble was second-rate; after Henderson's untimely death, Kemble rose to supremacy and then he could do no wrong. By the time he was writing for the *World* [1787–90], Este had become almost too much given to panegyric to be of much service. And at all times it is necessary to endure the most atrocious distortions of language in order to get at his few critical judgments. . . . At times the phrases are so distorted as to be unintelligible; there is almost never any grace of language; oddness is deemed sufficient justification.[18]

Este continued with the paper until it ceased publication in 1790, but afterward he wrote a very bitter account of his partnership with Topham. The *World* was a very profitable undertaking, and it was unfortunate for Este that he quarreled publicly with Topham. In June of 1789 there appeared a rival to the *World, The Oracle; or Bell's New World.* This time the editor was James Boaden—Mrs. Inchbald's James Boaden—and although he did not do all the theatrical criticism during 1791–1792, he probably did a group of items signed "Thespis."[19]

The beginning of the *World* in January 1787 had an even more important role to play than merely to give criticism of the theatres; the subtitle *Fashionable Gazette* promoted another, more contemporary role.[20] Moreover, it was another of John Bell's successful enterprises. Bell's first great success was his series of Shakespeare (11 volumes, 1774), and his second was *The British Theatre* (21 volumes); by 1792 he had published 109 volumes of *Poets of Great Britain from Chaucer to Churchill.* One day Topham, visiting Bell, discovered that Bell was about to begin a new journal, and Topham proposed himself as a partner. Topham cut quite a figure: he had beautiful horses and drove a special phaeton, and he dressed in a very curious and distinctive fashion, his coats cut to his design to show his fine figure. He was very prominent in the social life of London and, with his friend Miles Peter Andrews, was known in all the theatre circles. It is hardly surprising that the *World,* with Bell and Topham as partners, became a huge success.[21]

One authority says that Bell received four thousand pounds at the end of 1787 for his one-third share. It was said that three thousand copies of the first issue were sold at once and another thousand printed to fill the orders from the court. Those who contributed to the paper included almost everyone in the theatrical and fashionable world—such people as Sheridan, Miles Peter Andrews, Robert Merry, and two of the well-known sports figures, the boxers Humphries and Mendoza, who challenged each other by correspondence in the paper. Sheridan and Miles Peter Andrews were, of course, well known for their knowledge of the theatres, and Robert Merry contributed as a popular figure in London society. Merry had been part of the group in Florence, Italy, which included several other English gentlemen, who thought themselves poets. By the time of the *World*, Merry had become a leading member of the group that called itself the Della Cruscans; back in London the *World* became the chief publishing outlet for their work. The Della Cruscans became all the rage, and for a time were discussed everywhere in the literary circles of London.

One writer pointed out that "In spite of the fact that this verse was obviously and confessedly verse which laid no great claim to depth of thought and emotion, the London reading public regarded it with interest and enthusiasm." The group returned to London shortly after the publication of their collection *The Florence Miscellany* and discovered their fame, whereupon they began to regard themselves as poets of first rank and proceeded without delay to make their fame more widespread. "They wrote frenziedly for those who proclaimed them great."[22] The *World* was their "dumping" ground, and two of them, Parson and Bertie Greatheed, were steady contributors.

They all chose pen names; two of the women were "Perdita" Robinson, the prince's discarded mistress, now fallen upon hard times, whose pen name was Laura Marie; and the playwright Mrs. Cowley, who was Anna Matilda. Cowley had turned from writing for the stage to writing poetry, and when she wrote a poem in answer to one of Merry's, the stage was set for a series of romantic "love" poems answering each other in the pages of the *World*, where Este kept the series going. It has been said that although everyone knew their identity, they had never seen each other. These "platonic" lovers extended their correspondence from 1787 until March 1789, and everyone waited anxiously for them to meet, but when they did it was a disaster—she was forty-six and he was thirty-four! She returned to writing plays, and he to his usual not-very-profitable or -pleasurable social life: being a figure in London society along with Mrs. Piozzi. In 1791 the poetry was published in a separate volume. By that time, of course, the *World* had ceased publication.

Becky Wells, Mrs. Inchbald's friend, and Inchbald herself were a part of the group who put the paper together. Wells came to the Haymarket in 1781, and in 1784 she played Fanny in Inchbald's *Mogul Tale;* in 1785–1786, after she moved over from Drury Lane to Covent Garden, she was Lady Euston in *I'll Tell You What*, and in the fall of 1786, she created the role of Julia in *The Midnight Hour*, both Inchbald plays. Topham, a captain in the army who had stood guard on horseback at the royal residence during the Gordon riots, had met Wells when she came to rehearse a prologue he had written. His farce *The Fool* served as a vehicle for Wells, and he had written another, *Small Talk*, for her benefit; in 1786 and in 1787, she appeared in his *Bonds without Judgment*. Because he had used his work to feature her, it is not surprising that many people thought the *World* had been started to promote her; that was not the case, as even a brief look at the paper itself shows.

Wells and Inchbald herself helped with daily entries; Inchbald's were signed "The Muse." Several years earlier Twiss had given her the title "The Tenth Muse," now shortened to "The Muse." Wells supplied the daily paragraphs of news.

The "Fashionable Advertiser" section of the first issue included not only the announcements for the theatre productions but also advertisements for such things as "Floor cloths, jewelry, porcelain, fine old china, shells for grottoes," with a separate column, "The Fine Arts," that advertised new prints. There was a column about Shakespeare and the Shakespeare Gallery, and there were ads for foreign fruits and fencing lessons; there were horses for sale, ads for elastic gloves, waistcoats . . . muslin and calico, new novels—Mrs. Cowley's play—published by G.G. and J. Robinson, and the sermons of Hugh Blair in a new edition. It is obvious from even a brief look at one issue of the *World* that it was much more than a promotion by Topham of his mistress Becky Wells.

One of those who was a part of the *World* was the former Mrs. Thrale, Dr. Johnson's friend who in 1784 had married Piozzi, an Italian musician, much to the consternation of her family and friends. Soon after the marriage they went to Italy, and while there they made friends with several Englishmen who were also there. She, as James Clifford has said, had a weakness, an "inordinate love of praise . . . she always longed for adulation." After traveling for some time in various places, they settled in Florence and made friends with William Parson, who introduced them to Robert Merry. Both Parson and Merry thought of themselves as poets. James Clifford, in his account of the group, points out that Parson was "weak, unstable, inordinately conceited," and "thought of himself a talented poet"; his head was "full of grandiose literary schemes."[23] Clifford also states that their verse had political overtones, a characteristic that carried over when the group came to England and began to publish their verse in various periodicals. By 1787–1788, shortly after the establishment of the *World* and after their return from Italy, they began to publish in the *World*. Mrs. Piozzi, who was working diligently to reenter London society, was frequently featured in the "society columns" of various papers, and her social gatherings were often reported in the *World*. This is another interesting item, since such material in the paper was very much like the society columns of our own papers, columns used to promote charity events sponsored by prominent society women. Mrs. Piozzi did wish to promote various friends in their quest to be successful—and published—playwrights.

Whereas Parson and Merry thought of themselves as poets, Greatheed, another in the group, wished to be a playwright. The Greatheed family was very close to Sarah Siddons, because she had lived with the family before she was married, a connection she cherished and continued throughout her life. It was in this connection that Mrs. Piozzi began her association with Siddons.[24] Piozzi and her friends were all, as she said, "verse Mad." Together out of their association they had published a volume of verse, *The Florence Miscellany*. But now back in London, Piozzi pestered Sarah Siddons endlessly about sponsoring plays by various ones of their mutual friends. Once Siddons wrote to another of their friends, "Your friend, Mrs. Piozzi, may be an excellent judge of a poem possibly, but it is certain that she is not of a tragedy"; Piozzi sent an epilogue to be used in Greatheed's second tragedy (his first, *The Regent*, was produced at Drury Lane in 1788), about which she wrote, "I have written an Epilogue for Mr. Greatheed's Tragedy, but it won't do for Mrs. Siddons she says, so it must be changed I trow. Let nothing ever tempt me to write for the Stage, no Patience can hold out against their Objections and their Criticisms and their Mock-Importance—they teize Mr. Greatheed to Frenzy."[25]

When Merry came back from Italy, he was deep in debt, depending on friends to support him, but he resumed his part as a fashionable beau; when he went to the theatre, he saw Anne Brunton perform and fell in love forthwith. She had come from the Bath Theatre to Covent Garden in 1785 and had become quite successful; she played in Inchbald's *All on a Summer's Day* and was the original Amanthis in Inchbald's *Child of Nature*. She and Merry were married in August 1791, and Piozzi wrote, "Della Crusca [Merry's pen name] is married at last to Miss Brunton it seems, a pleasing young Actress of purely unsullied Character. Well! She may help maintain, if 'tis too late to reform him: poor girl I'm sorry for her."[26] His family did not approve of the marriage, and for a while she did not act, but in 1796, accompanied by her husband, she went with Thomas Wignell to New York and Philadelphia, where she made her American debut on December 5. Merry, who continued to live his society ways, was much admired in Philadelphia until his death in December 1798.

Beginning in 1785, before the *World* was started, Topham and Wells lived together at No. 15 Beaufort Buildings; they had four children, a son who did not survive and three daughters, but they were never married. In the end Topham deserted Wells and took the daughters to Scotland, leaving her to support herself. In 1788 Wells, Topham, and Inchbald saw each other frequently, both in the theatres and out. Wells frequently called on Inchbald, and no doubt there was much conversation about plays, players, and current events. Wells, known for her "imitations," helped to write the *World,* as her letters to London show. She spent the summers with her children at Topham's country house in Suffolk, where she managed the estate. She, like Sir Charles and Inchbald, attended the Hastings trial, and she reported it for one of the public prints. Her most celebrated performances, however, were not on stage but in the homes of friends, where she imitated the "characters" at the trial, especially Sheridan and the judge.

Next to Mrs. Whitfield, Mrs. Wells became Inchbald's best friend during these years, as everyone knew. Mrs. Whitfield was no longer acting in the winter season, and Mrs. Wells, who had come from Drury Lane to Covent Garden in 1787, was constantly associated with the players at Covent Garden. Boaden, writing long after the fact, found Inchbald's friendship with Wells rather "surprising." The "connexion," he says, "could proceed from no impure sympathy, or even indifference to worldly maxims, on the part of Mrs. Inchbald. She was above all suspicion herself, and her friend greatly below it. Topham himself was rather welcome to her than otherwise."[27] Boaden's prudish comments about Inchbald and her friends are evident throughout the *Memoirs.* It was almost as if he must defend Inchbald's "virtue." Inchbald herself told an amusing story about Farren and Wells. It seems that Farren came bursting into Inchbald's dressing room because Wells had entered Farren's. It was Farren who guarded her "virtue" constantly, lest she and Derby be "coupled" in adultery; Wells was far more relaxed about her "relationship" with Topham. Inchbald thought Farren's behavior amusing.

The years of the *World* and the people associated with it give additional evidence of the complexity of the press, the theatre, entertainment, and business in these last years of the 1780s. Inchbald's association with the paper shows again how much she was a part of the fashionable circles. All the people involved with the *World* were in the forefront of "fashion."

During October, while she was working on her play, Inchbald took new lodgings. This time she went to Frith Street at Mr. Grist's. The entries in the pocket-book about her decision to move, after she had earlier decided not to, say something about the players and their living accommodations as well as about Inchbald's indecision regarding lodging and daily living. Reviewing the entries also shows how dependent lodgers were on landlords. Inchbald's friend John Bannister and his wife, the former Elizabeth Harper, lived on Frith Street. Elizabeth Harper had been a member of the company at both Covent Garden and the Haymarket, where she not only acted but sang as well. Most of the parts she played were parts including songs. The Bannisters were married in 1783. They lived that year at No. 6 Great Russell Street, near both theatres; afterward they lived in Bow Street very near Covent Garden; and in 1788 they were at No. 4 Frith Street. The Bannisters—the father, Charles, and his son, John—were close friends of the Colmans. Charles Bannister was a celebrated singer as well as actor, and he and his future daughter-in-law had sung together in Marylebone Gardens before her theatrical debut. Inchbald's moving to Frith Street meant she was very close to them.

The entries in the pocket-book about Inchbald's search for new lodgings reveal her indecision, and after she moved, her fears about her landlady's illness suggest again the close relationships of landlord and tenant, perhaps indicating how crowded and close such quarters were. She had moved on a Saturday, October 11, 1788. Her entry for that day reads: "Fine—all day packing and denied—Sally came to help me and about four I came to my new Lodging in Frith Street Soho—very dull then till Davis came—he and Mrs. Grist supped with me." On the Tuesday before, she had written: "Mr. Texier calld—I calld at my new lodgings disliked them. . . . Davis here while I dined then I went to see his lodgings." The next day she began to pack her letters, and the day after that she writes, "Fine and cool at rehearsal of Suspicious Husband calld at Mrs. Whitfields looked over and burnt old letters." On Sunday she wrote, "Much better pleased with my change unpacked with pleasure a beautiful day." On Monday her entry said, "Better pleased with my lodgings yet," and on Tuesday, "better pleased with my lodgings still—dined at home for the first time." On Thursday she records that Mrs. Grist was ill, and the next day she heard first that Mrs. Grist was better and then that she was worse. On Saturday she went to "many lodgings in case of Mrs. Grist's death," but on Sunday she wrote, "Fine—heard Mrs. Grist was better till after dinner Mrs. Hunt teased me about my lodgings."

Her sister Hunt was among her most frequent visitors, though where Hunt lived is never mentioned. She frequently went with Inchbald to the theatre and various other places, but she is not mentioned as a member of the group who dined with Mr. Babb on Sundays. In the end it was Inchbald who supported Hunt. Boaden, using letters he had before him, no doubt, says that "her near connexions were this year [1788] excessively troublesome to her."[28] Her pocket-book does not indicate many references to the evidence Boaden gives. It is true that Mrs. Hunt's husband, John, died in April and that their brother George had evidently failed to make a success of the farm. Boaden says also that both of the sons "of her excellent husband besieged her by letter; but she refused to see either of them this year."[29] George had played in Edinburgh in the summers of 1780 and 1781 after Inchbald left Wilkinson, and he remained, according to Wilkinson, until May 1786. "He was a young man of great service in a theatre, though not so attentive always as he should be, but of good behaviour."[30] In the fall of 1786 he was in London at Covent Garden briefly, and in 1787 he was in Norwich, where he remained through 1789. Just what reasons he had for asking for help, Boaden does not say. Robert, the younger of the two, also acted in Edinburgh, but in 1788 he seems to have become a professional musician, playing both the violin and the cello.

One entry during the first week of November is both interesting and puzzling. It reads: "received a letter from Dolly and a note from Bunbury with one from Sir Charles enclosed." Bunbury was Sir Charles's brother Henry, and very likely he had come from Barton, where he had been with Sir Charles.[31] The Bunburys knew Inchbald and her brother George, and probably the letters from Dolly and Sir Charles were about the fact that George was obliged to give up the farm, leaving Dolly nowhere to live. From Boaden's point of view, Inchbald's family was a problem for her, especially since they all called on her for money. From the letters and her pocket-books, the family seems unusually close, and Inchbald, although she was sometimes rather sharp with them, was always supportive; she was not always so generous to Robert and George Inchbald.

Bunbury called again on Wednesday, and on Friday, November 21, Sir Charles came from the country and called on her very early and "staid till ten." She does not say what they talked about, but the next day, Saturday, she had a letter from Dolly saying that she was coming to her. On Friday Dolly arrived at noon and went to the theatre to see Inchbald's new piece, *The Child of Nature;* Inchbald records, "Mr. Texier was in the slips with Dolly at my piece . . . pleased at its reception Davis came to supper." The Saturday entry reads: "Dark and not so cold—pleased with what the papers said—at one went to the cutting of my piece angry Mr. Lewis objected Mr. Marlow called & Davis at dinner—behind at Child of Nature. . . . Mr. Marlow calld home with Dolly."

For several reasons Inchbald was upset about her piece. Her entry on Monday, December 1, reads, "Slept little Mr. Dive calld to offer me terms about the piece at 12 went to the rehearsal calld on Mrs. Whitfield—had high words with Mr. Harris. Mr. Lewis followed me home and settled it—Davis calld at tea— (play Reel & Duke and No Duke)—was behind a little and insulted by Mr. Barlow about Mr. Harris's order calld for Dolly in the pit—cry'd." Mr. Barlow was treasurer and a very strict administrator of his duties; it was said that he had a reputation for querulousness. His insult to Inchbald, for whatever reason, surely was unnecessary. *The Secret History* in another context said, "he is not remarkable for either flexibility or politeness; he exercises his power with an iron hand; nor do we find that he wishes to number *forgiveness* among his *many* virtues."[32]

These entries about *The Child of Nature,* though they are a puzzle, do, none-theless, add to our knowledge of the way the theatre—Covent Garden, that is—operated. Harris, Lewis, Dive, and Barlow were all involved in finances and various other decisions about which plays were put together with which farce or after-piece along with various kinds of extra "entertainment." By this time, well into December, the pantomimes were about to begin. On Tuesday, December 2, Inchbald wrote, "Fine and very cold—Mrs. Carter, Mrs. Hitchcock, Taylor and Mrs. Whitfield calld Davis here at dinner I in the pit with Dolly at some of Child of Nature then behind agreeing to withdraw it farce Poor Soldier my night." Al-though we have many of her accounts, we do not have one for *Child of Nature;* we cannot guess at the receipts for the night. Moreover, since she seems to have been discussing *Child of Nature* with the Covent Garden "board" for quite some time, perhaps she had made an agreement about her "night."

On the following Wednesday, she and Dolly went in a coach to a bookseller's "and many other places." She saw Holcroft at the bookseller's. On the next day, Thursday, she wrote: "Very fine and very cold—expected my bookseller. . . . I just calld at the house during Marian play Child of Nature . . . found they meant to cut my piece to a farce." Her report about her play continues on Saturday: "Cloudy and extremely cold—just calld at the house and many places began to correct many proofs. . . . Mr. Marlow calld and took Dolly to the play Axertes and Child of Nature—I at the later in the members Box." On Sunday she wrote, "A cold brown day hurried to correct the proofs and denied to all . . . calld on Mr. Lewis as I came home and wrote to my bookseller that my piece was to be playd first again." The next two days, Monday and Tuesday, she corrected proofs. On Wednes-day she wrote: "Fine and very cold. . . . Dolly and I went in a coach to Bow street up Pall Mall . . . in the pit with Dolly at some of Child of Nature then called on Mrs. Whitfield and behind and talking with Mr. Dive in the board room." The next entry reads: "Rather dark finished the last part of the Child of Nature Mr. Andrews called about the epilogue. . . . I in the pit at Midnight Hour other piece Child of Nature and Farmer." Two days later, on Sunday, she wrote, "my Books of Child of Nature came after being sent for." Evidently her "Books of Child of Nature" were just off the press and were of the four-act play, not the cut version.

On Monday, December 15, Ledger came to "settle" her accounts, and the next night *Child of Nature* was still playing. On Wednesday the entry reads, "Snowed

most of the day Dolly and I went in a coach to the bank and many other places
. . . after dinner we read the debates in the newspapers play Child of Nature Mrs.
Jordan's night at Drury Lane." But she was still not through with *Child of Nature;*
it was played on Thursday, and on Friday she received a letter from Lewis offering
her another night. Again her entry is puzzling. Does she mean she had another
night and thus made more money? Had her discussion with Harris and Lewis
when, as Boaden says, she was offered only fifty pounds resulted in a bonus when
the play proved to be popular?[33]

On Christmas Eve she and Mr. Marlow went to the rehearsal of a new pantomime and sat in the front boxes. On Christmas Day she wrote, "Christmas Day
warm and dirty Mr. Chambers calld at breakfast with a turkey, Sally my old maid,
after Sir Charles here from tea till supper reading pamphlets &." The remaining
entries are all about personal matters: it continued to snow and be very cold, her
landlady, Mrs. Grist, "was taken with a fit that made me expect every moment she
would die—we cooked our own dinner." She and Dolly and her sister Debby had
all had letters from their brother George. On this last Saturday in the year, Dolly
received a letter from "little" George that "confirmed all bad news." A week earlier
George had written that he could "never return home" (probably because of debts
he had incurred). During the last three days of the year, she was reading Gibbon,
sometimes aloud to Dolly; on December 31 she wrote, "A snow Mrs. Grist not so
well I read Gibbon to Dolly." All these entries toward the end of the year are, as
we see, a mixture of professional and personal concern, and in 1788 they attest to
the many interests and accomplishments she kept ongoing.

The pocket-books always include comments about her personal domestic
life; they also include information about her health, her food, her clothes. Although these subjects seem trivial, they add to our understanding of not only her
life but that of her friends and family as well. Most of the people in Inchbald's
circle were "middling" people, who, though they did not belong to the gentry or
the rich merchant class, were nevertheless not the poverty-stricken citizens of
London who wandered the streets or offered "favors" in Covent Garden. Indeed,
reading Inchbald's pocket-books over the years, with her long lists of people she saw
and had tea and conversation with, suggests that she was simply one of many people
who were becoming a part of the rising middle class, a class that in the 1780s was
the beginning of the dominant class of the nineteenth century and included theatre
people, writers, and those who wished to become writers or actors.

The people Inchbald worked with were also her personal friends—her publisher Robinson, her broker Morgan, Harris, and both the elder and the younger

Colman; references to dozens of people in the theatre and out suggest how closely associated her circle in London was, even including tradesmen and servants. Several times in the pocket-books she comments on the various maids she had. As noted earlier, she never had a permanent place of her own, and it is not quite clear sometimes exactly what her domestic arrangements were, but since she frequently talks of landladies, maids, food, cleaning, and entertaining visitors, the entries, put together, give an interesting account of the practices and customs of her group. She, of course, did not have a husband or children, which meant she could be far more casual about food and lodging than Mrs. Whitfield or Mrs. Siddons or the Kembles—Stephen and John Philip.

It is not clear just what Inchbald's situation about food was in London, where she seems to have been in rooms rather than the kind of boardinghouse she lived in with her husband on the York circuit, but the entries she makes in this 1788 pocket-book reveal a wide variety of circumstances and foods. The other impression revealed in the pocket-books, aside from the account of her work, is that she was constantly visiting and conversing with friends and colleagues. Indeed, there is no way that tea and conversation can be overemphasized, neither for her nor for her friends. Mrs. Siddons, having a family and a house of her own, had "open" house frequently; Inchbald, who never had proper accommodations, nevertheless entertained with conversation and tea almost every day during this 1788 year. In June 1789, after she had refused a new contract at Covent Garden, she moved into smaller quarters; that is, she gave up the dining room, but she continued to have tea and conversation with a wide variety of friends.

The topics of these meetings and conversations ranged from gossip to serious politics: from the news about the king's illness to miscarriages, from Farren and Lord Derby, Wells and Topham, Texier and his little girl, to successful plays and condemned plays, Covent Garden, Drury Lane, the Haymarket, assorted provincial theatres, especially Edinburgh, Norwich, York, Bath, and both theatres in Dublin—Smock Alley and Crow Street. Sometimes Inchbald indicates what the conversations were about, and sometimes she does not. The year 1788 was important for John Kemble, because he was made artistic director at Drury Lane; 1788 was also an important year for Hitchcock in Dublin, for it saw the publication of his first volume of *An Historical View of the Irish Stage from the earliest period down to 1788. Interspersed with Theatrical Anecdotes* (in the second volume, published in 1794, he ended his history at 1774).

Inchbald must have known about the history, since she records that she saw young Hitchcock frequently in 1788. She always had visitors from her past—if not her contemporaries, her friend's children. She saw young Woodfall and young Chambers, and of course she was very fond of Henry, Mrs. Siddons's son, and of Charles Kemble, who was a year younger than his nephew, Henry.

The 1788 pocket-book does not include her accounts, a listing that gave detailed information about the money she spent on food, clothes, and rent, as well as such things as washing and maid service. She shared a maid with Mrs. Grist, and she mentions Sally, the maid she had had before she moved. She does mention buying food and clothes, but in this pocket-book she is so absorbed with her work that she does not write in detail of her domestic affairs. She says she "walked to buy things to eat." Another time she reports that Davis "came to supper of a pigeon." On another occasion Etty brought her a piece of fish; Etty lived with Mrs. Whitfield. During this year Inchbald has several entries about servants. Such entries confirm our view that everyone went to the theatre and that Inchbald always enjoyed people for themselves, not for their rank or station. She mentions her new maid Sally, who came from Bury, and that Etty "called" on her. She says the next day that she and Sally talked of Bury. In another entry she says, "I played Dorinda—my maid there very well drest."

Sometimes she was not pleased with her servants; she wrote on a Sunday, "very fine and warm disliked my new maid or charwoman—worked." It was this entry that ended with the comment "I went out and bought my supper—read." She writes about going shopping, but this pocket-book does not include the details of the earlier ones. She went to buy handkerchiefs in Holbourn and was caught in the rain and "calld at Mr. Warren's for an umbrella."

Two very important national events happened in 1788—the Hastings trial began and the king became very ill. The Hastings impeachment and trial in one form or another was in the public prints from the time Hastings arrived back in England from India in January 1786. Now in 1788 Sir Charles gave Inchbald tickets to the trial, but having missed the opening, she went on Monday, February 25, and returned in a chair. The next day she wrote that she was "Fatigued with yesterday." But she did not go again, even though the trial went on and on. This was the trial that came about as a result of Sheridan's famous speech, when he so effectively argued before the House of Commons on February 7, 1787, and through his persuasion brought about the indictment of Hastings. In the months between February 7, 1787, and the beginning of the actual trial, on February 13, 1788, Sheridan spoke several times, but it was not until June 3, 1788, that he began the series of three speeches over the period of a week that made the trial appear "as a great moment in the history of international law."[34] This trial, like the Gordon riots, marked an important phase for the British government: in this case, in the end the East India Company came more directly under the control of the king and Parliament, and thus India took on supreme importance for the expansion of the empire. After England lost the American War for Independence, the affairs of the East India Company became even more important to the government.

The Hastings trial was actually initiated by the Whigs as an attempt to oppose Pitt, the prime minister. In 1783 Burke introduced bills aimed "to prevent and punish abuses of power by the East India Company, to ensure the observance of Indian rights and customs, and to place the company under the supervision of . . . commissioners . . . appointed by Parliament."[35] The company had had almost no control from the government, being administered by its own board of governors. By the 1780s it had brought a great deal of wealth to its administrators. Hastings had been made the first governor general, and although the Whigs accused him of corruption and in fact blamed him for everything that had gone wrong in India during his administration, he had been very careful of the Indian customs and had fostered the spread of the knowledge of their languages and cultures. Another of the political aspects of the trial was that a great many young men of the middle class had gone to India, made a fortune, and returned to buy estates and set themselves up as aristocrats, a consequence that many of the "real" aristocrats deplored. One such young man was Richard Griffith, son of the playwright and novelist Elizabeth Griffith, who returned with a fortune before he was thirty; this is only one example out of many. Having started in 1783, when Burke introduced his bills, the trial went on and on. It was not concluded until 1795, and in the end Hastings himself was exonerated.

Almost all the aspects of the trial are included in Inchbald's *Such Things Are* (1787). There are those seeking their fortune; there is the injustice of the administration and the comments throughout about corruption. The young man Twineall is a fool, and Lord Flint a corrupt and dangerous man. Inchbald did not reflect directly on any part of the trial, but both she and her audience were certainly aware of it, since it was printed everywhere—in newspapers, periodicals, and caricatures.

The other event of the year 1788 was the king's illness, which Inchbald mentioned twice in a special place at the top of the page; on November 3 she wrote, "The King's death expected." The king's illness made a difference for the theatres, since he, with his family, usually attended either Drury Lane or Covent Garden every week during the season. He was especially fond of comedy, and frequently Inchbald's plays were given "by the King's command." In the end the prince did not become regent until 1811, and the king did not die until January 1820.[36]

Although Inchbald used the pocket-books to remind her of the day's events, they include, buried in the names and recordings, interesting insights into other people and plays. The problems she had concerning *The Child of Nature* went on and on. While the play was in rehearsal, she was writing a speech, she says, for Edwin, and he did not come to receive it when she expected him. Edwin was John Edwin, the actor who had been in Inchbald's plays before, the original Humphuy in *Appearance Is against Them,* the original Nicolas in *The Midnight Hour,* and La Fleur in *Animal Magnetism.* He was praised by Reynolds and was a very close friend of the playwright O'Keeffe; he both sang and played comic parts. His death in 1790 on November 8 was the result of a breakdown; Boaden called him "the absolute victim of Scottish intemperance."[37] He did not come when Inchbald expected him, and she mentions him no more. These bits of references show Inchbald's involvement in staging her plays, and they also give significant information about the writing for certain players. Inchbald did only one play on commission for a set of players, a play commissioned by Kemble for Mrs. Jordan at Drury Lane; given the players and their contracts, she usually knew who would be available, and she must therefore have tailored some of the material, but she did not assign parts or schedule the time when her plays would be given. Because Covent Garden and Drury Lane were very much in the business of pleasing an audience, those who made the decisions about accepting a play were the ones who would oversee the productions. At Covent Garden, although the players and the authors could give their opinion, the plays were cast and produced by Harris and his staff, not by the playwrights themselves. The reference above to Edwin and his speech that he did not come for is perhaps an example of the way various players came to her to correct or add speeches for themselves. Another point that needs to be remembered is that in the summer the players came from both theatres, in addition to others who for one reason or another did not belong to either "winter" theatre, a circumstance that made the Haymarket especially interesting and important for the variety of players who came and went each summer.

    The Child of Nature, about which she had so many entries in the 1788 pocketbook, played more than thirty times in the next few years and became one of her most popular plays in the provinces. One later critic, writing about the revivals and importations of French comedies in England in the 1780s, said that Inchbald "occasionally departs from the polished but monotonous dialogue of Mme de Genlis' Zélie, from which it [*The Child of Nature*] was derived."[38] The original was a five-act piece, and Inchbald changed it to four acts. Moreover, her version had very abrupt transitions and rather unprepared-for plot changes, as, for example, when Amanthis's father suddenly appears out of thin air. Her lack of transitions and her abrupt changes in the plot structure may account for its becoming an afterpiece, but more likely it was simply Harris's decision, for whatever reason.

FALSE APPEARANCES: A SPECIAL PUZZLE

The time between the end of the 1788 pocket-book and the beginning of 1789 is not recorded in Boaden; he begins discussing 1789 by recording that in February 1789 Inchbald was working on a piece for the Haymarket when Texier brought her one to do for him. She left off working on hers and turned to do his, which was completed by March 7. On March 30 Texier brought her a letter from Horace Walpole and paid her for her work. Texier had already had her translate a piece for him; this time, Boaden says, "we feel confident that one was 'Les Dehors Trompeurs' of Mons. Boissy, called . . . 'False Appearances.'" It reappeared as *False Appearances* by Henry Seymour Conway and played at Richmond House as the last play of a long list given there. Boaden's report of Inchbald and Conway makes clear that, as Boaden said, "the Right Hon. Henry Seymour Conway" had no more than "nominal claims as a dramatist."[39] Boaden says that Inchbald did two translations for Texier. If one was *False Appearances*, what was the other? It is likely that Inchbald did others, too, since at this point she was working all the time and thought, no doubt, that she needed the money.

The way such a transaction was conducted is an example of how writers, players, and sponsors made theatre of special importance. Walpole would not have asked Inchbald directly to do the play; evidently, however, everyone knew Texier as a professional play master who would take a commission. French plays were the most popular ones to adapt in the 1780s, before the German plays of Kotzebue in the 1790s, and Walpole certainly knew Mrs. Inchbald, because she had been in *The Count of Narbonne,* an adaptation of his novel *Castle of Otranto,* when she was in Ireland. But because he would never have asked her himself, he employed Texier.

In addition to Boaden's information about Inchbald's part in this private theatre season, the reports in papers and letters of the people involved give insight into another important aspect of the knowledge and importance of plays. The Richmond House was one of many private theatres all over the country. For example, Sir W. Williams Wynne held private theatricals at his home, Wynnstay, in Derbyshire, from 1773 to 1790. It was here that the Colmans, father and son, spent Christmas more than once with Sir Charles's brother Henry Bunbury, the artist, and other friends. These private theatres imitated the professional ones in that they included the same "companies" year after year. Frederick Reynolds, upon his return from Switzerland, wrote, "I found the whole town infected with another mania,—Private Theatricals. Drury Lane, and Covent Garden, were almost forgotten in the performances at Richmond House; and the Earl of Derby, Lord Henry Fitzgerald, Mrs. Hobart, and Mrs. Damer, in the '*Way to Keep Him,*' and

'*False Appearances,*' were considered, by crowded, and fashionable audiences, equal, if not superior, to Kemble, Lewis, Mrs. Siddons, and the present Countess of Derby."[40]

The way the plays were presented at Richmond House this season illustrates how the private theatre worked. The Prince of Wales and the dukes of York, Gloucester, and Devonshire were all at the first performance on February 7. The first play was Centlivre's *Wonder,* with Lord Henry Fitzgerald playing the part of Don Pedro. He was very successful and was said to be as good as Garrick, especially since he had the figure for the part and "little" Garrick did not. Walpole wrote that he was "amazed Lord Henry is a prodigy, a perfection—all passion, nature and ease—."[41]

The costumes for *The Wonder* were sumptuous. Set in Portugal, the play lent itself to lavish display. Don Pedro—Lord Henry, that is—wore "a white satin vest and breeches with crimson slashes decorated with gold lace and with a richly embroidered cloak of crimson velvet; a blaze of diamonds shone from his hat." There were seven performances. The king and queen came on March 1, and it was reported that "the Great Theatric business going on is the subject of all fashionable conversation."[42]

The happenings at Richmond House and Inchbald's part in them, along with Texier, Walpole, and Farren, bring together the two worlds of the real and the unreal in the theatre. Farren, acting at Drury Lane during the seasons of 1778–1797, had by 1785 become "engaged" to Lord Derby; it was fitting, therefore, that she should direct the theatricals at Richmond House. Texier was well known in London, not only at Covent Garden, where he served as Harris's agent, but also through the evening entertainments that he arranged at his own house.

The various accounts of these plays at Richmond House give many details of the surroundings as well as the performers. There was no separate theatre as such, but rooms that were fitted up by James Wyatt. Tickets were issued as if they were invitations to an exclusive ball. The duke usually kept twenty tickets for himself and twelve for the duchess; each player was allowed twelve, also. Six were given to the writers of the prologue and the epilogue. The form of the tickets, to be filled in for each play, makes clear that the duke would know those who attended. It read: "The Duke and Duchess of Richmond present their compliments to Mr . . . and have the Honour of sending him His Ticket as a performer and four tickets at his Disposal for the Play of . . . for Thursday the . . . of . . . 178. . . . Mr . . . is requested to insert in his own Hand Writing, on each Ticket the Name of the Person to be admitted, and to sign and seal it with his Arms. Mr . . . is also requested to send to Richmond House on the Day before the Performance, a list of Persons for whom his tickets are made out, without which they cannot be admitted."[43]

The plays began at 8:00, with everyone seated by 7:30 except, of course, the Prince of Wales, who, with his friends, could admit himself at any time. Farren had a special alcove from which she watched and served as prompter. The costumes for these plays were in effect the very elegant clothes of the performers. Mrs. Damer's reflected her taste as a sculptress, and she and Mrs. Hobart wore their own clothes with their own jewels—"distinguished by a profusion of jewels arranged with great elegance and effect," according to a witness, as reported by Suzanne Bloxam. The men found an opportunity to indulge their elegant taste in rich and extravagant dress. One account reported that "'Lord Derby and Mr. Edgecumbe were most superbly habited. . . .' Lord Derby had four changes. 'A chintz nightgown; a brown morning frock; a dauphin colour embroidered with red and silver flowers and a very brilliant star; a rich vest with a light brown coat.'"[44] Mr. Edgecumbe wore richly embroidered crimson velvet with quantities of rings, seals, and diamond pins. The description of such elegance and beauty must have contrasted sharply with the reality of Lord Derby's appearance. He was short with a big head, and he wore his hair in a braid down his back. Exactly how he must have looked in a "chintz nightgown" is rather difficult to picture. Farren was tall and very thin, some two feet taller than Derby; they were a perfect pair for the caricaturist. One contemporary account of him is quite frank: "Lord Derby was a singular-looking man for a lover. Although at the time but 45 he looked fifteen years older. He had an excessively large head surmounting his small, spare figure and wore his hair in a long thin pigtail. This with his attachment to short nankeen gaiters, made him an easily recognized subject in numerous caricatures of the day."[45]

Derby was already married when he began to notice Farren. Three years earlier, in a round of fetes and parties, he had married Lady Elizabeth Hamilton, the only daughter of the sixth duke of Hamilton.[46] Her mother was one of the celebrated Gunning sisters who came to London from Ireland. Both Lady Elizabeth and Lord Stanley, as he was then, were young and a part of the fashionable set. It was known by all of her friends that Lady Elizabeth was in love with the duke of Dorset, who, it was said, had gone to Italy rather than become engaged to her. Among the various celebrations before the wedding of Derby and Lady Elizabeth, there was one magnificent "Fête Champêtre." One writer says it was the first of its kind in England; that was not quite true, perhaps, but it certainly was true that there had been nothing like it since the days of the Stuarts. The Adam brothers designed the pavilions; Garrick directed the players in Burgoyne's *Maid of the Oaks* (The Oaks was the estate of Lord Stanley's grandfather). It was said that the decorations cost five thousand pounds. So many people came from London that the prime minister could not raise a quorum in Parliament; thus, dismissing the remaining members, he himself went to the wedding.

In London the Adam brothers were building Derby House in Grosvenor Square (now the American Embassy). The marriage celebrated with such pomp and ceremony very quickly fell apart; the house on Grosvenor Street soon had no mistress, for Lady Stanley ran away with the duke of Dorset. The rumors went about: would he marry her if her husband would divorce her? It was said that when Derby heard the rumor, he said, "then by God, I will not get a divorce; I will not give her the opportunity of using another man so ill as she has done me."[47] Rumors and stories were reported in newspapers and in letters that speculated about the situation. Sarah Lennox (Sir Charles's wife) wrote: "It is imagined the Duke of Dorset will marry Lady Derby, who is now in the country keeping quiet and out of the way. There is a sort of party in town of who is to visit her and who is not, which makes great squabbles. . . . I am told she has been and still is more thoroughly attached to the Duke of Dorset, and if so suppose she will be very happy if the lessening of her visiting list is the only misfortune."[48]

At the time all these events were taking place at Richmond House, Farren was working hard at the Haymarket and at Drury Lane, and Inchbald had not yet been "coupled" with Sir Charles. It is something of an irony that Lady Sarah Lennox, who wrote about the scandal, would herself create just such a scandal when she ran away with her cousin and had his child shortly after she married Sir Charles. Subsequently, Sir Charles did give Lady Sarah a divorce, and afterward she married happily; Lord Derby did not give his wife a divorce, and the duke of Dorset deserted her, so that in the end she had a very unhappy life. Lady Sarah and Lady Hamilton are but two examples of the many tragedies of arranged marriages among the nobility in the closing years of the eighteenth century.

Those who participated in the Richmond House plays were quite experienced actors, even though they never appeared on stage at Drury Lane or Covent Garden.[49] There was a long tradition of private theatricals, and the players in these plays at Richmond House had acted before, giving yet another example of society's infatuation with plays. Mrs. Inchbald's part in the Richmond House plays adds to her professional work and gives an interesting insight into the London scene; Farren, who directed these plays, served as a link to the "real" theatre.

Burgoyne wrote the prologue for *False Appearances,* and his part in all these theatrical activities reminds us that he was quite involved in the theatre. By this time in 1789, he had had three plays produced at Drury Lane, one being *The*

Heiress, in which Farren created the role of the heroine, Lady Emily Gayville, a proper "Lady." The play created quite a sensation, becoming the hit of the season, and the part Farren played became celebrated as showing that she herself was a "Lady." It is not surprising that she became the directress for the Richmond House plays.

By 1786 Burgoyne had seemingly been forgiven for his disastrous part in the war in America, where he had begun serving in 1775; he was one of the three generals who arrived in Boston on the *Cerberus,* the others being Generals Gage and Howe. He was present at the Battle of Bunker Hill, and in June of 1777 he took Fort Ticonderoga, but he was not always so successful: in October, having lost his advantage at Ticonderoga, he retreated to Saratoga and surrendered to the American general Gates on October 17. In 1778, while his troops were imprisoned until the end of the war, he had returned to the life in England that fit his nickname, "Gentleman Johnny." He was Lord Derby's uncle by marriage, having eloped with Derby's aunt, Lady Charlotte Stanley, and thus was a part of the family.

Burgoyne's career in the theatre had an especially interesting episode in Boston in the winter of 1775–1776 while he and his troops remained after the Battle of Bunker Hill; he had organized amateur theatricals there and had written an original play. One officer called him "our David Garrick" and wrote, "we have plays, assemblies and balls." Faneuil Hall was used as a playhouse, and several popular plays were produced. Burgoyne's was entitled *The Blockade of Boston.* Benson Bobrick reports one account of this event:

As it happened, on opening night the play had a rude interruption. The Americans knew exactly when the performance was to begin, and they attacked the mill at Charlestown just as the curtain went up. Art and life traded places in a superior farce. As the introductory skit was ending, one of the actors, wrote an eyewitness, came onstage from the wings "dressed in the character of a Yankee sergeant (which character he was to play) desired silence, and informed the audience . . . that the rebels had attacked Charlestown, and were at it tooth and nail. The audience thinking this the opening of the new piece, clapped prodigiously; but soon finding their mistake, a general scene of confusion ensued. They immediately hurried out of the house to their alarm posts; some skipping over the orchestra, trampling on the fiddles, and every one making his most speedy retreat, the actors (who were all officers) calling out for water to wash the smut and paint from off their faces; women fainting, and, in short, the whole house was nothing but one scene of confusion, terror, and tumult."[50]

The significance of such "private" theatre performances as this one in Boston has not been examined extensively, but they were very popular in various places and under various circumstances, and frequently the playwrights who wrote such plays came from all segments of society; such information reaffirms the importance of theatre both in England and in America. Mrs. Inchbald was later to be a part of private performances with her friend Priscilla Kemble in another setting very much like Richmond House. The use of private theatricals as a point of reference was not limited to the "Great" houses, however, nor was it limited to the late eighteenth century. Jane Austen, for example, used Mrs. Inchbald's *Lovers' Vows* in her novel *Mansfield Park* to show the unseemly worldly behavior of Mary and Henry Crawford, the houseguests at Mansfield Park.[51]

False Appearances was the last play of the "season" and in fact the last play to be given at Richmond House, since the next year the room was dismantled and turned into accommodations for the duke's relative Colonel Charles Lennox and his wife Lady Charlotte. Richmond House burned just before Christmas in 1791 and was never rebuilt.[52]

It is interesting to speculate about how many people in the theatre world knew about the play. Willard Austin Kinne, discussing the adaptations of the French plays, follows his discussion of *The Child of Nature* (adapted from the French) with comments about Conway's *False Appearances,* little realizing that *False Appearances* was not Conway's but Inchbald's.[53] When it was given at Drury Lane, it played for only six performances. Inchbald has never been given any credit for her part in translating it, even though surely many of her friends and acquaintances knew she had done it. Perhaps her friends thought it not worth commenting about, and Conway's deception was made acceptable by the fact that doing translations had by 1789 become such a popular exercise for a great many people who wanted to publish or merely wanted to be known for their part in the literary world. It was a trend that extended into the 1790s and beyond, and it is probable that Inchbald did other such assignments that have gone unrecorded.

In the spring of 1789, when the time came to sign her contract at Covent Garden for the next season, Inchbald did not do so, and though she continued at the Haymarket, she acted very little—only once in her own *Mogul Tale.* In September she began what she called her poverty week by giving up the dining room and using only her quarters on the second floor. In the spring also she, along with all of London, rejoiced at the king's recovery. She was present when the queen and the three eldest princesses went to Covent Garden for their first appearance in public on April 15, and on April 23, St. George's Day, she and most of London saw the king go in procession to St. Paul's for a service of thanksgiving.

The Child of Nature, which had given her such trouble, continued to be played, now that it had become a farce, thus being played as an after-piece in second place

in the evening's entertainment. In the end, many years later when Inchbald selected farces for the collection entitled *A Collection of Farces and other Afterpieces
which are acted at The Theatres Royal, Drury-Lane, Covent Garden and Hay-Market. Printed under the authority of the Managers From the Prompt Book: Selected by
Mrs. Inchbald,* it was the first selection in the first volume. It remained a very
popular piece and continued to be a favorite of Inchbald herself.

Without having both sides of the correspondence about changing the play
from four acts to two, but surveying the four acts as compared to the two-act
farce, we see again the demands of the theatre to cut the scenes about Amanthis's
father, leaving out much of the story of his being in India and making a fortune
there. No doubt the references to the problems of Hastings and the East India
Company would have stirred mixed emotions among the diverse audience who
saw the play in its original form. The entries in Inchbald's pocket-book show that
she got her play published before it was cut, and repeated references to the fact
that it was played both as a main piece and an after-piece show how she regarded
her work. During April she was working on a play for Colman, another translation from the French. This new piece was *Le Philosophe Marié,* by Destouches.
She finished it and sent it to Colman on the fifteenth; she also sent a letter with
the manuscript, for Colman wrote on the seventeenth from Richmond:

Indeed, my dear Madam, I am rather surprised at your repeated declarations concerning the little drama you have sent me. It appears to me, on the first reading, both entertaining and interesting; with more rain and sun-shine than the month in which I write,
hitherto proverbial, has this year exhibited. Some alterations, however, especially in the
part of Sir John, (I don't like the name of Classic,) will I think be material. Early in the
next week I shall be in town, and hope to see you in the course of it, and to assure you that
I will, on this occasion, as usual, do all in my power to 'Speed the Plough,' and to convince
you that I am,

> Dear Madam,
> Your faithful and obedient
> Geo. Colman.

You have not communicated the French title, nor supplied any other. There have occurred to me three:—"The Perplexed Husband"—"The Perplexed Couple"—"The Married Man." The last, I believe, is the *very thing.*[54]

Boaden's comments about this piece again are significant, as he continues to
point out the way Inchbald worked: "Mr. Colman, as usual with him, suggested
alterations, and his fair friend's piece was read to the company on the 1st of July.
While it was in rehearsal Mr. Holcroft called upon her, and advised her to *with-*

draw it. The ground of this advice does not appear: what he said seems to have fortunately been disregarded, for on the 15th of the month it was produced with great success, and she was in a condition to pay Mr. Whitfield fifty pounds for some French piece which he had obtained for her."[55]

She had recorded in her pocket-book in 1788 that she had seen Holcroft on several occasions; she and he had been friends since those days in Canterbury in the summer of 1777 before she and her husband had gone to Wilkinson and York, but just when they became close friends in London is difficult to determine. Holcroft had been at Drury Lane from 1777 until 1783, and after he went to Paris in 1784, he returned with his adaptation of Beaumarchais's *Marriage of Figaro*, which he called *The Follies of a Day* and in which he played the part of Figaro. After 1784 he turned increasingly to writing, writing that began to be filled with his political and philosophical views. Inchbald was to be closely associated with Holcroft in the early 1790s, but at this point in 1789 she did not take his advice— or honor his request—and *The Married Man* came out on July 15. It was a great success, and Robinson bought the copyright immediately.

THE MARRIED MAN

The Married Man is another of the Inchbald plays that depend largely on dialogue, and Lady Classick, the married woman, is another "Inchbald woman." The opening scene sets the tone and theme of the play, and the title reveals the central concern. Sir John Classick is a "married man," but he does not want anyone to know it, and his wife, Lady Classick, finds it difficult to keep her marriage a secret; she has no reason to do so except that her husband wishes her to. Sir John's friend Dorimant had advised him to marry, suggesting the many advantages of the married state, and as the scene opens, Sir John, in his library, is complaining to himself: "A scholar, a philosopher to change his peaceful hours, his nights of study, and his days of fame!—And for what?—A wife!—A wife without a fortune too!— Where was my wisdom?—But young and handsome!—Where was my philosophy?—Where my pride, to do an act at which I blush?"

He does not hear Dorimant enter, and, still unaware of his friend, he continues: "Ah Dorimant, my friend, it is you I have to blame—You were the cause of my marriage—You painted wedlock with an eloquence that deluded me—Pictured my wife as soft, complying—." And when Dorimant asks, "And is not she?" Sir John has to admit that her only indiscretion is that she wishes to have her husband acknowledge her as his wife; her only indiscretion is the "secret" Sir John wishes to be kept. His speech places him in the situation of the play and also sets the action.

There are others in Sir John's household who know the secret, however, one of whom is the maid Lucy, and as Dorimant leaves, she enters. She speaks aside to the audience as she enters: "Always reading! And never thinking of his wife, day nor night," and then to him she says, "Sir, Sir, her Ladyship desired me to come—." Before she can give her message, he interrupts her—"Silence!—I thought, Mrs. Lucy, I had a hundred times forbidden you to make use of that name." She replies, "Yes, Sir—but when one forgets, I can't see what harm it can do."

> *Sir John:* You know you were amongst the few who were entrusted with the secret of our marriage.
> *Lucy:* And I have kept it a secret these two years!—Two years is a long time to hold one's tongue!

In his reply to this speech, Sir John reveals additional reasons for keeping the marriage a secret; his wealthy uncle would perhaps be very displeased. Lucy calls his hand. "I thought philosophers despised all such dirty dross as gold." But Sir John will not reply to that point. He says, "But Mrs. Lucy, although I may be of that opinion, perhaps my children may not, and I may one day be reproached for neglecting their fortunes." Whereupon she points out, "But Sir, your children are yet to come, and a philosopher's talent is to reform the world, but very seldom to people it."

Since he cannot be the "philosopher" to Lucy, he abandons that argument and threatens her: "Entrusting you with a secret, Mrs. Lucy, has given you a freedom that may very soon lose you your place." To which she replies, "Oh, Sir! I am sure you know better than to turn a servant away, whom you have been obliged to trust with a secret.—There are many better ways to keep a servant silent."

He gives her money, and she promises to be silent for a month. With this speech Lucy returns to her message, but she keeps referring to her Ladyship—"not your wife—but my mistress—." At this point Lucy leaves, and her mistress appears. Lucy is another of Inchbald's servant characters who adds pert dialogue to the situations but hardly moves the action along. Whereas in the earlier *Widow's Vow* and *The Midnight Hour,* the servants' parts advanced the plots, in this play Lucy's conversation is directed to Sir John and the other characters as a kind of commentary on their views, for example, her remark to Sir John about philosophers.

Sir John chastises Lady Classick for coming to his study, to which she replies, "And I have as many times obeyed you—but at present I want to speak to you upon a subject of so much importance, to us both, that I have ventured to disobey your commands."

Sir John replies, "'Commands.'—You talk to me as if I were your tyrant.—I have but one command—Keep our marriage secret." She knows that the world is talking—that she can no longer keep the marriage a secret, but again when he protests that her "joy" is a sign the secret is known, she replies, "To have you for a husband is a happiness so flattering—a felicity of which I feel myself so proud— that to have it known—would give me infinite delight." Here again, as an "Inchbald woman" she is blameless, but like Lady Euston in *I'll Tell You What,* she will manage her husband discreetly.

The "world" may not know the secret of their marriage, but Lady Classick's sister certainly does. The most pressing reason Lady Classick wishes her husband to acknowledge their marriage is that she is being courted by Lord Lovemore and must therefore declare her marriage—or have her husband do so. Sir John replies to her request: "The very person of all the world I would most conceal it from; for to him more frequently than to any person, have I declared my sentiments of the marriage state; and in what a despicable light, to him, must my inconsistency appear."

Sir John is more than inconsistent, or perhaps he is far too consistent, too full of his own "philosophy" to see anyone's view except his own, and he speaks again about Lord Lovemore. As his wife leaves, he picks up his book, pauses, and throws it down with the comment, "It is impossible for a married man to be a philosopher—and yet it is a state that requires more philosophy than any other."

Sir John is not the only one who is cynical about marriage, or perhaps the subject should be "relationships." Emily, Lady Classick's sister, appears to inquire for Lord Lovemore. Lucy appears with her and speaks as directly to her as she had done to Sir John, for when Emily asks if she (Lucy) thinks Lovemore likes her, Lucy replies "No, Madam."

> *Emily:* But I am determined to make him—and you know I will, if I say I
> will.
> *Lucy:* And if you should, what then?
> *Emily:* Then I shall have the pleasure to tell him I despise him, and that his
> title, birth, and fortune, could not recompense me for marrying a man
> who had previously offered himself, and been refused by my sister.
> *Lucy:* And I cannot help thinking he loves her still.
> *Emily:* As much as a beau, who loves nothing so well as himself, can love;
> and therefore it has long been my design to whisper to him, she is
> married.
> *Lucy:* Do you suppose he will love her the less for that?
> *Emily:* His love being but a mere compound of vanity and gallantry, I
> should suppose not—but at least the news will mortify his pride—and

why should not other people meet with mortifications as well as I, Lucy?

Lucy: And I am sure, Madam, it is not your fault if they do not—for you are ever doing all you can to tease every body you know.

With this dialogue between Emily and Lucy, we are presented with another view of love and marriage or, perhaps, of "relationships." We also here have the "other" woman that Inchbald creates, much like the foolish Lady Harriet in *I'll Tell You What.*

In this short opening in the first act, questions are raised that are surprisingly pertinent to our own society, for though the characters are somewhat stereotypical, the situations reveal the problems of relationships, not marriage; Emily is jealous and envious of her sister and of her marriage to Sir John. As Lucy and Emily continue to talk, Lucy says, "Ay, my mistress—the philosopher seems to have lost all his affection for her."

Emily: Pshaw! you know this pleases me—for it in some degree extinguishes that surprize I feel, while I cannot discover by what art she gained possession of a man of sense, of renown, in short, of such a man as Sir John.—If he were my husband—as you know I wished him to be—I should have expected him to love me—

Emily does not understand love and affection, and when Dorimant comes to call on her and declare his affection, she will not listen to him or his "romantic language." She accuses him of treating her like a child and takes his words as an insult: "This sneer is insufferable.—I tell you what, Dorimant, I wish to hate you—for indeed you have so many imperfections—."

Dorimant: What are they?—
Emily: Oh, innumerable!—You are vain of your person—ashamed of your birth—submissive to your enemies—insincere to your friends—with a thousand worse faults; and yet *with them all*—I can't help liking you.

To Emily's speech Dorimant replies with a list of his own: "As you call my *sincerity* in question, I will give you a proof of it immediately—You are haughty, envious, peevish, conceited, capricious, imprudent—with a thousand worse faults, and yet *with them all* 'I can't help liking you.'" Again Inchbald is using devices familiar to her audience, but with the contrast of the sisters and the men—Sir John and Dorimant—the speeches and replies make a kind of essay on marriage, on relationships.

With the set direction of the two couples, the impasse must have some incident to move the plot forward; that incident occurs with the entrance of Mr. Tradewell Classick, Sir John's uncle. Mr. Tradewell is wealthy and intends to make Sir John his heir; in doing so he has come to arrange a marriage for Sir John with a wealthy heiress, but it cannot be. At the end of this, the first act, we are left to solve the relationships of Sir John and Lady Classick, who are secretly married; Lord Lovemore, who has declared himself to Lady Classick, thinking she may be courted; Dorimant, who loves Emily; Emily, who loves no one but herself; and Mr. Tradewell, who is far more interested in wealth than in philosophy or romance.

This play, a true drawing-room comedy, is surprisingly like Wilde or Ibsen: like Ibsen, who said he asked the questions but did not answer them, or Wilde, who set up improbable situations of marriage or fidelity. And later George Bernard Shaw also would make independent women and their relationships with men the basis of his plays. Inchbald, using the outlines of the play she translated, has in her dialogue created a discussion of the many problems, the many angles, facing relationships in marriage and courtship. This play is about adults, not young ladies whose families seek to marry them to suitors not of their choice. It deals with men who are not conventional in their behavior—Sir John as a married man who wants to hide his marriage and Dorimant as a suitor who is honest and truthful about his faults and the faults of the woman he has chosen to be his wife. In addition to these questions, there are throughout the play recurring comments about "philosophers."

Acts 2 and 3 of *The Married Man* work out the puzzle. Sir John reveals his marriage, and his uncle accepts the situation and congratulates him. Dorimant and Emily agree to agree. The dialogue and the situations continue to the end on the subject of relationships, now of family relationships. Emily and Lady Classick quarrel, but they reconcile when anyone else interferes; Lord Lovemore cannot believe that Matilda (Lady Classick) is married to Sir John and not to Dorimant. The scene between Sir John and Lord Lovemore is a memorable one: Lord Lovemore enters laughing and attempts to tell "the secret," only to discover that Sir John *is* the secret. Again, as in the first act, there is a discussion of *the married man*. Sir John walks about in much confusion and distress while Lord Lovemore declares: "How strange, I could not perceive it before.—But my dear Sir John, pray forgive my having laughed—Upon my honour, had I known, had I conceived you had been the husband, I would not have laughed in your face—." But he cannot help laughing, and as he leaves it is clear that "the secret" is secret no more.

Lovemore: To the world, however, you may depend upon it, I will paint the circumstance in the most favourable light—I will say, your falling in love was but a weakness attendant on human nature—your shame of owning it; but—

Sir John: My Lord, my Lord, you'll make me forget myself.—

Lovemore replies, "Sir John, Sir John, you *have* forgot yourself," whereupon Lord Lovemore begins to leave, only to turn to Sir John and say, "I will [go] and I'll send your wife to you."

At the word "wife" Sir John is in a frenzy—he resolves to leave London instantly and never see Lady Classick again. His friend Dorimant tries to calm him; and when Lady Classick (Matilda), Emily, and Lucy enter, the subject of the secret marriage is discussed openly, with the conclusion that Sir John resolves to leave London. It is at this point that Dorimant reappears with the information that the uncle intends to annul the marriage, since he believes it took place abroad and therefore was not legal.

Mrs. Inchbald and her audience were quite familiar with all the circumstances of illegal and legal relationships, legal ones that frequently were not satisfactory, and illegal ones that were very satisfactory to both partners. Faced with the possibility of declaring his marriage illegal, Sir John does a total about-face, declaring: "Annul my marriage?—Let him—then openly, and in the face of day, I'll marry her again.—Annul my marriage?—Make void the happiest action of my life?—An act which gave to my gloomy mind a friend, a soothing partner to reform it."

The simple truth of the relationship between Sir John and his wife is not enough to solve the problem of marriage, since to sustain this public relationship requires the financial resources to do so. This dilemma is easy to solve in a play—much easier than in real life. It is done with dispatch although with no real solution, except that the uncle, Mr. Tradewell, gives his consent to the marriage, warning Sir John that if Lady Classick begins to act like her sister Emily, he will revoke his will. The play ends with Sir John saying, "I have been an impostor—for while I could equivocate with my friend, and blush at being the husband of such a wife as this, I usurped, like many others, the title of philosopher, without having a claim to it," to which his father replies, "And believe me, my son, while you fill the station as you ought to do, no title is more honourable than that of a MARRIED MAN."

As slight as the play is, it fits the discussions of marriage and the family found in many of Inchbald's other plays. Lady Classick is willing to indulge her husband's eccentric ideas, but she is also strong and insistent when he has gone too far with his "secret." Emily is a representative of those women who, envious of others' success, are, as Dorimant says, conceited, capricious, and imprudent. Emily is like Lady Mary in *Appearance Is against Them*. Lucy is another of the servants who, like Fish in *Appearance*, has an important role in explaining the plot.

Emily's conversation shows her to be another Inchbald example of a woman who would by any means have a husband; Dorimant deserves better. Lord Lovemore is the usual Inchbald character of the silly fop, used here, however, to offer a moment of laughter rather than to serve as a point of censure, as Major Cyprus does in *I'll Tell You What*. *The Married Man* contains one of the most direct analyses found in any of the Inchbald plays of relationships and marriage, especially since in this play the comments are specific and direct.

The dialogue in *The Married Man* is interesting in that the substance of the play lies in the conversations. It is tempting to speculate about how much is taken from the actual conversations that Inchbald had with her "philosopher," especially since Holcroft had suggested that she withdraw the play. By this time Holcroft and Godwin were close friends—did they talk to each other about marriage? Holcroft's third wife had died, and Godwin had never been married. Later they were both to be "married men" after each proposed to Inchbald and was rejected. The comments at the end of the play about usurping the title of philosopher and about the necessary money to finance a marriage were to be applicable to both Godwin and Holcroft, since neither of them had a stable financial base after they were married or indeed ever had one in any case, and Inchbald was determined to be financially secure.

THE HUE AND CRY

The new year found Harris again with an assignment for Mrs. Inchbald, brought by Le Texier. She set to work promptly, finished it by the end of January, and sent it to Harris, but he did not like it; in February she sent it to Colman. He kept it, and in August of the following summer he read it in the Haymarket; it was rejected, and when three years later it was played as a benefit, it was not successful. Called *The Hue and Cry*, adapted from Dumaniant, it was not published until the Backscheider edition in 1980.

The Hue and Cry is a farce set in Spain and filled with the usual situations. Don Lewis has found a prospective husband for his daughter; the daughter, Leonora, becomes attracted to Count Abeville, a Frenchman who met her at a carnival. Added to this situation is the fact that the count takes refuge in Don Lewis's house as he flees from the police for allegedly killing Leonora's cousin Don Juan. Leonora's maid conceals them and helps them escape. Meanwhile,

Don Juan is accused of killing his opponent. The four men—Count Abeville, Don Lewis, and their servants—meet in prison, where they discover no one has been killed, and all ends happily. The play includes Inchbald's use of the duel and a maid who facilitates the action. It is interesting to observe that although Inchbald continues to use such devices as duels and servants to advance the plot, she always contrives to make each use different and effective.

With the failure of two of her plays, we should examine again the way plays were brought to her to be adapted. Harris himself kept tight control of all the assignments and of the approval of any new play submitted to him that he accepted, but he had various people who helped him find suitable ones, people who understood Covent Garden and Harris's taste. As we have pointed out, during the decade of the eighties London was enamored with French plays; during the nineties, with German ones. Moreover, the plays of Shakespeare that Kemble presented in Drury Lane, the plays that Garrick had changed, and the plays that Colman adapted made up the repertory year after year. As for Inchbald, she did not select these plays but adapted them at the direction of Colman or Harris. Her experience with the adaptations shows her clever ability to follow the lines of the plays she was given and add her own touch. It is not possible in the limited space of a biography to document how the adaptation of French plays dominated the offerings in both Covent Garden and Drury Lane in the eighties, but the information we have from the pocket-books is a very significant comment on the whole practice of adapting plays for the theatres and on Le Texier, who evidently made a business of supplying the French ones. Considering the number of plays she worked with, it is not surprising that some of them did not succeed on stage.

A SIMPLE STORY

Between translations of one kind or another, Inchbald had been working on her own projects. She had picked up her novel that she failed to find a publisher for in 1780, and she had begun another at some time more than a year before. She was also working on her own new comedy. The novels became *A Simple Story*, and the comedy was *Every One Has His Fault*.

According to Boaden, in the midst of the rehearsals of *The Married Man*, "She had begun to copy her work [her novels] on the 2nd of July, when on the 25th she first thought of joining her two novels into one story."[56] Some critics have discussed *A Simple Story* as if Inchbald had sat down and written the whole of it in the last months of 1789 and the early months of 1790. Such was not the case, and the way she worked on what she had designed to be two novels explains a great deal about the final work. Moreover, remembering the way she revised and rewrote her plays, we may be certain that she followed the same pattern in writing her novels. There is also the fact that the novel as a form had become very popular with a wide reading public. From the first draft in 1777 to its publication in 1791, no doubt the changes had been read and discussed by friends; and most important for the final publication, William Godwin, who was working for her publisher Robinson, suggested that she change her original composition from letters to a "simple" narrative. At that time she did not know Godwin socially, but later Holcroft, Godwin, and she became close friends, and together they were to have a significant role in the theatre and fiction in the 1790s.

Now in 1789, no longer engaged as an actress, Inchbald especially enjoyed the freedom from her stage duties. Writing of this time, Boaden says: "her old list of notables [called on her], until the contraction of her lodgings made them discontinue what in her state of inconvenience was productive of more pain than pleasure."[57] She had given up the dining room to save money, but in doing so she had limited her visitors; perhaps only without visitors could she get her work done, but if someone very important called, she arranged for them to be shown into the drawing room and came down to see them. She continued to go about, however. Mr. Babb returned to Little Holland House after a trip to Italy, and she and the Whitfields resumed their Sunday dinners with him. She, the Whitfields, and the Kembles went to Billingsgate together on July 10 and after having a fish dinner returned by water to have tea with the Kembles at their house on Caroline Street. A fish house contrasts interestingly with the elegance of the Kembles' drawing room, but both she and the Kembles were free to conduct their social life as they saw fit; they did not have to conform to class and rank. She continued to see Stephen Kemble and his wife, and in October of this year, she went to visit her sister Bigsby in Bury. She was greeted by the local gentry—Lady Gage and Lady Blake—and sat with them at the theatre, and she saw many people she knew. She returned to London with her nephew George Huggins.

On another excursion she went to Mr. Woodfall's house and found it very beautiful. Her sister-in-law Mrs. Simpson came to see her alone for a brief visit, and on the twenty-fourth both her brother and she came and stayed at Charing Cross, and Inchbald saw them daily as long as they were in London. She sat for her portrait for Russell, who was a very fashionable artist at the moment. Working in crayons, Boaden says, he painted a very fine likeness of Topham and of John Palmer, two of Inchbald's good friends.

As always, she continued to read—this year Burke's *Reflections,* Jean-Jacques Rousseau's *Confessions,* Samuel Johnson's *Rasselas,* and some German plays given to her by a German acquaintance. She began a translation of the *Confessions* but did not finish it, and she continued to work on her comedy. At some point she turned all of her attention to her novel.

During November and December of 1789 Inchbald was ill, so ill that she did not write in her journal. She first sent for her apothecary and then for Dr. Warren. After the middle of January 1790, she was somewhat better, and on January 17 she sat up for most of the day; but then she developed a painful abscess on her leg, and Dr. Warren called again to remove it. In the following days he attended her, but it was March before she was able to be out; then she went to her friend Babb's residence in Kensington. She stayed for two weeks, being cared for by Mrs. Evans, the housekeeper. While she was there she did little work; perhaps she made a few alterations in *The Contrast* and thought about her novel. On March 15 she returned home to Frith Street.

By the eighteenth she began to work on her novel again. Without her pocket-book at hand it is impossible to follow exactly her progress in writing and combining her two novels. Boaden says she "finished, transcribed, and sold it to Mr. Robinson; received the first proof from the printer Woodfall on the 11th of November [1790]; but his newspaper seems to have caused delay in the progress, and she transferred her work to Cooper, who completed it."[58] It was published in four small volumes.

Writing more than two decades after *A Simple Story* was published, Boaden begins his discussion of it: "We are now arrived at the production which bears the highest testimony to the genius of Mrs. Inchbald. There are still living men of strong minds, who speak sincerely when they affirm her 'Simple Story' to be yet unequaled." He continues: "We conceive her interest, however, to be anything but *simple*, in any inferential use of that word. It is a story complicated with powerful character and the strongest passions."[59]

These two last terms—"powerful character" and "the strongest passions"—were the ways Inchbald's contemporaries viewed her novel. Interestingly enough, Boaden admits that as he wrote about the novel he was expressing his reaction to it from a recent reading. His testimony is the stronger in that it is the view of the novel that has continued, however the approaches to it may have varied over the years. It has remained a "story complicated with powerful character and the strongest passions."

In the 1790s *A Simple Story* brought unprecedented recognition to Inchbald, even though, as she revised and changed the editions, she continued to be dissatisfied with her work—and with herself. Her experience with the printers and with the work on the second edition formed another chapter in her ongoing struggle to be financially stable. She later said that writing novels was in no way profitable. When we remember that she had worked on the first part of Miss Milner's story in the winter of 1777 when she, her husband, the Siddonses, and the Kembles were forced to flee the magistrates and live without employment, it is not surprising that she felt the payment she eventually received was not worth the time she had given. The other side of her comment, however, was that she was determined that her novel would be published—if she had to change it—if she had to extend it—if she had to construct it in a different way—if she had to add tag lines to associate it with popular views and interests. In the end she did all of these things.

From the first publication of *A Simple Story*, readers have seen Inchbald as Miss Milner and Kemble as Dorriforth. Boaden quotes "an amiable critic" describing Dorriforth as "a Romish priest of a lofty mind, generous, and endued with strong sensibilities." Boaden himself continues, "When such a character gives himself up to celibacy, we are to expect that nature in him will some way *suffer* by the sacrifice. He becomes *stern* and *inflexible;* because, having commanded his own tendencies, he exacts from others the same performance of *duty*, however painful; and he literally avenges his own deprivations, when he punishes the errors or vacillations of those around him."[60]

Inchbald's contemporaries saw Miss Milner as a coquette, and since they saw Inchbald as a coquette as well, the equation of Kemble, the former Catholic in training for the priesthood, and Inchbald as a flirt who falls in love with him at first sight, was as intriguing as the story she invented. Proper young unmarried women did not converse with men as Miss Milner does, making pointed arguments that they cannot confute, and Mrs. Inchbald, a beautiful young widow, must surely have appeared in the green room as unduly vivacious and independent in her witty conversations.[61]

Boaden almost idolized Kemble, and he could not have imagined at any time that someone like Inchbald would not have been desperately in love with him, especially after her husband's death. But as we have seen, Kemble, who attempted to "regulate" her conduct in York, had hardly the attitude of a lover; in Ireland he was too timid and ambitious to declare himself, and she, concerned with other matters, went back to England to continue her writing. There is nothing in these years in the events of Inchbald's association with Covent Garden or in Kemble's with Drury Lane to give evidence for romance. Moreover, no one reading the novel and the comments of the contemporary audience has bothered to take into consideration the history of Kemble's and Inchbald's discussions about their writing. Kemble freely admitted that Inchbald's original work was far better than his, but we have no direct evidence about how he viewed *A Simple Story*. In

1791 he was busy attempting to keep Drury Lane solvent in the face of Sheridan's total disregard for financial matters. If the readers in the spring of 1791 wanted to discuss a possible "romance" between Kemble and Inchbald, they did so with no evidence except speculation, speculation that has, following Boaden, been repeated as a "romantic" story that is certainly fiction within fiction.

One of the important subjects in Miss Milner's part of the story is Dorriforth's eagerness to have her married and his selection of her "suitors" that he approved of and the ones he did not. This was not at all the true situation of Elizabeth Simpson. We may decide either that in her situation as a farmer's daughter she was left to be married to a man in her own community and become a housewife or that she made her own choice of a husband for reasons of her own. Whatever reasons she may have had for her choice, it is clear from her letters and later conduct that it was hers. The charming view of how Kemble read the service from the prayer book in 1777 when the Inchbalds, the Siddonses, and Kemble had been cast out of town as strollers breaking the law had by now been completely changed, and no use of this episode to make a "romance" of Inchbald and Kemble could survive. The question of Inchbald and her loyalty to the church in the late 1780s and the 1790s is certainly a part of her personal and professional life, but in 1791 all such matters were personal and not a part of her public—or for that matter her social—life.[62]

However important marriage is as a subject in the novel for Dorriforth, the feature of Miss Milner that is most like Inchbald is Miss Milner's independence, both in her actions and in her ideas; and the real dichotomy between the two sections of the novel lies in the fact that Sandford, whose views in the first part represent those of the Roman Catholic Church, has in the second part won his case to subdue Miss Milner, now Lady Elmwood, and now offers her only the comfort of escaping eternal damnation. By the time she published *A Simple Story,* Inchbald had had serious doubts about her religion and her relationship to the authority of the church. In the end she returned to the church, but in 1789–1790 she never records that she went to Mass. *A Simple Story* is not about the Catholic Church.

The second part of *A Simple Story,* written at least ten years later than the first, is quite a different matter. Looked at as a novel of the late 1780s and early 1790s, it is Inchbald's reading of a very dysfunctional family situation. Miss Milner/ Lady Elmwood is now a "fallen woman" and must suffer penance and hope for mercy. Sandford, the former harsh judge and accuser, is now, "his hair grown white, his face wrinkled with age, his heart the same as ever;—the reprover, the enemy of the vain, the idle, and the wicked; but the friend, the comforter of the forlorn and miserable."[63] The suggestions about what prompted Inchbald to join her two novels have been many. Boaden cites *A Winter's Tale* of Shakespeare, though he also suggests that the first part, the story of Dorriforth and Miss Milner, was really too short to be published as a novel. The devices Inchbald uses to join the two are rather slight, and the conclusions of both parts are quite ambiguous. The ideas about education are obviously added as an afterthought, brought about perhaps by various conversations Inchbald had with people like her friend Holcroft. She was to discuss education directly in her second novel, *Nature and Art,* but in *A Simple Story* her reader is left to decide just what she means in her parting comment: "what may not be hoped from that school of prudence—though of adversity—in which Matilda was bred?"[64]

Some critics have suggested various sources for the novel from her reading, but from the remarkable breadth of her reading—books, histories, pamphlets, newspapers, periodicals, poetry, letters, novels—no one source emerges. If there were one area in which she read the most, it was in history, and like her contemporaries, she believed that the Shakespeare plays were British history. To make any assessment of her use of her reading, we would need all the pocket-books in hand, but of course we do not have them and must rely on Boaden's report. We know she had read Samuel Richardson's *Clarissa;* she had also read Henry Mackenzie's *Man of Feeling,* Oliver Goldsmith's *Vicar of Wakefield,* and Alexander Pope's *Essay on Man,* and sometime in 1790 she had read Rousseau's *Confessions* and had begun a translation of it, work she abandoned before she completed it.[65]

No matter how much or how little we discover about Inchbald's reading or about her association with Kemble, however, we must conclude that the novel is fiction, her creation of two very strong characters and her view of what happens when neither understands the other. By the time she finished her novel, having written and rewritten and rewritten it, she was certainly not the young ingenue of 1777. *A Simple Story* is hardly a "fiction of her own experience" or even an imagined fiction of the people, events, or incidents of her life; instead, the novel is based on shrewd observation of her world, colored by the reading she had done; and by this time, having examined families and their various circumstances and problems in such plays as *Such Things Are* and *The Married Man,* she was quite ready to explore the experiences of a beautiful young girl brought up as a Protestant in the household of an older man who was a Catholic priest.

Maria Edgeworth, Inchbald's contemporary admirer and later close friend, was the critic who wrote the most penetrating and correct analysis. She wrote to Inchbald herself:

I have just been reading, for the third—I believe for the fourth time—the "Simple Story." Its effect upon my feelings was as powerful as at the first reading; I never read *any* novel—I except *none*—I never read any novel that affected me so strongly, or that so completely possessed me with the belief in the real existence of all the people it represents. I never once recollected the author whilst I was reading it; never said or thought, *that's a fine sentiment*—or, *that is well expressed*—or, *that is well invented.* I believed all to be real, and was affected as I should be by the real scenes if they had passed before my eyes: it is truly and deeply pathetic. I determined, this time of reading, to read it as a critic—or rather, as an author, to try to find out the secret of its peculiar pathos. But I quite forgot my intention in the interest Miss Milner and Dorriforth excited; but *now it is all over,* and that I can coolly exercise my judgment, I am of opinion that it is by leaving more than most other writers to the imagination, that you succeed so eminently in affecting it.... Writers of inferior genius waste their words in *describing* feeling; in making those who pretend to be agitated by passion describe the effects of that passion, and talk of the *rending of their hearts,* &c. A gross blunder! as gross as any Irish blunder; for the heart cannot feel, and describe its own feelings, at the same moment.[66]

This letter from Edgeworth is dated January 14, 1810. This "reality" that Edgeworth wrote about in 1810—almost two decades after the publication of *A Simple Story*—is the "simple" reason the book continued to be read and continued to be in print from that time to this.

A Simple Story begins in quite a "simple" way. Dorriforth, a Roman Catholic priest, is asked by his dying friend, Mr. Milner, to receive his daughter into his household, a household that includes Mrs. Horton, an elderly lady, the mistress of the house; her niece Miss Woodley, who at thirty is unmarried but whose cheerful temper and good nature keep her from ridicule, even from the use of the label "old maid"; and a frequent visitor, Sandford, who is Dorriforth's former tutor, another Catholic priest. Mr. Milner, a Catholic himself, married a Protestant; their only child, Miss Milner, was educated at a Protestant boarding school according to her mother's wishes. Mr. Milner's final request of Dorriforth is that he will "protect without controlling, instruct without tyrannizing, comfort without flattering, and perhaps in time make good by choice rather than by constraint." And that he will not "direct his ward in one religious opinion contrary to those her mother had professed, and in which she had been educated." His last words on the subject are that Dorriforth should "Never perplex her mind with an idea that may disturb, but cannot reform." We are told little about Dorriforth except that he shunned a cloister, that he has a more than adequate income, that he is related to one of the first Catholic peers, and that his income is "approaching to affluence."[67] Thus the church found his position with rank and property more important than a cloister. Inchbald's readers would hardly have needed any explanation of the situation, but for later readers the "instruct without tyrannizing" is perhaps more understandable with some brief comment about the positions of the Catholics at this time.

In Catholic households the sons were reared as Catholics, but if the mother was a Protestant, the daughters were brought up as Protestants. We remember, for example, that John Philip Kemble was a Catholic and his sisters were Protestants. The fact that Dorriforth was not cloistered was not unusual, since the church could not openly worship as an organized institution, and thus, although he was a priest, he had no duties to perform.[68] Sandford was tutor to Dorriforth and his nephew Lord Elmwood, and we are told that the young earl feared him and that Dorriforth was still very much under his influence. He becomes a central character in the story.

Before Miss Milner appears, we are told of her beauty, and after the passage about her beauty, Mrs. Hilgrave, Dorriforth's friend, appears and praises her character, but she cannot remember even whether Miss Milner was tall or short; and the next morning, when Miss Milner herself appears, both Dorriforth and Mrs. Horton are impressed not only with her beauty but also with her lively elegance and dignified simplicity. This combination of physical beauty and beauty of character is a theme examined throughout the first two books. With this introduction Miss Milner becomes the ward of Dorriforth—indeed the ward of Sandford and the extended family.

In 1791 Mrs. Inchbald's readers would have been very interested in "beauty," physical beauty. In her world of the theatre, there had been celebrated beauties— Margret (Peg) Woffington, for example; and in the 1780s and 1790s the Gunning sisters, the Lennox sisters, and Inchbald's own friends Sarah Siddons and Elizabeth Farren were celebrated beauties. The portraits of these beauties were widely admired, and Lady Sarah, Sir Charles's former wife, was much praised for her beauty in 1760 when the prince, shortly before he was to be the king, was widely known to be in love with her. At that time Horace Walpole wrote that Lady Sarah was "more beautiful than you can conceive." And shortly after we are told of Miss Milner's beauty we are told of the "beauties of her disposition." As always, Inchbald has set her work in the context of her own time.[69]

We follow Miss Milner as she becomes part of the household, and after some time we see Dorriforth becoming more and more aware of the growing intimacy between himself and his ward; he becomes increasingly concerned for the future. For although he wishes to act properly as Miss Milner's guardian and therefore arrange for Miss Milner to be married—that is, he wishes his ward in the protection of another rather than himself—he does not wish that man to be a young nobleman immersed in all the vices of the town. Thus Lord Frederick

Lawley, Miss Milner's professed admirer, and Dorriforth begin to be set against each other. Naturally Miss Woodley, who is always present as Miss Milner's chaperone, is very alarmed to hear Lord Frederick declare to Miss Milner, "By heaven I believe Mr. Dorriforth loves you himself, and it is jealousy makes him treat me thus." At this point Miss Milner, upon Miss Woodley's horror at such a sacrilegious idea, cries, "for shame," but Lord Frederick will not be put down. "Nay," he says, "if he be not in love for what but a savage could behold beauty like hers and not own its power?" To which Miss Milner replies, "Habit is every thing—and Mr. Dorriforth sees and converses with beauty, and from habit does not fall in love, as you, my lord, merely from habit do."[70] Their conversation ends with the entrance of Dorriforth, but the power of beauty, only just introduced, remains. We have now been told that Miss Milner is both beautiful and generous, and in her conversation with Lord Frederick, we see her loyalty to her guardian. Throughout the narrative of the first two books, Lord Frederick serves as a foil to Dorriforth. In a quite significant way, Inchbald makes his elegance and sophistication represent the best qualities of the society that Miss Milner and Dorriforth belong to; Lord Frederick has both the virtues and the flaws of that society. As always, in Inchbald's hands her characters are realized as belonging to her world. Lord Frederick's sophistication and wit make him as attractive as Dorriforth.

Soon after her arrival, Miss Milner begins to reveal her ability to have her own independent thoughts and ideas, to disapprove of certain actions of Dorriforth and of the restrictions Sandford attempts to place upon her; she does not feel that Sandford has any right to direct either her ideas or her actions. Indeed, it is this element in her character that dominates the whole of her relationship with Sandford and, at this point, with Dorriforth, for although in the beginning Dorriforth allows Sandford to place the restrictions, in the climactic scene after she returns from a masquerade that Dorriforth has explicitly forbidden her to attend, he, now Lord Elmwood and her declared lover, abandons her for no other reason than her continued independence. That is, Elmwood realizes just how independent she is and prepares to leave her, even though he has already designed her to be his wife.[71] Miss Milner, as we know, is not a Catholic, and although the methods of the church in exerting absolute authority extend far beyond the use of the patriarchal pattern in the novel and in Dorriforth/Lord Elmwood's exercise of his prerogative as a man, Elmwood's tactics are clearly reminiscent of his training for the priesthood and his accepting Sandford's "teaching." Boaden describes the scene when Elmwood is about to depart to Rome, the seat of Catholicism: "the lover," he says, "at last determines upon a foreign tour, and the destined moment of his *departure* is, by the most dramatic incident in the piece, rendered that of his *union* to the agitated ward." Immediately after this comment, Boaden writes: "Here again we have to notice the Catholic principle that pervades the interest. The tutor and bosom friend of Dorriforth is a Jesuit of profound discernment and rational attachment. He sees prophetically the mischiefs threatened by such an union, and systematically throws every impediment in the way of it. . . . But at the decisive moment, seeing his patron linger, unable to tear himself away, Sandford exclaims, 'Separate this moment, or resolve to be separated only by death.' . . . Cold indeed must be the bosom that does not sympathize with the bride."[72]

From the beginning Inchbald infuses her story with family. Miss Milner, having lost her father, has no one left. Dorriforth, as the senior member of his family, is the authority figure for his nephew, his sister, and her son, but having disapproved of her marriage, Dorriforth has also denied her child. These family relationships are very important not only for the story line but also for an understanding of the relationship between Dorriforth and Miss Milner. Dorriforth's heir, the Earl of Elmwood, who is to be married to Miss Fenton, is introduced, and almost at the same time, Sir Edward Ashton is introduced. Sir Edward is the man Dorriforth would like to select for Miss Milner's husband. "Sir Edward was not young or handsome; old or ugly; but immensely rich, and possessed of qualities that made him in every sense, worthy of the happiness to which he aspired." Perhaps it should be noted here that his qualifications to be Miss Milner's husband are that he is "immensely rich" and that he is "worthy of the happiness to which he aspired"—a significant comment on arranged marriage, which was still, of course, the practice at the time. But although Miss Milner declares her heart not given away, she refuses Sir Edward, and nothing can change her mind as she says, "Nor can I speak of love from experience . . . but I think I can guess what it is." But to disagree about suitors, however important, was only one small matter. Dorriforth, quite unaccustomed to govern, and Miss Milner, equally unaccustomed to be governed, inevitably faced serious problems. As we learn both from conversation and from conduct, Dorriforth had "in his nature shades of evil . . . an obstinacy"; Miss Milner was "the gay, the proud, the haughty." We find that Dorriforth refused to see his sister's son, whom Miss Milner tricked him into receiving only to see Dorriforth refuse him with "not one trait of compassion for his helpless nephew."[73]

At this point Dorriforth suggests Miss Fenton as a model for Miss Milner. Miss Fenton was beautiful, had elegant manners and a gentle disposition, and was in all ways, Dorriforth thought, a pattern for Miss Milner to emulate. "Not to admire Miss Fenton was impossible—to find a fault in her person or sentiments was equally impossible—and yet to love her, was very unlikely."[74] She had been selected by both Dorriforth and Sandford to be Lord Elmwood's wife, since Dorriforth, as Lord Elmwood's uncle, was in a position to arrange such a match.

Sandford, we are told, felt that "she [Miss Milner] was of no importance." Instead, Miss Fenton was given all his attention and praise. In confronting Miss Milner, he considered it his mission to humiliate her; he ignored her or reacted with vigor and ridicule to any conversation he had with her. Her wit and skill at repartee were quite equal to his. Again, as her beauty and innocence were counted as ciphers, her intelligence and wit were discounted. The struggle between the two makes up a good part of the conflict in the plot. Sandford had only authority to support his determination to make Miss Milner compliant; she had her independence and wit to keep her free. Dorriforth, who did not go out into society, did not forbid Miss Milner to do so, and inevitably she was surrounded by admirers; but very soon it was evident that Lord Frederick had became her favorite escort, and without consulting her wishes, Dorriforth and Sandford took Miss Milner into the country to remove her from him and the evils of the social whirl. Even so, Sandford continued to provoke her. "The air of the country has affected the young lady already . . . in the variety of humors some women are exposed to, they cannot be steadfast even in deceit." "Deceit," cried Miss Milner, "in what am I deceitful? did I ever pretend sir, I had an esteem for you?" "That had not been deceit, madam, but merely good manners." "I never, Mr. Sandford, sacrificed truth to politeness."[75]

Dorriforth's lack of understanding and Sandford's malicious teasing inevitably lead to a series of confrontations both in the country and in town. Having refused Sir Edward, Miss Milner also declares repeatedly that she does not love Lord Frederick. Back in the city, she rejoins her circle of society. She goes to the opera, to concerts, to the theatre; she defies Sandford and teases Dorriforth with her behavior about Lord Frederick.

The whole subtext of the conflict between Miss Milner and Sandford allows Inchbald to develop Miss Milner's character and to show Sandford as the most extreme example of the Catholic Church in his belief that he had absolute authority to regulate her conduct and to impose his views on her every move. Miss Milner, in turn, has been given the ability to confront Sandford with her intelligence and wit, so that for most readers then and now she represents the kind of independence that she deserves, whatever her age or station. She thus becomes another "Inchbald woman," one more fully developed than Lady Euston, Sir George's wife in *I'll Tell You What*, or Lady Classick in *The Married Man*. With more opportunity to develop her character, Inchbald has given a fully developed portrait; if in the end Miss Milner acts improperly, she does so for reasons of her own.

From the beginning the household is a unit, and when Miss Milner arrives, she is the outsider. One of the chief problems for Dorriforth and Sandford in understanding her is that neither can comprehend her participation in society. There is no indication that either attended any social function, attended the opera or the theatre, even though we are told that Dorriforth lived as a gentleman. Knowing so little of the social context, Dorriforth is puzzled beyond reason: he cannot understand her attitude about Lord Frederick or about himself. He does, however, understand the behavior of Lord Frederick, who in his presence, he believes, insults Miss Milner; he answers Lord Frederick's challenge, and when he is wounded in the duel that ensues, he begins to realize her concern for him and thus begins to see himself and Miss Milner in a new way. Here again, it is Dorriforth's lack of understanding of the society Lord Frederick represents that provokes him.

His kinsman Lord Elmwood, having died before his marriage with Miss Fenton, leaves the title and the obligation to marry to Dorriforth, who now as Lord Elmwood must continue the line; not to do so would mean that the property of a wealthy Catholic family would revert to the state. It is at this point that Miss Fenton appears again. Is it Lord Elmwood's duty to marry her now that her fiancé, his nephew, the former Lord Elmwood, has died? The question is a nice one that Dorriforth, now Lord Elmwood, must solve for himself, because after the duel with Lord Frederick, he realizes that he is Miss Milner's choice, not Lord Frederick; even so, he has little understanding of her feeling for him. Nevertheless, they become engaged, and upon their engagement she begins to act quite independently without consulting anyone.

Miss Milner's views of love and Lord Elmwood's are not at all compatible, and her view of how she should behave as his future wife is very different from his. He sees her engagement to be his wife as her commitment to him; she views love as being as much his commitment to her as her commitment to him. Again, as earlier, she reaches out into the real world. To test his love, she defies his wishes and goes to a masquerade even though he has made quite clear his disapproval. She, disguised as Chastity, and Miss Woodley, as a wood nymph, go with a group of wood nymphs and huntresses to make up a suit of Diana. Simply going against Elmwood's wishes is not the only thing that upsets him, however; her costume as Diana/Artemis, the virgin goddess, the protector of wild creatures and the protector of chastity, he finds very disturbing.

Her dress is hardly chaste, and in describing it Inchbald shows how a point can be made by being careful with details. We see Miss Milner through the eyes of Miss Woodley as she watches Miss Milner being dressed. She is "struck with astonishment at the elegance of the habit, and the beautiful effect it had upon her graceful person." But she wears buskins, "and the petticoat [is] made to festoon far above the ankle." She has left off powdering her hair and has had her hair curled in ringlets; she is both elegant and beautiful.[76] Buskins were a kind of soft boots that came slightly above the ankle; with a short skirt they would be seen as quite risqué. The whole costume was quite daring, and Inchbald's use of her striking appearance makes the reader a participant in the scene that follows when she returns.[77]

Elmwood, absent when Miss Milner and Miss Woodley leave, is totally overcome when he returns and finds her gone; he stays awake until the two return at four thirty, just as the sun is rising. But even before she returns, he questions the servants as to how she is dressed. This scene and the dialogue with the servants underscore the fact that he is still acting as her guardian and not as her lover; and Sandford, gleeful, holds court, finding the servants to testify against the still absent Miss Milner, "With all the authority and consequence of a country magistrate . . . with his back to the fire and the witnesses before him."[78] Moreover the servants are not questioned about Miss Milner's behavior but about her dress, a subject they have no real information about and certainly no judgment as to its consequence. Masquerades were ubiquitous. This episode not only creates the crisis in the action, but it also emphasizes again the basic theme of the relationship between Dorriforth/Elmwood and Miss Milner.

The masquerade incident has received a great deal of attention, far more in recent criticism than in Inchbald's time. Boaden's account of her going with the marquis of Carmarthen in 1780 was hardly remarked upon except by her own family, who, like Kemble at York, attempted to tell her how she should conduct herself. The marquis was a friend of the players in both theatres; he was never linked with Inchbald as a "keeper," and in the years after the incident of the masquerade, Inchbald continued to be his friend, remarking upon his marriage and many years later upon the death of his son, showing clearly their long friendship.[79] Moreover, one of Inchbald's favorite plays was Cowley's *Belle's Stratagem*, a play in which the whole action, not just an incident, turns on a masquerade ball. The device is used in countless plays and novels throughout the Restoration and the eighteenth century. To use the incident in *A Simple Story* as an autobiographical comment about Inchbald herself is hardly creditable, and the incident itself was of no great importance; it would have been read simply as a young lady going to a party without an escort. The focus on her dress would have been of more importance.

The real "story" of Dorriforth and Miss Milner, however, is not the implications arising from the masquerade but a far more important subject: the subject of love and its relation to marriage in a time and a society that viewed both in a very different way from his unfolding understanding as well as hers in the story. Inchbald's development of the subject in the episode of Dorriforth's duel with Lord Frederick speaks directly to the problem, far more directly than does the episode of the masquerade. When this examination is read as dialogue, the subject becomes immediate and dramatic. When Dorriforth returns from the duel with Lord Frederick, he confronts her:

> "You then still assert you have no affection for my lord Frederick?"
>
> "Not sufficient to become his wife."
>
> "You are alarmed at marriage, and I do not wonder you should be so; it shews a prudent foresight that does you honour—but, my dear, are there no dangers in a single state?—if I may judge, Miss Milner, there are many more to a young lady of your accomplishment, than were you under the protection of a husband."
>
> "My father, Mr. Dorriforth, thought your protection sufficient."
>
> "But that protection was rather to direct your choice, than to be the cause of your not choosing at all.—Give me leave to point out an observation which, perhaps, I have too frequently done before, but upon this occasion I must intrude it once again.—Miss Fenton is its object—her fortune is inferior to yours, her personal attractions less. . . . There is, besides, in the temper of Miss Fenton, a sedateness that might with less hazard secure her safety in an unmarried life; and yet she very properly thinks it her duty, as she does not mean to seclude herself by any vows to the contrary, to become a wife—and in obedience to the counsel of her friends, will be married within a very few weeks."
>
> "Miss Fenton may marry from obedience, I never will."
>
> "You mean to say, Love shall alone induce you?"
>
> "I do."
>
> "If, madam, you would point out a subject upon which I am the least able to speak, and on which my sentiments, such as they are, are formed alone from theory (and even there instructed but with caution) it is the subject of love.—And yet, Miss Milner, even that little I know, tells me, without a doubt, that what you said to me yesterday, pleading for Lord Frederick's life, was the result of the most violent and tender love."
>
> "The *little you know* then, Mr. Dorriforth, has deceived you; had you *known more*, you would have judged otherwise."[80]

When he suggests that he will submit her reply to Miss Fenton and Miss

Woodley, "'And yet, I believe,' replied she with a smile, 'I believe, theory, must only be the judge even there.'"[81]

At this point Sandford comes in, and the conversation turns to a discussion between Dorriforth and Sandford about Miss Milner in her presence, about Miss Milner's seeming frivolity in contradicting her declaration about Lord Frederick. Neither Dorriforth nor Sandford has any understanding of Miss Milner or of the situation; Sandford declares: "I was to blame, that on a nice punctilio, I left you so long without my visits, and without my counsel; in the time, you have run the hazard of being murdered, and what is worse, of being excommunicated; for had you been so rash as to have returned your opponent's fire, not all my interest at Rome would have obtained remission of the punishment."[82]

The Catholics were forbidden to fight a duel, to shed blood for such a reason. Turning the subject so abruptly from Miss Milner to Rome makes Miss Milner laugh through her tears. Sandford continues, "And here do I venture like a missionary among savages—but if I can only save you from the scalping knives of some of them; from the miseries which that lady is preparing for you, I am rewarded."[83]

The passage in the novel that follows this conversation is an extremely powerful comment on love as well as on Sandford himself. To love is to commit sin—to be a savage with scalping knives, and Sandford speaks with such force that the whole is a pronouncement of crime—of the sin of love. "'*The miseries which that lady is preparing for you,*' hung upon her ears like the notes of a raven, and equally ominous.— The words '*murder*' and '*excommunication*' he had likewise uttered; all the fatal effects of sacrilegious love.—Frightful superstitions struck to her heart, and she could scarcely prevent falling down under their oppression." Dorriforth brings the conversation to a close: "Say no more, Mr. Sandford." The end of the "chapter" is not the end of the subject, for Dorriforth, alone with Sandford, confesses "That the mind of a woman was far above or rather beneath, his comprehension."[84]

The discussions about love are scattered throughout the whole of books 1 and 2. In most of the passages, Miss Milner is the teacher and Dorriforth/Elmwood the pupil. His comment that love alone would be her only reason for marriage brings up the subject of Miss Fenton again, she who was merely passive with no will or even opinions of her own. Miss Woodley says, to comfort Miss Milner: "By no means do not suppose Lord Elmwood's marriage is the result of love—it is no more than a duty, a necessary price of business, and this you may plainly see by the wife on whom he has fixed.—Miss Fenton was thought a proper match for his cousin, and this same propriety, you must perceive still exists." To which Miss Milner replies, "And oh! could I but stimulate passion, in the place of propriety—

. . . do you think it would be unjust to Miss Fenton, were I to inspire her destined husband with a passion which she may not have inspired, and which I believe she herself cannot feel?"[85]

Following Miss Milner's declaration about "passion," Miss Fenton is the subject of conversation—she has returned to town. In the course of the conversation, Sandford begins to discuss the "different kinds of women . . . there is as much difference between some women, as between good and evil spirits." Sandford has been speaking to Mrs. Horton, but upon his pronouncement about good and evil spirits, he continues, "And beauty, when endowed upon spirits that are evil, is a mark of their greater, their more extreme wickedness.—Lucifer was the most beautiful of all the angels in paradise—."[86]

Such a pronouncement is more than Miss Milner can bear, knowing that while Sandford is speaking to Mrs. Horton he is really speaking about her. Miss Milner's beauty is a subject used to accuse her of pride, to suggest that she should not think of her appearance in any way to enhance the beauty she has been given as a natural birthright. Miss Milner challenges him: "How do you know?" He continues: "'But the beauty of Lucifer' (continued Sandford, in perfect neglect and contempt of her question,) 'was an aggravation of his guilt; because it shewed a double share of ingratitude to the Divine Creator of that beauty.'" Not to be silenced, she continues, "Now you talk of angels, I wish I had wings; and I should like to fly through the park this morning." To such a remark Elmwood says, "You would be taken for an angel in good earnest." Sandford, much upset with Elmwood's compliment, replies, "Then instead of the wings, I would advise the serpent's skin."[87]

It is at this point that Miss Woodley reminds him that he has promised to accompany Miss Milner to the opera. He replies that he will do so if the Fentons can be included, and she agrees, but although she goes, he does not. It is upon this occasion that Lord Frederick hands her to her carriage, and when her carriage brings her home, Elmwood's carriage arrives at the same time. He and Sandford have spent the evening with the Fentons, and Miss Fenton did not wish to attend the opera. The reader, deeply engaged in following the dialogue of this scene, is perhaps not aware that the discussion of beauty and charity revealed in Miss Milner's initial arrival is now reversed; these actions of Elmwood's and his evening with the Fentons underscore Miss Milner's dilemma: living without the family support that she deserves as a beautiful young, desirable belle in a proper social setting and at the same time being stifled in the tight-knit group of the household in which she is almost a prisoner.

Miss Milner, still very upset, says, "And she [Miss Fenton], with her gloomy disposition, chose to sit at home." Again Sandford reprimands her—"Gloomy disposition? . . . She is a young lady with a great share of sprightliness—and I think I never saw her in better spirits than she was this evening." Miss Milner: "Bless me, Mr. Sandford . . . I only meant to censure her taste for staying at home." "'I think,' replied Sandford, 'a much greater censure should be passed upon those, who prefer rambling abroad.'"[88]

When Lord Elmwood leaves, Sandford continues the conversation, which becomes even more heated when Sandford and she discuss love and marriage—or Sandford discusses marriage and Miss Milner love. Inchbald here, as in the earlier *Child of Nature,* has created a character who cannot accept the idea of a loveless marriage. As the conversation changes from love and marriage as the topic, Sandford speaks of Lord Elmwood, accusing Miss Milner of offending Elmwood by her remark that Miss Fenton's is a "gloomy disposition." A real dispute between the two develops:

> *Sandford:* Whatever her temper is, *every one* admires it; and so far from its being what you have described, she has a great deal of vivacity; vivacity which proceeds from the heart.
> *Miss Milner:* No, if it proceeded, I should admire it too; but it rests there, and no one is the better for it.
> *Miss Woodley:* Come, Miss Milner, it is time to retire; you and Mr. Sandford must finish your dispute in the morning.
> *Sandford:* Dispute, madam! I never disputed with any one beneath a doctor of divinity in my life.—I was only cautioning your friend not to make light of virtues, which it would do her honour to possess.
> *Miss Woodley:* I am sure Miss Milner thinks so—she has a high opinion of Miss Fenton—she was at present only jesting.

Whereupon Sandford continues: "But, madam, jests are very pernicious things, when delivered with a malignant sneer.—I have known a jest destroy a lady's reputation—I have known a jest give one person a distaste for another—I have known a jest break off a marriage."[89]

Sandford thinks that Miss Fenton and Lord Elmwood are formed for each other—their dispositions, their pursuits, their inclinations the same—"Their passions for each other just the same—pure—white as snow." To which Miss Milner replies, "And I dare say, not warmer." Miss Woodley responds, "how can you talk thus? I believe in my heart you are only envious my lord did not offer himself to you."

Sandford: To her! . . . to her? Do you think his lordship received a dispensa-
tion from his vows to become the husband of a coquette?

Miss Milner: Nay, Mr. Sandford, I believe my greatest crime in your eyes, is
being a heretic.

Sandford: By no means, madam—it is the only circumstance that can
apologize for your faults; and had you not that excuse, there would be
none for you.

Miss Milner: Then, at present there is an excuse—I thank you, Mr.
Sandford; this is the kindest thing you ever said to me. But I am vext
to see you are sorry, you have said it.[90]

For Inchbald's contemporary readers, all these discussions about love and
marriage, about "passions pure as snow" would have been read with careful attention, seeing Sandford as the restrictive Catholic he is and seeing Miss Milner as a
skillful polemicist as well as a clever, witty woman. It is here, if anywhere in the
novel, that Inchbald herself may be seen. From all accounts, she too could argue
cogently, and her witty repartee was widely admired. Sandford's claim that he
never disputed with anyone beneath him and his comment that "jests are very
pernicious things" that can even destroy a marriage are additional arguments used
to show Sandford's total lack of understanding of society, where gossip and wit
formed a part of the hundreds of "teas and conversations" that were an integral
part of society in the 1780s and 1790s, the setting of the novel. And again we are
reminded that Sandford is Catholic and lives outside of contemporary society.

The next morning after the discussion of "passions pure as snow," Lord
Elmwood engages Miss Woodley in conversation; again there is a very dramatic
scene. This time the conversation begins with Elmwood inquiring about the incident of Lord Frederick handing Miss Milner into her carriage; it ends with
Elmwood's realization that she is in love with him and he with her. As in the
scene with Sandford, the dialogue is especially subtle, leaving the reader to follow
the changes of emotions between Miss Woodley and Elmwood to bring about
the conclusion.

Had the story ended here, perhaps it would have been "a simple story," but
this is not the conclusion. The incidents that follow show how the whole of this
episode extends far beyond its action in the story; it begins much earlier, for Miss
Milner, having realized Elmwood's love for her, begins to behave not as his ward
but quite independently as herself. In this charming, whimsical episode, Inchbald
shows her skill in creating the "Inchbald woman" with her beauty, her wit, and her
lovable "faults." For example, Miss Milner spends a whole morning at an auction

where she "laid out" two hundred pounds "in different things she had no one use for; but bought them because they were said to be cheap—Among the rest was a lot of books on chemistry, and some Latin authors." The conversation that follows reveals again Miss Milner's wit and independence.

"Why, madam," cried Sandford, looking over the catalog where her purchases were marked by a pencil, "do you know what you have done? you can't read a word of these books."
"Can't I, Mr. Sandford? but I assure you, you will be vastly pleased with them when you see how elegantly they are bound."
"My dear," said Mrs. Horton, "why have you bought china? you and Lord Elmwood have more now, than you have a place to put them in."
"Very true, Mrs. Horton—I forgot that—but then you know I can give these away."[91]

At this point in the conversation, Miss Milner teases Elmwood by saying she will keep the present she had intended for him and give it to Lord Frederick. Her behavior, her speech, her teasing are by the standards of her society merely jesting in a happy, lighthearted way. Sandford makes it sinister. It is as if Sandford is an imp of Satan as he goes immediately to make Elmwood unreasonably jealous.

The incident of the masquerade follows immediately, and at the end, when Elmwood determines that he cannot live with Miss Milner as his ward—certainly not as his wife—he prepares to leave for Italy, never to return. Having made her characters act in very real situations, Inchbald must now make their actions match their inner feelings. This she does as Sandford marries Elmwood and Miss Milner.[92] This final section of volume 2 Inchbald again fills with detail—Elmwood looks for his hat, his gloves—he takes her hand and does not release it—she cries, "unable to suppress her tears as heretofore, suffer[ing] them to fall in torrents." Inchbald's readers must surely have imagined this scene on the stage as Elmwood "struck his forehead in doubt and agitation . . . fell upon his knees, and cried . . . 'will you, in possessing all my affections, bear with all my infirmities?'"[93]

Volume 2 having ended as a play, volume 3 begins with an epilogue and a prologue, an epilogue about the passing of time and place and a prologue that asks the reader to imagine that seventeen years have elapsed. After the marriage, we are told, there are four years of perfect happiness until Lord Elmwood "was then under the indispensable necessity of leaving . . . to save from the depredation of his steward, a very large estate in the West Indies." He is gone for three years, and when his absence continues, Lady Elmwood becomes at first suspicious and then indifferent. She turns to Lord Frederick. Lady Elmwood has always delighted in society, as when she as Miss Milner was upset when Dorriforth/Lord Elmwood would not accompany her. After the prolonged absence of her husband, it is hardly surprising that she and Lord Frederick find each other again. Nor is it surprising that Lord Elmwood considers property of more importance than family ties. When Lord Elmwood does return, Lady Elmwood flees from home alone, leaving her daughter behind. Only Miss Woodley accompanies her to a faraway isolated, dreary retreat. Elmwood vows revenge on Lord Frederick and sends his (Elmwood's) daughter to her mother.

Miss Milner/Lady Elmwood is "no longer beautiful—no longer beloved— . . . no longer—virtuous." Lord Elmwood, "the pious, the good, the tender Dorriforth, is become a hard-hearted tyrant. The compassionate, the feeling, the just Lord Elmwood, an example of implacable rigor and injustice." Their child, their daughter, he refuses to see "in vengeance to her mother's crimes." Sandford is said to be much the same; Miss Woodley grows old with grief. With this brief review we are brought into a very different world from that of volumes 1 and 2. As we have already learned, Inchbald, working on this second novel, found that perhaps the second needed to be constructed to fit with the first—the weaving together was not altogether seamless.[94]

Again, as pointed out above, it is society that is the temptation, although Inchbald does not describe any specific aspect of the social character of that society that is directly accountable for Miss Milner/Lady Elmwood's actions. The episode of the masquerade in book 2 is clearly about Miss Milner's defiance against Elmwood's wishes, but it is not merely the attendance at the party, but also the touch of how Sandford and Dorriforth summon the servants and inquire of them how Miss Milner is dressed and where she has gone, that makes an extreme example of how Sandford wants to control Miss Milner's every action, every dress, every idea. Elmwood's absence and seeming neglect when he is gone to the West Indies is for Lady Elmwood a return to those early days when Sandford and he either ignored her or instructed her about her sinful ideas.

The setting of books 3 and 4 is obviously gothic, with its gloom in a faraway dreary land, but as always Inchbald contrives to use the gothic tradition in her own way. The terror for Lady Elmwood is her fear for her daughter, who, after her mother's death, does indeed have her own terror in the gothic world of patriarchal neglect and power. And through the years of Lady Elmwood's exile, Sandford, now having her in his power after her sinful behavior, can keep reminding her by "prayer" that there is the very real possibility of eternal damnation. Here again Inchbald suggests the combination of the Catholic and Protestant worlds of sin and its consequences.

As for Elmwood, once he returns and grasps the situation, he vows revenge;

after maiming Frederick, now the duke of Avon, in the duel that follows, he declares that he will never see or speak of Lady Elmwood or their daughter, Matilda, a vow he extends beyond the death of Lady Elmwood and a vow that creates for him his own gothic world of gloom. The story of Matilda, then, is the story in volumes 3 and 4 of *A Simple Story*.

No review of Matilda's story is possible without reviewing what has happened to the characters of Lord Elmwood's household. Miss Woodley has gone with Lady Elmwood into exile. Sandford, "The reprover, the enemy of the vain, the idle, and the wicked; but the friend, the comforter of the forlorn and miserable," now grown old, is present at Lady Elmwood's deathbed, where he declares to the dying mother, "you were not born to die *the death of the wicked.*"[95] Sandford is also the messenger to Elmwood with Lady Elmwood's dying request that Elmwood receive his daughter. Elmwood refuses to see her but does allow her to live with Miss Woodley on one of his estates. The suspense created by his refusal to ever see her or hear anyone name her name or that of her mother sets up the incidents of Matilda's story. The chance encounter of father and daughter on the great stair, the introduction of Rushbrook, the abduction of Matilda, and her rescue make up a plot filled with many of the elements of the gothic novel.

Sandford and Miss Woodley remain, but Sandford, now placed in a different situation, plays a different role. "In the name of god," he urges Lady Elmwood to ask for mercy: "I bid you hope for mercy." Upon her deathbed Lady Elmwood is reminded to trust that "you were not born to die *the death of the wicked.*"[96] There is no longer a discussion of love or the sins of pride and vanity. If in the first two books Inchbald has used the tenets of the Roman Catholic Church, in books 3 and 4 she uses the teachings of the evangelicals. Her references to these groups is not specific, but she knew about them; she herself went to hear various preachers; she read evangelical periodicals; her maid was Baptist, and she must have discussed religion, even though Inchbald was frequently annoyed with her because she did not appear, probably because she drank. In the 1790s, of course, the Methodists were becoming more and more a part of the social fabric of London, and the Quakers also had a strong presence. Sandford in books 3 and 4 encourages Lady Elmwood to ask for grace, and to Matilda he implies that she will become at peace through travail and patience.

No discussion of the second part of *A Simple Story* can fail to admit that the first two books were one unit and the second two another, and no discussion can argue that the novel is one seamless production; otherwise it would fail to take into account the dates and circumstances under which Inchbald worked. As we have seen, Inchbald had some difficulty in bringing together diverse elements in a plot and creating unity and a proper closure. There are the unexplained circumstances in *I'll Tell You What* and the intricate plot of *Such Things Are*. The transition to the Lady Elmwood of books 3 and 4 is abrupt and in no way justified for the character created in books 1 and 2. One of the few consistent threads of the story is Dorriforth/Elmwood's failure throughout to understand the meaning of love or the need of his wife to be a part of society. He is, as in the days of his priesthood, never a member of any group; he refuses to go with Miss Milner when she is his ward; he almost leaves for Italy after she, in disguise, goes to the masquerade; and when he is obliged to go away on business, he sends no word for many long years.

By 1789–1790 the popular novel was being read by a large audience, especially women. Moreover, Inchbald's success as a playwright had taught her how to revise, how to adapt, how to shape plot and characters. Books 3 and 4 of *A Simple Story* show her skill. These last two volumes are about father and daughter, about the great need of a child for her father, an emotional need since nowhere in the story is there any discussion of money or possessions or the need for marriage to supply the one or the other. Given this situation, Inchbald continues her study of Elmwood's emotional life played against his daughter Matilda's need for a father's love, and as always, she fills the incidents with the need for family.

Matilda's story is actually Elmwood's—and Miss Milner's—in that all the events and characters are derived from their union. As if the reader, like Lady Elmwood, has forgotten Elmwood's character, we are reminded that he is "of a serious, thinking, and philosophic turn of mind" and that his religious studies "had completely taught him to consider this world but as a passage to another; to enjoy with gratitude what Heaven in its bounty should bestow, and to bear with submission, all which in its vengeance it might inflict." He resolves therefore never to hear the name of his daughter or her mother for "prudence he called it, not to form another attachment near to his heart; more especially near as a parent's which might a second time expose him to all the torments of ingratitude, from one whom he affectionately loved."[97] Again, as in Miss Milner's story, Elmwood must be taught about love. Learning the love of a parent is as difficult as learning the love of a mistress. There is never, anywhere in Matilda's story, any suggestion that Elmwood ceased to love Miss Milner/Lady Elmwood, simply that his love turned inward and became dangerous.

The psychological examination of Elmwood and Lady Elmwood provided a unique theme for a novel in its time. Later, when William Godwin's *Caleb Williams* came out in 1794, he too used such an examination to center his novel; his, however, was of the cold virtue of justice and not as appealing as that of lovers and the family. Moreover, Matilda's story offered Inchbald an opportunity to examine the family again, as she had done in several of the plays; it was one of her favorite themes. The reconciliation of Matilda's father to her and, by implication, to her mother is accomplished by a series of quite dramatic scenes. The first occurs between Sandford and Elmwood; in it Elmwood allows Matilda and Miss Woodley to reside in Elmwood Castle. This information, given by Sandford to Matilda, provides Inchbald another opportunity to recreate characters excited about the news:

They both loved him sincerely; more especially Lady Matilda; whose forlorn state, and innocent sufferings, had ever excited his compassion in the extremest degree, and had caused him ever to treat her with the utmost affection, tenderness, and respect. She knew, too, how much he had been her mother's friend; for that she also loved him; and being honoured with the friendship of her father, she looked up to him with reverence and awe. For Matilda (with an excellent understanding, a sedateness above her years, and early accustomed to the most private converse between Lady Elmwood and Miss Woodley) was perfectly acquainted with the whole fatal history of her mother; and was by her taught, that respect and admiration of her father's virtues which they justly merited.[98]

Matilda, having lived in the dark and gloomy house with her mother, finds Elmwood Castle astonishing and the idea that her father is the master almost more than she can comprehend. The restrictions her father has placed upon her, however, are the means by which the situation of her annihilation continues. Elmwood gives a fete on her birthday, but the guests are only heard and seen from a window. She and Miss Woodley live in silence for most of the time.

Rushbrook, Elmwood's nephew, now his heir, lives in the house also, and through a slight incident of a book borrowed from him by Matilda, we are introduced to the beginning of their relationship. Rushbrook, quite unaware of the presence of Matilda and Miss Woodley in the house, sees Matilda for the first time since they were infants. Rushbrook immediately reminds them that her mother found him as a child and first took pity on him. With this meeting the fate of both of them is sealed.

The most famous of the events in Inchbald's narrative is the chance meeting of Matilda and her father on the stairs, an episode always commented upon by readers and critics alike. Matilda, thinking her father has gone for the day, descends the great staircase, and as she does so, he appears about to ascend. Matilda, totally overcome, reaches for the banister, misses, and falls—into his arms. He catches her, as he would have anyone else, but she faints, and as he looks down at her in his arms, she murmurs, "Save me." "His long-restrained tears now burst forth—and seeing her relapsing into the swoon again, he cried out eagerly to recall her.—Her name did not however come to his recollection—nor any name but this—'Miss Milner—Dear Miss Milner.'"[99]

Elmwood has not seen his daughter since she was three years old; she only remembers that he gave her cherries. Inchbald here is dramatizing a situation that is central to her whole story, and because of this incident on the stairs, Matilda and Miss Woodley are sent away from Elmwood Castle.

The behavior of Elmwood is not enough to tell the whole of Matilda's story; there is Rushbrook's. Here again, as in Inchbald and countless other eighteenth-century writers, the subject of marriage is brought up. Because Rushbrook is his ward and heir, Elmwood believes that he must arrange his marriage, a rather ironic situation considering the past, when Elmwood abandoned his sister, Rushbrook's mother, because she married for "love." Using various devices to manage the time sequences, Inchbald allows Rushbrook to postpone a decision until the end. When Elmwood finds Matilda kidnapped and held by the wicked Lord Margrave, he rescues her and thereby receives her as his daughter, and thus the union of Matilda and Rushbrook can be brought about.

Here again the question of courtship and marriage makes up an important part of the story, but this time Elmwood's ward is his nephew, not the beautiful daughter of an esteemed friend; moreover, Rushbrook is a man, not a young woman, a man who will inherit Elmwood's estate, that is, if Elmwood does not disinherit him again, as he once did. This subject was of great importance for Inchbald's audience, far more than the psychological problems of father and daughter. In the end, of course, Elmwood allows Matilda to make the choice herself, and she does so, partly in the name of her mother.

The critics of the novel responded favorably for the most part. The *Analytical Review* reported, "The plan of this novel is truly dramatic, for the rising interest is not broken, or even interrupted, by any episode, nor is the attention so divided, by a constellation of splendid characters, as to make the reader at a loss to say which is the hero of the tale." Such a comment says perhaps as much about other novels of the time as about *A Simple Story*. The writer continues: "Mrs. I. has evidently a very useful moral in view, namely to show the advantage of a good education; but it is to be lamented that she did not, for the benefit of her young readers, enforce it by contrasting the characters of the mother and daughter, whose history must warmly interest them. It were to be wished, in fact, in order to insinuate a useful moral into thoughtless unprincipled minds, that the faults of the vain, giddy Miss Milner had not been softened, or rather gracefully withdrawn from the notice by the glare of such splendid, yet salacious virtues, as flow from sensibility."[100]

The writer of this review was Mary Wollstonecraft, who at this time was writing for the *Analytical Review*. Jane Spencer, commenting on the review, points out that "There is much more to *A Simple Story*, however, than its insistent but unintegrated moral tag." She suggests that Wollstonecraft wanted a "feminist moral," but the novel did not have one. "Miss Milner embodies the female sexuality that women writers of Inchbald's time were busy denying in the interests of their own respectability, and women's claims for better treatment." Spencer also says that "it is clear that education in this novel functions negatively, not adding wisdom but imposing taboos." Spencer in her discussion quite correctly examines Elmwood's use of power. "In fact the best key to understanding him [Elmwood] is his insistence on controlling any willfulness in his subordinates, especially in women. We see this from his treatment of Harry Rushbrook, son of his disobedient sister, as well as in his efforts to curb his ward's activities. Miss Milner's coquetry, and the warm-heartiness that supposedly makes up for it, are both expressions of her deep opposition to such control."[101]

Those who have written introductions to various editions present an unusual series of comments that reflect their own situations far more than any real understanding of Inchbald and her work. In Anna Barbauld's volume 28—the volume of *A Simple Story*—the introduction begins by observing that Dorriforth is the central character. But Dorriforth in the "latter volumes is become, from the contemplation of his injuries, morose, unrelenting, and tyrannical. How far it was possible for a man to resist the strong impulse of nature, and deny himself the sight of his child residing in the same house with him, the reader will determine; but the situation is new and striking."[102]

Because Inchbald was already well known for her work in the theatre, her novel became a sensation overnight. Having worked on it for weeks and months in the fall of 1789 and all of 1790, she finished it and submitted it to Robinson, who accepted it at once. The next information we have about this ongoing novel project is that she had intended to use Woodfall as the printer, only to find that he could not do it at once. She switched to Cooper. Again we are given significant information about the practice of publication. Boaden's account here is worth quoting in that Inchbald's situation about her work seems not to have been unusual:

Mrs. Inchbald . . . was busily engaged in correcting the press of her romance; a business which we apprehend to be much less burdensome at present, than it formerly was, to the author, as the following will prove:—She frequently sat up at this work till three in the morning, through the bitter nights of January. On the 10th of February, Robinson published her work; and on the 1st of March a second edition was ordered. While it was printing for the first fortnight she passed nearly the whole of her time at Mr. Cooper's, the printer, to forward the reimpression; and then to the close, Miss Cooper was nearly as constantly with *her,* till the 6th of April, when it was ready for delivery."[103]

Boaden's remarks about the process of publishing reveal more than Inchbald's intense labor. The first edition being so successful, Inchbald decided to change various elements of the text and in doing so set herself a rather formidable task, considering that the first edition had been sold out in less than a month. She and Robinson, and indeed everyone else, needed to have a second as quickly as possible. A second edition appeared in March, a third in 1793, a fourth in 1799. The reading public choosing one book after another in 1790–1791 would have found *A Simple Story* in the spring of 1791 long before Godwin's novel the *Adventures of Caleb Williams; or, Things As They Are* or Holcroft's play *The Road to Ruin* or his novel *Anna St. Ives.*

In the Oxford University edition of *A Simple Story,* J.M.S. Tompkins chooses to use the first edition because, she says, "It is now preferred chiefly because its combination of provincialisms, colloquial ellipses, and irregular grammar with pointed and eloquent expression brings us close to the 'piquant mixture of a milkmaid and a fine lady' as Godwin, on Mary Shelley's testimony, described Mrs. Inchbald."[104]

Moreover, she suggests that perhaps Godwin or some of her "classically educated friends" helped with the revision since even more emendations were added in 1810, the last edition Inchbald had a hand in. It may be true that Inchbald had suggestions from various friends for the second edition, but in February she was not yet an intimate friend of Godwin and Holcroft as she became later, and by 1810 she was not seeing either. It is far more likely that it was her friend Twiss with whom Inchbald talked.

In her introduction Tompkins compliments Inchbald for "the care [she] took to surmount the drawbacks of an imperfect education and to deserve her success by an improved presentation of her novel."[105] Although anyone may choose between the first edition and the second, there is no evidence anywhere that Inchbald does anything more than the kind of revision she always did, usually with the help of Colman or Harris, or sometimes with her friends in the green room. It is not that the final work was not hers, but as she clearly indicates in the pocket-books, she always asked other people to read and discuss her current projects; moreover, she was very much aware of the current literary discussions, which at this point were frequently about English grammar. It is indeed ironic that Tompkins chose to use the first edition for the Oxford University Press with its universal authority. Inchbald especially disliked the use of dialect in plays—she thought Mrs. Malaprop a disaster—and Godwin's comment repeated by Mary Shelley that she was a "piquant mixture of a milkmaid and a fine lady" was made long after she had ceased to be a friend of his; she would have written him a sharp letter, as she did more than once, had she heard such a remark. As for her "imperfect education," Tompkins reveals her own lack of understanding of Inchbald, for, as we have pointed out repeatedly, Inchbald was exceedingly well read—perhaps as much so, or indeed more so, than anyone in her circle. Does not being well read constitute being educated?

With Tompkins's comment about Inchbald's education, we are reminded again of the differences between the perceptions of Inchbald's eighteenth-century audience and a modern one. Inchbald's pocket-books are filled with mentions of the books she read, books of every kind and importance; and although such extensive reading does not fit a modern definition of "education," it certainly placed Inchbald in a special class. She has been labeled an autodidact, but she had a far more diverse "education" than Hannah More, for example, or Mary Wollstonecraft, who, although in later life she was associated with friends who had been educated at the universities, herself had only a very limited schooling. Tomalin says, "What formal education Mary received was in a day school, in Beverly or a neighboring village: there was a grammar school with a good library for Ned, but not for the girls. She was spared being set to master the dubious accomplishments of the boarding school miss. In fact she learned little more than reading and writing, but had enough wit to flourish under this sort of neglect."[106]

She perhaps had something more, but when she tried to establish a school, she was not successful. Inchbald, in contrast, frequenting the theatre, reading aloud at home, in the end had acquired a very "liberal" education.

NINE

A NEW CHAPTER

❦ Without having the constant attention to the theatre after the close of the season at the Haymarket in the summer and the conclusion of the work on the second edition of *A Simple Story,* Mrs. Inchbald could arrange her social appointments at her own pleasure; she continued to live in Frith Street and to see the Whitfields; Robinson, her publisher; and the Stephen Kembles, and she continued to be grateful to Dr. Warren, her physician—indeed, she almost revered him. Her continuing "crush" on Dr. Warren makes that part of her story as "physical" as Miss Milner's story.

Her new fame as the author of *A Simple Story* provided her with invitations from many people outside the theatre. Boaden wrote: "she had excited so much notice on the stage, as a respectable woman and a powerful dramatist, and had attracted so wide a circle of intelligent and zealous friends, that the '*Simple* Story' made its way to every heart, and the author was ascertained to be one of the greatest ornaments of her sex."[1]

Two of her new admirers became her friends, and through them she met others. Mrs. Dobson, one of the translators in the social circles of ladies interested in the arts, wrote to her and invited her to call. Inchbald did so, whereupon Mrs. Dobson presented Inchbald with an aeolian harp. Boaden's comments about their friendship are a kind of tableau of two eighteenth-century "ladies" who each represented a distinctive place among their friends. Mrs. Dobson's husband was "a physician of eminence," and according to Boaden Mrs. Dobson's carriage was frequently "at Mrs. Inchbald's service." Reading the pocket-books, no doubt, Boaden remarks, "but the elegant Troubadour was somehow capricious, and perhaps expected for her civilities greater homage than her new friend ever paid to any body. They disputed sometimes over a table of delicacies, and the adorer of Petrarch became cross, and then cool; but the occasional clouds passed away, and the intercourse between the ladies was not interrupted by their rival pretensions to either beauty or wit."[2]

Mrs. Dobson introduced Mrs. Inchbald to Mr. Phillips of Pall-Mall, who was surgeon to the king, and to his wife and family. Subsequently Mrs. Phillips became Mrs. Inchbald's close friend, and their correspondence provides a wealth of information about Mrs. Inchbald's life and opinions from 1791 until her death in 1821, when Mrs. Phillips became Inchbald's literary executor. As we have said, it was through Mrs. Phillips's instigation that Boaden wrote the *Memoirs*.

Many of the friends Inchbald now had the leisure to see were prominent members of the elite literary and political world in London. Among them were Horne Tooke, Lord Barrymore, and Lord and Lady Petre. During the year George Hardinge began a correspondence with her, giving some of the rare glimpses of her social behavior. Also during this year, she and Sir Charles had some kind of falling out; she did not see him until December, when she went to the Phillipses in Pall-Mall. Her friend Mrs. Phillips was Sir Charles's sister, and in 1792 she saw Sir Charles again when he called.

In June 1792 she went into the country with Mrs. Whitfield and Mrs. Morgan. Mrs. Morgan was the wife of Inchbald's broker; the theatre and London society were very closely associated. They went to a Quaker meeting and, joined by Mr. Follet, they went to Slough to dinner and returned through Eton and Windsor, where Boaden says they walked the Terrace with the king and the princesses. Follet was a "low comedy" son of a very popular "low comedian." Not only an actor, he was a singer and dancer as well, one of those players who played wherever he found work—in Covent Garden, in pantomime at the Royal Circus, in the Royalty in 1787 with John Palmer. As the *Biographical Dictionary* points out, he was "the utility harlequin, pierrot, clown, and scaramouch, singing, dancing, miming, and mastering the newest 'tricks' furnished by the devisors of pantomime." Boaden remarks, "We hope his Majesty *recognized* his favourites. Follet had greatly amused him in pantomime, which we may imagine was the inducement that led him to visit the Terrace on the present occasion."[3]

The party slept at Longford and went through Osterley Park on their way back to London. This outing was so successful that they went on another in August, this time to Hampton Court and the houses of Pope and Walpole. Sir Thomas and Lady Gage were in town in July and August, and Inchbald took them to see Carlton House and the Opera House. The tour of houses and parks was very much a part of English culture in the late seventeenth century and the eighteenth century; it continues to the present. Hampton Court and Osterley Park continue to give pleasure.

Inchbald's friend Dr. Parson took her in his carriage to dine with George Hardinge and his wife, a visit everyone found enjoyable. After she returned to town, she sent her picture to the Hardinges and began a friendship that lasted until Hardinge's death. Hardinge wrote about being introduced to her at a dinner party at Mrs. Siddons's where her friend Twiss was also one of the guests. About Twiss, Hardinge said that he

takes absolute clouds of snuff. . . . He is a kind of Dr. Johnson without his hard words; though he is often quaint in his phrase. Now for Mrs. Inchbald, who seems to be upon a footing of the most playful intimacy with him, and indeed with all of them. He calls her his Muse . . . her manners are gentle, easy, and elegant, as those of any person I could name. She is of the middle height and by nature fair. . . . Her figure is excellent, and her features pretty. . . . She is very near-sighted and cannot see three inches from her nose without a little round glass, which is a most graceful implement in her hand. She is perfectly modest; but arch, clever, and so interesting, that if she had no genius you would long to be acquainted with her.[4]

George Hardinge was a senior justice of the counties Brecon, Glanorgan, and Randmore. He was a conservative, though it seems that his wife was not. In any case, they lived apart for some time but were later reconciled. But after this introduction, both were loyal friends of Mrs. Inchbald, who knew them for many years.

In June of 1792, Inchbald moved from Frith Street to an unfurnished apartment in Leicester Fields. At first without a maid, she had a rather difficult time making everything clean and comfortable. After about two weeks, she had a maid who came every day to attend to household matters, leaving Inchbald to use her time in reading and writing and various professional duties.

In 1791, before she began to have tea and conversation with Godwin, Inchbald was working on another play for Colman, this time a combination of two French plays, *L'Indigent* and *Le Dissipateur,* and as always, in her hands the combination became a totally new production. Boaden found this little production, which Inchbald called *Next Door Neighbors,* to be an echo of *A Simple Story* in dialogue and to look forward to *Nature and Art.* Boaden's view this time is hardly correct, for the play is characteristically Inchbald, especially in the way she rather awkwardly combines two quite complicated sets of characters and plotlines.

The characters are stereotypical, which is immediately apparent in the "Dramatis Personae," with the men called names like Sir George Splendorville, Mr. Manly, Mr. Blackman, Lord Hazard, and Mr. Lucre. The women have such names as Lady Seymour and Lady Squander; only the two young people are called by their Christian names, Eleanor and Henry. The situations and details of the plot are also the stock-in-trade of the current interests. It is the way in which Inchbald uses wealth and poverty, family and inheritance, that gives the play its unique interest.

The play opens in the antechamber of Sir George's town house, where Bluntly and a servant are preparing for a ball. This society setting is in sharp contrast to the poverty next door, where Eleanor and Henry live in the most severe poverty. Their apartment is very cold, and the contrast between their situation and Sir George Splendorville's next door brings Henry near despair. Their father is in prison for debt, and they have been unable to find the relatives who they thought resided in London.

The setting of the ball provides background for one part of the plot, the cold bare apartment the other. Bluntly, responsible for the ball, is on stage as the play begins. He is anxious to see that everything is properly prepared in the ballroom. A servant has brought in a new chandelier; Bluntly questions the need for it and sends it back, only to have the shopman protest. Their dialogue, though it is the usual trite comment of trade, serves to begin the characterization of Sir George:

> *Bluntly:* Pray are you the person who was sent with the chandelier?
> *Shopman:* Yes, sir.
> *Bluntly:* Then please to take it back again—We don't want it.
> *Shopman:* What is your objection to it, sir?
> *Bluntly:* It will cost too much.
> *Shopman:* Mr. Bluntly, all the trades-people are more frightened at you than at your master.—Sir George, Heaven bless him! never cares how much a thing costs.
> *Bluntly:* That is, because he never cares whether he pays for it or not—but if he did, depend upon it he would be very particular. Tradesmen all wish to be paid for their ware, don't they?
> *Shopman:* Certainly sir.
> *Bluntly:* Then why will they force so many unnecessary things, and make so many extravagant charges as to put all power of payment out of the question?

As the tradesman goes away, Evans, Lady Caroline's maid, comes in. She is all excited about the ball and all the grand preparations. But Bluntly will not be cheered; he thinks Lady Caroline, who is engaged to marry Sir George, will not help his master even though she has a fortune and he does not; Bluntly thinks Lady Caroline is as extravagant as Sir George.

> *Evans:* For shame.—My Lady, I have no doubt, will soon cure Sir George of his extravagance.
> *Bluntly:* It will then be by taking away the means.—Why, Lady Caroline is as extravagant as himself.

Evans: You are mistaken.—She never gives routs, masquerades, balls, or entertainments of any kind.

Bluntly: But she constantly goes to them whenever she is invited.

Evans: That, I call but a slight imprudence.—She has no wasteful indiscretions like Sir George. For instance, she never makes a lavish present.

Bluntly: No, but she *takes* a lavish present, as readily as if she did.

Evans: And surely you cannot call that imprudence?

Bluntly: No, I call it something worse.

Evans: Then, although she loves gaming to distraction, and plays deep, yet she never loses.

Bluntly: No, but she always wins—and *that* I call something worse.

As the rapping at the door indicates the arrival of the party, Evans asks permission to stand in a corner and observe. Here, as in the earlier *Midnight Hour*, the servants give the play important material. Tradesmen and their practices, gambling, entertaining—whatever the practices were in real life on the stage, the questions helped make a drama more than the sentimental story or sentimental love plot.

Lady Caroline is the first to arrive, and Evans and she have a moment to speak. Lady Caroline asks her, "How do I look? I once did intend to wear those set of diamonds Sir George presented me with." When Evans replies that Sir George will make "the best of husbands," Lady Caroline says, "And yet my father wishes to break off the marriage—he talks of his prodigality—and, certainly, Sir George lives above his income." And when Evans says, "But then, Madam, so does every body else," Lady Caroline observes, "But Sir George ought undoubtedly to change his conduct, and not be thus continually giving balls and entertainments—and inviting to his table acquaintance, that not only come to devour his dinners and suppers, but him." Again, as in earlier plays, the question of money plays an important role in both characterizations and plot. In this play gaming is also central to the action.

As the company assembles, two of the guests, Mr. Lucre and Lord Hazard, speak privately to Sir George. Lucre says he cannot take part at pharo, for "I am not worth a farthing in the world." Lord Hazard, speaking aside to Sir George, promises to repay the debt he owes. As the company goes into the "ball-room," Mr. Lucre and Lord Hazard follow them after Lucre declares: "Oh! there never was such a man in the world as the master of this house; there never was such a friendly, generous, noble heart; he has the best heart in the world, and the best taste in dress."

Next door in the apartment of Eleanor and Henry, the two discuss their despair for their father and for themselves. Henry, unable to stay with the sound of music next door, goes out to walk the street, promising Eleanor, however, that he will not do anything desperate; he will not steal and in fact he will not take his own life, however desperate he becomes.

Hardly has Henry left by one door than a rapping on the other frightens Eleanor, even more so when she opens the door to see her landlord, Blackman, accompanied by Bluntly. Bluntly is looking for rooms, and Blackman has been searching to find some accommodation for him. Bluntly thinks that perhaps Blackman can put himself to a little inconvenience since Bluntly is acting for Sir George. Blackman is a lawyer, and he points out to Bluntly, "since I have been Sir George's attorney, I have gained him no less than two law-suits." Bluntly replies: "I know it. I know also that you have lost him four."

Ignoring Eleanor's presence, Blackman and Bluntly continue to look at the room. Bluntly asks why the cracks of the door have not been stopped up and the windows repaired. Blackman replies that at the paltry price he gets for the rooms, he can afford no repairs since he can hardly get his money every quarter. Bluntly obviously does not understand. "Is that the situation of your lodgers at present?" he asks. In Blackman's reply we begin to realize the situation:

> *Blackman:* Yes.—But they made a better appearance when they first came, or I had not taken such persons to live thus near to your master.
> *Bluntly:* That girl (*looking at* ELEANOR) seems very pretty—and I dare say my master would not care if he was nearer to her.

As the two men leave, Eleanor follows Blackman to plead for pity. Weeping, she says: "But are you resolved to have no pity? You know in what a helpless situation we are—and the deplorable state of my poor father." When Bluntly offers to pay Blackman, Eleanor refuses, saying, "I thank you for your offer, sir, but I cannot accept it. . . . My brother would resent my acceptance of a favour from a stranger."

As Blackman and Bluntly are about to leave, Henry returns, asking, "Who are these?" Blackman echoes, "'Who are these?' Did you ever hear such impertinence? (*Going up to him*) Pray who are you, sir?" To which Henry replies, "I am a man," and Blackman declares, "Yes—but I am a lawyer." Henry is not impressed with either the servant Bluntly or the lawyer Blackman.

Act 2 opens with Sir George in a violent passion. It is only just noon, and he inquires of Bluntly, "What am I to do with myself, sir, till it is time to go out for the evening?" Bluntly reminds him that he is to have company until then. Sir

George wants Bluntly to fetch Eleanor. Bluntly thinks to do so might not be easy, for he says, "But the young woman, Sir, has been so short a time in town, she has, seemingly, a great deal of modesty and virtue." Sir George: "And I am very glad to hear of that . . . for I am weary of that ready compliance I meet with from the sex." Bluntly continues: "But I might presume to advise, sir—as you are so soon to be married to her ladyship, whom you love with sincere affection, you should give up this pursuit." Sir George: "And I *shall* give it up, Bluntly, before my marriage takes place—for, short as that time may be, I expect this passion will be over and forgotten, long before the interval has passed away."

When Bluntly returns from next door, only Henry is with him. Henry is not very friendly, knowing instinctively that something is not quite as it should be. Sir George gives him a note for a hundred pounds, saying, "I mean to dispose of a thousand guineas this way, instead of fitting up a theatre in my own house.— That is a mere trifle; my box at the opera, or my dinner; I mean to dine alone to morrow, instead of inviting company."

Returning from seeing Henry to the door, Bluntly admonishes Sir George: "But I hope, sir, you do not mean to throw away any more thus—for although this sum, by way of charity, may be well applied, yet indeed, sir, I know some of your creditors as much in want as this poor family." Sir George is suddenly furious with Bluntly, ordering him not to speak another word and to bring Eleanor to him immediately now that her brother is gone. When Bluntly continues to argue with him, Sir George goes to the chimney piece and takes down a pistol and holds it up. Bluntly leaves at once, and Sir George puts the pistol down on the table.

While Bluntly has gone for Eleanor, Blackman comes in to speak to Sir George. He thinks that Sir George should go with him to Mr. Manly, the lawyer appointed by his deceased father to administer the estate. In the conversation it is clear that Sir George desperately needs to have the other half of his estate, which was left to his sister who has disappeared. Blackman has a scheme to bring the business to a conclusion, but before he can finish his conversation with Sir George, Eleanor arrives and Blackman is obliged to leave.

Eleanor's first words to Sir George are, "Pardon me, sir.—I understood my brother was here, but I find he is not." To this Sir George replies: "He is but this instant gone, and will return immediately.—Stay then with me till he comes." He takes her hand, and when she looks to the door and is about to leave, he goes and locks it.

> *Eleanor:* For heaven sake, why am I locked in?
> *Sir George:* Because you should not escape.

Eleanor: That makes me resolve I will—Open the door, sir.

Sir George: Nay, listen to me. Your sentiments, I make no doubt, are formed from books.

Eleanor: No, from misfortunes—yet more instructive.

Before anything more can be said or done, Bluntly tricks Sir George into opening the door, and when Eleanor says to Bluntly, "pray be so kind as to conduct me to my own lodgings" and Bluntly offers her his hand, Sir George says, "Dare not to touch her—or to stay another moment in this room.—Begone." And turning to her, "And now, my fair Lucretia—." He goes toward her as she picks up the pistol and points it at him saying, "No, it's not *myself* I'll kill—'Tis you." Sir George is frightened and trembling.

Sir George: Nay, nay, lay it down.—Lay that foolish thing down; I beg you will. It is charged—it may go off.

Eleanor: I mean it to go off.

Sir George: But no jesting—I never liked jesting in my life.

Eleanor: Nor I—but am always serious.—Dare not, therefore, insult me again, but let me go to my wretched apartments.

She passes by him, pauses at the door and presents the pistol again. With her departure, Sir George calls for Bluntly demanding, "Why did you break in upon me just now? Did you think I was going to murder the girl?"

Bluntly: Why, sir, if I may make bold to speak—I was afraid the poor girl might be robbed; and of all she is worth in the world.

Sir George: Blockhead! I suppose you mean her virtue?

Bluntly: Why to say the truth, sir, virtue is a currency that grows scarce in the world now-a-days—and some men are so much in need of it, that they think nothing of stopping a harmless female passenger in her road through life, and plundering her of it without remorse, though its loss, embitters every hour she must afterwards pass in her journey.

The scene that follows this conversation moves very rapidly. Henry, not knowing about the insult to Eleanor, thanks Sir George, but before he can finish, Eleanor and her father, Willford, enter. Eleanor tries to prevent Willford from thanking Sir George, and Willford, confused, is offended by Eleanor's silence. She explains that he must return to prison, because "The money that set you free, was given for the basest purposes—and by a man as far beneath you in principle, as you are beneath him in fortune."

Act 3 opens in the apartment of Sir George. He and the company there have been playing at cards all night, and now it is morning. Sir George has had very bad luck; he has lost everything—most of his fortune to Lady Caroline. The story of his attempted rape of Eleanor has now become the story of his gaming. Everyone begins to desert him; he appeals to Lady Caroline, if she loves him, to "give me my revenge in one single cut." She agrees, and he cuts the cards, but he loses the cut. He turns to her, "Cruel, yet beloved woman! Could you thus abuse and take advantage of the madness of my situation?"

> *Lady Caroline:* Your misfortunes, my dear Sir George—make you blind.
> *Sir George:* No, they have rather opened my eyes, and have shown me what you are.—Still an object I adore; but now I perceive you are one to my ruin devoted.—If any other intention had directed you, would you have thus decoyed me to my folly?—You know my proneness to play, your own likelihood of success, and have palpably allured me to my destruction. Ungrateful woman, you never loved me, but taught me to believe so, in order to partake of my prodigality.—Do not be suspicious, madam; the debt shall be discharged within a week.
> *Lady Caroline:* That will do, sir—I depend upon your word; and that will do.

Sir George has reached the lowest point of despair. He is deserted by all his friends, Lady Caroline has gone away, and his friend Lucre refuses to look into his face again. Only Bluntly, his servant, remains; he says, "I will never quit you; but serve you for nothing, to the last moment of my life."

Embracing him, Sir George declares, "I have then one friend left. And never will I forget to acknowledge the obligation." Bluntly's loyalty cannot solve the problem of Sir George's lost fortune, however. Blackman at this point enters and suggests that he has a scheme to finally get that half of the fortune that the will of his father has left him out of.

The scheme that Blackman proposes is that Bluntly, disguised as an apothecary, will swear that the death certificate of the lost young lady, Sir George's sister, is authentic. The scheme does not succeed, for as all the principals gather in Manly's office, the whole strange truth emerges. Sir George Splendorville changed his name from Blandford; Eleanor is his sister, and Henry her cousin; Willford's speech that clears the matter up is short: "Now, Eleanor, arm yourself with fortitude—with fortitude to bear not the frowns, but the smiles of fortune. Be humble, collected, and the same you have ever been, while I for the first time inform you— you are not my daughter.—And from this gentleman's intelligence add, you are rich—you are the deceased Blandford's child, and Splendorville's sister."

Eleanor's good fortune does not solve Sir George's misfortune. At this moment Lady Caroline appears; that is, her servant enters and declares, "Lady Caroline Seymour, sir, is at the door in her carriage, and will not be denied admittance." While Sir George and his new family retire into another room, Manly and Lady Caroline confer. From their conversation we discover that Lady Caroline has kept all her money won from Sir George; she has turned the expensive presents he has given her into payments for land that he foolishly sold to her agent; and when Sir George says to Eleanor, "Where is my fortune? Now *all* irrecoverably gone," she intervenes: "Behold a friend in your necessities—a mistress whom your misfortunes cannot drive away—but who, experiencing much of your unkindness still loves you; and knowing your every folly, will still submit to honour, and obey you. I received your lavish presents, but to hoard them for you—made myself mistress of your fortune, but to return it to you—and with it, all my own."

The play ends happily for everyone. Eleanor is rich; Henry, not her brother, becomes her future husband, and Sir George has in one "propitious morning" discovered "all [his] former folly" and "how to be in future happy."

In *Next Door Neighbors* Inchbald has done a great deal more than to translate and adapt two French plays. She has created an intricate plot situation; she has made of Sir George a character who is both hero and villain; she has commented about masters and servants, lawyers and clients; she has made the men weak or deceived. The dramatic scene of Eleanor and the pistol is another incident showing a determined, fearless woman to add to the list of strong women she created. The epilogue makes a plea for seeing the play as more than translation "by improving what was writ before, / Tho' Genius may be less, our Judgment's more." This is the comment to be added to all the plays that Inchbald adapted.

Boaden remarks about the performance of *Next Door Neighbors:*

A very lady-like and lovely creature, Mrs. Brooks, was Palmer's Lady Caroline. She wanted nothing but *force* to stand her ground in the profession, and looked perfectly *chaste* on the stage—the rarest accomplishment which it displays: yet this season it was in profusion at the Haymarket; for Mrs. Stephen Kemble was an impersonation of *purity*, and charmed with native innocence and tenderness of soul, which no successor among even the successful charmers yet seems to have rivalled. She acted the virtuous Eleanor, and from poverty is wafted into affluence, merely by ascertaining her real birth: a not very rare stage expedient.[5]

Boaden did not find Sir George an admirable character, saying he had "neither honour nor feeling in his mind, to atone for thoughtless extravagance." Boaden also remarks upon Lady Caroline's luck at cards: "But it does not appear by what *pass of practice* decent ladies become such absolute conjurers at cards; and how, when the beggared gamester asks for the slang *cut* of 'double or quits,' they can be so sure of their hand, always, as to indulge him and triumph."[6] Decent ladies "playing cards" was an incident Inchbald used again in a later play—*Wives As They Were, and Maids As They Are*—but in this later play they were not given so much triumph. Lady Caroline and Eleanor are among the strong women characters Inchbald created even from the early plays—Fanny in *A Mogul Tale* and Lady Euston in *I'll Tell You What.*

Tea and Conversation

Shortly after the publication of her novel, Mrs. Inchbald began to see William Godwin socially. He must certainly have known her, since Robinson was his publisher as well as hers. In fact, working for Robinson, he evidently saw her manuscript of *A Simple Story* and "edited" it. Godwin referred to his work for Robinson simply as "reading" and "revising," but the revising he did for Inchbald's novel changed it significantly; and in this case we have another puzzle about publishers, writers, editors, and printers. Without Inchbald's own account it is not possible to be certain what she did about revising her novel once again in 1789–1790 or just what the dates of the various submissions must have been or, indeed, to whom she gave her manuscript to read this time. She probably once again asked several friends, perhaps Holcroft for one, and perhaps this was the connection with Godwin.

The first reference Godwin makes to her manuscript is an entry in his journal between 1790 and 1791, turned crossways, that is just before 1791. He wrote, "It was in this year that I read and criticized this Simple Story in ms." Turned in the other direction, he wrote "The story/whole in alternate letters between two confidantes. / Miss Woodley relating the story of Dorriforth & other the story of Rushbrook," a curious reference since there is no mention of Miss Milner. No doubt Godwin was far more interested in the portrait of Dorriforth than in that of Miss Milner.[7]

By 1790–1791 Godwin had made a place for himself in London. During the eighties he had had some very unhappy times after deciding that he could no longer be a Dissenting minister. He had been trained at Hoxton Academy, a center for Socinianism under Dr. Kippis; but although he knew the strict polity of his own view, he could not explain his views in such a way that, as a Dissenting minister, he could hold a congregation, for each congregation could, and did, select its own minister. Moreover, he knew nothing of society, of the grace and understanding needed to lead a group of people, especially since the message he had to give was a very harsh one. Unsuccessful at Stowmarket in Suffolk, he resigned over a dispute about a minor matter of church discipline; he then moved to Beaconsfield, where, again unsuccessful, he finally determined to leave the profession he had been trained for and go to London. There, in the end, he became a part of the rapidly changing English radicalism, publishing one of the most discussed documents of the 1790s, his *Political Justice*. Before he published his book, however, he and Inchbald had become close friends, along with Thomas Holcroft and the publisher J.G. Robinson, the senior member of the firm of G.G. and J. Robinson. Godwin's friends have sometimes been said to belong to the "Godwin circle"; it would more properly be called the "Robinson circle."

Godwin's journal contains little more information of his daily life than do Inchbald's annual pocket-books, but in each case the entries about books and writing, about friends at tea and dinner, about the theatre and publishing, when put together, provide a significant picture of the people whose names appear. Beginning in 1788, Godwin kept his journal until long after his association with Inchbald.

When Godwin came to London in 1781, he earned a scant living as an independent writer, and in 1784 when he found employment as a writer on the *New Annual Register,* he did so as a kind of final desperate resort to find a place for himself in a society that he could tolerate. He was at that moment without funds, without a profession, and without friends. He still considered himself a Dissenter— a Dissenting minister like his father. But unlike his father, he had had years of training in the Dissenting academics, training that was rather more confusing than comforting, more cloudy than clear, whatever one's beliefs, and by this time Godwin had already changed his religious/theological beliefs not once but twice.

Godwin's two friends in London were James Marshall and Joseph Fawcett. Fawcett, who preached on Sunday nights at Old Jewry, always attracted packed congregations. Marshall, like Godwin, was a freelance journalist; unlike Godwin, he never advanced in his career. Both Marshall and Fawcett were Dissenters, but in 1791, when Inchbald became his friend, Godwin was already a nonbeliever, as was Holcroft. The decade of the 1790s was for both Holcroft and Godwin a turning point in both their religious and their political beliefs, as they became more and more associated with the "Radicals" in their views of society and government.

In these early days after he came to London, Godwin was desperately poor; his relatives, both in London and in Norwich, were frequently dependent on charity, frequently appealing for help. Godwin's sister was a seamstress, living in London also, and his mother always mentioned her in letters to Godwin, often asking him to help his brothers and his nephews as well. By the time Godwin began to see Inchbald socially, he had become firm friends with Holcroft.

Holcroft and Inchbald had been friends for quite a long time, in fact since they had acted together in Canterbury in 1777. They had both become successful as playwrights and as novelists, and living in London they saw each other frequently. Inchbald had acted in Holcroft's play *Duplicity* in 1781 and in *The Follies of a Day* in 1785. *Duplicity* was not successful on stage, even though John Henderson had the lead and Inchbald played as leading actress.[8] *The Follies of a Day* was an entirely different matter. It was played twenty-seven times during its first season, and the rewards of the printed version made it the most successful production of Holcroft's career.

Like Inchbald, Holcroft published both novels and plays; he was a fine musician and numbered among his friends many of the finest musicians in London. His friend Shields did the music for his plays, and Holcroft wrote the words for songs that Shields set to music. Holcroft was a special friend to Clementi, the music teacher whose exercises have been the assignments for hundreds of young pupils for more than two hundred years. Holcroft belonged to a musical club that included Shields and Clementi as well as the musical elite in London. At one time he owned two Cremona violins, one of which he gave to Shields. Holcroft was proficient in French, German, and Italian, having taught himself, and having lived in France, he was able to be aware of the rising interest in revolution that led to the execution of the king. Holcroft did not realize in the beginning the consequences of the views he promoted, but by 1792 he was deeply involved in English radicalism.

Robinson was a friend and patron to Inchbald, Godwin, Holcroft, and dozens of other writers who felt that the English public should be informed about the state of Britain. Robinson had been tried and fined for promoting the first part of Paine's *Rights of Man;* Holcroft himself joined the radical Society for Constitutional Information in 1793, the year of Louis XVI's execution. This was one of the strongest and most widely known of the popular radical societies and one that had important consequences for Holcroft.[9]

In 1792 Robinson had already published almost all the plays Inchbald had written before *A Simple Story.* His part in publishing Godwin, Inchbald, and Holcroft becomes very much a part of their association and their role in the public. The records of the Robinson firm, though very few and scattered, give a significant comment on Inchbald and Godwin and, perhaps to a lesser degree, on Holcroft.

In the Robinson archive, now in the Manchester Public Library, the entries show how important Robinson was to the publishing careers of Inchbald and Godwin and to their financial affairs. The entries also reveal how Harris did busi-

Elizabeth Inchbald, from *European Magazine,* ca. 1788. (Private collection)

A portrait Mr. Inchbald painted of his wife on ivory in 1776 after they returned from France. (Courtesy of the Folger Shakespeare Library)

Mr. Inchbald's portrait of Mrs. Inchbald's nephew, "Little George" (George Simpson). (Courtesy of the Folger Shakespeare Library)

Engraved for the Ladies Pocket Book.

B.M *LADIES in the Dresses of 1782.*

Two Ladies in the dress of the Year 1784

Dresses similar to those Mrs. Inchbald and her friends would have worn on social occasions. (Courtesy of the British Museum)

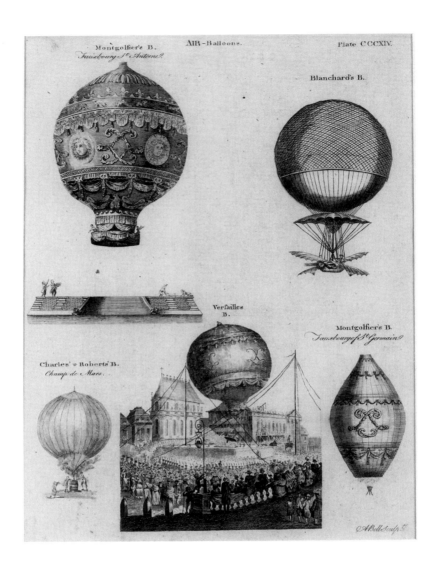

Early balloons. (Private collection)

Price One Shilling Coloured

MERMAID

by Thos. Tegg N° 111 Cheap Side

Prime Bang up at HACKNEY or a Peep at the BALLOON n. Aug^t

A celebration to mark the Regent's birthday on August 12, 1811. (Private collection)

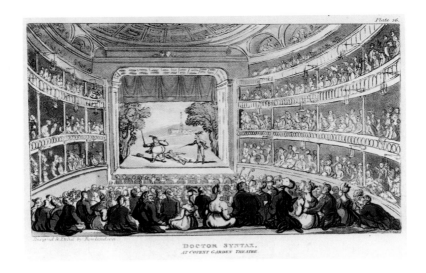

The interior of Covent Garden Theatre, showing the stage and side boxes. (Private collection)

Mrs. Inchbald in Nicholas Rowe's *Lady Jane Gray*. (Original in the Garrick Club, private collection)

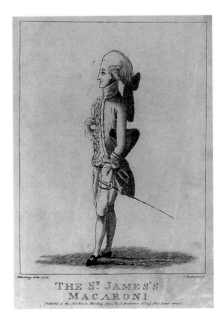

The St. James's Macaroni was one of a series Henry Bunbury did of young men affected in both dress and manner. Inchbald had several such characters in her plays. (Private collection)

After the great success of her play *Such Things Are,* Mrs. Inchbald became the "Celebrated Mrs. Inchbald." The books on her table are not those usually owned by a lady. Women did not read Aristotle, Rochester was wicked, Congreve risque. Her cat is sitting on *Pastorals,* and *Moll Flanders* was not proper for a dignified author. In fact, "puffing" was certainly not proper. (Courtesy of the Walpole Collection, New York Public Library)

L. Roberts del. Publish'd for Bell's British Theatre July 1st 1777. Thornthwaite Sculp.

Mrs. MATTOCKS *in the Character of* ELVIRA.

— but however I will not stand with you for a Sample.

Elaborate costumes were part of the pleasure of the plays. (Private collection)

J. Roberts del.   Publish'd for Bell's British Theatre April 1778.   Thornthwaite Sc.

Mrs BULKLEY in the Character of ANGELIN.

Sir you look Melancholy.

Stage costumes were widely copied as dress designs. (Private collection)

A comment on the theatre as a gathering place for both foreigners and Londoners. (Courtesy of the British Museum)

Sir Charles's horse, Diomed, won the first Derby. (Private collection)

Head dresses in the late eighteenth century. In 1781 feathers were becoming very fashionable. (Courtesy of the British Museum)

THEATRE ROYAL, DRURY-LANE.

This Evening, THURSDAY October 8, 1818,

Their Majesties' Servants will perform the Play of the

IRON CHEST.

Sir Edward Mortimer,	Mr. KEAN,
Fitzharding, Mr. POWELL,	Wilford, Mr. BARNARD,—
Adam Winterton,	Mr. MUNDEN,
Rawbold,	Mr. HOLLAND,
Samson,	Mr. COWELL,—
(From the Theatres Royal, York and Lincoln, his first appearance in London)	
Gregory, Mr. Minton,	Peter, Mr. Evans,
Armstrong, Mr. T. COOKE,	Orson, Mr. GATTIE,—
First Robber, Mr. COOKE,	Second Robber, Mr. J. SMITH,
3d Robber, Mr. MILLER, 4th Robber, Mr. SMITH,	Robber's Boy, Master Taylor—
Helen, Mrs. KNIGHT,	Blanch, Mrs. ORGER,
Barbara,	Mrs. BLAND,
Margaret, Mrs. COVENEY,	Judith, Mrs. HARLOWE.

To which will be added, the Farce of

The Midnight Hour.

The Marquis,	Mr. BARNARD,
The General,	Mr. WILLIAMS,—
(His second appearance in London)	
Sebastian,	Mr. OXBERRY,
Nicholas,	Mr. COWELL,—
Mathias, Mr. HUGHES,	Ambrose, Mr. WEWITZER,
Julia, Mrs. ORGER,	Cicely, Miss TIDSWELL,
Flora,	Mrs. GLOVER.

Doors open at 6 o'Clock. The Performance to begin at 7.

Boxes 5s. Second Price 3s.---Pit 3s. Second Price 2s.
Lower Gallery 2s. Second Price 1s.---Upper Gallery 1s. Second Price 6d.

Boxes and Places to be taken at the Rotunda, Brydges Street, from Ten till Four, where may be had a Private Box nightly ;---and, for the further accommodation of the Publick, the Box-Office will be open every Evening of performance from Ten till Eleven.

Vivant Rex et Regina.   No Money to be returned.   Rodwell, Printer, Theatre Royal, Drury Lane.

Madame BELLGAR,

On her second appearance at this Theatre, on Monday Evening, as *Don Carlos*, in the DUENNA, was again rapturously received, and honoured with the most unanimous applause ; as was also

Miss WITHAM,

(*From the Theatre Royal, Bath*) in the character of *Donna Clara*. Due notice will given of the next appearance of both these Ladies.

Mr. KEAN,

Will perform the Character of *Sir Edward Mortimer*, this Evening; *Sir Giles Overreach*, on Saturday; and *Hamlet*, on Monday next.

Mr. DAVID FISHER,

Whose successful performance of *Jaffier*, was honoured with so much approbation, will be duly announced for another Character.

On Saturday, Massinger's Play of A NEW WAY TO PAY OLD DEBTS.
Sir Giles Overreach,   Mr. KEAN.
With (*first time this season*) AMOROSO, KING of LITTLE BRITAIN.
And the WEATHERCOCK, Tristram Fickle, by a GENTLEMAN, (*his first appearance.*)
On Monday, Shakspeare's Tragedy of HAMLET, Hamlet, Mr. KEAN.
Ophelia, (*first time*) Mrs. MACKENZIE, (the Lady who was so favourably received in the character of *Juliet*,) being her 3rd appearance at this Theatre.
After which, (2nd time at this Theatre the Musical Entertainment of LOVE LAUGHS at LOCKSMITHS.
CUMBERLAND's revived Comedy of The FASHIONABLE LOVER, is unavoidably postponed for a few days.

A New COMICK AFTERPIECE,

Is in preparation, and will speedily be produced.

By 1818 Inchbald and Coleman's dispute had been forgotten, and *Iron Chest* and *The Midnight Hour* were played together. (Private collection)

Rowland's version of a bonnet shop where more than shopping goes on.
Inchbald lived above a milliner's shop when she was writing her Remarks
for *The British Theatre*. (Private collection)

DERBY & JOAN.
Long look'd for—Come at Last.
RICHES—HONOR—& TITLES, the reward of VIRTUE.

After the death of Lord Derby's estranged wife in March 1797, Elizabeth Farren and Lord Derby were married on April 8, 1797. This print shows them at the opera as "the constant couple." (Private collection)

Bunbury's joke about Lord Derby following Farren. A very fine horseman, Bunbury shows him here as very awkward and being unable to catch up. (Private collection)

H.W. BUNBURY ESQ.^R

Henry Bunbury, Sir Charles's artist brother. (Private collection)

Sarah Siddons, "Reynold's Tragic Muse," is pictured here in her role as Isabella in *Isabella; or, The Fatal Marriage.* (Private collection)

Mrs Inchbald.

A Lawrence portrait of his friend Mrs. Inchbald. The dress she wears here is of the 1790s, when the fashion of the high waist and the mob cap had been adopted from France. (Courtesy of the Folger Shakespeare Library)

ness with his playwrights, attempting to control the plays staged and then printed, illustrating once again the control he had over Covent Garden. It is only after examining these entries that Inchbald's shrewd business sense is revealed.

When she had her first success—*A Mogul Tale*—she made some attempt to find a publisher, but without success; given in the summer of 1784, it was not published until 1788 and then in a pirated edition in Dublin. She and Colman had some discussion about *I'll Tell You What*. He pointed out that if she released it to the public, neither of the theatres would use it.[10] It was published after the season was over in 1786, but *Appearance Is against Them*, given in 1785, was published in 1785. From that time on, her plays were published almost as soon as they closed on stage.[11]

Godwin's association with Robinson was in fact his professional career until after the publication of *Political Justice*. In 1793 Godwin had already written novels and a volume called *Life of William Pitt*, which was printed anonymously; he was briefly associated with Sheridan's short-lived *Political Herald*, and in 1785 he began to write the historical sections for the *New Annual Register*, a liberal journal edited by Dr. Kippis, his former tutor at Hoxton, and published by Robinson. It was in this way that he became associated with George Robinson. For his work on the *New Annual Register*, he was to receive sixty guineas, and he wrote that "the contract was sealed by a dinner in trio between Mr. Robinson, Dr. Kippis, and myself at the Crown and Anchor in the Strand." It was a happy circumstance for him, since he had said that in the previous year "for the most part I did not eat my dinner without previously carrying my watch or my books to the pawnbroker to enable me to eat."[12] The dinner with Robinson began a long and friendly relationship between author and publisher and ultimately a link to Inchbald.

Godwin's journal makes frequent reference to seeing Robinson, having conversation with him, and dining with him. The journal also serves as a record of Godwin's social life: reading, attending the theatre, working at writing, and attendance at a variety of political meetings on different occasions. In 1793 he signed an agreement with Robinson to undertake a major piece of writing. Godwin wrote, "My agreement with Robinson was, that he was to supply my wants at a specified rate, while the book was in the train of composition."[13] That book turned out to be *An Enquiry concerning Political Justice*.

Inchbald and Godwin had a number of mutual friends, and as Godwin became an admired spokesman for the political left after *Political Justice* was published, they frequently appeared in the same social groups—at the theatre, at routs, at tea with various friends. By 1792, when Godwin began to call on Inchbald, she already had a circle of her own, and frequently Godwin entered "nah," meaning "not at home" after the entry "Call on Inchbald." It was during these years that Inchbald became friends with the painters Thomas Lawrence and John Opie, and it was during this time that Amelia Alderson visited Godwin and Inchbald in London. As it turned out, Alderson became another link between Godwin and Inchbald.

Godwin grew up in a village just outside of Norwich; Inchbald's childhood home of Standingfield was only a little farther to the south of Norwich. They both knew Norwich very well—had been a part of the Suffolk and Norwich region for many years. Inchbald, knowing the players and the theatre, must have known a great many people; and Godwin, a part of the group of Dissenters and Jacobins, also knew a great many people. They must have known or known about many of the same people. And Godwin's first congregation was in Stowmarket, only a few miles from Standingfield.

Norwich, given its geographical situation and its nearness to the Continent, had always had a life of its own quite apart from London, and now that the French Revolution had become so disruptive, Norwich was one of the most liberal and independent cities in all of England. Amelia Alderson, born in Norwich, was the daughter of a physician; her mother died when she was only thirteen, and she became the mistress of her father's household. An only child, she was treated by her father as an adult, and although she and her father were stout Presbyterians, their friends the Gurney family were among the leading Quaker families in the area. Dr. Alderson was a cultivated man interested in books and music, and he surrounded himself with intellectuals—the elite of the surrounding area. He did a great deal of charity, and very early Amelia frequented his waiting room. She grew up with the Gurney family and remained friends with them all her life.

Even in her teens Amelia had verse printed in various periodicals; her first novel, *The Dangers of Coquetry,* was published in 1790 anonymously, but it was 1801 before her second, *The Father and Daughter* came out. It was an immediate success, with a second edition during the year, and by 1844 it had reached a tenth edition. In 1791 in January, while Mrs. Inchbald was hard at work seeing *A Simple Story* through the press, Amelia acted the leading role in a play she had written herself; it was performed in a private Norwich theatre. She came to London frequently and evidently had many friends to see and visit. She and her father were rather careful about their political views, and some of the comments in her letters are quite ambivalent. When she was in London in 1794 and wrote to her father about the Treason Trial, he destroyed her letters. Her friend Mrs. Taylor, to whom she wrote about quite different matters, had several accounts of her social life while she visited in London. She and Mrs. Inchbald became the two most impor-

tant women in the Godwin and Robinson circles. Inchbald and Alderson, however, were not the only women in Godwin's life. After he came to London, he
became a friend of Maria Reveley, the wife of William Reveley, the young architect who had drawn the blueprints for Jeremy Bentham's panopticon, a "modern"
prison never built but much discussed in certain circles. Maria Reveley was a very
accomplished woman; she spoke French and Spanish and was an artist (she had
studied under Angelica Kauffman) and a fine musician. Another of the women in
Godwin's life was Maria Hayes—Mary—who introduced herself to him on the
excuse of borrowing a copy of *Political Justice*.[14]

The time in 1791–1792 when Inchbald and Godwin began to see each other
was also the time when Godwin and Holcroft were virtually inseparable. Godwin's
journal, which documents his work and daily life, like Inchbald's pocket-books, is
filled with the people he saw, the way he worked, the books he read, the plays he
went to see, and the people he knew; many of those people Inchbald also knew,
saw, and went to the theatre with. It is through Inchbald's pocket-books, Godwin's
journal, letters from Holcroft and Amelia Alderson Opie, and visits with Robinson
that the relationships of a circle of friends become clear, relationships that became
a part of Inchbald's life and of Godwin's. And because of the close association of
Holcroft with Inchbald and Godwin, he too played an important part in their
work and friendship.[15]

In using Godwin's journal and Inchbald's pocket-book (there is only one of
the pocket-books in the 1790s, that of 1793), it is important to observe the ways
in which the relationships change from year to year and the way people and events
are recorded.

Godwin's journal begins in 1788, before he knew Inchbald and before he
"revised" her *Simple Story*. He was working for Robinson, however, and at this
time he was working on revising various manuscripts. On November 13, 1791, he
went to dine at Johnson's with "Paine, Shovet & Wollstonecraft, talk of monarchy,
Tooke, Johnson, Voltaire, feminist & religion. sup at Holcroft's." This entry marks
the famous dinner party with Wollstonecraft where she talked too much; it was
many years later, after many dramatic events, when Godwin became her friend
and lover. On September 22, 1792, he saw her again at tea at the Barlows' with
Jardine, Stuart, and Holcroft, where the talk was of "self love, sympathy & perfectibility individual and general." All the dates here are important. Wollstonecraft
in 1791–1792 had not yet gone to France.

On October 29 he wrote: "Write 2 pages. Call on Robinson, Davis, Holcroft,
& Mrs. Inchbald on massacres," and on November 2, "Write 3 pages: write to
Mrs. Inchbald, Holcroft calls." He called on Inchbald on the eighth with Taylor

and afterward "Sup at Nicholson's, talk of government, property, punishment." During these entries in the fall of 1792, he enters his page numbers for the manuscript he was working on for himself, a manuscript that became *Political Justice,* the number of pages in the books he was reading, and frequently the topics of the conversations he had at tea and dinner. Put together, these entries show how the three friends—Inchbald, Godwin, and Holcroft—discussed their ideas, ideas that reappear in their work.

In 1793 Inchbald's play *Every One Has His Fault* was performed at Covent Garden on January 29. It was performed thirty-four times that year. It is one of the most popular of Inchbald's plays, and it is tempting to see Godwin's and Holcroft's ideas on every hand. During the fall before the play was presented, Godwin makes several entries about her "comedy." On November 26 he called on her and, among other items for the day, records, "Revise Mrs. Inchbald's Comedy," which was followed by an entry in parentheses, "(Debating Society silenced.)" At this point Inchbald herself probably asked for his advice, or perhaps she read her play to him, as she had done to friends before.

Holcroft and Godwin were deep into political discussions at this time, and evidently Inchbald talked with them about their ideas and hers when they met for tea. Without her pocket-book we have no record of her part in their discussions; it is only through Godwin's journal and a scattering of letters from the three of them that we can construct a pattern, a pattern that for many months found the three of them not only at tea with one another but also at the theatre and various social events as they met and shared one another's friends. They became a "circle" within a circle of Inchbald's theatre friends.

In October 1792, while Inchbald was working on her play *Every One,* she had also been working on a play she called *The Massacre.* As always, she consulted various people whose judgment she trusted for advice, one of whom was Godwin. We do not have his letter that prompted her reply, but her letter addresses problems beyond his comments. This letter, dated November 24, 1792, speaks directly to her habits of work and makes a significant comment about writing for the stage and for the general trade market:

> Sir,—There is so much tenderness mixed with the justice of your criticism, that, while I submit to the greatest part of it as unanswerable, I feel anxious to exculpate myself in those points where I believe it is in you accuse me of trusting to newspapers for my authority. I have no other authority (no more, I believe, has half of England) for any occurrence which I do not see: it is by newspapers that I am told that the French are at present victorious; and I have no doubt but you will allow that (in this particular, at least) they speak truth.

2ndly. There appears an inconsistency in my having said to you, "I have no view of any public good in this piece," and afterwards alluding to its preventing future massacres to this I reply that it was your hinting to me that it might do harm which gave me the first idea that it might do good.

3rdly. I do not shrink from Labour, but I shrink from ill health, low spirits, disappointment, and a long train of evils which attend Labourious Literary work. I was ten months, unceasingly, finishing my novel, notwithstanding the plan (such as you saw it) was formed, and many pages written. My health suffered much during this confinement, my spirits suffered more on publication; for though many gentlemen of the first abilities have said to me things high in its favor, it never was liked by those people who are the readers and consumers of novels; and I have frequently obtained more pecuniary advantage by ten days' labor in the dramatic way than at the labor of this ten months.—Your much obliged humble servant E. Inchbald.

Leicester Square, 24th[16]

Inchbald's comment about the difference between the public prints and authoritative material is suggestive of her lifelong habit of reading the newspapers. The remarks about the public good being a part of her intention must have been a part of her conversations about their work with Godwin and Holcroft, conversations very frequent in 1792. But for us perhaps the most interesting comment in the letter is her reference to her novel, for it suggests not only her situation but also the problems of many other novelists, which in turn demonstrate again the differences between writing for the stage and for the reading public.

Her "3rdly" in the letter outlines again the history of her novel: "I was ten months, unceasingly, finishing my novel, notwithstanding the plan (such as you saw it) was formed, and many pages written" reminds us, as we now know, that Godwin had changed her manuscript from letters and thus no doubt caused her days and days of more work, as part of the "ten months, unceasingly, finishing" her novel. Just what she meant by "the plan . . . was formed" leaves the question of the second part of *A Simple Story*, books 3 and 4, with the story of Matilda, and Inchbald's work in the summer, when Boaden says she joined the two to make one story. Without the record in her pocket-book of her daily work, we cannot know precisely how she joined the two sections.

Finally, her comment "for though many gentlemen of the first abilities have said to me things high in its favor, it never was liked by those people who are the readers and consumers of novels": who are "those people who are the readers and consumers of novels"? Did she mean those who were reading the contemporary novels of the 1780s and 1790s? There were, of course, many references to novel-reading in the plays; did she, for example, feel that the "readers and consumers of novels" were like Lydia in Sheridan's *Rivals*? She later made witty remarks about writing novels in an article published in the *Artist,* a periodical conducted by her friend Prince Hoare, but at this point she was still uncertain enough of her audience to question her success.

Her reference to "more pecuniary advantage by ten days' labor in the dramatic way than at the labor of this ten months" underscores again the importance of writing and publishing plays. Her comments about her own situation were no doubt true of all those who tried to write in both forms. Holcroft wrote both novels and plays, but Godwin, although he was quite successful as a novelist, was never successful as a playwright. In the end only Inchbald profited enough from her work to be financially stable year after year. Considering the difficulty of maintaining financial stability in these years of the 1780s and 1790s, Inchbald's comments are especially notable. In the years to come, both Holcroft and Godwin had great difficulty about money, Godwin in the end being frequently in great distress.

With the date 1792 and Inchbald's comments in her letter to Godwin, it is important to remember the events she—and they—were reading in the newspapers and in the public arguments going on in the press. In July of 1789 in Paris, the Bastille was destroyed. On September 22, 1792, the French National Convention declared the monarchy abolished, and also in September 1792 some fourteen hundred innocent people were massacred. In 1793 in January the king was condemned and beheaded. The details of these months were in the newspapers, where no doubt Inchbald found the material for her play that she called *The Massacre.*

All this time Godwin was working on *Political Justice,* and, like Inchbald, he showed his work to various friends, those with whom he had tea and conversation. In the spring of 1793, he recorded in a notebook some of these conversations:

Dr. Priestley says my book contains a vast extent of ability—Monarchy and Aristocracy, to be sure, were never so painted before— . . . he admits fully my first principle of the omnipotence of instruction and that all vice is error—he admits all my principles, but cannot follow them into all my conclusions with me respecting self-love—he thinks mind will never so far get the better of matter as I suppose; he is of opinion that the book contains a great quantity of original thinking, and will be uncommonly useful.

Horne Tooke tells me that my book is a bad book, and will do a great deal of harm— Holcroft and Jardine had previously informed me, the first, that he said the book was written with very good intentions.

Horne Tooke was one of the leaders of the young men who saw themselves as reformers, those who wanted to create a more republican form of government, those who in 1794 would have to face a trial for sedition with Tooke himself; but in the spring of 1792, no one thought of trials.

Inchbald and Colman were working together all spring, and on June 30, 1792, Inchbald finished a play called *Young Men and Old Women*, but it was not a success, and she and Robinson agreed that it should not be published. She had also written a tragedy for which Colman wrote a prologue as she had requested. She called it *The Massacre*, and she sent it to Harris, but he declined it. Her tragedy, however, was not her summer farce, and she "resolved upon printing it with the name of the Robinson house, and the date 1792." For the advertisement before the play, she quoted from Horace Walpole's postscript to his *Mysterious Mother*, a part of which reads: "The subject is so horrid, that I thought it would shock, rather than give satisfaction . . . so truly tragic in the essential springs of *terror* and *pity*, that I could not resist the impulse of adapting it to the scene."

THE MASSACRE AND THE YEARS AFTER

The Robinsons did print *The Massacre*, but it was withdrawn and was not published again until Boaden included it in the *Memoirs*. Inchbald set it in France during the time of the persecution of the Protestants and the Massacre of St. Bartholomew's Day (1572). It is violent and bloody, introduced when the character Eusébe arrives from Paris and reports a terrible scene of horror. Eusébe has been an agent for the Protestants, and he, as well as Tricastin, another in the group, has a price set for his capture. The group plans to flee to England, but they become separated and instead are confronted with a mob; Mme. Tricastin manages to escape with her children. Eusébe is brought to trial and condemned, for his captors say "he does not think with us." A counterrevolutionary mob of soldiers intervenes to save him just as the slaughtered bodies of Mme. Tricastin and the children are brought in.

As dramatic as the incidents are in the play, the center of interest is the Tricastin family, father, son, and Madame Tricastin, the wife of the younger Tricastin. The play opens with her lament about her husband's delay in returning from the city. His friend Conrad, who appears, does little to console her, and when another friend, Menancourt, shows up, Conrad describes the horrors of the massacres: "Infernal massacre has been dealt to all our hapless party—bonds, vows, oaths, have been violated; nor even the prison-walls been a sanctuary for the ill-fated objects of suspicion. The report that's brought speaks of children torn from the breast of their mothers, husbands from the arms of their wives, and aged parents from their agonizing families." At this point Tricastin the younger—husband and son—appears. He is wounded; his report is vivid and detailed: "I fought with the assassins, and fell amongst my brethren—at that moment my senses left me.—When they returned, and I put out my arms to embrace my fellow sufferers, I found I clasped nothing but dead bodies.—I rose from the horrid pile, and by a lamp, discovered (all gashed with wounds) faces, that, but a few hours before I had seen shine with health and benevolence.—Rushing from the ghastly scene, I fled. I knew not where, about the town—my sword in my hand, reeking with blood, my hair disheveled, and my frantic features caused me to be taken for one of the murderers, and so I passed unmolested, once more."

He is in a state of shock, seeing still the horror he has escaped, and when his wife entreats him to "recollect" his "scattered thoughts," he again describes the scene: "No, I still hear the shrieks of my expiring friends, mingled with the furious shouts of their triumphant foes.—I saw poor females, youths, and helpless infants try to ward off the last fatal blow, then sink beneath it—I saw aged men dragged by their white hairs; a train of children following to prevent their fate, and only rush upon their own.—I saw infants encouraged by the fury of their tutors, stab other infants sleeping in their cradles."

After this speech there is a footnote at the bottom of the page explaining the connection with the St. Bartholomew massacre and citing the "late massacre at Paris." There is no doubt that Inchbald's descriptions were contemporary. The remainder of the play examines the efforts of the family to survive. They plan to flee the country, Madame argues that she will stay with her husband, and the younger Tricastin will not leave his father.

In the second act we find Madame Tricastin with her attendant Amédée and her children preparing to leave, to go to England, but the gates of the city are closed; they must remain in the house trusting to Providence, but the mob rushes in and the family flees to an inner room, leaving only the elder Tricastin on stage to speak. There follows a dramatic confrontation in which the leader of the mob cannot decide whether the elder Tricastin is, or is not, his son. As they are about to take him away, the son enters and is seized. The drama of this scene is heightened by the separation of the family—the father and son taken away and Madame Tricastin and her attendants taken off on the opposite side "as by stealth."

The third and final act of the play is quite unusual in that it shows a courtroom setting with a "President," not called a judge, presiding. Here, as earlier, Inchbald is using the events in Paris in a very direct way. In Paris as the bloody massacres were occurring on September 2 and following, one historian writes, "Even after it had become apparent that a massacre of appalling proportions was taking place . . . the only move made by the authorities of the Commune was to appoint *commissaries* to investigate what was happening. But those same men were mandated less with a mission to stop the killings than to give the violence a gloss of judicial respectability."[17]

For Inchbald the trial scene is used to make important pronouncements; Glandeve, the president/judge, will not allow Dugas, the accuser, to simply condemn Tricastin and his son without evidence. Glandeve says to him, "A few days ago, when I enquired, you told me, Dugas, you knew this man to be a peaceable citizen." To which Dugas replies, "I have since changed my mind." Whereupon Glandeve turns to the spectators saying, "Then, what do you think my friends, is it not better that we wait a few days longer before we put Tricastin on his trial; for in that time, the witness may possibly change his mind again."

When Tricastin is taken aside, Dugas says, "I thought, Glandeve, you were the sworn friend of liberty?" In reply Glandeve makes the key comment to the whole tragedy, "And so I am—liberty, I worship.—But, my friends, 'tis liberty to do good, not ill—liberty joined with peace and charity." To Inchbald "liberty joined with peace and charity" is the proper conduct of justice in any court, in any situation.

Glandeve, coming forward, says to Tricastin and his party: "My fellow-citizens! disperse your fears—I accepted the office of judge, not to condemn, but to preserve you; and, these [*pointing to the persons attending in court*] are a chosen set of men, whom I convened for the purpose of defeating the blind fury of your enemies." But such justice is not enough; Dugas's men have already slain Madame Tricastin and her two children. The bier is brought in as Eusébe and Tricastin stand by, horrified.

The closing action is Glandeve's command to his men to secure Dugas and his followers as prisoners "till our researches prove successful.—Then, the good (of all parties) will conspire to extirpate such monsters from the earth. It is not partly principles which cause this devastation; 'tis want of sense—'tis guilt—for the first precept in our Christian laws, is charity—the next obligation—to extend that charity, EVEN TO OUR ENEMIES."

This closing speech certainly represented Inchbald's own belief; unfortunately, charity toward one's enemies was not always the case in the world of 1792–1793. After the horrors of the massacres in Paris and the execution of the king, France found itself at war with Prussia, the Austrian Empire, Spain, Holland, and Britain. In 1793, with the declaration of war, the government in London was increasingly wary of "liberty," and the action and "charity" of Inchbald's play was not acceptable. The newspapers that provided her the materials for the play were also the source of the reasons it was withdrawn.

For her own future, early in 1792 Mr. Kemble and Mr. and Mrs. Twiss had urged her to accept an engagement to join the company at Drury Lane, but although she wrote a farce for Mrs. Jordan at Kemble's request, she refused the invitation. Boaden suggests that she would have been in competition with Sheridan to write for Drury Lane, since Sheridan wanted no rivals and Kemble supported the older, more traditional playwrights, especially Shakespeare in his own adaptations.

Boaden speaks of the offer and the state of the theatre in this year of 1792, observing that Kemble

never scrupled to declare his opinion that we had *plays* enough, and far beyond all modern competition; that these, carefully revised and well acted, with good farces and melodramas, with the aid of opera, now in the hands of Storace, and Cobb, and Hoare, constituted the proper attractions of a rational theatre. . . . We willingly suppose that Kemble would not have insulted her with Harris's thirty shillings or two pounds per week, nor have required the author of the 'Simple Story' to walk in a Christmas pantomime. He would have probably given her six pounds per week; but then he would not have expected that she should write for the *other* house, however she might be paralysed in *his*. These, and many other reasons more obvious, no doubt influenced the friends whom she consulted, when they advised her to *decline* the offer. They were people of discernment—Robinson, Woodfall, and the Whitfields.[18]

As 1792 came to an end, in the months of November and December Godwin was working with Inchbald on her comedy. On November 26 he wrote in his journal, "Call on Raine, Mrs. Webb & Mrs. Inchbald dine at Holcroft's. . . . Revise Mrs. Inchbald's Comedy. (Debating Society silenced)," and on the next day he wrote: "Revise Mrs. Inchbald's comedy; Letter from Robinson: call on Holcroft." On the twenty-eighth again he was busy revising her comedy, and the next day he had supper with Mrs. Inchbald. As December began, on the eighth he records, "Revise. Jardine at tea. Sup at Nicholson's Talk of abstraction. Hear from Mrs. Inchbald." On the twelfth he wrote eight pages, read, called on Inchbald, and had Holcroft at tea; on the eighteenth, a Tuesday, he notices Paine's trial and records, "call on Mrs. Inchbald, talk of Erskine, France and promise."

In the new year, 1793, Godwin continued to see Inchbald; on January 14 he called on her, on the eighteenth he had tea with her and on January 29 there is a special entry: "Call on Robinson & Davis. Finish Pol. Justice. Play, Everyone has his fault, with Robinson, Murphy, Davis, & Chambers. Sup at Holcroft's." Inchbald's play proved to be one of her most popular and, given her close association with Godwin and Holcroft, one of the most filled with new ideas, but although it reflects her "association" with Godwin and his efforts to "revise" it, it was very much her own play.

The whole of the year 1793 was an especially significant one for Inchbald, Godwin, and Holcroft. Godwin's *Political Justice* came out, Inchbald's play *Every One Has His Fault*, as we have said, was very successful and created quite a stir, and in the summer Holcroft evidently asked Mrs. Inchbald to marry him. Moreover, in the fall an entry in Godwin's journal reads, "talked of marriage." The three friends had evidently seen each other repeatedly.[19]

Godwin's journal entry on January 29, 1793, records the finish of his book *An Enquiry concerning the Principles of Political Justice, and Its Influence on General Virtue and Happiness,* called *Political Justice* as a short title; it was published in January by Robinson. Its immediate success justified Robinson's support, and it became one of the most talked about books of the 1790s; some of Godwin's ideas were extreme, and in the second edition, when he revised his work extensively, he did little to placate his critics. One commentator, examining the effect his ideas had, has said: "The statements which aroused the most clamor in his own era and continued to sound ridiculous to later commentators include these basic ideas: Truth is omnipotent. Vice is merely an error in judgment. Man is perfectible. Government is the great obstacle to human happiness. The operation of the law of necessity produces inevitable progress. The private affections block universal benevolence."[20]

Godwin claimed that truth, "when adequately communicated, must always be victorious over error." When he said that man is perfectible, he meant that man is susceptible of perpetual improvement.[21] His comments about marriage became notorious for his contemporaries. Viewed two hundred years later, however, perhaps his view is more reasonable—certainly more reasonable than the increasingly repressive views of the nineteenth century. He wrote:

marriage, as now understood, is a monopoly, and the worst of monopolies. . . . So long as I seek, by despotic and artificial means, to maintain my possession of a woman, I am guilty of the most odious selfishness. . . . All . . . arguments are calculated to determine one judgment in favour of marriage as a salutary and respectable institution, but not of that species of marriage, in which there is no room for repentance, and to which liberty and hope are equally strangers. . . . Certainly no ties ought to be imposed upon either party preventing them from quitting the attachment, whenever their judgment directs them to quit it. With respect to such infidelities as are compatible with an intention to adhere to it, the point of principal importance is a determination to have recourse to no species of disguise.[22]

Godwin's views about marriage, although they were certainly not what he intended to be central to his argument in *Political Justice,* became a point much cited and much discussed in the next years, and these views he would revise and defend later upon his own marriage. Working, as the journal shows, day by day, writing a page or two while he read or went to tea and the theatre, his views must have reflected conversation with his friends and associates, although only Godwin could have expressed his ideas about marriage so bluntly. Certainly Inchbald would never have agreed to a marriage in which the husband allowed no freedom and in which "liberty and hope are equally strangers." Inchbald's play *Every One Has His Fault* considers some of these ideas about marriage; it also makes sharp comments about such husbands.

Holcroft must also have had a part in the ideas of *Every One*. He and Inchbald saw each other frequently, and not always with their friend Godwin present. Holcroft, like Kemble in the early days, felt he could advise Inchbald about her work and ideas even when his advice was negative. Holcroft believed that everyone on all occasions should speak the truth. He felt sincerity was a cardinal virtue, untruthfulness a cardinal sin. He agreed with Godwin about the perfectibility of man, but the moral system he proposed had its foundation not only in reason but also in absolute sincerity and truthfulness on the part of each individual. Inchbald's play, although it is candid in allowing everyone to have at least "one" fault, is based entirely on having all the characters told they are loved, when actually such statements are, in the beginning, false. The play is a complex puzzle put together to discuss several aspects of love, marriage, and the family. In her play, which is far more complex than any such situations Holcroft presents in his plays, Inchbald discusses and largely refutes Holcroft's notion of complete sincerity and truthfulness.

The calendar years that divide the theatre seasons and the varied and outside interests of Inchbald, Holcroft, and Godwin came together in their discussions of their work over tea, prompted by events, not by the calendar. No doubt their conversations about their political world during these years of the 1790s, as the French Revolution created one disaster after another, had on occasion turned to the rise of the societies—a variety of groups representing opposition to the government of the king and his ministers, societies that became increasingly popular among those who wished to be reformers. Although it is not possible to know how much of the discussions of political and social ideas Inchbald participated in, we do know she had strong opinions.

The summer of 1793 was a very pleasant one for Mrs. Inchbald, especially the time she spent in the green room at the Haymarket. Her play *Every One*, presented in January, was still much discussed, and she was still being congratulated for her novel. It was here that she met Lord Guildford and Lord Barrymore, along with Lord and Lady Petre, all among the ton. As usual, she gave money to her sisters and one of her aunts out of the profit from her play and its publication. In August her friend Dr. Parson took her to dine with her new correspondent, George Hardinge; she and the Hardinges were immediately attracted to each other, and the correspondence in the years following this dinner party gives some important views of Inchbald's personal and professional life. The letters are not dated, though sometimes internal evidence suggests a date. One especially personal one reads:

Madam,

I have often heard the Siddons's and Mr. Kemble, and both Twiss's declare—but I would not believe it—that you were not only capricious, but ill-bred enough to look your friends in the face as if you never had seen them. I saw this, which I thought a calumny, demonstrated Monday last. It was near two o'clock, and in St. James's Park. You had on your black muslin, had a little umbrella in your hand, and a little dumpy woman in white as a foil. I passed as close to you as I am now to my pen, and you would not appear to know me.

I told my wife, and she said it was no surprise to her, as you had not answered her letter.[23]

The "little dumpy woman in white" was probably her sister Hunt, who frequently walked with her in St. James's Park, and as for her failure to speak and recognize him, perhaps it was because she did not have her glass with her. She was very nearsighted and kept her glass with her at all times. Hardinge teased her about her crush on Dr. Warren—everyone who knew her intimately knew she had a "weakness" for him—a word she herself used. She was thrilled if she saw him and frequently walked along Sackville Street on the chance to see him. Evidently she had asked Hardinge to inquire about Dr. Warren, who had been quite ill. His letter in reply is again a witty, teasing report:

My Dear, Dear Creature,

Your own words—your own hand—and the superscription to *me*. Oh how flattering! I thought Sir Charles looked yellow in the House of Commons last night; and when I arrived at home, I saw the reason for it in your *billet-doux* to me. The fairies told him that he was less beloved than me; and though I saw him fast asleep, I could easily discover that his dreams were feverish.

But alas! your affection to Warren makes you entirely overlook the invalid who suffered by it, and whom you don't even mention once. I have really no other intelligence of him than that my poor suffering angel was told he was ill, and that messages were not then (Saturday) permitted by Mrs. Warren to be delivered to her husband; except that Lord Bayham told me it was a complaint in his bowels and of no alarming nature; but for your sake, my dear, dear creature, I have sent a message to Mrs. Warren, and you shall learn the answer.[24]

This letter was followed by another:

Dear Muse,

I am just come from Lord Camden's where I learn that poor Warren is entirely out of danger, and will be in his chariot again very soon—in two or three days. This too comes immediately *from himself* in a message to Lord Camden.

For this I expect a kiss in your answer, at least by the bearer; and a good breakfast at nine, ten, or eleven, to-morrow morning, whichever of these hours you should prefer; though I should like the earliest of them: but I am,

Dear Muse,

Your ever affectionate though hated servant,

G.H.[25]

Hardinge continues, "If you don't think I deserve the expense, I'll bring a roll with me in my pocket." Boaden makes a footnote to this last remark, "A playful allusion to her systematic frugality," which shows again Boaden's lack of real understanding of Inchbald and her friends.[26] In all his biographies he is serious and rather dull. Many of Inchbald's friends were neither serious nor dull, and in these years of the 1790s she had the ideal combination of serious discussions with Godwin, social events with Sir Charles, tea and conversation in the green room with Holcroft, and letters and conversation with Hardinge. And she began to see such people as Horne Tooke and John Wolcot, better known as Peter Pindar, the poet who wrote satiric odes to the king, Mrs. Piozzi, James Boswell, and a great many other prominent figures.

Sometime soon after she began to work on the second edition of *A Simple Story*, she must have consulted Hardinge about language that Boaden calls "colloquial vulgarism"—about whether one should say "my sister Deborah is prettier than *me*." Boaden's footnote continues, "Hardinge, as a scholar, should have disdained to talk of determining such points as whether an *oblique* or a *nominative* case should be used, by a man's ear or good company. 'I am prettier than *she*,' he says, 'would shock every ear, and every optic nerve.' The *shock* is one from ignorant custom. The grammatical rule is perfectly simple, and a safe invariable guide. Take it therefore, ladies, from Dr. Lowth."[27]

Having expounded in a footnote, Boaden goes further and quotes from Dr. Lowth—that is, from the most recently revised edition of Lowth, an edition published more than forty years after Inchbald and Hardinge's discussion. But Boaden also invokes Horne Tooke for his "great discovery . . . which showed him the *manner*, of significations expressed by what are called particles in language."[28] These last years of the eighteenth century were important for the discussions of language and the beginning of scholarship about language and literature. These were the years of Edmund Malone and of the Variorum Shakespeare; Inchbald's friend Twiss, who was her friend and mentor in the 1780s, was still working on his Shakespeare concordance, and Boaden himself had been deeply into the scandal of the forgery of the Shakespeare play set up by the Ireland forgeries.[29]

Hardinge's wife, Lucy, also corresponded with Inchbald. One of her letters has a quite remarkable bit of comment about husbands and wives. She warns Inchbald not to send her letters directed in care of her husband, since he therefore feels they are for him as well, and the intimate quality of the letter is thus destroyed. The Hardinges lived in Sloane Street, and Lucy Hardinge, writing from there, apologizes for not being at home when Inchbald called. She then continues: "I wish . . . that I could *seduce you* into conquering *that bad habit* of *laying yourself up in cotton* after sunset in the winter—if *winter* this season can be called; but according to my opinion it has been put off till next year. I am not without hope of being able to persuade you to pick the *merry-thought* of a chicken with me, and the sooner the better after Tuesday next."[30]

The Hardinges' letters make the immediacy of Inchbald's life very real in ways that no comments about finances or plays can do. It is in one of Lucy's letters written from Twickenham that she comments about her husband's fearing that because she could not avoid showing Inchbald's letter to him he might make "some observations upon your letter. . . . It is contrary to my inclination to show my friends' letters in general; and for this reason, I universally desire they will *not* write to me *under cover to him;* for he always *makes a point* of *seeing every letter that is enclosed to him,* and is so apt to take offence (*entre nous,* without a cause,) that I am glad to avoid a *worry* by keeping them to myself."[31]

Lucy Hardinge had been nursing a sick friend who was dying of consumption, and afterward she went to Brandon and Hawstead to visit the Metcalfes, who knew and praised Inchbald. One of the Miss Metcalfes frequently visited Inchbald's sister in Suffolk, and after reporting about her visit, Lucy Hardinge continued: "I was very happy to hear the justice they did to your virtues, as well as your talents, and agreed with perfect sincerity in all they said. Talents *alone* would make me ambitious of your *acquaintance;* but your other perfections make me proud of you as a *friend.*"[32]

At one point Lucy Hardinge had separate maintenance from her husband; the comments in Inchbald's letter show one reason for her decision to be apart from him. But in a letter—not dated—Hardinge writes: "My wife and myself are happily re-united; she is goodness itself to me: I love her dearly, and wish to see you at the Castle again."[33]

Boaden included not only the Hardinges' letters but also letters Inchbald herself wrote about her work, letters that are very valuable for understanding her views of herself and her work. Writing of *Every One,* Boaden says, "Of the comedy itself, it is unnecessary to speak at large, since every body has seen it, or read it." It became so celebrated that after it was published in February, the *True Briton* made an attack "upon the doctrines it espoused, as tending to disorganisation. This journal was established for the avowed object of supporting Mr. Pitt in his endeavours to suppress the revolutionary spirit, then systematically exerting itself against the governments of all countries. They heard therefore with alarm anything like *liberal* opinions delivered with an emphasis upon the public stage, and caught up enthusiastically by the people, as sanctioning inferences that went still farther."[34]

Inchbald very cleverly used the attack not only to reply to their accusations but also to promote the theatre and the subsequent publishing of plays presented on stage. The whole episode is significant for the interaction of stage and print, quite beyond Mrs. Inchbald's experience. Her reply reads:

Sir,

    After the most laborious efforts to produce a dramatic work deserving the approbation of the town; after experiencing the most painful anxiety till that approbation was secured; a malicious falsehood, aimed to destroy every advantage arising from my industry, has been circulated in a print called 'The True Briton;' in which I am accused of conveying seditious sentiments to the public. This charge I considered of little importance, while an impartial audience were, every evening, to judge of its truth:—but my accuser having, in this day's paper, taken a different mode of persecution, saying I have expunged those sentences which were of dangerous tendency, the play can, now, no longer be its own evidence: I am, therefore, compelled to declare, in contradiction to this assertion, that not one line, or one *word,* has been altered or omitted since the first night of representation. As a further proof of the injustice with which I have been treated, had I been so unfortunate in my principles, or blind to my own interest, as to have written anything of the nature of which I am accused, I most certainly should not have presented it for reception to the manager of Covent-Garden Theatre.

E. Inchbald.

Leicester Square, Feb. 1st, 1793.[35]

Every One Has His Fault had been presented in January 1793 at Covent Garden with an especially fine and large cast. The prologue was spoken by Farren; using the title, it asks,

> O, be not in a frowning mood to-night!
> The Play, perhaps, has many things amiss:

> Well, let us then reduce the point to this,
> Let only those that have no failings, hiss.

The audience did not hiss, and the play, as Boaden remarked, became a universal favorite, perhaps because it included a whole range of "faults" and treated them with wit and charity.

If the title of the play suggests that the men are at fault, the first two lines of the prologue make clear that the women are at fault too. Farren began, "Our Author, who accuses great and small, / And says so boldly, there are faults in all ..." The "faults," moreover, cover a wide range of problems: problems of marriage, of husbands and wives, of families, of parents and children, of public and personal dilemmas. And these problems are concerned with a wide variety of social and personal problems, having to do with paternal authority, financial responsibilities, and moral obligations. The ideas of the play—the solutions offered—suggest somewhat revolutionary conclusions. No one member of a marriage or a family can impose absolute control, no one father or husband can deny independent judgments of a wife or a child. One of the constant features of the play as it is developed is the use of personal, individual judgments of the pairs of players, of the "faults" on the part of one or the other; in fact both have created the "problems," which are no single "fault" of either partner.

The faults are all examined in domestic situations, but for the time of the play it is not surprising that the *True Briton*, Pitt's supporting periodical, would find that the play suggested "disorganisation" by current standards of behavior; individual independence was not looked upon with any favor, especially for women and children. However, the women and children in the play are themselves at fault several times because they wish to exercise their independence, an independence clearly affecting the other members of the family—or the marriage—making for unhappy or, in some cases, dangerous incidents.

Another feature of the play that was apparent to Inchbald's audience but is not to ours is the device of using social—polite—lies or falsehoods to change an individual's perceptions and thus behavior. One of the most outspoken of the advocates of complete truthfulness was Holcroft, Inchbald's close friend and, in the summer of 1793, her suitor. Godwin also thought telling the truth in all situations was required of a "philosopher"; he learned after the death of Mary Wollstonecraft, his wife, in 1798 and his publication of her *Memoirs* just how devastating the "truth" could be.[36] Since Inchbald, Holcroft, and Godwin saw each other socially at tea, supper, and the theatre, it is tempting to see her play as a response to their conversations. Neither Godwin nor Holcroft was socially sophisticated, however, certainly not so much as Inchbald, Amelia Alderson, and the Kembles were, and the play suggests a more varied society than that of the pattern Godwin and Holcroft would have suggested. *Every One Has His Fault* shows the possibility of using social "falsehoods" to the advantage of "Every One," and "Every One" is included. The play is not a serious sociological study, not even a serious statement—it is comedy—but the characters representing themselves also represent their world, and they represent truth about the reality of human nature far beyond the ideas of Godwin and Holcroft. Moreover, Inchbald has filled this play with a detailed view of marriage and the family that is not found in any other one of her plays. Following the dialogue and the action, we find comments about marriage laws, the army, newspapers, coffeehouses, servants, women, men, husbands, wives, children, and families. Inchbald interweaves these subjects with such skill that it is only after the conclusion of the play that we realize what a wide variety of topics she has commented upon.

The play opens with a conversation between Mr. Placid and Solus in which they are arguing about Solus's desire to be married.

> *Placid:* . . . your singularity pleases me; for you are the first elderly bachelor I ever knew, who did not hug himself in the reflection, that he was not in the trammels of wedlock.
> *Solus:* No; I am only the first elderly bachelor who has truth and courage enough to confess his dissatisfaction.

Moreover, Solus declares that he wishes he had been married for thirty years and had "half-a-score" of children. Placid will not believe him: "Pshaw! You have in your time been a man of gallantry; and, consequently, must have made many attachments."

> *Solus:* Yes, such as men of gallantry usually make. I have been attached to women who have purloined my fortune, and to men who have partaken of the theft: I have been in as much fear of my mistress as you are of your wife.
> *Placid:* Is that possible?
> *Solus:* Yes . . . I have maintained children—
> *Placid:* Then why do you complain for the want of a family?
> *Solus:* I did not say I ever had any children; I said I had *maintained* them; but I never believed they were mine; for I could have no dependence upon the principles of their mother—and never did I take one of those tender infants in my arms, that the forehead of my Valet, the squint eye

of my Apothecary, or the double-chin of my Chaplain, did not stare me in the face. . . .

Placid: But those are accidents which may occur in the marriage state.

Solus: In that case, a man is pitied—in mine, he is only laughed at.

After this last speech of Solus, Placid reveals his problem: "I wish to heaven I could exchange the pity which my friends bestow on me, for the merriment which your ill fate excites."

Solus: You want but courage to be envied.

Placid: Does any one doubt my courage?

Solus: No. If a Prince were to offend you, you would challenge him, I have no doubt.

Placid: But if my wife offend me, I am obliged to make an apology.—Was not that her voice? I hope she has not overheard our conversation.

Solus: If she have, she'll be in an ill humour.

Placid: That she will be, whether she have heard it or not.

The dialogue between Placid and Solus sets the situation for the others to come, but as Solus is about to leave, another "situation," another concern develops. Placid reminds him that he would find more delight in his nephew and the nephew's family than he is likely to find in a marriage of his own at his age. The explanation that follows reveals that his nephew Irwin has married for love and has a large family as the result of his "indiscreet marriage," an indiscretion that has now brought him to destitution. With this final speech, Solus leaves and Placid's wife appears.

Mrs. Placid is hardly "placid"; on the contrary, she is constantly attempting to stir up her husband; she hates noise and will not tolerate any criticism of herself or the household. She speaks to her husband: "Pray, Mr. Placid, do not find fault with any body in this house. But I have something which I must take *you* very severely to task about, Sir." Placid tries to escape by summoning John to inquire about dinner, but his wife insists: "No, John. . . . Mr. Placid, you *shall* first hear what I have to say." What she has to say is that she wishes to have him promise that he will not lend money to Captain Irwin and Lady Eleanor. The Placids and the Irwins have been intimate friends in the past, but now that the Irwins are in distress, Mrs. Placid will have nothing to do with them, and she forbids her husband to even visit them. When the servant enters to say that dinner is served, Placid says, "Ah! I am not hungry now." And she replies, "What do you mean by that, Mr. Placid? I insist on your being hungry."

The play is filled with a certain kind of domestic farce, but the situations make very pertinent statements about marriage and the family. Scene 2 introduces Mr. Harmony and Miss Spinster; scene 3 introduces Mr. Irwin and his wife, Lady Eleanor. Harmony and Miss Spinster are characterized by their names; Mr. Irwin is the nephew of Solus and the friend of the Placids, the friend whom Mrs. Placid forbids her husband to help; Solus sees no reason to support the Irwins either.

As Harmony appears on stage, he is followed by Miss Spinster, who is upbraiding him: "Cousin, cousin Harmony, I will not forgive you for thus continually speaking in the behalf of every servant whom you find me offended with. Your philanthropy becomes insupportable; and, instead of being a virtue, degenerates into a vice." To which Harmony replies, "Dear Madam, do not upbraid me for a constitutional fault."

Miss Spinster: "Very true; you had it from your infancy. I have heard your mother say you were always foolishly tender-hearted, and never shewed one of those discriminating passions of envy, hatred, or revenge, to which all her other children were liable." Harmony is the kind of person who would befriend everyone, a trait Miss Spinster thinks is ridiculous. But Harmony says: "Nay, 'tis truth: and I sincerely lament that human beings should be such strangers to one another as we are. We live in the same street, without knowing one another's necessities; and oftentimes meet and part from each other at church, at coffee-houses, playhouses, and all public places, without ever speaking a single word, or nodding 'Good bye!' though 'tis a hundred chances to ten we never see one another again."

Miss Spinster thinks his "pretended philanthropy" makes him ridiculous, for she says that "There is not a fraud, a theft, or hardly any vice committed, that you do not take the criminal's part, shake your head, and cry, 'Provisions are so scarce!'" Harmony replies:

This is a weakness I confess. But though my honour sometimes reproaches me with it as a fault, my conscience never does: for it is by this very failing that I have frequently made the bitterest enemies friends—Just by saying a few harmless sentences, which, though a species of falsehood and deceit, yet, being soothing and acceptable to the person offended, I have immediately inspired him with lenity and forgiveness; and then, by only repeating the self-same sentences to his opponent, I have known hearts cold and closed to each other, warmed and expanded, as every human creature's ought to be.

Mr. Harmony's speech is followed by a series of demonstrations that prove the "truth," as he sees it, that in fact Miss Spinster finds objectionable: "I condemn that false humanity, which induces you to say many things in conversation which deserve to stigmatize you with the character of deceit."

Miss Spinster says, as the servant introduces Mr. Solus, that she cannot understand how Harmony can keep company with that old bachelor, and she leaves the room. When Harmony invites Solus to have supper with him and Miss Spinster, Solus refuses his invitation, saying, "to tell you the truth, your relation, Miss Spinster, is no great favourite of mine; and I don't like to dine with you, because I don't like her company." Harmony declares he is very surprised, but Solus explains: "Why, old bachelors and old maids never agree: we are too much alike in our habits: we know our own hearts so well, we are apt to discover every foible we would wish to forget, in the symptoms displayed by the other. Miss Spinster is peevish, fretful and tiresome, and I am always in a fidget when I am in her company."

To this speech Harmony replies: "How different are her sentiments of you! for one of her greatest joys is to be in your company. Poor woman! she has, to be sure, an uneven temper—." He continues, "I will assure you, I never see her in half such good humour as when you are here." Solus leaves, and when Miss Spinster reappears, Harmony insists that Solus is full of praises about her. When she insists—"What praises?" Harmony says, "he declared you looked better last night, than any other lady at the Opera." Miss Spinster believes him, saying she will not be guilty of ill manners, and as she leaves, "Come, let us go into the drawing-room to receive him"; Harmony, leaving, agrees, "Ay! this is right: this is as it should be."

The couple, Mr. Irwin and Lady Eleanor Irwin, demonstrate a different "fault." They have married for love, she being Lord Norland's daughter and he a former officer in the army. He speaks about his situation in poverty without money to support his family, as he says to his wife: "here, in London, where plenty and ease smile upon every face; where, by birth you claim distinction, and I by services:—here to be in want,—to be obliged to take another name in shame of our own,—to tremble at the voice of every stranger, for fear he should be a creditor. . . . To have no reward . . . to see our children looking up to me for that support I have not in my power to give." His uncle Solus had laughed at him and told him his distresses "were the result of my ambition, in marrying the daughter of a nobleman, who himself was too ambitious ever to pardon us." He has also seen Lord Norland, Lady Eleanor's father, who passed him in his carriage. Upon this speech a servant enters with a letter. It is from Placid, who, because of his wife, refuses to lend Irwin the money. Irwin is desperate, more even than his wife realizes.

The setting for act 2 is a coffeehouse. As the scene opens, Sir Robert Ramble appears on one side and Solus and Mr. Placid on the other. Sir Robert has been dining in public to meet with some good company. Solus agrees that he has now been "reduced to the same necessity which I frequently am—I frequently am obliged to dine at taverns and coffee-houses, for want of company at home." Sir Robert enjoys a public house where "a man may meet his friend without the inconvenience of form, either as a host or a visitor." Solus introduces Sir Robert to Mr. Placid; Sir Robert, greeting him, says: "Sir, I shall be happy in your acquaintance; and I assure you, if you will do me the honour to meet me now and then at this house, you will find every thing very pleasant. I verily believe, that since I lost my wife, which is now about five months ago, I verily believe I have dined here three days out of seven." He has not "lost" his wife but has divorced her and, as Placid plainly points out, "Divorced from a virtuous wife!" The only excuse Sir Robert can give is: "It may appear strange to you, Sir; but my wife and I did not live happy together." Solus understands when Placid remarks that that is not at all strange.

Sir Robert Ramble and his wife were married in Scotland, and he explains that by the law there, a wife can divorce her husband "for breach of fidelity; and so, though my wife's character was unimpeached, mine was not, and she divorced me." It soon develops that Sir Robert's fortune is much impaired as a result of the divorce and that he has "played very deep" lately; he would not have his situation known to anyone, least of all to his former wife and her guardian. Solus finds all this rather unbelievable. He inquires of Sir Robert why he and his wife separated, only to understand from Sir Robert that he wished her to oblige him.

When Solus declares her a "good woman," Sir Robert says "Very good—but very ugly." Solus replies: "She is beautiful."

> *Sir Robert:* I tell you, Sir, she is hideous. And then she was grown so insufferably peevish.
> *Solus:* I never saw her out of temper.
> *Sir Robert:* Mr. Solus, it is very uncivil of you to praise her before my face. Lady Ramble, at the time I parted with her, had every possible fault both of mind and person, and so I made love to other women in her presence; told her bluntly that I was tired of her; that 'I was very sorry to make her uneasy, but that I could not love her any longer.'—And was not that frank and open?

Sir Robert continues to justify himself. He is older than his former wife, "but the difference of sex makes her a great deal older than I am." But Solus will not agree that women lose their beauty so many years before the men lose their eyesight and can no longer judge beauty. With the discussion of beauty and fidelity and the present situation of Sir Robert and his loss of income after divorcing his wife, his "fault" is nullified, and the ability to correct it is far beyond anything he himself can do.

While Sir Robert has been speaking, Mr. Placid has been thinking—and remembering; he wishes to know how Sir Robert managed to escape. Solus, knowing Lady Placid, encourages the question when Sir Robert asks, "Sir, do you wish to be divorced?" He replies, "I have no such prospect. Mrs. Placid is faithful, and I was married in England." Sir Robert knows all the answers:

> *Sir Robert:* But if you have an unconquerable desire to part, a separate maintenance will answer nearly the same end—for if your Lady and you will only lay down the plan of separation, and agree—
> *Placid:* But, unfortunately, we never do agree!
> *Sir Robert:* Then speak of parting as a thing you dread worse than death; and make it your daily prayer to her, that she will never think of going from you—She will determine upon it directly.

Placid is very grateful, and Sir Robert asserts with great satisfaction that he has learned the art of "teasing a wife"; Solus concludes the scene with: "And now, Sir Robert, you have had the good nature to teach this Gentleman how to get rid of his wife, will you have the kindness to teach me how to procure one?"

Before any further conversation, Mr. Irwin, Solus's nephew, enters; it is he who is desperate for money and has been denied by both his uncle and his friend Placid. The subject having been matrimony—wives—the dialogue continues. Irwin has been in the army, out of the country. Sir Robert continues to celebrate the fact that he is being divorced, that, in fact, although his wife is the one with the money, he believes he has sufficient funds since he has no children. At one point Irwin remarks, "You are right to pay respect to fortune. Money is a necessary article in the marriage contract."

The discussion about lending Irwin money to support his wife and family becomes a discussion of borrowing and lending, of the definition of "rich" and the situation of the respectable poor. Sir Robert is quite candid: "And is it not very common to be rich without money? Are not half the town rich? And yet half the town has no money. I speak for this end of the town, the West end. The Squares, for instance, part of Piccadilly, down St. James's-street, and so home by Pall Mall. We have all, estates, bonds, drafts, and notes of hand without number; but as for money, we have no such thing belonging to us."

Irwin apologizes for being so direct in his questions about money, saying that Sir Robert misled him. Sir Robert continues: "I *am* in affluence, I am, I am; but not in so much, perhaps, as my hasty, inconsiderate account may have given you reason to believe," whereupon he explains that his wife has sued for the divorce (the divorce he has demanded), and he must return her fortune although he has two sisters to "portion off." He suggests, however, that he will speak to Lord Norland, Irwin's father-in-law, who in fact is Sir Robert's wife's guardian. Irwin knows such a contact will never prove successful, that Lord Norland will not forgive his daughter, Irwin's wife, and that Sir Robert is refusing any help in the most callous fashion by being excessively polite. Irwin follows Sir Robert's speech with a long soliloquy on his situation of leaving his brother officers who always shared their problems and returning to his nearest relations, ". . . so very civilized. . . . I could not take the liberty to enter under one roof, without a ceremonious invitation. . . . I may leave my card at their door, but as for me, or any one of mine, they would not give us a dinner; unless, indeed, it was in such a style, that we might behold with admiration their grandeur, and return still more depressed, to our own poverty."

At the end of this speech, he takes out a pistol—will he be a villain or a suicide? And at this point the question of money has been given another dimension, for Irwin's situation is a comment on the army as well as on his father-in-law. In spite of the sympathy of his fellows, the army has returned him to civilian life without any hope of an adequate income or position.

Irwin does not leave, but Harmony enters asking to see "half a dozen newspapers—Every paper of the day." To his request, the waiter says, "That is about three dozen, Sir," to which Harmony replies, "Get a couple of porters, and bring them all." Surrounded by newspapers, Harmony is not aware of Irwin at first, even though Irwin talks aloud about his troubles, and we are told in a stage direction that "*His mind [is] deranged by his misfortunes.*" The conversation between the two that follows finds Harmony offering to help Irwin and Irwin still deep in his prejudices—that no one in the "West end" will offer help; he adds, "Have you no sisters to portion off? no lady's fortune to return? Or, perhaps, you will speak to my wife's father, and entreat him to forgive his child."

Inchbald's juxtaposition of the newspapers, with their reality of current events, and Irwin's distracted wild behavior makes a striking contrast. Harmony offers to speak to Lord Norland, who is his good friend, but Irwin continues to be in a daze, "Well, Sir, if you should see him two or three days hence, when I am set out on a journey I am going, if you will then say a kind word to him for my wife and children, I'll thank you." Then Harmony says, "I will go to him instantly." Irwin replies, "No, do not see him yet; stay till I am gone. He will do nothing till I am gone."

Irwin is beyond reality, and when Harmony leaves to go to see Lord Norland at once, Irwin, vowing to curse his father-in-law, leaves also. The scene shifts to Lady Eleanor and Mrs. Placid, who has brought her home in her carriage. As they enter the house, Mrs. Placid is again teasing about her husband, leaving him in the carriage while she engages in conversation with Lady Eleanor, who discovers that her husband, Irwin, is not at home. Mrs. Placid finds fault with her husband on every mention of his behavior: "Mr. Placid, your behaviour throughout this whole day has been so totally different to what it ever was before, that I am half resolved to live no longer with you," to which Placid says aside, "It will do— It will do." Just as the Placids are about to leave, Irwin comes in; he has obviously been drinking.

The Irwins, left alone, are both distraught. Irwin gives his wife a pocket book from which he pulls a sheaf of paper. Lady Eleanor screams. It is clear that he has stolen—and from her father. Irwin must flee London; he asks his wife to accompany him, leaving behind their son. Lady Eleanor explains that in fact when they went abroad, they left their son, and now, returning to London, they have not found where his nurse has taken their child. At this point, at the end of the second act, the characters have not only been introduced but their relationships to each other have been established as well, and the incident of Irwin's drunken theft has set the action for the remainder of the play.

Every One Has His Fault, as a five-act comedy, is the longest of Inchbald's plays and one of the most intriguingly plotted. Act 3 is a drama within a drama, set in Lord Norland's library; he enters at once, followed by Harmony. Lord Norland is totally unforgiving of his daughter. Harmony, appealing to him, passes from his daughter to "those who possess" his love. He has adopted a boy—a child who, he says, he came upon accidentally. Harmony questions him closely, and in the conversation it is quite clear that the child is Norland's grandson, Lady Eleanor's son. Moreover, Harmony finds that the child was brought to Lord Norland some eight years before; feeling sorry for the half-starved boy, he brought him home, but when Harmony asks if his regard for the child does not plead for his mother, Lord Norland replies: "Never. For, by Heaven, I would as soon forgive the robber who met me last night at my own door, and, holding a pistol to my breast, took from me a sum to a considerable amount, as I would pardon her."

Upon this serious note, their conversation is interrupted by Miss Wooburn, who, we discover, is the former Lady Ramble, Lord Norland's ward. Although Harmony has been totally unsuccessful in changing Lord Norland's refusal to forgive his daughter, Harmony tries again, this time to make Lord Norland believe that Sir Robert has praised him in his absence.

Lord Norland: I wish he had sometimes done me the honour to have spoken
politely to my face.
Harmony: That is not Sir Robert's way;—he is no flatterer. But then, no
sooner has your back been turned, than I have heard him lavish in your
praise.

Lord Norland, while he banishes his daughter, is quite concerned about his
ward, the former Lady Ramble, now Miss Wooburn again after her divorce. She
is still very much in love with her husband, Sir Robert, so much so that Lord
Norland fears for her life. He says: "All my hopes of restoring her health rest on
one prospect—that of finding a man worthy my recommendation for her second
husband." If Lady Eleanor is the daughter who has married for love against her
father's will, Miss Wooburn has been equally foolish in allowing Sir Robert to
talk her into going to Scotland and contracting an illegal marriage, a marriage
acknowledged to the public but easily dissolved, as Sir Robert has done. Lord
Norland persuades Harmony that the solution to the problem is for him to be
Miss Wooburn's second husband, and Harmony seems to agree, but he says he
must discuss the plan with Sir Robert. Miss Wooburn appears, and the conversation between her and Harmony reveals that although she will agree to any plan
Lord Norland arranges, she will never, as she says, be completely his: "But it is in
vain to say, that, though I mean all duty and fidelity to my second husband, I shall
not experience moments when my thought—will wander on my first."
   Upon her speech about Sir Robert, she continues to ask Harmony to take to
him her bond that makes legal her "landed property" to "give him liberty; not
make him the debtor, perhaps the prisoner of my future husband." Harmony,
agreeing to take the bond to Sir Robert, asks if "the person on whom you bestow
your hand, may be a little surprised to find, that while he is in possession of you,
Sir Robert is in the possession of your fortune?" At this point Lord Norland
reenters the room, thinking Harmony has proposed to her; in fact, the subject has
not been brought up, and Miss Wooburn is very surprised, "He!, Mr. Harmony!—
No, my Lord, he has not told me; and I am confident he never will."

Norland: What makes you think so?
Miss Wooburn: Because—because—he must be sensible he would not be the
man I should choose.

Her reply to her guardian introduces an important dialogue about women and
marriage.

Lord Norland: And where is the woman who marries the man she would choose? You are reversing the order of society; men, only, have the right of choice in marriage. Were women permitted theirs, we should have handsome beggars allied to our noblest families, and no such object in our whole island as an old maid.

Miss Wooburn: But being denied that choice, why forbid to remain as I am?

Lord Norland: What are you now? Neither a widow, a maid, nor a wife. If I could fix a term to your present state, I should not be thus anxious to place you in another.

Miss Wooburn: I am perfectly acquainted with your friendly motives, and feel the full force of your advice.—I therefore renew my promise—and although Mr. Harmony (in respect to the marriage state) is as little to my wishes as any man on earth, I will nevertheless endeavour— whatever struggles it may cost me—to be to him, if he prefers his suit, a dutiful, an obedient—but, for a loving wife, that I can never be again.

In this exchange between Miss Wooburn and her guardian, Inchbald has introduced a new and surprising topic—the rights of personal, "romantic" response to the rational structure of society. Without being dramatic, Miss Wooburn has declared her independence, the independence of her heart if not of her hand.

Having set the parameters of her puzzle, Inchbald uses clever psychological strategies to examine the various responses to the "faults" everyone has. Harmony has given Sir Robert the bond Miss Wooburn, the former Lady Ramble, has sent. He is overcome with a kind of puzzlement that she should give him a fortune and that in doing so she proposes to marry again. He suggests several possibilities, including Solus, but when Solus enters, the talk turns to matrimony, not to Miss Wooburn.

Sir Robert: Ah! that I had never married! never known what marriage was! for, even at this moment, I feel its torments in my heart.

Solus: I have often heard of the torments of matrimony; but I conceive, that at the worst, they are nothing more than a kind of violent tickling, which will force the tears into your eyes, though at the same time you are bursting your sides with laughter.

Sir Robert: You have defined marriage too favourably; there is no laughter in the state: all is melancholy, all gloom.

Solus: Now I think marriage is an excellent remedy for the spleen. I have known a Gentleman at a feast receive an affront, disguise his rage, step home, vent it all upon his wife, return to his companions, and be as good company as if nothing had happened.

Among Sir Robert's requirements for a wife, he finds, "if ever a wife can be of comfort to her husband, it must be when he is indisposed. A wife, then, binds up your head, mixes your powders, bathes your temples, and hovers about, in a way that is most endearing."

Solus longs to have one hover about him. Sir Robert cannot escape the subject of his former wife and the plan he has discovered of her remarriage; he suspects Solus as being the designated husband. Solus leaves just as Placid appears with the announcement: "My dear Sir Robert, give me joy. Mrs. Placid and I are come to the very point you advised; matters are in the fairest way for a separation."

Sir Robert replies: "I do give you joy, and most sincerely.—You are right; you'll soon be as happy as I am. [*Sighing*] But would you suppose it? that deluded woman, my wife, is going to be married again! I thought she had had enough of me!" And when he says Solus is her intended husband, he describes him as "An old man—an ugly man. He left me this moment, and owned it—owned it! Go after him, will you, and persuade him not to have her."

But Placid says his advice will have no effect, and when Sir Robert suggests that Placid should suggest that Solus marry Lady Placid, since they are about to be separated, Placid replies, "Ours will not be a divorce, consider, but merely a separate maintenance. But were it otherwise, I wish no man so ill, as to wish him married to Mrs. Placid." This speech gives Sir Robert an idea—he will go to Lord Norland or Solus himself or Harmony, and afterward he and Placid will "take a bottle together; and when we are both free we'll join, from that moment we'll join, to laugh at, to contemn, to despise all those who boast of the joys of conjugal love."

At this point Inchbald has introduced and exhibited several features of the marriage laws current in England.

At the conclusion of act 3, all the situations and problems have been presented but not any solution; acts 4 and 5 provide some surprising turns, but in the end all the couples are united, brought together by Harmony's understanding, his clever "reading" of those involved, and his judicious use of subtle "falsehoods." His plans are not immediately successful, and Sir Robert is not immediately successful in regaining his wife; Solus vacillates between declaring that he will marry—someone, anyone, and Lord Norland remains steadfast in his commitment to finding the robber and punishing him without mercy. One of the most dramatic episodes in act 4 occurs when young Edward, Lord Norland's grandson, enters to report that the robber has been taken but is ill, too ill to be held responsible because he is not in his right mind. When Lord Norland says he will be "just," Edward says, "And that is being merciful, is it not, my Lord?"

Norland: Not always.
Edward: I thought it had been.—It is not *just* to be unmerciful, is it?
Norland: Certainly not.
Edward: Then it must be *just* to have mercy.
Norland: You draw a false conclusion. Great as is the virtue of *mercy, justice* is greater still. *Justice* holds its place among those cardinal virtues which include all the lesser.

After this conversation between Lord Norland and Edward, Harmony, who has been present, is about to abandon any hope of changing Lord Norland's views or behavior; speaking to him with great passion, he tells him that "amidst all your authority, your state, your grandeur, I often pity you." Lord Norland dismisses him and forbids him his presence until he apologizes.

Inchbald's ability to mix comedy, pathos, and tragicomedy is demonstrated in this play better than in any other of her five-act main pieces. After this serious and solemn dialogue, first with Edward and then with Harmony, Lord Norland exits, followed by Edward, and we find Sir Robert entering followed by a servant. Sir Robert has come to plead his case with Miss Wooburn. The scene is farce—comedy—throughout, as he tries to plead his case. She keeps reminding him of his past conduct, conduct that he cannot deny, and when he says he has come to "offer you advice that may be of the most material consequence, should you really be determined to yield yourself again into the power of a husband," his speech is interrupted by a knock at the door. Still unwilling to interrupt his plea, he kneels and continues, "you are no longer my wife, you are my Goddess; and thus I offer you my supplication, that (if you are resolved not to live single) amongst the numerous train who present their suit, you will once more select me."

Miss Wooburn: You!—You who have treated me with cruelty; who made no secret of your love for others—but gloried, boasted of your gallantries?
Sir Robert: I did, I did—But here I swear, only trust me again—do but once more trust me, and I swear by all I hold most sacred, that I will for the future carefully conceal all my gallantries from your knowledge—though they were ten times more frequent than before."

Before she can reply, Edward enters, almost immediately followed by Lord Norland, who reminds Sir Robert that he has broken his wedding oath. Sir Robert protests and kneels again: "But I am ready to take another oath; and another after that, and another after that—And, Oh, my dear Maria, be propitious to my vows, and give me hopes you will again be mine." Edward returns this time with both Mr. Solus and Mr. Placid. Sir Robert, unaware of their entrance, continues: "I cannot live without you.—Receive your penitent husband, thus humbly acknowledging his faults, and imploring you to accept him once again."

There follows a ludicrous scene, a gathering of all the people concerned—Solus, Placid, Sir Robert, Miss Wooburn, Mrs. Placid, and Lord Norland. Sir Robert thinks Solus has come to propose to Miss Wooburn and that Mr. Placid has also, since he is now thinking of a divorce. Mrs. Placid summons Placid to leave immediately, and Miss Wooburn goes to the door declaring: "Sir Robert, I have remained in your company, and compelled myself to the painful task of hearing all you have had to say, merely for the satisfaction of exposing your love, and then enjoying the triumph of bidding you farewell for ever." The ladies are not without their faults.

With all the couples in the same situations as at the beginning, there must be a resolution. Act 5 begins with the situation of Lady Eleanor and her husband, Irwin. As Lady Eleanor enters and asks to see Lord Norland, Edward, their son, enters. The dialogue between mother and son is in the best tradition of pathos. Edward offers to give her the pocket book he has taken from Lord Norland's desk, the pocket book the authorities found on Irwin when he was apprehended. As the two talk, Lady Eleanor realizes that Edward is her son, a miracle that is a good omen, promising another that will save her husband. Lord Norland enters; Lady Eleanor falls on her knees to thank him for saving her child and to ask for his love. Lord Norland summons the servant to send her away, and when she begs that for Edward's sake and hers, he will not pursue his father, he speaks to Edward: "Go, take leave of your mother *for ever,* and instantly follow me; or shake hands with me for the last time, and instantly be gone with her." Hesitating only a minute, Edward takes his grandfather's hand and says, "Farewell, my Lord,—it almost breaks my heart to part from you;—but, if I have my choice, I must go with my mother."

As Edward leaves with his mother, Mrs. Placid and Miss Wooburn enter, and shortly thereafter Mr. Harmony returns; his speech to the two women sets up the final situations, sets up Harmony's final use of "falsehood"; it is pure farce.

Harmony speaks to the two women: "My whole life is passed in endeavouring to make people happy, and yet they won't let me.—I flattered myself, that after I had resigned all pretensions to you, Miss Wooburn, in order to accommodate Sir Robert—that, after I had told both my Lord and him, in what high estimation they stood in each other's opinion, they would of course be friends; or, at least, not have come to any desperate quarrel:—instead of which, what have they done, but, within this hour, had a duel!—and poor Sir Robert—."

Harmony cannot finish his sentence before Miss Wooburn exclaims, "For Heaven's sake, tell me of Sir Robert—," and Harmony replies, "You were the only person he mentioned after he received his wound; and such encomiums as he uttered—." Harmony then tells Mrs. Placid that her husband was one of the seconds, and when she declares, "Then he shall not stir out of his house this month, for it," Harmony replies, "He is not likely; for he is hurt too." Harmony continues, "How tenderly he spoke of you to all his friends—."

> *Mrs. Placid:* But what did he say?
> *Harmony:* He said you had imperfections.
> *Mrs. Placid:* Then he told a falsehood.
> *Harmony:* But he acknowledged they were such as only evinced a superior
>   understanding to the rest of your sex;—and that your heart—
> *Mrs. Placid:* [*Bursting into tears.*] I am sure I am very sorry that any misfor-
>   tune has happened to him, poor, silly man! But I do not suppose
>   [*drying up her tears at once*] he will die.
> *Harmony:* If you will behave kind to him, I should suppose not.
> *Mrs. Placid:* Mr. Harmony, if Mr. Placid is either dying or dead, I shall
>   behave with very great tenderness; but if I find him alive and likely to
>   live, I will lead him such a life as he has not led a long time.
> *Harmony:* Then you mean to be kind?

Harmony then turns to Miss Wooburn to say that if he finds Sir Robert alive, he hopes she will "console" herself with the fact "that it was not your cruelty which killed him."

Thoroughly frightened, both ladies wish to go see for themselves, Miss Wooburn exclaiming, "Oh! how I long to see my dear husband, that I may console him!" and Mrs. Placid saying, "Oh! how I long to see my dear husband, that I may quarrel with him!" When Harmony conducts the two ladies to Sir Robert's house, they find Sir Robert and Mr. Placid at a table surrounded by a company of gentlemen. Sir Robert and Placid have had more than one bottle and are quite beyond reason. Sir Robert turns to his party, declaring, "Gentlemen, married men and single men, hear me thus publicly renounce every woman on earth but this; and swear henceforward to be devoted to none but my own wife." Placid follows him: "Gentlemen, married men and single men, hear me thus publicly declare, I will henceforth be master;—and from this time forward, will be obeyed by my wife." Such a speech calls for a response, and Mrs. Placid points out, "you will be sober in the morning." But he replies, "Yes, my dear; and I will take care that you shall be dutiful in the morning."

With the resolutions of the Placids and Sir Robert and his (now) wife again, only Solus and the Irwins must be considered. At this point Solus bursts in; he has been married, and his wife is in the carriage. Immediately after this announcement from Solus, Harmony announces that "A worthy, but an ill-fated man, whom ye were all acquainted with, has just breathed his last." Irwin is not dead, of course, and as the other couples prepare to leave, Harmony opens the door to reveal the Irwins. With everyone gathered, Lord Norland forgives his daughter, accepts her husband, and is reunited with his grandson.

Harmony ends the play with "Yes, my Lord,—and notwithstanding all our faults, it is my sincere wish, that the world may speak well of us—behind our backs."

Every One Has His Fault is quite the most directly ironic of Mrs. Inchbald's plays, yet she very cleverly uses the pathos of the Irwins to please her audience. Her skillful use of Edward would have been understood by those who had seen Mrs. Siddons in *Isabella, or, The Fatal Marriage,* where her son is an important part of her tragedy. The scenes in which Lady Eleanor kneels to her father would have been recognized as proper behavior for a daughter who had defied her father, and the scene in which Irwin kneels to Lord Norland would also have been familiar stage action. The popularity of the play is largely explained by the combinations Inchbald made, and when she wrote her *Remarks* about it some fifteen years later, she simply cited its popularity as proof of its value.[37]

With the success of her play, she was again "taken up" in various social circles, much as she had been after the publication of *A Simple Story.* And again, as before, she gave money to family and friends. Her nephew George Huggins asked to borrow four hundred pounds, and Mrs. Wells asked again for money. By the spring of 1793, Topham had taken their daughters to Scotland and left Wells to take care of herself, a situation Wells could not live with. Inchbald gave her a hundred-pound note and the money to pay her landlady. Topham had earlier settled four thousand pounds on her, but when she appealed to Inchbald again, she was in debtors' prison.[38]

In June and July Holcroft called on Inchbald repeatedly, wrote love letters and poetry to her, and saw her constantly. In the end she rejected his proposals, sent back his letters by his son, and felt that he unfairly reproached her for her behavior.[39] Boaden, using the pocket-book, lists a series of woeful tales. George Simpson, having failed to keep the farm and having little employment in the theatre, was put in prison for debt. George Inchbald appeared again to try to blackmail her by declaring "some improper conduct with Mr. Frank Hunt."[40] Mrs. Whitfield's daughter ran off with a Captain Dalton; when she returned, she accepted a theatrical engagement with Powell and went with him to America in September. Mrs. Grist, Inchbald's former landlady, came to tell her that her daughter had eloped and asked Mrs. Inchbald to write an advertisement for her for the daughter to return and be forgiven.

In July Inchbald was ill again and went to see Dr. Warren, but she continued to be subject to fainting spells. In November John Taylor, her oculist, removed something from her eye. Taylor and she had been friends for many years, and he, like Holcroft, felt he could advise her about her politics. Boaden says, "Taylor with great sincerity told her to beware of her politics, as their apparent leaning might injure her fortune."[41] Inchbald was always cautious, perhaps for several reasons; especially by this time she was very aware of the politics in the theatre, and she was also quite aware of the events on the Continent. She has two entries in her 1793 pocket-book about the French king—first that she heard he was condemned and then that he had been executed for certain.

Her play *The Massacre* and its "fate" is, as we have pointed out, clearly a part of her interest in the situation in France. All during this time in 1793–1794, Inchbald was working on her second novel, which she called *Nature and Art*. As usual, she discussed her work with her friends, and, as usual, they gave her advice—this time that her work was too extreme to be published under the circumstances of the unrest in England. Inchbald certainly knew that both Holcroft and Godwin were members of radical groups, and no doubt all such ideas were discussed at tea and dinner during the fall and winter of 1793.

Boaden says that in the month of January 1794, she began to copy her manuscript of *Nature and Art*, a work he found quite inferior to her *Simple Story*. Boaden says, "It is in fact the paradox of Rousseau's philosophy, dressed in the pointed smartness of Voltaire." Boaden's remarks pose the problem, the universal problem, of heredity and training, of innate and tutored, of the environments and the productions of church and state. Boaden thought her work had "its object to place the child of cultivation morally *below* the offspring of untutored nature. But this is an obvious fallacy, because it attributes to second causes what really belong to first, and supposes artificial life to be in fault, instead of the inherent bent of the individual. The goodness may be found in higher life, and the vice still more deformed in the lower stages of existence."[42]

A review of Inchbald's, Godwin's, and Holcroft's work in 1791–1792 and 1793 reveals a great deal about the interrelations among the three. Godwin argues that all authority is suspect, that individual freedom is of paramount importance; Holcroft, even more than Godwin, maintains that the government needs reformation; and Inchbald, with a wicked pen, reveals the corruption of church and state, the futility of education, the savage not noble, nature not benign, innocence corrupted by passion, the miscarriage of justice, and the hopeless plight of the poor. All three were agreed on the need for their world to be reformed.

Three of her friends, Godwin, Holcroft, and Hardinge, all read *Nature and Art* and either talked to her about it or wrote critiques of her work. In her pocketbook she says that Godwin encouraged her; Hardinge read the manuscript aloud to his wife and another lady and reported to Inchbald in a letter: "They were enchanted with it: and—I will do justice against myself, they were not offended by the *wig*, the *uplifted hand*, the *cut upon William in the pulpit*, and three or four passages against which I had protested. I begin therefore to believe, as well as to hope, that I was wrong. The eloquence, the simplicity, the wit, the sense, and the pathetic morality, enhanced them. I never gave more delight than in reading you, and I thank you for giving me so much consequence."[43]

From his letter it is obvious that he had objected to some key passages in the book, even though evidently his wife and her friend had not. Hardinge wrote Inchbald another long letter about a piece she had sent; the references are somewhat puzzling, and there is no date. Whatever the contents of her letter to him, his letter to her is revealing of his attitude toward her and her ideas. He calls her letter "absurd" but says he will not use it in judgment: "not because it is *ill-natured* and *unjust*,—not because it convinces me that your *temper* is *impracticable*, (because these are points that are becoming and rather interesting in a *petticoat*,) but from the delicacy which *I* feel for *you*, and which *you* little *deserve:* in other words, because it is a childish and weak letter."[44]

His characterization that follows of her friends and relatives draws a picture of her circle. In the letter Hardinge continues:

> Both of the Hunts would proudly disclaim it: Brother Simpson, at Lord Petre's, would say, "Thanks to the Holy Virgin that I am not an *original*, as Betty is." Martin would refuse your little parties with him upon a summer's day, to the King of Bohemia's Head, or the Paddington Bowling-green, if he could see a page of this letter to me. Good bye to the *Bob* Sundays!—and as to G***, the little atheist! he'd creep out of the key-hole, or even take his chance out of the window, if he could imagine you so *poor* and so *flimsy* a thing. Sir Charles would lift up his shoulders, and put his hands into his breeches-pockets, with more philosophy than respect or attachment, if I sent a copy to him of your philippics against me.[45]

Even more confusing are Boaden's comments and a letter to Godwin from

Inchbald. Boaden writes: "We have but little to say as to this last letter from Mr. Hardinge, and are thankful to him for refusing to our curiosity a sight of that to which it is an answer . . . 'The Satire on the Times,' which Mr. Hardinge refers to, is to us unintelligible: it must allude to some of those political writings which were of a temporary nature, and have happily perished in the furious season that gave birth to them."[46] The Inchbald letter reads:

I am infinitely obliged to you for all you have said, which amounts very nearly to all I thought.

But indeed I am too idle, and too weary of the old rule of poetical justice to treat my people, to whom I have given birth, as they deserve, or rather I feel a longing to treat them according to their deserts, and to get rid of them all by a premature death, by which I hope to surprise my ignorant reader, and to tell my informed one that I am so wise as to have as great a contempt for my own efforts as he can have.

And now I will discover to you a total want of aim, of execution, and every particle of genius belonging to a writer, is a character in this work, which from the extreme want of resemblance to the original, you have not even reproached me with the fault of not drawing accurately.

I really and soberly meant (and was in hopes every reader would be struck with the portrait) Lord Rinforth to represent his Most Gracious Majesty, George the 3rd.

I said at the commencement all Lords of Bedchambers were mirrors of the Grand Personage on whom they attended, but having Newgate before my eyes, I dressed him in some virtues, and (notwithstanding his avarice) you did not know him.

The book is now gone to Mr. Hardinge. Mr. Holcroft is to have it as soon as his play is over, and though I now despair of any one finding my meaning, yet say nothing about the matter to Mr. Holcroft, but let my want of talent be undoubted by his opinion conforming to yours.

And there (said I to my self as I folded up the volumes) how pleased Mr. Godwin will be at my making the King so avaricious, and there, (said I to myself) how pleased the King will be at my making him so very good at the conclusion, and when he finds that by throwing away his money he can save his drowning people he will instantly throw it all away for flannel shirts for his soldiers, and generously pardon me all I have said on equality in the book, merely for giving him a good character.

But alas, Mr. Godwin did not know him in that character, and very likely he would not know himself.[47]

We evidently cannot know exactly the details of her composition, but her letter does show her awareness of the current criticism of the king as he was said to be.

In January 1794 Godwin wrote in his journal: "Revise, Inchbald's 'Romance,'" and again on January 30 he worked on revisions; on the first day of February, he called on her, and on the sixth he went to the play *Love's Frailties* with her, Reveley, and Jennings.[48] He continued to call on her through the spring months—March, April, May—and all through the summer. In September and October he was reading Voltaire as he saw Inchbald and Holcroft. Evidently, sometime during these months, Inchbald was persuaded not to publish her new work—the novel that later (in 1796) became *Nature and Art*.

The year 1794 found Mrs. Inchbald with her family frequently. Her sister Dolly was a barmaid at the Staple-Inn Coffee-house, run by their friend Bob Whitfield, the Whitfield's son. Debby, who had earlier turned to prostitution, was now very ill and completely without money, which of course Inchbald supplied. Inchbald had earlier refused to see or have any association with her, and now all she could do was to make her comfortable and bring a priest to administer the last rites. According to Boaden, who had her pocket-book before him, "She could not help reproaching herself with cruelty for that severity which had driven her [Debby] from the door when she came a supplicant, perhaps a penitent too. She had, for almost strangers, disdained the world's opinion; and ought she to have done less for her own sister?"[49]

In May Mrs. Inchbald, Boaden says, "wrote a critique on Synonymy, probably occasioned by Mrs. Piozzi's volumes on the subject."[50] Since Boaden does not give the source of the critique, Inchbald's comments on Mrs. Piozzi's volume are not available. Mrs. Piozzi had become intimate with Mrs. Siddons by 1794, when her book was published, and although Mrs. Inchbald saw the Kembles, the Siddonses, and the Twisses, there is no direct reference to Piozzi. She had, of course, known her in 1787–1789 when Piozzi was very frequently written about in the *World*. In the small circles of Inchbald's London, everyone did know each other, whether they were close friends or not. In fact, there are many references in Piozzi's letters and in the public press about a great many of Inchbald's friends: for example, Piozzi thought Sarah Siddons one of her very close friends, and it is probable that Inchbald had continued to see Piozzi at Siddons's open-house occasions.

In August after Debby's death, Inchbald and her sister Hunt took a stage-coach to Bury. There they stayed with their brother George and on the next two days saw friends and relatives. She paid a visit to Lady Gage for a few days and then went to Sir Charles Bunbury's for a day or two, to her sister Bigsby's, and to the James Hunts'. On Sunday she went to chapel; she returned to London on Monday. The trip from three o'clock overnight to the next morning from London to Bury and from six o'clock in the morning until midnight was now not quite what it had been in 1772, when she had left her mother a note and gone to London alone, but it was still long and uncomfortable even though the roads were much improved. Upon her return she turned her attention to a play she had been commissioned to do for Drury Lane.

In two acts and entirely original, *The Wedding Day* is an exploration of the emotions of men—young and old—who think to have their own way in marriage and the family no matter the wishes of the women in their lives. It was presented on November 1 and, according to Boaden, "was very loudly applauded, and indeed few pleasanter farces have proceeded from her or any pen."[51] The part of Sir Adam Contest was played by King, and Lady Contest, played by Dorothy Jordan, became one of Jordan's favorite parts. Tomalin says the play is "mocking male vanity," and Boaden wrote in his *Life of Mrs. Jordan:* "The scenes between Sir Adam Contest . . . and Lady Contest . . . display some of the most pointed language in the drama, and Mrs. Inchbald fashioned every line to her peculiar manner of utterance. The interest was in a first wife's unexpected return on the very day that her old man had again united himself to a girl of eighteen. The new couple were of the Teazele family, well lowered to farce."[52] As everyone knew, Mrs. Jordan and Kemble did not always agree, and this play by Inchbald, written at his request, was especially gratifying. Earlier the play called *Anna* had created quite a contest between Kemble and Jordan. Again Boaden's account is revealing:

She [Jordan] did not appear in the season of 1792–3 until the 25th of February, in the Oratorio period; and then she carried her point against Kemble, and brought out a new comedy, called Anna, which the manager considered to be an outrageous insult to his authority. It was said to be written by a Miss Cuthbertson, with a few touches from Jordan's own pen. I never knew decidedly, that the play was rightly fathered upon either lady; Jordan, however, evidently brought it forth. Disputes ran very high about this play, Mrs. Jordan called for novelty—Kemble thought that she, like himself, and his sister, should be contented with the sterling drama, by which they had acquired their reputations; and that novelty should, only as entertainment, hold up the train. He threatened to resign his office, if that play was done; it was only done once, and thus the great disputants both triumphed—how far the reported displeasure of Kemble contributed to the fate of the play, may be a question; I should not be disposed to carry in this way, a point against him, or a slighter man, who was a manager.[53]

In discussing *Anna,* Boaden does not stop with his consideration of Kemble; he gives a summary critique:

There is not the slightest novelty in Anna. There is an amorous old dowager, and the more seasonable passion of two young ladies—but the whole family are Touchwood's. There was the old disguise for Mrs. Jordan's figure, and the charm which admitted of no disguise, a musical call upon her voice. To excite her lover's jealousy, she in the male habit sings a love song to herself, under her own window, and is, by the usual clear-sighted lover of the stage, immediately taken for a dangerous rival, and a challenge, and its consequence, a meeting follows, as things of course they rush on, but into each other's arms, and a most generous brother . . . makes a handsome provision for both parties. . . . Mrs. Jordan spoke an Epilogue of a very ponderous nature on the subject of novelty.[54]

It is interesting to note that for that February 25 Godwin wrote in his journal, "Tea at Marshal's with Holcroft & Cooper. Go to the comedy of Anna, with Inchbald."

It is also interesting to wonder just how Inchbald and Godwin happened to go to *Anna* when it was given only once and they did not go to Drury Lane for every new performance. Another biographer of Jordan gives a more detailed account of the discussion that went on over the play, a discussion that Inchbald probably knew about, especially since she was seeing the Kembles frequently this season. Tomalin's account of *Anna* centers around Jordan herself, not the play. In the summer of 1792, Jordan had had a miscarriage, and although she was too ill to act, she "spent the winter of 1792 writing, or helping to write, a play. It became the cause of one of the many quarrels that raged in a company full of strong-willed people with conflicting ideas: Kemble, a traditionalist; Sheridan, ready to try a novelty; Jordan, rather surprisingly appearing now as the assertive voice of female power. She wrote *Anna* in collaboration with another woman, a Miss Cuthbertson, who has left no other trace; and Tate Wilkinson credited it all to Dora, and reported 'that the whole town was on tiptoe for Mrs. Jordan's New Comedy!'"[55]

As we have said, Kemble threatened to resign, and Jordan refused to change her request to Sheridan. According to Tomalin, "the battle of wills flared up more fiercely because it was also a battle about the male manager being attacked by a female member of the company." The whole quarrel got into the public press—as might be expected—as Jordan threatened to get a lawyer to have Sheridan continue to support her, and she sent a letter to the press "accusing Kemble of trying to prevent her from appearing in new characters."[56]

From all the accounts, *Anna* turned out to be a point around which the whole town found an opportunity to gossip and speculate. Jordan and Kemble both complained that Sheridan never paid anyone on time; Sheridan's personal life had turned into a tragedy in this season of 1791–1792, as his wife Elizabeth, worn out with his infidelities, had taken a lover and had a child. Elizabeth died June 28, 1792, of tuberculosis, and her baby, Mary, died in October. Tate Wilkinson, in his *Wandering Patentee*, used *Anna* as an example of the play or performance that is "frivolous, absurd, and insipid; the birth and the death occur perhaps on the same night without the pain of a lingering departure. Indeed something too like what I have here mentioned has been often testified in the course of almost every theatrical season; as when the whole town was on tiptoe for Mrs. Jordan's New Comedy (as was the report); yet the first night it was frivolous—and alas! poor Anna dropped like an unfortunate young lady's pad."[57]

Inchbald's play *The Wedding Day* had a curious history of composition, quite aside from the history of its production, perhaps because of the ill-fated *Anna;* that is, perhaps Kemble thought to please Jordan and therefore went to Inchbald, who, he was sure, would write an acceptable piece. Kemble could only request; he could not offer her money. She, however, wrote in her usual rapid fashion, and Kemble in turn sent it to Sheridan, but she heard nothing from him for quite some time, until at length Kemble came again to say that Sheridan had lost the manuscript. Inchbald sent him another copy, and Sheridan paid her promptly—even before the play was put into rehearsal. Since Kemble had made the original arrangement about her piece, he "advised" her about the copyright. As the manager he certainly had the right to allow her to have it published at once, not to hold it for Drury Lane and Jordan, as Harris had held some of her early plays. Robinson published it at once.

Kemble and Inchbald both knew the professional ways of the theatre, both knew how to write letters and be polite, no matter how difficult the situation. Kemble finally left Sheridan because he found it impossible to deal with him financially, not only about his own salary but about the money to keep the theatre solvent. Inchbald's letter about her play illustrates her skill:

> Sir, there are few things that could give me so much pain as the being guilty of the impertinence of troubling you with a letter—but the necessities of another once more compel me. . . . Mr. Kemble many weeks ago purchased a farce of me in your name, at the same time assuring me it should be performed immediately—but, as I have now reason to apprehend, from the near approach to the close of the theatre, that it cannot be brought out this season. I take the liberty to . . . [second page missing][58]

THE WEDDING DAY

The Wedding Day is only two acts long, the dialogue is simple and direct, and the situation is easy to follow. As the play opens, the young Mr. Contest, returning from his travels abroad, is concerned and uncertain about his father's welcome. He is even more concerned when his friend Lord Rakeland tells him that his father is "lately married" and that the bride "is very young, extremely lively, and prodigiously beautiful . . . she has been confined in the country, dressed, and treated like a child, till her present age of eighteen, in order to preserve the appearance of youth in her mother."

The young Contest replies to the situation by revealing that he too has fixed his affections upon a widow of small fortune and that he will not forsake her even though his father might try to force him to do so.

The action of the play that follows reveals that his father has just come from the church where the marriage has been performed. Sir Adam, dressed as a bridegroom, appears alone, but when he summons his bride, she appears. Sir Adam is very morose, talking to himself: "Nothing is so provoking as to be in a situation where one is expected to be merry. . . . Now, notwithstanding this is my wedding day, I am in such a blessed humour that I should like to make every person's life in this house a burthen to them. . . . What a continual combat is mine! To feel a perpetual tendency to every vice, and to possess no one laudable quality, but that of a determination to overcome all my temptations."

He tends to have all the vices of "violent anger," "suspicion," and "malice," but he has conquered all these. He says, "I am addicted to love . . . that is a failing which always did get the better of *me*." And if Sir Adam is uncertain about his own responses, he is the more so of his bride, Lady Contest. He found her pale, pensive, and dejected at the church during the ceremony; he turns to her as he says, "Consider, every one should be happy upon their wedding day, for it is a day that seldom comes above once in a person's life." Lady Contest reminds him that this is his second wedding day.

Sir Adam had been married for many years when his wife was lost at sea, some fifteen years before the time of his second "wedding day." His first wife was young, beautiful, "possessed of every quality." He evidently talked to his new wife constantly of his former one. When he asked Lady Contest, "*Do* you love me? My first wife loved me dearly," she replies, "And so do I love you dearly—just the same as I would love my father, if he were alive." As the conversation continues, he tempts her by saying, "Your equipage will be by far the most splendid of any lady's you will visit. I have made good my promise in respect to your jewels too; and I hope you like them?" Even the jewels do not make her like him, and when he asks for further proof of her love, she lists first, "I will always be obedient to you," and second, "I will never be angry with you if you should go out and stay for a month—nay, for a year—or for as long as ever you like." Continuing to tease her, he is much upset when she declares, "how you and I differ! for I here declare, I do love a beautiful youthful face, better than I love any thing in the whole world." Their conversation ends with his reference once again to his first wife—"although I cannot say that you possess all those qualifications which my first wife did, yet you behave very well considering your age," and she replies, "And I am sure so do you, considering yours."

Shortly after this conversation, Lord Rakeland and the young Mr. Contest appear. Lady Contest is quite delighted to find Mr. Contest a young man, not a boy as she had expected. Sir Adam says he is in a rage "lest seeing my son a man, she should be more powerfully reminded that I am old." Rakeland and Lady Contest are left alone as the father and the son leave to confer, and Rakeland tries to tempt her. Their dialogue is made up of one-line witty flirtatious sparring. As Rakeland leaves, Sir Adam once again refers to his first wife, "But my first wife was a model of perfection," and to add another worry as the act ends, Lady Contest discovers that she has lost her wedding ring. The scene ends with Sir Adam saying, "But I must say this has been a very careless thing of you. My first wife would not have lost *her* wedding ring." And she replies, "But indeed, Sir Adam, mine did not fit."

In the second act we are introduced to a story Mrs. Hamford is about to tell. Again the conversation is quite brief and to the point. Mrs. Hamford does not wish to ruin Lady Contest's joy on this her wedding day. She tells Lady Contest that her message will "most probably, destroy [her] happiness for ever," upon which Lady Contest replies, "Oh! then pray don't—you'll break my heart if you do. What have I done, or what has happened to take away from me all my joys?—Where's my pocket handkerchief?" And when Mrs. Hamford says: "And now, my dear, I will inform you—and at the same time flatter myself that you will deal frankly with me, and not restrain any of those sensations which my tale may cause," Lady Contest replies: "Dear Madam, I never conceal any of my sensations—I can't if I would." Inchbald has created a beautiful young lady in the popular character of sentiment. She is the center of the play, even though Sir Adam thinks that all the people and events center around him and his grumpy ways. Mrs. Hamford announces, "I am Sir Adam Contest's wife—his wife whom he thinks drowned," and Lady Contest runs to her, hugs her repeatedly, and exclaims, "Dear Madam, I don't know any body on earth I should be happier to see!" Before Mrs. Hamford is brought to Sir Adam, Lady Contest warns her that he has changed, "greatly altered since that time," but "he loves *you* still—he is for ever talking of you; and declares he never knew what happiness was since he lost you. Oh! he will be so pleased to change *me* for *you!*"

The problems have not been worked out for Sir Adam. He is annoyed by his servants, who are slow, and he must meet Lady Contest's mother to be given her blessing on his marriage with her daughter. Upon announcing that her mother has arrived in town, Lady Contest begins to tease him with her knowledge of

Mrs. Hamford and her secret. She makes him guess what will give him joy. Has he another estate? "Has the county meeting agreed to elect me the representative?" No, she says he must guess again, but he has had enough and he says, "I hate such teazing—it is unmannerly—would my first wife have served me so?" The confusion for Sir Adam at this point gives the audience the pleasure of knowing what is about to happen while the situation on the stage is left unresolved. With the mention of the "first wife," Lady Contest tells him the story—like Robinson Crusoe, she has returned. With Lady Contest knowing what is about to happen and Sir Adam just about to see his first wife, the dialogue between the young Lady Contest, who is about to leave, and Sir Adam is a very clever bit of stage business. Sir Adam moves between his new wife and his concern for his former wife. He is very touched—about to cry—"I can't think to part with you—I can't think to turn a poor young creature like you upon the wide world." The "young creature" can take care of herself and will be very pleased to do so.

The problem of the two wives and his care of both upsets Sir Adam exceedingly. At this point in the action, Lady Autumn, the young Lady Contest's mother, and her mother's lover, Mr. Contest, Sir Adam's son, appear, and when Mr. Contest presents Lady Autumn as "the lady on whom I have fixed my choice," the young Lady Contest exclaims, "What, on my mamma! Nay, Mr. Contest, now I am sure you are joking—ha, ha, ha, ha,—ha, ha, ha, ha,—fixed your choice on my mother!" To which Sir Adam adds his "And my mother! your father's mother!—Why you are as bad as the man in the farce—fall in love with your grandmother." At this point the explanations begin. Mr. Contest brings his mother, the first Lady Contest, into Sir Adam's presence as he exclaims, "Oh my dear! If you knew what I have suffered, and what I still suffer on your account, you would pity me." To which Lady Autumn says, "Sir Adam, I give you joy of a wife that suits your own age." Lord Rakeland has been concealed all this time listening, and when Lady Contest brings him out on stage, she says, "Come, come, for you need no longer conceal yourself now, or be miserable; for I have no longer a husband to prevent my being your wife—or to prevent me from loving you—."

The remaining dialogue returns to the question of age. Mrs. Hamford, now returned to Sir Adam, suggests that Lady Autumn should find a husband more nearly her age than Mr. Contest and that Lady Autumn and Mr. Contest have both been wrong in their plans to wed each other. Sir Adam gives the young Lady Contest a handsome dowry and asks her not to marry until he dies; she agrees. "I will not—but then you won't make it long?" She concludes their dialogue and the play by saying, "And my next husband shall be of my own age; but he shall possess, Sir Adam, your principles of honour. And then, if my wedding ring should unhappily fit loose, I will guard it with unwearied discretion: and I will hold it *sacred*—even though it should *pinch* my finger."

The play was later staged and directed as a private theatrical performance by Priscilla Kemble, quite like the ones at Richmond House, but this time Inchbald was given full credit as the playwright.

1794: A Year Full of Happenings

The year 1794 was another very important time for Inchbald, Holcroft, and Godwin. Inchbald finished her second novel; Godwin finished his novel *Caleb Williams, Things As They Are: or, The Adventures of Caleb Williams;* Holcroft, having published two of his most successful pieces in 1792—his play *The Road to Ruin* and his novel *Anna St. Ives*—found himself deep into the discussions of politics. Two years before, in 1792, he had helped to see Paine's *Rights of Man* through the press, and he had lately joined one of the societies protesting the government.[59]

The year 1794 was also filled with various personal occasions for the three friends. Holcroft, having accepted Inchbald's refusal to marry him in the summer of 1793, had returned to their easy friendship when in the fall Amelia Alderson came to town, as she had done sometimes before. This time, Alderson wrote home to her friend Mrs. Taylor: "My Dear Mrs. T., At length I have found an opportunity of writing to you at my leisure, but now, though I have begun with the resolution of being very grave and very sentimental, I feel such an inclination to run into plain matters of fact and narration, that I shall beg leave to content myself with a recital of the events of my journey to town yesterday." Alderson was staying with friends out of town at Southgate, and she and her escort, Mr. J. Boddington, set off by way of Islington to visit Godwin at Somers Town. They arrived at Godwin's house at about one o'clock, where, she says: "we found [him] with his hair bien poudre, and in a pair of new sharp-toed, red morocco slippers, not to mention his green coat and crimson under-waistcoat."

They engaged in conversation, though from her report it is evident that Godwin directed the discussion in a barrage of questions:

[He] wondered I should think of being out of London;—could I be either amused or instructed at Southgate? How did I pass my time? What were my pursuits? and a great deal more, which frightened my protector, and tired me, till at last I told him I had not yet outlived my affections, and that they bound me to the family at Southgate. But was I to acknowledge any other dominion than that of reason?—"but are you sure that my affections in this case are not the result of reason?" He shrugged disbelief, and after debating some time, he told me I was more of the woman than when he saw me last.

Never having any social grace, Godwin seemed quite unable to be entertaining, and the picture of his appearing to receive his guest at one o'clock in the afternoon in powdered hair, red slippers, green coat, and crimson waistcoat reveals his lack of taste. He had changed a great deal from the early days in London, when he dressed in sober black as if he were still a Dissenting minister, but in the change he had not acquired any taste, had not learned the social skills of dress and conversation to match the social grace of Alderson.

Her letter continues: "Rarely did we agree, and little did he gain on me by his mode of attack; but he seemed alarmed lest he should have offended me, and apologized several times, with much feeling, for the harshness of his expressions. In short, he convinced me that his theory has not yet gotten entire ascendancy over his practice." Her friend Boddington was disgusted with Godwin's behavior, though they were both "charmed" with Barry, upon whom they had called the week before.

Alderson's letter was quite long, covering several days and several visits—one to Mrs. Siddons, whom she found nursing her little baby "and as handsome and charming as ever." She saw Charles Kemble there at Mrs. Siddons's and "thought him so like Kemble, Mrs. Twiss, and Mrs. Siddons, that it was some time before I could recollect myself enough to know whether he was a man or a woman." They went from the visit with Mrs. Siddons to Mrs. Inchbald's; Godwin had reported that Mrs. Inchbald remembered her and wished to see her. Remembering that this was 1794, sometime after Inchbald's letter to Sheridan, Alderson reports: "She is in charming lodgings, and has just received two hundred pounds from Sheridan, for a farce containing sixty pages only."[60]

The farce was *The Wedding Day,* and the "charming lodgings" were in Leicester Square. In July of 1794 Mrs. Inchbald became acquainted with a young physician, Dr. Gisborne, by his writing to inquire about her novel; his letter is a model one from an admirer to an admired author:

> Dr. Gisborne presents his compliments to Mrs. Inchbald, and would be much obliged to her if she would let him know the *name* of a novel which she wrote, and *where* it is to be *bought:* and, if it were not too troublesome, if she would give him leave to call upon her for five minutes, at any time this morning after twelve o'clock, or at any time to-morrow morning before that hour, to ask a question or two of the like kind, he should be still more obliged to her.[61]

Inchbald, in her usual fashion, sent him a packet of her books, whereupon he replied:

Dr. Gisborne presents his compliments to Mrs. Inchbald, and has received the packet; but is sorry to observe a considerable disadvantage which arises to himself on that subject, for she has so executed his commission as that he thinks he shall never trouble her on a similar occasion again. In short, she has managed it to be so entirely to his satisfaction, and so exactly what he wished for, as that he fears she must have given herself much trouble about it. There is a disadvantage, also, arising to herself from it, which is, that he must call upon her again (if but for a minute) to thank her, and to reimburse her the expense. He has so many things to do, as is always the case when he is about to leave London, that he confesses himself quite bewildered by the multiplicity of them.[62]

The result of this note is that he came to tea and met her; their subsequent meetings make another Inchbald "matrimonial speculation" as Boaden called it. In one of his notes to her, dated November 11, 1794, Dr. Gisborne writes:

Believe me, dear Madam, that it was with no small concern you were heard to say, the other day, that you were low-spirited. This is a disorder of a dastardly nature, which generally retreats on being opposed. I must therefore beg of you to use all exertions to baffle it; in which, I am persuaded, you will find great assistance in the company and conversation of your relations, and of those with whom you are familiar; for too much hurry or solitude are seldom of use. By this note you will assure yourself that you are thought of by your friends when you do *not* see them, and I will assure you that you are thought *well* of by them; and, give me leave to add, that this is no bad reflection for one who endures your complaint: I am therefore in hopes that these lines will be of more use to you than ever so long a prescription. You would have had them a day or two sooner, but that I have been a good deal engaged; and yesterday, for my sins, had the misery to dine with about a hundred apothecaries, and to sit at table by one of the most noisy of them all.[63]

His understanding of her moods is quite perceptive, and his comment "you are thought *well* of by [your friends]" is a rather strange remark if he wished to be counted among them. His understanding also reveals her mercurial moods, what some of her friends felt was uncertain behavior. In a letter less than a month later, on December 1, Gisborne wrote:

You know, my dear Madam, that my ears are very dull and fallacious, so that I could hardly believe the report they made to me when Mrs. Mattocks *seemed* to say, yesterday at dinner, that Mrs. Inchbald desired her compliments to me; for, when I last had the honour of seeing you, you dismissed me with so severe a speech, twice uttered, that, if you heard my reply to it, you must be convinced it was received by me as the words seemed to import you meant it should be received, viz. that you desired I should never call upon you again; which sentiment was so completely confirmed to me by the words of a note I had the honour to receive from you a few days afterward, that I really thought I must first wait till

I was absolutely forgotten ere I presumed again to be introduced to you. However, on the encouragement above, I beg your permission to drink a dish of tea with you on Friday, soon after six; but confess that I should be very happy to receive a *line* from you, in the mean time, to let me know what sort of reception I may expect.[64]

His request received a somewhat "bewildering" reply. A rather correct and earnest young man, he certainly did not understand Inchbald's "teazing" him. She had written, according to his letter of December 3, that she had "greater regard for those who *relinquish* [her] acquaintance, than for those who endeavor to preserve it." As their correspondence and friendship continued, Gisborne began to play her game when he reported in a letter that among his friends he recently had been "strangely treated" and requested her advice and assistance. "All at once, and without the smallest change of behaviour or diminution of friendship on my part, I am received with the utmost contempt and disregard . . . they shall like me better by knowing me less; that they wish never to see me again," a veritable echo of Inchbald's frequent sending friends away only to have them return as if nothing had been said.[65] By this time the reinstatement of her old friend Davis, who was very often sent away only to return, had become an annual ritual. While this correspondence was going on, the Treason Trials were being held. The events and interests of her personal life had come together with the public concerns of her friends.

THE TREASON TRIALS

As we have pointed out, the year 1794 was a significant year for Inchbald's friends Holcroft and Godwin. Not surprisingly, in October Holcroft had been indicted for high treason along with Horne Tooke, John Thelwall, Thomas Hardy, and several others. Everyone knew that Holcroft and Godwin had been closely associated with several of the radical groups and that Holcroft had contributed to several periodicals and journals, signing his name variously.

It was remarked upon that Godwin was not censored for *Political Justice*. According to the story, popularly reported, Pitt had said, "a three guinea book could not do much harm in the class which was dangerous, precisely for want of guineas"; such a book was unlikely to promote treason.[66] The book had had a tremendous sale, however, passing about from one hand to another, no doubt, and in October as the Treason Trials were about to begin, Godwin wrote a pamphlet called *Cursory Strictures*. One writer discussing this work found it "a brilliant brief that would have raised any fledgling barrister to the height of his profession, but . . . instead of imparting legal fame, it damaged the reputation of the writer." Again Godwin did not sign his name, although many accounts of the events surrounding the trial stated that "quite probably it saved the lives of twelve public-spirited Englishmen."[67]

The background of the trial was complicated and serious. It included defendants of several different persuasions and classes, from the cobbler, Thomas Hardy, to Horne Tooke, "the veteran democrat." As one commentator has explained, "High treason . . . included not just explicit threats to the life of the King but all attacks on the constitution. Anyone advocating a republican form of government was effectively attempting to remove the King from power and was therefore treasonous."[68]

English Jacobinism manifested itself, therefore, in different ways. Some Jacobins were organized in societies, such as the London Corresponding Society, founded in January 1792 mainly for artisans and led by Thomas Hardy, with whom Thomas Holcroft was charged. Their gospel was Thomas Paine's *Rights of Man*, the second part of which Godwin and Holcroft had helped to have published in February 1792.[69] Then there was the Society for Constitutional Information, which Holcroft attended regularly for two years, starting in October 1791. This organization had a more genteel membership than the Corresponding Societies and was founded in 1780 to promote political knowledge and gradual reform; but when Holcroft joined, it was taking a more radical turn.

The Dissenters or those of Dissenting background, such as a great many of William Godwin's friends of the 1780s and 1790s, belonged to the Revolution Society, which aimed to celebrate the Glorious Revolution of 1688 but which also celebrated the revolution in France. Godwin had dined with that society on the day after Richard Price delivered the famous "Discourse on the Love of Our Country," which was the occasion of Burke's *Reflections*. Finally, there was the Whig politicians' club, the Friends of the People (founded April 1792), of which Fox and Sheridan were the leading ornaments; and it was to them that Holcroft and Godwin had delivered their hortatory "Letters" in April of 1791.

Under the circumstances it is not surprising that all of the Robinson circle and their friends and acquaintances were present at the trial. Set to begin on Saturday, October 24, it was adjourned until the following Tuesday. Godwin's letter to the *Morning Chronicle* had already appeared on October 21 and had been widely read and discussed. As the trials began, it was agreed that each defendant would have a separate trial, the first one being that of Thomas Hardy, an earnest, poor young man who felt that he had a sacred duty to promote his views. It was not Hardy that interested Robinson, Inchbald, and Godwin, however—it was Horne Tooke and Holcroft.

By the definition of the attacks on the constitution, several of those on trial deserved to be there. Being tried for sedition also meant that all these prisoners, if convicted, could be executed. Like the Hastings trial, this "sedition trial" was the result of governmental fear in the very volatile aftermath of the tragic events in France, where both the king and the queen were executed 1793. Nevertheless, the trial was entertainment and drama as well as law; all the important people in the theatre and the literary world came for Horne Tooke, and some, like Godwin and Inchbald, came for Holcroft. Godwin's note about the trial is an indication of his view of the importance of the event:

The year 1794 was memorable for the trial of twelve persons, under one indictment upon a charge of high treason. Some of these persons were my particular friends; more than half of them were known to me. This trial is certainly one of the most memorable epochs in the history of English liberty the accusation, combined with the evidence adduced to support it, is not to be exceeded in vagueness and incoherence by anything in the annals of tyranny. It was an attempt to take away the lives of men by a constructive treason, and out of many facts, no one of which was capital, to compose a capital crime. The name of the man in whose mind the scheme of this trial was engendered was Pitt.[70]

As the trial began, the court was packed with people who knew Holcroft and even more who knew Horne Tooke, whose trial followed Hardy's. Among those present were Amelia Alderson, Inchbald's friend; Coleridge, the poet; and Crabb Robinson, a friend of both Holcroft and Godwin. Present also was the painter Opie. The Old Bailey opened for spectators at seven o'clock in the morning that first day in October, and the opening attorney general's speech lasted for nine hours. At the end of the speech there was the business of papers presented and witnesses sworn in, whereupon Erskine, for the defense, requested that the court adjourn until morning; his request was granted, and the trial resumed the next morning. Altogether, the trial lasted until December.

Godwin, who was present that morning, had been in Norfolk when he learned of Holcroft's impending trial; he was also concerned about Horne Tooke. Tooke was a friend of his with whom he had dined frequently and with whom he and Holcroft had supported the Corresponding Societies. No doubt many people in the audience were there for Tooke and not Holcroft, Thelwall, or any of the other less-well-known prisoners. There were twelve of them: Thomas Hardy, John Horne Tooke, John August Bonney, Stewart Kydd, Jeremiah Joyce, Thomas Wardle, Thomas Holcroft, John Richter, Matthew Moore, John Thelwall, Richard Hodgson, and John Baxter.

Horne Tooke spoke before the proceedings began: "My Lord, I beg leave to represent to the court that we have just come out of a very confined and close hole, and the windows now opened to our backs, expose us to so much cold air that our health, particularly my own, will be considerably endangered and most probably we shall lose our voices before we leave the place."[71] The Old Bailey had been rebuilt after the Gordon riots in 1780, and now, unlike the old building, it was large with a lofty ceiling, a design that attempted to help avoid the spread of gaol fever, which was a hazard to judges, lawyers, and spectators spread by those prisoners brought up from the horrible quarters in the prison below.

Inchbald was a friend of Tooke, having gone with other friends to enjoy his hospitality at his house at Wimbledon. Godwin had been entertained there also, usually with other men interested in political matters, men who were a part of this trial and others sympathetic to them and their cause.[72] Tooke was an eccentric: an ordained clerk in holy orders, he had never served formally in the church. He had been unsuccessful in his bid for Westminster in 1790 and later was disqualified to serve as a clerk in holy orders. He was a philologist and one of the leading amateurs in what later would be called semantics. There is an interesting association in that many of these friends shared the rather fashionable interest in language. Holcroft had once read a copy of Lowth's *Grammar* along with Pope's *Homer* when he and his friend Shields, both lacking a place, even in a strolling company, walked from Durham to Stockton-upon-Tees. Twiss belonged to the group interested in languages, having worked on his Shakespeare concordance in the time he had between cases as a circuit judge, although he would not complete it until many years later. Tooke also had written a volume that he called *Diversions of Purley*. In the intellectual circles in London, all of these men were acquainted with each other; Holcroft, Tooke, Godwin, and Twiss were all friends of Inchbald, Twiss and Holcroft for a very long time, since before her success in London.

Tooke and the others who were to be tried had been in the damp of the prison for quite some time—for Tooke, six months, and at his age his health had suffered even though his friends had been attentive. On the morning of the trial, he was dressed as the gentleman he was, with lace cuffs and a powdered wig—in marked contrast to Hardy, Holcroft, and the others. Holcroft's presence in the group was rather odd, since he had almost forced himself on the prosecution; he was better known for his work for the stage and his novels than for any political pamphlets, partly because he had not signed most of the pieces that had appeared in such periodicals.

The trial itself lasted most of the months of October and November, from the "true bills" found against the defendants on October 2 until early December, when John Thelwall was acquitted. After Thelwall's acquittal, three other defendants were released, Holcroft among them.

These months of October and November 1794 were the turning point for both Godwin and Holcroft. Godwin was at the height of his popularity. As the trial came to an end in December, after Thomas Hardy, John Thelwall, and Horne Tooke were acquitted, Holcroft became an "acquitted felon." He never recovered from the judge's refusal to allow him to speak and defend himself, and Godwin never again had an opportunity to appear so prominently in public upon so important an occasion.

In the end Holcroft, denied a public trial, could not relinquish his martyrdom: "My judgment tells me that it is my duty to address a few words to this Court and to gentlemen of the jury."[73] Eyre paused, but when Holcroft said he would not take more than half an hour, the weary judge demanded that he withdraw. Thelwall's trial was short, with a foregone conclusion; and with cheering inside and out, the whole occasion came to an end. Amelia Alderson, seeing Horne Tooke just ahead of her, went forward and flung her arms around him; he was her hero. She would never forget his triumph. Many years later, she wrote of her experience:

The occurrences of the year 1794 have lately been pressing with such power on my remembrance, demanding from me a decided confession that it was the most interesting period of my long life, or nearly such, that I am inclined to give an account of what made it so, and acknowledge that it was the opportunity unexpectedly afforded me of attending the trials of Hardy, Horne Tooke, and Thelwall, at the Old Bailey, for High Treason. What a prospect of entertainment was opening before me when (while on a visit at Southgate, near London) I heard that at these approaching trials, to which I hoped to obtain admission, I should not only hear the first pleaders at the bar, but behold, and probably hear examined the first magnates of the land; and on the event depended, not a nisi prius cause, or one of petty larceny, but interests of a public nature, and most nearly affecting the safety and prosperity of the nation; aye and much personally interesting to myself. Yes! how often (as I said) do I recall with all these alternate emotions of pain and pleasure, of disappointment and fruition, the last days of October, and the first five days of November, 1794.[74]

Some of the other spectators at the trials were to be a part of the rest of the story of the 1790s. Thomas Lawrence had made a sketch of Godwin and Holcroft as they sat together at Thelwall's trial; the artist James Northcote was there, and John Opie, sponsored by John Wolcot (Peter Pindar).[75] Inchbald knew all these people as well as, if not better than, Godwin and Holcroft. Sheridan was among the principal speakers who defended the accused, and after the trials, Sheridan spoke against the whole idea of treason as the government had defined it. All these people were friends of Mrs. Inchbald.

After the trial ended, both Holcroft and Thelwall wrote pamphlets, Holcroft to vindicate himself and Thelwall to continue to spread his political opinions. Holcroft entitled his "open letter" "A Letter to the Rt Hon William Windham" (Windham was the home secretary), and in it he said, among other vindications of his position, "I do not charge you with intentional guilt. It is a thing indeed with which I believe no man can be truly charged; and in your case, I find abundant proofs that your intentions have been virtuous. It is your ignorance, your errors, your passions only that are wicked and destructive."[76]

Holcroft's behavior is difficult to understand until we remember his zeal to reform the world, to move everyone toward "perfection," as Godwin said was possible. The trial itself was far more significant than the acquittal of any one of the accused; it was in fact a triumph for the societies. In June the London Corresponding Society held a great celebration in St. George's Fields, with thousands in attendance. On the morning of the rally, baskets of biscuits stamped with "Freedom and plenty, or slavery and want" were distributed to the poor. Thanks were voted to Sheridan as well as to Thomas Erskine, who had defended two of the accused, Hardy and Thelwall.[77] This Treason Trial in 1794 was not the only one Sheridan had a hand in; he also was involved with William Jackson's trial in Ireland. Jackson was found guilty of high treason, but when the time came for the sentence, he collapsed, having put arsenic in his tea that morning. His last words to his lawyers were, "We have deceived the Senate," the parting words of Jaffier, who commits suicide in Thomas Otway's play *Venice Preserved*. In the fall after this trial, at about the time Parliament was to begin, Sheridan presented *Venice Preserved* with Kemble as Jaffier. There was a great flurry of criticism in the press, but Sheridan and Kemble persisted, and on the night it was to be played for the third time, dirt and stones were thrown at the king's carriage and the license for the play was withdrawn for seven years.[78]

The end of the trial meant also that Godwin, Inchbald, Alderson, and Holcroft resumed their social rounds of tea and suppers. Alderson wrote of one of these occasions:

To-morrow I am going to enjoy "the feast of reason and the flow of soul," with Mrs. Barbauld and Dr. Geddes, at Mrs. Howard's. . . . Godwin drank tea and supt here last night; a leave-taking visit, as he goes to-morrow to spend a fortnight at Dr. Parr's. It would have entertained you highly to have seen him bid me farewell. He wished to salute me, but his courage failed him. . . . "Will you give me nothing to keep for your sake, and console me during my absence," murmured out the philosopher, "not even your slipper? I had it in my possession once, and need not have returned it!" This was true; my shoe had come off, and he had put it in his pocket for some time. You have no idea how gallant he is become;

but indeed he is much more amiable than ever he was. "Mrs. Inchbald says, the report of the world is, that Mr. Holcroft is in love with her, she with Mr. Godwin, Mr. Godwin with me, and I am in love with Mr. Holcroft!" This report Godwin brings to me, and he says Mrs. I. always tells him that when she praises him, I praise Holcroft.[79]

The friendship of Inchbald and Alderson, Holcroft and Godwin is an interesting one in what it reveals about the men. Godwin had no social presence at all; he remained very awkward in social situations all his life. He never understood the give-and-take of social conversation. Always the philosopher, he was much admired by those who thought his *Political Justice* was a handbook for the future. Inchbald is being witty when she tells Alderson the pattern of Godwin and Holcroft and herself. Holcroft had already proposed to her in the summer of 1793 and Godwin in the fall soon after. Godwin, as usual, hardly committed himself when he "talked of marriage," but from all the evidence, he wished to have Inchbald for himself in some way or another; not that he wished to seduce her—he was not capable of seducing her, or anyone else for that matter, but he was so naive as to suppose she would never withdraw herself from their friendship, a friendship based on their mutual association with Robinson and their mutual interest in writing and publishing. He was to learn the bitter lesson of how independent she was and how unwilling to support his unreasonable, selfish demands.

If Godwin did not understand Inchbald, with whom he was intimate, he never understood other people either. He had never liked Thelwall, for example, and refused to visit him in prison. He wrote in reply to a letter from Thelwall: "I am sorry to see in your letter a spirit of resentment and asperity against your persecutors. . . . How senseless and idiot-like it is to be angry with what we know to be a mere passive instrument, moved according to certain regular principles and in no degree responsible for its operations."[80]

Godwin's insistence on "sincerity" was very difficult for other people to understand, especially since sometimes he had a rather difficult time himself deciding what "sincerity" meant. Never consistent, because his belief—and his writing—changed as his circumstances and his friends changed, he revised all his work extensively—both *Political Justice* and *Caleb Williams*. He revised not for better style or better narrative but for a better exposition of "truth." These changing views he would have seen as becoming more and more aware of "truth," but his friends found such changes puzzling and uncertain.

Inchbald's September entries for these years of 1793, 1794, and 1795 are very revealing, as they parallel the events that she found significant. In 1793 she wrote, "London; after 'Every One Has his Fault'—*quite happy*"; in 1794, "London; after receiving two hundred pounds for a farce, not yet performed—extremely happy but for poor Debby's death"; and in 1795, "London; after 'The Wedding Day;' my brother George's death, and an intimate acquaintance with Dr. Gisborne—not happy."[81]

Her brother's death was a tragedy, the result of a quarrel that led to a duel. Boaden not only records the fact but also provides the letters that Inchbald received when she became alarmed at not having heard from him. Perhaps he was not so regular in writing letters as she—hardly anyone was so prompt, but after she had had two letters that reported the death of a George Simpson and she had not heard directly from him, she was puzzled until her friend Bonnor wrote that he had died in a duel at Hamburgh. The letter from Bonnor included a letter written to a friend of Bonnor in response to an inquiry about Simpson. The letter that was enclosed is as follows:

I recollect the Mr. Simpson you inquired about perfectly well, and particularly the melancholy circumstance of his death, which happened in January last, in the inn to which you say his letters were directed. He lodged there with a Mr. Webber, with whom I believe he had lived some time in the greatest friendship; but an unfortunate quarrel took place between them, (arising, I know not from what cause,) which ended in a duel; and, unhappily, in it Mr. Simpson was shot dead almost upon the spot, or at any rate expired that same evening. Mr. Webber got off, and had saved himself some days, and at some distance from this, but was found out, arrested, and brought back here, where he was put in prison, and remains still, I believe, without any decision in his case.[82]

Inchbald's brother George introduced her to the stage. He was in Norwich, where she went to see him, and it was here she met her future husband. Always uncertain about his career, George and his wife were very close to Inchbald; they were in Scotland with Digges and the company before the Inchbalds left to go to France. George Simpson was never a very successful actor, though he had the usual lists of parts and the usual places to perform. He was in Dublin in the year after the Inchbalds were married, before he went to Edinburgh. The Simpsons were frequently in London during the days when Mrs. Inchbald was acting at Covent Garden. Although they never had a secure place on the London stages, they got up benefits for themselves on two occasions and acted in special performances at the Haymarket in the winter of 1784–1785. George had first acted in Norwich in 1770; in 1771 he married Miss George, who was herself a provincial actress. Wilkinson found her very attractive—more so than her husband—when they came to the company upon Mr. Inchbald's death. They remained with Wilkinson until the spring of 1783.

The Simpsons were frequently in London in the 1780s and 1790s, as Inchbald's pocket-book indicates. Simpson knew Inchbald's friends—in fact, several of them had been his friends first, among these Francis Twiss and the Kembles. The Hardinges also knew the Simpsons, as did Sir Charles Bunbury and Mrs. Phillips. Simpson tried to keep the farm after his mother's death, but he fell into debt and was forced to give it up; he was in prison for debt at one point, though the details about this prison episode are not clear. Boaden merely mentioned it in passing, along with a comment about how Inchbald supported every member of her family at one time or another. As close as they were, both in the family and on stage, Inchbald certainly did help them, though Boaden is rather cryptic and judgmental when he reports:

He [Simpson] had not always met the just expectations of his sister; was by no means calculated for business, and frequently involved in his affairs, beyond the *measure* of her assistance. She well discriminated, even in her love, between a lavish bounty that injured the giver, without saving the receiver; and that moderated benevolence which added to the comforts at least of the unfortunate, and left the bestower in a condition to give *again*, to that subject, and to others.[83]

In this August of 1795, after she had learned of her brother's death in June, her friend Mrs. Whitfield became seriously ill, and Mrs. Inchbald went almost every day to be with her until she died on December 19. Mrs. Whitfield had been as close to Mrs. Inchbald as her sisters; since they had both been completely oriented to the stage and their friends who were players, Mrs. Whitfield had occupied a special place in Mrs. Inchbald's life. The Whitfields, after having been at both Drury Lane and Covent Garden, went abroad in 1784, and upon their return in 1786, he joined Covent Garden again, but she did not act in either theatre; instead she acted in the Haymarket every summer until two years before her death.

The Whitfields had met in Canterbury, where he was acting; they fell in love and eloped to France to be married in 1771; in 1772–1773 they were in Norwich, the year after the Inchbalds were married, and with Digges in Scotland. When Mrs. Inchbald came to Covent Garden in 1780, she and the Whitfields were very close, and Mrs. Whitfield's death in 1795 as the year closed affected Inchbald in a special way; she never again had such a close friend and colleague with whom she had shared so many experiences on stage and in her daily life. Boaden called theirs a "protracted friendship."

The death of Mrs. Whitfield was a great sorrow for Inchbald and created a very great void in her days. She had depended on Mrs. Whitfield for all the conversations about family and friends, for all the gossip of the green room, for all the concerns of the theatre. Another friend, Mrs. Dobson, had died in October, leaving Inchbald a mourning ring. Dobson, whose husband was a doctor, had been introduced to Inchbald by their mutual friend Mrs. Phillips, and afterward Dobson and Inchbald became close friends, Dobson offering Inchbald the frequent use of her carriage and an invitation to dine whenever she chose.

In 1793 Kemble had taken a house in Harrow Weald near the Abercorn family, the Kembles' intimate friends. Abercorn was Viscount Hamilton, and on October 15, 1790, he became marquis of Abercorn. He married Cathrine Corley in 1779, but when she died in 1792, he married his cousin Lady Cecil Hamilton. They were separated in 1798 and divorced in 1799. In 1800 he married Lady Anne Jane Hatton. Abercorn purchased the estate of Bentley Priory in 1788 and employed Sir John Soane to rebuild the house, which he filled with a fine collection of paintings and other works of art. According to one authority, the architect extended a small mid-eighteenth-century house, to which he added a library, a breakfast room, and a circular "tribune" space for displaying pictures and sculpture. Later a drawing room, a dining room, and a music room with an organ were added.

The marquis entertained lavishly, and his guests included men and women from government and the theatre—artists, statesmen, writers. Weekends were organized as house parties, with music and entertainment as well as food and drink. It was here that Inchbald was frequently a guest, and it was here that she enjoyed the mixture of social and professional people that made up the very special interclass of the late eighteenth century and early nineteenth, that special time before the onset of the Victorian Age. In September 1795 Inchbald went as a guest with the Kembles, and on November 14 she and Mrs. Kemble went on another visit to Stanmore, where they found that Sir George Beaumont and Mr. Steele of the musical Steele family were also guests. On the following Monday, they returned to London, where Inchbald dined with Mrs. Kemble in Caroline Street and afterward they went together to the theatre. The whole family of the Kembles, the Siddonses, and the Twisses usually gathered on Sundays, and frequently Inchbald was their guest. These were the people who were her friends and who remained in the center of her world, no matter if she sometimes went to tea and had conversation with the "philosophers"—Holcroft and Godwin.

At the beginning of 1795, in the middle of the 1794–1795 theatrical season, Mrs. Inchbald continued her correspondence with her friend Gisborne. On January 14 she slipped down on Gerard Street and dislocated her shoulder. She was attended by a surgeon, and by the end of February she records that she dressed herself. She continued her work, however, while she remained at home. She was writing her "life," copying out her novel, and working on a new comedy. She was introduced to the painter Thomas Lawrence at one of Mrs. Siddons's routs— Godwin said he introduced them; at any rate both Godwin and Inchbald sat for him this year.

Early in January, after the excitement of the trials was over, Godwin continued to see Inchbald for tea, sometimes with other people. On January 8 he reports in his journal, "call on Inchbald," on the twentieth "call on C. Moore, Davis & Inchbald." On February 7, a Saturday, "Call on . . . Inchbald with (adv.) Taylor; and King." He called on her on the twenty-first and on the fifth of March. On the thirteenth he called on "Miss Alderson nah, Inchbald and Mrs. Jardine; sup at Fenwick's." On the twenty-fifth and the thirty-first Wordsworth called on him, and on April 9 Wordsworth had breakfast with him. The next day Godwin called on Inchbald. On April 11 he called on Inchbald, and the next day, a Sunday he called on "Siddons, [with] Alderson."

All during these months when Godwin called on Mrs. Inchbald, she was working on her novel, and no doubt they discussed it while they had tea and conversation. Godwin usually worked in the morning and afterward dined with various friends, most frequently with Holcroft. Inchbald now lived in very comfortable quarters in Leicester Square, and although her apartment did not afford her a special "room" for her work—she never had "a room of one's own"—she did not always require total solitude to do her work, and from one project to another she varied her work habits to fit her "project." Translating a play given to her was far less demanding than revising and reworking her novel that she had worked on for years. Sometimes she shut herself up, closed the shutters, and was "denied" to everyone, including her friends Holcroft and Godwin. There are frequent references in Godwin's journal of "nah" meaning "not at home," and sometimes "nah" follows "call on Inchbald."

One entry in Godwin's journal reads: "Write 6 pages, Call on . . . Inchbald, Radcliffe nah, Ritson nah, & Nicholson nah. Virgil 148, Rheumatism 24 hours." Does he mean he had rheumatism for 24 hours? Three days later the entry reads in part, "Breakfast at Lawrence's; talk of God: call with him on Inchbald." And what had they said about God? Did they continue their conversation when they called on Inchbald? It is tempting to explore all these notes, but to do so is hardly possible in so brief a discussion.

During the summer Godwin continued to call on Inchbald, and on July 14 and August 15 Wordsworth called on him, a call he returned on the eighteenth, calling on Inchbald the next day, the nineteenth. Boaden does not mention

Wordsworth's name among Inchbald's friends, but he does not fill in her daily life in these months of 1795. Evidently he was more interested in the series of letters he found in her correspondence with Gisborne than her work or her social tea and conversations with Godwin. At this point Wordsworth had returned to London from France and, according to his recent biographer, had become a friend of Godwin's.

On October 20 Godwin writes: "Sit to Lawrence, talk of Cassius: call on Inchbald & Cooper; Fenwick & G. Cooper dine. Play Development, w. Inchbald & Marlowe; adv Taylor & King." Again on the twenty-fourth, "Sit to Lawrence, talk of Shakespeare & equality." Shakespeare and equality make a puzzling combination. Perhaps Godwin knew about equality, or thought he did, but he knew little of Shakespeare except the versions he saw on the stage. His association with the stage continued to be interesting. Cooper was Thomas Abthorpe Cooper, Godwin's relative, the son of his first cousin Mary Grace Cooper. Godwin had assumed the care of Thomas when his father, Dr. Cooper, died in India in 1787. At sixteen Thomas decided he wanted to be an actor, and Holcroft was asked to introduce him to the profession.[84]

Early in 1796, on January 2, Inchbald and the Kembles were again the guests of the marquis of Abercorn at Stanmore. The gathering was a distinguished one, including Lord and Lady Seymour, the artists John Singleton Copley and Gavin Hamilton, and Mrs. Kemble's niece Miss Sharp. The Sharp family were distinguished musicians; Miss Sharp was the daughter of Michael and Elizabeth Sharp, and her mother was the first daughter of William Hopkins and his wife Elizabeth. Priscilla Kemble was Elizabeth's younger sister. The company must have had plenty of entertainment at hand.

Boaden, as usual, had a comment to make: "On Sunday the Marchioness went to church; Mrs. Inchbald stayed at home, employed upon her novel. If curiosity should be at all tempted to inquire how a party so distinguished got through the day, we are fortunately in a condition to gratify them. A little more *gold leaf* was really all the difference between them and their humblest neighbors. After dinner they conversed on *religion* and *politics,* and after supper they played at *Crambo.*"[85]

The Kembles and Inchbald went to Stanmore again for Good Friday; this time Dr. Howley, who later became the archbishop of Canterbury, was a guest.

During the early months of 1795, Godwin was revising *Political Justice,* a much changed version. His journal entries of "Revise and Call on Robinson" perhaps referred to his work on this revision. In it he changed some of his most radical statements and amended others to make them more reasonable. The first edition had been a best-seller, and this second edition, published in octavo (the first had been a quarto that sold for three guineas), was sold for eighteen shillings. It was published on November 14, 1796. There was a third in 1798 with even more changes. It is this third edition that has been the basis for the modern editions.

Political Justice, for all its extravagances, has remained an important document, especially important to an understanding of the 1790s in England. One writer discussing the period observes:

Published at a moment when human hopes had reason to be at their highest, *Political Justice* caught the spirit of the age. At a time when religion was increasingly recognized as an agglomeration of primeval fears and superstitions, it offered a reassuring modern scientific explanation to put in its place, many former Christians being relieved to find that the morality which is recommended differed little from superseded Christian ethics. The New Philosophy—as the ideas which Godwin collected and codified were quickly called—was firmly in the tradition of religious dissent, appealing strongly to those of an inflexible, worrying, and puritanical disposition. At the same time it was wonderfully liberating and refreshing. If men and women are blown from perception to perception by the breezes of experience, they need feel no strong obligation to be consistent between one action and another. Provided each individual is sincere, every new situation can be judged afresh, and the practitioner is disencumbered from guilt. It may often be a clear and pleasing duty to burst out from the fetters, whether they are political obligations, economic contracts, or the more personal bonds of marriage. Indeed, a unique satisfaction attends those who know when to do so, for they are the privileged few whose improved perceptions accelerate perfectibility.[86]

After the Treason Trials, Godwin was introduced to a great many new admirers, a situation he very much enjoyed, especially if he was allowed to be the center of the conversation at tea or dinner. He once wrote, "There is a vivacity and . . . a richness in the hints struck out in conversation that are with difficulty attained in any other method." Godwin's and Holcroft's definition of conversation was all too often a kind of argumentative discourse not always pleasing to everyone. One member of the Philomaths, a club where both frequently held forth, remembered them as "among the most diffuse and tiresome of speakers." The speeches were supposed to be limited to fifteen minutes, but the committee that was responsible for the procedure was obliged to buy two fifteen-minute hourglasses to limit the length of the speakers; only Godwin and Holcroft always turned them over.[87]

Certainly both Godwin and Holcroft found conversation with Inchbald, whether in private or in public, an important part of their lives during these two years of 1795 and 1796, but for Inchbald there were several events that gave her great concern. By 1796, when Inchbald was about to publish her second novel, *Nature and Art,* the whole political and social context had changed from the time two years before when she had written it. Again, as in the case of *A Simple Story,* there is no way to make an exact assessment of the changes she made. And again, as in her earlier novel, she worked with the publisher Robinson. *Nature and Art* was published early in the new year; in May a second edition was brought out.[88]

As before, indeed as with all of her work, her various friends and relatives registered their opinions. Mr. Twiss, Mr. Whitfield, Mrs. Mattocks, and Inchbald's sister Dolly praised it; Holcroft and her friend Charles Moore did not. Holcroft probably felt that she was too cynical, too neutral. By 1796 he had become even more vehement in his views of the wrongs in his world than in 1794 and the Treason Trials, for since he was denied a public forum at the trials, he had turned to the theatre to make his views known.[89]

TEN

NATURE AND ART, A SECOND NOVEL, AND NEW PLAYS

☙ *Nature and Art* is a short novel of some fifty thousand words. Robinson paid her £150, and he brought it out on January 11, 1796; a second edition was called for in May. In his account Boaden remarks, "To be sure this branch of literature was then greatly underrated; and this would be felt by no one so sensibly as the *dramatic* writer; to whom, a lucky farce, (a fortnight's labour perhaps,) by the humour of the times, or the rage for some favourite actor or actress, would produce considerably more than a long-meditated work, the epitome of the author's whole intellect."[1]

His view was one that Mrs. Inchbald herself subscribed to, and perhaps, considering all the trouble she had had before *A Simple Story* was accepted and published, she might simply have made a play of her material. She had worked on this second novel in 1793, completing it in 1794. Since it is short and since we do not have the 1794 pocket-book extant, we must depend on Boaden's report. There is one entry in her 1793 pocket-book (September 3) in which she records that Godwin called and "encouraged the plan of my new story." She must have discussed her book with a number of friends in the usual way with tea and conversation. Among the public, of course, the news of the French Revolution was all the talk, and in 1794 the Treason Trials were reported everywhere in periodicals, books, pamphlets, and certainly in the circles in which Mrs. Inchbald moved. Godwin also would have played a part in any decision, for they were still close friends, discussing their work with each other. Godwin's *Caleb Williams* had been published in 1794, and Holcroft's imprisonment that same year certainly would have been a part of Robinson's consideration—not that *Nature and Art* is the kind of revolutionary work that Robinson had been called to court for when he was fined for his association with Paine, for Inchbald's novel is narrative, not polemics, and though some of the incidents and comments are clearly subversive, the presentation is such that the reader must respond for himself.

Nature and Art was never so popular as *A Simple Story* or her plays; it was admired, not loved, and viewed as somehow risqué, not quite proper for a popular female playwright to produce. It was indeed so different from *A Simple Story* that it can hardly be considered the work of the same writer. Because it was published in 1796, after many of the "revolutionary" ideas were beginning to fade, her readers were no longer inclined to consider the scandals of church and state, of their rapidly changing society as they approached a new century. In any case *Nature and Art* has not had as much attention as it deserves, most critics either considering it a sociological statement or, at least, a curiosity again full of the dramatic touches expected of Inchbald. Such a view is quite unfortunate, both for Inchbald's time and for the present, for it obscures the features of the whole story, which is quite a direct commentary on some of the major characteristics of the 1790s, Inchbald's contemporary world, as that world was revealed in the newspapers, prints, plays, and most of all, in the hundreds of conversations that floated about London.

Nature and Art is the story of two brothers, teenagers, who upon the death of their father set out for London to seek their fortunes. William, the elder, is a bookish young man; Henry, the younger, is outgoing and friendly. During the first year in the city, they search in vain for some way to find an establishment for themselves. The opening paragraph gives a hint of what is to follow:

"At a time when the nobility of Britain were said, by the Poet Laureate, to admire and protect the arts, and were known by the whole nation to be the patrons of music,—William and Henry, youths under twenty years of age, brothers, and the sons of a country shopkeeper who had lately died insolvent, set out on foot for London, in the hope of procuring by their industry a scanty subsistence." But the "arts" and the patrons of music were fickle patrons. During the first year the brothers were in London, they managed on "the precarious earning of half a crown or a shilling in the neighborhood where they lodged, by an errand, or some such accidental means." They looked for more permanent employment but without success. "If they endeavored for the place even of a menial servant, they were too clownish and awkward for the presence of the lady of the house;—and once, when William (who had been educated at the free grammar-school of the town in which he was born, and was an excellent scholar) hoping to obtain the good opinion of a young clergyman whom he solicited for the favor of waiting upon him, acquainted him 'That he understood Greek and Latin' he was rejected by the divine, 'because he could not dress hair.' But suddenly Henry remembered and 'once remembered and made known' changed the whole prospect of wretchedness placed before the two brothers and they never knew want more. Reader, not to keep you in suspense concerning this attribute—Henry could play upon the fiddle." And thus "he had the honour of being admitted to several tavern feasts of which he had also the honour to partake without asking of the expense." He thus was introduced into "many companies where no other accomplishment could have introduced him."[2]

William, however, could not play the fiddle and share Henry's good fortune. Instead, one evening when Henry came home from a dinner and offered him food and wine, he behaved in a very churlish fashion, throwing the food at Henry's head. Henry's kindness and patience with William's surliness finally resulted in Henry's support for William to go to university, where he prepared to enter holy orders.

One of the striking features of this very first episode is how filled it is with precise contemporary attitudes. As a musician Henry could earn a living, but he could never attain a proper social standing. Professional musicians could, in the late eighteenth century, become quite celebrated, for this was the period when the opera flourished and concerts were a part of both public and private entertainment. Handel, who died in 1754, was still very much a part of the annual Oratorio season; there had been a series of memorial concerts at Westminster Abbey and the Pantheon beginning in 1784. Moreover, Inchbald's stepson Robert is listed as a second violinist at these memorial concerts in May and June of 1784. In creating a character who is a "fiddler," Inchbald comments on her familiarity with the world of the theatre and the London social circles that she knew well.

Early in the story, when William is denied a position with a young clergyman because he cannot dress hair, Inchbald uses reverse discrimination to show how foolish popular prejudices can be. By the 1790s hairdressing was far more in favor than Greek and Latin. Inchbald's contemporary comments about her very present world continue, after these two early examples, throughout *Nature and Art.*

Henry continued to be successful; "he became so great a proficient in the art of music, as to have it in his power not only to live in a very reputable manner himself, but to send such supplies to his brother, as to enable him to pursue his studies." Moreover, through one of his patrons, Henry obtained a living of five hundred pounds a year for William. And within a year or two Henry presented William a deanery.[3] Full of pride and never really approving of Henry's profession, even though it was the source of his own advancement, William, accepting the deanery, "at once placed between them an insurmountable barrier to all friendship, that was not the effect of condescension, on the part of the dean." William began to call Henry's profession "his useless occupation," and the brothers became estranged.

This episode about the deanery is the beginning of one of the central points in the story. From this comment on until the conclusion, the separation of the two brothers moves along class lines. The musician, no matter how successful or celebrated, could never be equal to a dean in the Church of England. This subject, along with its corollary of the corruption in the church, extends to the end of the story.

Finding himself quite alone, Henry marries a "public singer," whom William finds quite unacceptable. He says to Henry, "do you imagine I can ever introduce her to my intended wife, who is a woman of family?" Henry is invited to William's wedding, but his wife is not, and Henry does not attend. William resents his absence; "the brothers once inseparable, whom adversity had entwined closely together, prosperity separated."

Henry's wife dies shortly after the birth of a son, and by the time William can bring himself to offer condolence to Henry, Henry has taken his infant son and set sail for Africa with a party of Portuguese to live on the uninhabited part of an extensive island. The dean, discovering his brother's departure, is for a time very distraught, but he too has an infant son and a gratifying position; he soon forgets his brother and goes about pursuing his ambition—to associate with the nobility in church and state. He spends his time attending levees and talking politics, practices Inchbald herself must surely have observed.

Some thirteen years pass. Young William is tutored in history and religion. He speaks learnedly on politics; he learns to "imitate the manners of a man."

One morning while the dean, his wife, and young William are at breakfast, the dean receives a letter, a message from his brother Henry asking that the child, young Henry, be taken into the household to save him from the fate of his father, who is in prison on a distant island. The dean does welcome him and thereupon begins to instruct him in proper behavior and proper ideas.

Again the years pass while young William and his cousin Henry apply themselves to studies of literature and customs and manners. And as they become men, they each remain themselves—Henry has a kind of natural simplicity; William has the bearing of good breeding and the proper manners of a gentleman.

About the time William and Henry are age twenty, they begin to spend their summers in the country near the residence of Lord Bendham, a peer of the realm. The dean has bought a summer residence in the village nearby, and while they spend their days in idle pleasures, the two young men fall in love, William with Hannah, the daughter of a cottager, whom he sets about to seduce, and Henry with Rebecca, the daughter of the curate of the parish. Henry and Rebecca share books and conversation; William, unwilling to leave Hannah alone, finally persuades her to make "so precious a sacrifice to him" as to lose her "honour."

The winter after the pleasures of summer, William has an engagement made for him by his father to marry Lord Bendham's niece, Miss Sedgeley. Summer follows, and Hannah, now totally ignored by William, gives birth to a baby boy secretly in the wood. Henry, coming upon the scene, finds the baby just as Hannah flees upon hearing him approach. Because of the mist of the early morning, Henry sees only a shadowy figure fleeing. Henry takes the baby to Rebecca, who, faced with keeping it secret from her father and sisters, is frightened and uncertain as to how she can care for the infant.

Her fears are far too real; she is accused of having the baby. Her father will not believe her story about Henry, and she, pressured beyond her limit, says the baby is hers. Again Henry is the one who must protect her, and to do so he agrees that the child is hers and his. At dawn, when he is taking the child to a caretaker whom he has engaged so that he can go to sea, he discovers Hannah wandering in the woods and preparing to drown herself in the lake. Not having seen her when he found the baby, he is quite stunned at her behavior as she acknowledges the truth and tells him about William. All these events coincide with William's wedding, and in the end, though the dean learns that William, not Henry, is the father and Hannah, not Rebecca, is the mother, both Henry and Hannah are obliged to leave and go out into a harsh and cruel world without assistance from anyone—family or friends. Henry can survive—indeed prosper; Hannah cannot. From this point on, the story line is Hannah's tragedy.

The years pass; William becomes a judge, and his father, the dean, becomes a bishop. Hannah, trying desperately to find food and lodging for her child and herself, spends years in poverty, finally turning to prostitution. Through a set of ironic incidents showing the inhumanity of man to man, Hannah is brought to court and tried before William, the judge; he sentences her to death and sends her away before he discovers that she is Hannah and that her son is his son, but it is too late for him to acknowledge his son, who follows his mother in death.

Meanwhile, Henry leaves Rebecca to go in search of his father, and after quite a long journey, he does find the elder Henry, who has changed much during the years between their parting and their reunion.

As the two Henrys return, they find themselves on the road in front of the bishop's seat just as his funeral procession is beginning. The elder Henry is much affected, while young Henry continues to inquire anxiously about Rebecca. Passing through the village where her father had been curate, they come upon his grave in the churchyard and meet her older sister. Rebecca is alive and well. The story ends with Henry the elder, his son Henry, and Henry's wife, Rebecca, living contentedly in a small cottage subsisting on fish they catch and vegetables they grow in their cottage garden. They agree, "it is not upon earth we are to look for a state of perfection—it is only in heaven—."

The whole of *Nature and Art* is so completely interwoven that it is not possible to speak of one pattern without pulling apart another. The plot incidents develop a good story, but without the wit and irony of the narrator's voice and opinions, the reader's interest would certainly not be sustained. It is within the context of the narrator's voice that the reader comes to understand how the story line is significant in the world of ideas as well as in the more visible world of society. The narrator remains, throughout, a guide for the reader, not a political orator or a preaching churchman or a reformer or a romantic poet or writer. Instead, the narrator so skillfully weaves all the social, political, and moral threads together that in the end the reader is left to respond for himself.

Mrs. Inchbald does not identify herself as narrator; she simply narrates the events and speaks out through the narrator's voice, thus creating distance for herself. Although most critics of this novel, as well as those of the earlier *Simple Story*, have emphasized its dramatic qualities, by now Mrs. Inchbald had mastered her craft of writing in such a way that she kept firm control and gave to her brief novel a life of its own. Moreover, the topics presented for the reader's judgment are so embedded in the story as to go unnoticed until the plot incidents have been worked out.

Since the story begins with the two brothers, Henry and William, leaving a small village and going to the city to find positions and perhaps fortune, the city-country contrast is immediately evident; very shortly, as Henry becomes associated with entertainment and the theatre and William displays scorn and intellectual pride, the subjects of taste and education become a major concern, weaving in and out of the narrative until the very end.

Although the two brothers have lived together in the same small village and have been devoted to their father and each other, they are quite different in important ways. Henry is innately musical; William has no "ear." Henry finds William's sermons incomprehensible. Henry's gift is "Nature," even to soothing the savage breast in the remote reaches of Africa; William's gift is "Art" of a high order as he wins praise for his sermons and his pamphlets. But both Henry and William operate in a flawed and unjust world, as the story makes quite clear.

William and Henry both were in a sense quite successful by certain worldly standards. And both reflected their different lifestyles; *Nature and Art* has as many diversions as it has parallels. William, the elder, obliged to depend on Henry for his daily bread, was understandably resentful. As he said, "I am eldest brother; obliged to my younger, an illiterate man." And William was "enraged . . . when, after taking him [Henry] to hear him preach, he asked him "how he liked his sermon and Henry replied (merely with pleasantry, and in the technical phrase of his profession) 'You know brother, I have no ear.'"

When the subject of education was to be considered for the young William and the young Henry, their circumstances were far different from those of the two brothers who had left their village and gone to London. The young Henry, after his mother's death while he was still an infant, was taken away to live in an uncivilized, primitive environment. It was not until his return to his uncle, now Dean William, that his true education in the ways of society began, and then there were frequent anomalies. For William the course was more clearly marked: "Young William passed his time, from morning till night, with persons who taught him to walk, to ride, to talk, to think like a man—a foolish man, instead of a wise child, as nature designed him to be."

"This unfortunate youth was never permitted to have one conception of his own—all was taught him—he was never once asked 'what he thought?' but men were paid to tell him, 'how to think.' He was taught to revere such and such persons, however unworthy of his reverence; to believe such and such persons, however unworthy of his credit; and to act so and so on such and such occasions, however unworthy of his feelings."

The young William was called "Mister Norwynne," and considering the labor that was taken to spoil him, "he was rather a commendable youth," but "although he could talk on history, on politics, and on religion . . . he merely repeated what he had heard, without one reflection upon the sense or probability of his report." He was also taught the manners of a gentleman and "thoroughly void of all the sentiment, which gives grace to such tricks."

When young Henry arrived at the dean's, having escaped the savages, he did so with a letter from his father, in which the elder Henry wrote:

Pray, my dear brother, do not think it the child's fault, but mine, that you will find him so ignorant . . . not having any books here, I have only been able to teach my child by talking to him. I have never taken much pains to instruct him in the manners of my own country; thinking, that if he ever did go over, he would learn them soon enough! and if he never did go over, that it would be as well, he knew nothing about them.

His father had taught him, however, "to love and do good to his neighbor, to hold in contempt all frivolous vanity, and to abhor all falsehood of any kind."

Being received by his uncle, the young Henry was immediately struck by the wig the dean wore; he had "never seen as unbecoming a decoration either in the savage island from whence he came, or on board the vessel in which he sailed." He found his uncle to be much like his father except for his enormous wig; the dialogue that ensued is not only memorable for the subject but is also an apt illustration of Mrs. Inchbald's skill in making serious ideas dramatic:

"Do you imagine" (cried his uncle laying his hand gently on the reverend habiliment) "that this grows?"

"What is on my head grows," said young Henry, "and so does what is upon my father's."

"But now you are come to Europe, you will see many persons with such things as these, which they put on and take off."

"Why do you wear such things?"

"As a distinction between us and inferior people: they are worn to give an importance to the wearer."

"That is just as the savages do; they stick brass nails, wire, buttons, and entrails of the beasts all over them to give them importance."

When young Henry was introduced to his cousin William, he was almost as astonished as he had been about the dean's wig. He found William's manners incomprehensible: "A little man! as I am alive, a little man! I did not know there were such little men in this country! I never saw one in my life before!" he exclaims, only to be told twice over that he and William are the same age and are cousins.

Lady Clementina and William used young Henry's ignorance as a subject for sport, while Henry himself "expressed without reserve . . . and felt little care what construction was put upon his observations." The dean's wig continued to puzzle him. Coming into the dean's dressing room, Henry "appeared at a loss which of the two he should bow to—at least he gave the preference to his uncle; but afterwards, bowed reverently to the wig." He found Lady Clementina's jewelry puzzling as well, until he "gave up his reason to his faith: and becoming, like all converts, over zealous, he now believed there was great worth in glittering appearances, and respected the ear-rings of Lady Clementina almost as much as he respected her."

Henry proved to be a difficult pupil; he found it impossible to accept the obvious and glaringly false arguments of his cousin and his uncle:

Observing his uncle one day offended with his coachman, and hearing him say to him in a very angry tone "You shall never drive me again."

The moment the man quitted the room, Henry (with his eyes fixed in the deepest contemplation) repeated five or six times in a half whisper to himself, "You shall never drive me again."

The dean at last asked "what he meant by thus repeating his words?"

"I am trying to find out what *you* meant by thus repeating his words?" said young Henry.

"What! do not you know," cried his enlightened cousin, "Richard is turned away?—he is never to get upon our coach-box again, never to drive any of us any more."

"And was it pleasure to drive us, cousin?—I am sure I have often pitied him—it rained sometimes very hard when he was on the box—and sometimes Lady Clementina has kept him a whole hour at the door all in the cold and snow—was that pleasure?"

"No" replied young William.

"Was it honour, cousin?"

"No," exclaimed his cousin with a contemptuous smile.

"Then why did my uncle say to him as a punishment "he should never"—

"Come hither, child," said the dean, "and let me instruct you—your father's negligence has been inexcusable—"

"There are in society" (continued the dean) "rich and poor; the poor are born to serve the rich."

"And what are the rich born for?"

"To be served by the poor."

"But suppose the poor would not serve them?"

"Then they must starve."

"And so poor people are permitted to live, only upon condition that they wait upon the rich?"

Henry found it very difficult to understand why, as the dean concluded this conversation by saying that after death there would be no distinction between rich and poor, that all persons would be equal. Was the world after death better? Why could not this world be so? The dean explained, "In respect to placing all persons on a level, it is utterly impossible—God has ordained it otherwise." Henry still did not understand: "How! has God ordained a distinction to be made, and will not make any himself?"

If Henry had problems explaining for himself the distinctions of class, he had many more about the language. He "had an incorrigible misconception and misapplication of many *words*." This along with "his childish inattention to their proper signification still made his want of education conspicuous." For example he called compliments lies; stateliness, affection—and for the monosyllable *war* he constantly substituted the word *massacre*. In vain did his uncle, the dean, try to explain the difference between battle and massacre. The dean ended the discussion by saying: "Consider, young savage, that in battle neither the infant, the aged, the sick or infirm are involved, but only those in the full prime of health and vigor." The argument ended with a frown on the part of the dean, "and Henry was awed by the dean's tremendous wig, as much as Pater-noster Row is awed by the attorney-general."

Learning the ways of society was a chore Henry tried desperately to understand, but frequently he was very confused. Moreover, he kept coming back to the subject of the poor, the unjust ways of the rich even within the church, among those his uncle counted as friends. As he learned one lesson after another, the deception in the ranks of the church became more and more evident.

The deception in the church and the obvious corruption in its ranks is a topic frequently referred to throughout the whole of the novel. Sometimes comments about the church become a part of the narrative, sometimes of the dialogue. But the repeated pattern of these references depicts an institution that is unjust, hypocritical, and full of arrogant, pompous officers, who look to their own careers and use anyone they can command to assist their climb to the top, to make for themselves fame and fortune.

William, the elder of the two brothers, as we have said, was enabled to go to university through the generosity of Henry, who, using his skill to play the violin, was able to send funds to keep him there. Moreover, one evening after a concert, a great man, moved by Henry's music, shook Henry's hand and promised a living of five hundred pounds to William as thanks for the entertainment Henry had given him. William accepted the offer and with the position assumed a majestic walk and a stern brow. Always full of pride, William as a priest became more and more filled with his own self-importance, especially so when, a year or so later, Henry was again able to help him by presenting him with a deanery. The gift of such an important position "at once placed between them an insurmountable barrier to all friendship, that was not the effect of condescension, on the part of the dean."[4]

William's decision that Henry's wife was not worthy of Lady Clementina, the wife he had chosen, again shows his pride of place, not an understanding of mutual affection. Lady Clementina was the daughter of a poor Scotch earl, and William had selected her "merely that he might be proud of her family"; she in turn was so full of vanity that she quite matched her husband's pride. And when she presented him with a child, her vanity was the equal of William's pride in his son.

William's pride was not that of a job well done; it was the pride of the deadliest of the seven deadly sins, the pride that in the end condemned Hannah while protecting his son William, the pride that set him up as judge in the prejudiced court of the church.

Soon after he became dean, William began to entertain a bishop as his most intimate friend. The story of their friendship is the story of professional deception, of using the offices of the church to promote personal fortunes and to seek, find, and keep rank in the corrupt, uncaring organization that had nothing to do with true religion. Nor did it have anything to do with true esteem and admiration. Instead, their friendship became a conduit for the publishing of sermons and pamphlets with false names given, as the clergy—especially "the patrician part"—

claimed what in fact was the dean's work. If he did not fashion the whole of their work, he did "blot out some uncouth phrases, rendered some obscure sentiments intelligible, and was the certain person, when the work was printed, to correct the press." The bishop delighted in publishing his works; "or rather the entire works of the dean which passed for his—and so degradingly did William, the shopkeeper's son, think of his own honest extraction, that he was blinded, even to the loss of honour, by the luster of this noble acquaintance; for though, in other respects, a man of integrity, yet, when the gratification of his friend was the concern, he was a liar, giving entire credit to the bishop, his learned friend."

If William, now the bishop, was a sycophant, his brother Henry, abroad among savages in Africa, did nothing to promote himself, his son, or the welfare of his native land. His virtue was quite negative, even though he was a good man and wished beyond all else to serve his neighbor—except, of course, when his neighbor turned out to be the savages among whom he lived and they, rejecting any help from him, imprisoned him. When, after a time, they allowed him to leave the prison, he was left to spend his lonely days and nights to find subsistence for himself, never having a friend or a companion. Young Henry found him thus when, having left Rebecca behind, he returned to Africa. He found his father, but they spent many years and endured many hardships before they came home again, years wasted in "the crosses at a land, and the perilous events at sea" before young Henry saw Rebecca again. Although he declared her to be as young and beautiful as when he left, her sisters were old and ugly, the bishop—William—dead; any denial of time on Henry's part was simply a reminder that he, like his father, was a romantic, not a realist.

The way in which Henry went off to Africa "to people there the uninhabited part of the extensive island" is worthy of a mind of "singular sensibility." More-over, as William recollected the way his brother had responded to him all his life, he realized that it was not the question of Henry's sensibility but the circum-stances in which Henry's sensibility could be exercised that became the focus of his story, of his role in representing "Nature." It was obvious to the first readers of *Nature and Art* that Henry's journey into Africa was especially ludicrous. That as a musician—an entertainer—he should go out to "people the uninhabited part of an extensive island" made no sense at all. In the letter sent with young Henry when he returned to his uncle, Henry explains that he lost the use of his right hand by a fall from his horse, and thus unable to play his violin and entertain his friends, he lost their friendship. He was imprisoned, his son's life was endangered, and only after he partially recovered the use of his hand was he allowed to leave prison. Even then, he could only live a solitary, lonely life without friends, without the comfort of any other person from the world he had left and the world to which he sent his son back. Nature offered very little pleasure and no profit, however tempting the idea of escaping the evils of civilization might appear.

The fate of Hannah/Agnes, the beautiful innocent whom William seduced, and her child offer the most dramatic example of the real tragedy of relying on "Nature"—pure innocence without the constraint of the "art" of reason. Although her situation is certainly tragic, her lack of reason and resolution, in the end, create the circumstance in which the sentence of death is inevitable. Her steps downward into finally breaking the law and standing before her lover, the father of her child, while he passes judgment are at least partly her own doing. Even in the last days before her trial, she seeks out William's town house to catch a glimpse of his carriage. She is certainly to be pitied, but the careful reader sees her actions and her fate as yet another comment on the foolishness of sentimentality, on the tragedy of not using reason.

The women in *Nature and Art* are not all portraits of the ideal woman; none of them fit even the "Inchbald woman" of the plays. Lady Clementina was almost forty when she was married. She was rather handsome except for the fact that she wished to be much younger and thus "Her dress was fantastically fashionable, her manners affected all the various passions of youth, and her conversation was perpetually embellished with accusations upon her own 'heedlessness, thoughtlessness, carelessness and childishness.'" Everything she said or did was turned to herself, a product of her own immoderate vanity. She had been an old maid before the dean found her, thinking no offer for her hand was worthy of her; her vanity was such that she would never have understood, since she felt that in her own thoughts she undervalued herself.

Her vanity made her a totally empty, pretentious person. She is described as living only within this charade: "If she complained she was ill, it was with the certainty that her languor would be admired; if she boasted she was well, it was that the spectator might admire her glowing health; if she laughed, it was because she thought it made her look pretty; if she cried, it was because she thought it made her look prettier still.—If she scolded her servants, it was from vanity, to show her superior knowledge to theirs; and she was kind to them from the same vice, that her benevolence might excite their admiration."

Lady Clementina has very little to do with the narrative of *Nature and Art;* her role is rather one of stereotype. Since her husband, the dean, cared very little for her and seldom required her to be a part of his life, she was free to do as she pleased, which meant that she "went out when she liked, dressed as she liked, and talked as she liked." While her husband attended to his interests, "she ran from house to house, from public amusement to public amusement, but much less for the pleasure of *seeing* than for that of being *seen*."

In one or two incidents, Lady Clementina serves as a focal point around which comments can be made and actions taken by other people, as for instance when she comes home one day weeping that she had lost her reputation. It seems she had been accused of "playing deep" at her own house and "winning all the money." Moreover, she had been accused in print, in a newspaper. Her husband was at that moment with his bishop for whom he wrote the material the bishop published under his own name. The irony is well placed:

> This bishop now exclaimed. . . . "It is a libel, a rank libel, and the author must be punished."
>
> "Not only the author but the publisher," said the dean.
>
> "Not only the publisher, but the printer," continued the bishop. . . .
>
> "My Lord, it is a pity we cannot try them by the ecclesiastical court," said the dean with a sigh!
>
> "Nor by the India diligent bill," said the bishop with vexation.

Young Henry, present in the conversation and not understanding, asked the meaning of the word *libel:*

> "A libel," replied the dean, in a raised voice, "is, that, which one person publishes to the injury of another."
>
> "And what can the injured person do (asked Henry) if the accusation should chance to be true?"
>
> "Prosecute," replied the dean.
>
> "But then what does he do if the accusation is false?"
>
> "Prosecute, likewise," answered the dean.
>
> "How, uncle! is it possible that the innocent behave just like the guilty?"
>
> "There is no other way to act."
>
> "Why then, if I was the innocent, I would do nothing at all, sooner than I would act like the guilty. I would not persecute—"
>
> "I said *prosecute*." (cried the dean in anger) "Leave the room, you have no comprehension."

As the years passed, Lady Clementina continued her ways, self-centered and unaware of anything not directly concerned with herself. In the end a stranger reported to the two Henrys: "Yes . . . she caught cold by wearing a new-fashioned dress that did not half cover her, wasted all away, and died the miserablest object you ever heard of."

The conclusion for the two Henrys and Rebecca is another use of "Nature," for like Voltaire's Candide, they settle peacefully on a small plot of land and are content with what Nature offers, "cultivating their garden."

If the readers of Mrs. Inchbald's *Simple Story* expected this second novel to exhibit the same characteristics and pleasures of her first, they were greatly disappointed; the two are not alike in any way. *Nature and Art* is more nearly related to the prints—the caricatures she found in the print shops. The pattern of the plot is the simple progression of anticipated events, and the commentary in the voice of the anonymous author resembles the brief identifications on the prints, especially in a series such as those of Hogarth, whose work would have been familiar to her audience. She herself went to the print shops, bought prints, and saw friends there. From the time she stole the picture of Griffith as a teenage stagestruck girl to the time she went out before breakfast to see a print of Dr. Warren in a print shop window, she had understood the appeal of the visual. *Nature and Art* is filled with little vignettes.

Almost every episode in the narrative could be "read" as a print: Lady Clementina's attention to dress, her "playing deep" and thus finding her name in the public prints, even her death caused by a chill because she adopted the fashionable style.[5]

In Boaden's comment that *Nature and Art* had something of both Rousseau and Voltaire, we have a key to the way the "savages"—the clergy, the rich and the poor, primitive society and the upper class in London—are all discarded as useless. As in *Candide* Voltaire created a character who found "this the best of all possible worlds" throughout his adventures all over the world, encountering wars, savages who were cannibals, and missionaries who were greedy adventurers, Inchbald with young Henry has created a similar character—good but untutored, devoted to his father but with no solution for the situation among the savages, loving his Rebecca but leaving her for years while she grows old. *Nature and Art* has been seen as a dissertation on education and a commentary on language, but we might do well to see it as Inchbald's ironic view of everything in her world. She was able to make a subtle comment (subtle enough that she would escape censure) that would for the discerning reader constitute a very serious and damning set of observations.

Mrs. Inchbald's contemporary Barbauld remarked that Henry should have ended more happily. "One can not help wishing the author had been a little more liberal of happiness to poor Henry, who sits down contented with poverty and his half-withered Rebecca."[6]

Nature and Art has been strangely neglected by most of the commentators on her *Simple Story,* perhaps because it is so unlike the earlier novel. Gary Kelly reviews it briefly, but the best assessment of it is in Mona Scheuermann's *Her Bread to Earn*. Scheuermann compares it to Mary Wollstonecraft's *Maria or the Wrongs of Woman*, pointing out that Inchbald expresses her "anger at social inequities with irony and amusement," whereas Wollstonecraft focuses on "the destruction of woman by a social system that gives her no power to act to save herself." Further, she suggests "that for Inchbald, as for many of her male peers, woman is not born victim but has, whatever her class, essentially the same social profile, for good or bad, as her male consort."[7]

In his recent edition, Shawn L. Maurer writes an introduction that is a careful review situating the work, including references to Inchbald, Godwin, and the Pantisocrats, who thought to find an earthly paradise. He finds that "Inchbald does not delineate the ideal man in relation to—and in distinction from—the model woman; rather, goodness in any character, whether male or female, is marked by that character's possession of significant attributes, including benevolence, nurturance, compassion, the capacity for intimacy, and the ability to think of others before oneself."[8] Inchbald seldom creates "perfect" characters. She rather depicts characters with a mixture of characteristics that make them real. She condemned the Williams, but she also showed the Henrys to be lacking in common sense—reason—in their mission to live on the "uninhabited part of an extensive island" where the elder Henry's benevolence has no object.

There are two subjects that have had the attention of recent commentators: "education" and the use of "language." Maurer writes cogently about both. He says that "the satirical attack on the English mores provided by the contrasting upbringings, attitudes, and behaviours of the two cousins [young Henry and young William] and the pitiful tale of the seduced and abandoned cottager's daughter . . . are inextricably bound by Inchbald's penetrating critique of language." Moreover, quoting Inchbald about young William's education, which "taught him to walk, to ride, to talk, to think like a man—a foolish man, instead of a wise child," Maurer finds that "William commands our sympathy because the novel has demonstrated exactly how external circumstances made him what he is. Indeed the novel's ultimate power emanates more from Inchbald's complex and ambivalent rendering of William and his father than from her more monochromatic portrait of the benevolent Henry and his son."[9]

After her novel was safely out of the press, Inchbald turned to work on her play *Wives As They Were, and Maids As They Are*. By October she offered it to Harris, but because he already had plays for which he had contracted, he gave it back to her. Wroughton, now the acting manager of Drury Lane, offered to review it, but in the end it was done at Covent Garden on March 4, 1797. It was one of her most successful plays.

GODWIN, COLMAN, AND *THE IRON CHEST*

The year 1796 was an important one for Mrs. Inchbald's friends Holcroft and Godwin. Godwin, who had not been very busy since the trials except to revise his work and hers, had had a play adapted by Colman from his novel *Caleb Williams.* It became one of the most celebrated productions of the 1790s, in part because of its failure in the hands of Kemble—or at least that was Colman's version. Inchbald, with her own knowledge of both Colman and Kemble, and even more so of Godwin, had an interesting part in the controversy. It continued for almost a decade, and Inchbald renewed the quarrel in her *Remarks* in 1808. The whole episode, moreover, is an interesting example again of how the theatres operated. In 1796 Covent Garden and Drury Lane still had a monopoly; the Haymarket was still the only recognized summer theatre.

Colman called his play *The Iron Chest.* It was produced on December 3, 1796, at Drury Lane, with Kemble playing the part of Sir Edward Mortimer, the principal role in the play. It was a complete failure; Colman was furious and blamed Kemble completely, a strange reaction to those who saw the play, many of whom had no doubt read the novel with its melodramatic tale of the mysterious chest and the pursuit of justice. In the novel Caleb, having discovered the secret that Falkland had murdered a man, his enemy, who really deserved to die, discovered also that Falkland had laid the murder upon an innocent man and his son, both of whom were executed. Caleb fled, and the rest of the novel is a pursuit plot interlaced with long passages about the government and injustice.

The play was roundly condemned on its first night, and that might have been the last of it except that Colman had it published, and in the preface to the published play, Colman castigated Kemble. Moreover, Colman said that Sheridan had promised him a great sum for the play. But evidently Colman did not hand him a completed script, writing the scenes in piecemeal so that there was never a complete rehearsal. Colman complained "that not once was the entire company present and that their conduct was more slovenly than that of a barnstorming company."[10] Colman got sick with a bad chill and blamed his illness on the workplace of the newly redecorated Drury Lane. Kemble fell ill also but insisted that the rehearsals go on without him. One account of what then happened clearly foretold disaster: "Kemble, as soon as he was better, took a look at the play as it then stood and decided that they would produce on the date announced, now but a couple of days hence. The news was taken to the sick Colman, and scared him. Nor were his fears allayed when he received a note from Kemble telling him to transpose two of the most important scenes in the play—the request being made only three hours before the curtain went up! The reason given was that the machinery required by the master carpenter was not yet ready and that if it could not be altered, there would be a wait of ten minutes between scenes. Colman refused to do it."[11]

Colman, in spite of his illness, went down to the theatre and to Kemble's dressing room and found Kemble taking opium pills. Colman said he was drinking as well.

In the beginning the play went very well—until a long dull scene, which the actor Dodd played very poorly. When Kemble came on, he looked the part perfectly, but when he began to act, he fell apart. Colman tried to stop the play, asking Kemble to make an apology; Kemble refused, and although an apology was made to the audience by the management, the play went on. When Dodd returned for another long dull scene, the audience would have no more of it. Kemble apologized and said it was all his fault, but when the announcement came that there would be another performance, the audience screamed their derision. This, however, was not the end of it. After a week passed, allowing Kemble to recover and Colman to make cuts in the long dull scenes, the play was put on again, but to no success. Colman was furious; he wrote:

The devil a trick did Mr. Kemble play but a scurvy one. His emotions and passions were so rare and so feeble, that they seasoned his general insipidity like a single grain of wretched pepper thrown into the largest dish of water gruel ever administered to an invalid. For the most part, he toiled on, line after line, in a dull current of undiversified sound, which stole upon the ear far more drowsily than the distant murmuring of Lethe, with no attempt to break the lulling stream, or check its sleep inviting course. Frogs in a marsh, flies in a bottle, wind in a crevice, a preacher in a field, the drone of bagpipes, all, all yielded to the inimitable and soporific monotony of Mr. Kemble. The most miserable mummer that ever disgraced the walls of a theatre could not have been a stronger drawback than Mr. Kemble.[12]

Colman did not admit even to himself that he was responsible for the dull speeches given to Kemble that produced the "sleep inviting course," and no doubt Kemble was reluctant to work at making the play a success by his acting alone; in fact, given the script, he could not possibly have done so, especially since the plot of the play had been completely changed from Godwin's novel. Caleb in the novel became Wilford, and as one commentator said:

Mr. Godwin has represented him (Caleb/Wilford) as a character unconquerably inquisitive indeed, but a thousand circumstances are introduced first to awaken, and then to heighten his curiosity. He is hurried on by a multiplicity of little incidents, all combining to justify his suspicions of the guilt of his master. . . . His was not the curiosity of wantonness, but an irresistible impulse, which drove him on to an involuntary, because an inevitable, act.

The curiosity of Wilford is wanton and indecent; he hears in one scene that there is a secret, and in the next, like both a fool and a madman, proceeds to open his master's chest . . . what cause he has, in the first place, to suspect Sir Edward of having committed murder, and in the next, to imagine the chest should contain any thing to establish his guilt, we are not told: for the want of this information, we feel no more anxiety, when Wilford proceeds to open the chest, than if he were a sugar toothed boy, watching his opportunity to filch some of mama's prohibited sweetmeats. We know, however, he is doing a mean action, and if Sir Edward were to shoot him in the first paroxysm of his rage, he would fall an unpitied victim to his own willful and unwarrantable impertinence.

Using the example of a dinner party, the commentator says in the "Appendix" to his discussion, "When a company are invited to supper it is not expected they should find fault with their entertainment; they must take what is set before them, whether suited to their palate or no." He continues by giving his personal testimony for what happened at the revival, when the play was given again: "I was present at this revival and must confess I never heard such rapturous applause; such congratulatory uproar, and acclamation: but I suspected immediately the sincerity of these extravagant acknowledgments." He adds, "Mr. Colman had no common incitements to make him attempt this revival.—To redeem his lost fame— to gratify his malignity—to impose on the public a belief that all he had said in his preface was true, and that Mr. Kemble had really been the bane of his production, it required that the play should be again acted, and should succeed."[13] Still determined to make his play a success, Colman produced it at the Haymarket, his own summer theatre.

The writer did not stop with the first productions at Drury Lane; he also analyzed the Haymarket production by discussing the actors and the acting, which he found much more suitable to the parts than those in the first productions. But in the end he makes some very sharp comments about Colman and his work, saying that at Covent Garden and Drury Lane, the winter theatres, the spectators come expecting to see a play "that will inform the mind: at the Haymarket we seek only the gratification of the eye and ear. We go to the former to be instructed as well as amused, the latter only to idle away time." After his remark about the differing merits of the three theatres, he turns to a discussion of Colman's plays that have been presented in the "winter-houses," not giving a favorable view of

Colman's work. Finally he returns to Colman and his presentation at the Haymarket:

> Mr. Colman must have been conscious of the weakness of his play, otherwise he would not have suffered tickets to be issued on its second representation, by the underlings of the theatre. To those who are unacquainted with the mysteries of management, it may be necessary to observe, that when there is a prospect of a bad house, on any particular night, it is a common practice to make it what is called a ticket night:—Now, a ticket night is something similar to a waiter's benefit at Ranelagh, when the public are admitted at re-duced prices—That this was the case on the second night of the Iron Chest I am very well assured:—pit tickets were hawked at the door at half a crown, and box tickets at four shillings each.

Colman, in the writer's view, had for his vanity and revenge filled his benches to "make Kemble mad to hear that it is acted," a comment about how Colman packed the house with friends and free tickets.[14]

The story of *The Iron Chest* did not end with the two dreadful performances at Drury Lane. It continued in the printed edition, Colman insulting Kemble in every way he could think of in the preface. It was shortly after its publication that the commentator who is quoted just above published his pamphlet. The adver-tisement begins: "The author (anonymous) of these slight remarks is aware that there is little excuse to be made for appearing abruptly and carelessly before the public; he claims, therefore, no other indulgence than that which has usually been granted to such as exercise their pens on subjects of a temporary nature."[15]

The "Comparison" annexed to the "Remarks" was written immediately after the first representation of the play. It appeared to the writer that Mr. Colman had "injudiciously treated his subject and he was led, for the sake of amusement and curiosity, to ascertain more distinctly the cause of his failure; he has subjoined it, therefore, to the remarks, as a further confirmation of his opinion, that Mr. Kemble is not, in the remotest accountable for the ill-success of the Iron Chest. . . . that the political sentiments in Caleb Williams have no share in this comparison ei-ther one way or the other. He has looked to the characters and incidents of the novel, purely as characters and incidents susceptible of DRAMATIC application and effect." Discussing Colman's preface, he makes some witty and pertinent com-ments: "To the irritability of authors much is allowed; we know how apt they are to quarrel with the decisions of an audience, and we grant them the occasional indulgence of softening the aspirates of their chagrin by animadversion and com-plaint; but, to splenetic effusion there should be some boundary. If a man writes a bad play, let him do all he can to make it a good one, or to make the public think it a good one, which is the same thing; but Personal Abuse is not among the privileges of irascible dramatists."

After such a positive declaration about authors, he continues:

no one can attribute the condemnation of the Iron Chest to Mr. Kemble, since the bare perusal to the character he had to sustain will convince him that the finest actor that ever trod the stage, by the most powerful exertions of his talents, could never produce, from such a subject, any dramatic effects on the minds of an audience:—besides it need not be told to any person conversant with the affairs of the stage, that the mal-performance of any one character, however prominent and important, could not be the means of damning a play so completely as the Iron Chest was damned. Sir Edward Mortimer, whatever the author in the vanity of his heart, may think was not the only opiate in the piece. Adam Winterton is perhaps, a paragon of prolixity and dullness; and I appeal to every auditor on the first night, whether the general disposition to solmnolency were not manifested previous even to the appearance of Mortimer.

Farren had played Helen, and Bannister had played Wilford. No one of them had a part competent to yield "vivid effects," according to the writer of the pamphlet. He continues, "Nor will it be said that Mr. Kemble was accountable for all the trash which was put into the mouths of Samson and Blanche, not to mention those dreadful incitations to languor—Fitzharding, Armstrong, Orson, and Judith." He goes on to call Colman a "poor weak man" who "mistook the secret whisperings of his own inordinate vanity . . . up he starts, big with the imaginings of pride and affectation, and hastens . . . to satisfy the suppositious cravings of popular desire . . . he finds, too late, that he had been the dupe of his own conceit."

Colman had not only blamed Kemble; he writes of his fellow dramatists that he had the unparalleled audacity to elevate himself above his more diffident brethren whose productions he stigmatizes with the appellation of "mere lining for chests," while his *Iron Chest*, he says, "will be found to hold together, and to be fit for all the purposes for which it was intended." Colman had called his "brother bards" sans-culottes and accused them "on the account of the largeness of the sum he was to receive for his labors, of having 'been vapidly industrious to level to the muddy surface of their own Castalian ditch. . . .' Is this to be matched in the records of pride and impertinent self-sufficiency?—Here is a man, rising Phoenix-like out of the ashes of his own disgrace, and calling on the world to bind the garland of bays round his head, for that he is the 'Dieu de la chanson,' and none can sing like him! that he alone has attained the summit of Parassus, while his poor stupid competitors are floundering in the ditch at the bottom!!!—"[16]

Colman blamed Kemble for "suffering the piece to be produced, uncut, to drag its slow length along," a totally absurd accusation, for Kemble would never have dared to change another's play, not Colman's at any rate; and given the circumstances, there was no time to rewrite it. The account of the circumstances in this first performance finds the audience as active as ever, notwithstanding the new, "vast" stage. At the beginning of the third act, the audience began to voice its displeasure: "It took place in the scene between Helen and Sir Edward Mortimer;— a scene it will be recollected altogether extraneous and inconceivably dull. On the appearance of Adam Winterton, a character very obnoxious to the house from the beginning, the disapprobation increased." The writer then, after he offers additional support for Kemble, discusses Kemble's style of acting and Kemble's personal appearance as "Tall and very handsome," whereas Colman had called Kemble "Of a tall stature, and of a sable hue, Much like the son of Kish, that lofty Jew." Colman must really have been beside himself about the whole episode to have so written about Kemble, especially since he, Colman, was quite small of stature. "Whereas he [Colman] is known to be a little priggish, dusky man."[17]

If the "Remarks" were worth our attention, the "Summary Comparison of the Play of The Iron Chest With the Novel of Caleb Williams" is even more important to our discussion of Inchbald, Godwin, and their friends. Godwin's novel is an intricate psychological study, many portions of which would be difficult to put in a dramatic setting. And Colman certainly could not transfer the characters from the page to the stage. Colman has "mistaken the source of the compunction of Falkland, which he has imagined to proceed from the murder of Tyrell; instead of the execution of the innocent Hawkinses. That Falkland ever regretted for a moment his murder of Tyrell is not to be supposed." Falkland killed Tyrell to satisfy his "high sense of honour"; he allowed the Hawkinses to be executed because he remained silent about the true facts.

The writer thought that in the novel Godwin had a real problem in developing the character of Falkland, in making it interesting and complex enough to keep the reader involved:

He [is] obliged to inform the reader, by amplification, of what he could not do abstractly;—in the first volume he appears an object of admiration, in the second of pity, and in the third of pity and terror combined.

The Sir Edward Mortimer of Colman is a creature of a different kind. For want of the necessary palliatives which are so ingeniously contrived in the novel, the murder he has committed appears to be the result of a dastardly malignity—his oppression of Wilford, of tyrannical caprice—his remorse is despicable, and his penitence ludicrous—instead of pity, he excites contempt, and instead of terror, merriment. In the novel, we are led on by degrees to admire a character who interests by his peculiar perplexities, conciliates by his benevolence, awes by the weight of his talents, and alarms by the formidableness of his power. In the play, we are introduced at once to a murderer without a plea to justify his crime a moody solitaire, who croaks about the loss of honour, which it does not appear he ever possessed: a trembling coward, who dreads rather the infliction of punishment, than the entailment of ignominy.[18]

The play took on a life of its own when Colman revised it and presented it in his own Haymarket in the summer of 1796. Here again, Colman was determined to be vindicated; he prepared carefully for the presentation, he rehearsed it himself, and he coached his new "find," Robert Elliston. This time the production was a success. Perhaps there were several reasons for such a change. The Haymarket was much smaller than Drury Lane, and the speeches were therefore more forceful. Elliston, new to the Haymarket, had come from Bath, having had some experience with Tate Wilkinson.

In spite of the success, the *Mirror* reported: "Had Mr. Kemble played Mortimer infinitely better than he did, *The Iron Chest* would, nevertheless, have been condemned at Drury Lane. Had Mr. Elliston not played half so well as he did *The Iron Chest* would have been successful at Mr. Colman's *'own theatre.'*" Perhaps Colman did see to it that his friends attended, but he probably did not engage a claque. No doubt the ill success at Drury Lane with Kemble had made such a mark in the minds of the theatregoing public that they came out of curiosity. Elliston, not associated with anyone else, played the part in a fresh and engaging performance, and the play became a stock piece for many years.[19]

In his journal Godwin simply wrote, "The Iron Chest." Inchbald certainly saw one if not both of the performances at Drury Lane. Later, in 1808 when she wrote her *Remarks* to accompany the play, there followed a paper war with Colman, who published a long and insulting letter about her criticism of his father and of his own plays. In 1796 Inchbald was not writing criticism, but she would certainly have agreed with some of the "Comparison." She had complimented Godwin extravagantly about his novel, and she must therefore have agreed that "There never was a copy perhaps so miserably varied from want of conception, or want of skill, or both, I will not pretend to determine; but surely there can be no stronger instance of consummate ignorance, or of corrupted taste." The writer continued: "If Mr. Colman meant to follow his author, I must impute his perversions to the former: if he did not, they proceed most indubitably from the latter."[20] Considering that Inchbald had become very successful in adapting material for the stage, she would be acutely aware of how Colman had failed.

As concerned as Godwin and Inchbald would have been about a new play at Drury Lane made from Godwin's novel and played by Kemble, they certainly must have known some of the circumstances both before and after the performance. Inchbald's practice with regard to her own plays is quite evident: she went to the first reading; she considered the response of the actors; she and Harris agreed or sometimes disagreed, and she took the play back and worked on it again. This was the pattern of her work, whether the play was an adaptation or entirely original, and, as we have said, sometimes her plays were not successful or were only moderately so. Perhaps it can be argued that she was merely the writer and therefore had not so much control over the presentation as Colman, who was the proprietor of the Haymarket and therefore could command more control. In any case Colman was very bitter about the result of the two performances at Drury Lane. Perhaps he should have been more careful of the situation at rehearsals, but both he and Sheridan were very careless about their own work, even though they required a higher standard in others.

Another factor in Colman's bitterness had to do with the financial difficulties he faced. Thinking to make quite a large sum of money if the play ran for several nights, he made very little when it did not succeed. In his Haymarket, where he could make all the decisions and where he very carefully coached a new young actor, Robert William Elliston, it is not surprising that *The Iron Chest* was a great success, playing for the rest of the summer season in 1796, and that afterward it became a stock piece, playing for many years into the nineteenth century. Colman made his profit after all.

Godwin, always short of funds, was exceedingly annoyed when Colman did not even send him a ticket; he really felt he should have had a box, especially since Colman freely acknowledged that the play was adapted from Godwin's novel. Perhaps it was just as well, since the play turned out to be so complete a failure. Whether Inchbald or Godwin saw the production in the summer at the Haymarket is not recorded. By August, when *The Iron Chest* was played with Elliston as Sir Edward Mortimer, Godwin, though he still continued to see Inchbald and their circle of friends—going to the theatre and to tea—had begun an affair with Mary Wollstonecraft. In August they had become lovers.

GODWIN AND WOLLSTONECRAFT

Early in January 1796 Godwin had met Mary Wollstonecraft again when he went to tea at Mary Hayes's, invited there by Hayes, who, as a friend of Mary and an admirer of Godwin, wished to introduce them again. The entries in Godwin's journal from this Friday, January 8, reveal a fascinating and, in the end, tragic story of two people who had led lonely and frustrating lives. At this point Wollstonecraft was only beginning to recover from her vain attempt to be reunited with Imlay, and Godwin, never accepted fully into any social group, was ready to accept the attention of someone who would share an emotional partnership.

After Godwin's first encounter with Mary at Johnson's dinner party, he had hardly seen her again; but he knew her work, and he also knew the gossip about her personal life. He knew that she had quite recently attempted to commit suicide by jumping off Putney Bridge, only to be rescued and taken to a public house, the Duke's Head, where a doctor was called and she was revived. The experience was physically very painful, quite unlike her first attempt, when, having taken an overdose of laudanum, she was roused and talked back to consciousness. This first time, in April 1795, she had recently returned from France with her baby, only to find that her "lover," Gilbert Imlay, had deserted her, in fact had found another mistress and would not call her his "wife"; indeed, she was never his wife, although she continued to use his name. It is significant to notice that in his journal Godwin calls her Imlay frequently.

After the tea at Hayes's, Godwin did not see Wollstonecraft again for some time; she had gone to the country to visit a friend and recover. Godwin and Inchbald, with Robinson and frequently Merry and Holcroft, continued their associations. On January 12 Godwin records, "dine at Robinson's w. Inchbald, Merry Chalmers, Ht & C. [Holcroft]." On February 13, a Saturday, "Call on Wolstencraft, nah: meet Mrs. Cristie." Ten days later, "Call on Lauderdale n[?] & Inchbald; adv Mattocks, C. Kemble & H. Siddons." C. Kemble was Charles Kemble, and H. Siddons was Henry; and before he went to see *The Iron Chest*, he had called on Inchbald with "C and Opie." It is not until April that the entry reads "Wolstencraft calls: call on AA: Theatre, Jane Shore: sup at Carr's." The next day Godwin records that he called on O'Connor, talked with Northcote about acting, and had tea at Wollstonecraft's with Christie.

For all of Godwin's entries in April, he perhaps knew something of Wollstonecraft's social affairs; Imlay had returned from Paris, and she found him one night at the Christies', where she had come with Fanny. Warned as she came into the house, she "entered the room determinedly and led Fanny up to him where he sat. Confronted in public by a bewildered little girl and a reproachful woman, he suggested that all three should retire to another room for a talk."[21] He promised to have dinner with her the next night, but nothing came of it. She saw him only once more, quite by chance as he passed along on horseback; he dismounted and they talked for the last time. It was after this, on April 14, that

Godwin records "Wolstencraft calls." By this time Mary had moved from Finsbury Place to Cumming Street, where Mary Hayes lived nearby, and from there she called alone and uninvited on Godwin.

Their courtship was strange and secretive, each attempting to direct the other and each attempting to live and work alone. The record in Godwin's journal is obviously transparent, even though he made some attempt to keep it secret, and the record of his days continues as before, filled with references to people he had been seeing since the publication of *Political Justice* and *Caleb Williams*. If he was rigid and harsh toward some of his admirers, he was in 1796 still a commanding voice in the intellectual and political circles of London.

One writer describing him at this point says:

He had a large circle of friends; scarcely a day passed without his being consulted, or receiving admiring callers, or being invited out. He had in fact stepped in to fill the position of intellectual leadership left vacant amongst the English democrats by the death of Price and the emigration of Priestley. He fell short of the moral majesty of their generation: where they had been innocent, he sought, strenuously and sometimes embarrassingly, to be candid; where they were sustained by faith in God, he found himself increasingly disappointed with mankind. Where they had been scientists, mathematicians and ministers, leading quiet personal lives, he was that more vulnerable figure, the man of letters dependent on his pen for his bread.[22]

By this spring of 1796, Godwin was still the mentor of a circle of young men—Wordsworth and Coleridge, for two—and his friendship with the Parrs flourished, even though he and Parr argued loudly and often. He sometimes had tea with Mrs. Robinson, as he calls her, though she was popularly referred to as "Perdita" from the role she had played in Shakespeare's *Winter's Tale*. When she appeared as Perdita, she so enchanted the Prince of Wales that he took her as his mistress, only to find that his interest did not last; he very shortly cast her aside. Godwin continued to see Wollstonecraft with other friends, Twiss, Joseph Ritson, and Wolcot. Godwin's other "interests" continued. When he went to Norfolk in July, he saw Amelia Alderson again and probably considered asking her father for her hand. She would never have married him, and perhaps at this point he came to understand that. He wrote a long letter to Mary, and when he returned home, he discovered she had moved quite near his place.

In early August they wrote letters back and forth, some of Mary's revealing her jealousy of both Alderson and Inchbald. She called Mrs. Inchbald "Mrs. Perfection" and teased him about her. Godwin at forty had never courted a woman, and Mary, denied again and again by Imlay, was at this point very much in need of a lover. Tomalin, in her judgment of the situation, observes, "probably he had never made love to a woman who was a friend before he became Mary's lover, and possibly he had lived a life of absolute chastity, guarding himself as best he could against the assaults of the imagination and the women in the streets." With regard to Mary, she "was clearly sexually curious, inflammable and enthusiastic. She had already enjoyed one affair with a lover singularly free of inhibition and had been living in torment ever since. However little emotional confidence she had, she was sexually confident and unashamed."[23]

All her life from her childhood onward, Mary had been unhappy, and very early she had voiced that unhappiness to her friends and family; her family paid little attention, her friends little more. It is true that her father was abusive and the family very dysfunctional, but Mary had always sought control, always sought power over those around her. She had lost all control over Imlay, even though she took quite a long time to acknowledge how completely he had escaped her. Even as a teenager she had tried to impose her views on her family and friends. Tomalin calls this her "natural dominance." She virtually broke up the marriage of her sister Eliza, and when she became a governess for Lord Kingsborough and his Lady, she acted very unwisely. Again discussing Mary's problems, Tomalin explains, "Caroline Kingsborough and Mary, though their positions were officially unequal, had something in common: they both needed to establish ascendancy over their companions in order to be happy." It was here in her situation as governess that she found she could not be equal in the drawing room conversations and be a servant. Lady Caroline was very kind to Mary, but after some months it was clear that the situation was impossible on both sides. According to Tomalin: "From Caroline's point of view Mary's fault as a governess was not just that she won the affections of the children too obviously or even attracted the attention of her [Caroline's] own admirer. It was that she allowed herself to behave with all the capriciousness and displays of sensibility that were meant to be the prerogative of the leisured classes. If she thought Caroline had been rude she would sulk in her room. In March a deputation of Mrs. Ogle, her sister and Caroline herself had to persuade Mary to come downstairs in order to meet the old Earl, and they had considerable difficulty with their mission."[24]

The early part of Mary's behavior was not generally known, but some of her behavior while she was in London working for the publisher Johnson was widely known and commented upon. Johnson's friend Henry Fuseli dominated all the gatherings he frequented. Among other of his talents, he was an artist; "he despised mere technique in art just as he despised the merely decorous life." Johnson is said to have told new guests at his dinner parties when Fuseli appeared, "If you wish to enjoy his conversation, you will not attempt to stop the torrent of his words by contradicting him."[25] Since Mary liked to dominate the conversation, as she had done when Godwin had wished to hear Paine, one wonders what she must have done when Fuseli made himself the center of attention. He was a friend of William Blake, who was another of the Johnson circle and another link to Mary, for Blake had illustrated the second edition of her *Original Stories* in 1791.

Fuseli was from a family of writers and artists in Zurich. He studied theology at the insistence of his family and was for a brief time a clergyman. He became embroiled in political affairs in Zurich and left to go to Berlin. He spoke eight languages, and for a time he supported himself by doing translations. In 1766, after returning from France, where he met Jean-Jacques Rousseau, he went to England. Joshua Reynolds encouraged him to devote his time entirely to painting, and taking Reynolds's advice, he spent eight years in Italy: in Rome, Florence, Venice, and Naples. Already a very learned man, he used the classical myths and the stories of Greece and Rome as the subjects of his paintings. His version of these materials, however, was unique, and he became famous for his interpretation of Milton and Shakespeare. In 1788 he contracted to do several paintings for the Shakespeare Gallery, and he also became a member of the Royal Academy.

When Mary came back to London after being discharged by the Kingsboroughs, she returned to Johnson; it was then that she became closely associated with Fuseli at Johnson's dinners, and upon Fuseli's invitation she visited him in his studio.[26] At this time Fuseli had just married, at forty-nine; his wife, Sophia, was an attractive though uneducated girl. As time went by, Mary fell passionately in love with him; he probably found her attention flattering but nothing more, even though there was speculation later about the contents of the letters she wrote to him. In the summer of 1792, Johnson and Mary, with Fuseli and his wife, planned to go to France; they got as far as Dover but turned back, returning to London. It was at this time that Mary wrote to the Fuselis to suggest that she become his "spiritual" wife. What Fuseli said about this proposal is not recorded, but his wife had had enough of Mary's flirtation, and Mary was denied. In December 1792 Mary went alone to France.

Godwin's friends and hers all knew each other; some were associated with the Johnson circle and some with the Robinson circle. There is very little evidence that Mrs. Inchbald knew intimately those who attended Johnson's dinner parties; she certainly knew who they were, as did her friend Amelia Alderson. Alderson knew both groups very well, partly perhaps because of her father and her friends in Norwich, many of whom were Dissenters and in favor of Paine, Godwin, and the Treason Trial group. Just when Amelia and Mary met is not recorded, but

Amelia's comment that only two experiences in her life had lived up to her expectations, Mary and the Lakes of Cumberland, has been quoted by every commentator about Godwin and Mary. Amelia had been corresponding with Godwin about writing for the theatre, a strange correspondence since neither knew the theatre except as spectators.

In 1796, when Wollstonecraft began to see Godwin, those days in August just before they became lovers, she was once again working for Johnson and slowly recovering from Imlay. She gradually became a part of the Robinson circle, and though not everyone welcomed her enthusiastically, she quickly was added to some of their social gatherings. She began to attend the Twisses' dinner parties on Sundays, where she saw the other members of the Kemble family—sometimes Mrs. Siddons. She began to go to the theatre; on one occasion she sat alone and watched Godwin having a theatre party in a box nearby with Inchbald and their friends.

When Amelia wrote to Mary about Godwin, her tone was somewhat different from that in the letter she had written to Mrs. Taylor about Godwin's red slippers and powdered hair. She wrote, "I found him indeed eloquent, entertaining, and luminous in argument even beyond my conceptions of his abilities, but my fancy had so long delighted to picture him a man after his own heart that I shrunk back almost displeased from a man after the present state of things."[27]

On April 22 Godwin records that he had a dinner party. His journal reads: "F. Imlay calls: call on Mrs. Mackintosh: Dinner, 3 Parrs, Mackintoshs, Inchbald, Imlay, Deathy, & Ht [Holcroft]." About his little dinner party he wrote, "In my little deserted mansion I received on the 22nd of April a party of twelve persons the most of whom good humorously invited themselves to dine with me, and for whom I ordered provisions from a neighboring coffeehouse. Among this party were Dr. Parr and his two daughters, Mr. and Mrs. Mackintosh, Mr. Holcroft, Mrs. Wolenstcroft and Mrs. Inchbald."[28] The guests at this party were not friends of Mrs. Inchbald's except for Holcroft. The Parrs came from Warwickshire and were longtime friends of Godwin's, visiting in London. The Mackintoshes were, like the Parrs, Dissenters and very conservative. The conversation over the coffeehouse fare must have been interesting, especially since Wollstonecraft/Imlay had certainly not seen the Parrs or the Mackintoshes or, for that matter, Mrs. Inchbald under such social circumstances.

On April 26 Godwin's journal entry reads, "sup at Machintosh's, w. Parrs, Inchbald, Ht [Holcroft], G. Moore, Deathy, Scarlet & Burroughs." The Parrs were still in town. This time Mrs. Inchbald was not present but on the twenty-ninth he called on Parr at the Mackintoshes', and he lists Montague, J. Hollis, and

Inchbald. It is always difficult to determine exactly how the entries in the journal are to be read—did he mean that Mrs. Inchbald went to the Mackintoshes' with him? Probably not. In the same entry he says he went to tea at "Wolstencraft's." By this spring of 1796, Godwin and Holcroft were enjoying a busy social life. In May Godwin called on Inchbald, Mrs. Robinson (Perdita), Montague, and Mackintosh one day and on a Friday, May 27, on Northcote and Inchbald; on the next day the entry reads, "call on Wolstencraft's; adv. Wolcot & Twiss." On June 1 he called on Inchbald and had supper with Wollstonecraft and Twiss. Following this supper, on June 2, a Thursday, he begins his entry, "Wolstencraft's Comedy." Mary had joined those who wished to be playwrights. Her attempt, like many another, was a failure.

That Mary should have consulted Godwin about a play is not surprising, since he did work for Robinson, advising him about manuscripts—what we might call editing. He continued to see Inchbald and to see Wollstonecraft the next day or the day after. These entries suggest that some of these "calls" were about professional matters as well as social. On Sunday, June 19, Wordsworth and his friend Stoddart, along with Godwin, had supper at Montague's. In July Godwin paid a visit to Norwich, where he visited Dr. Alderson and Amelia; it was on this visit that he very likely proposed to Amelia or told her father that he would like to marry her. Both daughter and father were too polite to make such a proposal known, but Amelia, allowed to make her own choices among suitors, would never have chosen Godwin, even though she admired his learning and his ability to speak. When Godwin returned from his trip to Norwich, he began to see Mary every day. On the first of August he called on Inchbald and on the seventh on Hayes and Inchbald; on the fifteenth he records the first of the "chez moi's." The "chez moi" and "chez elle" continue almost every day until March 29, 1797, when Godwin and Mary were married.[29]

They told no one of their plans, taking only Godwin's friend Marshall as witness and going to St. Pancras Church; Godwin's only reference to the occasion is buried in his journal entry identified only by the abbreviation "Panc." Old St. Pancras was their parish church, since they both lived very near, and after walking across the fields, they made legal a relationship that for Godwin was hardly the view he held of marriage but for Mary finally made her unborn baby legitimate. However the two of them felt, their friends—indeed the public of London—had a new topic to discuss. Neither Mary nor Godwin ever understood that they could not be public figures and still be private. Neither could they reconcile for themselves their views of the world, their zeal to reform, and their ambition for glory with the reality of themselves and their world. In the end, of course, after her death Mary had no decision to make, and Godwin went through a pathetic decline.

At the moment, in the spring of 1797, the immediate problem was how to tell their friends—indeed all of London and beyond—of what they had done. Godwin acted as if nothing had happened for the next few days. He wrote a silly letter to Mary Hayes, but it seems he did not write to Holcroft, nor did she. Both Mary and Godwin certainly behaved in a very crude way, as if to announce the marriage was somehow saying he had become her keeper. Mary, pregnant with his child, knew the situation perhaps better than he, but she was unable to be "smart" about her own position. Perhaps her attitude is to be understood, since, having married, she had succeeded in acquiring a kind of stability and respectability that she had never known. Her letters to Godwin while they still lived apart show a serenity she had never had. For their friends and the public, the fact of their marriage was another matter altogether.

Godwin was the "philosopher" who had written that marriage was simply a convenient arrangement and if the couple tired of the convenience they could simply break off the relationship and move on to another. Actually, of course, Godwin did not believe that such a relationship as he and Mary had formed was temporary, but he had argued in *Political Justice* for logic, not for an emotional response between two people, and when their friends heard the news, there was much comment and gossip. To compound their problem, they did not find a graceful way to announce the marriage, and as the spring months moved to summer, Mary's "condition" was evident. Moreover, the two of them had made an agreement to go their separate ways socially, which for Godwin meant he could keep recording in his journal the times he went to tea at Mrs. Inchbald's or to sup with Holcroft and Robinson, to go to the theatre and behave in his usual way of agreeing or not with Inchbald or Alderson or have an opinion of Siddons or Mrs. Mattocks. Mary, an outsider in the group, soon discovered that being "Godwin's femme" did not exempt her from the wit and sarcasm of Mrs. Inchbald or from the gossip in London circles.

When she had returned to London expecting to have Imlay acknowledge her as his wife and Fanny as his child, she had called herself Mrs. Imlay, and after moving to Charlton Street, she had continued to use his name. It is interesting to note that in Godwin's journal he calls her Imlay sometimes and Wollstonecraft in other entries. He spelled Wollstonecraft one way or another rather carelessly, although the journal was his own private record. The public was not so indulgent as Godwin. If she was really Mrs. Imlay, how could she be Mrs. Godwin? Divorce was difficult to obtain, costly, and very public. The marriage to Godwin obviously made her an unwed mother of little Fanny and Fanny an illegitimate child. After the announcement, the group that had been Godwin's and the friends that were especially hers broke up, leaving the Robinson circle now broken. When Inchbald met them at the theatre soon after the marriage was announced, there was a great "to do." Evidently Mary had not understood Inchbald's place in the circle, nor had she understood Inchbald's "wit"; there were words exchanged; Godwin thought Mary was insulted. Whether or not she was insulted, Inchbald certainly embarrassed her, even though she brought the situation on herself both by her actions and her comments. Many of the people Mary knew—Sarah Siddons, for example—refused to see her socially again. Holcroft wrote to complain that he was hurt to have been "teased," and Mrs. Inchbald wrote a "witty" little note to Godwin: "I most sincerely wish you and Mrs. Godwin joy, but assured that your joyfulness would obliterate from your memory every trifling engagement, I have entreated another person to supply your place. . . . If I have done wrong, when you next marry, I will act differently."[30]

Her reference to "when you next marry" was aimed directly at Mary in the note Mrs. Inchbald had addressed to Godwin, since if he followed his own announced principles, he would change wives; and indeed, more to the point, she, having called herself Imlay as if she were married, had now "changed husbands." Both Mary and Godwin were furious; both appeared that night in the box at the theatre. There were several others present, including Mrs. Reveley, Amelia, the Fenwicks, and others.

Mary wrote a long letter to Amelia the next morning justifying herself:

My Dear Girl,
    Endeavoring, through embarrassment, to turn the conversation from myself last night, I insensibly became too severe in my strictures on the vanity of a certain lady, and my heart smote me when I raised a laugh at her expense. Pray forget it. I have now to tell you that I am very sorry I prevented you from engaging a box for Mrs. Inchbald whose conduct, I think, has been very rude. She wrote to Mr. Godwin to-day, saying, that, taking it for granted he had forgotten it, she had spoken to another person. "She would not do so the next time he was married." Nonsense! I have now to request you to set the matter right. Mrs. Inchbald may still get a box; I beg her pardon for misunderstanding the business, but Mr. G. led me into the error, or I will go to the pit. To have done with disagreeable subjects at once, let me allude to another I shall be sorry to resign the acquaintance of Mrs. and Mr. F. Twiss, because I respect their characters, and feel grateful for their attention; but my conduct in life must be directed by my own judgment and moral principles: it is my wish that Mr. Godwin should visit and dine out as formerly, and I shall do the same; in short, I still mean to be independent, even to the cultivation of sentiments and principles in my children's minds, (should I have more,) which he disavows. The wound my unsuspecting

heart formerly received is not healed. I found my evenings solitary; and I wished, while fulfilling the duty of a mother, to have some person with similar pursuits, bound to me by affection; and beside, I earnestly desired to resign a name which seemed to disgrace me.

Her letter continues to say, "I am proud perhaps, conscious of my own purity and integrity"; "I wish to live as rationally as I can."[31]

Amelia, who was a very kind and gentle person, must have soothed Mary, but she wrote to her friend in Norwich:

by the bye, he never told me marriage or not; but now I remember, it was written before that wonder-creating event was known. Heigho! what charming things would sublime theories be, if one could make one's practice keep up with them; but I am convinced it is impossible, and am resolved to make the best of every-day nature.

I shall have much to tell you in a tete a tete, of the Godwins, & so much that a letter could not contain or do it justice; but this will be entre nous; I love to make observations on extraordinary characters; but not to mention these observations if they be not favorable.[32]

The Fenwicks, Saunders, Hamilton, Phillips, Leeds, and C. Moore: the list is from Godwin's journal, and again, as in other gatherings where Inchbald was present, she spoke in her usual witty (some would say sarcastic) way; Godwin later called her "joke" "base, cruel, and insulting."

After the episode at the theatre, Mrs. Inchbald seems to have refused to see Mary socially, for in a letter after Mary's death, Godwin wrote bitterly:

I must endeavor to be understood as to the unworthy behavior with which I charge you towards my wife. I think your shuffling behavior about the taking places to the comedy of the "Will" dishonorable to you. I think your conversation with her that night in the play base, cruel, and insulting. There were persons in the box who heard it, and they thought as I do. I think you know more of my wife than you are willing to acknowledge to yourself, and that you have an understanding capable of doing some small degree of justice to her merits. I think you should have had magnanimity and self-respect enough to have shewed this. I think that while the Twisses and others were sacrificing to what they were silly enough to think a proper etiquette, a person so out of all comparison their superior, as you are, should have placed her pride in acting upon better principles, and in courting and distinguishing insulted greatness and worth; I think that you chose a mean and pitiful conduct, when you might have chosen a conduct that would have done you immortal honour. You had not even their excuse. They could not (they pretended) receive her into their previous circles. You kept no circle to debase and enslave you.[33]

Godwin's letter is dated September 13, 1797, only three days after Mary's death; Inchbald's reply is dated the fourteenth and reads:

I could refute every charge you allege against me in your letter; but I revere a man, either in deep love or in deep grief; and as it is impossible to convince, I would at least say nothing to irritate him.

Yet surely thus much I may venture to add. As the short and very slight acquaintance I had with Mrs. Godwin, and into which I was reluctantly impelled by you, has been productive of petty suspicions and revilings (from which my character has been till now preserved), surely I cannot sufficiently applaud my own penetration in apprehending, and my own firmness in resisting, a longer and more familiar acquaintance.[34]

The two letters show again Godwin's lack of understanding and Inchbald's firmness in managing her own affairs. No matter how close their friendship, she and Godwin did not always move in the same social circles. The Kembles would never have invited Godwin to a weekend at the marquis of Abercorn's. Inchbald never again was intimate with Godwin, and when two years later he wrote to her sending his new novel, *St. Leon,* she wrote again:

In respect to the other subject, you judged perfectly right that I could not have expressed any resentment against you, for I have long ago felt none. I also assure you that it will always give me great pleasure to meet you in company with others, but to receive satisfaction in your society as a familiar visitor at my own house I never can.

Impressions made on me are lasting. Your conversation and manners were once agreeable to me, and will ever be so. But while I retain the memory of all your good qualities, I trust you will allow me not to forget your bad ones; but warily to guard against those painful and humiliating effects, which the event of my singular circumstances might once again produce.—Your admirer and friend.[35]

Between the lines of the comment "but warily to guard against those painful and humiliating effects" lies the implication that she would never again risk his publicly naming her for whatever reason. His letters to her shortly after Mary's death were not the end of his personal attack, for when he remembered her refusal to admire Mary as Mrs. Godwin, he wrote about it in the *Memoirs.*

Godwin's writing his *Memoirs of the Author of a Vindication of the Rights of Woman* only made the scandal of Mary and their marriage more apparent than ever. Godwin was unable to understand that his readers could not perceive Mary in the same way he did, and his recounting her love for Fuseli, her affair with Imlay, her attempted suicides, the gynecological details of the circumstances of her death, and his use of personal references to Mrs. Inchbald, Mrs. Siddons, and others of his friends was not acceptable to those who were mentioned or to the public, who found the book a scandalous account of a wicked woman.

Godwin never understood why the public was shocked or why Mary's publisher Johnson tried to warn him that much of his recounting of Mary's experiences should be left to memory. He refused to listen, and he soon found that the *Memoirs* created a contention in which he himself was attacked again by those who did not agree with his views in *Political Justice,* although he had once again revised his book. This version of 1798, the year of the *Memoirs,* is the one that afterward became the standard one.

It is the irony of fate that Mary, who had twice tried to leave this world for another, died at just the time she most wanted to live. If Godwin did not understand the reasons his *Memoirs* did not celebrate her life for his readers, he also must have used his account to help his guilty feelings for neglect, the neglect he had been guilty of in the summer before the birth of their child. When Godwin took literally their agreement to go their separate ways, his diary shows some very interesting entries. In May and June he called on Inchbald, and in August he went to visit his friends the Parrs and the Wedgwoods. Mary, left at home, was more than a little annoyed, especially when he wrote that his return was delayed because he and his friend Montague went to the Coventry fair and visited gardens along the way. When Godwin returned, he not only returned to Mary and little Fanny, to whom he brought a mug from the Wedgwood factory, but he also called on Inchbald on July 25 and August 9. On August 28 he called on Fuseli and Inchbald and went to the theatre, where he saw *The Merchant of Venice.* Two days later the baby was born, and on September 10 Mary died of childbed fever.

Godwin's reaction, as we have seen, revealed again that he little understood the world he lived in and little understood Mary or her world. The events that immediately followed her death were typical of the world he had now made for himself. Inchbald was not the only one who refused him. He was attacked by his friends Mackintosh and Dr. Parr, attacks he bitterly resented, and with his usual awkwardness, he replied to them publicly; his views now made little difference to Mackintosh or Parr, or indeed to the public.

Inchbald's summer of 1797 had been a busy one, filled with problems about her family and with the shock of the unexpected death of Dr. Warren. She records in her pocket-book that she "Talked of Dr. Warren's death," and once on June 28, when she and her sister Dolly had dinner together, she read the burial service. When it was appropriate to do so, she wrote a poem, "Lines by Mrs. Inchbald to Mrs. Warren, on the Loss of Her Husband, Richard Warren, M D." Her aunt Haslandine died this year too, as well as Mr. Frank Hunt, her cousin's husband. Mrs. Pope, who had acted in Inchbald's *Such Things Are* and in *Every One Has His Fault,* died also. She had been at Covent Garden with Inchbald since 1786.

In a letter to Mrs. Phillips after Mary Godwin's death, Inchbald wrote:

She was attended by a woman, whether from partiality or economy I can't tell—but from no affected prudery I am sure. She had a very bad time, and they at last sent for an intimate acquaintance of *his*, Mr. Carlisle, a man of talents. He delivered her; she thanked him, and told him he had saved her life: he left her for two hours—returned, and pronounced she must die. Still she languished three or four days. This is the account I have heard, but not from *him;* he has written to me several times since; but they are more like distracted lines than any thing rational.[36]

WIVES AS THEY WERE, AND MAIDS AS THEY ARE

Whereas the years 1794–1795 and 1796 were the disturbing years following the French Revolution and the Reign of Terror, the year 1797 was the year of one of Mrs. Inchbald's greatest successes. In her "Septembers" for 1797, she wrote: "London; after 'Wives as they Were and Maids as they Are;' after an alteration in my teeth, and the death of Dr. Warren—yet far from unhappy." In the year 1796 she had published her *Nature and Art,* recording this year in her "Septembers": "in prosperity, and at times very happy; at times not in perfect health, and sometimes very low-spirited."[37] *Wives As They Were, and Maids As They Are* was first played on January 25; that is, on that date she read her play in the green room at Covent Garden. There was some discussion, not all of it pleasant, and Boaden says she was "greatly" offended. On the twenty-eighth, however she had a contract from Harris, and on the thirty-first her play was read again. This second reading did not please her, and on February 9 she took back her script, recalled the parts from the performers, and refused to go to rehearsal on the next day.

The behavior of Harris and Inchbald, the reaction in the green room, and the discussion of terms again reveal valuable insights into the procedures of the production of plays, especially those that Harris sponsored in Covent Garden. By this time Inchbald's success made her able to be firm about her own play.[38] On February 15 Inchbald and Harris came to a mutual agreement, and the rehearsals were resumed. The play was performed on March 4.

There are several features of the play that were not the usual view of the public or, for that matter, of the players. The two young women, the "Maids As They Are," are extremely independent by the standards of 1797, and the part of the "Wife" of "Wives As They Were" becomes, in the action of the play, equally independent. In contrast to the three women, the men are weak or dictatorial or shallow. Miss Dorrillon and her friend Lady Mary Raffle are the characters around which the action of the play turns, and in the end the two of them bring about the conclusion.

The play begins with the appearance of Mr. Norberry and Sir William Dorrillon. Sir William is actually Miss Dorrillon's father, who has been away for many years and has only just now returned, not revealing his true identity. In his long absence abroad, Miss Dorrillon has been cared for by Mr. Norberry's sister until, upon her death, Mr. Norberry himself has become her guardian.

In the first scene, Sir William complains about his disappointment in his daughter's behavior and her response to him. Miss Dorrillon, unaware that Sir William is her father, is very impolite and has no patience with his peevishness. Moreover, we soon discover that Miss Dorrillon is deep into "play." She has lost all her money and all her jewels. Her father has not sent her any money for two years, and the very day of the play she must pay a debt that can no longer wait. Lady Mary, to whom she appeals, has no money; she too needs money to discharge her debts. She complains that Miss Dorrillon gives her money away when she has it and that she (Mary) has this very day to ask for some.

The two young women are caught in a difficult situation; without money to pay their gambling debts, they are "ruined." It is at this point when Lady Mary suggests that Miss Dorrillon marry and "throw all your misfortunes upon your husband." But to this suggestion Lady Mary protests that she has "no Sir George Evelyn with ten thousand pounds a year—no Mr. Bronzely." With the mention of Bronzely, we discover that he once paid his addresses to Lady Mary, but now Lady Mary says, "And you have the vanity to suppose you took him from me?"

As Lady Mary and Miss Dorrillon discuss their problems, Sir William and Mr. Norberry appear, and when Miss Dorrillon asks Mr. Norberry a "favour" to use his carriage, the contest between Sir William (Mr. Mandred) and Miss Dorrillon begins. Miss Dorrillon is rude and witty; Sir William, impatient and surly.

Sir William, in answer to her request for a favor, replies, "I never confer a favour, of the most trivial kind, where I have no esteem." And Miss Dorrillon replies, "[*Proudly.*] Nor would I receive a favour, of the most trivial kind, from one who has not liberality to esteem me."

With no resolution to their dilemma about money, the conversation turns to tickets for the fete about to be given. When the servant admits Sir George Evelyn, the subjects of tickets, friendship, and "supreme happiness" become the topics to be considered. But such topics must be discussed with all three gentlemen—Sir William, Sir George, and Mr. Norberry; Miss Dorrillon must ask permission. The complication of Sir William's concealed identity, concealed from Miss Dorrillon, not the audience, is but one of the problems. Sir George has tickets to the fete, but Miss Dorrillon must ask permission of Mr. Norberry to go, and when he is reluctant to give her that permission, she says, "Nay, my dear Sir, do not force me to go without it." Sir William interrupts, saying, "[*With violence.*] Would you dare?" To which she replies:

> *Miss Dorrillon:* [*Looking with surprise.*] "Would I dare," Mr. Mandred!—
> and what have *you* to say if I do?
> *Sir William:* [*Recollecting himself.*] I was only going to say, that if you did,
> and I were Mr. Norberry—
> *Miss Dorrillon:* And if you were Mr. Norberry, and treated me in the
> manner you now do, depend upon it I should not think your approba-
> tion or disapprobation, your pleasure or displeasure, of the slightest
> consequence.

Miss Dorrillon refuses to apologize for her speech, even though Mr. Norberry asks her to do so, for she has offended Mr. Mandred. To this request she speaks again: "No, no apology. But I'll tell you what I'll do. [*Goes up to Sir William.*]—If Mr. Mandred likes, I'll shake hands with him—and we'll be good friends for the future. But then, don't find fault with me—I can't bear it. *You* don't like to be found fault with, yourself—You look as cross as any thing every time I say the least word against you. Come, shake hands; and don't let us see one another's failings for the future."

When Sir William and Mr. Norberry leave, Sir George remains. They speak of Sir William. Lady Mary remarks: "Oh! if he was not rich, there would be no bearing him—Indeed he seems to have lost all his friends; for during the month he has been here, I never found he had any one acquaintance out of this house."

> *Miss Dorrillon:* And what is very strange, he has taken an aversion to me.—
> But it is still more strange, that although I know he has, yet in my
> heart I like *him*. He is morose to an insufferable degree; but then, when
> by chance he speaks kind, you cannot imagine how it soothes me.—He
> wants compassion and all the tender virtues; and yet, I frequently
> think, that if any serious misfortune were to befall me, he would be the
> first person to whom I should fly to complain.

For Inchbald's audience this speech of Miss Dorrillon's is a very signifi-cant one, since it represents the belief that blood relatives recognize each other unconsciously.

With the subject of Mr. Norberry, Sir George turns the conversation to the "misfortune" of "last night." The complications of the conversation that follows among the three—Sir George, Miss Dorrillon, and Lady Mary—turn to matters of "happiness," happiness, that is, of men and women, of the relationships of the three and Mr. Bronzely. Sir George warns Miss Dorrillon, "I will not affront you by supposing that you mean seriously to receive the addresses of Mr. Bronzely; but I warn you against giving others, who know you less than I do, occasion to think so."

Sir George's warning Miss Dorrillon about Bronzely reveals yet another way in which Miss Dorrillon must assert her independence, since Sir George wants to dictate to her about her friends and lovers; for although she has not accepted either Bronzely or Sir George, they each, jealously, warn her against the other. Sir George offers his steward to help Miss Dorrillon out of her financial crises, but she refuses.

Sir George knows that Miss Dorrillon's father has not sent her the usual moneys he has pledged, and here again, Sir George is inclined to blame Sir William and the situation he finds; he declares: "I . . . have always regarded you with a compassion that has augmented my love. In your infancy, deprived of the watchful eye and anxious tenderness of a mother; the manly caution and authority of a father; misled by the brilliant vapour of fashion; surrounded by enemies in the garb of friends—Ah! do you weep? blessed, blessed be the sign!" But Miss Dorrillon is angry with herself; she does not want Mr. Norberry or Mr. Mandred (Sir William) to find her more indiscreet than the true situation warrants—that is, she has lost money but not her reputation.

The second act introduces the "wife" of the "Wives As They Were." Lord Priory has accepted the invitation to be a guest at Mr. Norberry's in order to shelter his wife from the public. We very soon discover that Lady Priory is totally dominated by her husband—or at least at this point we think she is, complying with his wishes in everything. When Lady Mary suggests that they have tea, Lady Priory says she has already had tea. Miss Dorrillon protests, "Already! It is only nine o'clock." Then occurs the following dialogue:

> *Lady Priory:* Then it is near my hour of going to bed.
> *Lady Mary:* Go to bed already! In the name of wonder, what time did you rise this morning?
> *Lady Priory:* Why, I do think it was almost six o'clock.
> *Lady Mary:* And were you up at six this morning?
> *Lady Priory:* Yes.
> *Miss Dorrillon:* At six in the month of January!
> *Lady Mary:* It is not light till eight: and what good, now, could you possibly be doing for two hours by candlelight?
> *Lady Priory:* Pray, Lady Mary, at what time did you go to bed?
> *Lady Mary:* About three this morning.

Lady Priory: And what good could you possibly be doing for eleven hours
   by candlelight?
Lady Mary: Good! It's as much as can be expected from a woman of
   fashion, if she does no harm.
Lady Priory: But I should fear you would do a great deal of harm to your
   health, your spirits, and the tranquillity of your mind.

Upon meeting Lord Priory, Lady Mary continues: "Oh, my Lord Priory, I
really find all the accounts I have heard of your education for a wife to be actually
true!—and I can't help laughing to think, if you and I had chanced to have married together, what a different creature you most likely would have made of me, to
what I am at present!" He replies: "Yes; and what a different creature you most
likely would have made of *me,* to what I am at present."

This dialogue at the beginning of act 2 presents yet another concern of the
play: husbands and wives do interact—no matter if on the surface it would seem
that Lord Priory has fashioned his wife after his own expectations.

As the conversation continues, Lady Mary points out to Lord Priory, "Upon my
word, my Lord, your plan of management has made your wife unfit for company."

Lord Priory: So much more fit to be a wife.
Lady Mary: She is absolutely fatigued with hard labour—for shame!—How
   does household drudgery become her hand?
Lord Priory: Much better than cards and dice do yours.

With the introduction of Lord and Lady Priory, we have met all the principal characters except Bronzely, even though he has been discussed from the beginning. Here, as Lady Mary and Lord Priory leave and Sir George enters, Bronzely
is discussed again; Sir George thinks Miss Dorrillon is in love with Bronzely. He
says, "She loves him." Speaking to Mr. Mandred (Sir William), "Sir—I have reason to believe—to know she loves him. Thus she gives up my happiness and her
own, to gratify the vanity of a man who has no real regard for her; but whose
predominant passion is to enjoy the villainous name of a general seducer."

Miss Dorrillon is summoned, and she must defend herself before Sir George
and Sir William. In their conversation she sets up a "court" to judge treating a
"heart." From the beginning, when we are introduced to Miss Dorrillon, we are
reminded of Miss Milner in *A Simple Story.* Both have been left without a mother
and without a father's care, both are independent, both are very attractive, and
both are part of a society that their guardians denounce without providing any

direction or offering any substitute. The discussion of gaming, late nights, cards, and dice made this play contemporary for Inchbald and her audience.

In the midst of the discussion about Bronzely, he appears. He bursts into the room begging Sir William/Mandred to exchange coats. When the trick is revealed, it seems that Bronzely has encountered a woman in a dark hall and kissed her, thinking her to be either Lady Mary's or Miss Dorrillon's maid, only to discover that it was Lady Priory, who exclaimed, "Help"—"Murder!" and cut off a piece of his coat; she always carried her scissors by her side, as a proper wife and housewife should.[39]

With this farcical silly incident, we understand that Bronzely is a fool, but not the only one. Sir William, discovering the episode, protects Bronzely, because, he says, "I think the punishment of death, in the way that a man of Lord Priory's temper might inflict it, much too honourable for your deserts." As Bronzely is presented, he is not only a fool but a stupid coxcomb as well. But the mischief he causes is not over: Miss Dorrillon appears to report that it was Sir William who kissed Lady Priory.

The conversation and incidents in this part of the play, though they are farce, are nevertheless based on the view of "society" found in many of the plays and novels with which Inchbald's audience would have been familiar. The delight in the "trick" and in the episode that follows, when Lady Priory agrees to meet Bronzely alone, keeps the suspense of the incident and allows Lady Priory to show that she will not be seduced and that she will not be dictated to by her husband. She meets Bronzely, or rather she agrees for him to meet her, and when in the end he tries all his usual ways to entrap her, she remains unaffected. The fashionable "seducer" is humiliated and Lady Priory's character proved, not only by her refusal but also by her ability to show him as the fool he is.

Through the coat incident, Bronzely has become quite involved with Sir William; in turn, Sir William has now seen clearly that Bronzely is a fool in no way deserving of Miss Dorrillon. But since he has not revealed his identity as her father, there is little he can do to influence her. At this point in the action, Sir William has no way to escape Bronzely, who now volunteers to make an apology for Sir William to Lord Priory.

As the incidents of the play continue, Oliver, Lord Priory's servant, enters carrying the piece of cloth and matches it with the coat Sir William is wearing; Bronzely persuades him to hold his tongue, and Oliver, agreeing at first, is resolved not to tell his master, but when Sir William does not even acknowledge him—Oliver: "Why, he never so much as once said he was obliged to me."

In act 3 Bronzely appears in Lord Priory's apartment very early, not to see him but to see Lady Priory. He pretends to tell her that he needs her help in avoiding a duel between Sir William and her husband, but in truth he wishes to tempt her, to suggest that she meet him for an assignation and to arrange the time and place. Their conversation, brief as it is, suggests his constant pursuit of women—any woman, married or unmarried—a game he must play for his own self-esteem; surprisingly, she agrees.

Meanwhile, Bronzely is alone on the stage, and he speaks to the audience: "I'll do a meritorious act this very day. This poor woman lives in slavery with her husband. I'll give her an opportunity to run away from him. When we meet, I'll have a post-chaise waiting." Before he can finish speaking of his plan, Miss Dorrillon enters. Surprised to see her, he turns the situation into a protest—"I could not sleep all night, but am come thus early on purpose to complain of your treatment of me during the whole of yesterday evening. Not one look did you glance towards me—and there I sat in miserable solitude up in one corner, the whole time of the concert."

Seeing Bronzely so early, she says, "I protest I did not see you!—and, stranger still! never thought of you." To her he replies, "You then like another better than you do me?" She says, "I do." But when he says, "You tell him you like me the best," she replies, "Yes." Their game seems strangely out of place in the context of the action of the play; it underscores again the emptiness of Bronzely and of her foolish flirtation. Here, as in *A Simple Story,* the question is whom she will marry, not whether she will marry. We are reminded of the several discussions of suitable marriages in *A Simple Story.*

Sir William appears just as Miss Dorrillon leaves. Surprised to see the two of them in close conversation, he is quite upset. Bronzely ushers Miss Dorrillon to the door and turns to speak to Sir William. At once Bronzely announces, "Well, Mr. Mandred, I believe I have settled it. . . . At least I have done all in my power to serve you." But Sir William is not interested in settling his affair; he wishes to know about his daughter.

> *Sir William:* Without farther preface, do you pay your addresses to the
>   young lady who lives in this house?
> *Bronzely:* Yes I do, Sir—I do.
> *Sir William:* You know, I suppose, which of the two ladies I mean?
> *Bronzely:* Which ever you mean, Sir, 'tis all the same; for I pay my addresses
>   to them both.
> *Sir William:* [*Starting.*] To them both!
> *Bronzely:* I always do.

Sir William: And pray, which of them do you love?

Bronzely: Both, Sir—upon my word, both—I assure you, both.

Sir William: But you don't intend to marry both?

Bronzely: I don't intend to marry either; and indeed, the woman whom I love best in the world, has a husband already. Do you suppose I could confine my affections to Lady Mary or Miss Dorrillon, after Lady Priory appeared? do you suppose I did not know who it was I met last night in the dark? wherever I visit, Mr. Mandred, I always make love to every woman in the house: and I assure you they all expect it—I assure you, Sir, they all expect it.

Sir William is very angry and upset, but he continues to question Bronzely.

Sir William: And you really have no regard for this girl who parted from you as I came in?

Bronzely: Oh yes, pardon me—I admire, I adore, I love her to distraction: and if I had not been so long acquainted with my Lady Mary, nor had seen my Lady Priory last night, I should certainly call Sir George Evelyn to an account for being so perpetually with her.

Sir William: Do you think *he* loves her?

Bronzely: Yes, I dare say, as well as I do.

Sir William: Do you think she likes him?

Bronzely: I think she likes *me*.

Sir William: But, with your method of affection, she may like him too.

Bronzely: She may, she may.—In short, there is no answering for what *she* likes—all whim and flightiness—acquainted with every body—coquetting with every body—and in debt with every body. Her mind distracted between the claims of lovers, and the claims of creditors,—the anger of Mr. Norberry, and the want of intelligence from her father!

Sir William: She is in a hopeful way.

Bronzely: Oh, it would be impossible to think of marrying her in her present state—for my part, I can't—and I question whether Sir George would.—But if her father come home, and give her the fortune that was once expected, why then I may possibly marry her myself.

At the mention of her father and his fortune, Sir William says, "She will never have any fortune—I came from India lately, you know; and you may take my word her father is not coming over, nor will he ever come." Bronzely asks, "Are you sure of that?" and Sir William replies, "Very sure."

At this point the audience, knowing Sir William's identity, and now understanding Miss Dorrillon's position, must be directed to some conclusion about the whole situation. Bronzely tells Sir William that he must keep the secret about her father—"poor thing! it would break her heart. She is doatingly fond of her father!" And when Sir William asks how that can be true, since she could have no remembrance of her father, Bronzely explains: "Not of his person, perhaps: but he has constantly corresponded with her; sent her presents, and affectionate letters—and you know a woman's heart is easily impressed." And when Sir William says, "I never heard her mention her father," Bronzely replies: "Not to you—but to us who are kind to her, she talks of him continually. She cried bitterly the other day when the last ship came in, and there was no account of him."

Sir William may now have no fear that Miss Dorrillon will choose Bronzely for a husband, but he is certainly not satisfied that she cares for him or that as a coquette she will not choose someone quite unsuitable, at least in his view of the society she moves in. He next encounters Sir George, who upbraids him for his rudeness to Miss Dorrillon. Sir George: "Mr. Mandred, permit me to say, I have ever wished to treat you with respect. . . . Yet, I must now take upon me to assure you, that if you think to offend *every* lady in this house with impunity, you are mistaken." Sir William responds by calling Miss Dorrillon an "unworthy object." When Sir William refuses to apologize, Sir George speaks again in Miss Dorrillon's favor: "Were they not unjust?—Is it a reproach, that, enveloped in the maze of fashionable life, she has yet preserved her virtue unsuspected? That, encumbered with the expences consequent to her connections, she has proudly disdained even from me the honourable offer of pecuniary aid? that her fond hope still fixes on the return of an absent parent, whose blessing she impatiently expects?"

As the two men quarrel, Miss Dorrillon herself comes in and stops their discussion. After she leaves, they stand silent until Sir George says, "Why is it in the power of one woman to make two men look ridiculously?" And Sir William: "I am at a loss to know, Sir, whether you and I part friends or enemies.—However, call on me in the way you best like, and you will find me ready to meet you either as an enemy, or as a friend."

Act 4 finds Bronzely preparing for Lady Priory as he comes to see her. His plans do not work out quite as he expects, but she does agree to go with him. Before he can leave for the meeting, Lord Priory appears. He wishes to advise Bronzely: "A man of your pursuits, Mr. Bronzely, is of a very late date; and to be shamed out of them by a wife like mine." Little does he know of his wife's plans, but when he is left alone, he speaks: "I am passionate—I am precipitate—I have no command over my temper.—However, if a man cannot govern himself, yet he will never make any very despicable figure, as long as he knows how to govern his wife."

Before the continuation of the Bronzely–Lady Priory–Lord Priory episode, we see Miss Dorrillon; very upset, she enters and runs to lock the door. Sir William, who has come in, will not allow her to do so, and in the end, although she hides behind the bookcase, an officer of the law knocks. Sir William opens the door and asks to see the writ. It reads: "Elizabeth Dorrillon for six hundred pounds." Sir William: "Pray, Sir, is it customary to have female names on pieces of paper of this denomination?" The officer replies: "Oh yes, Sir, very customary. There are as many ladies who will run into tradesmen's books, as there are gentlemen; and when one goes to take the ladies, they are a thousand times more slippery to catch than the men." Even at this point Sir William will not bail her out.

While Miss Dorrillon is being taken away to prison, Lady Priory is making a fool of Bronzely; and Lord Priory, discovering that Lady Priory has run away, is making a fool of himself. Mr. Norberry comes to tell Lord Priory, "About a quarter of an hour after you left them, they stole softly out at the back of your house, ran to a post-chaise and four that was in waiting, and drove off together full speed." Lord Priory: "Gone! eloped! run away from me! left me! left the tenderest, kindest, most indulgent husband, that ever woman had! . . . I was too fond of her—my affection ruined her—women are ungrateful—I did not exert a husband's authority—I was not strict enough—I humoured and spoiled her!—Bless me! what a thick mist is come over my eyes!"

Act 5 opens with Lady Priory and Bronzely alone. Lady Priory is at all times in command of the situation, and nothing Bronzely can say or do frightens her or persuades her to take him seriously. He confronts her to ask that she forsake "a churlish ungrateful partner, never return to him more—but remain with me." To this she replies: "And what shall I have gained by the exchange, when *you* become churlish, when *you* become ungrateful? My children's shame! the world's contempt! . . . Come, come; you are but jesting, Mr. Bronzely! You would not affront my little share of common sense by making the serious offer of so bad a bargain. Come, own the jest, and take me home immediately."

He threatens her: "Lady Priory, you are in a lonely house of mine, where I am sole master, and all the servants are slaves to my will." At this speech Lady Priory takes out her knitting and calmly sits down. Lady Priory has defended herself, but Lady Mary and Miss Dorrillon are still in trouble; they have not learned the wisdom of common sense.

Sir William goes to the prison where Miss Dorrillon is being held and offers to pay her debts to release her, but in his offer he tries to exact a promise from her that she will mend her ways—live in the country away from temptation—but she refuses. She feels that she could not live up to her promise, and she does not want to break her word. Sir William, totally exasperated, gives her a thousand pounds; and as he turns to leave, he refuses even her gratitude, saying, "I will not hear you." But when she discovers he is returning to India, she pleads with him to search for her father. In his reply he says her father will never return to England, for he is now destitute. Overcome with emotion, she refuses to take the money, asking that he give it to her father to relieve his "severe affliction," and she begs to be taken to him.

This scene between Sir William and Miss Dorrillon is full of his admonition to persuade her to leave the social scene, to leave the fashionable circles of London; if she cannot be strong enough to live there without engaging in balls and routs, he demands that she not return to her "former follies and extravagances." From the beginning Sir William represents the very rigid views of a very dictatorial father. He allows Miss Dorrillon no judgment, no choices of her own. He is rude to her and exceedingly peevish and censorious. She is willing to be friends, given any opportunity, but he steadily refuses any suggestion of friendship. When she calls him "my benefactor" and asks him, "bid me farewell at parting—do not leave me in anger," he replies, "How! will you dictate terms to me, while you reject all mine?" Inchbald has contrived to match the dramatic situation of the father concealed and the daughter deceived with a powerful lesson for fathers, a lesson she did not explore in the relationship of Matilda and her father, Lord Elmwood, in *A Simple Story*.

Finally, when Miss Dorrillon appeals so sincerely to be taken to her father, Sir William, in the presence of Mr. Norberry, acknowledges his true identity. With the reunion of father and daughter, the other situations of the play conclude quickly. Lady Mary, who has been with Miss Dorrillon, is released, Sir William explains his "fictitious name," Sir George is selected by Sir William to "become the subject of a milder government" than his, and Lady Mary agrees to take Bronzely rather than have "no chief magistrate at all."

Miss Dorrillon speaks the last sentence—"A maid of the present day shall become a wife like those—of former times." And with this sentence we return to the parting remarks of Lord and Lady Priory. She has demonstrated that although she will no longer be her husband's slave, she will not be seduced by gallantry even though she has been touched by sentiment.

In the *Remarks* Inchbald writes for her play in *The British Theatre*, she speaks directly about the character of Miss Dorrillon: "[She] is by far the most prominent and interesting one in the piece; and appears to have been formed of the same matter and spirit as compose the body and mind of the heroine of the 'Simple Story'—A woman of fashion with a heart—A lively comprehension, and no reflection:—an understanding, but no thought—Virtues abounding from disposition, education, feeling:—Vices obtruding from habit and example."[40]

Inchbald's own view of her society was an ambivalent one, but in Miss Dorrillon she has created a witty and independent woman. In fact, Miss Dorrillon becomes one of several such women Inchbald created in the plays who resemble herself, since she felt sometimes that she had little "reflection."

1798 AND *LOVERS' VOWS*

Inchbald's entry for her "Septembers" in 1798 found her happy, except that she added, "but for suspicion amounting almost to certainty of a rapid appearance of age in my face."[41] By this September Mrs. Inchbald had had her forty-fourth birthday, and she was beginning to realize her age. In January of 1798 she had been ill again; she had a severe cold that seemed to continue until in early February she had a high fever. This time Dr. Phillips attended her, coming for several days twice a day. Boaden records that on the twenty-fifth she wrote in her pocketbook, "In the evening prayed, cried, and felt purely." It is difficult to make an assessment of her illness, but when we learn that her sister Dolly became ill as well as their cousin Mrs. Hunt, who died, we are left to wonder if some kind of virus had swept London. Mrs. Inchbald herself had been very susceptible to such a siege since the long-ago Aberdeen days when her life was despaired of and the priest came to give her the last rites. Inchbald's experience is only one of the recorded ones; there must have been many more, considering the circumstances of the crowded conditions in London and the way any virus could spread.

In June Harris brought her a translation of Augustus Kotzebue's *Child of Love* and asked that she adapt it. According to Boaden, she found the work very difficult, and later evidence suggests that this time the adaptation was actually so far from the original that it became virtually her own work. Moreover, with her version she once again became a rival of another translator, Anne Plumptre, a vicar's daughter, who made a career of translating various writers, especially Kotzebue. With the publication and success of Inchbald's *Lovers' Vows,* she published her own translation. Printed by R. Phillips, the title page read

The NATURAL SON;

A Play,

In Five Acts,

By
Augustus von Kotzebue,
Poet laureate and Director of the Imperial Theatre in Vienna
Being The Original of
LOVERS' VOWS, Now Performing, with universal Applause, At The
THEATRE ROYAL, COVENT GARDEN.
Translated From The German
By Anne Plumptre,
(Author of the Rector's Son, Antoinette, &)
Who has prefixed
A PREFACE
Explaining the Alterations in the Representation; and
A LIFE OF KOTZEBUE.[42]

Plumptre's translation reached a revised fourth edition in 1798 and did underscore the great success of Inchbald's play. Plumptre begins her preface: "The flattering Reception which the Natural Son, under the adopted Title of LOVERS' VOWS, has experienced from an English Audience, in an abridged and mutilated State, affords Reason to believe that a complete Translation of so admirable a Drama will entitle itself to a still higher Degree of Public Approbation."[43] In her own explanation of her work in her preface that is reprinted along with the play in the Backscheider edition, Inchbald pointed out that although she was "wholly unacquainted with the German language, a literal translation of the 'Child of Love' was given to me by the manager of Covent Garden Theatre to be fitted, as my opinion should direct, for his stage." She continues: "This translation, tedious and vapid as most literal translations are, had the peculiar disadvantage of having been put into our language by a German—of course it came to me in broken English."

After explaining the situation of the translation, she points out that some of the changes she made from the original were done because of her regard for an English audience, saying in the preface: "by the consideration of its original unfitness for an English stage, and the difficulty of making it otherwise—a difficulty which once appeared so formidable, that I seriously thought I must have declined it even after I had proceeded some length in the undertaking." Inchbald found the character of the count not to the taste of her audience, at least according to her view, and she found the butler not properly presented—"the dangerous insignificance of the Butler, in the original, embarrassed me much." She felt that if the part of the butler were to be included, "something more must be supplied than the author had assigned him." She therefore asked her friend John Taylor to add the verses the butler spoke, she herself supplying only the seventh and eleventh stanzas in the first of his "poetic stories."[44]

Inchbald worked on *Lovers' Vows* all the summer of 1798 and until the first week of October, when rehearsals began, and she attended them to oversee her work. The first performance was on October 11, and Boaden says it was "received with unbounded applause."[45] It had forty-five performances at its initial presentation and became a standard play all over England and Ireland for many years. Robinson printed it with thirteen printings in the next five years.

Lovers' Vows is a tale of families, wronged women, class division, and young lives dictated by family circumstances. The play opens with Agatha being led out of the inn by the landlord. She has no more money to remain, and the landlord is expecting a full house for fair day. Agatha refuses to beg, but the landlord thinks she had better learn to do so; he shows her how as a countryman, a farmer, and a country girl pass by; only the country girl, on her way to market, responds. Before she has time to return, Frederick appears. He is dressed in a soldier's uniform and appears in high spirits as he stops at the inn. Seeing Agatha leaning against a tree, he stops to give her a piece of money, and as he stands close beside her, she cries out his name, recognizing him as her son. The ensuing dialogue reveals that he has been away for five years and has now returned to search for his father or to find his father's name, since he cannot be discharged from the army to be apprenticed to a master and begin an apprenticeship. He and his comrades find his lack of a birth certificate puzzling; his comrades laugh at him, but his captain gives him leave to come home to find it.

Agatha's explanation is the usual one of a poor girl gone astray; it differs somewhat, however, by the account she gives of herself. Her parents were poor but reputable farmers; the lady of the castle asked for her to live with her and promised to provide for her. She went at age fourteen to the castle, where her mistress treated her kindly and taught her "in all kinds of female literature and accomplishments." She spent three happy years until her mistress's son, an officer in the army, came home. He spoke to her of love, "his flattery" made her vain, and he promised marriage. He made repeated vows, and in the end she says, "I was intoxicated by the fervent caresses of a young, inexperienced, capricious man, and did not recover from the delirium till it was too late." Turned away from home by her parents, she sought the help of the old clergyman of the parish, and he helped her. Through his care she went to another town and, after the birth of her baby, began to teach children in the neighborhood. She continued to do so until she became ill. Her explanation to Frederick, however, does not reveal his father's name, which she has refused to reveal to anyone; she must now reveal it to her son, and with her explanation Frederick inquires about the castle and Baron Wildenhaim, his father. The castle has only been kept by servants after the death of the baron's mother, Agatha's long-ago mistress.

The conversation has been too much for Agatha, but the innkeeper will not admit her and Frederick, even though now Frederick offers money. Left alone on a wooden bench, Agatha faints from hunger. Finally they find shelter in a cottage across the road. The second act opens with the cottager, the cottager's wife, Agatha, and Frederick inside the cottage. Frederick is in despair. He has no more money, and the cottager, kind as he is, has no money either. There is nothing to be done but for Frederick to go and beg, leaving his mother in the care of the cottager and his wife. Agatha gradually regains consciousness and listens, learning that her friend the parson died two years before and that the new parson is a young man who instructs the baron's daughter as well. With the name of Baron Wildenhaim, Agatha begins to ask questions. She finds out that the baron has returned to his estates and that his wife is dead, and the cottager's wife reports the baron was never happy in his marriage. When the wife begins to praise the baron and speak ill of his now-dead wife, she begins to tell the story of how as a young man the baron fell in love with Agatha and then left her. When the cottager's wife comments, "Who knows what is now become of that poor creature," Agatha faints again.

In scene 2 breakfast is set in an apartment in the castle. Baron Wildenhaim enters first, and his daughter, Amelia, soon follows. They talk about their guest, Count Cassel, who has come at the baron's invitation to meet Amelia. Even in this introduction, the baron is annoyed with his guest, but he inquires of Amelia as to her feelings about the count. Amelia does not respond in any of the ways her father supposed she might. Their dialogue sets the situation for the love/family plot of the story.

> *Baron:* Do you like to hear the Count spoken of?
> *Amelia:* Good, or bad?
> *Baron:* Good. Good.
> *Amelia:* Oh yes; I like to hear good of every body.
> *Baron:* But do not you feel a little fluttered when he is talked of?
> *Amelia:* No. [*Shaking her head.*]
> *Baron:* Are not you a little embarrassed?
> *Amelia:* No.

Baron: Don't you wish sometimes to speak to him, and have not the courage to begin?
Amelia: No.
Baron: Do not you wish to take his part when his companions laugh at him?
Amelia: No—I love to laugh at him myself.
Baron: Provoking! [*Aside.*] Are not you afraid of him when he comes near you?
Amelia: No, not at all.—Oh yes—once.
Baron: Ah! Now it comes!
Amelia: Once at a ball he trod on my foot; and I was so afraid he should tread on me again.
Baron: You put me out of patience. Hear, Amelia! [*Stops short, and speaks softer.*] To see you happy is my wish. But matrimony, without concord, is like a duetto badly performed; for that reason, nature, the great composer of all harmony, has ordained, that, when bodies are allied, hearts should be in perfect unison. However, I will send Mr. Anhalt to you—
Amelia: [*Much pleased.*] Do, papa.
Baron: —He shall explain to you my sentiments. A clergyman can do this better than—

The baron is interrupted by the arrival of the servant and thus breaks off in midsentence. The servant is sent for Anhalt, and the conversation turns to the count. He is late; the baron finds that "The Count is a tedious time dressing." When the count does appear, he begins to call Amelia Hebe or Venus and says that she is very beautiful, very unsuitable comments at breakfast—or indeed at any time. The baron is rather angry and says, "Neither Venus, nor Hebe; but Amelia Wildenhaim, if you please." The count protests, "I have traveled, and seen much of the world, and yet I can positively admire [her]." And when Amelia replies prettily, "I am sorry I have not seen the world," he continues, "I am an epitome of the world. In my travels I learnt delicacy in Italy—hauteur, in Spain—in France, enterprise—in Russia, prudence—in England, sincerity—in Scotland, frugality—and in the wilds of America, I learnt love." Amelia asks: "Is there any country where love is taught?"

Count: In all barbarous countries. But the whole system is exploded in places that are civilized.
Amelia: And what is substituted in its stead?

Count: Intrigue.
Amelia: What a poor, uncomfortable substitute!
Count: There are other things—Song, dance, the opera, and war.

With the word "war" the count rises and says, "Ay, we like to talk on what we don't understand."

Count: [*Rising.*] Therefore, to a lady, I always speak of politics; and to her father, on love.
Baron: I believe, Count, notwithstanding your sneer, I am still as much of a proficient in that art as yourself.
Count: I do not doubt it, my dear Colonel, for you are a soldier: and since the days of Alexander, whoever conquers men is certain to overcome women.

The baron and the count agree to go hunting, and Anhalt, pastor and tutor, goes with Amelia. Before Anhalt leaves with Amelia, the baron instructs him to help with the situation of the proposed marriage. The baron says he will not "command" Amelia, and he appeals to Anhalt to instruct the count; he says, "when you find a man's head without brains, and his bosom without a heart, these are important articles to supply. Young as you are, Anhalt, I know no one so able to restore, or to bestow those blessings on his fellow creatures, as you. The count wants a little of my daughter's simplicity and sensibility." Anhalt replies: "With your permission, Baron, I will ask one question. What remains to interest you in favor of a man, whose head and heart are food for nothing?" "Birth and fortune," the baron replies. Anhalt is left, however, to instruct Amelia for the moment, as the baron and the count prepare to go hunting.

In act 3 the scene shifts to Frederick as he is prepared to beg for his mother's needs. He almost immediately encounters the baron and the count, and approaching the two, he speaks, "Have pity, noble Sir, and relieve the distress of an unfortunate son, who supplicates for his dying mother." The baron gives him a coin, but looking at it Frederick declares, "What you have been so good as to give me is not enough." When the baron refuses to give more, Frederick draws his sword and exclaims, "Your purse, or your life." Calling for help from the gamekeepers in the baron's party, they seize Frederick and take him away to be imprisoned in the castle.

The scene next revealed is a room in the castle where Amelia awaits Anhalt. Amelia and Anhalt greet each other in formal terms, but their conversation becomes personal immediately; it is obvious at once that Anhalt finds it difficult to follow the baron's instruction to explain the marriage state to Amelia, and for her part it is quite clear that she needs no such instruction—it is Anhalt who should be instructed. They discuss the count in an oblique fashion, Anhalt asking if she knows that the count has arrived and for what reason he has come. She knows, and to the second question she says, "He wishes to marry me." In the ensuing discussion about marriage, both Anhalt and Amelia indicate their understanding of love and marriage and of the sentiments of each other. It is a delicate and beautiful scene, showing both truth and beauty, a scene far different from the one in the earlier play *The Child of Nature* when Amanthis instructs her guardian and teacher about love.

Anhalt begins by saying, "I am sent to you to explain the good and the bad of which matrimony is composed." And with her reply, "Then I beg to be acquainted with the good," he describes an ideal relationship:

When two sympathetic hearts meet in the marriage state, matrimony may be called a happy life. When such a wedded pair find thorns in their path, each will be eager, for the sake of the other, to tear them from the root. Where they have to mount hills, or wind a labyrinth, the most experienced will lead the way, and be a guide to his companion. Patience and love will accompany them in their journey, while melancholy and discord they leave far behind.—Hand in hand they pass on from morning till evening, through their summer's day, till the night of age draws on, and the sleep of death overtakes the one. The other, weeping and mourning, yet looks forward to the bright region where he shall meet his still surviving partner, among trees and flowers which themselves have planted, in fields of eternal verdure.

When Amelia says, "You may tell my father—I'll marry," Anhalt insists on giving the "bad of matrimony." He continues:

When convenience, and fair appearance joined to folly and ill-humour, forge the fetters of matrimony, they gall with their weight the married pair. Discontented with each other—at variance in opinions—their mutual aversion increases with the years they live together. They contend most, where they should most unite; torment, where they should most soothe. In this rugged way, choaked with the weeds of suspicion, jealousy, anger, and hatred, they take their daily journey, till one of these *also* sleep in death. The other then lifts up his dejected head, and calls out in acclamations of joy—"Oh, liberty! dear liberty!"

Following this speech, Amelia declares, "I will not marry."

Anhalt: You mean to say, you will not fall in love.
Amelia: Oh no! I am in love.
Anhalt: Are in love! And with the Count?

As Amelia denies she is in love with the count, the dialogue that follows circles the questions of love, teaching, and matrimony, both good and bad. Anhalt begins to understand, but he cannot face the truth about Amelia. She continues, "Come, then, teach it [love] me—teach it me as you taught me geography, languages, and other important things." He turns away, and again she continues, "Ah! you won't—You know you have already taught me that, and you won't begin again." Anhalt replies: "You misconstrue—you misconceive every thing I say or do. The subject I came to you upon was marriage." To which Amelia says, "A very proper subject from the man who has taught me love, and I accept the proposal." Anhalt protests, "Again you misconceive and confound me." At this point Amelia repeats his words, turning his teaching upon itself, as she says,

Ay, I see how it is—You have no inclination to experience with me "the good part of matrimony:" I am not the female with whom you would like to go "hand in hand up hills, and through labyrinths"—with whom you would like to "root up thorns; and with whom you would delight to plant lilies and roses." No, you had rather call out, "Oh, liberty, dear liberty."

Anhalt is very agitated; he replies: "Why do you force from me, what it is villainous to own?—I love you more than life—Oh, Amelia! had we lived in those golden times, which the poets picture, no one but you—But as the world is changed, your birth and fortune make our union impossible—To preserve the character, and more the feelings of an honest man, I would not marry you without the consent of your father—And could I, dare I propose it to him?"

Before their conversation is concluded, the butler bursts in. He has come to tell them about the incident of the encounter between Frederick and the baron, but he is slow and tedious. It is this part that Inchbald transformed into the kind of farcical character her audience expected. Comedies such as this one required some such element. Sometimes it was better than it is here: the butler insists on giving his story in "poetry," composed, as he says, while he was crossing the fields. If this episode breaks the talk of love and matrimony, perhaps it is dramatically acceptable, but it is awkward and silly, a part of the play far inferior to the other stage devices.

At first, when Amelia and Anhalt learn that the baron is safe and the young man imprisoned, she asks, "And the young prisoner, with all his honest looks, is a robber?" Amelia turns to Anhalt and begs him to plead for the young man, but the baron, more interested in the subject he has assigned to Amelia and Anhalt, asks her, "Amelia, have you had any conversation with Mr. Anhalt?" Both Amelia and Anhalt speak in confusing terms, and the scene ends with Amelia going to take food to the prisoner, refusing to take the butler's verses with her.

At the beginning of act 4, the "Lovers' Vows" have not been resolved; acts 4 and 5 are concerned with doing so. In act 4 Frederick confronts the baron, discovering that it is his father whom he has threatened. At the end of the act, Frederick has so accused him of cruelty and deceit to Agatha that the baron is the one suing for mercy. In this act, also, Amelia makes quite clear to her father that she will not marry the count, who leaves declaring, "for me to keep my word to a woman, would be deceit: 'tis not expected of me. It is my character to break oaths in love; as it is in your nature, my Lord, never to have spoken any thing but wisdom and truth." At the moment, however, the baron finds it hard to act with "wisdom and truth."

After the count has left, Amelia and the baron return to discussing the problem of her marriage. If she will not marry the count, and if she must marry, to whom must she be given? Amelia admits that she and her tutor, Anhalt, have discussed the matter and that Anhalt said he would not marry her without her father's consent. When asked how the conversation started, Amelia says, "*I* brought it up," and when her father asks, "And what did you say?" she replies: "I said that birth and fortune were such old fashioned things to me, I cared nothing about either: and that I had once heard my father declare, he should consult my happiness in marrying me, beyond any other consideration." The baron's reply reminds her again that "Lovers' Vows" are not enough: "I will once more repeat to you my sentiments. It is the custom in this country for the children of nobility to marry only with their equals; but as my daughter's content is more dear to me than an ancient custom, I would bestow you on the first man I thought calculated to make you happy; by this I do not mean to say that I should not be severely nice in the character of the man to whom I gave you; and Mr. Anhalt, from his obligations to me, and his high sense of honour, thinks too nobly—." And Amelia herself reports that Anhalt "talked of my rank in life; of my aunts and cousins; of my grandfather, and great-grandfather; of his duty to you; and endeavoured to persuade me to think no more of him."

Before the scene ends, Anhalt enters to conduct Frederick into the baron's presence. It is in this last part of act 4 that Frederick tells his story and that of his mother. At first it is only a story, but then the baron asks, "What is your father's name?" After Frederick replies, "He took advantage of an innocent young woman, gained her affection by flattery and false promises; gave life to an unfortunate being, who was on the point of murdering his father," the baron hears his own name in reply to his question, "Who is he?"

Frederick is especially bold and articulate as he accuses the baron, his father, of seducing his mother, Agatha. "In this house did you rob my mother of her honour; and in this house I am a sacrifice for the crime. I am your prisoner—I will not be free—I am a robber—I give myself up.—You *shall* deliver me into the hands of justice—You shall accompany me to the spot of public execution. You shall hear in vain the chaplain's consolation and injunctions. You shall find how I, in despair, will, to the last moment, call for retribution on my father."

Anhalt appears at this point, and hearing the baron speak to Frederick, "Stop! Be pacified—," Anhalt says, "What do I hear? What is this? Young man, I hope you have not made a second attempt," to which Frederick replies, "Yes; I have done what it was your place to do. I have made a sinner tremble."

Act 5, the last act, returns to the cottage, where we hear again of the goodness of the baron and Pastor Anhalt. The baron has sent Agatha a purse of gold, but she refuses it saying, "Tell him, my honour has never been saleable. Tell him, destitute as I am, even indigence will not tempt me to accept charity from my seducer. He despised my heart—I despise his gold."

The scene shifts to the castle and the baron with Frederick. The baron tells Frederick that he will acknowledge his son and that he will establish Agatha, his mother, in a nearby castle he owns. Such arrangement is totally unacceptable to Frederick, and again he protests, "My Lord, it must be Frederick of Wildenhaim, and Agatha of Wildenhaim—or Agatha Friburg, and Frederick Friburg." The baron is very confused between his "conscience" and himself. When Anhalt reappears, he finds only one way—"conscience"—which leads to marriage.

Anhalt has already brought Agatha to the castle, and the baron agrees to marry her. Anhalt, mindful of the disgrace Agatha has suffered, will not agree to a private ceremony; the village must be witness. When Amelia enters, she is told the news, and, turning to Anhalt, the baron says: "My obligations to you are infinite—Amelia shall pay the debt." With this speech the tableau of the ending is assured, as Frederick and his mother forgive the baron and the baron and Agatha embrace.

The final stage directions read: "[Frederick *throws himself on his knees by the other side of his mother—She clasps him in her arms.* Amelia *is placed on the side of her father attentively viewing* Agatha—Anhalt *stands on the side of* Frederick *with his hands gratefully raised to Heaven.*]—*The curtain slowly drops.*"

Lovers' Vows, like earlier plays, shows unmistakably Inchbald's views of the family—of husbands and wives, sons and lovers, women and their role in making marriage successful. Here also is another extended discussion of love, echoing the passages in *A Simple Story*. Inchbald's version of the play is very different from the translation as Plumptre did it. All the parts in Inchbald's play are fashioned out of her own world, out of the world of her audience. The baron is an Englishman, blunt and direct, seeking to do his duty to his daughter and her future happiness. He is not haughty or severe, although he reminds her—and the audience—that he knows as the father he has the right to arrange her marriage advantageously. He is kind and loving, and he repeatedly tells her that he will not force her to marry a man she does not love.

Both the baron and Amelia agree that the count is not suitable for a husband, that he is vain and silly and not the kind of man to make a good husband. Amelia herself is perhaps the most remarkable character in the play. Inchbald has taken the situation in the original play and made it believable. Amelia is a loving and dutiful daughter, but she is also independent and outspoken. She inquires several times if she may speak her mind—speak the truth as she sees it. She is among the most independent of the "Inchbald women," especially since she is kind and charming. She is gracious to the count and obedient to her father, and when Frederick is a prisoner, she is the one who orders that he be cared for.

In her preface to *The Natural Son,* Plumptre sharply criticizes Inchbald's Amelia, making clear the real difference between the character in her adaptation and Plumptre's translation, in which she wished to show the "Merits of the Author." According to Plumptre, "The Amelia in 'Lovers' Vows,' so far from being the artless, innocent Child of Nature, drawn by Kotzebue, appears a forward Country Hoyden, who deviates in many Instances, from the established Usages of Society, and the Decorums of her Sex, in a Manner wholly unwarranted by the Original. The most amiable traits in her Character are distorted and disguised, by a Pertness which greatly detracts from the Esteem which her benevolent Conduct would inspire."

She continues to make a distinction between the stage and the closet, a distinction perhaps warranted if the reader wished a more careful rendering of the original, for Kotzebue is a romantic and the Plumptre translation is filled with the language of sensibility, especially in the conversation about marriage between Amelia and Anhalt. Plumptre admits, however, that "Perhaps the latter [the pertness] may be better suited to Representation before an English Audience, but in the Closet the Amelia of Kotzebue must excite the stronger Degree of Interest." Just why there would be this "stronger Degree of Interest," Plumptre does not explain. Plumptre's other objection was to the character of the count:

The most essential Deviation respects the important comic Character of the Count von der Mulde, or Cassel, which scarcely possesses a single Feature of the Original. As it stands here, the Reader will observe that it is an exquisitely finished and highly-wrought Portrait of a German Coxcomb. Whether this Character might have been relished by an

English Audience the Translator will not pretend to decide; her own Judgment, however, leads her to think that it would have had much more Effect in its original, than in its altered State. Divested of all its marked Features as a German Coxcomb, particularly of the French Phrases so appropriate to that Character, yet not wholly transformed into an English *Petit Maitre,* we scarcely understand among what Description of Persons he is intended to be classed. The Baron indeed calls him a complete *Monkey,* but the smart Rertartees put into his Mouth, seem wholly inconsistent with the small Talents bespoken by the Appellation.

Plumptre finds the character of Frederick "plain and grave, but elevated." She also finds "Some interesting Scenes and exquisite Touches of Nature omitted."[46]

Anyone reading the two versions—Plumptre's *Natural Son* and Inchbald's *Lovers' Vows*—will find the greatest contrast between the two in the language.[47] Plumptre's is the Language of Sensibility, Inchbald's the Language of Sense.[48] The focus of Inchbald's play is the situation of the family. Both Amelia and Frederick are dutiful children who are far more sensible than their parents. Amelia's insistence to her father, the baron, that neither class nor money is to be the basis of marriage and Frederick's insistence that his father, the baron, must do more than provide physical comfort for his mother, Agatha, place them in the real world, not the world of romance.[49]

Inchbald's *Lovers' Vows* had almost the longest initial run of all of her plays; only *The Midnight Hour,* with its forty-six performances, surpassed the forty-five of *Lovers' Vows,* and the publication of Plumptre's version in the same year suggests that the rage for Kotzebue was dominating the current "charts." Much as certain writers and themes are repeated in the movies in our time, Kotzebue had displaced the French playwrights of Inchbald's work with Le Texier. This time Harris had brought her the play, and the situation was quite different from that of her work with Le Texier. When the time came for him to pay for her work, Harris refused to allow her the same amount as for an original work. He also held over her, perhaps, the threat of claiming the work as his for publication. All the circumstances are not clear, but Boaden remarks that "Harris seems now to have adopted the less liberal style of paying for an altered play differently from an original one. . . . He desired her 'to make a demand for her *trouble:*' but after some chaffering, he unconditionally put the MS. into her hands."[50]

She sold it immediately to Robinson, who published it on December 28. She sold it for 150 pounds, and at the same time Robinson published a fourth edition of *A Simple Story.* She was again successful both professionally and financially.

Always liberal to friends and family, Mrs. Inchbald, as usual, gave presents after the success of *Lovers' Vows,* in a kind of reverse custom from ours. She gave five- and ten-pound notes to her family members and presents to the two Mrs. Shakespears, her landlord's sisters. This year of 1798 had brought a good many changes among her friends. Amelia Alderson had married John Opie in August and had come to live in London. The Kemble family, especially Mrs. Siddons, had been of considerable concern; Mr. Siddons himself came to tell her that he had disengaged Mrs. Siddons from Drury Lane, and on October 7 Maria Siddons, their eldest daughter, died. In the fall the Twiss family, Mrs. Siddons's sister and her children, moved out of town. Twiss had been host to Sunday evening gatherings for many years, but evidently there were financial reasons for leaving the city. Boaden says, "this year [Twiss] experienced some check to his commercial prosperity; and found, in consequence, that it would shortly become necessary to retire into the country, to abridge the expenses which a town life had drawn him into, with his liberal habits and splendid connexions."[51]

Siddons and Kemble had by 1798 come to be very upset with Sheridan, with whom they almost never had agreed about moneys. Kemble as manager did what he could for himself and the other players, but with little success. Sarah's husband, William Siddons, continued to be her agent, as he had been since they came to London in 1783. He never acted on the London stage, and although he was a part of several ventures in theatres, Sarah was the one who supported the family. By 1798, when their daughter Maria died, they had already lost two daughters, both as young children. But for whatever reasons, when William spoke to Inchbald and Inchbald spoke to Harris, nothing came of the conversations, and Mrs. Siddons continued to be at Drury Lane in the winter and in various places in the summer. Her summer money, coming as it did from theatres outside of London, not only amounted to large sums, but also the money was paid to her, in contrast to the situation with Sheridan and Drury Lane.

A letter from Siddons written in 1799 deals with this season of 1797–1798. Addressed to Robert Peake, it lists the last account as Siddons had it. Siddons writes: "My account and yours agree exactly as to the number of nights of last season and to the £970 received from you—but I wish before we start again to have all the accounts drawn upon a sheet of paper, or this filled up will do— signed by Mr. Sheridan and you that we may fairly understand what they are—." The account as he gives it includes, among other things, "Due to her at the end of 97–98, 1307.15.6" and "Interest upon the two notes of 1677.15.6 from March 23 1797 to the same date 1799, somewhere about 167.14.0." He also includes, "Total before last season 1516.9.6" and "Last season deficiency of Salary 610.0.6."[52]

It is interesting to notice that a play in which Mrs. Siddons acted some twenty-six times in 1798 was Kotzebue's *Stranger*. It had been translated by Benjamin Thompson, but Sheridan took Thompson's adaptation and made it his own.[53] The part Siddons played was that of Mrs. Heller, who serves as housekeeper in the castle of Count and Countess Waldbourg. The Waldbourgs discover her story— that she is an aristocrat as are they and that she has deserted her husband and children because she has been seduced by a man she fancied herself in love with. Her husband—"the stranger"—comes to take her back, but at first she refuses, and not until she sees her children is she willing to return to her family.

Mrs. Inchbald's remarks on this play show that she was very aware of the "moral" elements necessary in a successful play:

> There seems to be required by a number of well-meaning persons of the present day a degree of moral perfection in a play, which few literary works attain. . . . In the general failure of human perfection, the German author of this play has compassionated—and with a high, a sublime example before him—an adulteress. But Kotzebue's pity, vitiated by his imperfect nature, has, it is said, deviated into vice; by restoring this woman to her former rank in life, under the roof of her injured husband. To reconcile in the virtuous spectator this indecorum, most calamitous woes are first depicted as the consequence of illicit love. The deserted husband and the guilty wife are both presented to the audience, as voluntary exiles from society: the one through poignant sense of sorrow for the connubial happiness he has lost—the other, from deep contrition for the guilt she has incurred.

Kemble was the injured husband, and Mrs. Inchbald says, "Kemble's emaciated frame, sunken eye, drooping hair, and death-like paleness; his heart-piercing lamentation, that—'he trusted a friend who repaid his hospitality, by alluring from him all that his soul held dear,'—was potent warnings to the modern husband." Inchbald, however, is always the realist. She concludes her essay by asking, "What woman of common understanding and common cowardice, would dare to dishonor and forsake her husband, if she foresaw she was ever likely to live with him again?"[54]

The Stranger was played in the spring of 1798 at Drury Lane; its success perhaps prompted Harris to acquire *Lovers' Vows*, a very different and far more "moral" play, but Inchbald, as always, was aware of the effect of her adaptation on her audience at Covent Garden; thus she made Amelia into a different character from that in Kotzebue's original. About this change she says:

> The part of Amelia has been a very particular object of my solicitude and alteration: the same situations which the author gave her, remain, but almost all the dialogue of the character I have changed: the forward and unequivocal manner, in which she announces her affection to her lover, in the original would have been revolting to an English audience: the passion of love, represented on the stage, is certain to be either insipid or hateful,

unless it creates smiles or tears: Amelia's love, by Kotzebue, is indelicately blunt, and yet, void of mirth or sadness: I have endeavored to attach the attention and sympathy of the audience, by whimsical insinuations, rather than coarse abruptness. She is still the same woman, I conceive, whom the author drew, with the self-same sentiments, but with manners conforming to the English rather than the German taste; and if the favor in which this character is held by the audience, together with every sentence and incident, which I have presumed to introduce in the play, may be offered as the criterion of my skill, I am sufficiently rewarded for the task I have performed.[55]

With the new year of 1799, Harris came with another of Kotzebue's plays; this time Kotzebue had himself sent it to Harris, and it was called *The Writing Desk, or Youth in Danger*. Inchbald began work on it in February, calling it *The Wise Man of the East*. For this task Mrs. Inchbald wrote to Harris: "According to your desire I send you the terms, as fairly as my calculation can make them, on which it will be worth my while to hazard the success of the German play I have been altering; and if there should be any thing in my demand which does not meet with your perfect concurrence, I will most willingly submit to the arbitration of any two persons you and I shall appoint, and suffer that our agreement be regulated by their judgment."[56]

After this introduction she sets out the financial terms:

I ask one hundred pounds on the third, one hundred on the sixth, and one hundred on the ninth night of the representation of the play; making in the whole three hundred pounds. For every night it is played after, during twenty-one nights, which will exactly include the thirtieth, I ask twenty pounds a night.

This will make my demand on the theatre three hundred pounds for the first nine nights, five hundred and twenty on the twentieth night's performance, and seven hundred and twenty pounds should the play be so fortunate as to run thirty nights.[57]

Harris, however, refused her terms, as she wrote to Mrs. Phillips on September 17:

I once more date from home, where I am returned with most grateful remembrance of the hospitality I received at your house; but so long had I been kept from my own lodgings that I was glad to return. The complaint of weakness and excessive pain in my legs is returned, and I now consider it as the effect of sitting fifteen hours a day, for ten weeks past, at the German play of Kotzebue's, in which I have exerted all my strength, both of body and mind. At the end, Mr. Harris has not treated me as I expected. My verbal agreement was, that I should have the same reward as if the piece had been wholly my own; but having *once* sold a play of my own, before it was acted, to him for five hundred pounds, he wished to make that sum the estimate of my present payment. After some contention, I this day gave up my altered manuscript for that price; though had I run the risk I wished to run, the sum in case of success had been *double*.[58]

It is perhaps just as well that Mrs. Inchbald agreed to Harris's terms, for when it was acted on November 30, it was not a success. Boaden thought the "*depravity* of the hero ought to have destroyed it outright." But the day after Mrs. Inchbald spent cutting and altering it, and on December 2 it was accepted. In her letter to Mrs. Phillips, she made a significant statement about her financial matters: "I now have nothing to fear or hope from pecuniary reward for my labour; still, I have anxiety as to discredit; and as I am not in want of money, I had rather have hazarded both together. But where money is the subject, I feel great delicacy, and had rather receive too little than too much: but not any thing can pay me for the loss of health."[59]

She had been very shrewd in her finances, and although she continued to help her family, she did not have as many obligations as she had had formerly. Since the play ran only fourteen nights, she would hardly have had more than five hundred pounds. The other part of her letter to Harris addresses the subject of the copyright: "For the above proposals I reserve to myself the sale of my own altered manuscript; but which manuscript, whatever good success may attend the play, you may purchase of me, at any time previous to the third night, for two hundred pounds; which is the sum I received for 'Lovers Vows,' at the late date of the twenty-third night, when it was first published, and had many original manuscripts published six weeks prior to it to injure the value."[60]

By the middle of December it was published by Robinson.

THE WISE MAN OF THE EAST

The Wise Man of the East is a dark comedy using many of the situations popular in the theatre; disguise, poverty, unexpected returns of persons thought dead, unexpected fortune. It is the story of a young man, Claransforth, who, thinking his father has died in India, leaving him a fortune, is determined to spend money as he pleases. Bankwell, his father's longtime friend and financial adviser, has attempted to advise him, but to no avail, and his request asking him to help his father's old friend, Metland, is also denied. Claransforth, however, is a young man rather uncertain of his place in London, for he had been abroad before he learned about his father. As the play opens, Claransforth has been introduced to a "Wise Man from the East," who has known his father. The Wise Man, "Ava Thoanoa," claims to know all about Claransforth and his lifestyle—about his gaming at Lady

Mary Diamond's pharo table and about his designs on Ellen Metland, who is Metland's daughter and Lady Mary's waiting maid.

At first Claransforth is very skeptical, but as the "Wise Man" talks of his father and reveals his father's last testament, spoken to his mother, Claransforth begins to believe, only to protest as he says to Ava, "No—no . . . I won't believe it.— . . . you have only dreamt a dream, that has by chance revealed." Scene 2 is in a room in Metland's house, where Mrs. Metland is alone knitting when her son Ensign Metland enters; he has brought her half his pay. The Metlands are desperately poor, and the son's half pay and a bit of money Ellen can save are their only means of subsistence. Brother and sister are happy to see each other, though publicly, as we discover, Ellen as a maid does not acknowledge her brother lest she embarrass him and her family; indeed, their father Metland does not know that the brother and sister give their mother money. Their mother cautions them: "But I entreat you both not to make known to your father the assistance you give us. His mistaken pride wou'd rather let him perish than live on your bounty." Metland enters as she speaks.

The "Metland" story must have been of interest to Inchbald's audience. By 1799 there were many of the rising middle class, the "middling" class, who shared some if not all of his story. His character and actions to and about his family also bring up a significant number of questions. As he enters, he greets his son and daughter, asking "How do you do?" Ellen says, "Very well, dear father," but his son replies, "Tolerable. . . . You know, Sir, that I want—" Before he can finish his sentence, his father speaks, "A good and courageous heart is all that a soldier wants; and that I am sure you possess."

> *Ensign:* It is my paternal inheritance.
> *Metland:* If that is true, you are a rich heir, although my purse is empty, and these walls almost bare.
> *Ensign:* But—inconveniences at your time of life.
> *Metland:* What do you call inconveniences? Those who can supply their wants are well supported.
> *Ensign:* Can you do that?

Metland's reply to this question is significant for his character: "Oh yes, for I am content.—Do you think your mother and I go fasting to bed? No—no—What my industry daily produces, her dear hands daily prepare; and our homely fare is made delicious by her constant cheerfulness and serenity. If ever you perceive tears in her eyes, the smoke of the kitchen fire is the cause of them."

The dialogue that follows this speech reveals even more of the situation, as his wife remarks, "Yes, my dear husband, I should be contented, quite satisfied, if only—." He interrupts: "No one lives whose contentment is not, at times crossed by an 'if only.' Let us hear the tendency of your 'if only.'" She replies, "If only— Ellen were not obliged to be a servant."

Again, his speech reveals his character and the servitude of his wife and children as they continue to listen to him without protest. Metland: "And what is her servitude? Your daughter is a waiting-maid, and obliged to humour the whims and caprices of another woman, which prevents her having leisure to indulge her own."

Metland has brought home a "large heap of papers," and when Mrs. Metland remarks upon it, he replies: "Yes; heaven be thanked! there is work for a whole month; and 'if only'—There, now, I have caught myself at an 'if only.'" With Mrs. Metland's "Explain it—instruct its meaning to your family," he replies: "I was going to say, 'if only' my debts were paid—then anxiety would not alone be cast from my heart, but, what would please me much more, from the hearts of my creditors."

Mrs. Metland speaks to their present situation. They are poor, but through work and thrift they amassed quite a small fortune, which was put in the hands of the merchant Claransforth the very night Claransforth's house burned. Now they have nothing.

The scene in the family's home with mother and father, son and daughter, underscores Metland's ruin. The two women—Mrs. Metland and Ellen—suffer the most, Ellen because she must be a servant and her mother because she chooses to protect her husband's false pride. When her father asks Ellen what time she goes to bed, she hesitates to tell him the exact time. It is obvious that she fears he will find out that she participates with Lady Mary in her "pharo scheme," and when her mother declares her a good girl, Metland says, "I take her to be such, or she would have no business here, though she is my daughter."

As he reveals himself, he shows his character as rigid, though honest, and traditional without any thought of an alternative lifestyle. His son, the ensign, is proper. His wife and his daughter, the women in his world, must conform to his expectation, must be judged by his rules. After Ellen and her mother leave, Metland says to his son:

Charles, I have spoken something warmer to your sister than I intended. I did not mean to make her weep, especially as she comes so seldom to see us. Follow her, Charles, and your mother, and say I was a little hasty. Go—it does not become me to own myself to blame. But invite Ellen to stay, and take some dinner with us, and I'll come in by the time you are all sat down. You know, Charles, I am often harsh with you; and yet I love you.— You know I am sometimes even severe with your mother; yet, heaven is my witness! this world would be nothing to me without her mild society.—You know my temper, Charles—you know, too, that irritable temper has met with some sharp trials.

If Metland is too realistic to be pitied, he is too genuine to be dismissed lightly. A scene such as this one about the family may be placed in the current literary fashion. Wordsworth and Coleridge had published their *Lyrical Ballads* in 1798, and in them the public had read of ordinary characters, characters that played an important part in the content and view of the poets. Metland, a ruined business man, could perhaps be forgiven for an "irritable temper." And although his is the life of toil in the city, he and his situation are somewhat like Wordsworth's view

> that pride is littleness. . . . True dignity abides with him alone
> Who in the silent hour of inward thought,
> Can still suspect, and still revere himself,
> In lowliness of heart.[61]

Metland had little "lowliness of heart."

Act 2 is set in the household of the Starch family: Rachel Starch, her husband Timothy, and their daughter, Ruth. We discover immediately from their speech that they are Quakers. From the conversation we also learn that they are worldly and scheming. The opening dialogue reads:

> *Rachel:* Timothy, Timothy, I say unto thee, that Claransforth, the merchant, is the man whom I have chosen, from amongst all other of her suitors, to be the spouse of thy daughter Ruth.
> *Timothy:* What will our elders say to such a marriage? For neighbour Claransforth is not one of the faithful.
> *Rachel:* But he is one of the rich.
> *Timothy:* It is asked by pious speakers, "Of what value are riches?"
> *Rachel:* And it is answered by other pious speakers, "Of a great deal."— How can a man give to the poor, while he is poor himself?
> *Timothy:* Thou art right. What can a man give who possesseth nothing? What produceth alms but money?—Verily, what doth money not produce? And, that my daughter shall be wedded to a rich husband, maketh me content.

The daughter, Ruth, is not so sure that Claransforth will suit her. Like her father, she is devoid of any emotion; indeed, her father says: "And it is a precept thou art bound to follow, in imitation of thy father, who has never, since he came to man's estate, suffered himself to feel either joy or sadness, grief or merriment;

but has passed his life in an uniform dullness, and insensibility to all around.—And I am thankful that it is so; for, though I never felt love, I have likewise never known hate. Though I am steeled to pity, I am also proof against anger: and I never in my life did any harm, though I never did any good."

Ruth says of her father, "Verily, to the cold of which my father is composed; for I liken him unto a *snow-ball,* and myself unto a *snow-drop.*" Her mother will not be silenced as she continues to speak on the subject of marriage, but before she can get an answer from Ruth, a servant appears with a letter. Addressed to Ruth, it proves to be from Ensign Metland, who immediately follows. His conversation with the father, the mother, and Ruth is more "wit" than "sense," and when Rachel dismisses him, the scene ends; its only value lies in the comments the Quakers make to each other and the knowledge that Ensign Metland and Ruth are perhaps something more than acquaintances.

In scene 2 of this second act, we are in a room at Lady Mary Diamond's. Claransforth has come hoping to see Ellen; she enters, and in the dialogue that follows, he tells her that she is the only reason he comes to Lady Mary's establishment, that the cards and dice are not the true attraction. She is very upset and protests that his conversation about her—a servant—degrades him; he replies: "Why not be the mistress of me, and of all that is mine? . . . Why these doubts and suspicious of a man who loves you?" Ellen is used throughout the play as an example of a dutiful daughter and an ideal young woman. Claransforth's suggestion that she become his mistress frightens her; "You have no mercy, no pity for me,—and you change my love to hate." Both Ellen and Claransforth exit, and then Ellen reenters with Lady Mary.

Her situation is made worse as Lady Mary explains quite directly that Ellen is her employee to be used to entice the men to her table—"Why do you think I suffered you to ride by my side through London streets, but that you might be followed by unthinking fools, who enrich our pharo-bank?—You are the allurement of half those madmen who lose to me their fortune." Claransforth is the richest and least suspicious, she says, and Ellen, replying, reveals that he has tried to seduce her. Lady Mary thinks this all the better, and she gives Ellen the means to make him poor—"poor as you are." Without his fortune, "reduced to poverty, he will offer you his hand in marriage." Ellen, caught in this whole scheme of evil as she is, refuses to follow Lady Mary's scheme. Lady Mary, furious because Ellen refuses, threatens her. If she will not entice him to the table that night, Lady Mary declares, "I will send you home to your parents, as unworthy of staying a moment longer in my family—as one devoted to Claransforth: and the very degradation which you dread shall be the stigma with which I will return you to your parents."

Left alone, Ellen reviews her options. She is more appalled with Lady Mary's wicked scheme to ruin Claransforth than she is with the danger to herself. She considers sending him a letter, only to think he might consider it to be "some new artifice . . . to draw him back to me.—Unprincipled as he is himself, he is wholly unsuspecting of the wicked gamesters who visit this house." She finds that Lady Mary has given her loaded dice and a signed paper plotting Claransforth's destruction. She decides to take the proof to him and "with my own hands safely place them in his—then, bid him farewell for ever."

At this point in the play we have three situations set up—Claransforth; Ellen and her brother, the ensign; and the poverty and distress of Metland. At the end of the second act, we have been told about these situations; we have had only a very little action. It is as if Inchbald has anticipated Ibsen when it was reported that he said, "I ask the questions I do not answer them." Acts 3 and 4 then can almost stand alone as a two-act melodrama. At the beginning of act 3, Ava is again predicting Claransforth's future; as Ava leaves, Ellen enters and seems to fulfill the prophecy that Ava has predicted of Claransforth's finding a pretty young woman. As Ellen enters, she hands Claransforth the paper revealing the scheme against him. He calls her "Dear lovely being—My guardian angel!" He seems not to understand that by giving him the papers she can no longer return to Lady Mary and that if he will take her to her father's, she will "plead my own cause to my dear parents—tell them I have only done my duty to you; then promise them faithfully never to see you more."

Ellen does not want to be identified, and he does not know her name or where she lives; Claransforth goes for a hackney coach and in her hearing tells the coachman to go to the "City-road" but whispers to him to go to the "corner house" instead—a house of ill-repute. Ellen, leaving, exclaims, "You are very good, I thank you for your trouble. Oh! that my parents may receive me kindly." That her parents, her father, might not "receive" her "kindly" reintroduces the family and the interaction of parents and children, of parents and their attitude, of the outside world and the dilemma of the children and parents, of obeying and commanding, creating the situation of how love and honor on the part of a child can be destroyed. Ellen, faced with the choices she must make, has been caught and sees no way to escape. Claransforth's duplicity is criminal, for he has directed the coachman to go to a brothel, where he intends to follow and to have her on his own terms. When the coachman leaves her, she realizes the situation and flees. As she is leaving, Claransforth speaks: "[*Aside, as he leads her off.*] Oh, passion! passion! what a fiend art thou!—While I practice cruelty, my heart is torn with pity."

Scene 2 returns to Metland's house, where a clerk appears with a letter informing Metland that his creditors are about to come to seize his goods—a warning that includes the proviso that he will have the night in which to remove his furniture. Mrs. Metland enters to hear him declare that in a few minutes they will have nothing left; they will have to sleep on straw. When Lawley, the clerk, comes to check their possessions and asks Metland to identify his papers, Metland explains that the writing desk once belonged to Claransforth, the late Claransforth, and that after his death his old clerk, Bankwell, gave it to him. Metland hands over the key; Lawley opens the desk and finds a secret drawer filled with banknotes. The find is astonishing—the money is Metland's twelve thousand pounds that he carried to Claransforth on the evening before he died. But Metland is not ready to claim the money without the consent of young Claransforth, even though Lawley warns him that young Claransforth is unthinking and dissipated. The scene is not over; at this moment Lady Mary appears to tell them that since Ellen is not at home, "where I did hope, (though I must own I feared I should not find her), confirms me that she is—" Mrs. Metland: "Not dead?" Metland: "Not worse than dead?"

Lady Mary's explanation is in fact an accusation of Ellen, an explanation that leaves herself blameless but makes it seem that Ellen has indeed "fallen." Lady Mary refuses to name Claransforth as the lover, fearing, she says, that Metland and he would fight a duel and one or both be killed. The scene ends with Metland saying, "Our daughter is gone for ever—and all the gold and gems contained in the whole world, would not repay us for her loss."

Act 4 returns us for the first time to the lodgings of Ava Thoanoa—actually the elder Claransforth, whose disguise we know but the younger Claransforth, Ellen's would-be seducer, does not. In a repeat of the story about Ellen's warning and his dastardly behavior, Ava questions Claransforth carefully. In the retelling, Claransforth admits his actions and tells Ava that Ellen is not just another pretty girl: "I have a thousand—but they are none of them to compare with her I have lost."

Turning to Ruth and Ensign Metland, we pick up their story. The ensign begins: "At length I have watched your father and mother from the house.—And now, Ruth answer me—Is the report true of their intention to marry you to Mr. Claransforth?" Ruth replies: "It is their intention, but not my will." As they speak, Claransforth enters, and Metland retreats to another room. The dialogue between Claransforth and Ruth hardly moves the action along, but it does make points about love and marriage, about children and parents, about true feeling and pretense. And again we have a discussion of love—a far different discussion from that in *Lovers' Vows* or *A Simple Story*.

He presses her hand; she calls it an impertinence and wishes her parents were present to tell him so. He declares, "Impertinence!—Why, that's my love, my adoration of you." To which she replies, "Why dost thou come to me, neighbour, to make professions of thy affection? For thou dost not love me, I can perceive by thy vacant eye, thy absent thought, and careless manners.—Verily, these are no arguments of the lover." Claransforth, mocking her language: "'Verily,' what maketh thee such a connoisseur in judging of love?" But Ruth will not retreat, "Verily, from the first dawn of my understanding, I have had an ear for music, an eye for painting, a taste for poetry, and a heart for love."

As they speak, her mother, Rachel, enters. The dialogue between her and Claransforth makes clear that the parents want his money and will do anything they can to force him into a marriage contract. Claransforth, determined he will not agree to any such union, is interrupted by Metland, who enters and declares: "Hold, Sir!—make no rash promises. That young woman has suffered no disappointment on your account; but she is constrained to silence.—Nor had she ever a man of fortune for her suitor.—I am her only lover; and I am not worth a guinea.—Ruth! do you love this gentleman?" She replies with an emphatic "No."

In performance the various scenes move rapidly, with Claransforth as the center keeping the conversation about the young couples moving forward and the question of money and the parents a part of the drama. In the end, as no doubt the audience expected, Ava turns out to be the elder Claransforth, and the young couples are united. Metland is convinced that the money is his own when Ava reveals himself, and Ellen and the young Claransforth are united as he says to her family, "I will deserve to be related to this family, whose virtues I have proved." And immediately when the Starch family—Rachel, Ruth, and Timothy—appear, Claransforth the elder, in the role of the "Wise Man of the East," declares, "I am permitted to revisit this world, to dispose of my riches worthily; and I mean to give this young Ensign a fortune, in addition to that which his father will give him." Timothy, turning to his daughter, says, "But, Ruth, what say'st thou to this man?" and is answered, "Verily, I should like to become unto this man such as my mother became unto thee." Timothy replies: "Then, take her, young man.—But I say unto thee, love her only with that discreet love with which I have lov'd her mother—and which made me content to marry her, and would have made me equally content if I had not," a reply that makes yet another comment about parents, children, and marriage. The play ends with a set speech by Claransforth the elder: "What various manners and passions have I witnessed since my disguise gave me the power of judgment on the failings of my neighbours!—I now, in my turn, am to be judged;—and, in order to support the title of a Wise Man, I most humbly submit my character to the approbation, or censure, of—Wiser Heads than my own."

Inchbald was disappointed with the reception of *Wise Man of the East*, since she had spent an inordinate amount of time working on it. The epilogue, written by her friend John Taylor, is spoken by Ruth, the Quaker, and is a comment on both marriage and the Quakers, making a final statement for the young couples:

> Friends, peradventure, ye may deem it strange,
> That, from my peaceful sect, I thus should range,
> And chuse to join in wedlock, undismay'd,
> A suitor in terrific red array'd.
> But, verily, my feelings to confess,
> I trust when marry'd he'll put off that dress.
> And when my loving helpmate shall require,
> I, too, perchance, may cast off this attire.

As a Quaker she continues to say she will accept the fact that he is a soldier:

> And tho' in marriage he should hold a truce,
> And turn his sword to some domestic use,
> Yet since his purpose with my doctrines suits,
> I e'en may give him leave to raise recruits.

Remembering the great success of *Lovers' Vows*, it is not surprising that Inchbald was disappointed, but *Wise Man* is really a very different play, a complex study of situations not usually combined, and although it has the kind of stage situations that keep an audience interested, the supposition that all the various moral and social questions it poses can be worked out in so brief a time is a challenge both for the audience and the players. It is in some ways a play to be read and considered, not merely seen for one performance on the stage. The questions it poses make up a list of social questions that were in 1799 becoming more and more relevant to the middle class, the patrons of the theatre.

The 1790s had been a turbulent time in England as well as in France, and the questions raised in *Wise Man* were no doubt seen as yet another discussion in the closing months of the century. Thomas Paine had published his *Age of Reason* in 1794–1795, Burke his *Reflections on the Revolution in France* in 1790, and Godwin his *Political Justice* in 1793. There had been severe food shortages in 1795 and in 1797. The Bank of England suspended payment. And in 1798 the Irish Rebellion brought added tension to an already disturbed society. In 1799, the year of Inchbald's *Wise Man,* Sheridan's *Pizarro,* another adaptation of a Kotzebue play, was very successful, but *Pizarro* raised no such domestic questions as those in *Wise Man.*

The years around the turn of the century were rather unsettled ones for Inchbald. In the late summer of 1799, she visited her friend Mrs. Phillips in Barton, and writing to her upon returning to London, she thanked her for the hospitality and reported that the manuscript for *Wise Man of the East* had been delivered to Harris. Her complaint about her long hours of work was underscored even more when the play was read for the first time on September 25, for it was postponed to make way for Reynolds's play *Management* and did not appear until November 30. To add another footnote to her work on this play, although it was not successful on the opening night, she immediately began cutting and altering it, so that when it was played again on December 2, it was quite successful. It was not repeated as many times as she had hoped, however, thus adding less to her funds.

Since Twiss had moved his family to the country in April of this year, the "Sundays" there were no more. With the departure of the Twiss family and the end of their hospitality, Mrs. Inchbald turned more and more to the Phillipses, who welcomed her as a part of their family circle. She continued to go to her friend Lady Milner's parties, and she occasionally attended the parties assembled by Samuel Rogers, the poet, in his chambers in the Temple. She went to the Opies' to see her friend Amelia, who held open house while her husband painted; there Inchbald met the Fuselis; it is tempting to speculate about whether Fuseli and she spoke of Godwin and his "dinner."

In the spring Mrs. Inchbald had written Mrs. Phillips a letter in which she made arrangements about her sister, who was ill in Barton, near the Phillipses. Her comments are revealing both about the care of her sister and her continuing responsibility for all the members of her family:

I am more apt than most people to start at expense, but believe me 'tis only when I witness expenses that are superfluous. Upon an occasion like the present, with you for the manager of my purse, I shall consider every farthing expended as indispensably necessary, and from my heart rejoice that I have earned and saved a little money for so good a purpose.

I have no one direction to give you, because you perfectly understand my wishes— every thing requisite to the comfort and decency of her and those about her, and nothing further. I will add, it would be more satisfactory if the weekly expenses, after you come away, could be ascertained; and that no bill of any kind should be run on her account, an immediate demand sent to me, or an immediate statement of any thing taken up on an emergency. . . . Whatever money is weekly wanted shall be most punctually sent.[62]

At Christmas she gave her sisters—Dolly and Mrs. Hunt—ten pounds each, having already paid Dolly's medical bills. During the year she helped Mrs. George Inchbald, her stepson's wife, obtain a place in Collins's company at Portsmouth. George Inchbald had married Sarah Riely in 1792 while they were acting in the provinces. She was the widow of another provincial actor; her mother and father were Isabella and Bredge Frodsham, two of Wilkinson's favorite performers. Sarah herself became a member of the company at York and played subsequently in Norwich, Dublin, and Cork, and in 1783 she came to the Haymarket. In the 1785–1786 season, she frequently played the role of Bloom in Inchbald's *I'll Tell You What*. George Inchbald died on October 28, 1800, and left her a widow again.

In this year Inchbald's landlord, Mr. Shakespear, had the good fortune to inherit a considerable sum from a cousin, whereupon he gave up the house on Leicester Square to a Mr. Brookes, who with his new wife had lived there since Christmas 1799. When Mr. Shakespear left, the Brookeses took the lease, and Mrs. Inchbald and Mrs. Brookes shared a maid between them. General Martin, who had lived in the house since before Inchbald moved there, gave up his apartments and went to live at his country house, where he died, and in the first week of May, Mrs. Inchbald, writing to Mrs. Phillips, reported: "I have passed a most melancholy week, and have sustained a great loss in the death of General Martin. He was a very polite man, and had every requisite to render my abode here perfectly comfortable: and most of all, his extreme parsimony made every creature in this house look up to me, (with all my economy,) as the most munificent of human beings."[63]

Inchbald continues to point out that Martin left his poor housekeeper nothing after she had served him virtually as a slave for twenty years, and therefore upon his death, she, at seventy-six, was obliged to go to the workhouse. General Martin never married, but he had the reputation of having "a greater number" of the women on the town "than ever any one man did." His mistress, "whom he seduced many years ago, and visited to his death, and whom, while living, he allowed seven shillings a week, (the ancient board wages,) he has left without a farthing." This combination of Inchbald's awareness of her own "economy" and his "avarice beyond the grave," as she calls it, is evidence, if need be, which speaks of both her generosity and her practice of carefully managing her funds.[64]

During the illness of her stepson George Inchbald, she gave money for his care several times; Mr. Morrell, her former landlord on Hart Street, came to beg "a few shillings," and she sent John O'Keeffe a guinea by Thomas Morton. By this time O'Keeffe was dependent on friends, for although his plays were presented in the theatres, he was blind and destitute; Morton, his friend, helped make his plight somewhat easier than when O'Keeffe worked alone.[65]

In one of her letters to Mrs. Phillips, Inchbald reported that she had gone to see Joanna Baillie's *De Monfort* on its opening night. She found the play "both dull and highly improbable in the representation; and sure it is, though pity that it is so, its very charm in the reading militates against its power in the acting."[66]

The play was a tragedy, one of the series on the passions, and in her *Remarks* about it for *The British Theatre*, Inchbald writes chiefly about Baillie herself: "Amongst the many female writers of this and other nations, how few have arrived at the elevated character of a woman of genius! The authoress of 'De Monfort' received that rare distinction, upon this her first publication." Leaving aside the fact that Inchbald's definition of the author as a "genius" may be her own, she is quite complimentary about the play itself. "There was genius in the novelty of her conception, in the strength of her execution; and though her play falls short of dramatic excellence, it will ever be rated as a work of genius."

Inchbald felt that Baillie's play was better as a closet drama than a stage one. In fact, she felt that staging the passions was very difficult, that "Authors may think too profoundly, as well as too superficially—and if a dramatic author, with the most accurate knowledge of the heart of man, probe it too far, the smaller, more curious, and new created passions, which he may find there, will be too delicate for the observation of those who hear and see in a mixed, and, sometimes riotous, company." Moreover, she felt that "This drama, of original and very peculiar formation, plainly denotes that the authoress has studied theatrical productions as a reader more than as a spectator; and it may be necessary to remind her—that Shakespeare gained his knowledge of the effect produced from plays upon an audience, and profited, through such attainment, by his constant attendance on dramatic representations, even with the assiduity of a performer."

Inchbald was always, both inside the theatre and out, aware of the stage; it was the most important factor in the success or failure of a drama, no matter what judgment might be made of it in the closet. It is this constant attitude toward theatre that sets her apart from many of her friends and contemporaries who thought themselves deserving of seeing their work presented at Drury Lane or Covent Garden and could not understand why they were not accepted or why, when they had a play accepted, it failed by the disapprobation of the audience.

ELEVEN

A NEW CENTURY

❧ The year 1801 was a kind of sabbatical for Mrs. Inchbald: she spent much time in visiting, she walked in the enclosed part of the garden that belonged to Leicester House, she played with her landlord's baby, and she attended the theatre. She had no new play presented during the year, and her suggestion to translate one Harris turned down. Her domestic life had its problems; the maid she shared with Mrs. Brookes was withdrawn, since Mrs. Brookes needed her full time. Mrs. Inchbald attempted to use her sister Dolly for help, but Dolly refused, and Inchbald was left to perform her own domestic chores. When her former maid became ill, it was Mrs. Inchbald, not Mrs. Brookes, who fetched the doctor, who sat up at night with her, and who provided Mrs. Pearce, General Martin's former housekeeper, to nurse her.

Inchbald's family and friends continued to depend on her care and generosity: her sister Hunt had an abscessed arm; her brother Edward, who lived in Barton, wrote to tell her about the death of his wife. In June her special friend and publisher George Robinson died suddenly. In August his brother, John Robinson, came to present her a mourning ring to be worn in remembrance. It is unlikely that she would ever forget Robinson. They had gone together on many excursions and had frequently visited with friends in the circle we have called the Robinson circle. He had always promoted her business interests and had, in fact, recently repurchased her two novels for six hundred pounds and the extended copyright.

Robinson had been not only her publisher; he had published work for most of her friends in the theatre as well. He had actually supported Godwin while he wrote *Political Justice*; no one else would have permitted Godwin to proceed as he did and then risk the publication of a book he knew would be censured by the government.

By 1801 Inchbald knew a great many of the "society" people in London, especially those who attended the theatres; and although she continued to present her plays at Covent Garden—indeed, by now she was virtually a playwright in residence there—she also knew and attended Drury Lane. She knew about Kemble and Sheridan, about Sarah Siddons and Mr. Siddons, who managed his wife's contracts, and about the deplorable financial state of Drury Lane. By this time Sheridan had almost completely stopped paying any of the expenses of the theatre to the actors and actresses, or the whole body of stage people, dressers, money takers, or indeed any of the people necessary to keep Drury Lane open. Like everyone else, however, Inchbald was reluctant to make judgments about Sheridan, for, like everyone else, she very much admired him.

It was also during these early years of the 1800s that she went with the Kembles to various places and social events; she went to their country house, they took her to a masquerade, and she was with them at a dinner at Sheridan's with the marquis of Lorn, Sir Francis Burdett, and others. Boaden, recording the names of those who entertained her, remarks that these years were "the years of visits." Reading this part of the *Memoirs* reminds us that by this time the theatre and the players had become integrated into the social fabric of London. There Jordan had represented a kind of amalgamation of theatre and society, of theatre and government. Sheridan was still an important figure in the government, and Mrs. Inchbald's friend Sir Charles was still in Parliament. Within a decade, however, there were to be great changes in the theatre, in government, and in Inchbald's personal and domestic life.

For all the active social life Inchbald enjoyed, she continued to be concerned with her profession and with writing. She reported that "The beautiful play of 'Deaf and Dumb,' just performed with universal admiration at Drury Lane, was sent a few months ago to me in French as performed in Paris. I was struck with the novelty and beauty of the story, and more particularly with the exquisite taste with which it was simply and pointedly told. I was charmed to have my author in a language I could read, instead of being in the dress of a miserable translator, as my *German* plays had been." She went to Harris, but she says, "he, who is for ever tormenting me to write or translate for him, positively refused 'Deaf and Dumb,' as a play that must infallibly be condemned." Her friend Le Texier also "gave it as his decided opinion it would not be suffered by an English audience." Her next comments are revealing of her relationship with Harris, "I argued, I contended, I scolded, I stampt; I almost tore my hair to convince them. All in vain, Mr. Harris *'dared not venture it.'*" And then it proved to be a great success at Drury Lane. She probably exaggerated when she declared, "he [the author, Herbert Hill] will get a thousand pounds, and the managers ten thousand by it. Mr. Harris is ready to shoot himself, and I am too unhappy to write another word."[1]

Boaden, making comments about this letter, reveals an interesting situation when he suggests that the author was Holcroft, not Hill, and that he begged in vain for fifty pounds. John Doran in his book *"Their Majesties' Servants": Annals of the English Stage*, in fact, lists it as Holcroft's in the new plays at Drury Lane for 1801, along with only two other new plays of the season. John Kemble, Charles Kemble, Miss DeCamp, and Miss Pope played in it, and the success was assured. Harris, having missed the opportunity of presenting it, did not "shoot" himself, but he must have regretted his decision.

While Inchbald was seeing such people as the countess of Cork and Orrey, she received an invitation from the Pic-Nics.[2] She did not attend one of their performances, for, she said, "The acting would tire me to death, and the hour of returning home totally disqualify me for the next day." Her letter continues with a discussion of her own involvement with an amateur theatrical group. Her report is very revealing of the rage for private theatre that was sweeping the country:

To my extreme sorrow I am at present under the dread of being a party in a private theatrical myself. I was surprised into a promise, and now go every morning to attend rehearsals; still I foresee many impediments, which I will as far as in my power increase. One is, the drama on which they have fixed has a supper in it, and I have represented that the hurry of clearing away the table, which is a part of the comic incidents of the piece, will probably break the wine bottles and throw the hot dishes against the beautiful hangings and furniture of the room. This observation gave Mr. Monk Lewis, M.P., (who is one of the performers,) an opportunity of saying an excellent thing to the lady of the house, who, alarmed at my remark, immediately cried out she would not have a *real* supper, but that every thing should be *counterfeit*. On which she rang for her butler, and ordered him to go and bespeak a couple of wooden fowls, a wooden tongue, wooden jellies, and so forth. "Nay," cried Monk Lewis, "if your ladyship gives a wooden supper, the audience will say all your actors are STICKS."

It was not less entertaining to see the surprise of the butler or house-steward (a good-looking grave elderly man). He knew there was a supper to be given to the company after the play; and not knowing there was a supper to be *in* the play, he was confounded at the orders given him, said he would see them executed as far as in his power, but with great humility represented, that, "he thought the company would like a *real* supper better."[3]

By the early 1800s the debate about private theatricals had become an ongoing protest by those who would regulate morals and manners, especially the morals of young women—indeed of all women. The Reverend Plumtre, in his instructions for young ladies, *On Amusements in General*, writes:

For some years past the custom of acting in private theatres, fitted up by individuals of fortune, has occasionally prevailed. It is a custom liable to this objection among others: that it is almost certain to prove, in its effects, injurious to the female performers. Let it be admitted, that theatres of this description no longer present the flagrant impropriety of ladies bearing a part in the drama in conjunction with professed players. Let it be admitted that the drama selected will be in its language not always reprehensible. Let it even be admitted, that eminent theatrical talents will not hereafter gain admission upon such a stage for men of ambiguous, or worse than ambiguous, character. Take the benefit of all these favorable circumstances; yet what is even then the tendency of such amusements? To encourage vanity; to excite a thirst of applause and admiration on account of the attainments which, if they are to be thus exhibited, it would commonly have been far better for the individual not to possess; to destroy diffidence, by the unrestrained familiarity with persons of the other sex, which inevitably results from being joined with them in the drama; to create a general fondness for the perusal of plays, of which so many are unfit to be read; and for attending dramatic representations of which as many are unfit to be witnessed.[4]

The Reverend Plumtre was not the only one to make comments on private theatricals; there were those who saw private theatricals as the extravagance of the rich and those like Gillray, who satirized them in his print *Dilettanti Theatricals, or a peep at the Green Room*, which "has a wealth of allusion which apes the cultural pretensions of its aristocratic subjects." As one commentary pointed out, "the jarring inappropriateness of the players to their chosen roles—in physique and social class, ability and gender—symbolizes a false and vulgar taste which is a function of their decadence."[5]

Mrs. Inchbald's assignment was certainly not of such magnitude as to threaten the morals of any of the young ladies of her acquaintance, and no doubt she pleased her friends, for she does not mention her own earlier play that General Conway—and Walpole—claimed.

In another letter of this summer, she tells her friend Mrs. Phillips of a far more disappointing event:

The dramatic mortification I have sustained is merely a passing grief, though a renewal of it is likely in the winter. Mr. Harris engaged me to translate a little three-act serious drama (M. Caigniez' 'Jugement de Solomon'): I sat up, after all my work was over in the day, and did it in the nights of Easter week. Accident (after all the haste I had made) made it almost necessary to defer the representation till next winter; but lest the Haymarket theatre should procure another translation in the time, Mr. Harris had a promise from Mr. Colman he would accept of none; and on those terms only Mr. Harris deferred performing mine. Another was offered Mr. Colman, and Mr. Harris was *prevailed* on to consent to its being acted; resolving to bring mine out all the same, in which I have to contend with a first impression, and a plot already discovered.[6]

Inchbald's letter gives only one side of what happened, for thirty years later,

Boaden, writing and arranging the *Memoirs*, tells his side of the story; he was the one who translated the piece and persuaded Harris to agree to Colman's request to present it. Boaden's account is worth quoting:

What Mrs. Inchbald alludes to was this:—Perfectly unconscious that she had translated the 'Jugement de Solomon' of M. Caigniez, Mr. Boaden had rendered it, with alterations, suitable to the English Stage, and offered 'The Voice of Nature' to his friend Colman
for the summer season. To his great surprise, that gentleman told him that he would act it
with much pleasure, *but* that Mr. Harris having had it done for Covent Garden, and not
being able to produce it last winter, he had engaged Mr. Colman by promise not to fore-
stall him, by letting it appear at the Haymarket, before the next winter season of Covent
Garden. Mr. Boaden, who had worked for Mr. Harris with success, went to him on the
business, and represented the hardship of authors in being left only a *single* market, by this
compact between managers; and that it was doubly hard to be denied a small summer
pavilion, when they were not permitted to occupy the winter palaces. Harris, one of the
best men we have ever known, said that he had "*paid* his author unfortunately; however, he
had no right to turn Mr. Boaden's cart out of the *Hay*-market; and therefore he had no
objection to release Colman from his promise; provided the author would consent not to
print his piece till the rival play had been acted." Mr. Boaden consented: 'The Voice of
Nature' was eminently successful.[7]

Boaden continues the report of what happened: "The following season, when Mrs. Inchbald's version was called into preparation, the *company* decided against it, on several grounds, and it was given up; which Mr. Harris immediately notified to the *fortunate* author, who then printed his play."[8] Boaden was not always so fortunate. Doran in his *"Their Majesties' Servants"* tells the story of Boaden's *Aurelio and Miranda*. It seems that when Boaden was reading his play to the actors, he "re-marked that he knew nothing so terrible as having to read it before so critical an audience. 'Oh, yes!' exclaimed Mrs. Powell, 'there is something much more terrible.' What can that be Boaden foolishly asked. 'To be obliged to sit and hear it.'"[9]

The author who printed his play was Boaden himself, a fact that adds an-other comment about playwrights and their profession and, in this case, a com-ment about the composition of the *Memoirs*, reminding us again that Boaden himself was a part of the scene, that he knew Mrs. Inchbald, and that he was writing many, many years after the fact.

In another letter of this period, written to Mrs. Inchbald by Priscilla Kemble, Kemble gave her version of "theatricals" under her direction at the Priory, the seat of Lord Abercorn. "Nothing could be more brilliant: the whole theatricals under my direction, and, I do assure you, most excellently acted. Lady Cahir admirable in *Lady Contest*, and she was a blaze of diamonds!"[10] This is an echo of the theatricals at Derby House when Mrs. Damer wore her jewels and Farren directed, an echo also of Gillray's print, which in fact is peopled with those who made up the Prince of Wales's circle. Mrs. Kemble said there were some forty persons to dine and sleep in the house; the audience consisted of some seventy people. Lady Cahir, in her diamonds, played the part of Lady Contest, the principal part in Inchbald's *Wedding Day,* the play written for Mrs. Jordan. The part of Lady Contest would have fitted nicely into such a setting. This fete was reported in the papers, but since Mrs. Kemble was in the center of it as the directress, her lists of important people represent an interesting selection. There were "the Prince of Wales, Duke and Duchess of Devonshire, Lady Melbourn and family, the Castlereaghs, Mr. and Mrs. Sheridan, Lady Westmoreland, and the Ladies Fane, Lady Ely, &c."[11]

Priscilla Kemble was quite familiar with *The Wedding Day,* since she must have seen it when it was first presented at Drury Lane, and she certainly knew the players who played in the first performance with Mrs. Jordan as Lady Contest and Mrs. Hopkins as Mrs. Hamford.[12] Mrs. Kemble could use it for a private performance because it was short—only two acts—and had genteel characters suitable for the guests at the Priory. Sir Adam was played in the original performance by Thomas King, one of the leading actors at Drury Lane. Mr. Contest was played by Charles Kemble, John's younger brother, who was in his second season at Drury Lane. Rakeland was played by William Barrymore, also a member of the Drury Lane company for some years, one of those who filled out the parts and spoke prologues.

As we have said earlier, the play was commissioned by Sheridan for Jordan and played in 1794. Since it was published at once, no doubt copies were immediately available, and the fact that it was being played at the Priory in 1803 is evidence of its continuing popularity. Sir Adam's part in the play is nicely written to be a gentle satire on all such gentlemen, several of whom were probably present in Priscilla's audience. His total self-concern and his constant references to his "humour" make a portrait of personal responses and public behavior ideal for the domestic world of the 1790s.

INCHBALD, THE KEMBLES, AND COVENT GARDEN

The letter from Mrs. Kemble to Inchbald contained far more serious business, however, than a report of a private theatrical; it was really prompted by the fact that she and Inchbald were arranging with Harris for Kemble to buy into Covent Garden. After twenty years Kemble had finally left Drury Lane, leaving for a tour in Europe in July of 1802; he was gone until March of 1803. In Mrs. Kemble's letter dated November 28, 1802, she enclosed a letter from Kemble himself to Harris; it was not sealed, and she asked Mrs. Inchbald to "be so good as to read it" and send it to Harris "if you think it . . . properly worded."[13] Moreover, Mrs. Kemble had written to Mr. Morris, Kemble's agent, and requested that he call on Inchbald, who would in turn introduce him to Harris. Through Mrs. Inchbald and his wife, Kemble arranged to buy into Covent Garden for a sixth share; he was also made the manager. Harris's son Henry remained the principal share-holder, and Harris himself was still active, very much a part of the decisions about the plays to be given in the season of 1803–1804 and the members of the Kemble "company," even though Kemble had a great deal of authority and influence. In the fall after Kemble returned from Spain, he came to Mrs. Inchbald with a par-ticular request; she wrote to Mrs. Phillips:

> When Kemble returned from Spain (1803), he came to me like a madman,—said Mrs. Siddons had been imposed on by persons, whom it was a disgrace to her to *know;* and he begged me to explain it so to her. He requested Harris to withdraw his promise (of engag-ing Mrs. G, at Mrs. Siddons's request). Yet such was his tenderness to his sister's sensibil-ity, that he would not undeceive her *himself.* Mr. Kemble blamed ME: and I blamed HIM for his reserve; and we have never been so cordial since. Nor have I ever admired Mrs. Siddons so much since; for though I can *pity* a dupe, I must also *despise* one. Even to be familiar with such people was a lack of virtue, though not of chastity.[14]

Kemble, always mindful of his sister, was appalled when he learned of the allegations published in the papers that Mrs. Siddons had had an affair with an Irish actor whom she sponsored. It is probable that she was only indiscreet and that the jealous wife published her story to blackmail the Siddonses. It is not clear from Inchbald whether she did anything about his request, but given her usual way of exaggeration, she seems to have continued her friendship with the Kembles and the Siddonses.

In June of 1803 Mrs. Inchbald left her place in Leicester Square and went to Annadale House at Turnham Green, where all the tenants were Roman Catholic women. She had a separate room, where breakfast and tea could be served, with all the "sisterhood" meeting together for other meals. In July she wrote Mrs. Phillips:

> I have thought and said to myself a thousand times since I came, that it was impossible I could have gone from London, and have been half so agreeably situated as I am here. The house and gardens are quite as beautiful in my eyes as when I first saw them. I sit down every day to a far better table than ever I enjoyed for a constancy at any period in my life. Every thing is clean in perfection—and even MY HANDS; which, Heaven knows, they

have not been before for many a day; and I don't know whether this does not constitute one of my first comforts.[15]

But her pleasure did not last, for Mrs. Wyatt, the manager, proved to be impossible, and Mrs. Inchbald left at Christmastime. During the last weeks she was there, she was in London frequently seeking suitable lodgings; on November 20 she left Annadale House and came to lodge with Miss Baillie, a milliner, in the Strand, where she remained for some five years.

During 1804 she continued to work on her *Life*, a project like *A Simple Story* that she had worked on for many years, and in early May she sent it to Mr. John Robinson, but he declined to take it; Boaden points out that perhaps it was just as well, since he shortly thereafter went bankrupt. She sent it then to Phillips of St. Paul's Churchyard, who also declined it.[16] She was not without other writing, for she was busy on a play, first called *Modern Love*, that in the end was her play *To Marry or Not to Marry*. It was to be her last play.

To Marry or Not to Marry, like the earlier *Married Man*, is a study of a confirmed bachelor who has no intention of changing his status or of allowing anyone to disturb the simple pleasure of his household and his library. Inchbald's construction of incidents includes her familiar devices: a beautiful young girl in need of charity, a sister—a gentlewoman of impeccable manners, a forgotten incident of a long-ago duel, a black servant who is excessively devoted, and the reappearance of a man from the distant past. Making such a list of the incidents in the play suggests something of the "romantic," but in the hands of Mrs. Inchbald, it is hardly even sentimental; rather it is another study of the family and the subject of marriage, especially the choices the young sons and daughters have and do not have with regard to their own future.

In the beginning of the *Remarks* for *To Marry or Not to Marry*, she makes a kind of summary of her ideal "writer": "It appears as if the writer of this play had said, previous to the commencement of the task, 'I will shun the faults imputed by the critics to modern dramatists; I will avoid farcical incidents, broad jests, the introduction of broken English, whether Hibernian or provincial; songs, processions, and whatever may be considered by my judges as a repetition of those faults of which they have so frequently complained.'"

A NEW ASSIGNMENT: THE *REMARKS*

Again, as usual, she found that she did not altogether succeed to her own satisfaction. Her ideal was "Simplicity, the first design in the accomplishment of theatrical success, the most difficult of all attainments." She realized that the delight of the stage rather than the "ear" appealed to the audience, and she continued, "Incidents, too, must be numerous, however unconnected to please a London audience; they seem of late, to expect a certain number, whether good or bad. Quality they are not judges of—but quantity they must have."

The pleasure of the audience and their expectations were the major consideration in the *Remarks,* Inchbald's new assignment. The other two themes that Inchbald included in the majority of the essays that made up her *Remarks* were her concerns that the plays be "moral," or at least not indecent by her standards, and that the leading characters not be "low." As Katharine Rogers has written: "The critical principles of Inchbald's prefaces reflect the assumptions of her time. . . . Late eighteenth-century critics prized interrelated values of naturalness or probability, gentility, and morality."[17] Perhaps the presence of "naturalness" was the first characteristic Inchbald looked for in a play, a characteristic she sought from Shakespeare and for her own plays, but this was only one of the things she expected; she also thought that the language of the play should be "moral"—that at least it should not celebrate immorality and that the characters not be "low," and that the dialogue not be dialect or crude.

The very nature of the task that Inchbald undertook required her to speak to the audience of theatre patrons, an audience she knew both personally and professionally. The circumstances of her assignment have been entirely misunderstood by many readers and scholars in our time. Her publisher, the Longmans, came to her with the request that she write "remarks" for a series of plays to be published as *The British Theatre;* it was a series that the Longmans had bought from Bell, who had been publishing *Bell's British Theatre* since 1775, for more than a quarter of a century. Bell had followed the success of his series of Shakespeare plays with a more varied collection of plays that included contemporary ones as well as historical ones. When the Longmans came to Inchbald, they had already selected the plays to be included, and they had already set the procedure.[18]

Inchbald signed a contract with them in early 1806, and she finished the work in 1808; it was a long and difficult task, longer and more difficult than she had thought in the beginning. Her 1806 pocket-book is not extant, but those for 1807–1808 are, and the entries constitute a history of her writing and the methods she and her publisher used to make a great commercial success of their project.

Inchbald had nothing to do with selecting the plays to be published; they were merely sent to her.[19] Furthermore, there seems to be no pattern of publishing by date or genre; a tragedy by Shakespeare came out one week and a contemporary comedy the next. A second circumstance frequently misunderstood by recent scholars is that she did not select the text to be used. The texts were the ones as performed at Covent Garden, the Haymarket, and Drury Lane; occasionally the theatres were cited on the title page. The cast of characters is included in every case, usually the contemporary cast, with again sometimes two sets of casts, one for each theatre.[20] In the end there were 125 *Remarks;* that is, in the collected edition published in 1808 there were twenty-five volumes with five plays in each volume. Inchbald's achievement was monumental.

Collecting and writing about plays was not unique to the Longmans and Inchbald; it had been done before and would be done extensively in the nineteenth century. No other series, however, was so successful, and no other prefatory "remarks" were nearly so serious and professional as Inchbald's. Moreover, the fact that this edition was actually an extension of *Bell's British Theatre* gave it an advertisement from the beginning. It was designed also for a wider public than the earlier *Bell's;* the widening market for inexpensive publications of plays, novels, and tracts created a market for the plays that the Longmans selected.

There is no information as to who selected the plays or who decided the schedule of publication. Inchbald's pocket-books record the plays as they came out in 1807–1808; she also records working as she read, wrote, and checked her *Remarks,* and here, as earlier, she seems to have been responsible for copyediting her work. The entries in the pocket-books always include a jumble of personal, domestic, and professional items. By the time of the 1807 book, she is working hard at her task of writing the *Remarks,* and again, as always, the disparate items show the circumstances in which she worked.

Early in 1807 she writes in her pocket-book, "'The West Indian' came out," and continues in the same entry, "accosted Mr. L.—at a print shop in Pall Mall we talked a little—after I read my news paper." On Friday of this first week in January, she writes, "Admired that the French had been defeated in Poland After read . . . and had a proof." She was still living in the Strand, but she had been told by her landlady that she must find other lodging; and on Sunday she went to Berkeley Square "to seek Lodgings and met with Mr. Kemble." On the next day she records that it was very cold and that her maid Baptist came and after dinner her friend Mr. Hood. On the Saturday following she learned that Mr. Hood's news that the French were defeated was false; she had already spent the early part of the day "correcting old remarks." The next day she corrected two old remarks, and at about three Mr. Robinson called and she "went down and had much talk with him." This Mr. Robinson was one of the younger members of her former firm, G.G. and J. Robinson, now working in the Longman firm.

On Saturday she writes, "Fine and mild—corrected 'Distressed Daughter' . . .

corrected old proofs—wrote to Mrs. Phillips." At the top of the page, she writes, "had my coals of a new coal man," and across the page in the margin, "Longmans sent for all his books." In the midst of her entries, mixed with a new coal man and the weather fine and mild, it is difficult to know quite what she means by "Longmans sent for all his books." From reading entry after entry of the pocket-books, it is evident that her work was a part of her daily routine, that the publishers brought her the plays to work on, and that they came to pick up the proofs and consult about the publishing.

On Monday, January 12, she writes, "Gloomy and cold day, busy with proofs & . . . 'Every One Has his Fault' came Out," and on Saturday, January 24, her sister came and they rode to Paternoster Row and called on Longmans, and afterward Robinson called on her. There is never a complete record of how much she was paid for her *Remarks*, but evidently such a mention of going to Paternoster Row meant that she collected her money. She continues in this entry, "then we walked to the Bank and I bought stock and we walked home." Later in the week, on Friday, the day of King Charles's Martyrdom, she writes, "Mr. Longman sent me my last two books to Remark and also six of my own as a present." On Sunday, February 1: "Cold and some snow on the ground that fell in the night— at a proof and corrected the last of [the] remarks in the evening read 'Know Your Own Mind.'" At the top of the Monday, February 2, entry, "The Orphan came out," and across the page, "Wrote 'Know Your Own Mind & Count of Narbonne' . . . my concluding remarks." On Monday, the sixteenth, *Belle's Stratagem* came out. That she read *Know Your Own Mind* in the evening and wrote her *Remarks* for it and *Count of Narbonne* the next day suggests that the reading of the play and the writing about it followed immediately and also suggests that she worked steadily.

While the record of the writing, correcting, and submitting of the *Remarks* continued, she remained for most of 1807 in the Strand, living in very close quarters with few comforts. She writes:

My present apartment is so small, that I am all over black and blue with thumping my body and limbs against my furniture on every side: but then I have not far to *walk* to reach any thing I want; for I can kindle my fire as I lie in bed; and put on my cap as I dine; for the looking-glass is obliged to stand on the same table with my dinner. To be sure, if there was a fire in the night, I must inevitably be burnt, for I am at the top of the house, and so removed from the front part of it, that I cannot hear the least sound of any thing from the street; *but then,* I have a great deal of fresh air; more day-light than most people in London, and the *enchanting* view of the Themes; the Surrey Hills; and of *three windmills,* often throwing their giant arms about, secure from every attack of the Knight of the woeful countenance.[21]

The setting and circumstances under which she worked were difficult indeed, although, except for the cramped quarters, perhaps hardly more so than other writers she knew. Her reference to "more day-light than most people in London" reminds us that she and her contemporaries worked in semidarkness much of the time and that as she wrote and copied at night, she did so with only candlelight.

In the collected edition, the Shakespeare plays are gathered in the first five volumes; for the Shakespeare, we must remember that the promptbook texts she used were those altered texts of Dryden, Garrick, Tate, and Cibber—such texts as that of *The Tempest* with its added pair of lovers, of *Lear* with its happy ending, and of *Romeo and Juliet* much chopped up by Garrick. It is only after taking into consideration these varied circumstances that we are able to understand her comments, however strange they may seem to us.[22]

Inchbald said of *The Comedy of Errors*: "of all improbable stories, this is the most so. The Ghost in 'Hamlet,' Witches in 'Macbeth' and Monster in 'The Tempest' seem like events in the common course of nature, when compared to those which take place in this drama." And the incidents are even more impossible than the fable. She considered the plot of *Much Ado* a trivial one, for, she said, "all the incidents of note, which arise from it, are connected with persons of so little consequence in the piece." "Hero and Claudio are only *said* to be in love," and "If Benedick or Beatrice had possessed perfect good manners, or just notions of honour and delicacy, so as to have refused to have become eves-droppers, the action of the play must have stood still, or some better method have been contrived—a worse hardly could—to have imposed on their mutual credulity." She did not admire Dogberry.

Being herself almost wholly oriented to the theatre and dramaturgy, she frequently reflected in her judgments the interpretations given to certain roles by her contemporaries. She demanded that the reality of the action upon the stage support any reality of plot or character in the plays. For example, she did not think *As You Like It* suitable for the stage except in the hands of an unusually skillful cast. The character of Rosalind required an actress "of very superior skill," she says, since "she has so large a share of the dialogue to deliver; and the dialogue, though excellently written, and interspersed with various points of wit, has still no forcible repartee, or trait of humor, which in themselves would excite mirth, independent of an art in giving them utterance." Moreover, each of the other characters required a most skillful actor, "to give them their proper degree of importance." Her judgment was that John Kemble's Jaques, highly applauded by the public, was "one of those characters in which he gives certain bold testimonies of genius, which no spectator can controvert" and that Mrs. Jordan "is the Rosalind both of art and nature; each supplies its treasure in her performance of the character, and renders it a perfect exhibition."

In some of the plays Inchbald felt that even the skill of good performers could not conceal the incredible occurrences Shakespeare used from the old tales he adapted. In her *Remarks* on *Measure for Measure,* she says: "Had the plots of old tales been exhausted in his time, as in the present, the world might have had Shakespeare's foundation as well as superstructure, and the whole edifice had been additionally magnificent."

Even though Inchbald very much admired Siddons in the role of Isabella in *Measure for Measure,* she felt that it was a "character of declamation, rather than of passion." She also found the play full of incredible occurrences. The effect of the duke's disguise she found possible perhaps, but "there still remains a most disgraceful improbability, in representing the deputy Angelo, a monster, instead of a man."

In *The Winter's Tale* she found this same improbability in the character of Leontes. His unfounded jealousy of Hermione was, she says, "a much greater fault, and one with which imagination can less accord, than with the hasty strides of time, so much censured by critics, between the third and fourth acts of the play." Two other occurrences that she thought equally improbable were that "the gentle, the amiable, the tender Perdita, should be an unconcerned spectator of the doom which menaced her foster, and supposed real, father" and "that the young prince Florizel should introduce himself to the court of Sicilia, by speaking arrant falsehoods." This play, like *As You Like It,* she considered more suitable for the closet than the stage.

Inchbald's attitude toward the Shakespeare history plays is the predictable one, that she saw in them "faithful history . . . combined with transcendent poetry." Her judgment of their dramatic qualities is again put in terms of the dramatic reality of stage performances. Her view that the plays are accurate accounts of history makes for us, however, a second notable emphasis of her criticism, especially instructive since it is certainly not our understanding of history or, for that matter, of Shakespeare's handling of ideas.

In writing about *Richard III* she felt Garrick to have been "the actor, of all others, best suited for this character.—His diminutive figure gave the best personal likeness of the crooked-back king. He had, besides, if tradition may be relied on, the first abilities as a mimic; and Richard himself, was a mass of mimicry, except in his ambition, and cruelty."

Regarding *Henry IV, Part I,* she observed that even the most delicate readers, although they might be offended by the "revolting expressions in the comic parts" and by Falstaff's "unwieldy person," may receive "infinite entertainment and instruction." Moreover, she felt that the "Second Part of Henry the Fourth, like the First, has different effects, in producing pleasure or distaste, to different auditors." Always aware of the audience, she said, "few can appreciate the merit of Shakespeare's plays, so as to be greatly moved, where neither love nor murder is the subject of the scene." She felt, therefore, that many of the spectators failed "to feel and enjoy, as perfectly natural, those actual occurrences, and true touches of nature, with which the plot and the dialogue of this drama, as well as its foregoing part, abound." In fact, she thought that in *Henry IV, Part I* every character was "a complete copy of nature" and that to admire what she terms the delinquency of Falstaff, Hotspur, and the errant Prince Hal was to admire the skill with which Shakespeare handled the "creatures of his fancy," for she suggested that the realistic characterizations of such creatures required far more skill in execution than giving them "that false display of unsullied virtue, so easy for a bard to bestow."

Her comments about *Henry V* show that she took seriously her view that Shakespeare retold accurately the events of history. She closes her brief essay by pointing out that "the hero of Agincourt was in declining health, the effect of former intemperance, even on the spot where he gathered his laurels. . . . He lived no more than three years . . . and left no more than one child, who was dethroned and murdered."

In several of the *Remarks,* she makes comments about political topics. Her Roman Catholic views are evident in the comparison of Lear and his daughters' situation with that of James II and his daughters. Shakespeare, she thought, did not make Lear very affectionate toward his daughters, whereas "James's daughters were . . . under more than ordinary obligations to their king and father, for the tenderness he had evinced towards their mother, in raising her from an humble station to the elevation of his own; and thus preserving these two princesses from the probable disgrace of illegitimate birth." Inchbald, knowing history as she did, is here commenting on the fact that James II married Anne Hyde, daughter of Edward Hyde, earl of Clarendon, and with her had two daughters, Mary and Anne. Hyde was not a Royal, but by marriage Anne's two daughters both became queens of England; Mary married William of Orange and ruled jointly with him, and upon William's death, her sister Anne became queen. The whole story of

James II and his brief reign is the story of his failed attempt to restore Catholicism in England. In 1688 James fled to France, and William of Orange came over from Holland; he and his army restored order in England, a triumph spoken of as the Glorious Revolution.

The popularity of *Coriolanus* she saw as "joyful evidence—that the multitude at present are content in their various stations; and can therefore, in this little dramatic history, amuse themselves with beholding, free from anger and resentment, that vainglory, which presumes to despise them." In the part of Coriolanus she thought Kemble reached "the utmost summit of the actor's art," but she quite understood the political implications of certain passages in the play that she found provocative. She said, "When the lower order of people are in good plight, they will bear contempt with cheerfulness, and even with mirth; but poverty puts them out of humor at the slightest disrespect." And with this same understanding of the relationship of the stage to political topics, she saw why "it has been thought advisable, for some years past 'Julius Caesar' should not appear upon the stage." These two plays did have a history of political provocation in Kemble's career. His acting of Coriolanus was thought to be too condescending, too haughty.

From her own experience as a dramatist, Inchbald had an eye for the stage effects of the various dramatic details of the plays. In *Cymbeline* she thought Shakespeare fell short of creating characters of enough importance to make a real impression upon the audience. She says, "when the curtain is dropped, they immediately discourse upon the splendor of Imogen's bed-chamber, the becoming dress she wore as a boy and the dexterity with which Iachimo crept out, and crept into his coffer." She felt that the magic necessary to transform reason to imagination was lost in this play; perhaps, she suggested, the air of Italy has infected it with what she calls "that nation's predominant crimes."

In her comments on *Macbeth,* about which she says, "So conspicuous are the various excellencies contained in this tragedy, there is no cause whatever to point them out to the reader; for if he cannot see them at once, it is vain to direct his sight," she again discourses upon the "effect wrought by theatrical action and decoration." Her view is so inclusive of the theatrical effect of the play as she saw it that perhaps it is worth quoting in its entirety: "The huge rocks, the enormous caverns, and blasted heaths of Scotland, in the scenery;—the highland warrior's dress, of centuries past, worn by the soldiers and their generals—the splendid robes and banquet at the royal court held at Fores;—the awful, yet inspiring music, which accompanies words assimilated to each sound;—and, above all—the fear, the terror, what remorse;—the agonizing throbs and throes, by Kemble and

Mrs. Siddons, all tending to one great precept—*Thou shalt not murder,*—render this play one of the most impressive moral lessons which the stage exhibits."

Discussing *Antony and Cleopatra,* she again points out how Shakespeare has used the scenes of the play "to admit the spectator to see men and women as well as emperor and queen; the Triumvirs of Rome as men in their domestic habits; one toying with his mistress, another in the enjoyment of his bottle; a third long-ing, like a child, for a gaudy procession . . . the Queen of Egypt, in her undress, as well as in her royal robes; he is . . . admitted to her toilet, where in converse with her waiting-woman, she will suffer him to arrive at her most secret thoughts and designs; and he will quickly perceive, that the arts of a queen with her lover, are just the same as those practiced by any other beauty."

She felt that the theatrical effects in *The Tempest* made the play more spec-tacle than drama. She concluded her *Remarks* by saying, "The senses are, indeed, powerfully engaged by the grandeur of the spectacle in a London theatre—and the senses highly gratified, are sometimes mistaken, by the possessor himself—for the passions."

She was always aware of the view that the stage should present material of real situations, as a medium for displaying the proper lessons to be learned by the audience. For example, she thought that the duping of Malvolio in *Twelfth Night* was hardly the material for high comedy. Moreover, she says, "The imprudence of women, in placing their affections, their happiness, on men younger than them-selves, cannot be better described, nor the sex more powerfully warned against such propensity, than, by the Duke Orsino, in this very play."

Inchbald thought Volumnia in *Coriolanus* one of Shakespeare's greatest cre-ations, and she felt that both Volumnia and her son "talk so well, and at times act so well that their pitiable follies, couched beneath such splendid words and deeds, raise a peculiar sympathy in the heart of frail man; who, whilst he beholds this sorrowful picture of human weakness, discerns along with it his own likeness, and obtains an instructive lesson."

In her conclusion about *Antony and Cleopatra,* Inchbald felt that "There is scarcely a person now existing or a present occurrence in politics, to which some observation in this drama . . . will not apply." She saw in this play "lessons—multifarious, and enforced by great example—for, monarchs, statesmen, generals, soldiers, renegades; for the prudent and the licentious; the prosperous and the unfortunate; the victor and the vanquished."

Unfortunately, she did not discuss *Hamlet,* merely giving a short account of Shakespeare's life. She herself had played Hamlet, as had Mrs. Siddons; it would have been instructive to have her view. It is in her *Remarks* for *Othello* that we find her unqualified praise of Shakespeare's skill. She begins her essay on the "life" by pointing out that Shakespeare himself was a player as well as "The Pride of Britain." Moreover, he was unlearned in just the way she herself was, and "to the shame of the vain and petulant author, he was meek and humble." About *Hamlet* she concludes, "This is one of Shakespeare's dramas, in which all criticism has been absorbed in the tribute of praise."

Mrs. Inchbald did not care for *Romeo and Juliet*. She found their love contrived and unreal, having no basis of development over a period of time, and in her *Remarks* she observes: "But, with all the genuine merit of this play, it seldom attracts an elegant audience. The company, that frequent the side-boxes, will not come to a tragedy, unless to weep in torrents—and 'Romeo and Juliet' will not draw even a copious shower of tears." But she testified to the power of Shakespeare's pen, in *Othello*, to show "the rise and progress of sensations in the human breast, that a young and elegant female is here represented, by his magic pen, as deeply in love with a Moor,—a man different in complexion and features from her and her whole race,—yet without slightest imputation of indelicacy resting upon her taste." The contrasts that run throughout the play, even to the inferior characters, show to her Shakespeare's consummate art, not only in the malignant spirit of Iago, "so reverse from the generous mind and candid manners of Othello," but in the others as well. She felt that it was "the very zenith, of the poet's genius to have conceived two such personages" as Othello and Iago; and, she continues, "not only for the same drama, but to have brought them on the stage together in almost every scene," is, combined with "the admirable fable, incidents, and poetry, to rank the composition among the very best of Shakespeare's plays."

Inchbald herself had, of course, played in many of the Shakespeare plays, though there is no record of her playing in *Othello*. She and all her readers were very familiar with the players who interpreted the roles, and they all had opinions about the interpretations of the characters. Because the plays that follow the Shakespeare plays in the collected edition were not so frequently performed, she was more general in her comments.

The volumes that follow the Shakespeare ones are in a somewhat loose chronological order. Volume VI includes plays of Francis Beaumont and John Fletcher and of Massinger, Nathaniel Lee's *Royal Queens*, and John Dryden's *All for Love*. Mrs. Inchbald's *Remarks* on Dryden are chiefly about Dryden's life and politics, an interesting choice since he, like Inchbald, was Catholic. Garrick had altered Beaumont and Fletcher's *Rule a Wife and Have a Wife*, which she found had an "unpleasing" fable; *The Chances* had also been altered by Garrick. Massinger, she says, is considered to be second only to Shakespeare; although he may be inferior to Beaumont, Fletcher, and Ben Jonson in "purity of style, and delicacy of manners, he has surpassed them all."

She considers the plays she writes about each in its own place, especially as it relates to the current theatres. Her readers had seen Garrick play Don John in *The Chances;* they had seen Henderson in the part, and now Robert Elliston. Her *Remarks* were for the playgoers of 1807, as we are reminded when she writes: "Garrick was perfectly humorous in Don John and made the play a favorite, when he performed the part. So did Henderson. Elliston can do the same at present." About Dryden and *All for Love,* she explains, "the author was an advocate for tragic-comedy, and held, that all theatrical productions required alternate scenes of grief and joy, to render the whole a more perfect picture of nature, than could be given by one continued view of either." She reports, however, that some of his biographers said that he changed his opinion in his later days and "was convinced, that tragedy and comedy should never unite . . . it is consolatory to reflect, that this great man was as apt perhaps to change his mind upon all other subjects, as upon that in which his political interest was concerned." With this comment about Dryden's dramatic views, she turns to politics and religion. "In politics . . . [he] was so inconstant, that he wrote funeral lamentations on the death of Oliver Cromwell, and hymns of joy on the restoration of King Charles. He wrote 'The Spanish Friar' to vilify the Roman Catholic religion, whilst that religion was persecuted; and translated an ancient Father, to prove it the true faith, when the King on the throne professed himself one of its members." In conclusion she makes a rather cryptic comment: "So distinguished a believer might have done honour to that Church—but Dryden believed also in astrology." That a belief in astrology canceled Dryden's honoring the church reveals Inchbald's own regard for her church.

Volume VII begins with Thomas Southerne's *Isabella*, a play and a part that Siddons made her own, and Inchbald uses the *Remarks* to praise Siddons and to analyze the character of Isabella as it is developed by the characters around her, comments that again show Inchbald's understanding of dramatic composition.[23] She also understood the psychology of the character of Isabella and of Siddons's interpretation. "Beyond the deepest pain, felt by an audience for Isabella's grief, there is a pang almost insupportable, which proceeds from her gratitude. The author has in no part of the tragedy more effectually wrung the hearts of those, who possess nice sensibility, than when this poor widow is overcome by kindness." These remarks about Southerne here and also about his *Oroonoko* develop an idea that Inchbald thought of great importance: that the proper development of character was essential in any play, whatever the plot.

Oroonoko follows *Isabella* in volume VII. In her *Remarks* here, Inchbald cites Aphra Behn's account of the ill-fated lovers and says, "The repulsive qualities of some of those characters, joined to the little which has been allotted for the heroine to perform, have been obstacles to the attraction of this drama, and it is seldom acted." Yet, she says, her friend Alexander Pope played Oroonoko as his first role and was so successful that he made the play successful by his acting. Remembering Pope as Oroonoko must have given Inchbald a rather strange feeling when she read the cast printed with the play this time. Master Betty, the child actor, is listed as Oroonoko. Another comment Inchbald makes about the play is significant for date and place: "But could the ancient Roscius ascend from his grave to personate the hero of this piece, there is a great mercantile town in England, whose opulent inhabitants would not permit the play to appear in their magnificent theatre. The tragedy of 'Oroonoko' is never acted in Liverpool, for the very reason why it ought to be acted there oftener than at any other place—The merchants of that great city acquire their riches by the slave trade."

Mrs. Inchbald included a wide range of comments and ideas in *Oroonoko*, but she included even more in her review of *Zara*, in this same volume VII, the tragedy by Voltaire that was translated by Aaron Hill. In writing Hill's "Life," she examines his travels at the age of fourteen to visit his relative Lord Paget, the ambassador from England at the Ottoman court. Inchbald thought his book about this travel was "puerile" and "made all he had seen of less use to his reputation than if he had staid at home and seen nothing." Soon after his travels, he began to write plays and was made manager of Drury Lane and of the Opera Theatre then in the Haymarket, but his involvement there was very short-lived, and he turned to other projects, such as making oil from beechnuts; writing poetry; and establishing a periodical, the *Prompter*, in which he gave "directions" for actors. Inchbald mentions all these activities, including his scheme to cut timber in Scotland.[24] *Zara* was first performed in 1735 after a long history of failures to have it produced. In this first professional production, Mrs. Cibber, who was known as a singer, was introduced in her first dramatic role; Cibber's playing the role of Selima was a great success, foreshadowing her very important acting career.[25] Having discussed Hill and his work, Inchbald turns to the play itself, saying, "It is impossible to read this play without being delighted, or to see it without being weary. Love is seldom the passion, or religion the subject, which pleases greatly on the stage—the one is hard for the actors to describe, the other is difficult for the auditors to reflect upon."

Volume X includes four plays of Nicholas Rowe—*Tamerlane, The Fair Penitent, Jane Shore,* and *Lady Jane Grey.* The volume is completed with *The Siege of Damascus,* by John Hughes. The Rowe plays were very popular from the time they were written until the time Inchbald was writing. By one account *The Fair Penitent* was presented more times than any other play on the two winter stages in London and was very popular in the provinces. *Tamerlane,* Rowe's play celebrating William III, was acted for many years on November 5, William's birthday, the day he landed in England in 1688, but by the time Inchbald wrote, it was seldom given. In the play Tamerlane represented William, and his enemy Bajazet represented Louis IV, but by the early nineteenth century the custom had ceased, and Inchbald says "but as the political fire, no longer blazes, it is now seldom acted, and never with strong marks of approbation." The part of Arpasia was one Siddons played, both in London and in the provinces. Of this part in the play, Inchbald says, "The sorrows of love . . . are interesting to read, but childishly insipid in the action."

The title of *The Fair Penitent* was much debated, since many of Rowe's critics thought that, as Inchbald says, "Calista is not penitent, in a religious acception of the word; for though she laments her fall from virtue with all the anguish of degraded pride, she is still enamored of the cause from whence her guilt originated, and feels deeper sorrow from her lover's abated passion (the natural consequence of her frailty) than from motives of contrition."

The part of Lothario, Calista's lover, was so celebrated that his name passed into the language, but Inchbald's version of Calista and Lothario reveals her own views and the views, no doubt, of many of the women she knew. Always aware of the setting of a play, she finds the ladies in Italy quite lacking in judgment—"But certain it is, that, since the ladies of Great Britain have learnt to spell, and have made other short steps in the path of literature, the once highly favored Lothario of illiterate times has sunk in estimation, and there is scarcely a woman in this country who can sympathize in the grief of the fair penitent."

Her comment is more radical than it seems to us and reveals once again the problem of judging her criticism. As we commented about the Shakespeare criticism, she took setting and history in the most literal terms, as did her readers and her audience. Although she did not promote feminism as much as Barbauld or Catherine Macaulay did, she believed that a woman who "learnt to spell" and to read literature would not be weak enough to yield to her lover, whatever the circumstances. Lothario, telling of his triumph to his friend, recounts the circumstances:

Once, in a lone and secret hour of night,

When ev'ry eye was clos'd and the pale moon

And stars alone shone conscious of the theft,

Hot with the Tuscan grape, and high in blood,

Hap'ly I stole unheeded to her chamber . . .

I found the fond, believing love-sick maid

Loose, unattir'd, warm, tender, full of wishes . . .

I snatched the glorious golden opportunity . . .

Till with short sighs, and murmuring reluctance,

The yielding fair one gave me perfect happiness. (act 1, scene 1)

Even though by the time Inchbald was writing about Lothario the play was not so frequently performed in London, she continued to discuss the character: "that party of critics, in opposition, who extol this play for its moral purport, should recollect, that, on account of present modes and fashions, its power of example is much confined. Loss of maiden innocence is now limited to the poor female domestic and orphan apprentice. Women of fortune and quality, for whose instruction the style and manners of this tragedy seem most designed, are scarcely assailable in the state of spinsters. The great will preserve importance even in their crimes; and a woman of superior rank in life is rarely guilty of a breach of chastity—beneath the sin of adultery." This is a comment indicative of Inchbald's world, not merely her opinion.[26]

The Fair Penitent is followed by another very popular play—*Jane Shore*, also by Rowe. Jane Shore, the wife of a goldsmith, had been the mistress of King Edward IV, but upon the accession of Richard III, she was accused of witchcraft and condemned to do public penance by walking barefoot through the streets with a burning taper in hand to St. Paul's, and the public was forbidden to give her food or drink. In the old version of the story, she starved to death, but Inchbald, always interested in history, begins her *Remarks* by pointing out that "Jane Shore perishing for hunger is the fiction of an old ballad." After the death of her royal lover, it is said that she became the mistress of Hastings, Edward's friend and courtier, who in turn became a player in Richard's scheme to destroy the young Edward V and his brother. Hastings wanted to save them, but another courtier, Gloucester, used his knowledge of Jane and Hastings to accuse Hastings of treason and to condemn him to death.

The role of Jane was a favorite one for the "stars," from Mrs. Oldfield, who originated it, to Siddons, who was currently playing it at Covent Garden as the play and Inchbald's *Remarks* came out. The other role in the play that was equally famous and sought after was that of Alicia, Hastings's mistress, who, although a friend of Jane's, becomes insanely jealous and betrays both Jane and Hastings. Alicia's mad scene was justly famous, and again the part was one that all the "star" actresses played, or wished to play. Inchbald leaves the reader to decide which character, Jane or Alicia, is the more tragic.

Lady Jane Grey, Rowe's third "she tragedy," follows *Jane Shore*, but this time Inchbald's *Remarks* review the history of the "Nine days Queen"; she declares: "Rowe, who melted every heart at the sufferings of the low-born and guilty Shore, has not here even touched the strings of commiseration, not withstanding he has softened the real character of Lady Jane, in hopes of producing that effect." She felt that neither "reader nor auditor ever sheds a tear for the unhappy fate of Lady Jane Grey!"

A new edition of *The Works of Nicholas Rowe* had come out in 1792, giving Inchbald's readers an opportunity to judge Rowe's work for themselves. The readers of these plays in the new edition or in the Inchbald version would have understood an element not evident to later readers. Rowe, as the champion of William and Mary, wrote as an advocate of the Glorious Revolution, that is, the revolution that brought the Protestant William to the throne after the Catholic James II fled to France. The Glorious Revolution had been celebrated in 1788 upon the one-hundredth anniversary, the government using it as an example in praise of England's history in contrast to that of France, especially to call attention to what was happening in France—the French Revolution. The theatre, as always, played an important part in shaping public opinion. According to his 1792 journal, Godwin had been reading Rowe. It is interesting to speculate about what effect the new, cheap editions of these four Rowe plays had on the reading public; indeed, it is interesting to speculate about the whole undertaking and the public response to the earlier plays. Surely, for many of those who bought and read the plays, the publication offered an advantage to purchase plays that they had seen or in which some favorite actor or actress had performed. The whole enterprise was commercial; that Mrs. Inchbald included as much solid criticism as she did is quite extraordinary and for us quite valuable.

Volume XII begins with two plays of Thomas Otway and ends with *The Beggar's Opera*. It also includes Richard Steele's *Conscious Lovers* and Edward Young's tragedy *The Revenge*. Inchbald thought *The Orphan* taught some "wholesome lessons," even though it was a very "faulty work." Her *Remarks* suggest that she felt all the characters were guilty of "speaking falsehood," that this could be said of every one of the characters; thus "it is proper it should be a tragedy." *Venice*

Preserved was the favorite of Otway's plays and was presented "repeatedly every year; except when an order from the Lord Chamberlain forbids its representation, lest some of the speeches of Pierre should be applied, by the ignorant part of the audience, to certain men, or assemblies in the English state"—another example, like Shakespeare's *Julius Caesar* and *Coriolanus* and the Rowe plays, of the political implications in a popular play. There is only one actress in the play, Belvidera, a favorite part for Siddons, a part she made her own, and Inchbald must have seen her in this part many, many times, making her remark about "speaking falsehood" a response she made from experience and not merely from writing her essay.

When she writes about the plays that were more nearly contemporary, especially those that were written by actors, Inchbald's comments become very direct, combining play and writer, as, for example, Macklin and his *Man of the World* and Holcroft's *Road to Ruin* and *The Deserted Daughter* in volume XIV.

In writing about the Macklin play, she remembers Macklin's performance as Shylock the Jew in *The Merchant of Venice,* which she says was "so perfect a representation of malignant human nature; so congenial were the countenance and manners he gave to this black character, which Shakespeare's genius formed, that every other part, in which he appeared, is seemingly forgotten, in the minute remembrance of all he did in Shylock." And when she turns to *Man of the World,* she writes: "That the author of this comedy had a capacious understanding, this production, as well as his skill as an actor, will testify. His [play] could only be written by one, capable of making the nicest observations on all he saw there. It is an excellent lesson for politicians and courtiers."

In writing about Holcroft's plays, she was making judgments of her friend and fellow actor and of plays she herself knew and had acted in. The first paragraph of her *Remarks* for *The Road to Ruin* reads: "This comedy ranks among the most successful of modern plays. There is merit in the writing, but much more in that dramatic science, which disposes character, scenes, and dialogue, with minute attention to theatric exhibition; for the author has nicely considered, that it is only by passing the ordeal of a theatre with safety, that a drama has the privilege of being admitted to a library." In the end she concludes: "*The Road to Ruin* is a complete drama; resting its power on itself alone, without adventitious aid; neither music, song, dance, or spectacle, such as authors fly to, when, like Shakespeare's Orlando, 'they are gravelled for lack of matter,' is here introduced. This is an example that should ever be pursued, when it can be done with safety. But good plays are difficult to produce; and those, who write often, must divide the materials, which should constitute one extraordinary, into two ordinary dramas."

The *Remarks* for *The Deserted Daughter,* which follows in the collected edition, are concerned almost entirely with comments about the characters and their portrayal of society. In fact, this essay reveals quite precisely Inchbald's views of her own society and of her own portrayal of the society she created. Although this was a very successful play and "worthy of admiration," it was not equal to "the author's more fortunate works." She finds that the deserted daughter "is not of so high importance in the drama as the author might have made her—she is interesting, but not sufficiently so"—and that Lady Anne "too often calls to the recollection Cibber's Lady Easy." She thinks that Mordent, Item, Grime, and Clement—minor characters in the play—are characters "of general instruction." In fact, she says, "The praise, indeed, so justly bestowed on all the works of Mr. Holcroft is—that instruction and information ever accompany amusement," a sentiment Inchbald always commended.

Joanna Baillie's *De Monfort* is included in the same volume as Holcroft's plays; *De Monfort* is one of the plays that Baillie published in a volume called *Plays of Passion* in 1798; performed in 1800 with Kemble and Siddons in the principal parts, it was a great success. Baillie wrote a long preface to this, her first publication, in which Inchbald says she "displays knowledge, taste, and judgment, upon the subject of the drama, to a very high degree; still as she observes, 'theory and practice are very different things;' and, perhaps, so distinct is the art of criticism, from the art of producing plays, that no one critic so good as herself, has ever written a play half so good as the following tragedy." Inchbald thought Baillie "a genius." Considering the "passion" of hatred that Baillie exhibits in the play, Inchbald analyzes the character of De Monfort. She finds the origin of hatred in pride and observes, "The proud man yielding to every vice which pride engenders, descends, in the sequel of his arrogance, to be the sport of his enemy, the pity of his friends, to receive his life a gift from the man he abhors, and to do a midnight murder!" She concludes that "though her play falls short of dramatic excellence, it will ever be rated as a work of genius."

It is interesting to note that Baillie's play was published in the same year as Inchbald's *Lovers' Vows* and Wordsworth and Coleridge's *Lyrical Ballads*, three publishing events that had an enormous influence into the nineteenth century; Inchbald's *Remarks* end by prophesying that "other dramas may yet proceed from her pen, to gratify every expectation which this production has excited." In fact, Baillie had brought out another volume of plays in 1802, one play in which, called *The Election*, was the companion "passion" to *De Monfort*. Refused at first, it was given finally as a musical "with a huge cast and indifferent reception."[27]

There are four plays of Arthur Murphy's with Inchbald's *Remarks* in volume XV. Murphy's career as a playwright was only a part of his work, which also included the periodical press, acting and managing with Foote, and the law. Murphy's success—or lack of it—in the theatre began with Garrick, with whom he alternately quarreled and was reconciled. Mrs. Inchbald's *Remarks* discussing the four plays reflect Murphy's experiences and relationships in the theatre and comment about the plays themselves.[28]

The Way to Keep Him, a comedy, had an interesting history of composition, having been played as a three-act production and later as a five-act play. In changing the play, Murphy added the character of Sir Bashful. Inchbald found this character somewhat ambivalent, remarking, "It is impossible to attend to characters destitute of sense; and delightful to observe particular follies usurping the reason of those, who, in all other respects, are wise. Fools who accidentally have sapience, are too despicable to be heeded;—but the wise man, who is accidentally a fool, is an instructive picture of human nature."

All in the Wrong, another comedy, Inchbald considered one of his best. She found the dialogue of the play especially fine—"a species so natural, that it never in one sentence soars above the proper standard of elegant life; and the incidents that occur are bold without extravagance of apparent artifice, which is the criterion on which judgment should be formed between comedy and farce." Murphy's last play, *Know Your Own Mind,* is also a comedy; in its prologue he declared it to be his last dramatic production. Its reception was very favorable; it was much discussed by the critics and playgoers because of its resemblance to Sheridan's *School for Scandal,* which made its appearance just at the time *Know Your Own Mind* was at the height of its popularity at Covent Garden. In the theatre world of London, with patrons attending the theatres every night—at Drury Lane one night, Covent Garden the next, and back to Drury Lane the next—the circumstances of the two plays and their productions created just the proper context for opinions. Moreover, as Inchbald points out, the two plays are very similar. "The reader will observe, before he has proceeded far in the following play, that an inclination to scandal is the prominent trait of the first character of the piece, Dashwould; that the wit of the composition depends chiefly upon descanting on the faults of the absent; and that the hypocrisy of Malvil, joined to his love of slander, gives him many of the features, in miniature, of Joseph Surface and Mrs. Candour."

The fourth of Murphy's plays to be included with *Remarks* is a tragedy, *The Grecian Daughter.* Inchbald's essay here is especially well written, illustrating both her style and her judgments. Too long to be quoted in its entirety, it deserves a special commendation. The first paragraph reads: "This tragedy has been so rapturously applauded on the stage, and so severely criticized in the closet, that it is a task of peculiar difficulty to speak either of its beauties or its defects, with any degree of certainty. To conciliate both the auditor and the reader, both the favorable and the unfavorable critic, the 'Grecian Daughter' demands a set of Remarks for each side of the question—and the good Natured side shall have precedence."

The play was very successful upon its first appearance, and Inchbald sees in it "a splendor of decoration, a glow of martial action, events of such deep interest, and above all, a moral of such excellent tendency which concludes the performance, that its attraction can readily be accounted for, without the slightest imputation upon the judgment of the public." She continues to praise the "flowing verse," "the wonderful events" that take place naturally, and the smooth progression of incidents. She also finds that this tragedy has passages that "excite tears, whilst certain high-sounding sentences, with meaning insignificant, are irresistibly risible."

The story of the play was a very popular one, and the part of Euphrasia was first played by Mrs. Barry and then by Siddons, but Mrs. Inchbald felt that the men's characters had been sacrificed "to the valour of the woman," so much so that "no actor likes to appear in the part" of Evander and that the man "most talked of, most praised, and by far the most perfect character in the whole drama, should never make his appearance!" Inchbald concludes her *Remarks* by observing that Otway wrote "miserable comedies" and that it was no disgrace to Murphy to having written an "indifferent tragedy."

In the *Remarks* on Murphy's plays, we see a review of his work, not simply of a single play. For some of the plays Inchbald was given, however, there are only single ones of a writer. This is the case for William Wycherly's *Country Wife*, altered by Garrick and called *The Country Girl*, in which Jordan made her first appearance on the London stage as the character of Peggy. Another single entry was *The Countess of Salisbury*, by Hall Hartson, which was first acted in Ireland and then in the Haymarket during the management of Foote. It was one of the few plays attributed to the Haymarket in the *Remarks*.[29] *Douglas*, by Home, another of the "single" plays, is famous for its history, which Inchbald reviews by quoting the poet Thomas Gray, who said that "it retrieved the true language of the stage, lost for three hundred years." This was the play that Inchbald says was "written by the only living author of a living tragedy." She also comments on the actress Mrs. Crawford, who, as Lady Randolph, "displayed, in this part, dramatic powers which at times electrified her audience," but she says it was given to Mrs. Siddons "to unite the same bursts of pathetic tenderness, so wonderful in her predecessor, to that maternal beauty of person, and dignity of action, wherein it was denied Mrs. Crawford, to paint this exquisite drawing by Home, in faithful colors." Home, a minister of the church of Scotland, was stripped of his benefice because of his play; at the time Mrs. Inchbald wrote, he was living on a pension, given by the Prince of Wales, now George IV.

Two important plays by George Colman the elder are included in volume XVI, *The Jealous Wife* and *The Clandestine Marriage;* Inchbald's *Remarks* on these two plays became the basis of the attack against her by George Colman the younger after her *Remarks* on his plays. *The Jealous Wife* was in part based on Henry Fielding's novel *Tom Jones*. As Inchbald points out, the characters in *Tom Jones* are minor characters compared to those Colman created for his play. Inchbald repeats that Colman "submitted the play for inspection in its first 'rude state'" to Garrick, who "gave him advice in many particulars as to its fable and characters." Inchbald's discussion of the making of Colman's two plays is quite significant, because it was Colman who gave her advice, sponsored her first play, *Mogul,* and for the second gave her encouragement and direction both in writing and in conversation. Colman, like Garrick, did more adaptations than original plays, and the question of how much collaboration there was between Garrick and Colman in the important *Clandestine Marriage* was an ongoing dispute. Inchbald gave no judgment of her own about *The Jealous Wife*.

Inchbald begins her *Remarks* on *The Clandestine Marriage* by calling it a play of "joint authors," Colman and Garrick, "The one, a scholar, a man of general and acknowledged talents, and—not among the least of his honors—the father of Colman the younger. The other is a well known name as affixed to the greatest actor that ever appeared on the English stage, and the stage's best reformer."

With such an introduction she reviews the life of each—Colman and Garrick—repeating the fact that Colman was a near relation to the earl of Bath and that Garrick was the pupil of Dr. Johnson. Both facts were surely known to most of her readers. Although she discusses Garrick rather more than Colman in her brief *Remarks,* she says that "Garrick did no more as a writer to this work than cast a directing hand and eye over the whole."

The composition of *The Clandestine Marriage* was much disputed by those who wished to give Garrick credit for a greater part in writing the play than did those who championed Colman. The Colman "friends" were very positive in their support; Inchbald's rather brief comments on the subject are surprising considering her association.[30] These two plays of Colman the elder and her *Remarks* were part of Colman the younger's disaffection, part of the controversy he stirred up after she wrote *Remarks* on his plays, a controversy provoked in part by her comments about Garrick.

The comments she does make about the play are instructive in that she makes judgments as a playwright: "Though the Clandestine Marriage may rank as a modern comedy, yet it is pleasanter to read than to see. The characters are well drawn; but the speeches are too long for the attention of a listener, though not for a reader. A London audience are become a very impatient multitude; and tragedy alone has the prerogative of being tedious."

The whole of volume XVIII in the collected edition contains plays by Richard Cumberland. The five are *The Brothers, The West Indian, The Jew, First Love,* and *The Wheel of Fortune.* Among these five plays, Inchbald makes several comparisons. *The Brothers,* which she praises for its refined language, is not so nearly perfect as *The Jew* and *Wheel of Fortune; First Love* is slight in comparison to the others, though each play has merits of its own.

Following her interest in language, she writes of *The Brothers:* "The language . . . is wholly refined, and every idea it contains, perfectly delicate. The youthful parts are there rendered brilliant, as well as interesting; and wit and humor are not confined as here, to the mean, or the vulgar, but skillfully bestowed on persons of pleasing forms and polite manners." Discussing *The West Indian,* she writes, "Remarks, which precede a work, must be written with infinite restraint, lest an observation carried too far upon any one part of the fable or characters should reveal secrets which it is the reader's chief amusement, in the perusal of the play, himself to find out. It cannot be, however, any diminution of the pleasure of reading this comedy, to be told—that, although it may bestow no small degree of entertainment in the closet, its proper region is the stage."

In *The Jew* she praises the character of Sheva that Cumberland has created; she says that although as a Jew there is the novelty of his professing his faith, "still his character would be new to the stage, common as it is in real life, were he the follower of any other doctrine—A virtuous miser is as much a wonder in the production of a dramatist, as a virtuous Jew; and Mr. Cumberland has in one single part, rescued two unpopular characters from the stigma under which they both innocently suffered." She continues, "indiscriminate profusion has been the dramatic hero's virtue in every comedy, till Cumberland showed to the long blinded world, that—the less a man gives to himself, the more it is probable, he bestows upon his neighbor."

Inchbald found *First Love* "not deep, nor the events forcible." She considered it inferior to the others, even though it was quite successful, posing "much merit."

For Inchbald and her readers, *The Wheel of Fortune* was quite a remarkable play, in several ways. It was based loosely on a play by Kotzebue, *Misanthropy and Repentance* (as was *The Stranger*), but so clever was Cumberland that Inchbald says the two plays can be read in one evening and both enjoyed or played on the stage on succeeding nights and be applauded, with some spectators unaware of their mutual origin. This brief discussion here by Inchbald comments on the popularity of adapting plays—especially plays by Kotzebue, who for some three years in the 1790s dominated the London stages, Mrs. Inchbald having done both *Lovers' Vows* and *The Wise Man of the East* from Kotzebue.[31]

Each play had a "star" character; Kemble acted the "star" in *The Wheel of Fortune,* and Siddons was the "star" in *The Stranger.* Inchbald remarks about Kemble in *The Wheel of Fortune:* "Perhaps, in no one character, he performs, does Kemble evince himself a more complete master of his art than in Penruddock. The dignity of mind and mien, which appears under his old coarse clothes, and the tenderness of his love, beneath the roughest manners, are so wonderfully impressive; that an audience . . . commiserates his passion, and feels its power in every fiber with himself."[32]

Inchbald's ability to make her readers respond to the plays even when the play was in hand, not on stage, was one of the features of these volumes that made them so successful and so memorable that they became standard classics throughout the nineteenth century and into our own. We who are unfamiliar with the players she writes about can only imagine from the illustrations in the volumes and from reports, memoirs, and biographies of the period how powerful Kemble was as Penruddock or Siddons as Isabella.

The judgments Inchbald makes about the various merits of the plays, their relations to other plays, and the current theatre audience form a significant commentary on the early-nineteenth-century London theatres. The theatre audiences were changing rapidly, which meant that the plays presented were changing; the classic ones like *Douglas* or *All for Love* were dropped from the repertory, and the new "entertainments" became the standard repertory. In one sense the *Remarks* preserved history while giving the reader direction for reading and, if it reappeared at either Covent Garden or Drury Lane, seeing a play.

Inchbald's own plays fill volume XXIII; included are *Such Things Are*; *Every One Has His Fault*; *Wives As They Were, and Maids As They Are; Lovers' Vows*; and *To Marry or Not to Marry.* She does not include any biographical material about herself, but she does make comments about how she felt when the plays were written and sometimes about the circumstances when they were produced. For *Such Things Are* she writes about Howard, the prison reformer who appears in the play as Haswell, and she points out that Twineall's character was based partly on Lord Chesterfield's *Letters* to his son. Howard died in 1790, and Inchbald writes, "Death having robbed the world of that good man's active services . . . a short account of the virtuous tendency of his inclinations, and success of his charitable pursuits, is at present requisite for some readers." As we have commented about other plays and *Remarks,* Inchbald keeps in mind the contemporaneity of her essays.

The essay for *Every One Has His Fault* is neither a comment about composition or characters nor an analysis of structure. Instead, it is a discussion of the dramas current on the London stage and the criticism that "modern dramas are the worst that ever appeared on the English stage." She says: "When it is inquired, 'Why painting, poetry, and sculpture, decline in England?' 'Want of encouragement,' is the sure reply—but this reply cannot be given to the question, 'Why dramatic literature fails?' for never was there such high remuneration conferred upon every person, and every work, belonging to the drama." She follows such a statement by analyzing the economies of playwrights, managers, and the whole financial situation of the drama: "if the stage be really sunk so low as it is said to be, that patronage and reward have ruined, instead of having advanced genius, or is it more likely that public favor has incited the envious to rail; or, at best, raised up minute inquirers into the excellence of that amusement, which charms a whole nation."

For this play, *Every One Has His Fault,* she says, "It has been productive both to the manager and the writer, having on its first appearance, run, in the theatrical term, near thirty nights; during which, some of the audience were heard to laugh, and some were seen to weep." Whatever she thought of the use of the stage to "teach," to be morally engaged, she always wanted her plays to make the audience laugh and cry. Any review of her plays finds that there is a possibility in each of engaging the emotions.

The *Remarks* for *Wives As They Were, and Maids As They Are* are written in the third person. Calling herself "the writer" or "the authoress," she analyzes her own play in as objective a fashion as possible. She says the first act "promises a genuine comedy," but since she failed of "true comic invention," she turned to farce at the end of the second act. She continues: "Aware of this consequence and wanting humor to proceed in the beaten track of burlesque, she then essays successively, the serious, the pathetic, and the refined comic; failing by turns in them all, though by turns producing chance effect; but without accomplishing evident intentions, or gratifying certain expectations indiscreetly raised."

A part of her essay then turns to the characteristics of "a good play," characteristics not all found in *Wives As They Were, and Maids As They Are.* She says, however, "There are some just sentiments, some repartees, a little pathos, and an excellent moral in this production;—but there are also vapid scenes, and improbable events, which, perhaps, more than counterbalance those which are lively and natural."

The *Remarks* for *Lovers' Vows* follow a reprint of the preface to the first publication, in which she explains the changes she made from the original *Child of Love,* by Kotzebue. She examines the relationship of the baron and his son, addressing the behavior of the son when he discovers the cruel injuries that have been inflicted on his mother. This is an especially interesting passage, since one of the main features of Inchbald's adaptation is her changing the character of the baron to make him more sympathetic and allow the patriarchal features of his character to be more humane and sentimental. In observing how Frederick should speak to his father, she says, "Irony and sarcasm do not appertain to youth: open, plain, downright habits, are the endearing qualities of the young. Moreover, a son, urged by cruel injuries, may upbraid his father even to rage, but if he contemn or deride him, all respect is lost, both for the one and the other."

Inchbald says that "the grand moral of this play is—to set forth the miserable consequences which arise from the neglect, and to enforce the watchful care, of illegitimate offspring; and surely, as the pulpit has not had eloquence to eradicate the crime of seduction, the stage may be allowed an humble endeavor to prevent its most fatal effects."

In the *Remarks* for her *To Marry or Not to Marry,* she actually takes herself to task, pointing out not beauties but flaws, finding only "a degree of interest in the fable of 'To Marry, or not to Marry' which protected it on the stage, and may recommend it to the reader."

Several times in her pocket-books for 1807–1808, she complains about how tiresome her task has become, sometimes because she is ill, sometimes because someone has criticized her sharply. In the pocket-book for 1807, she mentions the various plays as they came out, and she writes about continuing to correct and to write more *Remarks.* On January 2, a cold and gloomy day, she corrected old *Remarks;* on Sunday she writes: "Fine and not so cold as yesterday—corrected two old Remarks—about three Mr. Robinson call'd, I went down and had much talk with him." The entries for the next week continue the same pattern, "at my corrections." On Friday her own play *Every One Has His Fault* came out, and on the next day she corrected two *Remarks.* On Monday the nineteenth, "At my corrections . . . young Robinson brought me in the morning a novel to read." On Friday the thirtieth, "King Charles's martyrdom—gloomy and cold—Mr. Longman sent me my last two books to Remark and also six of my own as a present." On Saturday following, "at a proof and corrected the last of [the] remarks . . . read 'Know

Your Own Mind & Count of Narbonne' my concluding remarks." These two plays were evidently the last ones she had been sent, and she had begun at once to write. On Tuesday she had been "at Remarks on 'Know Your Own Mind'"; on Wednesday she read *The Count of Narbonne* in the morning, and young Robinson had called to tell her "how extremely bad Miss Lee's comedy was." At the top of the page for February 9–15, she has written "'Cato' came out" on the left, and on the right "Lent came in." In this week she was "at a proof" and "corrected my last two remarks." She could not foresee at this point that she would do some very significant *Remarks* in the future and that it would be into 1808 before she was finally done with her task.

Never without "projects," she began a new one during this winter of 1807. It was begun in quite a casual way, but in the end it became a serious essay on her views of writing the novel. It was published in a periodical called the *Artist* and came out in June. Her report of this assignment gives an example of how she was regarded by the proprietors of the periodical press. She was later offered an assignment to join the staff of the *Quarterly Review*, but she refused.

Just before Lent, on Monday, she wrote, "Mr. P. Hoare caught me in the Shop and proposed to me to become one in the new periodical publication." On February 26 she writes, "received a most flattering Letter from Mrs. Hoare on the subject of my consenting to write in her Brothers periodical work," and on March 3, "Cold and gloomy—try'd to write an essay for Mr. Hoare." On March 9 she notes, "First number of 'The Artist' came out," and on the fifteenth, "Had the first number of the periodical work of 'The Artist' sent me." Her essay was a part of the third issue. Later she wrote an unsigned article, published in issue number 9 in 1809, after fire had destroyed the theatres.

The essays for the *Artist* are, like her *Remarks*, witty and to the point. In the essay about the novel, she begins by denying that she knows anything about writing a good novel but she says she will show "how to avoid writing a very bad one." She gives a number of things to avoid: the hero and the heroine should be "neither of them too bountiful." Neither Mrs. Radcliffe nor Maria Edgeworth are to be imitated, for "you cannot equal them; and those readers who most admire their works, will most despise yours." Always aware of speech, she cautions: "Take care to reckon up the many times you make use of the words 'Amiable,' 'Interesting,' 'Elegant,' 'Sensibility,' 'Delicacy,' 'Feeling.' Count each of these words over before you send your manuscript to be printed, and be sure to erase half the number you have written;—you may erase again when your first proof comes from the press—again, on having to revise—and then mark three or four, as mistakes of the printer, in your Errata."[33]

She suggests that actions should be counted—the times the heroine blushes and the hero turns pale—"the number of times he has pressed her hand to his 'trembling lips,' and she his letters to her 'beating heart'—the several times he has been 'speechless' and she 'all emotion,' the one 'struck to the soul;' the other 'struck dumb.'" She points out that when the heroine is about to drown, be burned, or her neck "broken by the breaking of an axle-tree—for without the perils by fire, water, or coaches your book would be incomplete," you should be careful that she not be rescued by a handsome young man, lest "the catastrophe of your plot is foreseen, and the suspense extinguished." She believes that to introduce too many characters is distracting. And then when you have written "as good a novel as you can—compress it into three or four short volumes at most; or the man of genius, whose moments are precious, and on whose praise all your fame depends, will not find time to read the production, till you have committed suicide in consequence of its ill reception with the public."

Having considered the writing of the novel, Inchbald discusses the readers; they are as significant as the writers, and throughout the essay Inchbald is gently —most of the time gently—ironic. She says there are two classes of readers, one hostile to originality and another

so devoted to novel-reading, that they admire one novel because it puts them in mind of another . . . by them it is required, that a novel should be like a novel. The true novel reader, especially "of the female sex" is indifferent to the fate of nations, or the fate of her own family, whilst some critical situation in a romance agitates her whole frame! Her neighbor might meet with an accidental death in the next street, the next house, or the next room, and the shock would be trivial, compared to her having just read—"that the amiable Sir Altamont, beheld the interesting Eudoeia, faint in the arms of his thrice happy rival."

Inchbald thought the intelligent novel reader could profit by reading: "if they are wise they will know how to profit." In the last section of her essay, she turns to the difference between writing a novel and writing for the stage. The novelist, she asserts, is "a free agent. He lives in a land of liberty, whilst the Dramatic Writer exists but under a despotic government.—Passing over the subjection in which an author of plays is held by the Lord Chamberlain's office . . ." Moreover, the playwright is obliged to be careful of the characters he creates. At a time when the upper class, the rich, the privileged were frequently the subject of discussion in novels, books, and periodicals, she says, "What dramatic writer dares to expose in a theatre, the consummate vanity of a certain rank of paupers, the boast of that wretched state as a sacred honour, although to show to an audience, the privilege of poverty debased into the instrument of ingratitude? 'I am poor and therefore slighted'—cries the unthankful beggar; whilst his poverty is his sole recommendation to his friends; and for which alone, they pay him much attention, and some respect." Such a comment reminds us of her novel *Nature and Art* and its ambivalent attitude to both rich and poor, no one of whom acted with Christian charity.

Her conclusion repeats: "A dramatist must not speak of national concerns, except in one dull round of panegyrick. He must not allude to the feeble minister of state, nor to the ecclesiastical coxcomb. Whilst the poor dramatist is, therefore, confined to a few particular provinces; the novel-writer has the whole world to range, in search of men and topics. Kings, warriors, statesmen, churchmen, are all subjects of his power. The mighty and the mean, the common-place and the extraordinary, the profane and the sacred, all are prostrate before his muse. Nothing is forbidden, nothing is withheld from the imitation of a novelist, except—other novels."

Writing this piece gave her some trouble; she says more than once that she is not pleased. On Easter Sunday she wrote, "Cold and cloudy—all day at my Essay for the 'Artist' in the Evening read in 'The Tatler.'" Again the next day, Easter Monday, "Very cold & gloomy—wrote for the 'Artist' & received the 3rd number"—on Thursday "at the Artist" till Dolly "came to dinner on Friday . . . wrote much for the 'Artist.'" She continued to be dissatisfied with her piece, and all the next week she continued to work. She read an article by Cumberland in one of the issues and "altered my own." The next day: "At my artist and made a new copy of it." The next day, a Tuesday, she read it to Dolly, and Dolly read "other Artists c&c." Finally, on Thursday, April 16, her entry read, "Cold and gloomy rose early—Dolly called at breakfast and read my 'Artist' with observations—I completed the whole copy of it by dinner, and sent a letter about it to Mr. P. Hoare—he called for it after I was in bed and I rose and went to him." The day following this entry, she wrote, "at dark received a letter from Mr. Hoare in high praise of my 'Artist,'" and when Dolly came, she showed her the letter.

A review of the ideas in her essay makes clear that she herself had followed the pattern she suggested. Always concerned about language, Inchbald made certain that both her *Simple Story* and *Nature and Art* use clear, direct language; she never in any of her work uses the language of sentimentality. Also, both novels have relatively few characters, and both have simple, straightforward plotlines. Moreover, it is significant that she was reading the *Tatler* as she was writing her essay; in structure, language, and tone, her work echoes the essays in the *Tatler*.

All during the time she was working on her piece for the *Artist*, she was recording the publication of her *Remarks*. This series of records makes an interesting comment on the publishing project. A bound copy of the original plays certainly reveals the random—not chronological—sequence of publication and confirms her report of the publications. Doubtless some of these bound copies done for individual readers did not follow exactly Inchbald's report, but to discover that volume X in one collected edition follows Inchbald's "this week came out" entries confirms her pocket-book entries as accurate and lays a basis for the next incident in her project, the controversy she had with George Colman the younger.

GEORGE COLMAN THE YOUNGER AND THE *REMARKS*

On December 19, in a box in the margin of her pocket-book, Inchbald wrote, "Had a letter that caused me anxiety," and the next day she wrote "at two Mr. Reeves came and I saw him in the parlor—found that a preface by Colman against me was his business." The next day she wrote a letter to Mr. Reeves. These are the entries that began the series in the 1808 pocket-book that followed her work on her response to Colman's "complaints."

　　Boaden's account of this quarrel—dispute—written more than a decade later, is interesting for his own views about one of the points in the discussion, a point Colman found fault with Inchbald about, and a point that again brings up the question of the composition and production of plays in the last half of the eighteenth century. In one of the essays, Inchbald had written: "In thus acknowledging my obligations to Mr. Colman the *Elder*, let it be understood, that they amounted to no more than those usual attentions which every manager of a theatre is supposed to confer, when he first selects a novice in dramatic writing, as worthy of being introduced on his stage to the public."[34]

　　Boaden, as usual, takes this opportunity to give his own opinion of the matter. He writes: "'*Supposed* to confer'—by *whom* supposed, dear lady! 'Those *usual* attentions!'—with Garrick they *were* usual, and he was *able* to confer them; but, except by *him*, any thing like the labour of re-modeling the whole piece, never either was done or could be done, for reasons referring to inability, or indolence, or other occupation, all of which will occur when the managers are thought about."[35]

　　This remark, "for reasons referring . . ." to the managers, is rather uncomplimentary on Boaden's part, since he had worked with both Harris and Kemble, who as managers had presented his plays. Perhaps he did not know until he wrote in the *Memoirs* to what degree Colman the elder had worked with Inchbald. Garrick and Colman had, as friends, worked together; and later as managers, Garrick at Drury Lane and Colman at Covent Garden, and during the 1760s, they continued to do so. In 1776, when Colman became the proprietor of the Haymarket, they each sponsored new playwrights, one of whom, as we have said, was Mrs. Inchbald. Boaden himself must have had some firsthand experience with both Garrick and Colman.[36]

Colman the younger's complaints about Inchbald's *Remarks* on his plays are quite "picky," showing him more jealous of her success than annoyed by the criticism, a view confirmed by his opening comments. He begins: "When I lately sold the copy-right of 'The Heir at Law,' (with two or three other dramatic manuscripts,) I required permission to publish any prefatory matter, which might appear eligible to me, in the first *genuine* impression of the plays in question. I had reason to suppose that they would be put forth in a series of dramas, with *Critical Remarks by Mrs. Inchbald.* On this account I more particularly urged my *postulatum.* I make no apology for writing Latin to you, Madam; for, as a scholiast, you, doubtless, understand it, like the learned Madame Dacier, your predecessor."[37]

If the references to "a scholiast" and Madame Dacier were a slap at the ladies, his reference to "the first *genuine* impression of the plays in question" is a complaint against the publisher, and he continues by making his letter current when he writes: "did it not absolutely fall in my way, I should have been silent: but as your *critique* on the present play, will, probably, go hand in hand with this letter, I would say a little relative to those dramas of mine which have, already, the honour to be some what singed, in passing the fiery ordeal of feminine fingers;—fingers which it grieves me to see destined to a rough task, from which your manly contemporaries in the drama would naturally shrink." Not content to present himself as a "manly contemporary," he makes a smart remark about the classics, adding to his "no apology for writing Latin." "Achilles, when he went into petticoats, must have made an awkward figure among the females; but the delicate Deidamia never wielded a battle-axe to slay and maim the gentlemen."[38]

Colman should have made a better judgment of Inchbald's abilities; to be so childish about his own accomplishments and so scornful of hers was a real mistake. She had no trouble in replying.

The pocket-book for 1808 continues her story from the December entry of 1807. On Sunday, January 3, she writes, "Read over my various addresses at the end of my Remarks on my answer to what Mr. Colman should publish against me . . . in the evening read an Evangelical Magazine." On Monday, the eleventh, she had a letter from the Longmans asking that she do four more *Remarks,* and she agreed. Colman's *Battle of Hexham* must have been one of the four, for on Sunday, February 14, she read the play, and the next day she wrote her *Remarks* on it, but this was only the beginning; she continues to work on her essay. On Tuesday she had done "a sketch." On Wednesday she writes, "A general frost—cold with a gloomy thaw—all the day at my Remarks on the Battle of Hexham—in the evening read Enigmas &." On Thursday the snow was all gone, but it was a "damp gloomy & dirty" day, and again she was at her remarks; the next day the weather had improved, but she was still "busy with my Remarks." Finally, on Sunday, she writes: "Fine frosty & cold—completed my remarks on Battle of Hexham. Mr. Robinson called about them & I went down to him for sometime—afterwards read Roscoe's pamphlet on Peace with France."

For the next two weeks she "had a proof" or she was "busy with proofs." The plays continued to come out—*Provoked Husband, Distress'd Mother, Duenna.* Just after Ash Wednesday, she wrote that she had finished reading "Calais," another play of Colman's, *The Surrender of Calais.* By Sunday she had finished writing her *Remarks,* and on the following Tuesday she reports, "at tea Mr. Colman's 'Heir at Law' was brought me—far from displeased with his published address to me." On Wednesday she was "at my answer to Colman," on Thursday, "at my reply to Colman," on Friday, "Gloomy, windy, dry and excessive cold—at my reply to Colman all day again," and by Sunday she writes, "finished my reply in the rough to Mr. Colman, Mr. Robinson called." On Monday, March 14, Mrs. Opie called on her, Mrs. Opie read Colman's address, and they "talked much." By Sunday she copied her "Reply," and on Tuesday she began copying it; the next day "busy at copying and by dusk completed my Reply to Mr. Colman."

While Mrs. Inchbald was busy with proofs and writing her "Reply" to him, Colman was busy as well, though his problems were far more worrisome than hers. The year 1808 was a disastrous one for him, and by the summer, when his Haymarket season began, he was in debtor's prison, and his partners at the theatre were quarreling among themselves and with him. Evidently, during 1807 Colman had made a contract to republish his plays, or at least some of them, and since this was the very time Inchbald and the Longmans were publishing their series, he saw an opportunity to have a bit of extra advertisement. The occasion he chose was the publication of his *Heir at Law.* At the first presentation of this play in 1797, it was a great hit, playing twenty-eight times that season. The character Dr. Pangloss made the play quite amusing. A character that became a favorite with actors and audiences, Dr. Pangloss is a tutor hired to teach Baron Duberly to speak English; the baron says, "Odsbobs, my lady! that's the man as learns me to talk English." In the character of Pangloss, Colman has created a pedant who talks about Milton, Congreve, and Virgil, mixes such words as "vernacular" and "vermicular," "concert" and "consort," and sprinkles his conversation with Latin phrases that the baron (who is really a tradesman) does not understand. The use of Latin phrases is the cue for Colman's letter, printed with the play.

After his introduction, in which he complains about his contract for his copyright, Colman attempts to place Inchbald with women who did not have an understanding of Latin and the classics.[39] It was actually a cliché of the male chauvinist view, used especially to assert male superiority. For example, Henry Fielding, writing the preface for his sister Sarah's novel, pointed out that he had not been present to correct her grammar. Greek and Latin, moreover, were the possessions of those men who had gone to university. Colman's language here reminds his readers that he and his father were educated gentlemen and Mrs. Inchbald was merely a female writer, an irony on his part, since, in spite of his father's insistence, he had dropped out of school and made a secret and unfortunate marriage. It is true that his father, George Colman the elder, was a fine scholar, having published a translation of Horace's *Epistola ad Pisones, de arte poetica,* but his father's work had been published many years before. Colman the younger, though he had written successful plays, had never done a translation of anything, classic or otherwise.

Continuing to speak of his own work, he says he could have pointed out "*twenty* of my blots, in the *right* places, which have escaped you, in the labour of discovering *one* in the wrong." Such petty comments, without any examples of his "blots" and her "wrong places," set the tone for the remainder of his "complaint." He objects to her criticism of his father's play *The Jealous Wife* for "mixing, *ad libitum,* the biographer with the critic. Oh, Madam! is this grateful? is it *graceful,* from an ingenious lady, who was originally encouraged, and brought forward, as an authoress, by that *very man,* on whose tomb she idly plants the poisonous weed of remark, to choke the laurels which justly grace his memory?"[40]

He next reprimands her for not consulting him about his father's *Clandestine Marriage* and the part Garrick had in it. He then turns to his own plays—"allow me merely to ask a few questions." To later readers his review of her criticism of his plays is largely unintelligible without reading the play in question and her comments and his. But his comments bring up several interesting points that would have been understood by current readers. The whole of the series now entitled *The British Theatre; or, A Collection of Plays* was published by the Longmans, but they had bought the right to do so from Bell, whose *Bell's British Theatre* had been immensely successful for many years. A great many publishers and writers were very jealous of Bell's success; moreover, copyright laws were difficult to enforce. It should be pointed out, however, that Bell's edition included more plays by Colman the younger (eight in all) than by any other writer except Shakespeare and that Inchbald is on the whole very complimentary of Colman's work. The *Remarks* in volume XX on his plays show her usual concerns; for example, she calls him to task for setting *Inkle and Yarico* in America rather than in Africa and for the language used by Irish bog-trotters and Yorkshire clowns in his *John Bull*. Colman concludes his letter with:

> You really clothe your Remarks, Madam, in very smooth language. Permit me to take my leave in a quotation from them, with some little alteration:—
> "Beauty, with all its charms, would not constitute a good *Remarker*. A very inferior *Dramatic Critique* may be, in the highest degree, pointed."
> I have the honour to be, Madam, (With due limitation,) Your admirer, and obedient servant, George Colman, the Younger. January, 1808.[41]

Mrs. Inchbald's reply begins gracefully: "My Dear Sir, As I have offended you, I take it kind that you have publicly told me so; because it gives me an opportunity thus openly to avow my regret, and, at the same time, to offer you all the atonement which is now in my power." She then explains the assignment of writing the *Remarks:*

> The judgment on which I placed my reliance on this occasion was,—that many readers might be amused and informed, whilst no one dramatist could possibly be offended, by the cursory remarks of a female observer, upon works which had gone through various editions, had received the unanimous applause of every British theatre, and the final approbation or censure of all our learned Reviews; and that any injudicious critique of such female might involve her own reputation, (as far as a woman's reputation depends on being a critic,) but could not depreciate the worth of the writings upon which she gave her brief intelligence and random comments.[42]

At this point in her apology, she turns to personal matters—she had been ill; she had to meet a deadline; she had other distractions. She reminds him that for his *Mountaineers* she had reported what he had said to her; her comments about his opera *Inkle and Yarico* are addressed directly to him as a person she has long known, known intimately as a friend, who knows his explosive nature. She writes: "The admiration I have for 'Inkle and Yarico,' rendered my task here much lighter. Yet that very admiration warned me against unqualified praise . . . and to beware lest suspicions of a hired panegyrist should bring disgrace upon that production, which required no such nefarious aid for its support."[43]

Thus she felt she should not be altogether complimentary of everything in the play. At this point she addresses his comment that he could have found many "blots" had she asked him to do so. It is obvious that his objection is nothing more than mere pique, and Inchbald, as she continues her comments, makes clear that she knew him very well indeed: "Sir, had I exposed any fault but such as you could easily argue away, (and this, in my Preface, I acknowledged would be the case) you would have been too much offended to have addressed the present letter to me; your anger would not have been united with pleasantry, nor should I have possessed that consciousness which I now enjoy—of never having intended to give you a moment's displeasure." As for his father, George Colman the elder, she writes:

Of your respected father I have said nothing that he would not approve were he living. He had too high an opinion of his own talents, to have repined under criticisms such as mine; and too much respect for other pursuits, to have blushed at being cloyed with the drama. . . . But, in thus acknowledging my obligations to Mr. Colman the *Elder*, let it be understood, that they amounted to no more than those usual attentions which every manager of a theatre is supposed to confer, when he first selects a novice in dramatic writing, as worthy of being introduced on his stage to the public.[44]

This last remark about the obligations of the manager her readers would have understood, for it was widely known that Garrick had trained many a novice; and as we have seen, Harris had certainly done the same careful reviews of the plays he produced. Her final paragraph is her final witty rejoinder to his comments:

Permit me, notwithstanding this acquiescence in your contempt for my literary acquirements, to apprise you, that in comparing me, as a critic, with Madame Dacier, you have, inadvertently, placed yourself, as an author, in the rank with Homer. I might as well aspire to write remarks on 'The Iliad,' as Dacier condescend to give comments on 'The Mountaineers.' Be that as it may, I willingly subscribe myself an unlettered woman, and as willingly yield to you all those scholastic honours which you have so excellently described in the following play.

She signs herself:

I am, dear Sir, (With too much pride at having been admitted a dramatist along with the two Colmans, father and son, to wish to diminish the reputation of either,) Yours, most truly and sincerely, Elizabeth Inchbald. March, 1808.[45]

Boaden's only comment after he has included the letters is another acknowledgment of the importance to the men of "scholastic honours." He writes: "The *comic* writer breaks out most in her conclusive sentence, where she willingly yields to the author of the 'Heir at Law' all the *scholastic honours* he so excellently describes in Pangloss."[46] Pangloss is a very exaggerated comic character; Inchbald's remark is surely ironic.

Boaden's attitude is the predictable one, since, even though he was writing more than a decade later, he remained the male chauvinist. Boaden says she had "slender preparation" for the task and that doing so was "a measure not sufficiently weighed by her, and calculated to open various sources of displeasure against a person whose interest it assuredly was to conciliate every body." Just why she should conciliate everybody is not clear—Boaden does not explain, but he continues to comment: "There is something unfeminine, too, in a lady's placing herself in the seat of judgment. Criticism has been commonly supposed more nearly allied to LEARNING than to GENIUS; and although the posterity of the latter may consist of nearly an equal number of both sexes, yet, as learning but seldom appears in the female garb, it is commonly thought that criticism requires something beyond genius to arm itself fully for its awful task."[47]

With such comments Boaden was supporting the idea that women were not capable of acquiring "classical" learning; such learning was an area of male education in the eighteenth century. As Linda Bree points out in her study of Sarah Fielding, "it provided 'a code of culture, a privileged discourse' upon which the public and political world depended; but for that very reason it was regarded as entirely inappropriate for women, whose lives were led in the private and domestic sphere. Women skilled in Greek and Latin found themselves regarded as unfeminine, not to say unnatural."[48] Charles Howard Ford, writing about Hannah More, observes, "To the Georgians women who attempted to master this road [classical learning] their status were therefore unladylike."[49] Boaden's "smart" remarks about Inchbald were not even original, however witty he intended them to be. She had shown herself sharper than either Boaden or Colman when she pointed out that if she were compared to Dacier, the leading French classicist of the period, Colman would be the translator of Homer—he was far from it, and to remind him at this point must have caused him to contrast his father, who had a real classical education, with himself, who failed to complete his university years.

Inchbald's pocket-books of 1807 and 1808 give a far more accurate picture of the problems she had with her *Remarks*. Because she had virtually completed her assignment when the Colman "complaint" appeared, she was obliged once more to take on an additional task. The entries after she found Colman's letter did not end after she completed her reply. She had worked on her response over a period of some three weeks, copying it twice before she finally recorded "Put by my reply as complete." And on a Wednesday, a week later, she writes: "Fine and warm—all day seeking out & reading those remarks which Mr. C has alluded to in his address to me; & they gave me pleasure and contained nothing objectionable."

The entries about her "letter" continued for some time. On Monday, June 6, in an extra box at the top of this week, she recorded, "My Remarks on 'Heir at Law' & reply to Colman sent for and printed," and the next day, "sent my Remarks on 'Heir at Law' to the printer." The next day, Wednesday, she wrote: "Gloomy & cool—Dolly called before breakfast with the Edinburgh Review. Read in it and cooked a mackerel—my answer to Colman returned by the printer with a couple of words altered by Longman for my approbation." On Friday she wrote, "Cloudy & cool—read in Edinburgh Review all day—Dolly called in the Evening—I sat up till morning correcting the proofs for the 'Heir at Law' & my answer to Colman." The next day was fine and warm, and she rose early and worked on her proof again. On Tuesday the fourteenth she wrote, "Corrected my revision of 'Heir at Law' and my reply to Colman before breakfast," and on Saturday she wrote, "'Heir at Law' came out."

Even with the conclusion of her reply, she was not yet finished with the whole project. She began to work on an advertisement "to conclude my remarks." She had been feeling very "low"; adjusting to days without her "work" made her, she said, "Low even more than usual." Her sister Dolly called to report that *Heir at Law* had come out and that "Miss Crunkshanks did not like it." Over the next several weeks, she continued to be "low"; in one entry she wrote, "Fine and warm— Baptist here—very Low till two then I went to shop in Oxford street."

Mrs. Inchbald never again took on a major project; she continued to work on her memoirs, on a comedy that was never completed, and on a translation of a Corneille play, which in the end she gave up.

There is no way to separate Inchbald's work from her social life. One of the pleasures of following her activities from one day to another, one season to another, is to go along with her and her friends. In the summer of 1807, in the midst of work, she went with her friends Sir Charles, Mrs. Phillips, and Mr. Nassau to see the collection of the marquis of Stafford, especially admiring the *Holy Family* by Raphael. In August she went with her friend Mrs. Morris to Hampstead.

The Morrises had a beautiful cottage there, and later, writing about her visit to Mrs. Phillips, she said, "The uncommon beauty of the house at Hampstead quite overpowered my faculties." Her friends had let the cottage, furniture and all, from the former owner, who had recently beautified "the whole like an Arcadian palace." Mrs. Inchbald continued, "This proves what I observed to you very lately, that the person who has many houses cares for none of them; while I love my own little apartments so well, I would not have let them for the five weeks I was at your house for five hundred pounds, and had my furniture *used* into the bargain."[50] These friends, Mr. and Mrs. Morris, were closely associated with the government, she being the daughter of Thomas, Lord Erskine, and he a master in chancery.

Mrs. Inchbald had talked of putting some of her money into a property—she called it "a small purchase of *land*"—and thus not keeping it all in the funds. She did not find a suitable piece for a small property, but her report is interesting for what she says of herself: "I do not care how small a farm I am the mistress of, provided it will only keep me a cow, a sheep, a pig, and a donkey, in case of invasion or other equally perilous event to the Bank of England."[51] She knew about animals from her childhood, and Mrs. Phillips, who lived in Suffolk when she was in the country, would have quite understood. As she investigated the matter, however, she found that property near London was expensive and that she should look farther out. When she did find a farm on the Edgeware road selling for one hundred pounds an acre, she was tempted to buy it but learned that it was already sold.

During this year she subscribed to Bell's circulating library for the first time for 8s. 6d. a quarter. Her own version of this new pleasure reads, "I never subscribed to a circulation library before; and I began now for the sake of reading *Marmontel.* And so, for this trifle of money, I have had four volumes at a time in my house of choice books, that I have read at my leisure."[52] As the year was coming to a close, she was invited to join the group who were beginning to publish the *Quarterly Review,* but although John Hoppner and John Murray tried to persuade her, she refused; the *Remarks* had been enough of criticism for her. Her "Septembers" for 1807 and 1808 show her depression; 1807: "London; after a certainty that my remarks were disliked—very unhappy"; 1808: "London; after all my remarks completed, and my public reply to Colman the Younger's address to me; Dolly very ill, and I hesitating whether to go to Aldborough, to Margate, or where—extremely unhappy."[53] One of her most pressing problems had always been that she found it difficult to find suitable quarters, and over the years she had moved in London to various places, almost as if she were still on the circuit.

So important had she become in the literary world that she was asked to continue various kinds of criticism. Not only was she asked to be a part of the *Quarterly Review;* she was asked to join the *Edinburgh Review* staff as well. She was also asked by Robinson to read a novel of Burney's, which she did, though what she wrote about it to Robinson she does not record in her pocket-book. When John Murray wrote to ask her to do a review of Tobin's after-piece *The School for Authors,* he explained: "As it is desirable to study subjects as well as books, and to generalise as much as to criticise; if, in your review of this production, you could take an excursive view of the present state of theatrical literature from your own knowledge and observation, the Editor conceives this play would be rendered a more interesting article; but he leaves it to your better experience to manage as you please."[54]

In response to Murray's letter, Boaden comments: "Mr. Murray has well explained the principle of modern reviewing, by which a three-act comedy may become the hint to a criticism of four times its extent . . . this will best display the *critic*, and *may* most instruct the public; but the poor author is, for the most part, but a 'stalking-horse,' from whose back the critic deliberately levels at distant and surrounding game, giving his steed a lash or two as he ends his diversion."[55]

Boaden's comments throughout the *Memoirs* remind us that he, too, was a playwright, sensitive about his work as were others about theirs. The *Review* very quickly became a powerful tool for any critic since, as Murray wrote, "the most inviolable secresy will always be observed respecting the writer of a particular article."[56] But after her long task of writing the *Remarks*, Inchbald refused to accept another assignment as a critic—writing criticism for publication, that is.

THE GREAT FIRE

On Tuesday, September 20, 1808, Inchbald's pocket-book entry reads, "A beautiful summer day—had slept little—as soon as I was up heard that Covent Garden Theatre was Burnt to the ground—Harris called immediately to confirm it— Greatly concerned—many lives lost," and on Wednesday she wrote, "Thought much on the Fire of yesterday—the whole account in the newspaper."

Perhaps the best short account of the fire is to be found in a letter that Mrs. Siddons wrote to her friend James Ballantyne, in Scotland. She describes her personal loss:

The losses to the proprietors are incalculable, irreparable, and, of all the precious and curious dresses, and lace, and jewels, which I have been collecting for these thirty years, not one article has escaped. The most grievous of these, *my* losses, is a piece of lace which had been a toilette of the poor Queen of France. It was upwards of four yards long, and more than a yard wide. It never cou'd have been bought for a thousand pounds, but that's the least regret. . . . It is as true, as it is strange and awful, that everything appeared to be in perfect security at *two* o'clock, and that at six . . . the whole structure was as compleatly swept from the face of the earth as if such a thing had never existed.[57]

And to Mrs. Piozzi she wrote about the loss of all her jewels, all her lace; and of the point lace, she said: "I us'd to wear it *only* in the Trial Scene of Hermione in the Winter's Tale, it covered me all over from head to foot. I suppose my losses could not be repaid for Twelve hundred pounds." Not only the structure of the theatre was destroyed, but many houses and properties around as well, and the most tragic part was that there were many lives lost—firemen and spectators who stood too close when the roof collapsed. It was said that the wadding of a gun that had been fired during the play *Pizarro* had gone undetected until about four o'clock in the morning, when the fire was already engulfing the structure.[58]

The original building had been built on the site in 1692, and the extensive alterations had been done in 1792. It was in this structure that Inchbald's plays of the 1790s had been performed and it was the green room here that she had frequented. Here too her last play, *To Marry or Not to Marry,* had been presented.

With the help of his friend the duke of Northumberland, Kemble began at once to build another—even larger and grander—theatre in the same place. The cornerstone of the new structure was laid by the Prince of Wales on Saturday, December 31, 1808.[59] Designed by Robert Smirke, the new theatre was ready in September for the first performance of the season, a performance of *Macbeth.* The new structure was elegant both inside and out; the interior had been redesigned in such a way that the boxes were especially comfortable and beautiful. Kemble, as always concerned about financial matters, both professionally and personally, now announced new prices for boxes, pit, and upper balcony, but the pit and the balcony would have no such scheme. Neither the prices nor the less accommodating places, some of which were so far away that the actors on stage were hardly visible without a glass, were acceptable.

Beginning the first night in the new theatre, the audience rioted, and the riots continued all season. Known as the OP (old price) riots, they were organized demonstrations against the new prices; sometimes they became violent, and from the first no spectator could hear any of the speeches from the stage.

Sarah Siddons played Lady Macbeth to Kemble's Macbeth in this first performance in the new theatre; Thomas Campbell's account of the scene is very dramatic:

The interior of the house was brilliantly lighted up, and served most impressively to display the beauteous order of the edifice, raised, by the creative power of the architect from a late dismal chaos. The groups of admiring spectators, as they entered, burst into the warmest expressions of applause; and, for some time, no sentiment obtruded but that of self-complacency, and the satisfaction arising from novel enjoyment. Before six, the house was overflowingly full, and yet at least three times the number of those admitted, remained in the entrances and lobbies, making vain endeavors to obtain farther entrance. Mr. Kemble made his appearance in the costume of Macbeth, amidst volleys of hissing, hooting, groans, and catcalls. He made an address, but it was impossible to hear it. His attitudes were imploring, but in vain.

The actors all came on as they properly should and spoke as they properly should, but none could be heard; Campbell says, "Perhaps a finer dumb show was never witnessed." The end of this first performance was only the beginning of the riots.[60]

Boaden described a typical OP rioter in his biography of Kemble:

The efficient O.P. rioter, dressing for exhibition in the theatre had to pass, though unsearched, at the doors, and to squeeze himself through an iron or wooden hatch, of our usual width, encumbered as he might be with his watchman's rattle, or dustman's bell, or post-boy's horn, or French-horn, or trombone, with a white night cap in his pocket, his placards of a dozen feet in length wound about his body, and his bludgeon for close action with the enemy . . . he, at the hazard of his limbs, had to make the central *rush* from the back of the pit down to the orchestra, which trembled at every nerve of catgut it contained. And, in addition to all this, he became skilled in the most seemingly desperate sham-fights, ending with roars of laughter, or real combats, to maintain his position in the field.[61]

The riots went on from September until the meeting between Kemble and one of the ringleaders of the OP faction, and many people felt as Siddons did when she wrote: "Surely nothing ever equalled the domineering of the mob in these days. It is to me inconceivable how the public at large submits to be thus dictated to, against their better judgment, by a handful of imperious and intoxicated men."[62] In the end there was something of a compromise with the OP faction, but no compromise could change the physical features of the new building. The boxes were more closed to the view of the audience, the upper range of seats were so constructed as to obscure the sight lines to the stage, and the vast size of the whole enclosure made the stage unfit for domestic drama, such as the social drama of Mrs. Inchbald or Mrs. Cowley, drama that depended on hearing dialogue and seeing gesture.

In the fall of 1809, Mrs. Inchbald was out of town, but she of course knew about the riots. She wrote a letter to Mrs. Phillips dated November 12, in which she commented:

I am rather angry that you seem to doubt whether an Englishman has any right over his own property. The favourite song of the rioters is, 'Britons never shall be slaves;'—but they seem to think the managers of a theatre are to be condemned to the vilest slavery—the will of the mob. As players were out of the pale of the Church under the late government in France, so WE would now exclude them from the protection of our laws. Yet such variety of views have the dissatisfied, that revolutionary principles seem the guide of the public indignation at present; and if they force the managers to reduce their prices, a revolution in England is effected—with this difference, that in France it began by enmity to the Priests, and here by hatred to the Players. Both those orders of persons have been too much idolized in each of the nations, no doubt; but, in destroying false gods, objects of true worship, I fear, will tumble here, as they did under Lewis the Sixteenth.[63]

Mrs. Inchbald had given Mrs. Phillips's son an order to go to the theatre, and she wrote, "Before I gave your son Harry the order, I asked him particularly if he had his father's leave to go, and I represented to him the danger which I thought was to be apprehended. Charles [Phillips] called last night and submitted with a most excellent grace to my warnings; for I told him, he, that had escaped all the horrors of Walcheren, would be *disgraced* to receive a wound or a scratch, a fall or a push, in a mob at the theatre."[64]

On the night of February 24, 1809, Drury Lane Theatre burned. This second destruction prompted many of the pious to proclaim that both theatres had been destroyed by the hand of God. Inchbald's second essay for the *Artist* appeared in 1809 in support of the players and the theatres who stood against this view. The introduction, a kind of prologue to the essay, reads: "The late extraordinary conflagration of our two great Theatres appears to have given rise to many rash speculations of the nature above alluded to. In the visions of the zealot and the enthusiast, the hand of Divine vengeance has been seen, stretched forth to cut short the growth of impieties, which Theatres have been accused of nourishing; and the conviction of some superstitious spirits has been so violent, as to lead them to foresee, and perhaps even to foretel, the recurrence of similar chastisements, already suspended over the vain attempts at rebuilding edifices, mysteriously delivered to destruction."[65]

After this introduction Inchbald, writing in May 1809, argues vigorously against those who fostered "defamation," which is, "unhappily, a vice of most persuasive eloquence; and to the low, the laborious, and vulgar part of community, its allurements are wholly irresistible. There is a certain solace for the minds of such persons in having them impressed with the transgressions of their refined and wealthy neighbours. They are cheered by comparison,—and the expected joys of heaven are inexpressibly enhanced by the assurance, that very different regions are in reserve for those who, in this world, are styled their superiors."

Declaring that of late the English theatres have flourished and their adherents have prospered, she wishes to "counteract the zealot's furious persecution, and to vindicate the literary amusement which inspired the pen of Britain's highest boast—the Poet and the Player." After citing sermon and Scripture, she not only defends drama but also argues that the stage is as powerful for teaching morals and manners as is the pulpit. She deplores those who "libel theatrical representations," for this means "to libel all its patrons; and those defamers seem to forget that their king, their virtuous, pious sovereign . . . those females that form his domestic circle . . . are warm admirers, benevolent protectors, and frequent spectators at the Theatre."

Having made clear her views, she cites the *Evangelical Magazine*, "wherein, the gift of prophecy is presumptuously ascribed to certain inhabitants of London, solely to gratify an uncharitable triumph upon an event, of infinite calamity to hundreds of their fellow-creatures. After giving a precise and apparently malicious account of a late dreadful conflagration, the writer adds—that pious persons, as they passed Drury Lane Theatre, while it was building, exclaimed, 'This house can never prosper.'"

Following this example she remembers the burning of the Catholic chapels in 1780. She follows that reminder by pointing out that both Catholic and Methodist clergy persecute the "poor player." After cautioning the player to be careful of his language and conduct, she concludes "that when these, his two powerful foes, the intolerant Catholic, and the gloomy Methodist (their errors fully pardoned) shall meet in heaven,—they will neither of them be so much surprised to behold *him* there,—as they will on seeing each other."

The experience Kemble had with the OP riots very much lessened his pleasure in managing Covent Garden, even though he planned the remaining season in the spring of 1810, and in the season of 1810–1811 he returned with his usual roles of Macbeth, Hamlet, Wolsey, and Octavian. In June of 1812, he acted Macbeth in Mrs. Siddons's farewell performance. In the spring of 1812, he had resigned as manager of Covent Garden. In January of 1814, he returned to act Coriolanus at Covent Garden after an absence of two years. He was received with great applause, but in that same January, Edmund Kean appeared in Drury Lane playing Shylock. It was in many ways the end of an era and the beginning of another. The theatre world of London became the *Theatre in the Age of Kean*.[66] In the years after 1800, the competitions among the entertainment world of the theatres, the pleasure gardens, the concerts, the opera, and the circus created an entirely new combination for those seeking entertainment. It was a quite different world from the one Mrs. Inchbald found when she came in 1780 as an actress at Harris's Covent Garden.

TWELVE

THE LAST YEARS

✆ After the new Covent Garden theatre opened and the OP riots were over, Kemble finished the season, but the changes that had already begun when he became the manager became more and more marked. Mrs. Inchbald's life in 1809 continued to include seeing friends, working on various projects, and reading. Having refused to be a part of the *Quarterly Review,* when the Longmans came to her in January and proposed that she should select the plays for an edition of "modern" farces, she agreed to take the list she was given and make the selections; the selections were for the most part the popular two-act plays that were given after the main pieces. The title page of volume 1 reads:

A

Collection

of

FARCES

and other

Afterpieces

which are acted at

The Theatres Royal, Drury-Lane, Covent-Garden and Hay-Market.

Printed under the authority of the Managers

From the Prompt Book:

Selected by

Mrs. Inchbald.

In Seven Volumes

London: Printed for Longman, Hurst, Rees, and Orme,

Paternoster-Row.

1809.

In the first volume, Mrs. Inchbald's plays *The Child of Nature, Wedding Day,* and *Midnight Hour* are the first three plays. There is no preface of any kind to *The Wedding Day*, but before *The Child of Nature* there is an advertisement:

ZÉLIE, the French piece, from which the Child of Nature has been taken, was, with great taste, selected from the dramatic works of the Marchioness of Sillery (late Countess of Genlis) by a Lady, who presented the Manager of Covent-Garden Theatre with a *literal translation*—but however correct or elegant, *a mere translation* must have precluded all prospect of success—the Manager therefore sent the play of *Zélie* to the present translator, who with much care and attention, prepared it for the English stage—That care has been amply recompensed by the reception the piece has met, and more especially in those parts of it which she has taken the liberty to add from her own invention.[1]

The advertisement before *The Midnight Hour* in the Longman *Collection* reads:

The translation of *Guerre Ouverte; or, Ruse contre Ruse*, has been given by several hands; but particularly by one, who has printed it under the title of "The Midnight Hour, or War of Wits, as in rehearsal at the Theatre Royal, Covent Garden." This, the present translator thinks proper to mention, as it may tend to mislead the Public in regard to the present piece, which has alone been performed at any of the London Theatres.

These two advertisements remind us of the dozens of translations that were made in the 1780s and 1790s by writers who hoped to have them turned into plays accepted at one or another of the theatres or at the very least have them published. As we have pointed out in discussing Inchbald's *Lovers' Vows*, when she defended herself and her translation in light of Anne Plumptre's published comments, rival translations were a very frequent part of a year's publications.[2]

THE YEARS AFTER

Mrs. Inchbald had never found permanent lodging; she had moved from one boardinghouse to another—from one rented room or one rented apartment to another. She had lingered at the little place on the Strand even when her landlady had told her she must move. Finally she moved to a place on St. George's Row close to Regent's Park. This house was owned by her friend Este—"Parson" Este of the days when she was a part of the group supporting the *World,* but some twenty years had passed, and she was no longer intimate with her former friends; consequently she was very frightened one night when someone pounded on the door and shouted her name. Boaden explains this happening by reporting that Mr. Clarke, Mrs. Inchbald's landlord, had not paid the rent, and Este wished to evict him.[3] Mrs. Inchbald was very distressed about the situation and moved shortly thereafter to another place nearby.[4]

This area, somewhat removed from the bustle of the city, was beautiful; she wrote, "The scene is more beautiful than ever. The trees tipped with golden leaves, and the canal peeping through their branches, which are half stript, with the grass of the extensive ground as green as in Spring, all delight my eye, and almost break my heart. I must have *London,* combined with the sun, the moon, and the stars, with land or with water, to fill my imagination, and excite my contemplation."[5]

These places on St. George's Row were quite near two Roman Catholic chapels, one in Spanish Place and another at Farm Street. After Mrs. Inchbald refused to write for any of the periodicals, she turned more and more to the church, going to mass and confession several times a week and observing the rituals of the church. By 1810 she had withdrawn almost entirely from society, seeing only those friends who sought her out. She no longer went to the theatres; instead she turned to reading and writing letters and conversing with her immediate neighbors. The pocket-books for 1814 and 1820, though filled with incidents of her daily life, hardly mention the theatre or her plays.

Mrs. Inchbald's health had always been uncertain after the years in Scotland and York when, as a player on the circuit, she traveled in all kinds of weather and in all kinds of circumstances, from deplorable roads to stormy seas. In these last years, she had some "complaint" as she called it. The symptoms she records in her pocket-books are not specific enough to make any conclusive judgment about what it might have been, but in both the 1814 and the 1820 books she writes a diary of her feelings about her "complaint." She consulted several physicians, and gradually she felt better, but she continued to record her feelings. She consulted Dr. Phillips, and after her condition returned, she consulted Dr. Baillie; afterward she reported that "my complaint is much less troublesome." These entries about her "complaint" extend over several years and remain a puzzle, the symptoms suggesting some kind of stomach problem. Boaden suggests that her undergarments were too restricting—too "laced up," he called it, speculating that she had a habit of drawing too closely the strings of her underapparel. In her pocket-book she says she began to wear an elastic waist. In the end some of the symptoms suggest that she might have had liver problems rather than a stomach "complaint."[6]

The pressure and frustrations of being a public figure became especially great in 1808 when the *Remarks* were published and Colman attacked her in public. Her records for the years 1807 and 1808 show that she worked very hard. Day after day she wrote, corrected, returned, and checked and consulted with her publisher, Robinson. She also records the various flattering and unflattering comments friends made about these pieces of hers. In the midst of such entries, she also records over and over her various physical complaints. She was upset with her sister Dolly and "had a bad dinner." She was taking medicine, this time evidently by her own prescription, and she became so weak that she could hardly walk. Her friend Phillips called to say his sister was sick to the point of death, and her maid Baptist was sick and could not prepare her food. Among comments such as "had a proof," "corrected my reply to Colman," and "rose early, to a proof—much fatigued," there are statements like "my weakness encreased" and "—something better after Hollies Bowen call'd and came up to my room—went to Bed by daylight." The next day she rose better and continued so, and the day following was "nearly strong again." But the next week she "Had a pain and swelling in my Instep" that continued for several days; there were also such accounts as "Dolly call'd in the morning and told me Mr. Underhill had died suddenly. Went to bed at dusk without Supper."

Although Inchbald herself did not seek out people to meet socially, many people refused to allow her to be a recluse. One of the most interesting of the friendships she formed in these last years was with Maria Edgeworth—indeed with the whole Edgeworth family.[7] Their correspondence was initiated by the Edgeworths, but Mrs. Inchbald responded, agreeing to read and criticize their work and to see them when they came to London. Maria's father, Richard Lovell Edgeworth, was an original member of the Lunar Society of Birmingham; his fellow members included James Watt, Josiah Wedgwood, Erasmus Darwin, and Joseph Priestley, who were all very much interested in current scientific projects. The Edgeworth letters to Inchbald are from different members of the family, not always from Maria, showing how much they admired her and asking for her help.

Another memorable person she met was Madame de Stael, who was at the time a refugee in London, having fled France. In a letter to her friend Mrs. Phillips, Inchbald gives an account of her meeting de Stael. Mrs. Opie had introduced them, and according to Mrs. Inchbald's account, they talked quite easily to each other.[8]

In 1819 Mrs. Inchbald went to live at No. 4, Earl's Terrace, opposite Holland House Kensington.[9] Her search for a suitable place is rather amusing; it also gives an example of "house hunting" that is quite like the present. One of the places she looked at was in Kensington Gore, where the landlady was obviously impolite, asked a guinea and a half a week, and kept the second floor for herself. Mrs. Inchbald says, "Her furniture is crazy, and she would not suffer one bit of mine to come in;—indeed, one of my large trunks only would take up half the bedchamber." When Mrs. Inchbald refused this place on Kensington Gore, she went to Earl's Terrace, where most of the residents were Roman Catholics. Here there was a private chapel where she could attend Mass every day, and it was here where Kemble came to visit her the last time he was in England. When she took up residence there, her artist friends the Cosways were also residents, but they left soon after she arrived, having found a house of their own.[10] Boaden, with the pocket-books before him, observes that she attended Mass regularly and that though the "society" changed rather frequently, the members of the group were "extremely genteel."[11]

Living in Kensington House, Mrs. Inchbald was quite isolated from the usual society she had known, but she continued her correspondence, and she continued to read the daily papers. She also continued her negative views of the government and was especially appalled at the treatment of Queen Caroline; Boaden says she refused to have the shocking writings "read aloud before her, in any mixed society of ladies and gentlemen."[12]

Caroline had been married to the Prince of Wales in 1796 after he had agreed to forsake his "wife," Mrs. Fitzherbert.[13] The marriage was a disaster for everybody concerned. Their only child, Charlotte Augusta, was born on January 6, 1796. George III congratulated his son, the Prince of Wales, but the child did nothing to reconcile the prince to his wife, the princess. She was accused of adultery; they were separated, and she went to live on the Continent; in February 1811 the prince became the regent, and on the death of his father in 1820, he became George IV. Caroline had earlier refused to meet the king when he was the prince regent, and when he became king, he refused to have her crowned queen. The whole sorry mess was in the public prints on and on for more than a decade. It is not surprising that Mrs. Inchbald would have nothing to do with it.

At the close of 1820, Kemble came to bid her farewell as he was leaving England for Switzerland. Kemble had been living in Lausanne but had returned upon the death of Harris; in the letter of farewell he wrote: "When I left you before, dearest, it was to visit Spain, and you managed for me in my absence; now, I think I shall make out my tour to Italy, and end perhaps like an old Roman."[14]

In early July of 1821, Richard Cosway died, another of her friends lost. She continued to attend Mass at the chapel in Holland Street, and frequently during the week she heard Mass in the chapel of Kensington House. She continued to keep her pocket-book, and on July 26 she recorded that she had a sore throat and that her old "complaint" had returned; on Sunday, a day of gloom and cold, she read and walked in the field behind her windows.

She walked out no more. On the following Wednesday, August 1, 1821, at nine o'clock in the evening, she died. On the following Saturday she was buried in the Kensington churchyard. The rites and ceremonies of the Roman Catholic Church were administered, and the two Roman Catholic priests who lived in Kensington House attended the Church of England funeral service. In the end she had two ceremonies, just as she had had two ceremonies when she and Joseph Inchbald were married.

Mrs. Inchbald's friend Mrs. Phillips was left her papers and pocket-books. Her nephew George Huggins and her niece Ann Jarrett were left the bulk of her fortune, in the words of the will "to be divided equally between them both, share and share alike; that share which devolves on my niece to be possessed by her free entirely from any control of her husband."[15] Frances Phillips and George Huggins the elder were the joint executors of her will. Mrs. Inchbald's will, like her plays, was properly written out, stating clearly her wishes.

After her death Mrs. Inchbald's friends wrote about her to each other, and many of them wrote special remembrances in their own memoirs. Although she never found a publisher for her own memoirs, she left in her letters and her pocket-books an unusually detailed account of her private life and the life in the theatre that she shared with many friends, an account that is an invaluable source for understanding the world she lived in, especially the world of London after she went to Covent Garden in 1780. That she burned her memoirs on the advice of her priest is not surprising, because she had long since left the world of the theatre and of all the gossip she had known. By 1821 that world had changed so completely that it was hardly recognizable to those left in it. Though remembered by her friends, she was given little notice in the many times and places where her plays were performed. Her novels remained in print for one generation after another, but with the changed social culture of the nineteenth century, the novels were read in an entirely different fashion from that of the 1790s when they were first published. As is always true of literature that is valuable, her work has remained to be read and judged by the ever-changing but ever-important readers.

In the twentieth century, she and her work were judged variously. Allardyce Nicoll, in reviewing the whole of her work, remarks, "we cannot deny the fact that her plays are as good as any of her time, and that one, at least, *I'll Tell You What*, really challenges comparison with the comedies of Goldsmith and Sheridan. Her sense of construction is perfect. Scene follows scene with absolute precision. Nor are her plots simple. She usually manages to confuse and mingle two or three themes delightfully, disentangling the webs at the end with a skillful hand. Towards this her own love of situation led her surely. She has little comedy of character, but she excels in the comedy of situation."[16]

Many of the feminist critics examine her work in comparison with other women writing in the eighteenth century, usually discussing her novels rather than her plays.

In the 1908 edition of *A Simple Story,* Lytton Strachey begins by observing, "*A Simple Story* is one of those books which, for some reason or other, have failed to come down to us, as they deserved." He continues by pointing out that Inchbald's obscurity is not the only reason for her neglect: "The merits of *A Simple Story* are of a kind peculiarly calculated to escape the notice of a generation of readers brought up on the fiction of the nineteenth century." He found that "The spirit of the eighteenth is certainly present in the book, but it is the eighteenth century of France rather than of England. Mrs. Inchbald no doubt owed much to Richardson; her view of life is the indoor sentimental view of the great author of *Clarissa;* but her treatment of it has very little in common with his method of microscopic analysis and vast accumulation. If she belongs to any school, it is among the followers of the French classical tradition that she must be placed. *A Simple Story* is, in its small way, a descendant of the Tragedies of Racine; and Miss Milner may claim relationship with Madame de Cleves."

It is perhaps ironic that Strachey, like most of his readers, considered Inchbald quite artificial, especially if we remember how she felt about reality and how Maria Edgeworth felt about Inchbald's portrait of Dorriforth. Strachey says: "For in spite of Mrs. Inchbald's artificialities, in spite of her lack of that kind of realistic description which seems to modern readers the very blood and breath of a good story, she has the power of doing what, after all, only a very few indeed of her fellow craftsmen have ever been able to do—she can bring into her pages the living pressure of a human passion, she can invest, if not with realism, with something greater than realism—with the sense of reality itself—the pains, the triumphs, and the agitations of the human heart."[17]

As attention has turned to her plays, in recent criticism of the drama there have been several examinations of settings, characters, and plots as they reveal her interest—and the interest of her theatre—in a wider context than the social world of London. As interesting as these suggestions may be, the critic should always be aware of the time the play was produced and the other plays on stage that season, as well as the fact that setting a play in Spain or in the Mogul's Seraglio was merely a theatrical device to make a background for setting and costumes. No matter the setting, the characters are always contemporary English men and women, characters Inchbald had known and observed and about whom she had opinions.

RUM AND A LEMON FOR A SHILLING AND A PENCE

Over the period of Mrs. Inchbald's records, the conditions of travel and the necessity of coping with the weather—enduring the endless hardships of rain and cold, storm and calm—create an important physical pattern of the life she and her friends led, first as strolling players and later as they acted year-round in London or the provinces. The various indispositions brought about by these circumstances fill her pocket-books and the reports of many of her professional friends.

In the early days in Scotland, she twice barely survived because of the severe weather, and on the trip to France in 1776, when they were becalmed, she suffered severely from the heat. She records that when they arrived finally in Paris on July 21, they bought melons, apricots, and plums; on the way back after an evening at the theatre, they had walnuts and pears, and in one entry she says that Mr. Inchbald bought grapes and pears.

Again on their way back to London, their voyage was rough, and she was very sick until they were on land; and she records on several occasions that since they had no money and could find no work, they did without supper or dinner, or both.

The illnesses Mrs. Inchbald records seem usually to have been colds or the ague; at one point so frequently was she ill in Scotland that her doctor thought perhaps she had consumption. After she came to London, she continued to have days when she was too ill to go to rehearsal. Sometimes she used her own remedies. Once she "took an Emetic" and her sister stayed the night with her. The next day she was sick, the next "still poorly and low spirited"; the next day the doctor came and "staid all morning," but by Friday she felt "very well." She records that she paid three pence for "Brandy for my medicine." In the early accounts she almost always lists lemons and brandy, entries that suggest she used lemons and brandy as medicine, not for food or drink. Boaden felt that much of her ill health was the result of her frustration in not placing the plays and farces she had been working on before she came to London and the heavy schedule she kept for herself.

Along with her own physical problems, Mrs. Inchbald was concerned with her family and friends. She fulfilled all of her responsibilities with admirable care, particularly with regard to her two sisters Dolly and Debby. For some years she attended to both, neither of whom had conformed to the usual means by which one obtained proper or public security. When Dolly was ill, Mrs. Inchbald was asked to respond to Dolly's landlady, even though Mrs. Inchbald hardly felt obliged to give an accounting of the funds she herself had spent. Dolly was better at the end of the year, and she received a set of instructions in a letter from her sister that show clearly Inchbald's awareness of the basis of good health:

> Take chocolate for breakfast. If you be faint, wine and toasted bread between breakfast and dinner; and thus vary your dinner each day:—Sunday, a joint of meat; Monday, two lean mutton chops boiled but not stewed, with an onion, a turnip, and a carrot; Tuesday, a beef-steak, preferably beef roasted; Wednesday, a broiled mutton chop; Thursday, a veal cutlet; Friday, stewed oysters or eggs; Saturday, nice boiled beef from the cook's shop, or a pork chop, a rabbit, or anything more novel you can think of.
>
> Eat, whenever you have an appetite, but never eat too heartily, especially of different things. Have cake or what you please at tea; a light supper; but go to bed satisfied, or you will not sleep.[18]

These instructions are interesting for several reasons, especially since Dolly was advised to eat meat every day. By the turn of the century, there were writers advocating vegetarian diets of various kinds; among these writers was Inchbald's erstwhile friend Pratt, who wrote a poem titled "Humanity, or the Rights of Nature" and another called "Bread; or, the Poor," published by Inchbald's publisher, Longman.[19]

Inchbald's own account of various foods that she ate is recorded, as we have found, in her pocket-books and in her letters. The entries in the pocket-books are filled with references to food and drink mixed with comments about her work and the people who came to call. She drank tea and coffee, she went to bake shops, and her mother sent her food from the farm. In her accounts she mentions eating fruit, wine, a trifle cake. In January of 1781, she had a turkey from the farm, and there are several entries about sending it to her sister. At another time someone sent her venison. She frequently ate fish, and once when she was living on the Strand, she and her landlady had a live chicken that they dressed in the attic.

Inchbald also kept up her interest in fashion. From the first accounts we have in the 1776 pocket-book to the final one in 1820, she makes reference to dress and fashion.

When she came to Covent Garden, one of her first concerns was constructing her hat for the part of Bellario. By 1780 in London, fashion dictated quite elaborate dress for both men and women, and the design of costumes for the stage was a carefully worked out part of the productions. We, as later reviewers of stage setting and costume design, may find great inconsistencies, but we are examining the material long after the fact. A visitor from Germany who saw Inchbald's play *Lovers' Vows* wrote to complain that "the worst feature" was the costumes, that "The landlord and the servants are dressed in the German style of Charlemagne's time, and the others in Hungarian attire."[20] An often repeated story about Inchbald's friend Digges and his acting Cato in 1777 at the Haymarket describes his costume as of "the stiffest order, decorated with gilt leather upon a black ground with black stockings, black gloves, and a powdered periwig." When Kemble became manager at Drury Lane, he tried to use costumes of the period of the plays he was producing. This was sometimes rather strange, since the audience did not understand the various historical periods.

In the description of Inchbald's *Wives As They Were, and Maids As They Are* published in the *Remarks* for the play in 1834, the costumes were described. Lord Priory wore a blue plain coat, waistcoat, and breeches, with a star; a grizzled wig, with a tail; and white stockings, shoes, and buckles. In contrast, Sir George wore a blue coat, a white waistcoat, very light drab breeches, and silk stockings to match. Mr. Bronzely, who needed two coats since the first had a piece cut off, had first a blue coat with a piece of the skirt cut off and second a black coat lined with buff, with figured gilt buttons; and he wore a white waistcoat and breeches.

After she was no longer an actress, Inchbald adopted the fashions of the 1790s as the elaborate designs gave way to the more simple dress that evolved in the years of the French Revolution and the Napoleonic era. In the print published in *La Belle Assemblée* in 1821 (from an earlier plate in the *Monthly Mirror* in 1797), she wears a high-waisted sheer gown with a dark shawl, and in her hair she has plumes. And in the print published in the *European Magazine* in 1807, her gown is low-cut with a draped neckline of light material in contrast to the body of the dress. In wearing the plumes in her hair, she was following the current fashion for hair ornaments. Perhaps it is worth noting that hats—hair ornaments—were very much in vogue during the 1780s and 1790s, as numerous portraits attest. For example, Reynolds's portrait of Sarah Siddons in 1785 shows her hat decorated with plumes, and she is wearing a low-cut dress and a fur muff.[21]

Boaden records that on August 2 in the summer of 1781, Mrs. Inchbald "absolutely appeared without powder; still, however, the natural shape of the human head was only to be guessed at, as at present, winged out by certain side-boxes of curls, and the head thus describing an equilateral triangle, of which the base was uppermost. Still to be rid of the *larded meal* was something."[22]

Unlike some of her friends, Inchbald remained slender and, according to several accounts, beautiful until into middle age. Wilkinson wrote about her in his *Wandering Patentee:* "but to her praise be it spoken she was then and is beautiful still, and that beauty like her understanding, unfaded, and if possible, more impressive."[23] She found it very difficult to face the passage of time, and she laments her aging in both the pocket-books and her letters. Age was as constant a subject for women in the eighteenth century as in the twenty-first, though perhaps their attempts to use paint and powder were sometimes more destructive to their complexions than is the use of cosmetics in the present. Mrs. Inchbald did not use heavy makeup, although she records buying powder to use on stage. One of the problems of retaining a youthful appearance was the state of one's teeth, since losing teeth changed the structure of the face. Once after losing a tooth and looking into the mirror, Mrs. Inchbald was especially aware of aging.

PARTIES, EXCURSIONS, MASQUERADES

Making friends and becoming a member of a social circle was always easy for Inchbald, and when she came to Covent Garden, she found the green room a place to meet and converse with interesting new people. The green room was a special kind of "club" for the actresses, who, of course, could not become members of the social clubs that were exclusively male. This first year in London, she met the marquis of Carmarthen in the green room, and it was he with whom she attended a masquerade, an episode much discussed by later writers, since she included a masquerade in her *Simple Story*.[24] Her own pocket-book account of this occasion is not very dramatic. In the week of February 4, 1781, she records "a comb and dressing tongs 1s/4p. Hair dressing for the Masquerade 3s, a Black Mask 3s, my ticket 11s, coach hire 1s." On Wednesday of this week, she had "sent to ask Mr. Harris for a Masquerade dress c&c." The next day, Thursday, she writes: "A wetish day—read c&c—Miss Satchell calld. I went with her to look at masks and to my hair dresser—wrote a note to Mr. Sheridan . . . in the pantomime— after some consideration went to the masquerade." The next day she writes, "not till morning in bed." On January 30, a Wednesday, she writes, "My cousin Hunt came before I was up and sat and worked till after dinner . . . in the Pantomime— read after and very sorry I did not go to the Masquerade." Since the masquerades were frequent, she perhaps had had to decide whether she would work or enjoy company. She records once that she went to her sister's "frolic," and in the 1780s and 1790s she went to Mrs. Siddons's "open house" frequently. Inchbald and her friends did not have movies, television, or "charity balls," but they had many opportunities to entertain themselves, and they frequently did so. As we have pointed out, the pocket-books are filled with excursions of one kind or another.

Among other gathering places, the artists' studios were popular places to meet friends and acquaintances of the artist. When she lived in Leicester Square, Reynolds lived just opposite; his was an especially popular gathering place. Sarah Siddons's two daughters, Sally and Maria, were there often, and after the Opies were married, Mrs. Inchbald visited them frequently, conversing with Amelia while her husband worked.[25]

In the last two decades of the eighteenth century, the practice of going to shops became something of a social occasion. It was, for example, at this time that Oxford Street was developed, after the Tyburn gallows were removed. One visitor, Mrs. Booth, described various shops:

We strolled up and down lovely Oxford Street this evening, for some goods look more attractive by artificial light. Just imagine . . . a street taking half an hour to cover from end to end, with double rows of brightly shining lamps, in the middle of which stands an equally long row of beautifully lacquered coaches. . . . First one passes a watchmaker's, then a silk or fan store, now a silversmith's, a china or glass shop. The spirit booths are particularly tempting, for the English are in any case fond of strong drink. Here crystal flasks of every shape and form are exhibited: each one has a light behind it which makes all the different colour spirits sparkle. . . . Up to eleven o'clock at night there are as many people along this street as at Frankfurt during the fair.

In another letter she wrote:

This afternoon I took a walk up that lovely Oxford Street. . . . I found a shop here . . . containing every possible make of woman's shoe; there was a woman buying shoes for herself and her small daughter: the latter was searching amongst the doll's shoes in one case for some to fit the doll she had with her. But the linen shops are the loveliest; every kind of white wear, from swaddling-clothes to shrouds, and any species of linen can be had. Night-caps for ladies and children, trimmed with muslin and various kinds of Brussels lace more exquisitely stitched than I ever saw before.[26]

Having friends for tea and conversation was a daily entertainment where Inchbald saw friends and not always players. One friend, for example, who often came to have tea and report "news," was Mrs. Booth, whose husband, Cockran Joseph Booth, was acting at Covent Garden with Inchbald, but Mrs. Booth, even though she was not a member of the company, was a valuable friend.[27] All of the Siddonses and Kembles were Mrs. Inchbald's friends—John Philip, Sarah Kemble Siddons, Stephen Kemble, Frances Kemble Twiss, and Charles Kemble. In the pocket-books the visits of the Kemble family included all these members, from the mother and father Kemble, who now lived in London, to their grandchildren as well, Henry Siddons and his sisters. Charles, the Kembles' youngest child, and his nephew, Henry, were very nearly the same age. The Stephen Kembles appear over and over in her books. In fact, much of the time Stephen and his wife continued to play at Covent Garden with Inchbald until they left and went to various places in the provinces in the winters, but they returned to the Haymarket in the summers and Inchbald continued to see them.

MRS. INCHBALD AND THE ARTISTS

In the small circles of London in the 1780s and 1790s, it is not surprising that the writers and the artists all knew each other, especially since many of the artists were employed to illustrate novels and plays. Mrs. Inchbald knew most of the artists who were her contemporaries. Moreover, the plays in her *Remarks* edition of *The British Theatre* are illustrated, and she herself appears as the abbess in *The Comedy of Errors*. There are several entries in the pocket-books about having her portrait done, and, of course, Mr. Inchbald painted several of her. The only one of Mr. Inchbald's that has survived is an early one, painted on ivory, which is now in the Folger Shakespeare Library.

In an essay, "Herself as Heroine: Portraits as Autobiography for Elizabeth Inchbald," Cecilia Macheski says, "the autobiographical impulse was strong for Elizabeth Inchbald, but her gender and by extension her limited education re-quired that she shape the product of that impulse to suit her own voice, and to conform with the prejudices of her day."[28] Thus, Macheski maintains that her autobiography is to be found in a series of her portraits, an intriguing idea but one difficult to support. The fact is that most of the portraits of Inchbald are a part of a much larger number of theatrical and commercial portraits done of hundreds of actors and actresses for all kinds of publications—for periodicals, for books, for private collectors, for print makers.

From Joseph Inchbald's miniature to the pastel in the Garrick Club, the portraits may be read as stage and literary history, with some of the late ones as illustrations in such periodicals as *La Belle Assemblée*. If we use the entry in the *Biographical Dictionary* as a source, the portraits fall roughly into three types: those that are a part of the illustrations for *Bell's British Theatre;* those that were done for the public, that is for the periodical press and as artists' examples; and those that were done for her friends. For example, her portrait was among those in Thomas Harris's picture gallery.

The selections of Mrs. Inchbald's portraits in *Bell's British Theatre* were as the abbess in Shakespeare's *Comedy of Errors* and as Lady Jane Grey in Rowe's *Lady Jane Grey*. The illustrations in *Bell's British Theatre* were then used in various periodicals. For example, the print of Inchbald as the abbess was used as a print in the *New Lady's Magazine* in 1786, with a print of her friend Mrs. Wells as Lady Jane Grey on the same page. Originally Inchbald's Lady Jane Grey was published in the 1785 edition of *Bell's British Theatre*. This example is only one of many that could be cited. Rose Emma Drummond did a portrait of Inchbald that was published in the *Monthly Mirror*, and Boaden reports that in March 1794 she sat for her portrait to Mrs. Douce.

Both Lawrence and Opie did portraits of her, although these are hard to place; they were probably done for friends. Lawrence may have done one of her to display in his studio, as he did of several prominent people. Because Mrs. Inchbald was an intimate of the Opies, Opie's portraits of her were probably privately commissioned and are perhaps the most accurate ones of the way she looked, for he was especially noted for painting real likenesses, not enhanced, decorated ones as Reynolds and Gainsborough sometimes did.

THE PLAYS AS COMMENTS ON THE SOCIAL SCENE

Reading the plays separately as they appeared from 1784 to 1805, one cannot easily find any consistent "message" for those who attended the performances or who read the plays in the closet. For us, some two hundred years later, it is much easier to consider them in their entirety. For the most part they present an ongoing commentary on Inchbald's contemporary society; in doing so they created for her an important following both of those who went to the theatre and those who read the plays as they came out. In general she was concerned with the problems of marriage and the family, but each play dealt with a special situation, usually having to do with women and their position in some specific problem of her world. Those problems, however, are universal and timeless.

In her first play, *A Mogul Tale*, Fanny is caught up in a situation in which both her husband and the doctor are entirely naive; she is the only one of the three who has any sense of reality. In *I'll Tell You What*, only the second Lady Euston faces the real situation and brings about a solution, not only for her husband, Sir George, but for Lady Harriet Cyprus, Sir George's first wife, as well. In *Appearance Is against Them*, Miss Angle, who tries and fails to catch a husband, presents direct and cynical comments not only about the men but also about herself and other women.[29]

The more serious *Such Things Are* extends the considerations from the relationships between men and women to include government, charity, intrigue, and tyranny. Even though the figure of Haswell as an "Angel of Mercy" structures the serious social commentary of the play, the characters of Lady Tremor and Meanright form the underlying situations of pretense and deception.

For the plays that she adapted, she contrived ways to continue to develop her views of her contemporary society. Even when she was given the task of turning a French or a German play into one suitable for Covent Garden and her audience, she always picked up some current interest to serve as a focal point, as she did in her own plays. For example, she used the balloon craze in *A Mogul Tale*, the Persian shawl in *Appearance Is against Them*, the celebrated Howard in *Such Things Are*, and mesmerism in *Animal Magnetism.*

Another device she used was divorce, and it is interesting to discover how many of the friends she knew were divorced. Since divorce was expensive and difficult to obtain, it is also surprising how frequently she made reference to it. Of course the divorce she was most familiar with was that of Sir Charles Bunbury and Lady Sarah. The scandal of Lady Sarah's affair with her cousin was widely reported at the time, and because she refused to reconcile, she and her baby continued to be the talk of the aristocratic circles in London. In 1769 Bunbury was granted a separation, but it was not until 1776 that he sought and obtained a divorce, which allowed Lady Sarah to marry again. By 1780, when Inchbald came to London, he was again a popular man about town and a very eligible bachelor.[30]

Another divorce Inchbald was quite familiar with was that of John Opie. He was married when he came to London, but the story was that his wife was unfaithful and that she was in love with an army officer. After their divorce she did marry, but in the early months after he came to London, he had had an affair with one of his pupils. It was only after these events that he met and married Amelia Alderson, who was already a friend of Inchbald's.

Women could not sue for divorce. For many wives, whatever their views of marriage, their future was entirely governed by the wishes—the whims—of the husbands they had married as an arranged family agreement. This was the case of Lord Derby, who, in spite of his devotion to Elizabeth Farren, refused to divorce his wife.

Lord Abercorn was another friend of Inchbald's who was divorced. She wrote of him, "Since the very few years which I have known him he has lost his wife (by the worst of all disorders, love for another) two grown-up children by death; he has had his castle in Ireland burnt to the ground; and has broken both his legs."[31] She concluded, however, that he probably had happy days nonetheless.

THE MEN AND THE WOMEN: THE CASE FOR EQUAL JUSTICE

Inchbald has few "perfect" characters. Both men and women belong to the flawed humanity of her *Simple Story*. With the possible exception of Amanthis in *The Child of Nature* and Hester in *To Marry or Not to Marry*, they are willful, naive,

contriving, excessively independent, and self-centered, creating, or at least allowing, the unpleasant situations in which they find themselves. They have run away
and married without paternal permission; they have been persuaded or provoked
into unsuitable marriages, sometimes marriages that have failed. Almost all of the
women are independent and therefore create problems, as, for example, Miss
Dorrillon does in *Wives As They Were, and Maids As They Are.*

The men have perhaps the most unseemly flaws; that is, they are, in most
cases, unwilling to propose to or marry the women in their lives. This reluctance
is especially notable in *The Married Man* and *To Marry or Not to Marry.* Inchbald
also created a whole list of "fops," for example, Twineall in *Such Things Are* and
Bronzely in *Wives As They Were, and Maids As They Are.* Allardyce Nicoll observes:

> She was too practical, perhaps, for idealism to carry her over-far; her English common
> sense pointed out to her one way, what seemed to her the only way, out of a position
> degrading and obnoxious—more degrading than the old fashioned subjection she would,
> no doubt temporarily, have substituted for it. The practical nature of Mrs Inchbald's mind
> is revealed, too, in one other minor matter where she again deviated slightly from her
> models. In her presentation of feminine innocence she kept much nearer to life as she
> knew it than did the authors of the French or German sentimental comedies. She saw that
> her period was a hypocritical and coquettish period. She saw, for example, that no girl
> would act as the original of Amelia in Kotzebue's drama acted, with a fearless sort of
> sincerity, boldly asking her tutor to marry her. This, she realised quite plainly, "would have
> been revolting to an English audience." Accordingly she has kept Amelia as an unspoilt
> child, while presenting her with just those coquettish touches, with just those little hints
> of civilised hypocrisy which would make her conform with life.[32]

THE WIDOW INCHBALD

One of the intriguing puzzles about Mrs. Inchbald's personal life is that she never
married again after her husband's death, even though she had many proposals.
The pocket-books and her letters offer some clues to her determination to remain
free and independent, but perhaps the situation she found herself in London
motivated her to refuse any formal arrangement, for, as time went by and she
became more and more successful, she saw no need to change her status.

We have discussed her relationship with Kemble, a friendship that continued
through all the years after they met in 1777. Long after they were celebrated figures
in the theatre world of London, she is reported to have said she "would have jumped
to have him." S.R. Littlewood gives perhaps the best opinion of their relationship
after Mr. Inchbald's death when everyone expected them to marry:

It is just possible that, although there was still a certain amount of sentiment between them, Kemble and Mrs. Inchbald had already found each other out. Mrs. Inchbald herself must have seen through him, and known the self-love that underlay his undoubted manliness and high ideals and genuine grit. One gathers as much from her portrait of Dorriforth in *A Simple Story*. At the same time, it is pretty certain that Kemble, who would never brook a rival to himself by his own throne, would have found it very difficult to put up with the independence of mind and the freedom of action that Elizabeth demanded all through her life. In short, they would most certainly have both wanted their own way, and a satisfactory match for either could hardly have resulted without a desperate conflict, and a crushing defeat on one side or the other. Even as it was, though they remained friends to the end of their days, there were continual little controversies and coolnesses between them.[33]

There are the several acquaintances she mentions in the pocket-books, some no doubt serious, some casual. There was a Mr. Monson, a Mr. Berkeley of Aberdeen, and there of course was Suett. He and she remained good friends until his death, a tragic tale of alcoholism. For all his talent, he was a shy young man when Mr. Inchbald died and he asked Kemble to present his case to Mrs. Inchbald. Later, in London, when he and she talked again, he must have realized that his case was hopeless, even though he was, along with Wilson, one of those she asked to help her find a place at Covent Garden.

Wilson was her friend for many years, but as we have seen, she refused to marry him, probably for several reasons. For one, he was more like her husband than any of the others, and she had had enough of having to be the stable partner in a marriage; he was always in debt, he was frequently drunk, as she records, and he seems not to have been able to find a permanent place in either Covent Garden or Drury Lane. She had had enough of such instability.

She refused both Godwin and Holcroft, Godwin in 1792 or 1793 and Holcroft in the summer of 1793. They remained good friends throughout most of the 1790s until Godwin's marriage, an event discussed in chapter 10, but it is interesting to note that Godwin never gave up his attempt to see her socially, even in the years after he married again. As late as 1817, he corresponded with her about her memoirs.[34] And in a letter dated February 11, 1820, Godwin wrote:

I have all my life been unwilling to put an ill construction on an ambiguous action; and therefore, though I was sent away in somewhat of a rude manner from your door some months ago, I would not believe that any thing unkind or unfriendly was intended. The repetition of the same thing last Monday seems to leave no room for doubt.

One reason of my confidence was the clearness of my conscience, and my perfect assurance, that since I had last the pleasure of seeing you at Earl's Terrace and Lennard House, I had done nothing that could give you the slightest occasion for displeasure. . . .

I have had the happiness to know you five-and-twenty years; and in all that time I can fully acquit you of any capricious action towards me. Is it worth while to change the tenour of your conduct towards me so late in the day? You, I have no doubt, can say with King Henry, in the song "God-a-mercy, I have a hundred as good as ever was he," and therefore can part with me without compunction. But I must take up the exclamation of King James, "Alas, and woe is me, such another England within, in faith, shall never be!"

Give me leave to subscribe myself, with much regard and attachment,

Very faithfully yours,
William Godwin.[35]

Godwin's letter perhaps had to do with his attempt to help her find a publisher for her manuscript, but it is interesting to notice the dates of these last two letters he wrote her and to realize that she had kept them.

Boaden's version about Sir Charles is that she finally refused to see him because he wished to have an affair with her, an affair that, considering his position, he wished to be public—he wished to be her "keeper," but he would not marry her. As we have pointed out, their relationship probably did evolve into an affair, but she was too clever and too discreet to allow it to be public; both she and Mrs. Siddons were very much aware of their reputations as virtuous women in a society where every actress was said to be tainted by the theatre—by being an actress. Although such gossip was in many cases just that, there was always Mrs. Bulkley, Mrs. Hartley, Becky Wells, and many another, who, while they remained devoted to a single man, did not have the blessing of church and state. Moreover, Sir Charles must have been dreadfully dull and stodgy, characteristics Mrs. Inchbald would surely have found extremely distasteful. And perhaps the real reason was that, like Lady Sarah, she would have been expected to live at Barton; she did not wish to return to Suffolk, no matter how grand the estate she was mistress of.

The two young men she became involved with—Dr. Gisborne in 1794 and Charles Moore in 1796—were both in love with her, and Charles Moore would certainly have married her if she had accepted him. Dr. Gisborne went to the Continent in 1795, and Charles Moore died. Boaden, writing about Moore, represents Mrs. Inchbald as feeling old and ugly before her time when he says: "the beauties still remaining were sufficient to inspire a very ardent love for her in a very young man, of very good family, considerable talents, and likely to become no inferior ornament of a brilliant and honorable profession. We allude to the attachment of the late lamented Charles Moore, whom we personally knew and esteemed; whose convivial powers were peculiarly fascinating, and whose melancholy close has already occupied the pen of the lady whom no disparity of years prevented him from wishing to be the GRACE and GUIDE of his existence."[36]

Moore was a friend of Sir Thomas Lawrence, and when Lawrence was proposing to do Mrs. Inchbald's portrait but, in his usual desultory way, had delayed, Moore wrote to her, "I saw Lawrence to-day; he expects you *for certain*." Moore was the author of "Character of Mrs. Inchbald by Mr. Moore," which Boaden published. In it Moore points out: "Her school was society; to which she gratefully returned, as an instructoress, what she had gathered as a scholar. Her passion was the contemplation of superior excellence; and though her personal charms secured her admirers, which flattered her as a woman, she preferred the homage of the MIND, in her higher character of a woman of genius. A little disposition to coquetry perhaps she had, but the frankness of her nature disdained it; and when necessity called for the choice of the one or the other, sincerity was sure to triumph."[37]

Moore's view of her character is perhaps the view of most of her friends. He commented that "Her conversation was easy and animated." It was said of her that when she came into a room and took her seat, all the men gathered around her to talk, so animated was her conversation. That skill is evident in all her plays.[38]

Mrs. Inchbald's relationship with Thomas Harris is the most puzzling of all her connections. Harris has not had a good press; he has been found to be severe and unsympathetic to his players and his authors, but the truth of the matter is that he kept tight control of the business of Covent Garden, making it far more successful than either Drury Lane or the Haymarket. Neither Sheridan nor Colman the younger ran so successful an operation. He has been accused of being excessively interested in finances and very little interested in the substance of the plays he presented. Neither accusation is true. He did make a financial success of Covent Garden, and perhaps he paid too much attention to the "popular culture" of his time, but he paid his players on time, and he paid his writers reasonable fees, unlike Sheridan, who was always in debt and who never paid his players on time—in fact, Sheridan never paid them, creating the situation that resulted in Kemble's and Mrs. Siddons's departure from Drury Lane for Covent Garden.

Throughout Boaden's *Memoirs* and Inchbald's pocket-books, there are repeated references to Harris and their relationship, which in the end was very personal. In the early days he teased her; she knew his reputation as an admirer of beautiful women, but she certainly knew how to have her own way, and the evidence in the pocket-books indicates that she had frequent conversations with him about her work, but scattered here and there are personal comments about him. He teased her by taking her "spying glass"; he gave her a watch, which she returned. And she no doubt saw him daily during the season, both when she was an actress and later when she worked on her plays. Some of the social situations in both theatres occurred in the green rooms, and here Harris certainly associated with all the players.

Boaden was himself somewhat puzzled as to how the professional and the personal relations between Inchbald and Harris must have developed in the years they worked together. In discussing *Wives As They Were, and Maids As They Are,* Boaden quotes a letter to Inchbald from Harris; Boaden's comments precede the letter, pointing out that Inchbald and Harris had words at the rehearsal, and he continues:

Managers seldom really excuse such interferences with their arrangements. On this subject it is probable that there might pass what she calls an *insult* to her in the green-room by Mr. Harris, before Mrs. Mattocks. This, oddly enough, in April he followed by a kind of *love-letter,* to which on the day following he sent for an answer. The sort of answer he would get may be easily imagined; and Harris explained himself out of his dilemma with the address of an experienced general.

TO MRS. INCHBALD.

"I came into the Square to-day, meaning to protest against the *insult* with which I am charged; but I durst not trust my feelings, and passed your door. I wish you knew my whole heart! but it has sensations that are too keen, and is obliged to take refuge in stubborn *silence,* or reasoning, or (if you will) *compelling* itself to APATHY. 'Intentional insult?'— No: not to you.

Shall I take places for the new opera at D.L. on Saturday? Will you go? T.H."[39]

It is interesting to observe that this is one of the letters Inchbald kept for over twenty years and several "removes."

In town Harris had a house in Bow Street very near the theatre; he also had a house in Wimbledon. Harris was a very sophisticated, educated man, and although from the beginning of his part in Covent Garden, he intended to make the operation profitable, he was not insensible to the quality of his players and the suitability of the plays he accepted.

From his early affair with Jane Lessingham, he had three sons, one of whom, Henry, succeeded him as proprietor of Covent Garden. Harris commissioned a large collection of theatrical portraits, Inchbald's among them, a collection that was sold in 1819 shortly before his death. The collection was housed at his country estate, Belmont, in a building constructed specifically for it, which one contemporary source called a "mimic hermitage."[40] These portraits included most of the principal actors and actresses from Garrick to 1800, and no doubt when Inchbald visited Belmont, she was given a tour of the gallery.

The Success of Being a Professional

Without realizing it, perhaps, Mrs. Inchbald became one of the first professional writers to succeed in writing both plays and novels in her time. Fanny Burney wrote plays and novels, but only her novels were successful; her one play that was produced survived for only two nights. Mrs. Cowley, Mrs. Inchbald's only contemporary rival, did not write novels, and when Jane Austen began writing in the 1790s, the only plays she wrote were for her family performances.

Certainly Inchbald's experience as an actress gave her a basis for writing; her constant attention to rewriting and revising created a context for submitting her work to her friends and colleagues, thus using their criticism to improve her work. Twiss was an especially fine critic, and she listened to him and Colman the elder in her early career. Even so, her success was quite remarkable considering the competition she faced. It is surprising to realize how few new plays were presented each season. Because her friends Holcroft, Colman, Morton, and Reynolds were all presenting successful plays during the years she was writing, because only Drury Lane, Covent Garden, and the Haymarket were licensed, and because of the repertory system, the number of new plays each season was limited, especially if one play was very successful. Her friends Godwin and Mrs. Opie hoped to have plays presented; both were unsuccessful.[41]

Colman, writing about his first experience after he became a manager, explained:

> People would be astonished if they were aware of the cart-loads of trash which is annually offer'd to the Director of a London Theatre. . . .
> The very first manuscript which was proposed to me for representation on my undertaking theatrical management, was from a nautical gentleman, on a nautical subject:—the piece was a trageck description, and in five acts;—during the principal scenes of which the Hero of the Drama declaim'd from the main-mast of a man-of-war without once descending from his position.[42]

Perhaps Godwin's experience with his play *Antonio* will serve as an example of "important" people who were totally unsuccessful in their attempt to write plays that were accepted. Writing about Godwin's disappointment, Charles Kegan Paul says:

> The failure of *Antonio* was a very serious matter. . . . His pecuniary circumstances had long been increasingly unsatisfactory, and he was of all men least fitted to manage such a household as his own, the expenses of two little girls and their attendants lying quite

outside his experience. In play-writing he had found, as he considered, an occupation peculiarly suited to his genius, one, moreover which could more quickly yield definite results, and bring at once fame and money. The disappointment of his hope brought matters to a crisis, and many letters of this year, not interesting in their details exhibit him in the position, so sad for any man, saddest of all for a man of great ability and lofty aims, of appealing to one friend after another for money and of making excuses for non-payment, and neither in applications or refusals, was he or could he perhaps be quite straightforward.[43]

Mrs. Inchbald wrote Godwin a witty but quite unsympathetic letter that prompted Paul to remark, "Mrs. Inchbald certainly excelled most of her sex in the power of saying a disagreeable thing in the most irritating manner."[44] In one of his digressions, Boaden wrote: "I hope that I do not digress at all when I thus unfold the beauties of our great authors. I will not repeat the criticisms of others; but if my own reading and taste suggest what may lead to sound criticism, I will avow that I never intended to write a mere chronicle of events or a cold catalogue of even good qualities among the professors of the stage. The skill of an actor operates upon the primary skill of the author."[45]

In the case of Godwin and *Antonio,* the actor was Kemble; Herschel Baker's account is yet another footnote about Godwin, Inchbald, and Kemble, as well as a comment about Sheridan and Drury Lane. Baker, writing about the financial difficulties Kemble was having with Sheridan, adds:

These financial difficulties—nothing new in a theatre controlled by Sheridan—were accentuated by other vexations. William Godwin, in an evil hour, had written his dolorous *Antonio* and had persuaded Sheri to produce it, and poor Kemble . . . was faced with the thankless task of staging and acting in a play he had nothing but contempt for. Godwin, rather declined in fortune since his *Political Justice* had set all the young intellectuals agog seven years before, was offensively generous with his suggestions: he expected to make £500 by the venture and was not reluctant to favor Kemble with his advice as to details of the production. But the actor, sadly wise in the ways of the inexperienced authors, protected none of Godwin's illusions. He sharply demanded a final version at once and told the aggrieved playwright that *Antonio* "may be acted five or six or seven nights, but that kind of success would at once be a great loss to the theatre, and I daresay a great disappointment to your expectations." . . . The one and only performance (December 13) proved an unmitigated failure.[46]

Another would-be playwright was Mary Robinson. Robinson was Perdita, the discarded mistress of the prince who in the end turned to writing to support herself. Her poems had some success, but again, although she had been successful as an actress before she had become the prince's mistress, she did not have the skill to become a playwright; her only play, *Nobody*, was played at Drury Lane. It was about fashionable ladies who gambled and their footmen, and it is not surprising that it failed.[47]

THE FRUITS OF HER LABOR

Though always careful to record the sums she earned for her work, Inchbald did not leave a detailed account, but in the end she was comfortably well-off. In fact she kept a basket of guineas at the door of her apartment, so that any visitor who needed money could simply take it without having to ask. After she came to London, she was never seriously in debt, but many of her friends were, and she quite understood their predicament. In a society in which shopkeepers extended credit and everyone was free to buy and not pay immediately, almost all her friends in the theatre were constantly in debt. She used gaming in several of the plays, for example in *Next Door Neighbors* and *The Wise Man of the East*, to point out the evils of gambling.

As we have found, she virtually supported her family—her sisters, her brother, and his wife after his death. She arranged for her sister Mrs. Bigsby to be cared for in Barton, and she herself supported both Dolly and her sister Hunt in their last years. In spite of the moneys she spent for her relatives, she continued to prosper, buying into the annuities until in the end she lived on the interest and left the annuity to her niece and her nephew, Ann Jarrett and George Huggins.[48]

Boaden discusses her finances in scattered places, pointing out that in the year when the Bank of London was caught in the interruption of the impending war with France, she left her funds there when many people were withdrawing theirs for fear the bank would fail. She never withdrew her funds, and in the end she left some five thousand pounds in her estate.

One interesting task is to collect the comments various people made about the money that Inchbald made from the plays, that is, the plays that were produced. One visitor to London wrote, "Mrs. Inchbald received 705 pounds sterling in the winter of 1786 for her mediocre comedy *Such Things Are*. Hence it is worth while to compose a play."[49]

During her lifetime Inchbald was severely criticized for being miserly. Her friend John Taylor wrote: "Mrs. Inchbald was censured and ridiculed by many of her former theatrical connections, and even some of her private friends, for her thrifty habits, which were imputed to her extreme love of money, as she had derived much profit from her plays and other productions. Having a sincere friendship for her, I told her in a letter what I had heard."[50]

Mrs. Inchbald's answer to his letter is significant not only for her own defense but also for the examples she gives of what she "might of done," examples that reveal the practices of some of her friends and acquaintances:

> I am now fifty-two years old, and yet if I were to dress, paint, and visit, no one would call my understanding in question; or if I were to beg from all my acquaintance a guinea or two, as subscription for a foolish book, no one would accuse me of avarice. But because I choose that retirement suitable to my years, and think it my duty to support two sisters, instead of one servant, I am accused of madness. I might plunge in debt, be confined in prison, a pensioner on "The Literary Fund," or be gay as a girl of eighteen, and yet be considered as perfectly in my senses; but because I choose to live in independence, affluence to me, with a mind serene and prospects unclouded, I am supposed to be mad.[51]

In his discussion Taylor wrote, "Such a letter does honour to her feelings and I am proud of having tempted her to write it." Like Kemble and Godwin, he felt he had the obligation to admonish her, to write: since "hearing her character arraigned for avarice and meanness among the theatrical community, I deemed it right to adopt an intrepid sincerity, such as friendship demanded."[52]

It is because of Taylor that we have some account of her Memoirs, information found only tentatively in Boaden, who, unlike Taylor, did not know her intimately. Taylor writes:

> As far as I can recollect, I advised her to suppress it. With respect to her memoirs, the following is authentic and ludicrous. The manuscript was submitted to the judgment of my friend Mr. Alexander Chalmers, and a more liberal and judicious critic could not have been found. As the work consisted chiefly of that portion of her life which passed in provincial theatrical companies, before she came to London, and nothing of what occurred after she was engaged at a London theatre, when her mind was expanded, and her knowledge augmented by an intercourse with literary and other enlightened connections, Mr. Chalmers advised her to suppress it.[53]

Taylor continues to relate the story of a publisher who consulted her and Chalmers, but when Chalmers told him that he disapproved of the publication, the publisher, observing that Chalmers was a "grave character," thought the work "might savour too much of youthful levity, and be of too piquant a nature for him to relish." He "started from his chair, seized his hat, left the room abruptly, and hurried to Mrs. Inchbald, telling her that he declined purchasing the work."[54]

It is tempting to suggest that this "publisher" might have been Phillips. Taylor must surely have known his name, but he says only, "Yet this man has come forward as a moral and political reformer, and perhaps is one of the Society for the Suppression of Vice and Irreligion." Taylor's comment, made many years after the fact, can be viewed as the ongoing moralizing of the early nineteenth century, reminding us of the comments about Inchbald's play *Wives As They Were, and Maids As They Are* in Dolby's *British Theatre.*[55]

Taylor certainly knew how generous Inchbald was, for she insisted on paying him for his help in creating the "rhyming" butler's part in *Lovers' Vows,* and when he insisted that he would take no money, they went together and bought lottery tickets; Taylor had better taken the twenty guineas she wished him to have, for their "fortune" turned out to be only three pence each.

Over the years as her plays were presented, a great many spectators made comments about them, especially after the initial run, when they could be presented anywhere. We have discussed Wilkinson's experience with her *Such Things Are,* and when Jordan played in *Child of Nature,* it was her acting, not the play, that was admired.[56]

In recent years various writers—various critics—have sometimes made slighting remarks about her plays, often placing her in the rather mediocre group of playwrights writing in the last two decades of the century. Such discussions usually occur in the context of the years after Garrick's death. For critics who evaluate the plays of this period against the plays of the Restoration or the later Victorian period, the comedies presented from 1780 to 1810 are slight, mere entertainment perhaps, and Inchbald is included along with Reynolds, Cumberland, and their contemporaries.

Judith Phillips Stanton has made an important statistical survey of the work of women dramatists, both of the plays produced and of the plays printed. Inchbald is listed as the third most successful dramatist by number of plays both staged and published, after Centlivre and Behn.[57]

Cheryl Turner, in *Living by the Pen: Women Writers in the Eighteenth Century,* includes Mrs. Inchbald in various discussions along with other women writers.[58] Dale Spender, editor of *Living by the Pen: Early British Women Writers,* includes an essay by Katharine M. Rogers entitled "Elizabeth Inchbald: Not Such a Simple Story," in which she examines both *A Simple Story* and *Nature and Art.*[59]

Doran has asserted that Mrs. Inchbald "exhibited a skill and refinement" remarkable for a farmer's daughter; he says, "In her plays, the virtues are set in action; and there is much elegance in her style."[60] Littlewood, commenting on her plays, says, "Mrs. Inchbald could devise bright comedy-scenes, but her dialogue never had that natural, brisk staccato which her predecessor, Mrs. Centlivre—undoubtedly a finer dramatist,—had at command." He felt that *Such Things Are* was couched in too obviously stilted an eighteenth-century jargon for toleration by an average audience.[61]

Allardyce Nicoll, in his *History of Late Eighteenth Century Drama*, described Inchbald as "an authoress who, considered from the historical point of view, is one of the most interesting figures of her time." After reviewing her plays that were adapted from the French and the German, he says: "her best works of individual inspiration are more nearly allied to the French and German humanitarian dramas than to the sentimental English plays immediately preceding them. They are full of the same air of serious purpose, the same *naiveté*, the same earnestness, the same improbabilities." Nicoll cites Burke for his view that "a great part of the French upheaval was due to the continuous and seemingly innocuous stream of fanciful plays and romances that flowed from the time of *Le Fils Naturel* to the last years of the century." He continues, "She was destructive in her attacks on contemporary foibles of society . . . [she] is not always wholly destructive in this way. All but the worst of her characters are amenable to reason, all are capable of being touched by conscience or by good counsel."[62]

WRITING FOR THE THEATRES IN LONDON

The plays Mrs. Inchbald wrote were all done for the London theatres, that is, for Covent Garden, Drury Lane, and the Haymarket. Several of the critics examining her work and that of other women writers for the theatre in the last part of the eighteenth century have not taken into consideration the structure of the monopoly long maintained by the government. Although almost all of those who discuss women and playwriting know that the plays were submitted to the government examiner, several of these critics fail to understand the way in which plays were accepted and produced. Theatre was big business, certainly from Garrick's time until the turn of the century, and if a play was considered unsuitable by Sheridan, or Harris, or Colman, or Kemble, it was unlikely to be accepted in the first place. In addition, no matter who sponsored it, to be successful a play had to be performed at least four nights for the writer to be paid his or her part of the profit. As Inchbald became successful, she was given an advance—her manuscript was "bought"—and if she had been given the commission to adapt a play, she was given an advance and could profit even more if the play, like *Lovers' Vows*, had a long run; but a long run kept another play waiting, a circumstance that happened to Inchbald more than once. Some of the most valuable information in the pocket-books makes clear the situation for playwrights in the last years of the eighteenth century.

THE POLITICAL SCENE

As we have pointed out, Mrs. Inchbald had a wide knowledge of the political scene from 1780 to 1810, but she is never outspoken about the government, nor does she discuss the views of her friends who were involved; for example, she must have heard over and over the views of both Holcroft and Godwin, and for that matter she must have heard both Kemble and Sheridan make comments. Throughout the *Memoirs,* Boaden suggests that he felt she was somewhat radical, even though, as he also continued to point out, she was very fond of the king and the royal family.

Moreover, it is not at all clear just what she did think of the views of either Godwin or Holcroft and their insistence on certain points of social structure and political positions. She certainly paid no attention to Holcroft's outspoken views of insisting on the absolute truth in social situations; he objected, for instance, to the polite "not at home" when one was busy or not inclined to see a visitor. Godwin's journal repeatedly records "nah," meaning "not at home," when he has indicated that he called on Inchbald. Sometimes Holcroft was with him, sometimes not. Godwin's and Coleridge's part in the Treason Trials from their place in the audience does not say anything very bold about either of them. Godwin actually was never an important political figure. Holcroft was much more willing to defend his views than was Godwin, and neither of them had an important role in the actual political events of the 1790s; only Holcroft's unfortunate experience in the Treason Trials and Godwin's letter of defense made a political footnote.

Mrs. Inchbald occupied an enviable position in that she knew, but was not asked to support, most of the players in the political games of the government during the 1780s and 1790s. Sir Charles, though not a very effective member in Parliament, was there for a very long time, and she no doubt supported him in general if not actively. She knew Sheridan and his part in the East India controversy; she knew Horne Tooke; she knew Peter Pindar (John Wolcot, that is), who was very sharp in his views of the king and the government.

Her rejected tragedy *The Massacre* revealed her view of the tragedy of the French Revolution—she was certainly not interested in telling people they should go to France and fight for "liberty," as Mary Wollstonecraft did, but in 1787, when she was a part of the periodical that Topham and Este produced, she must have gone along with Topham's very conservative stance. She, like many others in her circle, deplored the behavior of the prince regent, prayed for the king's recovery, and went to St. Paul's Cathedral to give thanks when he did recover. She very much objected to England's war with France, and like many others, she admired

Napoleon. She followed the news carefully and did not rejoice very much after the Battle of Waterloo. From her perch on the Strand, she saw Nelson's funeral cortege, but it was only a public event.

Reviewing the events at the time of the war at sea and on land with the Pitt coalition involves trying to understand an overwhelming set of events, with the English sometimes overcoming the French, sometimes losing in various places and times, until June 18, 1815, when at Waterloo the English were finally victorious over Napoleon and his army. Lacking the resources of the twenty-first century, the readers in London were unable to have instant access to information and thus could do no more than become informed after the fact. Moreover, there was not as yet a single authoritative voice in the world of print, and though it is interesting for us to read the various periodicals of the time, it must have been difficult for someone like Mrs. Inchbald to come to any reasonable conclusion about the far-flung events reported.[63]

In *Nature and Art* Inchbald discusses directly many of the social conditions, the state of the church and the courts, where she again, as in the plays, takes a detached and ironic view. As we have pointed out, the novel is full of detailed analysis of Inchbald's own world in the 1790s, and the fact that her friends and Robinson delayed the publication from 1793–1794 to 1796 is, of course, an important political statement. Precisely how much of the decision was hers and how much her friends' cannot, however, be discovered. The date 1793 is a very important date for those English interested in the French, who were in the midst of the aftermath of the execution of the king and the attempt to organize a government.

Thomas Paine had fled to France in the summer of 1792, just barely escaping with the help of William Blake, who got him out of the house of Johnson, where he had been when the authorities issued a warrant for him. By the summer of 1793, he had, by lucky chance, escaped again after attending the convention in June in Paris, and later he experienced a very dramatic escape from prison when he was condemned to the guillotine. As we have pointed out before, Inchbald's publisher Robinson had already been in trouble for selling Paine's work.

This year 1793 was the date of the publication of Godwin's *Political Justice*, and in a strange convergence of the fates, it was in the summer of 1793 that Mary Wollstonecraft became the mistress of Gilbert Imlay.

It was in the election of 1796 that Horne Tooke stood again for Westminster; he had two opponents—Charles James Fox and Admiral Sir John Gardner. There was no hope for Tooke to win, but his speeches confirmed his freedom to inveigh against the government, a freedom dearly bought during the Treason Trials. Mrs. Inchbald's friend Amelia Alderson, later Mrs. Opie, wrote to her friend Mrs.

Taylor: "I heard H. Tooke and Fox speak. And that's something. To be sure I had rather have heard Bonaparte address his soldiers, but I may still hope to hear him when the *bonnet rouge* has taken the place of the tiara and a switch from the Tree of Liberty dangles from that hand which formerly wielded the crozier."[64]

One writer reviewing these years observes: "The Corresponding Societies, which had survived Government repression better than those with a less broadly-based membership, had educated their members politically, and their influence continued to work in widely diffused forums and other cultural associations. In these Paine and his works were still fervently discussed and so was Godwin."[65]

It was at this time in April that Godwin gave his dinner party for Dr. Parr and his daughters, Mr. and Mrs. Mackintosh, Mr. Holcroft, Mrs. Inchbald, and, as he wrote, Mrs. Wollstonecraft, although at this time she was known as Mrs. Imlay. All of his visitors were considered "Jacobins," Mrs. Inchbald included, and it is tempting to wonder if they talked of any of the subjects in *Nature and Art.*

The years from 1793 to 1796, then, when Inchbald finished *Nature and Art* and when it was published, were years when she was surrounded with political commentary and Jacobinism. As we look back on Inchbald's life and work, it is not possible to speak definitely about her political views, especially since those were the years when England became embroiled in the war with France. By the time it was over in 1815, Inchbald had retired from the public world of both art and politics.

AND FINALLY

The first decade of the nineteenth century was especially difficult for Inchbald, for those years included not only the burning of the two theatres, Covent Garden in 1808 and Drury Lane in 1809, but also her indecision about her domestic life—moving from the Strand—her work on the *Remarks,* her involvement with Kemble's leaving Drury Lane and moving to Covent Garden, her failed attempt to have her memoirs published, and her loss, one by one, of relatives and close friends.

After the death of her friend Mrs. Whitfield and her sisters—Mrs. Hunt, Debby, and Dolly—Inchbald was frequently lonely, and toward the end of her life she found no solace in reading; even so, Boaden says, "To the last she studied so intensely, that many who loved her affectionately thought it almost a cruelty to interrupt what she made the business of life, by their, as they feared, tiresome solicitude about her health."[66] Her friend Mrs. Wells wrote about the early years: "When she was at the theatre, at such a low salary, she conducted herself with so much propriety that even the very scene-shifters and dependents about it treated her with the most marked respect; and every person there declared there was a something in her which they found it impossible to ascertain; but her pen has since accounted most amply for it."[67] Always independent, she remained so, and there was "something in her" which is "impossible to ascertain."

Toward the end of the *Memoirs*, Boaden writes a kind of appreciation of Mrs. Inchbald, a kind of conclusion of the view of her friends and his view of her as a person, quite aside from the honors she had received and quite apart from her work. This essay is perhaps a fitting conclusion for any review of Inchbald and her world.

As the Kembles pursued the brilliant course which led them into the first societies of this country, they carried the "amiable Muse" with them into high life; and she became an object of anxious request among all who could admire powerful talent, graceful manners, and the urbanity of native wit. To her lasting honour, she could live in this higher atmosphere without disdaining that from which she had no wish to remove—*that* in which her relations and humbler friends received her kind offices, and her darling independence was alone secure! Prosperity in every shape smiled upon her. She accumulated a fortune of some five thousand pounds. . . .

To those who remember her in private, she seemed to possess many of the qualities of Swift: like the Dean, "she told a story in an admirable manner;" she absolutely painted while she spoke, and her language started into life. Her sentences, like HIS, were "short and perspicuous; her observations piercing." She too had seen much of the world, and had profited much by experience. She had not the least tincture of "vanity in her conversation, and in truth was too proud to be vain." She was decidedly polite, but in a manner entirely her own. She resembled Swift too in her frankness, for she spoke strictly what she thought. . . . The materials of this biography are entirely her own.[68]

And it is from these materials that *this* biography is fashioned. Independent, witty, and determined, Mrs. Inchbald serves as an example for anyone who is willing to work without self-pity, willing to work without physical comforts to accomplish the tasks set for themselves, all the while giving generously to family and friends. Mrs. Inchbald belonged to her own time and place, but she also serves as an example for anyone at any time and place.

NOTES

1. IN LONDON TO FIND A FORTUNE

1. She was there some three days before she went to her sister's, and during this time she had little to eat and became confused wandering about to find a place to stay. Boaden, *Memoirs of Mrs. Inchbald*, 1:12, 18–24. Some of the stories of finding a place by saying she was a traveler were probably not true or at least were very exaggerated.

2. Much of the material on the various players mentioned throughout this study is to be found in Highfill, Burnim, and Langhans, *Biographical Dictionary*, hereafter cited as just *Biographical Dictionary*.

3. John Taylor, writing about this episode years later, gives a very dramatic version, which he had from Elizabeth Inchbald, no doubt. In fact, this story appears in one form or another in almost all of the early accounts of Elizabeth's trip. One such account reads in part: "Indignant at his proposals, and not being perfect mistress of her temper, she availed herself of the tea equipage which lay on the table, and discharged the contents of a bason of scolding water in his face. This spoke sufficiently plain her resentment." Gilliland, *Dramatic Mirror*, 2:399–402.

4. Both Elizabeth and Joseph Inchbald were Roman Catholics and were therefore required to be married by the rites of the Church of England, as well as by their own priest, for their marriage to be legal.

5. These *Remarks* were written in 1806 as a part of a series; perhaps Elizabeth was not quite so aware of "passion" in 1772 when she was only eighteen. See vol. X of *The British Theatre*, hereafter cited as Inchbald, *Remarks*.

6. Additional Mss., British Library, London, 46611 ff., 260–63. The list included 66 pocket-books, 14 letters from Mr. and Miss Edgeworth, 20 letters and notes of Mr. and Mrs. George Hardinge, and 24 letters from Mr. George Colman.

7. Boaden had not only written books about Jordan, Kemble, and Siddons; he himself wrote plays—musical romances and melodramas. See *Dictionary of National Biography* (1917), s.v. "James Boaden."

8. These three theatres were the three patent theatres in London. Licensed by the government, they had exclusive rights to the performance of plays in London. Drury Lane and Covent Garden were the winter theatres, and the Haymarket was the summer one.

9. Cecilia Macheski, in her chapter "Herself as Heroine: Portraits as Autobiography for Elizabeth Inchbald," dismisses James Boaden as "a mere recorder." She says his is a

compilation "of mere facts" and that he "lacks sympathy, insight, or any attempt at constructing an analysis." Moreover, Macheski feels that Inchbald's pocket-books "disappoint the avid biographer because they too are little more than *annuals*" and because she "had little space to comment." Schofield and Macheski, *Curtain Calls*, 37.

10. See *Notes and Queries*, vol. 29, no. 3 (1982), 220–24.

11. Standingfield is now spelled Stanningfield on the map of Suffolk.

12. Pevsner, *Buildings of England*, 435. See also Boaden, *Memoirs of Mrs. Inchbald*, 1:3–4.

13. Boaden, *Memoirs of Mrs. Inchbald*, 1:10.

14. See Hodskinson, *County of Suffolk Surveyed*; Scarfe, *Shell Guide—Suffolk*; and Thrisk, *Suffolk Farming in the Nineteenth Century*, vol. 1 (Redstone Memorial Volume), for further information.

15. Boaden, *Memoirs of Mrs. Inchbald*, 1:6.

16. Inchbald stuttered all her life. At some times her speech problem was more obvious than at others: for example, when she was under stress she stuttered badly; when she was with family or friends she stuttered very little. The acting style of her theatre as a declamatory presentation made it more possible for her to act than would the present realistic method of acting. There have been many famous stutterers, including such people as Isaac Newton, Somerset Maugham, Marilyn Monroe, Jimmy Stewart, and Winston Churchill. Among Inchbald's own friends, the famous comic Dicky Suett (also her suitor) was a stutterer.

17. Boaden, *Memoirs of Mrs. Inchbald*, 1:7.

18. Perhaps the fact that Elizabeth stuttered made her all the more determined to fulfill her ambition to be an actress. In 1772 acting was still very formal, consisting of declamation and very little "natural" performance. Under such circumstances the chief requirement for a player was to be a quick study and have a good memory.

19. Boaden, *Memoirs of Mrs. Inchbald*, 1:8–9. Even at this time the print trade was flourishing. Theatre prints of actors and actresses were easy to find.

20. Grice, *Rogues and Vagabonds*, 48–50.

21. The text of the plays used for this study is from Backscheider, *Plays of Elizabeth Inchbald*. The text for the *Remarks* is from the first collected edition, *The British Theatre; or, A Collection of Plays, Which Are Acted at the Theatres Royal, Drury Lane, Covent Garden, and the Haymarket, with Biographical and Critical Remarks, by Mrs. Inchbald* (London: Longman, Hurst, Rees, and Orme, 1808). The plays have been cross-checked with the originals, which came out earlier in single pamphlet editions.

22. The double wedding ceremony was required by law because the Roman Catholic Church was not recognized as lawful in England.

23. The knowledge of such an affair was spread into all the theatre circles. When Dodd and Bulkley came back from Dublin, Garrick refused to hire them both, employing only Bulkley at Drury Lane. See the entries in *Biographical Dictionary*, 2:393–98, 4:412–40.

24. Boaden, *Memoirs of Mrs. Inchbald*, 1:34–35. In this same passage, looking ahead

in time, Boaden tells the story: "It was for this woman that Smith of Drury Lane, at his maturity, made a fool of himself—deserted his wife, with the greatest respect for her all the time, and, like a green boy, would have given up the whole world, as he told Garrick, 'rather than desert his *Rose.*'"

25. Ibid., 1:37.

2. Scotland and the Perils of Travel

1. See *Biographical Dictionary,* 4:401–11; quote from 406. Information from the *Biographical Dictionary* is supplemented by Boaden and later by Mrs. Inchbald's pocketbooks.

2. Quoted in *Biographical Dictionary,* 4:408.

3. They sailed up the North Sea and into the Firth of Forth, coming into the harbor of Leith, which was some thirty to forty miles from Glasgow. Boaden says they rested for a day and on the nineteenth took a chaise for Glasgow. A chaise would have been the fastest and most comfortable means they could have chosen.

4. Rosenfeld, *Strolling Players,* 35–95.

5. Ibid., 72–73.

6. The Garrick version had a happy ending. Much later, in her *Remarks,* Mrs. Inchbald said she did not think his version—or indeed the play itself—was of much value. See below, chapter 11.

7. Rosenfeld, *Strolling Players,* 72–73.

8. Gilliland, *Dramatic Mirror,* 1:235. See 248 ff. for the Edinburgh stage.

9. Families with children counted on using them for the children's parts in the plays, thus adding to the salaries of the adults. Bob Inchbald would have had such parts when they were available.

10. Boaden, *Memoirs of Mrs. Inchbald,* 1:46.

11. See the *Biographical Dictionary* entry on Richard Wilson, 16:162–63, for the account of his five "wives." See also Boaden, *Memoirs of Mrs. Inchbald,* 1:46, for Boaden's account of this "cold night."

12. Boaden, *Memoirs of Mrs. Inchbald,* 1:43. A benefit night meant the actors could select their own play and reap the "benefits" of the tickets sold. In the early days the players went about and sold tickets for their own benefits. Later this practice was changed, but the cost of the production was deducted from the tickets sold. Sometimes the cost was more than the money taken in.

13. Ibid., 1:48–49.

14. Ibid., 1:52.

15. See *Life of Thomas Holcroft,* 2:107. See also *Biographical Dictionary,* 2:232–33.

16. Boaden, *Memoirs of Mrs. Inchbald,* 1:60.

17. Wilkinson, *Wandering Patentee,* 1:231–32.

18. Boaden, *Memoirs of Mrs. Inchbald,* 1:63.

19. For information about Younger, see *Biographical Dictionary*, 16:364–68. See also Manvell, *Sarah Siddons*, 47–49, for an account of Younger and this season at Liverpool; see also Siddons's letter to Inchbald (50).

20. Boaden, *Memoirs of Mrs. Inchbald*, 1:72; see 1:47 ff. for an account of Younger and the season at Liverpool.

21. Boaden, *Memoirs of Mrs. Inchbald*, 1:71.

22. See Price, *Theatre in the Age of Garrick*, 191–95, for an account of the Manchester Theatre and Younger and Mattocks. The debate in the House of Lords (191) may help explain why the company later was dismissed. See Boaden, *Memoirs of Mrs. Inchbald*, 1:69–84.

23. Boaden calls this novel "a brief outline of her 'Simple Story,'" *Memoirs of Mrs. Inchbald*, 1:81.

24. Boaden, *Memoirs of Mrs. Inchbald*, 1:77–78.

25. Ibid., 1:77.

26. Ibid., 1:81.

27. For a discussion of the practice of benefits, see Hogan, *London Stage*, cxxxiii–cxxxvi. Boaden gives no information about benefits for the Inchbalds until they were in the York Company.

28. Boaden, *Memoirs of Mrs. Inchbald*, 1:81.

29. Boaden was so intent in recording all he knew or thought about Kemble and Mrs. Siddons that he constantly includes his own opinions about their conduct and their associates. These entries about the time the Siddonses and Kemble were with the Inchbalds come from Mrs. Inchbald's pocket-book—Boaden includes very little about Kemble's early time in his *Life of John Philip Kemble*.

30. Boaden, *Memoirs of Mrs. Inchbald*, 1:83.

31. Both Younger and Mattocks were to be a part of the Inchbald-Siddons-Kemble group for many years to come.

32. Quote from Boaden, *Memoirs of Mrs. Inchbald*, 1:87. Thomas Holcroft had already been in Dublin and in Kemble's company as a strolling player. He must therefore have already known the Siddonses and John Philip, and he had been in Scotland with the Inchbalds at some point; although he wrote about his strolling days later, it is difficult to be certain exactly when and where he acted. See *Life of Thomas Holcroft*, 1:170–71.

33. It was with Booth that he met the Inchbalds, but it is not clear just how long he was in Booth's company. After the summer season, the Inchbalds went their own way, and evidently Mrs. Inchbald was not associated with Holcroft until after her husband's death.

34. For Holcroft see *Biographical Dictionary*, 7:358–63. See also *Life of Thomas Holcroft*, only the first part of which is by Holcroft himself. It was continued from his papers by William Hazlitt and edited by Elbridge Colby in 1925.

35. This is probably the occasion when Inchbald painted the child's portrait that is in the Folger Shakespeare Library. It is a charming picture of a boy wearing a hat; someone has written "Master Inchbald" on it, but Mrs. Inchbald did not have a child, and the age of the child in the portrait does not fit either of Joseph Inchbald's two sons.

3. WILKINSON AND THE YORK COMPANY

1. See below for an account of Inchbald's playing in *The Belle's Stratagem*.

2. Boaden, *Memoirs of Mrs. Inchbald,* 1:87.

3. Wilkinson's *Memoirs of His Own Life* was published in 1790, his *Wandering Patentee* in 1795. In the *Memoirs* he records some of his early adventures.

4. See *Biographical Dictionary,* 16:97. Quarrels about pirated productions were frequent, brought about usually by the attempt of the playwright to protect his property. Later Wilkinson had a quarrel with Mrs. Inchbald when he produced one of her plays. For Peg Woffington's anger, see Dunbar, *Peg Woffington and Her World,* 215–20.

5. *Biographical Dictionary,* 16:102.

6. Sherington's *York Chronicle or The Northern Post and General Advertiser,* Jan. 1777. It is important to note that the time between the events in New York and the report in the paper was almost a year.

7. Ibid., Feb. 7, 1777.

8. Ibid., Feb. 14, 21, 1777.

9. This report and the following reports of the Inchbalds' playing in the York Circuit are taken from the playbills that Wilkinson kept, which are to be found at the York Minster Library. The playbills reveal a wealth of material beyond the listing of plays and performers. For example, a review of the playbills over a period of several years not only gives information about the plays and entertainments but also includes a great deal of information about Wilkinson and his management of the theatre in terms of the players he hired, the ones who left him, and the problems with finances and personnel. Playbills at the York Minster Library.

10. Johnson, *Lives of the English Poets,* 2:106–7.

11. Linda Fitzsimmons, "Theatre Royal York," *York History,* no. 4. (York, n. d.): 169–91. See also Wilkinson, *Wandering Patentee,* 2:72 ff.

12. See *Biographical Dictionary,* 14:330–37.

13. The experiences of the Inchbalds, the Hitchcocks, and Griffith illustrate players' interlocking careers between the provinces and the London theatres. Griffith had acted in Dublin and London before he went to Norwich, Hitchcock was to leave Wilkinson for Daly and the Smock Alley Theatre, and Mrs. Inchbald succeeded Griffith's sister, Elizabeth, as one of the women playwrights in London after 1765. For information about Elizabeth Griffith, see *Biographical Dictionary,* 6:374–80; for her brother Richard Griffith, see 6:372–74; and for the Hitchcocks, see 7:340–42. Elizabeth Griffith is chiefly remembered for writings and translation, not for the theatre; see Todd, *British Women Writers,* 296–300.

14. The players not listed in the *Biographical Dictionary* remained in the provinces. Wilkinson mentions all of them in his *Wandering Patentee.*

15. Boaden, *Memoirs of Mrs. Inchbald,* 1:89.

16. Ibid., 1:90.

17. Sheridan's play had been presented on May 8, 1777, not a year before the Inchbalds joined Wilkinson; Mrs. Abington created the role of Lady Teazele.

18. This is the first mention of Burgoyne, called "Gentleman Johnny."

19. Kemble had written a long letter to Inchbald about his—and Siddons's—rejection for not being approved by the Royal Patent. See Boaden, *Memoirs of Mrs. Inchbald,* 1:91–93.

20. Ibid., 1:92.

21. Ibid., 1:93. It was in this letter that Kemble reported a riot that had occurred while he and the Siddonses were still in Liverpool; he wrote: "our affairs here are dreadful. On Monday night . . . before the play began, Mr. Younger advanced before the curtain, if possible to prevent any riot, with which he had publicly been threatened for presuming to bring any company to Liverpool who had not played before the King. In vain did he attempt to oratorize; the remorseless villains threw up their hats, hissed, kicked, stamped, bawled, did every thing to prevent his being heard. . . . They next extinguished all the lights round the house; then jumped upon the stage; brushed every lamp out with their hats; took back their money; left the theatre, and determined themselves to repeat this till they have another company" (1:91–92).

22. Wilkinson, *Wandering Patentee,* 2:11–12.

23. Ibid., 1:250. Wilkinson's allowing his son to play reminds us that there were several children in the troupe, Mr. Inchbald's son Bob, for example. Later we learn that Mrs. Siddons's son, Henry, was in several plays with her.

24. Boaden, *Memoirs of Mrs. Inchbald,* 1:95.

25. Ibid. Wilkinson wrote a very dramatic account of Mr. Inchbald's death: Mrs. Wilkinson went to the Inchbalds to invite them for tea in the afternoon, and when she returned, she reported they were "both well and in high spirits" and would be delighted to come. Tea being later than dinner, Wilkinson wrote, "Our dinner was instantly produced, the duck not half dissected, nor the green peas begun with, when a servant came in breathless and pale, wildly exclaiming that Mr. Inchbald was dead!" Thinking her husband had colic, Mrs. Inchbald had suggested he lie down; he evidently expired in her arms, a scene that Wilkinson suggests was a banquet turned suddenly into grief. This whole passage in Wilkinson, written when Mrs. Inchbald was the "Celebrated Mrs. Inchbald," is very much in his joking style, and unfortunately it has been used by later writers as a risqué account of the Inchbalds' relationship. *Wandering Patentee,* 2:56–60.

26. Boaden, *Memoirs of Mrs. Inchbald,* 1:96.

27. Ibid.

28. Wilkinson, *Wandering Patentee,* 1:277.

29. Ibid., 1:76.

30. Boaden, *Memoirs of Mrs. Inchbald,* 1:95.

31. See Annibel Jenkins, "John Dunton and His Post-Angel" (Ph.D. diss., University of North Carolina, Chapel Hill, 1965), 223.

32. See *Biographical Dictionary*, 3:502–7, for an account of Cornely's remarkable career.

33. "Spouting" was the term used to refer to amateur stagestruck gentlemen's declaiming in public—frequently at taverns or such places. The practice was declamatory and fitted nicely into the style of acting frequently practiced in provincial playhouses and, for many of the actors, on the stages in London. Boaden writes that soon after the Inchbalds arrived in Edinburgh, they walked on the hills and by the seashore "to spout aloud." Boaden, *Memoirs of Mrs. Inchbald*, 1:41. See Baker, *John Philip Kemble*, 56–57. Baker suggests that this was the first time Kemble had been in London.

34. For information about Henry Bate, see *Biographical Dictionary*, 7:160.

35. See Wilkinson's account of the quarrel he had with Mrs. Inchbald about her play *I'll Tell You What* (*Wandering Patentee*, 2:59–61), and see his account of seeing *Such Things Are* and then playing it for his benefit (3:32–33).

36. See the Wilkinson playbills at the York Minster Library in York, England. These playbills contain a wealth of information for anyone interested in theatre management as well as scholars interested in Wilkinson.

37. For a discussion of the Covent Garden theatre in this period, see Burling, *Summer Theatre in London*, 138–55.

38. *Biographical Dictionary*, 3:417.

39. Hibbert, *Redcoats and Rebels*, 217–25, quote on page 217. See also O'Toole, *Traitor's Kiss*, 160–65; and Foreman, *Georgiana*, 81–83.

40. Hibbert, *Redcoats and Rebels*, 217–25.

41. Boaden, *Memoirs of Mrs. Inchbald*, 1:107.

42. Ibid., 1:106.

43. Unfortunately, Suett was an alcoholic and died in 1805 in his forties.

44. Boaden, *Memoirs of Mrs. Inchbald*, 1:102.

45. Manvell, *Sarah Siddons*, quotes from 47, 23.

46. There is a watercolor of Siddons as Hamlet, done by Mary Hamilton, in London at the British Museum.

47. See *Biographical Dictionary*, 14:26.

48. See ibid., 6:235–41, for Glover; and 12:143–48, for Powell quotes.

49. This is the first of the three letters in "Three Letters from Elizabeth Inchbald to Tate Wilkinson," located in the Public Library in York.

50. Wilkinson, *Wandering Patentee*, 2:97.

51. Ibid., 2:93.

52. Baker, *John Philip Kemble*, 49.

53. Wilkinson, *Wandering Patentee*, 2:93–94.

54. Ibid., 2:94.

55. James Boswell, *Laird of Auchinleck—1778–1782*, ed. Joseph W. Reed and Frederick A. Pottle (New York: McGraw-Hill, 1977), 47–50; see also 80–81 n. 5.

56. Boaden, *Memoirs of Mrs. Inchbald,* 1:109–12.

57. Wilkinson, *Wandering Patentee,* 2:95–96.

58. Ibid., 2:81 ff.

59. Ibid., 2:85–86.

60. Ibid., 2:88.

61. Ibid., 2:88–89.

62. For David Ross, see *Biographical Dictionary,* 13:103–10.

63. Kelly, *Thespis,* 20.

64. Manvell, *Elizabeth Inchbald,* 188.

65. Wilkinson, *Wandering Patentee,* 2:97–98.

66. Ibid., 2:131. See also *Biographical Dictionary,* 14:166–67.

4. LONDON AT LAST

1. In her *Remarks,* 3:3–4, she wrote about *Measure for Measure:* "Had Shakespeare been the inventor of the fable (the story was taken from an old tale) he would assuredly have avoided the incredible occurrences. . . . Allowing the Duke's disguise could possibly conceal him from his friends . . . there still remains a most disgraceful improbability." She felt that "the grave scenes . . . are tedious and dull."

2. It is obvious from the way she used the room that the furniture was of the kind to push back against the wall and make the room suitable for entertaining guests and engaging in conversation for pleasure or business. Inchbald frequently held both kinds of conversation, as for example with Texier, who sometimes came on business and sometimes brought his little girl with him.

3. The Shambles were used in the early days for the butchers. Near the market, this area had become in the Inchbalds' time an inexpensive housing section. It was a suitable place for the players to board because of its proximity to the Minster and the theatre. Wilkinson, of course, had his own house.

4. In the Strand when she had very cramped quarters, she had a coal fire—she records going to get coal and carrying it up flights of stairs, for she lived in the "attic."

5. Taylor, *Records of My Life,* 1:398, 400.

6. See entry in her pocket-book for February 12, 1780. In her accounts for 1776, she enters moneys for washing every week. She must surely have had it done, but see Mrs. Barbauld's poem "Washing-Day," quoted in Messenger, *His and Hers,* 186–93. The contrast between Inchbald's "washing" and Barbauld's is a striking difference between the domestic and the professional.

7. In her "Description of me," Inchbald says, "Hair—of a sandy auburn and rather straight as well as thin." Boaden, 1:175–76.

8. *Biographical Dictionary,* 10:23; see 10:2–27 for the entire entry on Macklin.

9. See George Colman's advertisement that precedes the play printed in *Philaster: A*

Tragedy. Written by Beaumont and Fletcher. With Alterations As It Is Acted At The Theatre-Royal In Drury Lane (Dublin: P. Wilson, J. Exshaw, S. Price, E. Watts, J. Potts, and A. McCulloh, 1763).

10. Ibid.

11. The Woodfalls were proprietors of important journals in Mrs. Inchbald's London years. The elder William Woodfall was the conductor of the *Morning Chronicle;* Mr. Henry Sampson Woodfall and his son George Woodfall were both journalists with the *Public Advertiser.* See Taylor, *Records of My Life,* 2:252–55.

12. Wilkinson, *Wandering Patentee,* 1:304–5.

13. Ibid., 97.

14. Boaden, *Memoirs of Mrs. Inchbald,* 1:128.

15. The three letters from Wilson are quoted in ibid., 1:128–32.

16. Ibid., 1:135.

17. Ibid., 1:138.

18. Boaden, *Memoirs of Mrs. Siddons,* 137.

19. *Biographical Dictionary,* 14:88.

20. Grice, *Rogues and Vagabonds,* 145.

21. Ibid., 143 ff.; quote from 146.

22. Manvell, *Sarah Siddons,* 55–56.

23. Boaden, *Memoirs of Mrs. Inchbald,* 1:138–39.

24. Ibid., 1:139.

25. Ibid.

26. It is clear in the pocket-books that her friends all knew each other and all went to the theatre.

27. Altick, *Shows of London,* 121.

28. Ibid.

29. Boaden, *Memoirs of Mrs. Inchbald,* 1:138.

30. Wilkinson, *Wandering Patentee,* 2:105–7.

31. An interesting comment about her part. Does this mean she was given the permission to give over her part to Wells? In any case by this time she and Harris could have "much talk."

32. Both Boaden quotes are from *Memoirs of Mrs. Inchbald,* 1:141.

33. Doran, *"Their Majesties' Servants,"* 2:235–40. See also Macqueen-Pope, *Haymarket,* 136–44; and the *Biographical Dictionary.*

34. Boaden, *Memoirs of Mrs. Inchbald,* 1:142.

35. Sherington's *York Chronicle,* Feb. 21, 1777.

36. Wroughton was Richard Wroughton, who had been at Covent Garden since 1768. In the 1780s he was connected with Sadler's Wells, but it was not until 1784 that he became a manager there. When Inchbald wrote her letter, he was still a principal player at Covent Garden; later he had a quarrel with Lewis and left Covent Garden. Did Inchbald

think he had influence to help her gain a place at the Wells? See the *Biographical Dictionary*, 16:297–304.

37. In the spring of 1781, Wroughton was one of the leading members of the Covent Garden Company; later he was to be part owner and manager of Sadler's Wells. See *Biographical Dictionary*, 16:299.

38. Borer, *Illustrated Guide to London*, 43, 48–54. Inchbald usually chose a stagecoach.

39. Wilkinson, *Wandering Patentee*, 2:119, 132; and *Biographical Dictionary*, 14:89.

40. Boaden, *Memoirs of Mrs. Inchbald*, 1:149–50.

41. Ibid., 1:154–55.

42. Ibid., 1:155.

43. Ibid., 1:161.

44. Ibid., 1:162.

45. Ibid., 1:3. For more information on the Wilsons, see the *Biographical Dictionary*. Mrs. Wilson is listed as "Mrs. Wilson" in vol. 16 of the *Biographical Dictionary;* see 16:175, where she was first Sarah Adcock, and 16:146, where she is called Mrs. Wilson. She acted in Inchbald's plays, creating the role of Fish, for example, in *Appearance Is against Them*.

46. Boaden, *Memoirs of Mrs. Inchbald*, 1:157.

47. Ibid., 1:163.

48. Ibid., 1:119.

49. *Biographical Dictionary*, 16:175–78.

50. Boaden, *Memoirs of Mrs. Inchbald*, 1:158. See also Manvell, *Sarah Siddons*, 55 ff. Palmer was the proprietor of the Bath Theatre Royal and was a close friend of Harris. Siddons went to Bath in 1778 from Liverpool while the Inchbalds were still in York.

51. "Four Letters from Mrs. Inchbald the Actress to Tate Wilkinson," York Public Library, Y927.92.

52. Colman, *Random Records*, 2:600–601. Also quoted in Macqueen-Pope, *Haymarket*, 154–55.

53. *Biographical Dictionary*, 16:177.

54. Boaden, *Memoirs of Mrs. Inchbald*, 1:160.

55. Manvell, *Sarah Siddons*, 150–52.

56. Bloxam, *Walpole's Queen of Comedy*, 52.

57. Macqueen-Pope, *Haymarket*, 21.

58. Stephen Kemble was John Philip's brother called "the Great one."

59. Macqueen-Pope, *Haymarket*, 126–27.

60. Ibid., 140; see also 133–34 for an account of Farren in *She Stoops to Conquer*.

61. Boaden, *Memoirs of Mrs. Siddons*, 161.

62. This play is not included in the collection of Burney's plays edited by Sabor; in fact, he does not believe it was hers, but Boaden certainly knew about contemporary performances, and his comment about India adds to our understanding that Inchbald did know about India when she wrote her *Mogul Tale*.

63. Boaden, *Memoirs of Mrs. Inchbald,* 1:162–63.

5. TO IRELAND WITH HITCHCOCK

1. Baker, *John Philip Kemble,* 65.

2. The Crawfords were Thomas Crawford, called Billy, and his wife, Ann Dancer Barry Crawford, the widow of Spranger Barry. She was some sixteen years older than he, but she was very much in love and encouraged him to act; he was never very successful. When they returned to Dublin from London in 1781, they did so in part because Ann had established her husband as part owner of the Crow Street Theatre. His tenure as manager was not successful, and the theatre was closed in December 1782 and rented out for 150 pounds. At this point Ann separated from her husband, continuing to support him, however. After she returned to London in the fall of 1783, she was at Covent Garden for two seasons, where she and Inchbald were in the company together. See *Biographical Dictionary,* 1:339–51 for her and 4:34–36 for him.

3. *Biographical Dictionary,* 4:129.

4. Baker, *John Philip Kemble,* 66–67.

5. Jephson was the favorite playwright of Walpole, and according to Doran, Jephson always "improved" the passages Walpole objected to—Doran says, "Walpole gave orders for alterations in Jephson's plays, as he might for the repair of a cabinet." Doran, *"Their Majesties' Servants,"* 2:145.

6. Baker, *John Philip Kemble,* 69–70.

7. Boaden, *Memoirs of the Life of John Philip Kemble,* 1:38–39.

8. Baker, *John Philip Kemble,* 75–76.

9. A series of entries in the pocket-book such as these, including references to Mrs. Melmoth, Pratt, Kemble, and Daly, give a vivid picture of the reality of the interaction of players and their lives backstage—offstage. It is also important to remember that this is 1783, before Kemble had become the leading actor he became in something less than nine months when he played Hamlet at Drury Lane. After that memorable night, his relationship with both Inchbald and Daly changed.

10. Mrs. Melmoth was Pratt's wife, though at this time their relationship was uncertain.

11. Boaden, *Memoirs of Mrs. Inchbald,* 1:170–71.

12. Ibid., 1:171.

13. Did Pratt's letter have to do with his wife, Mrs. Melmoth, whom Inchbald had just seen in Dublin?

14. The Whitfields usually were at the Haymarket in the summer, but this time they were not there when Inchbald returned and began to act. Perhaps they had gone to France, for they had eloped there to be married in 1771. Their house, where Inchbald was staying for the summer, was in Leicester Court, Castle Street, Leicester Fields.

15. Ann Kemble, the seventh child of Roger Kemble, born in 1764, was nine years

younger than Sarah. She was bitter about her family, claiming that because she was lame they neglected her in her childhood. Although she wrote a play that was performed at her father's theatre, she declared that her family ridiculed her. In 1783 she published a notice in the London press that her lameness prevented her from playing on the stage and that she was unable to earn a living by her needlework (she had been apprenticed to a mantua maker). Her husband, Curtis, proved to be a bigamist, and their marriage was therefore illegal. In November 1783 she published a notice that as Mrs. Siddons's youngest sister she would read a lecture at the Temple of Health. She was not Mrs. Siddons's youngest sister, and her "lectures" were for the quack doctor James Graham. See *Biographical Dictionary*, 7:171–75; and Manvell, *Sarah Siddons*, 117–18.

16. Precisely what Inchbald means about Mrs. Bulkley "reading" a play is not clear, but according to the *Biographical Dictionary*, 2:395–96, Bulkley had just managed to have her current "gallant" employed at the Haymarket this 1783 season; he was John Williamson, who had succeeded Dodd, who, as we remember, had run away with her to Dublin after that summer in Bristol when the Inchbalds were in their company. A check of Bulkley and Dodd in the *Biographical Dictionary* shows that they were in Tate Wilkinson's York Company for Race Week in 1777.

17. See *Biographical Dictionary*, 13:386. The story is that as a child, when he first played the part, he was overcome when he thought his mother had actually died. Manvell, *Sarah Siddons*, 324 n. 2, quotes the account printed in the *Morning Post* for Oct. 10, 1782: "Mrs. Siddons of Drury Lane theatre has a lovely little boy, about eight years old. Yesterday, in the rehearsal of *The Fatal Marriage*, the boy, observing his mother in the agonies of the dying scene, took the fiction for reality, and burst into a flood of tears, a circumstance which struck the feelings of the Company in a singular manner." It is in this part that Henry appears with his mother in the print in *Bell's British Theatre*. For a reproduction of this print, see Manvell, *Sarah Siddons*, ill. 6, following p. 116. See also Asleson, *Passion for Performance*, 54, for three illustrations of Henry and his mother.

18. Boaden, in *Memoirs of Mrs. Inchbald*, 2:258–60, records Inchbald's retrospective chronicle of a portion of her life that she calls "My Septembers Since I Married."

19. Ibid.

20. Boaden, *Memoirs of Mrs. Siddons*, 127.

21. Ibid., 17–20. The suggestion that Harris's agent would have mistaken Stephen for John Philip seems very unlikely. Campbell's comment, "The messenger, mistaking the large for the great brother, unfortunately engaged the former: and Stephen made his first appearance at Covent Garden as Othello, in 1785," was made long after the facts. See also Kelly, *Kemble Era*, 34–37.

22. Boaden, *Memoirs of Mrs. Inchbald*, 1:177.

23. On Mrs. Pitt (Harriet Pitt, actress, singer, and dancer), see *Biographical Dictionary*, 12:16–17.

24. A significant comment when it is remembered in connection with *Such Things Are*, written some four years later.

25. Morison, *Edward Topham*, 14.

26. In the pamphlet entitled *An Address To Edmund Burke, Esq. On His Late Letter Relative To The Affairs of America*, Topham takes Burke to task and concludes, "As for yourself, Sir, though you possess a very uncommon share of understanding, you have unfortunately been led into the only line where that excellent understanding could be perverted and lost. Formed to examine men and things with metaphysical precision, the heat and violence of Parties have distracted your attention, and made you a florid speaker without winning the passions, and a laboured writer without convincing the understanding."

27. George Colman the younger, *Random Records*, 2:60–61, quoted in Macqueen-Pope, *Haymarket*, 154–55.

6. 1784

1. Boaden, *Memoirs of Mrs. Inchbald*, 1:183–84.

2. These notes and letters from Colman are from Boaden, *Memoirs of Mrs. Inchbald*, 1:185–86. Jewell had long been associated with the Haymarket as treasurer and in other capacities. That both the younger Colman and Jewell recognized Inchbald's hand shows their acquaintance with and awareness of her work.

3. Macqueen-Pope, *Haymarket*, 155, 157 ff.

4. See Foreman, *Georgiana*, for the chapter "The Westminster Election: 1784," 136–59.

5. See Macqueen-Pope, *Haymarket*, 154–57.

6. Colman, "Prologue," in Colman, *Election of Managers*.

7. Gillispie, *Montgolfier Brothers*. For Reveillon, see 12, 26, 37, 46; see also ill. 7 and fig. 26, p. 65.

8. Gillispie has written an account of both the family and the development of their version of the balloon. See ibid., 3, for the first ascent, on June 4, 1783, after many experiments; see, e.g., 38, for one of the failures. On Sept. 19 the successful flight from Versailles was staged. This flight had a sheep, a rooster, and a duck aboard; see ibid., 40. Then on Friday, Nov. 21, two men, Pilatre de Rozier and François Laurent, marquis d'Arlandes, went up in the first manned flight (51–52 ff.).

9. Ibid., 29–32. See also Altick, *Shows of London*, 85.

10. Reynolds, *Life and Times*, 1:255–58.

11. Altick, *Shows of London*, 85.

12. Foreman, *Georgiana*, 173.

13. *Memoirs of Mrs. Sumbel Late Wells*, 2:199–201.

14. Hogan, *London Stage*, lxxxi–xciii.

15. See *Life of Thomas Holcroft*, 1:265–66. See also the editor's preface, by Elbridge Colby, vii–xiv. The dates and places of the plays and their productions have been listed, but the opinions about Holcroft's "Political Interests" are largely Colby's. See 2:26–80.

16. Boaden, *Memoirs of Mrs. Inchbald*, 1:186.

17. Ibid., 1:187.

18. Ibid., 1:187–88; see also Boaden, *Memoirs of Mrs. Siddons*, 127–28.

19. *European Magazine* 6 (July 1784): 74.

20. Boaden, *Memoirs of Mrs. Inchbald*, 1:189.

21. Macqueen-Pope, *Haymarket*, 129. See his discussion of this 1784 season, 154–60. He makes brief comments on the 1785 season. After the close of the season of 1785, while he was on vacation at the seaside resort of Margate, Colman the elder had a stroke, and although he continued to manage the Haymarket for some time, he never fully recovered. See the account of this episode, 160 ff. It is interesting to note that Dr. Warren was called but could not leave his patient in London, so Colman was left to the mercy of a local doctor. Warren was Inchbald's doctor. By 1786 Colman had returned for the season.

22. *Biographical Dictionary*, 4:110; for the entire Cuyler article, see 4:108–12.

23. Dialogue was always—in all the plays—very, very important since it was the center of Inchbald's society. She herself was celebrated for her conversation and her wit, and this characteristic is obvious in all the plays. In both of the novels, *A Simple Story* and *Nature and Art*, the dialogue accounts for a major feature of their composition. For any reader the dialogue throughout her work is the key to understanding her views; therefore I have quoted extensively in discussing the plays, especially since Backscheider's edition is the only one extant.

24. All quotations from all of Inchbald's plays throughout this study are taken from Backscheider, *Plays of Elizabeth Inchbald.* The quotations are in order of their occurrence in the plays.

25. Gillispie, *Montgolfier Brothers*, 52, 95, 97. Franklin's comment was reported with slight variations in several places at the time he made the comment.

26. See Hibbert, *George III*, 237–42 for the prince's affairs; see 250–51 for his affair and "marriage" with Mrs. Fitzherbert. His attempt to kill himself over her reluctance to please him is recounted in Foreman, *Georgiana*, 162–64, 177–79, a discussion of Georgiana's part in the "wedding."

27. Boaden, *Memoirs of Mrs. Inchbald*, 1:192.

28. Ibid., 1:193. Boaden includes a long letter and then another to Inchbald from Twiss. See 1:201–22. Twiss probably had more influence on Inchbald's writing than anyone else, except perhaps Colman the elder. Twiss was her friend—her longtime friend—whereas her association with Colman was professional. She seems never to have resented his criticism, and she certainly talked to him about her work.

29. Ibid., 1:198–99.

30. Ibid., 1:199.

31. Ibid.

32. Ibid., 1:200.

33. Quotes from Donald, *Age of Caricature*, 75, 80–81.

34. Boaden, *Memoirs of Mrs. Inchbald*, 1:222–23.

35. Ibid., 1:221–22.

36. The entire poem is quoted in Bloxam, *Walpole's Queen of Comedy*, 59.

37. Adolphus, *Memoirs of John Bannister,* 1:121.

38. Boaden, *Memoirs of Mrs. Inchbald,* 1:218–19.

39. See Boaden's remarks about this play in his *Memoirs of Mrs. Siddons,* 161–62.

7. New Plays and a Publisher

1. The king loved comedy, and he and his family went to Covent Garden frequently. See Hogan, *London Stage,* ccx–ccxi.

2. Boaden, *Memoirs of Mrs. Inchbald,* 1:222–25.

3. The permission granted by Colman meant that he had exclusive use of the plays he presented in the Haymarket. The arrangement among the three theatres was a complicated one, since all of the theatres needed whatever income they could find to make a profit.

4. Tillyard, *Aristocrats,* 121. See also 111–18 for the discussion of Sarah and George III; see also 108 ff. for Sarah's early life at the court of George II.

5. Ibid., 124.

6. Ibid.

7. Ibid., 128.

8. Ibid., 131. See also *Life and Letters of Lady Sarah Lennox.*

9. Tillyard, *Aristocrats,* 131–32.

10. Ibid., 240.

11. No doubt sometimes divorce was denied for various reasons. See Reynolds, *Life and Times,* 1:159–71, and his report of a divorce that his father handled.

12. The Persian shawls had become very fashionable by this time, since the commerce with India had become very important. It was said that the Empress Josephine collected them. The Rhode Island School of Design has a collection in its museum.

13. Boaden, *Memoirs of Mrs. Inchbald,* 1:236–37.

14. Ibid., 1:237.

15. Ibid., 1:236.

16. Adolphus, *Memoirs of John Bannister,* 1:139.

17. The Robinson firm was a family business, and over the years, as various members left or others were added, the imprint varied; for example, in the first edition of Inchbald's *Next Door Neighbours,* it is listed as "printed for G.G.J. and J. Robinson." Beginning with *The Wedding Day* it became G.G. and J. Robinson. In 1805 for *To Marry or Not to Marry* it was Longman, Hurst, Rees, and Orme.

18. Throughout Boaden's account of Inchbald's professional dealings, there are many puzzles, perhaps because the circumstances were so familiar to him and his public that he omitted certain details. One "puzzle" is about the publication of her work. From the little evidence available, it seems that Harris held the copyright of the plays that he produced, that is, in the early days. There is an archive in the Manchester Public Library of some of

the Robinson accounts, in which Inchbald's accounts were paid through Harris. Here also are significant entries for Godwin and Holcroft. The Holcroft one includes the expenses of paper. The archive is listed as the Robinson Archive.

19. Boaden, *Memoirs of Mrs. Inchbald,* 1:240.

20. Ibid.

21. The advertisement for *Such Things Are* is reprinted before the play in the Backscheider edition of the collected plays.

22. See O'Toole, *Traitor's Kiss,* 212 ff.

23. See Donald, *Age of Caricature,* 84, 90–91.

24. Boaden, *Memoirs of Mrs. Inchbald,* 1:242.

25. Quotation from ibid., 1:244. Since we have only very incomplete records of Inchbald's financial affairs, it is not possible to know precisely how she handled her money. Harris did perhaps give her extra money unofficially, without the knowledge of his other writers. The king sometimes rewarded writers, and he and his family certainly enjoyed this play. Inchbald, moreover, always followed the advice of her stockbroker, and perhaps he, for some reason, felt that she should invest only a part of the nine hundred pounds.

26. Ibid.

27. Ibid.

28. Ibid., 1:245–46.

29. The very popular play *The Marriage of Figaro* by the French playwright Beaumarchais had in the fall of 1784 been translated and adapted by Inchbald's friend Thomas Holcroft. See *Life of Thomas Holcroft,* chap. 4, 272–79. Figaro became the most famous of the "servant" characters on the eighteenth-century stage, especially after Mozart's opera.

30. Boaden, *Memoirs of Mrs. Inchbald,* 1:247.

31. Ibid., 1:247–48.

32. Ibid., 1:249–50.

33. See Backscheider, *Plays of Elizabeth Inchbald,* vol. 1, the prologue to *All on a Summer's Day,* the transcription of the play (1–53), and the epilogue.

34. Altick, *Shows of London,* 82–85; see also caricatures, 83. Information on Graham and Katterfelto may be found in Taylor, *Records of My Life,* 1:209–10. Also see Macqueen-Pope, *Haymarket,* 153, for Colman's play *The Genius of Nonsense* and his burlesque of Graham. Graham himself was present, giving out handbills advertising his "Temple of Health." Bannister as the harlequin was perfect as Graham, much to the delight of the audience.

35. Altick, *Shows of London,* 82–85.

36. Quotations are from act 3, pp. 42–43 and 33 of *The Tempest, adapted to the stage, with additions from Dryden and Davenant, by J.P. Kemble, with Remarks by Mrs. Inchbald.* It is important to note that Inchbald was using the current play texts of the late eighteenth century. In this version of *The Tempest,* Miranda has a sister named Dorinda who, in addition to Miranda and Ferdinand, has a "story."

8. 1788–1789

1. Edwin was frequently drunk on stage and frequently late, and he frequently spoke extemporaneously instead of giving the speeches assigned. See *Biographical Dictionary*, 5:20–28.

2. Boaden, *Memoirs of Mrs. Inchbald*, 1:259. It is interesting to observe that her friend John Taylor wrote the very popular verse "story" *Monsieur Tonson*. It was purported to have been a prank played by Tom King on an unsuspecting Frenchman by knocking on his door and asking if "Thompson lodges here." There was no Thompson, of course, and the Frenchman's pronunciation of "Thompson" became "Tonson." King repeated the trick until he was obliged to leave London. Six years later, when he returned, he again knocked on the Frenchman's door. And again the Frenchman came to answer the knock; this time, thinking he had seen a ghost, he ran away. The last verse—verse 28—reads: "As if some hideous spectre struck his [the Frenchman's] sight, / His senses seem'd bewilder'd with affright, / His face, indeed, bespoke a heart full sore— / Then starting, / he exclaim'd in rueful strain, / "Beggar! here's Monsieur Tonson come again!" / Away he ran—and ne'er was heard of more." The amusing text was illustrated by R. (Isaac Robert) George Cruikshank. The little pamphlet went through several editions. The one used for this reference is the one published in 1830 in London by Marsh and Miller and in Edinburgh by Constable and Co. Before the poem itself, there is a "Life of Tom King." King, in addition to his other positions, was in Covent Garden, Sadler's Wells, and Drury Lane in the summer of 1788, when Inchbald tried the knocking trick; King had just given over the management of Drury Lane and had received a contract with Covent Garden. See *Biographical Dictionary*, 9:26–43.

3. Mrs. Morgan was the wife of Inchbald's broker. That she went to her house is another comment on how everyone knew everyone else.

4. The reference "from breakfast to dinner" indicates that her visitors were there from breakfast, at about ten o'clock, to dinner, about four—quite long visits.

5. O'Toole, *Traitor's Kiss*, 220.

6. These references about pain in her face strongly suggest that she had a toothache. Since she was always subject to sinus problems, she must have found the combination quite painful; she complained all spring and into the summer.

7. For a detailed account of the king's illness, see Hibbert, *George III*, 254–81; for an account of the doctors, see 282–87; and for his recovery, see 288–91. For a discussion of the king's illness and the regency crisis, the Prince of Wales, and Sheridan, see O'Toole, *Traitor's Kiss*, 235–51.

8. See the account of this election in Foreman, *Georgiana*, 205–6.

9. *Biographical Dictionary*, 9:257–60. Texier is listed as Le Texier. He has been called "this mysterious and eccentric figure," but in Inchbald's pocket-books he seems to be another friend. He came to see her on business and stayed to tea, and more than once he brought his little girl. Texier's association with those who had private playhouses and used

him both to act and to organize the theatricals partly explains his work with Inchbald. When we realize that Harris used him as a procurer of plays, especially French ones, we begin to understand that he, Inchbald, and Harris had business with each other.

10. Boaden, *Memoirs of Mrs. Inchbald,* 1:256.

11. *Biographical Dictionary,* 9:258–59.

12. Altick, *Shows of London,* 120–22.

13. See O'Toole, *Traitor's Kiss,* 200.

14. Boaden, *Memoirs of Mrs. Inchbald,* 1:257.

15. Ibid.

16. Gray, *Theatrical Criticism,* 258–60. Gray reviews the *World* on 258–66.

17. Taylor, *Records of My Life,* 2:289–94.

18. Gray, *Theatrical Criticism,* 256.

19. Ibid., 290–93.

20. For information about Bell and Topham, see Morison, *John Bell.*

21. Topham was very proud of his figure; he was one of the men who helped to promote the new fashions of the 1770s. See Ribeiro, *Art of Dress,* 45.

22. Quotations are from Hargreaves-Mawdsley, *English Della Cruscans,* 2–3.

23. See Clifford, *Hester Lynch Piozzi,* 237–38, 249–54, for the quotations and for the group and their association in Florence.

24. Ibid., 231–32, for an account of Greatheed's play and Mrs. Piozzi's attendance at the Richmond House plays. See above for Mrs. Inchbald's play that General Conway called his own. For Piozzi see Clifford, *Hester Lynch Piozzi,* 272 ff.; for Inchbald and General Conway see chapter 8.

25. Quotations from Manvell, *Sarah Siddons,* 127, 150.

26. See *Biographical Dictionary,* 16:72.

27. Boaden, *Memoirs of Mrs. Inchbald,* 1:251.

28. Ibid., 1:258.

29. Ibid., 1:258–59.

30. Wilkinson, *Wandering Patentee,* 1:76.

31. Henry Bunbury was Horace Walpole's favorite caricaturist. Bunbury was devoted to the theatre and was a participant in amateur theatricals. He married Catharine Horneck, a celebrated beauty; she was Goldsmith's "Little Comedy." They lived at Barton in a small house near Sir Charles's Barton Hall. See John C. Riely, "Horace Walpole and 'the Second Hogarth,'" *Eighteenth-Century Studies* 9, no. 1 (1975). Bunbury did "illustration" for Sterne's *Tristram Shandy.* He was celebrated for his work depicting horses and grooms. Living at Barton, he was very near Epsom, and since Sir Charles was the leading figure in the racing world, Henry had ample opportunity to portray all kinds of horses and their riders.

32. Quoted in *Biographical Dictionary,* 1:291.

33. These entries about *Child of Nature* are significant because they reveal the very close association between the stage play and the printed version. It is clear that at the

beginning *Child of Nature* was a full-length play that Harris and the "board" cut down to a farce—at least that they made it an "after-piece." Inchbald's dealing with the publisher in these entries indicates that she began to do so when the piece was a "main piece"; she agreed in the end to publish it as a farce when in 1809 she included it in her collection of farces and after-pieces. It is in volume 1, along with *Wedding Day* and *Midnight Hour,* which are clearly intended to be after-pieces.

34. O'Toole, *Traitor's Kiss,* 230. See 224–34 for a discussion of the trial.

35. Ibid., 177.

36. See Hibbert, *George III,* 254 ff., for the king's illness; on the regency crisis, 272–74; and on the king's recovery, 297–303.

37. See the entry on John Edwin in the *Biographical Dictionary* for the quote about him from Boaden. Inchbald's problems with *The Child of Nature* and her work with making it a three-act after-piece must have been the result of Harris's judgment that the play was too slight to be a main piece or that it needed to be short to leave time for the popular and elaborate holiday pantomimes.

38. Kinne, *Revivals and Importations,* 205.

39. Boaden, *Memoirs of Mrs. Inchbald,* 1:261–63.

40. Nicoll, *Late Eighteenth Century Drama,* 20.

41. Bloxam, *Walpole's Queen of Comedy,* 91.

42. Ibid.

43. Ibid., 83.

44. Ibid., 85.

45. Baron Wilson's account of Lord Derby is from *Mrs. Cornwell, Memoirs of Harriet, Duchess of St. Albans* (1839), as quoted by Bloxam, *Walpole's Queen of Comedy,* 97 n. 12.

46. This account of Lord Derby's "history" is found in many places. See Bloxam, *Walpole's Queen of Comedy,* 40–44; see also her account of Lord Derby and the private theatre at Richmond House, 80–96.

47. Ibid., 46.

48. Quoted in Foreman, *Georgiana,* 68.

49. Mrs. Piozzi helped one of the singers, a Miss Hamilton, with a special song, and afterward she was invited to the entertainments. See Clifford, *Hester Lynch Piozzi,* 332.

50. Bobrick, *Angel in the Whirlwind,* 163–64. For the account of his command at Saratoga, see 242–85. This account includes not only Burgoyne but also the events that led to Burgoyne's defeat and his return to England. For another account of the same events, see Hibbert, *Redcoats and Rebels,* 55–56, 72, 195–97. For Conway's part in the American war, see 254, 336. After the war Conway was appointed commander-in-chief by the king; in 1784 he resigned, and he died in 1785.

51. The use Austen makes of the proposed theatrical performance was, however, a good deal more than simply to show the worldly behavior of the Crawfords; by the early nineteenth century, private theatricals had been condemned as an extension of the preju-

dice against the social standing of the players. Both of the Crawfords in the end proved to be dissolute.

52. Holland House had been the scene of private theatricals for many years. Once Lady Sarah played Jane Shore, and in the summer after Sarah's marriage, private theatricals flourished both in the country and at Holland House; see Tillyard, *Aristocrats*, 144–45.

53. See Kinne, *Revivals and Importations*, 205–7.

54. Boaden, *Memoirs of Mrs. Inchbald*, 1:263.

55. Ibid., 1:263–64.

56. Ibid., 1:264.

57. Ibid., 1:266.

58. Ibid., 1:270.

59. Ibid., 1:274.

60. Ibid., 1:274–75.

61. See Jane Spencer's introduction to Tompkins, *A Simple Story* (London: Oxford University Press, 1967; The World's Classics paperback reprint, 1998), xii–xiii, on the subject of "the literary tradition of the coquette" and on female education. All quotations from *A Simple Story* come from this edition.

62. By this time it was well known that both Godwin and Holcroft were nonbelievers. See also Boaden, *Memoirs of Mrs. Inchbald*, 1:298–99, where he reviews Inchbald's "religious duties" and finds that "she was not exclusively Catholic in her attendances."

63. Ibid., 1:280.

64. Tompkins, *A Simple Story*, 338.

65. McKee, in his chapter "Origin and Inspiration of Her Novels," in his *Elizabeth Inchbald, Novelist*, discusses Inchbald's originality and finds that "what she borrowed was the manner of handling material, rather than the material itself" (49).

66. Boaden, *Memoirs of Mrs. Inchbald*, 2:152–53.

67. Tompkins, *A Simple Story*, 5–6.

68. See Clemit's introduction to *A Simple Story*, edited by Clemit, xxv n. 30.

69. Hibbert, *George III*, 30–31. There are portraits of Lady Sarah in Tillyard's *Aristocrats;* one portrait is especially interesting, as she is portrayed in her teens dressed for an amateur performance of *The Mourning Bride*, following p. 124; there is another when she was fifteen, done by Francis Cotes, and one after she was Lady Sarah Bunbury, both following p. 188.

70. Tompkins, *A Simple Story*, 20.

71. Ibid., 174–75.

72. Boaden, *Memoirs of Mrs. Inchbald*, 1:276.

73. Tompkins, *A Simple Story*, 23, 26, 33–36.

74. Ibid., 37.

75. Ibid., 40, 41.

76. Ibid., 154–55.

77. Ribeiro, *Art of Dress*, discusses masquerade costumes in several places. See, e.g., 183, 188–91, 213–15; on 213–15 is a discussion of the use of Diana in portraits; see esp. pl. 224.

78. Tompkins, *A Simple Story*, 159.

79. Boaden, *Memoirs of Mrs. Inchbald*, 1:141. Boaden says she went dressed in her Bellario costume as a boy and that she attracted some of the women.

80. Tompkins, *A Simple Story*, 84–85.

81. Ibid., 85.

82. Ibid., 87.

83. Ibid.

84. Ibid., 87–88. Inchbald's having Dorriforth introduce the "mind of a woman" here is significant in that he would see Miss Milner as having an intellectual quality that he did not comprehend.

85. Ibid., 115.

86. Ibid., 117.

87. Ibid.

88. Ibid., 121.

89. Ibid., 123–24.

90. Ibid., 124.

91. Ibid., 146.

92. They were required to be married legally according to the rules of the Church of England, and they were.

93. Tompkins, *A Simple Story*, 191.

94. Ibid., 194–95. Many of the women novelists use this situation to find that men care for property over the "care" of marriage and the family. Jane Austen, in *Mansfield Park*, makes the continued absence of the father a central turning point as the young people are about to put on a play—Inchbald's play *Lovers' Vows*.

95. Tompkins, *A Simple Story*, 200, emphasis in original.

96. Ibid.

97. Ibid., 201–2.

98. Ibid., 216.

99. Ibid., 274.

100. *Analytical Review* 10 (1791).

101. Spencer's introduction to Tompkins, *A Simple Story*, xiv, xix. In a note Spencer says, "I attribute this review to Wollstonecraft on internal evidence and because one of the initials she used, 'M,' is the next signature to appear in the issue."

102. Anna Laetitia Barbauld wrote introductions for a series of novels; this quotation is from her introduction to *A Simple Story, by Mrs. Inchbald, a New Edition*, vol. 28 of Barbauld's *British Novelists* (London: F.C. and J. Rivington, 1810).

103. Boaden, *Memoirs of Mrs. Inchbald*, 1:290–91.

104. Tompkins, *A Simple Story*, xxi.

105. Ibid.

106. Tomalin, *Mary Wollstonecraft*, 9.

9. A NEW CHAPTER

1. Boaden, *Memoirs of Mrs. Inchbald*, 1:289.

2. Ibid., 1:293.

3. *Biographical Dictionary*, 5:318; Boaden, *Memoirs of Mrs. Inchbald*, 1:297.

4. *Biographical Dictionary*, 8:84.

5. Boaden, *Memoirs of Mrs. Inchbald*, 1:295–96.

6. Ibid., 1:294–95. The *Monthly Catalogue's* review is rather more judicious: "Mrs. Inchbald's success in adapting French dramas to an English stage is well known; and, slight as many of these pieces are, yet, in an age so fond of novelty, they serve to add to the variety in request. . . . The present is a pleasing, and occasionally an interesting production . . . as it exalts honesty and depresses knavery, it may divert and amend those who look to the moral, without weighing the probability of circumstances and events by which it is produced."

7. The manuscript of Godwin's journal is in the Carl H. Pforzheimer Collection at the New York Public Library.

8. Holcroft and Harris had frequent disagreements, one of which was over Holcroft's play *Seduction* and his comic opera *The Choleric Fathers*.

9. See O'Toole, *Traitor's Kiss*, 425 ff., for a discussion of John Frost and William Cobbett and their part in the Society for Constitutional Information. Godwin and Holcroft knew both men. Two other prominent members were Sheridan himself and his friend Peter Finnerty.

10. Boaden, *Memoirs of Mrs. Inchbald*, 1:224.

11. Inchbald's concern about the publication of her plays continued until the last one, *To Marry or Not to Marry*. Evidently Harris himself "bought" the copyright from his authors and then sold it to a publisher. See, e.g., Cecil Price, "Thomas Harris and the Covent Garden Theatre" in *The Eighteenth-Century English Stage*, edited by Kenneth Richards and Peter Thomson (London: Methuen, 1972), 108–9.

12. Paul, *William Godwin*, 1:21. See also St. Clair, *The Godwins and the Shelleys*, 31–33.

13. Paul, *William Godwin*, 1:68. See also St. Clair, *The Godwins and the Shelleys*, 58–62, 65–66.

14. For a discussion of Inchbald's part in the Godwin/Reveley story, see St. Clair, *The Godwins and the Shelleys*, 155. See also 146–47 for Godwin's friendship with Mary Hayes.

15. This study of Inchbald's life is perhaps not the place to make a detailed account of the association of Inchbald with Godwin and Holcroft, but their friendship with each other is reflected in their work as well as in their personal lives, and a study of their friend-

ships reflects their subsequent behavior in the decade after 1790. Holcroft's wife had died in 1790, and both Godwin and Holcroft sought to "advise" Inchbald about her work, and both proposed marriage to her. Without a knowledge of their daily associations, writers have made false conclusions—usually derogatory to Inchbald and favorable to Holcroft and Godwin, as, for example, after Godwin's marriage to Wollstonecraft and especially after her death.

16. Paul, *William Godwin,* 1:74–75.

17. Schama, *Citizens,* 633.

18. Boaden, *Memoirs of Mrs. Inchbald,* 1:305–6.

19. In the summer of 1793, Holcroft asked that his letters be returned. He sent his son to get them from Mrs. Inchbald. Her entry simply reports that she gave them to him. Various sources suggest that Inchbald had love letters from several suitors. Evidently she burned the ones she did not return.

20. Smith and Smith, *William Godwin,* 23. See also *Political Justice,* bk. 1, chap. 5, quoted in Smith and Smith, *William Godwin,* 23.

21. *Political Justice,* bk. 1, chap. 5, quoted in Smith and Smith, *William Godwin.*

22. *Political Justice,* bk. 8, chap. 8. Appendix quoted in Smith and Smith, *William Godwin,* 25. See also St. Clair, *The Godwins and the Shelleys,* 81.

23. Boaden, *Memoirs of Mrs. Inchbald,* 1:316.

24. Ibid., 1:316–17.

25. Ibid., 1:318.

26. Ibid.

27. Ibid.

28. Ibid., 1:319.

29. The Ireland forgeries created a great discussion in theatre circles. Boaden at first maintained that the play was Shakespeare's; he later changed his mind. The play was given on Apr. 2, 1796, at Drury Lane. See Manvell, *Sarah Siddons,* 195, 197, for Boaden's views. See 193–98 for the discussion of the whole event. Kemble played a part in it; Siddons did not. The play was a total disaster.

30. Boaden, *Memoirs of Mrs. Inchbald,* 1:324.

31. Ibid., 1:326.

32. Ibid., 1:327.

33. Ibid., 1:323.

34. Ibid., 1:310.

35. Ibid., 1:311.

36. See St. Clair, *The Godwins and the Shelleys,* 182–84, for an account of what happened when Godwin published *The Memoirs of the Author of a Vindication of the Rights of Woman.* He omitted nothing; he told about her love for Fuseli and Imlay and the birth of Fanny. He also censured Mrs. Inchbald by name—in print. "Truth" would have been better left unsaid.

37. See Overbye's article "'Neither a Widow, a Maid, nor a Wife,'" 50–59. Overbye finds that although it is a comedy, a war of the sexes, "the play goes beyond this and

exposes attitudes of a more malignant nature" (51). She says that Miss Wooburn's "fault" is "her lack of position" that "threatens the status quo" (54). In her conclusion Overbye states, "Inchbald may not be considered as a radical in the struggle for women's rights, but she does use subversive tactics, tactics which could only be seen by those who were aware of and sympathetic to women's plight" (58).

38. Boaden, *Memoirs of Mrs. Inchbald*, 1:312.

39. Although the 1793 pocket-book is not as detailed as the others, the entries about Holcroft are included. Holcroft's son who was the courier committed suicide by shooting himself in the presence of Godwin and his father in 1794—see Paul, *William Godwin*, 1:63–64, for his account of Holcroft.

40. Boaden, *Memoirs of Mrs. Inchbald*, 1:313.

41. Ibid., 1:314. Taylor's *Records of My Life* is filled with information about the world of the theatre and publishing. This is not surprising, since he was editor of the *Sun*, a successful newspaper, but reading his opinions of Inchbald and her friends and acquaintances, we find that he, like ourselves, has a distinct prejudice against certain people. See, e.g., Taylor's discussion of Sheridan and Kemble in 2:262–65.

42. Boaden, *Memoirs of Mrs. Inchbald*, 1:315.

43. Ibid., 1:320–21.

44. Ibid., 1:328.

45. Ibid.

46. Ibid., 1:329–30.

47. Paul, *William Godwin*, 1:140.

48. Reveley was an artist and architect married to Maria Reveley, who, it seems, carried on a flirtation with Godwin. See St. Clair, *The Godwins and the Shelleys*, 154–56. St. Clair suggests that perhaps Mrs. Inchbald had a hand in this "friendship"; see 155.

49. Boaden, *Memoirs of Mrs. Inchbald*, 1:332–33.

50. Ibid., 1:331.

51. Ibid., 1:334.

52. Tomalin, *Mrs. Jordan's Profession*, 145; and Boaden, *Life of Mrs. Jordan*, 1:273.

53. Boaden, *Life of Mrs. Jordan*, 1:222–23.

54. Ibid.

55. Tomalin, *Mrs. Jordan's Profession*, 140.

56. Ibid.

57. Ibid., 140–41.

58. Quoted in Manvell, *Elizabeth Inchbald*, 187.

59. For Holcroft and the Society for Constitutional Information, see *Life of Thomas Holcroft*, 2:27, and the footnote on 27–28.

60. Amelia Alderson's letter to Mrs. Taylor is printed in Brightwell, *Life of Amelia Opie*, 41–43.

61. Boaden, *Memoirs of Mrs. Inchbald*, 1:335.

62. Ibid., 1:335–36.

63. Ibid., 1:337–38.

64. Ibid., 1:338–39.

65. Ibid., 1:340, 344.

66. Quoted in Smith and Smith, *William Godwin*, 51. See also St. Clair, *The Godwins and the Shelleys*, 85–86, for a discussion of publishing and price.

67. Quoted in Smith and Smith, *William Godwin*, 59; the full title of Godwin's pamphlet was *Cursory Strictures on the Charge Delivered by Lord Chief Justice Eyre to the Grand Jury, October 2, 1794,* and it was first published in the *Morning Chronicle* on Oct. 21 before being printed and sold by Daniel Isaac Eaton at the Cock and Swine, according to Smith and Smith, *William Godwin*, 59.

68. O'Toole, *Traitor's Kiss,* 301.

69. See Paul, *William Godwin,* 1:69, for Godwin's and Holcroft's association with Paine.

70. Ibid., 1:117–18.

71. Grylls, *William Godwin and His World,* 17–18.

72. *Life of Thomas Holcroft,* 1:104–5. See also 1:174–75, about Ritson.

73. Grylls, *William Godwin and His World,* 30–31.

74. Brightwell, *Life of Amelia Opie,* 49.

75. See St. Clair, *The Godwins and the Shelleys,* 288, for an illustration of this sketch.

76. See Thomas Holcroft, "A Letter to the Rt Hon William Windham," in *Life of Thomas Holcroft,* 1:xxxv, 2:71–75.

77. See O'Toole, *Traitor's Kiss,* 301–2, for Sheridan's part in the trial.

78. In her *Remarks* Inchbald observes: "Venice Preserved is the favourite work of Otway. It is played repeatedly every year; except when an order from the Lord Chamberlain forbids its representation, lest some of the speeches of Pierre should be applied, by the ignorant part of the audience, to certain men, or assemblies, in the English state" (vol. XII). By this time in 1808 Kemble was no longer playing the part of Jaffier, but in the double listing of the cast, Mr. H. Siddons (Henry, Sarah Siddons's son) was playing the part at Drury Lane, and Mr. C. Kemble (John and Sarah's younger brother, Charles) was listed at Covent Garden. Even though Charles was Henry's uncle, they were very near the same age, and both continued the Kemble-Siddons tradition in the theatre.

79. Brightwell, *Life of Amelia Opie,* 56–57.

80. Quoted in St. Clair, *The Godwins and the Shelleys,* 127. See also Grylls, *William Godwin and His World,* 51.

81. Boaden, *Memoirs of Mrs. Inchbald,* 2:259; these quotes are from Inchbald's "My Septembers Since I Married."

82. Ibid., 1:350–51.

83. Ibid., 1:351.

84. See *Biographical Dictionary,* 3:479–83. Cooper was one of the actors who came to America with Wignell along with Brunton and Merry.

85. Boaden, *Memoirs of Mrs. Inchbald,* 2:2.

86. St. Clair, *The Godwins and the Shelleys,* 90–91.

87. Ibid., 93.

88. The recent edition of *Nature and Art,* edited by Shawn L. Maurer, uses the second edition for the text. See *Elizabeth Inchbald: Nature and Art,* edited with introduction and notes by Shawn L. Maurer (London: Pickering and Chatto, 1997).

89. His plays continued to be successful at both Covent Garden and Drury Lane, but he never forgot that, as he said, he was an acquitted felon. See *Life of Thomas Holcroft,* 2:94–95.

10. *NATURE AND ART,* A SECOND NOVEL, AND NEW PLAYS

1. Boaden, *Memoirs of Mrs. Inchbald,* 2:3.

2. All quotations from Elizabeth Inchbald's *Nature and Art* are from the edition published in 1796 in 2 volumes for G.G. and J. Robinson, Paternoster Row. All quotations are in order of their appearance in that text and are easily found. Also, this is the first edition of *Nature and Art* in which the name Hannah—instead of Agnes—is used for the young woman William seduced and abandoned.

3. The structure of the Anglican Church began with a priest, ordained and taking orders after studying at university. Five hundred pounds was a very good living for a first-time priest.

4. The Church of England has three orders of clergy: deacons, priests, and bishops. A deacon is the first order to becoming a priest. A priest can be in charge of a parish, as rector or vicar. A bishop is in charge of an entire diocese made up of a number of parishes. A dean is in charge of the cathedral in the diocese. His is an important position since, as an assistant to the bishop, he has a great deal of authority.

5. See Donald, *Age of Caricature,* 102–4, for her discussion of the political and moral views of women's dress in the 1790s, especially in 1794–1796. See also Ribeiro, *Art of Dress,* 91–94, for the styles brought about in the 1790s with their high waists and bare arms, "skimpest of white dresses."

6. This quotation is from Anna Laetitia Barbauld's introduction to *A Simple Story,* as published in Barbauld's fifty-volume *British Novelists* (1808–1810), 28:iii–iv. The title page of the volume used for these quotations cites it as "A New Edition." See below the discussion of *Nature and Art* that Inchbald published in 1796.

7. Scheuermann, *Her Bread to Earn,* 169, 175–76.

8. *Elizabeth Inchbald: Nature and Art,* ed. Shawn L. Maurer (London: Pickering and Chatto, 1997), xxx–xxxi. See 149–50 nn. 35–40 for a discussion of the differences between the first and second editions. See also Maurer's "Variants: Changes to the Third Edition of *Nature and Art,*" 154–63, in the same work.

9. Ibid., xxxvii.

10. Macqueen-Pope, *Haymarket,* 171.

11. Ibid.

12. Ibid., 172.

13. These quotations are all from an anonymous pamphlet called *Remarks on Mr. Colman's Preface also a Summary Comparison of the play of the Iron Chest With the Novel of Caleb Williams* (1796). Costing a shilling, it had been "Originally Written for, and inserted in, *The Monthly Mirror.*"

14. Ibid.

15. Ibid.

16. Ibid.

17. Ibid.

18. Ibid.

19. Macqueen-Pope, *Haymarket*, 179–82.

20. *Remarks on Mr. Colman's Preface.*

21. Tomalin, *Mary Wollstonecraft*, 193.

22. Ibid., 197; see also 200 for a note about Inchbald.

23. Ibid., 206–7.

24. Ibid., 15, 46, 58.

25. Ibid., 83–84.

26. Artists' studios were popular places for social gatherings; for example, Reynolds arranged his in such a way that he entertained there frequently. See Wendorf, *Sir Joshua Reynolds*, 48–52. His house in Leicester Fields was a gathering place for fashionable friends to view his work and enjoy conversation.

27. St. Clair, *The Godwins and the Shelleys*, 165.

28. Grylls, *William Godwin and His World*, 104.

29. See appendix 1 of St. Clair's *Godwins and the Shelleys* for a discussion of their sexual encounters and a transcript of the evidence in Godwin's journal.

30. Brightwell, *Life of Amelia Opie*, 59–61.

31. Ibid.

32. Ibid., 62.

33. Paul, *William Godwin*, 1:278; see also Brightwell, *Life of Amelia Opie*, 62.

34. Paul, *William Godwin*, 1:279.

35. Ibid., 1:350.

36. Boaden, *Memoirs of Mrs. Inchbald*, 2:14–15.

37. Ibid., 2:259; quotations are from Inchbald's "My Septembers Since I Married."

38. Inchbald's friend Frederick Reynolds indicates in his *Life and Times*, 2:335 ff., 379 ff., that he very much admired Harris and was a friend of Harris's son Henry.

39. As the mistress of the household, she would have worn a chatelaine, a hook fastened to her belt with her keys, a watch, a small pair of scissors, and many times a seal, frequently one made of gold and precious stones; the whole chatelaine would have been decorative as well as useful.

40. *Remarks*, 23:2.

41. Boaden, *Memoirs of Mrs. Inchbald,* 2:259; quoted from Inchbald's "My Septembers Since I Married."

42. Quoted from Anne Plumptre, *The Natural Son,* 4th ed., rev. (1798), title page.

43. Ibid., preface, i–vii.

44. See Taylor's account of this assignment in *Records of My Life,* 1:403–4.

45. Boaden, *Memoirs of Mrs. Inchbald,* 2:22.

46. This review of Plumptre's *Natural Son* is taken from the preface, "Explaining the Alterations in the Representation," to the 4th edition, revised, of her *Natural Son,* i–vii. She dated her preface London, Oct. 15, 1798. Mrs. Inchbald's play had opened on Oct. 11. Plumptre certainly took advantage of Covent Garden and the success of Inchbald's play. Plumptre made her reputation by translating German plays.

47. See Boaden, *Memoirs of Mrs. Inchbald,* 2:20–21, for his version of Plumptre; he says "that no English reader has ever for a moment endured the rival publication of Miss Plumptre."

48. In the discussion here between Plumptre and Inchbald about reality and sensibility, we are reminded of Jane Austen's *Sense and Sensibility,* which was probably written in an early version in 1796–1797. Whatever the exact date, it, like Inchbald's *Simple Story,* was in its first form a series of letters. Austen worked on it for more than a decade, not publishing it until 1811, another example of how Austen, like Inchbald, considered the current fashions. Tanner, *Jane Austen,* in his introduction, finds the alternation of the antitheses "as an instrument for separating out of qualities to achieve ever greater clarification through ever finer differentiation" to be a dominant quality in much eighteenth-century literature (7–8). He uses Inchbald's *Nature and Art* as an example. See also Tomalin, *Jane Austen,* 154–55. Tomalin states that in *Sense and Sensibility* "Austen is considering how far society can tolerate openness, and what its effect on the individual may be. The question was keenly debated in the 1790s as a part of a wider political discussion, with radical writers like William Godwin and Robert Bage favouring the complete openness practised by Marianne" (155).

49. Nannette Johnston created the role of Amelia; she had come to Covent Garden in the fall with her husband, who, it seems, was engaged at 12 pounds a week and she at only 3 pounds a week. She and her husband had been in Dublin, where she had played Lady Contest in Inchbald's *Wedding Day.* The next year she created the role of Ruth in *The Wise Man of the East.* Sometime in 1811 while she was in Ireland, she separated from her husband. When she returned to Covent Garden, she lived with Henry Harris, Thomas Harris's son, an affair that lasted only until 1814, when she left him to live with a London banker. See *Biographical Dictionary,* 8:200–204. Notice also the illustrations on 202–3. The illustration of Zorilda is a detail of the larger print featuring Kemble—see 203.

50. Boaden, *Memoirs of Mrs. Inchbald,* 2:22.

51. Ibid., 2:23.

52. Manvell, *Sarah Siddons,* 202.

53. It has been suggested that Sheridan in turn got Plumptre to translate it or that at least he obtained a copy of her translation. Plumptre's translations were well known. See Durant, *Richard Brinsley Sheridan*. See also Loftis, *Sheridan and Georgian England*, 126–27, 155 n. 5; see the reference to Inchbald, 133–34.

54. *Remarks*, 24:3–5.

55. *Remarks*, 23:5–6 (preface). This preface is followed by the *Remarks* and another essay on how the performers would "read" the stage. See also Inchbald's discussion of "passion" here.

56. Boaden, *Memoirs of Mrs. Inchbald*, 2:24.

57. Ibid., 2:24–25.

58. Ibid., 2:26–27.

59. Ibid., 2:27.

60. Ibid., 2:25. Here again we have interesting evidence of the way publishing a play while it was being acted cheapened the copyright.

61. Wordsworth, *Poems*, 56.

62. Boaden, *Memoirs of Mrs. Inchbald*, 2:31–32. See also *Remarks*, vol. 24.

63. Boaden, *Memoirs of Mrs. Inchbald*, 2:34–35.

64. Ibid., 2:35. Mrs. Inchbald was constantly criticized even after she retired. See Taylor, *Records of My Life*, 1:404–5.

65. O'Keeffe and Morton were two of the most prolific and popular of the playwrights in the late eighteenth century and early nineteenth. Inchbald writes about O'Keeffe in the *Remarks* for his play *Wild Oats;* her opening review says, "The present comedy is written by O'Keeffe, who saw not the traces of his pen as he marked the paper; whose days pass away, uncheered by the sun or any visible object; but whose mind supports with resignations his bitter calamity, and is enlightened by imagination, whilst his eyes are shut in utter darkness." See also *Biographical Dictionary*, 11:97–98, for an entry about Mrs. O'Keeffe; O'Keeffe himself acted in Dublin before he came to London, where he became successful as a playwright. He did not act on the London stages.

66. Boaden, *Memoirs of Mrs. Inchbald*, 2:34.

11. A NEW CENTURY

1. Boaden, *Memoirs of Mrs. Inchbald*, 2:49–50.

2. The Pic-Nics was an amateur group that organized a club in Tottenham Street in 1802. It had a periodical in 1803, but the club and its publication were soon attacked, and its periodical ceased, even though Thomas Sheridan, Sheridan's son, was one of the managers. See Graham, *English Literary Periodicals*.

3. Boaden, *Memoirs of Mrs. Inchbald*, 2:56–57.

4. Reverend Plumtre, *On Amusements in General*, 173–75. See also Boaden, *Memoirs of Mrs. Inchbald*, 2:133–34.

5. Donald, *Age of Caricature*, 107–8. See especially the reproduction of Gillray's *Dilettanti Theatricals* on 107 and the reference to the Pic-Nics.

6. Boaden, *Memoirs of Mrs. Inchbald*, 2:59.

7. Ibid., 2:60.

8. Ibid., 2:61.

9. Doran, *"Their Majesties' Servants,"* 2:146.

10. Boaden, *Memoirs of Mrs. Inchbald*, 2:67.

11. Ibid. See also Bloxam, *Walpole's Queen of Comedy*, 122, 124 n. Lawrence was a part of this evening's entertainment, as he wrote to his sister Anne Bloxam: he reported on the lists of the guests—"The Prince, the Duke of Devonshire, Lord and Lady Melbourne, Lord and Lady Essex, with a long etcetera amongst the rest, Sheridan was present." He opened the play and found Sheridan rather intimidating, but, as he said, Lord Abercorn was a friend and had been kind to him. He pledged to her, however, "I am not going to be a performer in other families. I stick to Lord Abercorn's; and for the rest I pursue my profession as quietly and more steadily than ever" (122).

12. Mrs. Tidswell usually played supporting roles, but this time Lady Autumn was a principal role. See the *Biographical Dictionary*, 12:272, for information about her. She is featured also in the satirical print "Management—or—Butts & Hogsheads."

13. Boaden, *Memoirs of Mrs. Inchbald*, 2:64.

14. Ibid., 2:75. See also Manvell, *Sarah Siddons*, 270 ff. Manvell quotes Inchbald's letter and follows it with the explanation of the "affair," which he reviews, the events and the accusations of the Galindos, the Irish couple Siddons had befriended. It is probable, as Manvell suggests, that the money Siddons lent to them and Catherine Galindo's extreme jealousy prompted the bitter end after some four years of friendship. Manvell points out that Galindo was infatuated with Sarah and that she gave her affection to him in return. Manvell comments: "There are only too many precedents for such anomalous attachments between women in their forties or fifties who, lacking any firm emotional anchor in their lives, respond unwisely to the exuberance of a man much younger than themselves. As often as not, the young men involved in such relationships are unscrupulous and out to exploit both the affections and the fortunes of their victims" (268).

15. Boaden, *Memoirs of Mrs. Inchbald*, 2:72.

16. Phillips is the publisher who was said to have offered her a thousand pounds for her memoirs sight unseen, but she had been so elusive about giving a contract to anyone that when she sent it to him again, it is not surprising that he refused it. Boaden's account of this last dealing with Phillips is worth noting: "She immediately [after Robinson refused] went herself to Phillips, the gentleman who had so gallantly offered to buy in the *dark;* and left him with the impression that she had *sold* her work, and was soon to count over her thousand pounds. But whatever was the reason, on the 20th of June she received a *final* reply from St. Paul's Church-yard, which was unfavorable. Perhaps from their vicinity, the prior tender to Paternoster Row might have been buzzed some night in the

Chapter Coffee-house. Nothing in fact ever came of this work." *Memoirs of Mrs. Inchbald,* 2:76. Again, Boaden's remarks show his knowledge of the publishing business and Inchbald's determination to handle her own work.

17. Katharine Rogers, "Britain's First Woman Drama Critic: Elizabeth Inchbald," in Schofield and Macheski, *Curtain Calls,* 282.

18. See her discussion in the *Remarks.* There is no evidence in Inchbald's pocket-books that she knew anything about how the plays were selected or anything about the transaction between Bell and the Longmans. The procedure was a commercial one, and a very successful one in the end.

19. The fact that she was sent the text of the plays has misled some critics who accuse her of mutilating the plays. See, e.g., an extremely unfortunate essay, Fenstermaker, *"All for Love* and Mrs. Inchbald," in which he writes, "When comparing *All for Love* (1678) as originally written by Dryden with the version produced by Mrs. Elizabeth Inchbald in 1808 for *The British Theatre* series, one will find a clear indication of what being a nineteenth-century editor could mean" (40). As the headings for the plays clearly indicate, the texts are the acting versions as given in Drury Lane, Covent Garden, and the Haymarket. And as her pocket-books confirm, she was given the text—she did not edit any one of them— not even her own plays. Fenstermaker writes, "Mrs. Inchbald permanently excised much that is important in the play and subtly created a third and fourth category of variants" (43). His judgment throughout the article shows that he has missed the important point that the publication was designed for a contemporary theatre audience. And his conclusion, "But whether or not Mrs. Inchbald was, or could be, completely 'successful' in her attempt to render the play acceptable to the moral sensibilities of her day is not really the question. The fact remains that she vitiated Dryden's play, a very fine work of art; and, although no period can claim that its literary taste is better than another's, certainly no explanation by way of taste or morality can ever justify the 'doctoring' illustrated by this text of *All For Love*" (49), shows clearly that he did not know—or understand—the way plays were altered for the eighteenth-century theatre. Although the years from 1780, when Inchbald came to London, on into the nineteenth century saw an interesting mixture of altered and unaltered earlier plays, it was much later before Shakespeare, for example, was presented in something close to his original text. Kemble, of course, was very much interested in making the Shakespeare plays as authentic as possible.

20. A check of the collected edition as to which theatre manager gave permission for the use of the text reveals an interesting footnote about George Colman the younger, in that his plays that were given at Drury Lane are so listed, but *The Mountaineers* is listed as at the "The Theatre-Royal, Haymarket."

21. Boaden, *Memoirs of Mrs. Inchbald,* 2:91.

22. For a discussion of the Garrick alterations, see Stone and Kahrl, *David Garrick,* 247 ff. See 251–55 for *Romeo and Juliet.*

23. Inchbald spells Southerne's name without the final *e,* a reminder that there is a difference in spelling in many instances. In reviewing his life, Inchbald points out that he

was the first "who increased the advantage of dramatic authors, by obtaining, in addition to the first, a second and third night for their emolument." *Remarks*, 7:5.

24. See the *Biographical Dictionary* entry on Aaron Hill, 7:295–307. For an account of the acting history of *Zara*, see 7:302–3.

25. See ibid., 3:262–82, for information about Mrs. Susanna Maria Cibber's acting career.

26. Mrs. Inchbald's comments in this quotation point out both her view of the stage as a place of instruction and her view of upper-class women whose sexual misconduct was adultery, not the loss of chastity before marriage.

27. See Todd, *British Women Writers*, 30 ff., for the remaining works. In 1815 Byron tried to revive *De Monfort*, but his effort failed.

28. See the entry in the *Biographical Dictionary*, 10:391–99. Murphy published a *Life of Garrick* in two volumes in 1801. Murphy was a special friend of Dr. Johnson; in fact, he introduced Johnson to the Thrales. Taylor knew him very well over a long period of time. See Taylor, *Records of My Life*, 1:194–207. See also the entry in the *Biographical Dictionary* for Ann Elliot, 5:50–54.

29. Inchbald points out that the principal parts of *The Countess of Salisbury* were created by Barry and Mrs. Dancer, afterward Barry's wife, and that it was the acting that made the play a success, for when Siddons revived it, it failed.

30. See Stone and Kahrl, *David Garrick*, 242–46.

31. See chapter 10 for discussion of *Lovers' Vows* and *Wise Man of the East*.

32. See Boaden, *Life of John Philip Kemble*, 2:140–41, for his discussion of Kemble as Penruddock.

33. The whole essay from the *Artist* is printed in McKee, *Elizabeth Inchbald, Novelist*, appendix 1, 151.

34. Boaden, *Memoirs of Mrs. Inchbald*, 2:103.

35. Ibid., 2:103–4.

36. It is tempting to wonder whether Colman read Boaden's account of Inchbald's *Remarks*. By 1833 Colman had become "Examiner of all Plays, Tragedies, Comedies, Operas, Farces, or any other entertainment of the stage, of what denomination soever." See *Biographical Dictionary*, 3:427–28.

37. Boaden, *Memoirs of Mrs. Inchbald*, 2:104.

38. Ibid., 2:104–5.

39. Ibid., 2:105.

40. Ibid., 2:105–6.

41. Ibid., 2:106–8.

42. Ibid., 2:108–9.

43. Ibid., 2:110–11.

44. Ibid., 2:111–12.

45. Ibid., 2:113.

46. Ibid., 2:114.

47. Ibid., 2:84.

48. Bree, *Sarah Fielding*, 21.

49. Ford, *Hannah More*, 240.

50. Boaden, *Memoirs of Mrs. Inchbald*, 2:97–98.

51. Ibid., 2:98–99.

52. Ibid., 2:100–101.

53. Ibid., 2:260; quotations are from Inchbald's "My Septembers Since I Married."

54. Ibid., 2:116.

55. Ibid., 2:117–18.

56. Ibid., 2:117.

57. Manvell, *Sarah Siddons*, 292.

58. Ibid., 292–93. The fire was one of the worst in a city that frequently witnessed such. Many people perished, including some spectators and a number of firemen crushed by the falling roof. See Campbell, *Life of Mrs. Siddons*, 2:322–23.

59. Mrs. Siddons was present upon this occasion, dressed in formal attire with a plume of black feathers on her hat. The rain fell in torrents, but Kemble refused to have any of the ceremony shortened even though he had been very ill. Harris, his partner, was present also and, Boaden says, "laid the foundation of a paralytic disorder which conducted him to his grave." *Memoirs of Mrs. Siddons*, 442.

60. Campbell, *Life of Mrs. Siddons*, 2:325–27; see also Boaden, *Memoirs of Mrs. Siddons*, 449–51. Boaden's account here is interesting for his analysis, in that he said too much was attempted at one time. The prospect before the proprietors was an entire monopoly of the public. Covent Garden was to possess "every enviable convenience and display every kind of talent." The boxes were designed to be "as select and private as their own residences." The reference to every kind of "talent" included the Italian singer Catalani, about whom Boaden remarks, "Catalani was the grand theme of discount." As time went on, the protest became political, and also it became a point around which the religious fanatics gathered. See 451–52. A contemporary print entitled "The House that Jack Built" reads like a comic strip, with the facade of the new building, the boxes, the upper gallery followed by Catalani, the leader of the riots with his horn, and in the last square Kemble himself..

61. Boaden, *Life of John Philip Kemble*, 2:498–99, 499.

62. Manvell, *Sarah Siddons*, 296.

63. Boaden, *Memoirs of Mrs. Inchbald*, 2:143.

64. Ibid., 2:143–44.

65. All quotations from this essay, Inchbald's second essay for the *Artist*, are from her untitled article as printed in the *Artist*, May 1809, article no. 16, pp. 309–18.

66. See Donohue, *Theatre in the Age of Kean*. The second chapter, "The Theatre of the 1790s," includes a discussion of the audience in which he writes, "The most elementary fact about an audience is that it congregates in one place for purposes either aesthetic or social or, more likely, both. Riots or large-scale disruptions notwithstanding, the eighteenth-century audience was a homogeneous group, yet at the same time well aware of its own distinctive

components" (15). Donohue sees Inchbald's plays, along with those of her contemporaries Morton and Holcroft, as "hardly . . . radical experiments. Yet their works are marked by an overall attempt to come to terms with a freshly emerging consciousness of the way people think and behave under stress" (93).

12. THE LAST YEARS

1. This advertisement can also be found along with the play in the Backscheider edition.

2. Plumptre herself translated several of Kotzebue's plays, and in fact she made her reputation as a translator.

3. Boaden, *Memoirs of Mrs. Inchbald*, 2:158.

4. It was in this crisis that Inchbald wrote to Mrs. Phillips, in a letter dated Oct. 2, 1810, "I protest I envy Cobbett in jail; for he is safe, and knows where he shall rest his head for the winter." Ibid., 2:160. Cobbett, who believed passionately in the freedom of the press, had been tried for seditious libel and sentenced to two years in prison. Since he could afford to rent private quarters, he was relatively comfortable in rooms where members of his family could live with him and visitors could be entertained. See also Sambrook, *William Cobbett*, 76 ff.

5. Boaden, *Memoirs of Mrs. Inchbald*, 2:162. This whole episode with Mr. Clarke upset Inchbald immoderately, and her comments reveal again her feeling that she never had a permanent home of her own. Boaden, in his usual way, digresses to quote from Horne Tooke about the state of the country. Tooke wrote, "Good God! this country in a state of siege! Besieged collectively by France from without; and each individual at home, more disgracefully and daily besieged in his house by swarms of tax collectors, assessors, and supervisors, armed with degrading lists, to be signed under precipitate and ensnaring penalties; whilst his growing rents, like the goods of an insolvent trader, are prematurely attached in the hands of his harassed tenants, who now suddenly find that they too have a new and additional rent, beyond their agreement, to pay to a new and unforeseen landlord" (2:161).

6. Ibid., 2:262–63.

7. Boaden has included the Edgeworth letters. See ibid., 2:192 ff.

8. See Inchbald's account of her meeting de Stael in a letter to Mrs. Phillips dated Aug. 26, 1813, in ibid., 2:190–91.

9. Ibid., 2:215–16.

10. The Cosways were Maria and Richard Cosway, both artists. He was a court painter to the Prince of Wales and is now known especially for his exquisite miniatures. Their marriage was very much of the eighteenth century, not exactly one of convenience but rather of accommodation. They entertained lavishly. Maria was a famous beauty and a very accomplished artist. She sang and played the piano and the harp. She was gossiped about, as might be expected, especially when, after a childless marriage of many years, she

gave birth to a daughter. As artists and friends of the prince, they knew all the theatre people; indeed, Cosway's paintings of Perdita Robinson are especially celebrated. They are seen today in the Wallace Collection, and we are reminded of the beauty and fashion of the last years of the eighteenth century. Maria became a friend of Thomas Jefferson when they were both in Paris in 1786, and some writers have suggested they were more than friends, a doubtful conclusion from the evidence. After their time in 1820 in Kensington House, the Cosways moved into a place of their own, where Richard died soon after, another victim of tuberculosis. For Maria's association with Jefferson, see Shackelford, *Thomas Jefferson's Travels*, 65–74, 185 nn. 31, 32.

11. Boaden, *Memoirs of Mrs. Inchbald*, 2:261.

12. Ibid., 2:269.

13. The prince had married Mrs. Fitzherbert in 1786 even though by the Marriage Settlement Law, she as a Roman Catholic could not marry him. Because the marriage was not legal and because the prince was very much in debt, he was forced by his father, the king, to marry Caroline of Brunswick. See Hibbert, *George III*, 250–51; Foreman, *Georgiana*, 177–79; and David, *Prince of Pleasure*, 167–69. The prince married Princess Caroline of Brunswick in 1796. See Foreman, *Georgiana*, 296–97. See also an account of the whole affair in Fraser, *Unruly Queen*, chap. 3, "Matrimony," and 60–61 for the ceremony.

14. Boaden, *Memoirs of Mrs. Inchbald*, 2:270.

15. Ibid., 2:287. Boaden quotes her will in 1:284–87.

16. Nicoll, *Late Eighteenth Century Drama*, 150.

17. Strachey, introduction to *A Simple Story*.

18. Boaden, *Memoirs of Mrs. Inchbald*, 2:122.

19. For Pratt, see Morton, *Shelley and the Revolution in Taste*, 94, 95, 137, 209, 222–23.

20. Kelly, *German Visitors*, 154.

21. See Asleson, *Passion for Performance*, 31, fig. 24.

22. Boaden, *Memoirs of Mrs. Inchbald*, 1:173. Larded meal is a reference to the elaborate hair fashions that were finished with "lard" to preserve them for weeks.

23. Wilkinson, *Wandering Patentee*, 1:278.

24. See Taylor, *Records of My Life*, 2:242–43. Taylor found the marquis "one of the best bred gentlemen I ever knew." He quoted Kemble as saying that the duke "always reminded him of the higher characters in Congreve observing that he had their ease, courtesy, elegance, and sprightliness in his conversation, without any of their licentiousness and occasional grossness." In this same passage, Taylor contrasts the marquis with Abercorn, who, he said, "assumed a haughty dignity of demeanour, and looked around as if he thought he disgraced himself by condescending to cast a glance upon any person in the room. The performers, who are never wanting in humour, ridicule, and mimicry, on his departure, amply revenged themselves for his indignant neglect by amusing caricatures of his manner." Such a comment perhaps reveals more about Taylor than about Abercorn, since, although many of Taylor's own friends were friends of Abercorn, he was not.

25. Mrs. Opie was a very popular hostess, entertaining at tea with conversation so often that finally her husband found the noise and bustle distracting, and she was obliged to entertain less frequently. See Grylls, *William Godwin and His World*, 138.

26. Borer, *An Illustrated Guide to London*, 101, 102.

27. Mrs. Booth and her husband came to London in the seventies from the provinces. She acted only briefly in London, and her husband was at Covent Garden from 1775–1776 until 1788–1789.

28. Cecilia Macheski, "Herself as Heroine: Portraits as Autobiography for Elizabeth Inchbald," in Schofield and Macheski, *Curtain Calls*, 38–39.

29. See Miss Angle's conversation with Fish in Backscheider, *Plays of Elizabeth Inchbald*, 1:4–6.

30. See Tillyard, *Aristocrats*, 251–53, for an account of Bunbury's divorce. Sarah's family was torn apart over these events, and it was not until 1781 that she was married to George Napier. At the time of their marriage, he was an officer in the army, having seen action in America—in New York and Charleston. His first wife and children had accompanied him to America, but she had died in New York, and when Napier returned to England he was free to marry Sarah. It was a love match on both sides. One of their daughters married Sir Henry Bunbury, nephew and heir of Sir Charles and son of Sir Charles's brother Henry, the artist.

31. Boaden, *Memoirs of Mrs. Inchbald*, 2:124. Boaden adds the note that Abercorn's lost wife was "his Lordship's cousin . . . he was divorced by act of Parliament in 1799."

32. Nicoll, *Late Eighteenth Century Drama*, 149–50.

33. Littlewood, *Elizabeth Inchbald and Her Circle*, 40–41.

34. See Boaden, *Memoirs of Mrs. Inchbald*, 2:222–23.

35. Ibid., 2:355–56.

36. Ibid., 2:237.

37. Ibid., 2:248, 255.

38. Ibid., 2:255. See also 2:237–55 for Boaden's discussion of Moore and the reprinted letters to Inchbald from Moore. Boaden points out that he used the letters from Moore that Mrs. Inchbald had kept; there were none of hers. Moore was the younger brother of Sir John Moore, a lieutenant general who died in 1809 in Spain.

39. Ibid., 2:16–17.

40. See Hayes, "Thomas Harris," 221–27. Belmont was near Uxbridge (226). See also St. Clair, *The Godwins and the Shelleys*, 230–33.

41. Opie (Amelia Alderson) before her marriage wrote several letters to Godwin asking for advice about writing a play. She had done a play in Norwich and no doubt wanted to test the London theatres. At this point she did not know Inchbald well enough to ask her for advice. Later, after her marriage, she did not publish anything until after her husband's death and her return to Norwich. Godwin never wrote a successful play. See below for his experience with *Antonio*. See also St. Clair, *The Godwins and the Shelleys*, 147–48, for Amelia and Godwin.

42. Colman, *Random Records,* 2:60–61. Quoted also in Macqueen-Pope, *Haymarket,* 154–55.

43. Paul, *William Godwin,* 2:56.

44. Ibid., 2:56, 77. By this time, we remember, Godwin was no longer intimate with Mrs. Inchbald.

45. Boaden, *Memoirs of Mrs. Siddons,* 56.

46. Baker, *John Philip Kemble,* 240–41.

47. See *Biographical Dictionary,* 13:30–48. Notice how many of the prints having to do with her affair with the prince are listed.

48. See Boaden, *Memoirs of Mrs. Inchbald,* 2:284–87, for a copy of her will. She included very precise items for many people, including her hairdresser.

49. Kelly, *German Visitors,* 121.

50. Taylor, *Records of My Life,* 2:404.

51. Ibid., 2:404–5.

52. Ibid., 2:406.

53. Ibid., 2:408.

54. Ibid.

55. Ibid.

56. See Kelly, *German Visitors,* 156. He also found her *Every One Has His Fault* "not extraordinary," but redeemed by Mrs. Pope's stirring acting.

57. Judith Phillips Stanton, "'This New-Found Path Attempting': Women Dramatists in England, 1660–1800," in Schofield and Macheski, *Curtain Calls,* 325–54.

58. Turner, *Living by the Pen.* See 169 ff. for a discussion of *Nature and Art.* See Katharine M. Rogers, "Elizabeth Inchbald: Not Such a Simple Story," in Spender, *Living by the Pen,* 86–90.

59. Katharine M. Rogers, "Elizabeth Inchbald: Not Such a Simple Story," in Spender, *Living by the Pen,* 82–90.

60. Doran, *"Their Majesties' Servants,"* 2:149. Doran, like the visitor to London, found that "Sometimes success was owing more to the actors than herself."

61. Littlewood, *Elizabeth Inchbald and Her Circle,* 74.

62. Nicoll, *Late Eighteenth Century Drama,* 144–45.

63. See Plumb, *England in the Eighteenth Century,* the chapters "The War at Sea, 1793–1802" and "The War on Land, 1802–1815," 195–214, for a brief discussion.

64. Quoted in Grylls, *William Godwin and His World,* 102.

65. Ibid., 103.

66. Boaden, *Memoirs of Mrs. Inchbald,* 2:271.

67. *Memoirs of Mrs. Sumbel Late Wells,* 1:206–7.

68. Boaden, *Memoirs of Mrs. Inchbald,* 2:290–91.

BIBLIOGRAPHY

Ashton, Geoffrey. *A Catalogue of Paintings at the Theatre Museum, London.* London: Victoria and Albert Museum, 1992.

Adolphus, John. *Memoirs of John Bannister, Comedian.* London: Bentley, 1839.

Altick, Richard D. *The Shows of London.* Cambridge, Mass.: Harvard Univ. Press, 1978.

Asleson, Robyn, ed. *A Passion for Performance: Sarah Siddons and Her Portraitists.* Los Angeles: J. Paul Getty Museum, 1999.

Authentic Memoirs of the Green-Room; Involving Sketches of the Performers of the Theatres Royal, Drury-Lane, Covent Garden and the Hay-Market. London: J. Roach, 1806.

Backscheider, Paula R. *Spectacular Politics: Theatrical Power and Mass Culture in Early Modern England.* Baltimore: Johns Hopkins Univ. Press, 1993.

————, ed. *The Plays of Elizabeth Inchbald.* 2 vols. New York: Garland, 1980.

Backscheider, Paula, Felicity Nussbaum, and Philip B. Anderson, eds. *An Annotated Bibliography of Twentieth Century Critical Studies of Women and Literature, 1660–1800.* New York: Garland, 1977.

Baker, David E., I. Reed, and S. Jones. *Biographia Dramatica, or a Companion to the Playhouse.* London: Longman, Hurst, 1812.

Baker, Herschel. *John Philip Kemble: The Actor in His Theatre.* Cambridge, Mass.: Harvard Univ. Press, 1942.

Barker, Gerard A. *Grandison's Heirs: The Paragon's Progress in the Late Eighteenth-Century Novel.* Newark: Univ. of Delaware Press, 1985.

Bell, John. *Bell's British Theatre, Consisting of the Most Esteemed English Plays.* 20 vols. London and York: Etherington, MDCCLXXVI.

Biographical Dictionary. See Highfill, Burnim, and Langhans.

Bloxam, Suzanne. *Walpole's Queen of Comedy: Elizabeth Farren, Countess of Derby.* Ashford, Kent: Suzanne Bloxam, 1988.

Boaden, James. *Life of Mrs. Jordan.* 2d ed. 2 vols. London: Edward Bull, 1831.

————. *Memoirs of Mrs. Inchbald: Including Her Familiar Correspondence with the Most Distinguished Persons of Her Time.* 2 vols. London: Richard Bentley, 1833.

————. *Memoirs of Mrs. Siddons.* London, 1893.

————. *Memoirs of the Life of John Philip Kemble.* 2 vols. London: Longman, Hurst, Rees, Orme, Brown, and Green, 1825.

Bobrick, Benson. *Angel in the Whirlwind.* New York: Simon and Schuster, 1997.

Borer, Mary Cathcart. *An Illustrated Guide to London, 1800.* London: Robert Hale, 1988.

Boswell's Life of Johnson. Oxford Standard Authors. London: Oxford Univ. Press, 1960.

Bree, Linda. *Sarah Fielding.* New York: Twayne, 1996.

Brewer, John. *The Pleasures of the Imagination: English Culture in the Eighteenth Century.* New York: Farrar, Straus, and Giroux, 1997.

Brightwell, Cecilia. *Memorials of the Life of Amelia Opie.* Norwich, Eng.: Fletcher and Alexander, 1854.

The British Theatre; or, A Collection of Plays, Which Are Acted at the Theatres Royal, Drury Lane, Covent Garden, and the Haymarket, with Biographical and Critical Remarks, by Mrs. Inchbald. 25 vols. London: Longman, Hurst, Rees, and Orme, 1808.

Burling, William J. *Summer Theatre in London, 1661–1820, and the Rise of the Haymarket Theatre.* Madison Teaneck, N.J.: Fairleigh Dickinson Univ. Press, 2000.

Burnim, Kalman A., and Philip H. Highfill Jr. *John Bell, Patron of British Portraiture: A Catalogue of the Theatrical Portraits in His Editions of Bell's Shakespeare and Bell's British Theatre.* Carbondale: Southern Illinois Univ. Press, 1998.

Burton, Elizabeth. *The Georgians at Home.* London: Arrow Books, 1967.

Butler, Marilyn. *Jane Austen and the War of Ideas.* Oxford: Clarendon Press, 1975.

———. *Romantics, Rebels and Reactionaries: English Literature and Its Background, 1760–1830.* Oxford: Oxford Univ. Press, 1981.

Campbell, Thomas. *Life of Mrs. Siddons.* London: Effingham Wilson, 1834.

Cannon-Brookes, Peter, ed. *The Painted Word: British History Painting, 1750–1830.* Woodbridge, Suffolk: Boydell Press, 1991.

Choudhury, Mita. *Interculturalism and Resistance in the London Theater, 1660–1800.* Lewisburg, Pa.: Bucknell Univ. Press, 2000.

Claeys, Gregory, ed. *The Politics of English Jacobinism: Writings of John Thelwall.* University Park: Pennsylvania State Univ. Press, 1995.

Clayden, Peter William. *The Early Life of Samuel Rogers.* London: Smith, Elder, and Co., 1887.

———. *Rogers and His Contemporaries.* London: Smith, Elder, and Co., 1889.

Clemit, Pamela, ed. *A Simple Story,* by Elizabeth Inchbald. New York: Penguin Books, 1996.

Clifford, James. *Hester Lynch Piozzi (Mrs. Thrale).* 2d ed. Oxford: Clarendon Press, 1952.

Collins, A.S. *Authorship in the Days of Dr. Johnson.* London, 1929.

Colman, George. *T. Harris Dissected.* London: T. Becket, MDCCLVIII.

Colman, George (the younger). *The Election of Managers.* N.p., n.d.

Conger, Syndy McMillen. *Mary Wollstonecraft and the Language of Sensibility.* Rutherford, N.J.: Fairleigh Dickinson Univ. Press, 1994.

Craft-Fairchild, Cathrine. *Masquerade and Gender: Disguise and Female Identity in Eighteenth Century Fictions by Women.* University Park: Pennsylvania State Univ. Press, 1993.

Darby, Barbara. *Frances Burney, Dramatist: Gender, Performance, and the Late-Eighteenth-Century Stage.* Lexington: Univ. Press of Kentucky, 1997.

David, Saul. *Prince of Pleasure: The Prince of Wales and the Making of the Regency.* New York: Grove Press, 1998.

Dibbin, T.J. *Reminscences of the Theatre Royal.* London: Henry Colburn, 1827.

Donald, Diana. *The Age of Caricature: Satirical Prints in the Reign of George III.* New Haven, Conn.: Yale Univ. Press, 1996.

Donohue, Joseph. *Theatre in the Age of Kean.* Oxford: Basil Blackwell, 1975.

Doran, John. *"Their Majesties' Servants": Annals of the English Stage.* 2 vols. Philadelphia: David McKay, 1890.

Dunbar, Janet. *Peg Woffington and Her World.* London: Heinemann, 1968.

Durant, Jack D. *Richard Brinsley Sheridan.* Boston: Twayne, 1975.

Este, C. Clerk. *My Own Life.* London: T. and J. Egerton, 1787.

Fenstermaker, John J. *"All for Love* and Mrs. Inchbald." *Research Studies* 48, no. 1 (Mar. 1980): 40–49.

Fitzsimmons, Linda. "Theatre Royal York." *York History,* no. 4 (York, n.d.): 169–91.

Fitzsimmons, Linda, and Arthur W. McDonald. *The Yorkshire Stage, 1766–1803.* Metuchen, N.J.: Scarecrow Press, 1989.

Ford, Charles Howard. *Hannah More: A Critical Biography.* New York: Peter Lang, 1996.

Foreman, Amanda. *Georgiana, Duchess of Devonshire.* London: HarperCollins, 1998.

Fraser, Flora. *The Unruly Queen.* New York: Knopf, 1996.

Genest, John. *Some Account of the English Stage from the Restoration in 1660 to 1830.* Bath, Eng.: Carrington, 1832.

Gilliland, Thomas. *The Dramatic Mirror containing the History of the Stage, from the Earliest Period to the Present Time....* 2 vols. London: C. Chapple, 1808.

———. *Elbow Room: A Pamphlet containing Remarks on the Shameful Increase of the Private Boxes of Covent Garden.* London: Printed for the author, 1804.

Gillispie, Charles Coulston. *The Montgolfier Brothers and the Invention of Aviation.* Princeton, N.J.: Princeton Univ. Press, 1983.

Godwin, William. *Caleb Williams.* World Classics. New York: Oxford Univ. Press, 1986.

———. Journal manuscript. Carl H. Pforzheimer Collection, New York Public Library.

Gordon, Daniel, ed. and trans. *Candide,* by Voltaire. Boston: Bedford/St. Martin's, 1999.

Graham, Walter. *English Literary Periodicals.* New York: Thomas Nelson and Sons, 1930.

Gray, Charles Harold. *Theatrical Criticism in London to 1795.* New York: Columbia Univ. Press, 1931.

Grice, Elizabeth. *Rogues and Vagabonds: The Rise and Fall of the Theatre in East Anglia during the 18th and 19th Centuries.* Lavenham, Suffolk: Terence Dalton, 1977.

Grylls, Rosalie Glynn. *William Godwin and His World.* London: Odhams Press, 1958.

Hadley, Elaine. *Melodramatic Tactics: Theatricalized Dissent in the English Marketplace, 1800–1885.* Stanford, Calif.: Stanford Univ. Press, 1995.

Hardinge, George. *The Miscellaneous Works in Prose and Verse of George Hardinge, Esq.* London: J. Nichols, 1818.

Hargreaves-Mawdsley, W.N. *The English Della Cruscans and Their Time, 1783–1828.* The Hague: Martinus Nijhoff, 1967.

Harris, Tim, ed. *Popular Culture in England, c. 1500–1850.* New York: St. Martin's, 1995.

Hayes, John. "Thomas Harris, Gainsborough Dupont and the Theatrical Gallery at Belmont." *Connoisseur* 169 (1968): 221–27.

Hibbert, Christopher. *The Days of the French Revolution.* New York: William Morrow, 1980.

———. *George III: A Personal History.* New York: Basic Books, 1998.

———. *Redcoats and Rebels: The American Revolution through British Eyes.* New York: Avon Books, 1991.

Highfill, Philip H., Jr., Kalman A. Burnim, and Edward A. Langhans. *A Biographical Dictionary of Actors, Actresses, Musicians, Dancers, Managers, and Other Stage Personnel in London, 1660–1800.* 16 vols. Carbondale: Southern Illinois Univ. Press, 1973–1993.

Hodskinson, Joseph, ed. *The County of Suffolk Surveyed.* London, 1783.

Hogan, Charles Beecher. "A Critical Introduction." *The London Stage, 1776–1800.* Edited by Emmett L. Avery. Carbondale: Southern Illinois Univ. Press, 1968.

Hume, Robert D., ed. *The London Theatre World, 1660–1800.* Carbondale: Southern Illinois Univ. Press, 1980.

Inchbald, Elizabeth. *Nature and Art.* 2 vols. London: G.G. and J. Robinson, 1796.

Inchbald, *Remarks. See The British Theatre.*

Jobson, Allan. *Suffolk Villages.* London: Robert Hale, reprint, 1979.

Johnson, Samuel. *Lives of the English Poets.* World Classics. London: Oxford Univ. Press, 1972.

Kelly, Gary. *The English Jacobin Novel, 1780–1805.* Oxford: Clarendon Press, 1976.

Kelly, Hugh. *Thespis: or, A Critical Examination Into the Merits of all the Principal Performers Belonging to Covent-Garden Theatre.* London: G. Kearsly, 1767.

Kelly, John Alexander. *German Visitors to English Theaters in the Eighteenth Century.* Princeton, N.J.: Princeton Univ. Press, 1936.

Kelly, Linda. *The Kemble Era.* London: Bodley Head, 1980.

Kinne, Willard Austin. *Revivals and Importations of French Comedies in England, 1749–1800.* New York: Columbia Univ. Press, 1939.

Kramer, Lloyd. *Lafayette in Two Worlds.* Chapel Hill: Univ. of North Carolina Press, 1996.

Lee, Henry. *Memoirs of a Manager.* Tauton, Eng.: W. Bragg, 1830.

Levy, M.J., ed. *The Memoirs of Mary Robinson Written by Herself (Perdita) (1758–1800).* London: Peter Owen, 1994.

The Life and Letters of Lady Sarah Lennox. Ed. Countess of Ilchester and Lord Stavordale. 2 vols. London: John Murray, 1901.

The Life of Thomas Holcroft, Written by Himself. Continued to the Time of His Death from His

Diary Notes and Other Papers by William Hazlitt. Ed. Elbridge Colby. 2 vols. London: Constable and Co., 1925.

Littlewood, S.R. *Elizabeth Inchbald and Her Circle.* London: Daniel O'Conner, 1921.

Loftis, John. *Sheridan and the Drama of Georgian England.* Cambridge, Mass.: Harvard Univ. Press, 1977.

Lunardi's Grande Aereostatic Voyage Through the Air . . . London: J. Bell, W.J. Murray, 1784.

MacGregor, Margaret E. *Amelia Alderson Opie: Worldling and Friend.* Smith College Studies in Modern Languages, vol. 14. Northampton, Mass.: Smith College, 1933.

Macqueen-Pope, W. *Haymarket: Theatre of Perfection.* London: W.H. Allen, 1948.

Manceron, Claude. *Their Gracious Pleasure.* New York: Knopf, 1980.

Manvell, Roger. *Elizabeth Inchbald: England's Principal Woman Dramatist and Independent Woman of Letters in 18th Century London: A Biographical Study.* New York: Univ. Press of America, 1987.

————. Introduction to *Selected Comedies of Elizabeth Inchbald.* New York: Univ. Press of America, 1987.

————. *Sarah Siddons: Portrait of an Actress.* New York: Putnam's, 1971.

Marshall, Dorothy. *Fanny Kemble.* New York: St. Martin's, 1977.

Mathews, Mrs. Charles. *Memoirs of Charles Mathews.* London: Bentley, 1838–1839.

McKee, William. *Elizabeth Inchbald, Novelist.* Washington, D.C.: Catholic Univ. of America, 1935.

Memoirs of the Life of Mrs. Sumbel Late Wells. 3 vols. London: C. Chapple, 1811.

Messenger, Ann. *His and Hers Essays in Restoration and 18th Century Literature.* Lexington: Univ. Press of Kentucky, 1986.

Miles, Robert. *Ann Radcliffe: The Great Enchantress.* Manchester: Manchester Univ. Press, 1995.

Morison, Stanley. *Edward Topham, 1751–1820, Author of the Fool and Other Farces, Conductor of the World and Fashionable Advertiser . . . and a Gentleman of Fashion and Public Character.* Cambridge: Cambridge Univ. Press, 1933.

————. *John Bell: Bookseller, Printer, Publisher, Typefounder, Journalist.* Cambridge: Cambridge Univ. Press, 1930.

Morton, Timothy. *Shelley and the Revolution in Taste.* Cambridge: Cambridge Univ. Press, 1994.

Nicoll, Allardyce. *A History of Late Eighteenth Century Drama.* Cambridge: Cambridge Univ. Press, 1927.

Nixon, Edna. *Mary Wollstonecraft: Her Life and Times.* London: J.M. Dent, 1971.

O'Keeffe, John. *Recollections of the Life of John O'Keeffe.* London: Henry Colburn, 1826.

O'Toole, Fintan. *A Traitor's Kiss: The Life of Richard Brinsley Sheridan, 1751–1816.* New York: Farrar, Straus, and Giroux, 1998.

Oulton, Walley C. *The Drama Recorded.* London: J. Burke, 1814.

————. *History of the Theatres of London.* London: Martain and Bain, 1818.

Overbye, Karen. "'Neither a Widow, a Maid, nor a Wife': Miss Wooburn's 'Fault' in *Every*

One Has His Fault." Restoration and 18th Century Theatre Research, 2d ser., 8, no. 1 (summer 1993): 50–59.

Oxberry, William. *Oxberry's Dramatic Biography and Histrionic Anecdotes.* London: Virtue, 1825–1826.

Paul, Charles Kegan. *William Godwin: His Friends and Contemporaries.* 2 vols. Boston: Roberts Brothers, 1876. Facsimile reprint, New York: AMS Press, 1970.

Peake, Richard Brinsley. *Memoirs of the Colman Family, Including Their Correspondence.* London: Bentley, 1841.

Perry, Ruth. "De-Familiarizing the Family; or, Writing Family History from Literary Sources." *Modern Language Quarterly* 55, no. 4 (Dec. 1994): 415–27.

Pevsner, Nikolaus. *The Buildings of England: Suffolk.* Harmondsworth, Eng.: Penguin, 1961. Reprint, 1985.

Pindar, Peter (Dr. John Wolcot). *The Works.* Philadelphia: Woodward and Co., 1835.

Plumb, John Harold. *England in the Eighteenth Century.* Harmondsworth, Eng.: Penguin, 1974.

Price, Cecil. *Theatre in the Age of Garrick.* Totowa, N.J.: Rowman and Littlefield, 1973.

Reynolds, Frederick. *The Life and Times of Frederick Reynolds, Written by Himself.* 2 vols. London: Henry Colburn, 1827. 2d ed., reissued 1969, New York: Benjamin Blom, 1969.

Ribeiro, Aileen. *The Art of Dress: Fashion in England and France, 1750 to 1820.* New Haven, Conn.: Yale Univ. Press, 1995.

Rosenfeld, Sybil. *Georgian Scene Painters and Scene Painting.* Cambridge: Cambridge Univ. Press, 1981.

———. *Strolling Players and Drama in the Provinces, 1660–1765.* Cambridge: Cambridge Univ. Press, 1939.

Sambrook, James. *William Cobbett.* London: Routledge and Kegan Paul, 1973.

Scarfe, Norman. *A Frenchman's Year in Suffolk: French Impressions of Suffolk Life in 1784.* Woodbridge, Suffolk: Boydell, 1988.

———. *A Shell Guide—Suffolk.* London: Faber and Faber, 1976.

Schama, Simon. *Citizens: A Chronicle of the French Revolution.* New York: Knopf, 1989.

Scheuermann, Mona. *Her Bread to Earn: Women, Money, and Society from Defoe to Austen.* Lexington: Univ. Press of Kentucky, 1993.

Schofield, Mary Anne, and Cecilia Macheski, eds. *Curtain Calls: British and American Women and the Theatre, 1660–1820.* Athens: Ohio Univ. Press, 1991.

Shackelford, George Green. *Thomas Jefferson's Travels in Europe, 1784–1789.* Baltimore: Johns Hopkins Univ. Press, 1995.

Sheppard, Francis. *London: A History.* London: Oxford Univ. Press, 1998.

Smith, Elton Edward, and Esther Greenwell Smith. *William Godwin.* New York: Twayne, 1965.

Smith, John Thomas. *Nollekens and His Times.* 1828. Reprint, London: Century Hutchinson, 1986.

Spender, Dale. *Mothers of the Novel.* London: Pandora Press; New York: Methuen, 1986.

———, ed. *Living by the Pen: Early British Women Writers.* New York: Teachers College Press, Columbia Univ., 1992.

St. Clair, William. *The Godwins and the Shelleys: The Biography of a Family.* New York: Norton, 1989.

Stone, George Winchester, Jr., and George M. Kahrl. *David Garrick: A Critical Biography.* Carbondale: Southern Illinois Univ. Press, 1979.

Strachey, G[iles] L[ytton]. Introduction to *A Simple Story,* by Mrs. Inchbald. London: Henry Frowde, 1908.

Summerson, John. *Georgian London.* London: Penguin, 1945. Rev. ed., 1991

Tanner, Tony, ed. *Jane Austen: Sense and Sensibility.* London: Penguin, 1969.

Taylor, John. *Records of My Life.* 2 vols. London: Edward Bull, 1832.

Thrisk, Joan, ed. *Suffolk Farming in the Nineteenth Century.* Suffolk: Suffolk Records Society, n.d.

Tillyard, Stella. *Aristocrats: Caroline, Emily, Louisa, and Sarah Lennox, 1740–1832.* New York: Farrar, Straus, and Giroux, 1992.

Todd, Janet. *Mary Wollstonecraft: A Revolutionary Life.* New York: Columbia Univ. Press, 2000.

———, ed. *British Women Writers: A Critical Reference Guide.* New York: Continuum, 1989.

Tomalin, Claire. *Jane Austen: A Life.* New York: Knopf, 1997.

———. *The Life and Death of Mary Wollstonecraft.* New York: Harcourt Brace Jovanovich, 1974.

———. *Mrs. Jordan's Profession: The Actress and the Prince.* New York: Knopf, 1995.

Tompkins, J.M.S., ed. *A Simple Story,* by Elizabeth Inchbald. London: Oxford Univ. Press, 1967; paperback reissue, 1998.

Topham, Edward. *An Address To Edmund Burke, Esq. On His Late Letter Relative To The Affairs of America.* London: n.d.

Turner, Cheryl. *Living by the Pen: Women Writers in the Eighteenth Century.* London: Routledge, 1992.

Wendorf, Richard. *Sir Joshua Reynolds: The Painter in Society.* Cambridge, Mass.: Harvard Univ. Press, 1996.

Wilkinson, Tate. *The Wandering Patentee.* 4 vols. York: Wilson, Spence, and Mawman, 1795; facsimile ed., Menston: Scolar Press, 1973.

Wollstonecraft, Mary. *An Historical and Moral View of the Origin and Progress of the French Revolution; and the Effect It has Produced in Europe.* London: J. Johnson, 1794.

Wordsworth, William. *Poems.* Ed. George McLean Harper. New York: Charles Scribner's Sons, 1923.

Wyndham, Henry S. *The Annals of Covent Garden Theatre.* London: Chatto and Windus, 1906.

INDEX

Young, Edward: *The Revenge,* 465. *See also Remarks* (Inchbald)
Younge, Miss, 93, 114
Younger, Joseph: as actor, 29, 31; as theatre manager, 30, 34, 47, 102

Zara (Hill), 462. *See also Remarks* (Inchbald)
Zelie (Sillery), 258, 493